An Introduction to Perception

Irvin Rock

Institute for Cognitive Studies
Rutgers—The State University

Macmillan Publishing Co., Inc.
New York
Collier Macmillan Publishers
London

Dedication

To my friend *Carl Zuckerman* in appreciation
of his many contributions to this book.

Copyright © 1975, Irvin Rock
Printed in the United States of America

Macmillan Publishing Co., Inc.
866 Third Avenue, New York, New York 10022

Collier-Macmillan Canada, Ltd.

Library of Congress Cataloging in Publication Data

Rock, Irvin.
    An introduction to perception.

    Includes bibliographies and indexes.
    1. Perception.   I. Title.
BF311.R553   153.7   74-3806
ISBN 0-02-402490-2

Printing: 2 3 4 5 6 7 8   Year: 5 6 7 8 9 0

Acknowledgments

I wish to express gratitude and give credit to the following individuals and organizations whose illustrations have been included in this text:

Academic Press for figures 7-17, 7-18, 7-19, and 7-21, adapted from an article by F. Halper, T. Clayton, and myself, "The perception and recognition of complex figures." *Cognitive Psychology,* 3 (1972), 655-673.

Anstis, S. M., for figure 5-12, adapted from "Phi movement as a subtraction process." *Vision Research,* 10 (1970), 1411-1430.

Basic Books for figures 5-1, 7-23, 10-5, 10-7, and 10-14, adapted from my book, *The Nature of Perceptual Adaptation.* New York, 1966.

Bower, T. G. R., for figure 2-22, adapted from "The visual world of infants." *Scientific American,* 215 (1966), 80-92.

Brislin, R. W., and H. W. Leibowitz, for figure 2-21, adapted from "The effect of separation between test and comparison objects on size constancy at various age levels." *American Journal of Psychology,* 83 (1970), 372-376.

Cambridge University Press for figures 9-26, 9-27, 9-28, 9-30A, 9-31, and 9-32A from J. Fraser, "A new visual illusion of direction. *British Journal of Psychology,* 2 (1908), 307-310.

Chapanis, A., and R. A. McCleary, for figure 3-14 from "Interposition as a cue for the perception of relative distance." *Journal of General Psychology,* 48 (1953), 113-132.

Dinnerstein, D., and M. Wertheimer, for figures 3-45A and 3-46 from "Some determinants of phenomenal overlapping." *American Journal of Psychology,* 70 (1957), 21-37.

Escher Foundation, Haags Gemeentemuseum, for permission to reproduce 3 figures by M. C. Escher. The Hague, Holland.

Fantz, R., for figure 8-17, adapted from "The origin of form perception." *Scientific American,* 204 (1961), 66-72.

Fisher, G. H.. for figure 9-38, adapted from "An experimental and theoretical appraisal of the perspective and size-constancy theories of illusions." *Quarterly Journal of Experimental Psychology,* 22 (1970), 631-652, and for figure 9-57A, adapted from "Towards a new explanation for the geometrical illusions." *British Journal of Psychology,* 60 (1969), 179-185.

Gilinsky, A., for figure 2-18, from "The effect of attitude on the perception of size." *American Journal of Psychology,* 68 (1955), 173-192.

Goldmeier, E., for figures 7-12, 7-13, 7-14, and 7-16, adapted from "Similarity in visually perceived forms." *Psychological Issues,* 8 (1972), 1-135.

iv   Acknowledgments

Gregory, R., for figure 9–52, adapted from "Cognitive contours."
Nature, **238** (1972), 51–52.

Hale Observatories, for figure 3–5, from catalogue 258. 813 Santa Barbara Street, Pasadena, California 91109.

Harcourt Brace Jovanovich, Inc., for figure 6–22, from K. Koffka's *Principles of Gestalt Psychology*. New York, 1935, illustrating a figure used by P. Bahnsen in 1928.

Held, R., for figure 4–7, adapted from "Plasticity in sensory-motor systems." *Scientific American*, **213** (1965), 84–94.

Hershberger, W., for figure 3–47, from "Attached shadow orientation perceived as depth by chickens reared in an environment illuminated from below." *Journal of Comparative and Physiological Psychology*, **73** (1970), 407–411, copyright © 1970 by the American Psychological Association. Reprinted by permission.

Holding, D. H., for figure 9–58 from "A line illusion with irrelevant depth cues." *American Journal of Psychology*, **83** (1970), 280–282.

Hotopf, W. H. N., for figure 9–19B, adapted from "The size-constancy theory of visual illusions." *British Journal of Psychology*, **57** (1966), 307–318.

Inmont Corporation, for plate 6. 1133 Avenue of the America, New York, New York.

Julesz, B., for figure 3–28, from *Foundations of Cyclopean Perception*. Chicago: University of Chicago Press, 1971.

Kanizsa, G., for figure 7–4, from "Margini quasi-percettivi in campi con stimolazione omogenea." *Rivista di Psychologia*, **49** (1955), 7–30.

Linksz, A., for figure 3–20, adapted from *Physiology of the Eye*. Vol. 2. New York: Grune & Stratton, Inc., 1952.

Metelli, F., for figure 11–31, adapted from "Zur Analyse der phänomena len Durchsichtigkeitserscheinungen." *Gestalt und Wirklichkeit*. Ed. by R. Mühlher and J. Fischl. Berlin: Duncker & Humbolt, 1967.

Olson, R., and F. Altneave, for figure 6–12 from "What variables produce similarity grouping?" *American Journal of Psychology*, **83** (1970), 1–21.

Pick, A. D., for figure 8–23, adapted from "Improvement of visual and tactual form discrimination." *Journal of Experimental Psychology*, **69** (1965), 331–339.

Ratliff, F., for figure 11–23 from "Contour and contrast." *Scientific American*, **226** (1972), 90–101.

Robinson, J. O., for figure 9–30B from *The Psychology of Visual Illusion*. Hutchinson University Library, 1972.

Scientific American, for figures 8–24 and 8–25, adapted from an article written by C. S. Harris and myself, "Vision and touch," and published in *Scientific American*, May 1967.

Street, R. F., for figure 8–7 from *A Gestalt Completion Test*. Teachers College, Columbia University, 1931.

University Museum of the University of Pennsylvania, Philadelphia Collection, for figure 3–6.

Woodworth, R. S., for figure 3–41 from *Experimental Psychology*. Henry Holt & Company, 1938.

Zangwill, O. L., for figure 8–11 from "A study of the significance of attitude in recognition." *British Journal of Psychology*, **28** (1938), 12–17.

Preface

How does one write a textbook in a field such as perception, where there is still so little agreement among experts? There is certainly no widely accepted theory, and even the phenomena which an author considers important will reflect his bias. Of course, one could give equal weight to all the known facts, hypotheses, and theories, but that would make very dull reading.

Nonetheless, I have attempted to write a text in perception which would not simply be a personal statement of my views on the one hand or a mere cataloguing of facts and theories on the other. There is now fairly wide agreement about the central phenomena of perception—for example, the perceptual constancies, illusions of motion, and the like—and, once these phenomena are clearly understood, there is necessarily agreement about what the central problems are. There is even good agreement about the *kinds* of solutions to these problems that must prove correct. For example, most investigators would agree that the constancy of perceived size, despite variation in an object's distance, depends upon a "taking account" of distance by the perceptual system. Although not all investigators believe that neutral color constancy depends upon such a taking-into-account mechanism, there is wide acceptance of one particular alternative theory (the determination of neutral color on the basis of the relative luminance of adjacent regions).

Therefore, I have tried to concentrate on the central phenomena of perception and to make clear the problems to which they give rise. From this perspective I believe that Chapter 1, an introduction, Chapter 2, on size, Chapter 3 on the third dimension, Chapter 5 on movement and events, Chapters 6 and 8 on form, Chapter 9 on the geometric illusions, and Chapter 11 on neutral color can reasonably be said to fulfill the requirements one expects of a textbook. This is not to imply that these chapters do not reflect my own point of view and my critical analysis of various theories. They obviously do. For the most part, however, it will be clear to the reader where I introduce my own ideas, and if they disagree with prevailing views, those views and relevant references are given. Therefore, I hope I have protected the reader from reaching erroneous conclusions concerning what is and what is not accepted as true by most investigators in the field. On reading these chapters, the student should achieve an understanding of the central phenomena in each case, knowledge of the major direction (or directions) of the solution believed to be correct by the majority of investigators in the field, and an awareness of various criticisms, suggestions, and interpretations of the author.

There are, however, some chapters which are more idiosyncratic for one reason or another. Certain topics have been neglected in the experimental literature and in textbooks as well. For example, despite much research on adaptation to displacing prisms in recent years, one rarely finds an adequate treatment of the problem that such adaptation bears on, namely, the perception of direction. Despite much research on adaptation to an optically disoriented retinal image, one finds little in the way of adequate discussion of the problem this adaptation bears on, namely, the perception of egocentric orientation. These gaps have been filled here by a chapter on direction and a lengthy discussion of the problem of egocentric orientation in a chapter on orientation. Certain problems concerning form perception have also been neglected in the literature, perhaps because the Gestalt psychologists equated the problem of form perception with the problem of perceptual organization. More recently the problem of form perception has been equated with the problem of pattern recognition. These approaches, therefore, have failed to come to grips with the problem of phenomenal shape per se—the question of what accounts for the similarities and differences between forms. I refer to this problem as that of *specific shape* and devote a separate chapter to it.

My most clearly identifiable bias is one which runs counter to the prevailing Zeitgeist, my belief that it is premature to seek to explain perceptual phenomena in terms of neurophysiological mechanisms (despite my agreement that in the final analysis psychological facts are explicable in terms of brain events). Because we seem to be in the midst of a revolution within sensory physiology, based on the discoveries of so-called neural feature-detector units, many teachers may consider this bias very serious. Yet the fact is that those who are making these discoveries (let alone their disciples in psychology) are by no means certain of the precise role of these mechanisms in determining perception. It seems to me that a careful consideration of the perceptual phenomena these detector mechanisms are presumed to explain is necessary, timely, and valuable. For example, only when it is clear that the perception of movement often occurs without displacement of the retinal image and often fails to occur with such displacement are we in a position to evaluate the possible theoretical meaning of neural units that actively discharge when a contour displaces across the appropriate receptive field of the retina. In any event, I have not ignored these findings, but I have not placed them in the center of the stage either. And I have repeatedly tried to show that at this stage of our knowledge (with one possible exception) these mechanisms as presently understood cannot do justice to the phenomena under consideration. I would like to think that this book will be helpful for those who work or will work in sensory physiology by making clear the nature of the psychological facts which physiological theories must address.

When I began work on this book some years ago, there were few textbooks that provided detailed treatment of the present-day status of the field of perception. There were, however, various books that emphasized sensory processes, with only occasional references to the problems of perception. This is one reason why I have left out of this book any coverage of such traditional topics as the anatomy and physiology of the visual and other sensory systems, color vision, visual acuity, and the like. In the meantime, a few books have appeared which do treat the perception of objects and events in space, but for one reason or another the approach has not been such as to render this one unnecessary. As to justifying the neglect here of perception via modalities other than vision, I would argue that the central problems of perception are most clearly identifiable in vision, and much of the literature on these problems concerns visual perception. However, some discussion of perception through touch is included.

There are many people whose help I wish to acknowledge, but first and foremost is that of my friend, Carl Zuckerman. He worked with me on every stage of the book, from its initial inception some years ago to revisions only a few months ago, and on every level, from discussions of the fundamental problems of perception to the phrasing of sentences and the selection of illustrations. He read and made invaluable suggestions concerning each draft of the manuscript. I am very indebted to William Epstein, William H. Lichte, and Arien Mack for reading a draft of the entire manuscript and for their many helpful comments. Others such as Lloyd Kaufman, Sheldon Ebenholtz, Stanley Coren, Paul Whittle, Jacob Beck, and Peter Rock helped me with specific chapters. I also want to thank Professor Oliver L. Zangwill and others on the staff of the Psychological Laboratory at Cambridge University for their hospitality in the spring of 1973, enabling me to work very effectively on this book.

As every married author knows and customarily acknowledges, the contribution of one's spouse to the process of writing a book is beyond all reckoning. Not only did Sylvia Rock type, retype, and correct every draft of this book, but she provided the calm environment in which I could think, read, and write over a period of many years, and she repeatedly sacrificed her own time and interests in the process.

Irvin Rock

Contents

chapter 1

INTRODUCTION

Introductions to new disciplines should either be dispensed with entirely or presented *after* the student has come to grips with the concrete facts and problems of that discipline. Introductory comments try to generalize about a field, but since the beginner does not yet know that field, the general statements seem vague, unclear, and uninteresting. A field of inquiry consists of the problems that scientists actually have worked on and are working on, so if it is desirable to define that field, it makes a certain amount of sense to do so simply by referring to those problems. After the student has read this book he will know what the field of perception is all about.

Still, some more general considerations about a field such as perception are worth commenting on. What is the history of thought on the subject? How does it differ from related disciplines in psychology such as the study of thinking, learning, and memory? What unique methods are employed in its study? On what philosophical assumptions does it rest?

This introductory chapter has been written, but the reader is strongly advised to do one of two things. Either skip over the chapter now and come back to it later after first reading several other or all other chapters or read it now but don't dwell on it too long. Do not expect many of the points to be clear at this time, and above all do not let this chapter deter you from pushing on and getting into some of the fascinating problems that arise in connection with the specific topics covered in the rest of the book. Then reread this chapter. In the remainder of the book, it may be helpful to read the summary at the end of each chapter before as well as after reading the chapter.

1

The Field of Perception

Perception is a unique field of inquiry. In all other scientific disciplines, the purpose is to explain objective facts and events, be they the behavior of a honeybee or the movements of a planet. What we mean by *objective* is that the events we wish to explain are independent of the observer, are observable to all, and are not mere illusions. By *independent of the observer*, we mean that it can be safely assumed that these events are actually taking place whether anyone is observing them or not. If there is ever any reason to think our observation of what is happening is faulty or illusory, then we correct it. Thus, for example, the moon appears to be moving when it is visible through a cloud passing in front of it. However, we know that this is an illusion; the moon *is not* really moving through the clouds and so its apparent movement must be disregarded by the astronomer.

Of course, the objective facts with which science deals are known through perception. Although the relevant observations in some fields of modern science are indirect, as in the case of the path of a subatomic particle in a cloud chamber, many natural events are open to direct inspection. We can, for example, directly observe the strata of rocks, the constellations of stars, and the behavior and changes of plants and animals. In many cases, vision is aided by optical instruments, but that does not alter the fact that the starting point is what we perceive. As long as people agree about what they observe and as long as there is no reason to suspect that our senses are deceiving us, scientists are quite willing to assume the objectivity of the event. (Sometimes there is uncertainty about this, as in the case of the apparent color of a feature such as a "canal" on a planet that could be either the true color or the result of contrast with the surrounding region.) How we arrive at these perceptions is of no concern to the natural scientist, and, in fact, until fairly recently it was implicitly assumed that the world as we perceive it—barring optical illusions—is no more and no less than the world as it is.

However, in the field of perception, the interest is not in the objective event but in how things appear. Thus, in the case of the apparent motion of the moon through a cloud, it is this experience, namely, that it appears to be moving that is the focus of interest. Or to take another example about the moon, its color seems to be different at night, when it looks luminous, as if it is itself a source of light, compared to its appearance during the day, when it looks like a whitish object in sunlight. The objective fact is that the moon reflects the sun's light, by day or night, and to the same extent. The color of the moon, objectively speaking, or to be more precise, its reflectance property, is the same as that of a very dark gray rock. This property is a constant; this is what matters to the astrogeologist. But the apparent color of the moon at a given time and the change in its color under different conditions is precisely what interests the psychologist who studies perception.

Thus, in the study of perception, it is the appearance of things that is the focus of attention rather than the objective reality. The facts to be explained are the sensory impressions we have of the world about us, via the different sense modalities of vision, audition, and others, and the task is to account for these impressions. Whether a given perception is *veridical* (i.e., truthfully reflecting the objective state of affairs) or *illusory* (i.e., not in accord with the objective state of affairs) does not affect its status as a fact of perception requiring explanation.

The Real World and the Perceived World

The distinction we have made between a real world of objective events on the one hand and a subjective or perceived world of events on the other may seem legitimate and correct to the reader, but it raises many problems of a philosophical nature, some of which must be considered if the student's understanding of perception is to have some depth.

One problem that has concerned philosophers from the beginning of recorded history is this: What is real? What, the metaphysician asks, is the ultimate nature of being: The material universe or subjective awareness? The materialist answers: The world of physical objects and events is what exists and subjective awareness is no more than a special property of the brain, the brain itself being a physical object. The idealist answers: All we can be certain about is that we experience the world. Whether it exists or not is pure inference. Therefore, what is real is subjective consciousness, our ideas about the world, not the material world as such.

Others believe that there are two realities, or realms, the material and the mental. They acknowledge that the mental world depends upon or is correlated with events in a material object, the nervous system, but they are not willing to say, as some do, that mental events are thus nothing more than neural or brain events. After all, not *all* events in the brain lead to conscious mental states, so that brain event and mental event are not synonymous. Those holding this view are dualists, that is, they believe in two kinds of reality.*

A second and related problem is that of epistemology. How can we have knowledge of the material world? How can we be certain that what we think we know is correct? Problems arise if one acknowledges that the perceived world is essentially a "construction" of the mind. That is to say, what we have directly available are our sense impressions, our perceptions. Some, referred to as naive realists, simply say that our perceptions give us correct knowledge about the outer world; however, this answer is seen to be unsatisfactory when one considers illusions.

With the development of modern science, it has become increasingly clear that the physical world, as it might be described by the physicist, and the world as we perceive it are not one and the same thing. Thus, for example, the physicist tells us that material objects consist of countless numbers of atoms that themselves consist of nuclei surrounded by charged particles rotating about them. Between the nucleus and the rotating particles is empty space, so that one might say that much of the volume of an object reduces to such empty space. This description of things is sharply at variance with the way they *appear*. Or, to give another example physicists speak of electromagnetic waves but these are not perceptible. Since the world as it appears to us differs in so many respects from the physical world, it would seem that the world we perceive is the end result of events that occur in the nervous system and in this sense is a construction. It bears a certain kind of similarity to the real, material world, but is also very different from it. Our conception of the real world derived from physics is also a construction, but it is an intellectual and not a sensory construction.

That the perceived world and the world as described by physics that we assume to exist are qualitatively different is clearly evident if one considers perceptions such as color, taste, smell, or pitch. Where the physicist refers to electromagnetic vibrations of varying wavelength, we experience the hues, red, green, blue, and so on; where the physicist

---

*There are various species of dualists depending upon how they view the relationship between the material and the mental. The psychophysical parallelist argues that there are two parallel domains. Whenever a brain event of a certain kind occurs, there is a concomitant mental state or conscious experience of a certain kind. That is all one can say. On the other hand, there are those who, while remaining dualists, believe that the brain events cause the mental events. They believe this because the status of the two domains is not equal: there are brain events that do not yield conscious experience but, it is probably safe to say, there never can be a mental event without an accompanying brain event. Many contemporary psychologists and investigators in the field of perception fall in this category.

refers to certain chemical compounds, we experience tastes or smells; where the physicist refers to objects vibrating at varying frequencies, we experience tones of varying pitch. The point is that hues and tones have no existence other than as contents in the consciousness of living beings. The old philosophical problem of whether a sound exists if a tree falls in the forest with no one to hear it is not a problem at all. The vibrations in the air would exist, but a sound, which, by definition, implies the sensation evoked in an experiencing organism by such vibration, would not. Only if a living being is there to experience it can a sound be said to exist.

These sensations, namely, of hue, pitch, taste, and the like were distinguished by philosophers from those of size, form, and the like presumably because they were purely psychological events or constructions that as such do not exist in the real world. They were called secondary qualities. Primary qualities were those that directly correspond with the objects they represent. Thus a perceived triangle has the same formal properties as the real triangle being perceived, namely, three sides, three angles, and so on. Although the distinction between primary and secondary qualities is, therefore, of great interest, it must not be permitted to obscure the fact that all perception, of primary as well as other qualities, is the end result of events in the brain and, therefore, is at most a symbolic representation of objects in the real world. Whether what is perceived does or does not directly correspond with what is present in the real world is a further question.

If perception results from events in the nervous system of living beings, how do we obtain valid knowledge about the outer world? Clearly we obtain such knowledge from our perceptions. Granting that the perceived world is different from the world that is the object of perception, one can still say that there is a high degree of correspondence. We can determine whether or not a correspondence exists between a particular perception and an object in the world by performing certain kinds of operations. For example, we can measure whether two lines that appear to be the same length are indeed the same length. When we see a red triangle, it is a fair inference to conclude that there is an object of triangular shape present in the world and that it does reflect primarily particular wavelengths of light; when we see something move, it is a fair inference to conclude that an object is changing its position relative to other objects in the world and so forth. Of course, our perceptions, even if often veridical, are only the starting point for establishing knowledge about the world. These perceptions provide the facts that are ultimately dealt with by scientific theories.

But then the further question arises, how do these perceptions come about? How can we have perceptions such as of shape or movement?

Philosophers differed in the extent to which they believed that such perceptions were present at birth (or innate) or were only possible as the result of learning. Since this problem can be answered by study and experiment, psychologists began to study it when their discipline was born. We will consider it further when we briefly summarize the historical background of the field of perception.

Explanation in Perception

The task is to explain how we obtain the relevant information about the real world and how we use this information to construct the perceptual world. But there are differences of opinion concerning the level at which perceptual events should be explained. The diagram in Fig. 1-1 helps to make the issue clear.

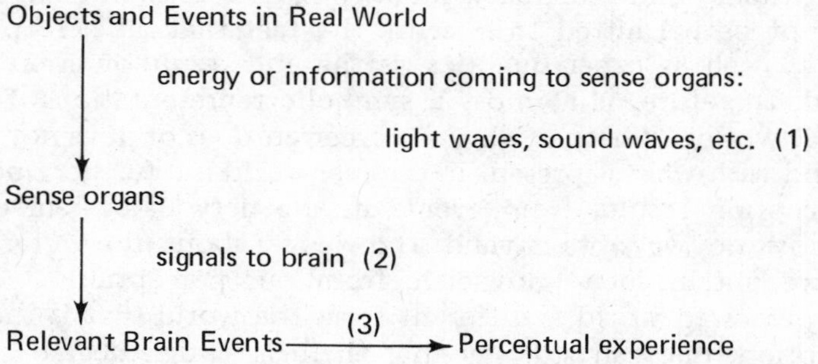

Objects and Events in Real World

> energy or information coming to sense organs:
>
> light waves, sound waves, etc. (1)

Sense organs

> signals to brain (2)

Relevant Brain Events ——— (3) ———> Perceptual experience

Figure 1-1

Some students of perception believe that the task in perception is to isolate the incoming energy or information that gives rise to a particular sensory experience. When Newton discovered that sunlight consists of a mixture of many components (later identified as electromagnetic waves of different frequencies) and that the sensory basis for experiencing a certain hue is that a light wave of a particular frequency reaches the eye, he thereby "explained" color vision. Similarly, it is an explanation of the perception of pitch to say that it is based on sound waves of varying frequency of vibration striking the ear. This kind of explanation is at level 1 in the diagram. One might say that the explanation consists of finding the proximal stimulus, stimulation at the sense organ (for vision, the retinal image), that correlates with a particular perceptual experience (or, in short, finding the stimulus correlate). As is evident throughout this book, we often do not know what this stimulus correlate is. For example, what is the stimulus correlate for a particular perceived shade of gray? The discovery of the stimulus property correlated with a particular shade of gray would constitute an explanation.

A different view is that the isolation of the proximal stimulus correlate is only the first step and in itself is not explanatory. This belief is particularly understandable in areas where the proximal stimulus has been known for some time. In the case of color vision, it no longer seems like an explanation to say that we perceive blue when a wavelength of 470 nanometers strikes the eye. We want to know *why* this is true, where *why* means what happens in the eye or in the brain. Some investigators, therefore, seek to discover the physiological events that occur in the sense organ. In the case of color vision, it is now known that some cells in the retina, the cones, are most sensitive to certain wavelengths of light. When a particular wavelength is reflected to the eye by an object, certain cells respond far more than others do. Thus, the explanation, at this level of analysis, consists in uncovering the particular mechanisms within the sense organ that mediate the perceptual experience under consideration. This would be at level 2 in the diagram.

But there are still others who believe that even this level of explanation is incomplete. Why do we perceive red when one set of cone cells, scattered randomly throughout the central part of the retina, are firing more actively than the remaining cones? These processes alone are insufficient to explain the perception of red. We need to know what happens inside the brain as a result of these processes that leads to the experience "red" (level 3 in the diagram). This is not the only reason why some investigators seek a more central explanation of perceptual events rather than one at the peripheral or sense-organ level. There are many phenomena in perception which, by their very nature, would seem to require a more central type of explanation. Thus, for example, the perception of Fig. 1-2*a* can alternate between that of a cube standing on its rear lower edge as shown in 1-2*c* and that of a cube resting on its base, as in 1-2*b*. Since the image of the reversible figure, as it is called, can remain unchanged on the retina while the perception changes, it is clear that we cannot possibly explain such perception merely on the basis of mechanisms inside the eye.

What precisely do we mean by a "central explanation?" Ultimately we mean an explanation in terms of the relevant events that occur in the brain that give rise to (or cause) the perception in question. But

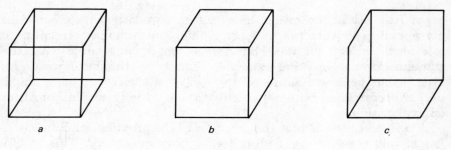

a   *b*   *c*

Figure 1-2

there are certain reasons why it may be wise to postpone attempts at an explanation of perception in terms of neurophysiology. First, our knowledge about the brain is still rather limited, so that it is unlikely that we could deal with the complex problems of perception in such terms at this time. Second, it is often not desirable in science to try to go directly from the phenomenon we wish to explain to the ultimate or deepest level of explanation. An example from the field of physics may be helpful here. Suppose we want to understand why an object falls to earth and accelerates as it descends. The ultimate explanation would be one that accounts for the pull of gravity. We still do not understand what lies behind gravitational attraction, but in the meanwhile we have advanced our understanding of gravitational phenomena on a different level. Thus, for example, we now know that all masses attract one another, that gravity behaves like other forces, that when a force acts on a mass it causes it to accelerate, that the farther away two bodies are from one another the weaker is the force of gravitational attraction, and so forth. In fact, these laws provide a more comprehensive picture of the nature of the facts that ultimately must be explained on a deeper level.

The same logic applies to the problems of perception. Suppose, for example, we wish to explain the basis of the perception of movement. We might try to theorize about how cells in the brain fire whenever we perceive an object moving, but, even if we could do that, it might prove to be an error in strategy. Alternatively, by examining carefully all instances where movement is perceived we may find out what they have in common. Suppose, for example, in all such instances the image of the object moves over the retina. This would then tell us to look for a neurophysiological explanation in which cortical cells are fired by an image that moves across retinal cells. But suppose, as seems to be the case, we often perceive movement when the image of the object is perfectly stationary on the retina? Such a physiological explanation would have been incorrect, at least as a general theory of movement perception.

Instead, by arriving at the general principles that govern all cases of movement perception, we will not only have attained an explanation on a certain level but we will have pointed the way toward the requisite kind of physiological explanation. Therefore, the strategy that is adopted throughout this book is to look for central explanations of perception by attempting to specify the kinds of events in the brain that must be assumed to be occurring. Generally these explanations are not couched in neurophysiological language.

The Phenomenal World

The word *phenomenal* is used synonymously with *perceived*. Although the phenomenal world is thoroughly familiar, we take it so much for granted that we rarely think about some of its characteristics. Since the task in perception is to explain how we come to perceive the world the way we do, the first step is to describe accurately just how it does appear to us.

Consider a puppy frolicking on the lawn. He has a certain three-dimensional shape and size and coloration; at any moment he is located in a certain place at a certain distance and in a given direction from us and he has a certain orientation, such as right side up; he is seen to move or to be stationary; he appears to be solid, that is, he looks like an object we can touch and not penetrate, unlike the appearance of water or the sky. The puppy's coloration is a property of the surface of his body, that is, the surface *has* a color. If he bumps into a small object, we have the impression he has *caused* it to move. All this is given through vision. But we also hear him bark and that sound has a particular pitch, intensity, and timbre, and it too is located in a particular place in space. In fact, it is located in the same place as the visually perceived puppy. We also can feel the puppy with our hands and when we do, we find that he has a certain texture, smooth or rough, depending upon where we touch him; his body is soft but still solid; and whatever we touch also has a certain shape, size, and location, and these qualities will also agree with those experienced by vision. We also can smell him, and the odor will have a unique quality and a certain intensity. The only sensory experiences not covered by this example are taste and those emanating from inside the body, sometimes grouped under the heading of *proprioception*. Proprioception would include the perception or "feeling" of where one part of the body is located with respect to the rest, *kinesthesis* or the feeling of movement of parts of the body, and forces related to the pull of gravity such as the pressure against our feet when we stand. There are also other internal states such as pain.

But it is not the intention here to provide an exhaustive catalogue of all aspects of the phenomenal world but rather to bring out certain general facts about this world. One such very general fact, discussed throughout this book, is that the perceived qualities such as color, size, and the like tend to remain *constant* despite the fact that the proximal stimulus, for example, the retinal image of objects, is continually changing. Thus, the puppy does not seem to change color when he runs under the shadows of a tree nor to change size when he approaches or recedes from us. With the exception of the few objects in the scene that are moving, the rest of the world remains stationary. Although the observer may be moving, thereby causing the image of the entire scene to displace across his retina, the world appears stationary and the objects in it remain constant. In fact, there is an implicit assumption that objects are permanent despite the fact that they may disappear from view from moment to moment, either because another object gets in the way or because we change our own position, turn our head, or close our eyes.

Another general fact is that within each sense modality there are both unique *qualities* perceived (colors, tones, and so on) and varying *intensities*. The qualities can often be arranged in a continuum, in which neighboring points are experienced as being most similar to one another, such as red, orange, yellow, and so forth in color (although red at one end of the spectrum is similar to violet at the other end).

The phenomenal world of objects is three-dimensional with ourselves at the center. In vision, there are limits to the field of view beyond which we cannot see for any given position of the head, but we are rarely aware of this. Instead, we have the impression that objects behind us are very much present so that there is a sense of continuity between that which is strictly visible and that which is not visible. Within this three-dimensional space are distinct segregated objects with definite shapes seen in front of backgrounds. At any single moment one such object, or a part of it, is perceived clearly. This is in the center of the visual field; more remote objects are blurred or unclear. But more often than not we are not very aware of this fact, perhaps because the eyes are in constant motion, and what had been blurred a moment ago is now clear. There is also the fact that at any moment we are attending to only part of the total field. What we are not attending to often has an entirely different status in our consciousness. For example, although we may hear the buzzing of other voices at a cocktail party, only the conversation we are attending to seems to be understood.

This last observation touches on the more general fact that by and large the objects in the world are perceived as familiar and meaningful. Of course, this is not always the case; obviously the very things that are now so familiar to us at one time in our lives were not.

In describing the way the world appears, we have employed what has come to be called the *phenomenological method*. By that is meant the attempt to describe the way things appear without any prejudices, biases, or theories. If we do not do this, if instead we describe things in terms of how we believe they *ought* to appear, taking into account what we think we know about sensory processes, we are in great danger of altering the very facts that it is our task to explain. By analogy, it would be a serious matter if in the field of physics one were to deny that the volume of water expands when it freezes to ice simply because it seems unlikely that volume could change in this way.*

In perception, it might seem unlikely that the world could appear stationary when we ourselves move, since the entire retinal image moves, and so one might be inclined to say, "the world *does* appear to move when we move, but since we know it doesn't move we ignore it." This error of assuming how things ought to appear can lead investigators to commit the further error of finding a suitable method to confirm their expectations. For example, one can isolate an object in the visual scene by covering over everything else with a screen. Or one can train observers to ignore certain aspects of their experience and to attend analytically to particular aspect. Titchener, one of the major figures in psychology at around the turn of the century, explicitly advocated substituting analytical introspection for the naive introspection described previously. (Introspection means the examination of one's experience and, in perception, means noting the perceptual appearance of objects and events.) Titchener argued that descriptions by untrained observers often committed what he called the *stimulus error*. By that he meant that observers erroneously include in their description of how an object appears what they *know* about the object. Thus, if we *know* that an object does not change its size when we move away from it, we erroneously claim that it appears not to change its size. More careful observation, so he thought, would reveal that it does appear to change. But

---

*Phenomenology is also a school of philosophy, and the reader should not confuse this with the phenomenological method employed by psychologists as outlined above. In scientific psychology, description is only the starting point. In order to *explain* perception, we postulate hypothetical mechanisms in the nervous system that themselves are *not* experienced, just as the physicist seeks to explain the observable behavior of matter by postulating hypothetical entities such as atoms that are not directly experienced themselves. It is this step beyond description that phenomenology as a philosophy does not take.

the danger of such methods is that the perceptual experience of the object may be altered in the process of isolating it. Occluding from view objects surrounding the one under study presupposes that these surrounding objects do not affect the perception of the object under study. And although careful, somewhat more analytical, introspection can be valuable and may occasionally be improved by training, here too there is the great danger of distorting the facts of perception in the process. In the example of size perception, Titchener's method would deny the phenomenon that now goes by the name of *size constancy* (see Chapter 2).

It is sometimes difficult to decide whether we are actually perceiving a certain property. For example, do we perceive pictures as three-dimensional or do we perceive them as two-dimensional but know that they represent a three-dimensional scene? What criteria can be used to resolve questions of this kind? The answer is that we must decide on the basis of naive introspection whether an experience is perceptual or not. Perception means the immediate experience of a stimulus object in terms of certain properties. A daffodil is perceived as, that is, it looks yellow, at least in daylight. But seen in dim light at night a daffodil no longer looks yellow although we know it is yellow. By this criterion, a picture of a landscape is *perceived* as three-dimensional in spite of the fact that we know the surface on which it is painted is two-dimensional. Occasionally, there are other useful criteria as, for example, the fact that certain perspective drawings may simultaneously appear to undergo a reversal of depth (see Fig. 1–2). Therefore, if such a reversal occurs, the observer must be perceiving the depth in the picture. But by and large, the ultimate criterion is phenomenal experience. The picture either *looks* three-dimensional or it does not.

This last example illustrates a very general fact about perception, that what we perceive is independent of or autonomous with respect to what we know. Perception follows its own independent laws. Proof of this fact is presented throughout the book. However, such independence does not necessarily imply that the mechanisms that lead to perception may not be similar to those that lead to conclusions in thought.

A Brief Historical Perspective

This is not the place for a thorough history of perception, but some understanding of previous thinking about the problems to be discussed in this book would be helpful.* Needless to say, many different historical contributions have played a role in the development of the field of perception as it exists today: broad philosophical theories, physiological discoveries, psychological findings, and advances in methodology. Only a few of these can be touched on here.

Long before psychology became a separate scientific discipline, philosophers grappled with problems of cognition. To the question "How do we have knowledge about the world?" one school of thought, consisting of many of the great thinkers of the seventeenth and eighteenth centuries, answered "through the senses." The theme underlying the thinking of men such as Hobbes, Locke, Berkeley, Hume, Hartley, and Mill was that knowledge is not only acquired through sensation but that it is acquired *only* through sensation. Thus Hobbes wrote in 1651, "There is no conception in man's mind which hath not at first, totally or by parts, been begotten upon the organs of sense."[4] This means, of course, that all knowledge is derived from prior experience; this school of thought is thus known as empiricism.

The question then arises as to precisely what is provided by the senses. After all, the stimulus reaching the sense organ is quite different from the qualities that we perceive. The retinal image might be described as a two-dimensional mosaic of bright and dim patches of light that ought to give rise to nothing more than a mosaic of corresponding sensations. In fact, if all knowledge is acquired, then perception itself must be learned. How does this learning occur? By association, according to Locke. In his famous *Essay Towards a New Theory of Vision*, George Berkeley in 1709 argued that we cannot directly perceive the third dimension of space because the retinal image is only two-dimensional.[5] Depth perception must, therefore, come about by learning that the world is three-dimensional. How do we learn this? We do so touching objects (and presumably also by walking toward objects); this information is tactual, not visual. More specifically, Berkeley suggested that in viewing an object at a certain distance the eyes converge for that distance. We directly sense the angle at which the eyes are turned, and this sensation thus becomes a sign of a particular distance. We also make use of the relative sharpness of the retinal image (based on the accommodation of the lens) as a sign of distance. These signs (or cues as they later came to be called) suggest specific distances because they have been associated with tactual information about distance. We see here an example of the doctrine of associationism.

*The reader is referred to books by E. G. Boring,[1] and N. Pastore,[2] and a chapter by J. Hochberg[3] for further reading on the history of the field of perception.

This way of looking at perception had a profound effect on all sub-sequent thinkers, and, in fact, it is still very much present in contemporary psychology. The central idea is that visual sensations themselves do not provide much knowledge about the world but that they do provide a basis for arriving at correct interpretations. They are signs or cues to which various associations or images can become attached, supplementing the sensations, although we are not aware that this is happening. Berkeley's notion that it is touch that educates vision has also endured over the centuries, although not all empiricists subscribed to that particular hypothesis. A distinction between sensation and perception is also implicit in Berkeley's thinking, since what we perceive (an object at a distance) is itself something different from the sensations (an image of a certain shape, size, and sharpness and a felt state of the eye muscles.)

In the following century, Helmholtz made great contributions to our knowledge about vision and hearing and also argued forcefully that most of perception is the result of learning.[6] In 1852, the German scientist and philosopher Lotze had suggested that each sensory region, for example each point on the retina, was qualitatively distinct from every other region.[7] We, therefore, are able to know when one region rather than another is being stimulated. But this *local sign* does not itself say anything about the location of the stimulus in the world that produces this image. That is learned. Helmholtz and other subscribed to this thesis and suggested that the learning is based upon movements of the eyes and information from touch concerning where the stimulus is. Thus to bring a retinal image into central vision we must move the eye until the image falls on the fovea. The magnitude and direction of such eye movements inform us of where in the visual field the object is. We learn the meaning of the direction of gaze of the eyes through simultaneous touch experience. Thus the perception of space—and therefore of form—is a matter of learning. According to Helmholtz, what we perceive, for example, a point in a particular place in space, is not the same as the sensation that leads to the perception, for example the unique stimulation of a given locus on the retina. Thus Helmholtz said; "The sensations of the senses are tokens for our consciousness, it being left to our intelligence to learn how to comprehend their meaning."[8]

The realization that the objects of perception remain relatively constant despite variation in the proximal stimulus was another reason for the belief by Helmholtz and others in the distinction between sensation and perception. It seemed self-evident that the sensation must be a direct function of the proximal stimulus. Thus, if the light intensity is high, the sensation must be strong. Therefore, if a black object continues to look black even when it is seen in sunlight, it must be that the

Read

sensation of it is indeed strong and the perception or interpretation of it must be based on taking certain other information into account. We realize that the object is in sunlight and so interpret the strong sensation coming from the object as resulting from the great intensity of light striking it, not the object's own color. According to Helmoholtz, past experience with how changes in overall illumination affect sensation is what makes such interpretation possible: "It is only by experience that we ever could have learned about the laws of illumination, shading, atmospheric haze, geometrical concealment of one body by another, the sizes of men and animals, etc."[9]

Wundt, who is generally credited with founding psychology as an experimental science during the second half of the nineteenth century, further developed the theory that perception is the end result of a process of interpreting our sensations on the basis of past experience.[10] Titchener[11] carried Wundt's psychology to America. The program of psychological inquiry for Wundt and Titchener was to uncover the "elements" of consciousness, the individual sensations. This was to be accomplished by analytical introspection. By that was meant, first, that we can arrive at a description of consciousness only by introspection and, second, that we must be careful to be analytical and report accurately the bare bones of the sensation. We must avoid the tendency to clutter the report with related experiences. Thus, for example, in the case of the black object in sunlight, the sensation to be reported is "intense" or "bright." That the object is interpreted to be black is beside the point when we are trying to describe accurately our sensations. As noted earlier, Titchener cautioned against the stimulus error. To avoid this kind of error, Titchener advocated the use of trained observers, those who knew how to report a sensation itself rather than the object that gave rise to the sensation. It is interesting to note that if one looks at a black object in sunlight through a hole in a cardboard so that only the object is visible (a reduction screen as it is now called), the object may no longer look black but may look very bright or even luminous. This kind of demonstration was taken as proof of the nature of the real sensation.

What is left today of this way of thinking about perception? The Gestalt school of thought criticized the distinction between sensation and interpretation (or perception) so effectively that with few exceptions—one being the transactionist point of view espoused by Adelbert Ames, Jr., and his associates in the 1940's and early 1950's—little has been heard of it since.[12] On the other hand, the belief that perception entails taking into account certain information in addition to the most relevant feature of the proximal stimulus is still widely held. That perception is to a large extent learned or that it develops is considered almost axiomatic by many investigators in the field, in spite of a number of recent findings that establish the presence of various perceptual attributes at the moment of birth or very shortly thereafter. The nature of such learning is still held to be associative.*

This brings us to the other mainstream in the history of the study of perception. Among the philosophers who asked how we attained knowledge about the world were those who felt that the human mind is more than an empty slate or *tabula rasa* that is written upon by experience. Descartes in the seventeenth century was explicit in his belief in two realms, the mental and the material.[14] What characterized mind was rational thought, and, in fact, it was the certainty about the existence of one's own thought that was the starting point in Descartes' philosophy of how knowledge of the world was attained. *Cogito ergo sum.* "I think, therefore I must exist." Among our ideas are those that are innate. For example, Descartes believed that our knowledge about properties such as form, size, and the like is based on certain innately determined ideas. So for Descartes, the mind brings a good deal of its own to bear on the sensations that come to it from the outside world.

This was precisely the point emphasized by Immanual Kant over a century later, by which time British empiricism was a firmly established point of view.[15] Consider the perception of objects as extended in space and having spatial locations with respect to one another. Even if it were proved that much learning enters into our perception of spatial relations, can one say that the very nature of perception as spatial is learned? No, Kant argued, the mind imposes spatiality on sensation. Space is a form of sensory experience that transcends the specific content of this or that momentary scene. Thus the location of things as separate from one another and of all things as outside of ourselves is in the very nature of visual experience and it makes little sense to say that *this* is learned. This is also true with regard to other modes of cognition such as the experience of time. If the mind did not innately work in such a way that events were apprehended as occurring either simultaneously or in succession, we could never learn temporal sequences. Thus, the notions of space and time are given *a priori*, before information that comes to us via the senses.

In the following century Johannes Müller[16] was able to provide some support for Kant's views when he developed the notion of the specific energies of the senses. It had previously been discovered that there were

---

*Not mentioned among the more recent thinkers in the empiricist tradition is D. O. Hebb who sought to develop a physiological theory to explain how our perception of the world could be based upon past experience.[13]

different nerves for sensation (ascending into the central nervous system) and for motor action (descending from the central nervous system). It was also known that there is a basis in the brain for the distinctive qualities of each sense modality, that is, that there is something unique about the neural pathways that mediate each type of sensory experience. Müller developed this idea into a formal doctrine. To be specific, the reason why experiences such as color and sound are so different is not that light energy and sound waves are different (although of course they are), and not even that the receptors in the eye and in the inner ear are specialized to respond to light and mechanical vibrations (although they are), but rather because the optic nerve is specific to vision and, when stimulated, produces the experience of color and light. The auditory nerve is specific to sound and, when stimulated, results in the experience of sound. Proof that this is true is given by the fact that mechanical stimulation of the eye, as by pressing against it with a finger, produces the experience of light. In the same way, a blow to the ear produces the sensation of sound, a "ringing" of the ears. We know that direct electrical stimulation of sensory nerves will elicit an experience typical for each nerve. Müller considered the possibility that the reason for these differences in sensation was not that the nature of the nerves for each sense differ ("specific energy"), but that all nerves work in the same way; what is crucial is where they terminate in the brain. He favored the specific energy idea (the word *energy* was perhaps unfortunate since Müller could equally well have used the word *quality*), but we now know that it is the terminal or projection area in the cortex that determines which sensory quality will be experienced.*

But whatever the precise physiological explanation, the unique character of each sense is a function of the way the brain works. This simple fact has important philosophical implications. It brings out very dramatically that the phenomenal world is a construction. We perceive on the basis of brain functioning and certainly not—as some of the early Greeks had thought—because objects in the world give off images of themselves that are projected directly to the senses and thus to the mind. Furthermore, it seems clear that we do not learn to have these distinctive sensory qualities. If vision is spatial and audition is temporal, this is innately determined by the nature of the sense organs and the neural pathways from these to the brain.

---

*To the unique sensations of each modality can now be added the unique sensations *within* a modality. Thus, for example, we now know that the nerve fibers associated with particular retinal cone cells mediate the experience of a specific hue. This was Helmholtz' extension of Müller's doctrine.

Hering,[17] who was a contemporary of Helmholtz, leaned toward explanation of many perceptual phenomena in terms of the inherited structure and functioning of the nervous system. Hering is well known for a particular theory of color vision, but when it comes to color vision no one has ever argued in favor of learning. However, Hering sought to explain a number of phenomena concerning color in terms of physiological mechanisms, whereas Helmholtz argued for an explanation in terms of past experience. Helmholtz tried to explain contrast (i.e., a medium gray looks darker surrounded by white and lighter surrounded by black) as an outcome of errors in judgment (as when a medium-sized man looks small standing next to tall men). Hering, however, thought in terms of the interaction between adjacent regions of the retina: the stimulus led to a certain chemical reaction in its own region but led to the opposite reaction in the adjacent regions. Today this "opposite reaction" would be called lateral inhibition. Again, in the case of the constancy of color of objects under varying illumination, where Helmholtz thought in terms of correcting for or taking into account the effects of illumination on the appearance of things based on past experience, Hering thought in terms of mechanisms such as the automatic change in the size of the opening of the pupil, adaptation of the retina to changes in light intensity, contrast effects, and the like.*

Hering also believed that the location of objects in the field need not to be learned because each retinal point (or the local sign associated with it) innately signified a particular location, either right or left or up or down with respect to vertical-horizontal coordinates that intersect at the center of the eye. However, he was aware that this location is a purely relative one, i.e., relative to the point in the field we are looking at. It says nothing about where a point will appear to be with reference to the self. This distinction has often been misunderstood so that certain experimental refutations of Hering's theory were directed at a theory that he never advanced. Since the eyes can change their positions with respect to the head, the determination of where objects will appear to be located in relation to the self is a further problem. (See the distinction drawn between field location and radial direction in Chapter 4.) Hering also believed that each retinal point innately signified a particular depth value.

There can be little doubt that Hering was an important precursor of Gestalt psychology, promulgated by Max Wertheimer, Wolfgang Köhler,

---

*However, Hering did suggest one possible effect of past experience, namely, that our memory of the color of a familiar object may serve to offset effects of very different conditions of illumination.

and Kurk Koffka, the founders of this school of thought.[18]   There were two aspects to the thrust of the Gestalt movement. The negative aspect was a devastating critique of the point of view advocated by Helmholtz, Wundt, and Titchener. First, the Gestalt founders criticized the distinction between sensation and perception. More often than not, what had been considered to be a sensation was not consciously experienced, and to speak of an unconscious or unnoticed sensation seemed like a contradiction in terms. For, example, they pointed out that it is not true that a black object in strong light is sensed as "intense" or "bright or white. Second, it is not true to say that we merely interpret our sensations in this or that way, but that the true sensory experience is a direct function of the proximal stimulus. The black object in sunlight looks black; it is not merely that we know it is black. The Gestaltists argued that the belief that perception must accord with the local proximal stimulus was a bias. They referred to this belief as the constancy hypothesis (not to be confused with the tendency toward constancy in object perception). The same proximal stimulus may lead to very different percepts depending upon other factors, and, conversely, different proximal stimuli can lead to the same percept. This fact is illustrated repeatedly in subsequent chapters. The central point made by the Gestaltists is that stimuli do not remain insulated from one another, going their own way until each local stimulus produces a separate sensation, so that sensory consciousness represents the sum of all the separate sensations. Rather stimuli interact. The relationship between them is what matters and these relationships produce perceptual effects that are not merely the sum of all the component parts. Third, we are unaware of making an inference, and to speak of an unconscious inference is a contradiction in terms by any reasonable definition of what inference means. It was also found that infants and animals perceived in terms of constancy (the black object is perceived as black even in sunlight) rather than in terms of the proximal stimulus, and it seemed improbable that they would be capable of making intellectual judgments of the kind implied. In fact, evidence that infants tend to perceive in this way also contradicted the assumption that past experience played an important role.

The positive aspect of the Gestalt thrust was the substitution of an entirely different hypothesis about the basis of our perceptions. These are not determined merely by the proximal stimulus, nor by inferences about what is producing the proximal stimulus, but rather by certain organizing events in the brain. A good example is the one that played a central role in Wertheimer's paper of 1912, which is credited with launching the Gestalt movement.[19] Wertheimer was examining a phenomenon known as apparent or stroboscopic movement in which perfectly stationary objects appear to be moving back and forth if they are flashed alternately at a certain rate. Thus, if first line *a* in Fig. 1-3 appears, and then disappears, followed a fraction of a second later by line *b*, which then also disappears and so on, one perceives a line moving back and forth. This effect is essentially the one that underlies our experience of movement in moving pictures. Now the point is that nothing is moving on the retina, so one can hardly say that the proximal stimulus is such as to lead to the experience of movement. And to say that movement is inferred but is not really perceived in this case is a distortion of the facts. Phenomenally one can hardly distinguish strobo-scopically generated movement perception from real movement percep-tion. Furthermore, it became known that various animal species seemed to perceive movement under these conditions. Also there was the fact that movement is perceived only when the rate of alternation and other conditions such as brightness and the distance between lines *a* and *b* have certain values. The importance of having just the right rate of alternation, separation, and the like suggested a direct physiological explanation. Wertheimer therefore speculated that the reason we per-ceive movement under such conditions is that some further event is occurring in the brain *between* the places where lines *a* and *b* are pro-jected to the visual cortex, something like a short circuit. It is this central event acting *upon* the incoming stimulation that is crucial for perception. Since this represents the spontaneous functioning of the brain, learning is not necessary. By and large, the Gestalt psychologists were nativists. Rather than merely referring to something mysteriously innate, they were suggesting the mechanisms that gave rise to percep-tions. However, they also acknowledged that past experience did have certain effects on perception.

a   b

Figure 1-3

One modern point of view does not fit neatly into either tradition (the empiricist or the nativist) but extracts certain features from each. The thesis developed by James J. Gibson is that for every percept there is some attribute of the proximal stimulus that can be said to be its cause, correlate, or determinant.[20] However the attribute in question is often not an absolute feature of the stimulus such as intensity, size, or the like but rather a more subtle, higher-order feature involving rela-tionships, gradients, and the like. This higher-order attribute of the proximal stimulus is uniquely related to a particular experience of the outer world. Examples are given in Chapter 3.

Gibson shares with the Gestaltists the belief that perception is a direct experience rather than an interpretation based on sensation, that past experience is not always necessary, and that certain relationships within the proximal stimulus rather than absolute properties determine perception. But he disagrees with the Gestalt view that perception must be explained by the events in the brain initiated by these stimulus relationships (level 3 in Fig. 1-1).   Gibson believes that it is a sufficient explanation to uncover the relevant feature of the stimulus, and for this reason this approach has been called a psychophysical theory (level 1 in Fig. 1-1).

Method in the Study of Perception

We wish to explain why things look as they do. This means that the starting point, the facts to be accounted for, are the various aspects of the phenomenal world. It has already been pointed out that to establish these facts calls for the phenomenological method. We first have to be clear about what we want to explain. Now that we have surveyed the history of perception, it should be evident how a particular theoretical outlook led investigators such as Titchener to deny various facts about spontaneous perception and to substitute other facts more in keeping with that outlook. This is to be avoided.

But is it a legitimate scientific enterprise to seek to explain subjective experience? The behaviorist point of view that has so dominated psychology during most of the present century has not been mentioned in the brief history of the field. It was not included because Behaviorists had little to say about perception, preferring instead to investigate the field of learning. But they did argue that whatever the problem under study, only that which is observable is a legitimate subject matter for science. Behavior is observable, but subjective experience is not.[21]

Yet it seems manifestly absurd that we should not think that our task is to study subjective experience. In fact, any other way of viewing the subject matter of perception would seem to be an obvious distortion. The fact that in all other scientific endeavors the subject matter consists of something externally observable may well be true. But it does not follow from this that the field of perception has to adapt itself to that prescription. Some psychologists have satisfied themselves on this score by suggesting that we can legitimately study the "perceptual response," since a response is supposedly something observable. However, it is not clear what that term is supposed to mean because perception refers to the sensory or input side of events rather than the response or output side. Some take it to mean a verbal report of what we are experiencing. Of course, we usually find out about what an observer is seeing by asking him to tell us about it. But does that mean that what we are studying is his verbal report? If one asks whether the moon on the horizon looks larger than when it is higher in the sky, and an observer tells us it does, then are we interested in his *statement* or are we interested in what we believe to be his subjective *experience* of size? Although we make use of verbalizations, we do so only to find out about sensory experience. Admittedly, the discipline of perception hinges on the assumption that the experience of others is like our own. But our own sensory experience is certainly directly available to us. It seems plausible to assume that the sensory experience of others is like our own.

Science always starts with publicly observable events, which means that observations are confirmable. Subjective experience per se is not publicly observable. No one can look at anyone else's experience. Nowhere else in the history of science have we encountered this problem. But then it seems very strange to deny a subject matter in order to conform with the pre-existing methodology of science. Methodology should be the servant of science not its master.

Aside from this very basic question of what we are trying to explain in perception, actual research in this field proceeds in a perfectly objective way. We usually start with a fact that most, if not all, observers agree upon, for example, an illusion. We may then introduce some change in the situation and try to find out what effect this has on perception. Generally, we measure this by requiring the observer to equate his impression of one object with another. Thus to the extent that we are striving to explain *general* facts of perception—rather than idiosyncratic or ephemeral subjective effects—we have a discipline that is as objective in terms of its methodology as any other.

When, in an experiment, we try to obtain a fairly precise indication of how something looks to an observer by having him equate it (often called the standard) with another object (called the comparison or variable object), various methods can be used. For example, if we want to find out how large a distant object appears, we can present the observer with a nearby object whose size can be varied. He then equates its size with the distant object. In investigating absolute sensory thresholds (the point below which a stimulus is too weak or small to be experienced at all) and relative thresholds (the minimum difference between two stimuli required before a difference can be detected), various methods were evolved.

We have omitted from our historical outline a discussion of the work of Weber and Fechner in the nineteenth century on the problem of the correspondence between the magnitude of sensation and the magnitude of physical stimulation, (the problem referred to as psychophysics), since it was not relevant to the issues under discussion.[22] In studying this problem, various methods of ascertaining sensory thresholds were perfected, the so-called psychophysical methods. These methods, or variations of them, are employed in many experiments in perception. They are concerned with the specific manner by which the observer makes his judgments: does the observer vary the comparison object or does the experimenter; is the comparison object varied continuously or in discrete steps, or are comparison objects presented in random order calling for "greater than" or "less than" responses in each case?*

Needless to say, there are some problems in perception that cannot be studied simply by comparing one object with another. For example, we might want to know what is perceived when a reversible pattern such as that shown in Fig. 1–2a is presented. In that case, we simply ask the observer what he sees. Of course, we must make certain that we know what his response means. Obviously, the response "cube" would not tell us enough and in this case we would have to question him further. Various other techniques that have been devised are encountered in subsequent chapters.

A particular problem arises in the study of perception in animals or human infants since they cannot talk or understand instructions. The usual procedure here is to require the animal to learn to discriminate one object from another. If such learning is possible, it implies that the difference between the objects is perceived. When and if the discrimination is learned, the conditions of presentation of one of the objects can be changed. For example, after the animal learns to run to a large circle rather than a small one, the large circle is now placed much farther away than the small one. Since the retinal image of the larger circle may now be smaller than that of the small circle, evidence that it is still preferred would indicate the presence of constancy of size for that species. Other techniques have been employed with animals and human infants, which make use of the fact that certain objects are desirable to them and others are aversive.

---

*For a thorough discussion of these psychophysical methods, the reader is referred to Engen.[23]

Sensory Processes, Cognitive Processes, and Perception

Although it is difficult—if not unwise—to draw a sharp line separating one field of inquiry from another, investigators who consider themselves to be specialists in perception have staked out certain problem areas that are more or less distinguishable from those of neighboring disciplines. The field of perception can be said to lie between the field of sensory processes on one side and of cognitive processes on the other. Investigators of sensory processes—and this would, of course, include vision as well as other sense modalities—typically are concerned with the psychophysical relationship between stimulation and sensation and with the physiological mechanisms that mediate sensation. Thus they search for the physical and physiological correlates of sensory experience but tend to focus on less complex aspects of sensation than investigators in perception. For example, they seek the basis of color vision in retinal cone cells that respond differentially to different wavelengths of light, or they seek to explain a phenomenon such as contrast on the basis of the inhibition of nerve cell activity by other neighboring nerve cell activity.

Although the distinction between sensation and perception has been effectively criticized, this criticism applies primarily to cases where the issue is how *an object* is apprehended. The question has been: Do we sense it in accord with the proximal stimulus and go on to interpret it on the basis of other information? But suppose we wish to study how a quality such as color is apprehended. We could study this question even without an object being present as, for example, the color of the sky. Therefore, in such cases there need not be any objection to the use of the word *sensation* and, in fact, it may be useful in distinguishing this field of inquiry from that which is more concerned with apprehending objects.

On the other "side," investigators of cognitive processes are concerned with problems that begin where perception ends, that is, they begin with the perceived object as given. These investigators are interested in processes such as recognition, recall, association, attention, abstraction, concept formation, understanding and meaningful learning, problem solving, and thinking.

In perception, the interest is in the representation of the world of objects and events that constitute our physical environment. Thus the concern is with the perceived shape, size, distance, direction, orientation, and state of rest or movement of objects. The determinant of each of these aspects of perception is sought and, invariably, the determinants prove to be difficult to isolate, as is made clear in ensuing chapters.

References

1. Boring, E. G. *Sensation and Perception in the History of Psychology.* Appleton-Century-Crofts, 1942.
2. Pastore, N. *Selective History of Theories of Visual Perception: 1650–1950.* Oxford University Press, 1971.
3. Hochberg, J. Nativism and empiricism in perception. Chap. 5 in *Psychology in the Making.* Edit. by L. Postman, Alfred A. Knopf, Inc., 1962.
4. Hobbes, T. *Leviathan.* Basil Blackwell, 1957 (originally published in 1651).
5. Berkeley, G. *An Essay Towards a New Theory of Vision*, E. P. Dutton & Co., Inc., 1910. First published in 1709.
6. Helmholtz, H. von. *Treatise on Physiological Optics.* Vol. III (Trans. from the 3rd German ed., edit. by J. P. C. Southall), Dover Publications, Inc., 1962. First pub. in the Handbuch der psysiologischen Optik. Voss, 1867.
7. Lotze, H. *Outlines of Psychology.* Trans. and edit. from the 3rd German ed. by G. T. Ladd. Ginn and Company, 1886.
8. Helmholtz, op. cit., p. 533.
9. Helmholtz, op. cit., p. 292.
10. Wundt, W. *Outlines of Psychology* (4th German ed.). Trans. by C. H. Judd, Stechert, 1907; *Grundzüge der physiologischen Psychologie*, 6th ed., III, W. Engelmann, 1911, pp. 530–736, especially 702–736.
11. Titchener, E. B. *A textbook of Psychology.* Macmillan Publishing Co., Inc., 1926.
12. Ames, A., Jr., Visual perception and the rotating trapezoidal window. *Psychological Monographs*, 1951, **65,** whole No. 324; See also W. H. Ittelson. *The Ames Demonstrations in Perception*, Princeton University Press, 1952.
13. Hebb, D. O. *The Organization of Behavior.* John Wiley & Sons, Inc., 1949.
14. Descartes, R. See F. Alquié. *Oeuvres Philosophiques de Descartes*, Vol. I (1618–1637), Garnier, 1963.
15. Kant, I. *Critique of Pure Reason*, Macmillan, 1929 (originally published in 1790).

16. Müller, J. Handbuch der Psysiologie des Menschen für Vorlesungen, II, Bk. 5, especially introduction section, J. Hölscher, 1838. Trans. from the German by W. Baly. *Elements of Physiology.* Vol. II, pp. 276–393, Lea and Blanchard, 1843.

17. Hering, E. Grundzüge der Lehre vom Lichtsinne. In Handbuch der gesampten Augenheilkunde, ed. Graefe-Saemisch, J. Springer, 1920. Trans. by L. Hurvich and D. Jameson. *Outlines of a Theory of the Light Sense,* Harvard University Press, 1964.

18. See for example, Köhler, W. *Gestalt Psychology.* Liveright Publishing Corp., 1929; K. Koffka. *Principles of Gestalt Psychology.* Harcourt Brace Jovanovich, Inc., 1935.

19. Wertheimer, M. Experimentelle Studien über das sehen von Bewegung. *Zeitschift für Psychologie,* 1912, **61,** 161–265.

20. Gibson, J. J. *The Perception of the Visual World.* Houghton Mifflin Company, 1950; *The Senses Considered As Perceptual Systems.* Houghton Mifflin Company, 1966.

21. See for example, J. B. Watson. *Behaviorism.* University of Chicago Press, 1930; C. L. Hull. *Principles of Behavior: An Introduction to Behavior Theory.* Appleton-Century-Crofts, 1943.

22. Fechner, G. T. *Elemente der Psychophysik.* Breitkopf und Hartel, 1860.

23. Engen, T. Psychophysics, Chap. 2 in *Woodworth & Schlosberg's Experimental Psychology, Vol. I: Sensation and Perception,* edit. by J. W. Kling, L. Riggs, et al. Holt, Rinehart & Winston, Inc., 1972.

chapter 2

THE PERCEPTION OF SIZE

An intelligent person who knew nothing about experimental work in psychology might well be puzzled to learn that our ability to perceive the size of objects is considered to be a problem by psychologists. After all, everyone knows that the eye works very much the same way a camera does. A picture taken by a camera records size more or less accurately, at least for objects that all lie at about the same distance from the camera. To be sure, objects that are far away from the camera appear small in the picture but such objects also look small to the human eye, don't they? That a distant object would "look" small to both camera and eye has something to do with optics; the picture or image focused on the retina at the back of the eye or on the film at the back of the camera would be smaller the farther away an object is. Therefore, size perception would seem to correspond perfectly with the size of the image cast upon the retina and that in turn can be explained in terms of optics and the structure of the eye. Why then should size perception pose a problem?

There actually are two problems. The first is that objects at a distance simply do *not* look as small as they ought to on the basis of the size of the image they cast upon the retina. In fact objects at a distance often appear to be the same size as when they are nearby. This is the problem of size constancy, which we discuss throughout most of this chapter. The second problem is a little more difficult to understand. An object at a specific distance yields an image on the retina of a specific size. In turn, that image, gives rise to a perception of a specific size. An image 1 millimeter square might yield an impression of an object the size of a house. The problem is, what is the relationship between the size of the image and the size of the object perceived? There has been essentially no discussion of this problem in the psychological literature. We return to it toward the end of the chapter.

27

A Brief Digression into Optics

In order to clearly understand the problem of size constancy, it is first necessary to understand how distance affects the size of the image focused on the retina. But before this can be understood, it is necessary to consider how the lens of the eye—or for that matter, any lens—creates an image.* The lens refracts or bends the incoming rays of light so that all light rays emanating from a given point A, which get through the pupillary opening of the eye are brought to a focus at one point on the retina, a. At least this is the case when the lens assumes the appropriate shape (or accommodates) for the distance of that point (see Fig. 2-1). The same will be true for any other point B, as shown in Fig. 2-2.

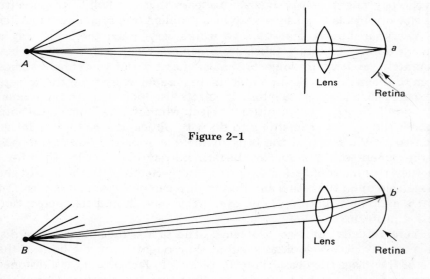

Figure 2-1

Figure 2-2

If we now think of points A and B, as the end points of an object A–B, then the size of the retinal image cast by A–B is ab (Fig. 2-3). The farther apart points A and B are—that is, the bigger object A–B is—the farther apart image points a and b will be. The reason for this is that the farther apart points A and B are, the greater is the difference in the

---

*The cornea of the eye cooperates with the lens in refracting incoming light to form an image on the retina. But it will simplify the discussion to refer only to the lens.

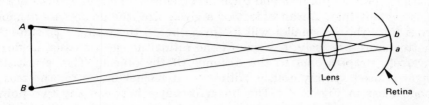

Figure 2-3

direction of the rays of light emanating from each of these points. It is the direction of the rays of light that affects the direction in which the lens will cause the rays to be deflected. Thus, for example, if point *B* were located as shown in Fig. 2-4, then point *b* would be imaged further from point *a* than is depicted in Fig. 2-3.

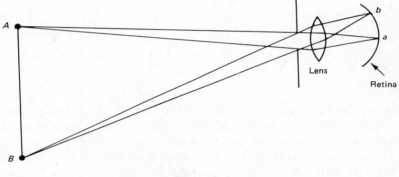

Figure 2-4

This now brings us to the effect of distance on the size of the image. If *A-B* as shown in Fig. 2-3 were to be moved much farther away, the situation shown in Fig. 2-5 would prevail. The difference in the direction of rays from points *A* and *B* would be less than it was before (Fig.

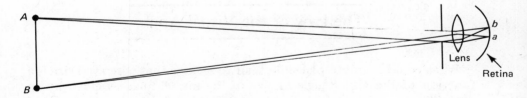

Figure 2-5

2-3). Therefore points *a* and *b* would be closer together. Consequently it is evident that, for an object of a given size, the greater its distance from the eye, the smaller will its image be on the retina. To state the matter more precisely, the size of the retinal image (or visual angle) is inversely proportional to the distance of the object. The term *visual angle* is used synonymously with size of retinal image for the reason made clear in Fig. 2-6. The linear distance between any two points measured along the retina, such as *a* and *b*, or *c* and *d* can also be considered as an angular separation, α or β.

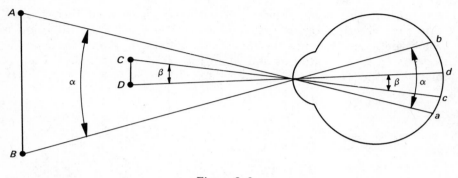

Figure 2-6

The explanation about the size of the retinal image can perhaps be stated even more simply and without any reference to a lens. Light travels in straight lines. If we imagine the pupil of the eye to be as small as a pinhole opening, then we can assume that only one ray of light enters the eye from any point. The angle formed at the eye by the rays from the ends of an object will then be greater for large objects than for small ones at the same distance (compare Fig. 2-3 and 2-4) and it will be greater for an object nearby than for the same object far away (compare Figs. 2-3 and 2-5).

The Law of the Visual Angle

What could be more plausible than to assume that perceived size is a function of the visual angle or size of the retinal image yielded by an object? As a matter of fact, if we restrict the analysis to objects all of which lie in a plane perpendicular to the observer's line of sight, then this assumption is essentially correct. The larger the object drawn on the blackboard, the larger will be its retinal image for a student sitting facing the blackboard, and, of course, the larger it will appear. What interferes with this state of affairs, however, is distance, since when differences in distance exist, it is no longer necessarily true that the larger object will yield the larger retinal image. If the larger object is far enough away it may well yield the smaller image as shown in Fig. 2-7.

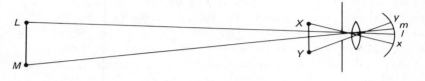

Figure 2-7

At this point, many readers may say, "Well the farther away an object is the smaller it *does* appear. Everyone knows that a person seen at a very great distance looks tiny. Therefore, it may be correct to say that perceived size is a function of visual angle." In fact, it is said that Euclid stated this as a law of size perception, the law of the visual angle. It implies that the perceived size of objects varies in direct proportion to the size of the retinal image.

As is brought out in later discussion, there is much truth in this assertion. Objects at a great distance often do look small. Nevertheless this law is, at least in certain important respects, false. The best way to illustrate its falsity is to examine the way objects appear in the immediate environment. Does a book seen across your study appear only one fifth or one tenth the size of a book lying nearby on your desk? Obviously not, although it may well be the case that the image it subtends is one fifth or one tenth the size of the nearby book because it is five or ten times as far away. Or, to take another example, hold your right hand fairly near on the right side of your head and your left hand as far away as you can stretch it sideways to your left. Ask yourself whether your two hands appear different in size. Most people would say "no" despite the appreciable difference in the size of the visual angle of the two hands in this situation. These are examples of size constancy.

Many experiments have been performed in the laboratory in which the observer is required to compare the size of objects at different distances. Typically the procedure is as follows. One object, such as a triangle, is considered the standard. It may be placed nearby. Another triangle is placed at a much greater distance, and is considered the variable, because its size can be either decreased or increased. (By using an object such as a triangle—which of course can be any size—this type of experiment gets around the difficulty that the size of many familiar objects is known.) The observer then adjusts the size of the distant triangle (or instructs the experimenter to do so) until it appears to him to be the same size as the nearby one. The size of the variable triangle selected by the observer is then recorded by the experimenter. Many such settings are made, half of which begin with the triangle being much too large (descending trials) and half of which begin with the triangle being much too small (ascending trials). It is also desirable to include a condition in which the standard object is placed at the greater distance and the variable one is placed nearby. The average of all these settings for a given individual and, in turn, of many individuals, is presumed to be a good index of the perceived size of the distant object—or at least of the perceived size of the two objects in relation to one another. By repeating this procedure for various distances, a curve may be plotted that characterizes size perception at various distances. As can be seen in the typical result shown in Fig. 2-8, apparent size does not diminish very much with distance. It remains more or less constant.

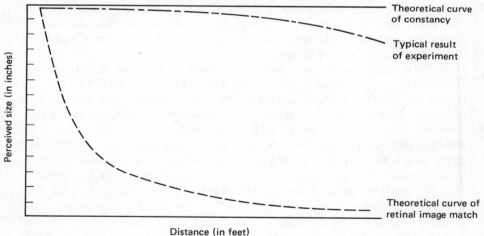

Figure 2-8

The Taking into Account of Distance

The traditional explanation of size constancy, which the author believes to be essentially correct, is that the perceptual system assesses size not merely on the basis of visual angle but on information concerning the distance of the object as well. By itself, visual angle is, a completely ambiguous indicator of the size of an object as is made clear in Fig. 2-9. There it is shown that a specific visual angle can result from objects of varying sizes at varying distances (*a*,*b*,*c*,*d*). Therefore, if size is to be perceived veridically, information concerning distance is also needed. If, for example, it is registered in some way that the object is at distance *Y*, then the visual angle must result from an object the size of *C*.

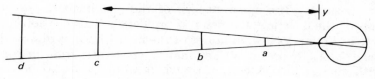

Figure 2-9

It is convenient to express this relationship as an equation, namely, Perceived Size = Visual Angle × Distance. All that this equation says is that the size perceived is a function of *both* the size of the retinal image (or visual angle) *and* the registered distance of the object. Thus, for example, if an object subtends a visual angle of 4 degrees when it is 10 feet away, it will subtend an angle of 2 degrees when it is 20 feet away. Multiplying the visual angle by the distance, we get 4 × 10 or 40 in the first case and 2 × 20 or 40 in the second case. In other words, the decrease in visual angle as the object recedes from the observer is exactly compensated for by the increase in registered distance. Therefore, if the perceptual system takes distance into account and the information concerning distance is accurate, the outcome would be constancy of size.

Emmert's Law

A corollary that follows from the equation given previously is as follows: if the visual angle were to remain constant instead of changing as an object is seen at varying distances, then the further away the object, the larger it will appear. This is illustrated in Fig. 2-9 where *a*, *b*, *c*, and *d* all subtend the same visual angle. Given information concerning distance, however, *d* would be seen as larger than *c*, *c* larger than *b*, and so on, which, in this case is veridical. It follows from the equation because the entry for visual angle remains constant while the entry for distance increases. Therefore the product of visual angle times distance increases with an increase of distance.

A convenient illustration of this corollary is to form an afterimage by fixating a sharply contrasting object for a few seconds (for example a small cutout placed in front of a light bulb). An impression of the object fixated will persist for a short while thereafter because of certain physiological changes in the specific area of the retina stimulated. The afterimage will naturally appear to be located on whatever surface the observer fixates. Clearly the size of the retinal region producing it will remain constant. The apparent size of the afterimage is, however, a function of the distance at which it is projected. This relationship is referred to as Emmert's law, in honor of the man who first observed it.[1]

Emmert's law expresses a fact that refers to *variation* in perceived size with change in distance. As such it would seem to be the very opposite of the typical situation in daily life where change in distance is accompanied by *constancy* of perceived size. Yet Emmert's law is an expression of the very same principle that leads to constancy, namely the taking-into-account of distance. If the perceptual system works like a computer and effectively multiplies the visual angle by the distance of the object in arriving at perceived size, then if visual angle decreases as distance increases, the product may remain constant (size constancy); if visual angle remains constant as distance increases, the product will increase (Emmert's law).

Physical Distance, Perceived Distance, and Registered Distance

The question now arises as to how to interpret the term *distance* in this equation. Obviously it cannot refer to the physical distance of the object. It must be some representation of the distance inside the organism that is crucial. The traditional assumption about this is that it is *perceived* distance that is taken into account by the perceptual system. This is often true, but there are certain reasons for suggesting a somewhat different answer.

In the next chapter we discuss the various kinds of information that permit us to perceive the distance of an object—the cues to distance and depth. This is the kind of information that must be taken into account in the perception of size. Thus, for example, the impression that a man is at a specific distance may be based upon cues such as accommodation of the lens, convergence of the eyes, binocular disparity, and perspective. Presumably, the greater the distance signified by cues such as these, the higher is the value of d (distance) taken into account by the perceptual system. Therefore, it should be possible to perform an experiment in which information about distance is varied and the effect on perceived size observed.

A simple way to vary distance information is to change the angle of convergence of the eyes. This can be achieved by means of a mirror stereoscope, as shown in Fig. 3-21 of Chapter 3. When the angle of the two mirrors is altered, the observer must change the angle of convergence of his eyes in order to continue seeing a single (fused) object derived from images to the two eyes. Since the physical distance of the object is unchanged, there is no change necessitated in accommodation of the lens. Thus the only change is in convergence. This procedure has been used many times by psychologists to study the effectiveness of convergence as a cue to distance. The question has been, when convergence is decreased (eyes more nearly parallel), is the impression of distance of the fused object increased and vice versa? By and large, the answer has been negative.[2] Observers are unable to say with any certainty or accuracy whether the perceived object appears farther or nearer as a function of the angle of convergence of their eyes. However, the observers do have a spontaneous impression of a change of size of the object. When convergence is decreased, as would occur naturally if viewing distance were increased, most observers experience the object as increasing in size, and, when convergence is increased, as would occur naturally if viewing distance were decreased, they experience it as decreasing in size. This is precisely what one would predict from Emmert's law because there is no change in the size of the retinal image. Therefore, one must conclude that the information about distance is "getting through," is registered centrally in the brain, despite the fact that the observer is unaware that this is happening.

It is not clear why this information does not lead directly to correct impressions of difference in perceived distance. A possible explanation is that the effect on size of changing convergence, a particular kind of distance information, is immediate. Therefore, with convergence decreased, apparent size is immediately increased. But size change is itself a cue to distance. Viewing this phenomenally larger object, the observer is now confused about distance. When a thing gets larger it usually is because it is moving nearer to the observer.*   Thus on this basis he may be inclined to say "nearer;" on the basis of the sense of distance derived from convergence per se, the observer would be inclined to say "further." Perhaps it is these conflicting tendencies that result in the ambiguous judgments.   The very same problem arises in connection with the moon illusion (see p. 39).

Another way of looking at the matter is to say that what is taken into account by the perceptual system in evaluating visual angle is not *perceived* distance, but registered information about distance, whether or not that information leads to awareness of the actual distance of the object.   This fact may explain the apparent failure of one experiment designed to confirm the proposition that perceived size is a function of taking distance into account.   In this experiment, the investigator sought to test the proposition by requiring observers to compare *both the size and the distance* of the standard and variable objects.   It was found that the judgments about distance were inaccurate whereas judgments about size were fairly accurate.   In general, there was little correlation between judged size and judged distance.[3]   Data of this kind have convinced many psychologists that perceived size is *not* a function of taking distance into account (or that the size-distance invariance hypothesis, which this relationship has been called in recent years, is incorrect).   The author believes that such a conclusion is unwarranted.   Judgments about distance may be inaccurate either because we are not accustomed to making distance judgments, because perceived size enters in secondarily as a determinant of distance, and leads to confusion about distance as in the experiment just described on convergence, or because the information about distance may not be represented in consciousness. Nevertheless, perceived size may be determined by cues to distance that are centrally registered in the nervous system.

*The careful reader may be puzzled by this statement. If in daily life an object approaches us, and if size constancy obtains, it should continue to appear the same size.   However as is brought out shortly, we also have impressions of size change of a certain kind associated with changes in visual angle.   Thus when an object approaches us we simultaneously experience it as remaining constant in size and also as expanding in size in the sense that it fills an increasingly greater extent of our visual field.   Prior experiences of this latter kind may lead the subject in the experiment under discussion to infer that the increase in apparent size of the fused object results from its coming closer to him.

Size Perception in the Absence
of Distance Information

If visual angle is an ambiguous indicator of objective size, the interesting question arises, what size will be perceived if all information concerning distance is eliminated? Some investigators have sought to accomplish this by using a reduction screen. The observer views a distant object through an aperture in a large screen placed directly in front of him. If all he can see is the object, he is deprived of certain information concerning its distance, such as perspective, the location of the object on the ground plane, interposition of other objects, and so on. However, certain cues are still present, such as accommodation and convergence, and parallax, if the observer is free to move his head.

The correct method for eliminating all cues to distance or rendering them ambiguous is to make the object luminous and present it in a totally dark room. The observer must view the object monocularly through a pinhole, with his head held stationary. This procedure deprives the observer of unambiguous information from accommodation and parallax, eliminates pictorial cues, and, of course, binocular cues (see p. 81). An object perceived under these conditions is indeterminate in size, precisely as we should predict, since the only information available is visual angle. In other words, the object does not appear to have a unique objective size. The observer has no basis for deciding whether it is 1 inch, 1 foot, or 1 yard in size. The question can now be asked whether the observer would be able to compare one such "reduction object" with another. Suppose after the observer views a square that subtends a visual angle of 1 degree in this way, he turns his head and looks through another artificial pupil at a square that subtends a visual angle of 5 degrees. Would the second square look larger? The answer is yes. In fact, observers are able to match visual angle quite accurately under these "reduction" conditions.[4]

The fact that visual angle matching is possible may seem paradoxical if size is indeterminate under such viewing conditions. However, it is not the case that the observer is matching on the basis of perceived objective size. Rather, the observer is detecting something that might be referred to as pure visual extensity, the proportion of the total visual field that an object subtends.* The reader can appreciate what is meant

---

*However, it should be mentioned that some investigators believe that we are only capable of comparing visual angles with one another because we unconsciously assume the objects are equidistant from us. If so, distance is taken into account, but equally for both objects. See the discussion of the equidistance tendency on p. 133. For further information see reference 5.

here by noting that when he holds a finger a few inches from his eye, it looms large, filling almost the entire visual field, despite the fact that it still appears to be the size of a finger. By contrast, a finger (perhaps someone else's) viewed at a distance, is sensed as filling only a small sector of the field, although its objective size is perceived to be the same as when it was viewed nearby.

Two Aspects of Size Perception

There are, therefore, two aspects of perceived size with which we must reckon. Without doubt, perceived objective or linear size is not only the more important of the two in everyday life, but it is directly present in awareness at all times. Conversely, perceived extensity or visual angle perception is of little practical importance in daily life, is either not present in awareness or, at least, is not attended to, and, therefore, it is difficult to explain what is meant by it. Nevertheless this aspect of size perception is important for a complete understanding of how objects in the world appear to us when seen at varying distances.

Consider, for example, what one experiences in looking down a railroad track or a road. Do the tracks appear to converge or do they seem to be parallel? On the one hand, one would say that the tracks seem to converge. Yet standing on the tracks, if we were to consider the apparent size of the wooden ties at different distances, we would say they appear to be about equal. If equal, the tracks must appear parallel. Hence the experience has been referred to as the paradox of converging parallels.

In one respect (perceived objective size), the tracks do appear parallel. If they did not, the engineer (or motorist on the highway) would see himself heading for trouble! In another respect, however (perceived extensity), we are aware that successively distant ties subtend smaller and smaller angles until, at the horizon, they become only a point. The reason why this second aspect of size perception obtrudes into our awareness in this example more so than in others in daily life is that the objects being compared are adjacent to one another in the field. The adjacency of the successive ties makes it quite apparent that their visual angles differ. If one tie were seen in one part of the field and the next in another part, they would be very difficult to compare in this regard. This fact explains why the artist often uses his thumb to compare visual angles of objects at different distances. He has the task of presenting the observer with visual-angle relations on his canvas that mirror those reaching the eye from the scene itself. Therefore, the artist must try to see the visual angle relationships in the scene and, since this is difficult, he lays off his thumb against the distant object. In this way he can see that the distant house subtends the same angle as, say, his thumbnail held at arm's length.

The presence of the two aspects of perceived size may explain why there is often disagreement about how an object at a distance actually *looks*. Some observers insist that a man at a distance of a few hundred yards does appear small. Others insist that he looks perfectly normal in size. Perhaps those who think the man looks small are emphasizing the fact that he subtends a small angle of the field at that distance, not that he actually looks like a diminutive person. Those who say he looks normal in size may not consider the small visual angle subtended to be relevant to the question of perceived size or they may be less aware of the visual angle subtended.*

The Moon Illusion

Since antiquity men have puzzled about the fact that the moon and sun appear larger over the horizon than when elevated in the sky. The distance to the moon is actually somewhat greater at the horizon, so the retinal image of the horizon moon is a fraction smaller than that of the zenith moon.† The phenomenon cannot be explained by differences in refraction based upon differences in the angle of incidence to the earth's atmosphere, as many people seem to think, because photographs of the moon in the different positions yield no measurable difference.

---

*These two aspects of size perception have been noted by many investigators over the years. Terms such as *bodily size, distal size,* and *visual-world size* have been used to refer to what is here called objective or linear size; terms such as *projective size, analytic size,* or *visual-field size* have been used to refer to what is here called the perception of visual-angle or perceived extensity. See reference 6.

Since perceived extensity is essentially a direct function of the size of the retinal image, the Gestalt critique of the constancy hypothesis discussed in Chapter 1, p. 19 is not entirely correct. The same point can be made with respect to other perceptual properties that seem to directly reflect features of the proximal stimulus. These are discussed in subsequent chapters.

†This is because the tangent to the earth is greater than the distance to the earth's surface along the line joining the centers of earth and moon.

We are, therefore, dealing with an illusion in which retinal images of approximately equal size yield quite different phenomenal impressions of size, based upon differences in perceived direction. There are, however, two ways of understanding the phrase "differences in perceived direction" in this context. In relation to the observer—that is, egocentrically defined—the horizon moon is "straight ahead," whereas, to view the elevated moon, the observer must raise his head or his eyes, or both (thus changing the angle of regard). When the observer changes his position—as when he is lying supine—the elevated moon, not the horizon moon, is egocentrically "straight ahead." On the basis of the egocentric definition of direction one would have to predict that the elevated moon would appear larger than the horizon moon to an observer lying in this position. On the other hand, from an objective standpoint, one can say that the horizon moon is seen at the point where the terrain meets the sky, whereas the elevated moon is seen surrounded by sky on all sides, away from terrain or horizon. Here the two positions of the moon are distinguished in terms of their geographical location relative to the earth's surface, and changes in the position of the observer's eye or head are considered irrelevant. The two ways of defining the difference in direction have led to different explanations of the moon illusion.

A theory based on the second approach was put forth by Ptolemy, among others, to the effect that the presence of the terrain creates the impression that the horizon moon is farther away than the zenith moon because the filled space between the observer and the horizon produces an impression of greater extensity than the unfilled space between the observer and the sky overhead. If this were true, it would follow that the horizon moon would look larger than the elevated moon, as shown in Fig. 2-10. Many people find this point hard to grasp because it seems paradoxical: If something is perceived as farther away shouldn't it appear smaller, not larger? The confusion lies in the fact that in this case the size of the retinal image or visual angle *remains unchanged.* It would require a larger object to yield the same image from a greater distance.

This theory can now be restated in the terms of our analysis of size perception. Where the visual angle remains constant but where the distances are registered as different, the apparent size will change. The moon illusion can thus be considered as a special manifestation of Emmert's law if the registered distance to the horizon moon is greater than the distance to the elevated moon, since the visual angle of the moon remains approximately constant. In fact, on the basis of such differences in registered distance, we would predict a moon illusion even if one had never been observed. Fig. 2-11 illustrated the effect of seeing an object in the horizon sky (*a*) as compared to one of the same size seen in isolation on a homogeneous background (*b*), the latter being

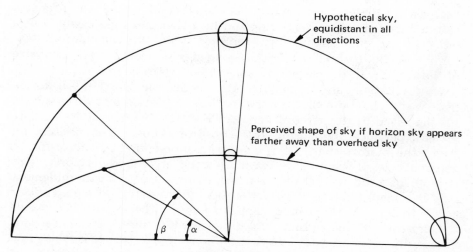

Hypothetical sky, equidistant in all directions

Perceived shape of sky if horizon sky appears farther away than overhead sky

β α

Figure 2-10

analogous to the elevated sky. Even in this illustration, with only the perspective cue operating, an illusion occurs.

But is it true that the horizon moon appears farther away than the elevated moon? A prominent psychologist, the late E.G. Boring, concluded not too long ago that quite the contrary is the case. He asked observers which moon appeared nearer and they were unanimous in saying that the horizon moon did. This led Boring to conclude that theories such as Ptolemy's were invalid and that the crucial difference

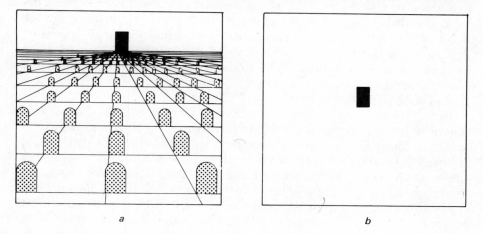

a   b

Figure 2-11

between the direction of the horizon and elevated moons is a difference in the angle of regard.[7]   Boring and his colleagues then carried out a series of experiments—the first thoroughgoing experiments ever performed on the moon illusion—that seemed to connect the apparent size of the moon with the elevation of the observer's eyes.

However, there are reasons for not rejecting the "apparent-distance" hypothesis. Suppose that the moon illusion is based on a difference in the perceived or registered distance of the two moons, and that an observer experiences the illusion. If the observer is now asked which moon seems the more distant, he is comparing moons that already differ in apparent size. It is natural to reason that the larger moon is closer. This is more of a judgmental than a perceptual reaction, and the judgment may dominate when the observer is asked this question. He may not be aware that the horizon moon appears larger to begin with because of the presence of the terrain. As noted earlier, the observer need not necessarily be aware that information concerning distance is registering and thereby affecting apparent size. When asked about the distances of the two moons, therefore, he may fall back upon what seems an obvious clue—namely, the different apparent sizes of the moons. A similar explanation of the failure of convergence change to produce expected change in perceived distance was suggested earlier (pp. 35–36).

The problem was, therefore, reopened by other investigators some years later.[8]   Two experiments were performed in support of the argument outlined in the previous paragraph. In the first experiment, the investigators sought to demonstrate that observers will report whichever moon is smaller as being farther away. Subjects were shown a horizon and a zenith disk or "moon" (by a method described later in more detail), one disk being set so as to yield a much larger impression than the other. The subjects were unanimous in reporting the small-appearing disk as being farther away, regardless of whether it was seen over the horizon or at the zenith. This finding shows that whichever moon appears larger will be judged nearer, quite apart from any other factors that produce differences in perceived distance.

In the second experiment, these investigators sought to show that if one does not use the moon itself (which so readily produces the effect just described) as the object with which to gauge apparent distance, it is possible to obtain direct evidence in support of the assumption that the horizon "sky" seems farther away than the elevated sky (assuming the moon to be in the same plane with the sky). Subjects, looking at a sky without moons, were asked to scan the sky and to try to perceive it as a surface. They were then to report whether an imaginary point over the horizon seemed nearer or farther than such a point at the zenith. Virtually all subjects reported that the horizon sky seemed farther away.

This finding corresponds to the belief, which goes back at least to the eleventh century, that the sky appears somewhat flat.*

Having shown that the apparent-distance theory is not really contradicted by reports of the distance to the moon in its different locations in the sky, these investigators then went on to devise a new method in experimenting on the moon illusion. Artificial "moons" were created that were seen against the sky and could be compared with each other. (The actual moon illusion involves the same sort of comparison, although the two real moons are separated by a considerable interval of time as well as space.) In the artificial moon apparatus, light rays from a lamp pass through a circular aperture and are made parallel by a lens. The parallel rays fall on a piece of glass or a half-silvered mirror tilted at an angle of 45 degrees. An observer looking into the glass sees a bright disk against the sky, which is also visible through the glass (see Figs. 2–12 and 2–13.

Two such devices were employed, one pointed toward the horizon and the other pointed toward the zenith sky. Each device was equipped with a set of circular apertures of different sizes; thus the aperture in one device could be changed until the subject said that the size of the "moon" matched that in the other. The ratio of the zenith aperture to the horizon aperture gave a numerical value for the illusion. A ratio of 1 would mean no illusion: a ratio greater than 1 would indicate that the illusion was present in its usual form.

The investigators first tested the eye-elevation hypothesis by their new method. In one experiment, subjects viewed the artificial horizon moon normally and compared it with an elevated "moon" that they saw either with eyes elevated or by tilting their heads with their eyes level. They obtained a very appreciable illusion both ways. The ratio of the horizon "moon's" apparent diameter to that of the elevated "moon" was 1.48 with eyes elevated and 1.46 without eye elevation—an insignificant difference. No illusion was obtained inside a completely darkened room such as the Hayden Planetarium in New York, a finding that is consistent

*Smith, in 1738, actually tried to determine the degree of flatness by measuring the half-arc angle.[9] The observer points to that spot in the sky that is perceived as bisecting the arc of sky connecting the horizon with the zenith. The angle that this direction forms with the ground is the half-arc angle. A hemispherically shaped sky would yield a 45 degree angle (β in Fig. 2–10), but a flattened sky would yield a smaller angle (α). The most recent attempt to determine this angle was made by Miller, a student of the meteorologist Neuberger.[10] Miller found this angle to be in the neighborhood of 30 degrees and to vary inversely with the distance of the horizon and directly with the elevation. In other words, his data supported the hypothesis that the apparent flattening is a function of perceived distance along the ground plane. The reader is also referred to an interesting laboratory demonstration of the effect of an artificially created terrain by McNulty and St. Claire-Smith.[10]

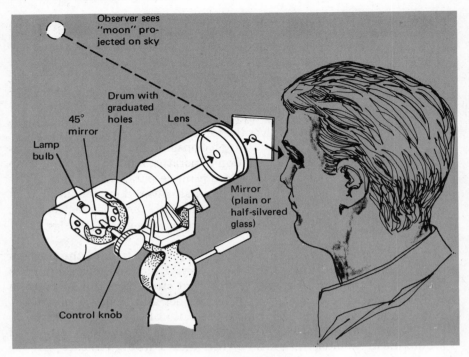

Observer sees "moon" projected on sky

Drum with graduated holes

Lens

45° mirror

Lamp bulb

Mirror (plain or half-silvered glass)

Control knob

Figure 2-12

with the view that the presence of the visible terrain is crucial but is inconsistent with the view that eye elevation accounts for the illusion.

In another experiment, observers viewed the horizon "moon" through a hole in a sheet of cardboard that masked the terrain; the elevated "moon" was unobstructed. Under these circumstances the illusion vanished: the horizon "moon" looked no larger than the elevated "moon." In a variation of this experiment, both devices were pointed at the horizon; in one the "moon" was viewed through a mask and in the other the "moon" was seen over unobstructed terrain. The illusion appeared just as the apparent-distance theory predicts. These experiments tend to support the conclusion that the elevated moon is more or less a reduction object, that is, an object seen without cues to distance.* The horizon "moon" on the other hand is not a reduction object. It is seen at the end of the terrain so that virtually all the known cues to distance can be assumed to be operating.

*It would seem likely that only accommodation and convergence can serve as cues to the distance of the elevated "moon." As is made clear in chapter 3 (pp. 119ff), these cues are ineffective beyond a relatively short distance.

Figure 2–13

The investigators further reasoned that if the horizon moon looks larger only because it is seen over terrain, it should be possible to reverse the illusion by moving the terrain overhead with a mirror or prism. They arranged a mirror at a 45-degree angle so that by looking into the mirror a subject could see the horizon and its "moon" high in the sky. By looking straight ahead into another mirror the subject saw an image of the elevated sky and "moon" in a horizontal direction. As the investigators had expected, the illusion did reverse: the "moon" on an overhead horizon appeared to be larger than the "moon" at a horizontal zenith.

One final test of the apparent-distance theory was provided by turning the scene of the horizon upside down with prisms. Inverting a picture of a landscape has the effect of lessening the impression of distance, and so it was expected that inversion would reduce the size of the moon illusion. Here too the expectations were confirmed: with the scene of the horizon inverted the ratio of horizon to zenith "moon" was 1.28, for the same set of observers under normal conditions it was 1.66.*

In summary, this research demonstrated that the moon illusion depends on the presence of terrain and specifically on the distance effect of the terrain. Eye elevation evidently has nothing to do with the illusion. In other experiments it was shown that differences in color or apparent brightness between horizon and zenith moon that sometimes occur also have nothing to do with the illusion.

The apparent-distance theory should not be confused with a deceptively similar explanation that has often been suggested. The horizon moon, it is said, can be compared with adjacent objects along the terrain. If the moon is seen next to a distant house and if its image is about the same size as the house, then it appears as large as a house; since the house is quite large, the moon must be large.[11] This explanation is incorrect because the illusion can also be obtained over water or desert, where there are no familiar terrestrial objects for comparison. The apparent-distance theory, on the other hand, stresses the impression of distance created by the terrain considered merely as a plane extending outward from the observer—a distance impression that in turn affects the moon's apparent size because the perceptual system takes distance into account in evaluating visual angle.†

One fact not yet mentioned about size perception may be related to the moon illusion. Objects seen from an airplane, high point, or tall building generally look very small, smaller than they would if viewed from the equivalent distance along the ground. Some have thought that this failure of constancy is a function of the vertical direction of viewing. However, another possible explanation of poor constancy when looking down in this way is that there is no filled space between observer and object as there is when viewing along the ground. Thus all the cues provided by the terrain are eliminated. The reversal of the moon illusion described previously, when a visual terrain was provided between observer and elevated "moon," supports this interpretation. It should be possible to test this hypothesis by investigating size perception from a tall building when the observer is positioned in such a way that he can see the entire side of the building between himself

---

*The result probably explains why people have noted a reduced illusion when they view the moon with head down, looking backward between their legs. The retinal image would be inverted.

†However one might reformulate this comparison theory by saying that the horizon moon is compared with an *extent* on the horizon subtending an equal visual angle. If that extent appears large because it is perceived as very far away, so too must the moon.

and the ground as, for example, placing him on a scaffold about 5 feet out from the building.

Is Size Constancy Judgmental Rather than Perceptual?

Many students, on first learning about the problem of size constancy, say, "I *see* the distant object as small but I *know* it is much larger." If this were an accurate description of the subjective experience of size at a distance, then strictly speaking, there is no such phenomenon as size constancy. Perception would follow the law of the visual angle. Based on experience moving about in the environment we, of course, learn that distant objects are larger than they appear and, therefore, we would come to judge them in this way. Are the data of experiments on size constancy merely a reflection of an intellectual act of judgment?

There is a great appeal in this interpretation, and, in fact, this is the view proposed by Titchener and others. In one respect at least, that of perceived extensity, it is true that an object looks smaller when it is far away than when it is near. Furthermore, there are occasions when even the impression of the objective size of a distant object is that it is smaller than when it is nearby, namely when cues to distance are lacking or are inadequate. Nevertheless, there are good reasons for maintaining that size constancy is a perceptual fact. In the final analysis this is a question that can only be directly answered by phenomenological description. Things at a distance either do or do not *look* the same size as when seen nearby. The following arguments are intended to clarify the nature of our experience of size.

If the perception of size followed the law of the visual angle, then nothing should be easier than to match size with respect to visual angle. Suppose, therefore, we place a circular cutout, 12 inches in diameter, across the room, 24 feet away from the observer. Alongside the observer we place a large cardboard with circles of varying sizes pasted to it, from ¼ inch to 3 feet in diameter. The cardboard is 2 feet from the observer. We ask the observer to select the nearby circle which appears to subtend the same angle in the field as the distant one, that is, the circle that would exactly cover the distant one if it were directly in front of it. We must take pains to make clear that we do not want the observer to select the circle that is the same size but rather the one that looks like the same extent ("since as you know things at a distance look smaller . ." we might add). The correct match of visual angle would be a 1-inch circle since the distant circle is twelve times as far away. Few observers will select so small a circle. Most observers will find the instructions confusing and will be unable to resist the impression that a 12-inch circle matches the distant one. Except at very great distances (a situation that is discussed shortly) and except for people skilled at drawing, it is difficult to perceive size in terms of visual angle when normal conditions of illumination prevail.

This fact can even be observed in some drawings and photographs, despite the fact that only certain cues to depth are present and, in fact, other cues (accommodation, convergence, and binocular disparity) are registering the two-dimensional character of the picture's surface. For example, in Fig. 2-14A, the distant man, although not appearing to be the same size as the near one, does not appear as small as the reduced

Figure 2-14A

visual angle would warrant.   In Fig. 2–14B the distant man is placed
in the foreground and here one *does* see him as diminutive. This is the
way the man would appear in A if size perception were based purely
on visual angle. Fig. 2–15, on the other hand, illustrates what happens
when the depth cues in pictures are poor. The boy's feet appear disproportionately large. By contrast, if we actually viewed the boy from
the vantage point of the camera, his feet would not look this way. That
is because adequate depth cues would then lead to constancy with respect to the rest of the boy's body. There are other instances in daily
life where cues to distance are lacking or are relatively poor. There is
no stimulus information to do justice to the great distance of an air-

Figure 2–14B

Figure 2-15

plane. Hence it actually does look very small and, therefore, in this case it *is* an act of judgment when we conclude that it is larger. Such judgment would not be necessary if the plane were seen on the ground at an equivalent distance; it would look appropriately large.

It is interesting to consider the problem of drawing in the light of this discussion. As noted earlier, the artist has the task of putting down on paper the visual angle relations that prevail in the retinal image, just as they would be captured by a photograph. The viewer of the picture then receives the same retinal image as he would if he viewed the scene represented. Providing the pictorial cues in the drawing yield an adequate impression of depth, the viewer will then achieve a degree of constancy in the picture he perceives. At any rate, the problem for the artist is to draw in terms of the visual angle relations given by objects in the scene. But if we perceive size in terms of visual angle, why should this be difficult? It should be the easiest thing in the world. Yet few of us are able to do it and, in fact, this is one of the major difficulties in drawing. After all, would we find it difficult to draw if the task were nothing more than copying a two-dimensional shape? The difficulty arises because of the third dimension in the scene *since we tend to perceive primarily in terms of constancy and not in terms of visual angle.* This can be understood when we consider the kinds of errors we make in trying to draw, particularly the errors of a child. The drawing in Fig. 2–16 is an example of how a child might draw a table viewed from one end. Rather than drawing the far end smaller— which its image on the retina is—he draws it the same size as the near end for the simple reason that it looks to be the same size. Thus, size constancy gets in the way of portraying the visual angle relations re- required for correct pictorial representation.

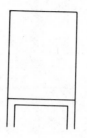

Figure 2–16

Another argument is that when the *same* visual angle is subtended by objects at different distances, these objects *look* very different in size. The perceived size of an afterimage located on surfaces at different distances is a case in point. Another example is shown in Fig. 2–17 where the three equal-size pennants look strikingly different in size. A final example is the moon illusion. In all these illustrations, if the thesis is to be maintained that we perceive size on the basis of visual angle and only judge size by taking distance into account, it would have to be argued that the objects compared do look alike but we only judge them to be different. Immediate experience contradicts this claim. The very meaning of the illusion in Fig. 2–17 is that the pen- nants *look* different in size although they are not.

A convincing demonstration along this line is the following. With one eye closed, hold a pencil vertically at arms length, with the top at about eye level. Hold it in front of an object across the room, such as a book. Focus your vision on the pencil so that the book appears blurred. Continue focusing on the pencil but attend to the book as you slowly move it nearer to your eye. Now move the pencil slowly out again. The book will appear to grow smaller as the pencil approaches and grow larger as the pencil recedes. The explanation of this effect would seem to be that the size of the distant object is very much affected by the accommodation cue to distance. It is the near object

Figure 2-17

for which the lens is accommodating. As the pencil gets near to the eye, accommodation of the lens increases markedly, thus requiring a reduction in phenomenal size as is predictable from Emmert's law. The visual angle of the book remains more or less constant. The diminutive appearance of the book is in marked contrast to the way it looks when we accommodate correctly for an object at this distance, as we normally do. Yet the visual angle is the same in both cases. The contrast serves to make clear that normally the way things *look* entails taking distance into account.

Then there is the fact, not yet mentioned, that many animals behave as if their perception of size does not vary with distance. Since an animal cannot directly tell us what it sees, it is necessary to deduce this from its behavior. The technique usually employed is as follows. First the animal is taught to discriminate between two objects on the basis of size. For example, the larger of two squares is always rewarded regardless of the side on which it is presented. Thus the animal learns to go to the large square. Then, in the critical test, the larger square is presented at a much greater distance than the smaller one, such that the visual angle it subtends is now actually smaller than that subtended by the physically smaller square. If size is perceived on the basis of visual angle, the animal should now select the smaller square; if size is perceived by taking distance into account, the animal should continue to select the large square (even though it has farther to go to get to it). Using this kind of technique it has been shown that species such as rats, chickens, monkeys, and chimpanzees seem to react in terms of size constancy.[12] Although we cannot rule out the possibility that size constancy in animals is learned (see p. 62), it would seem unlikely that the animals learn to make judgments. A judgment by definition is an intellectual act we would think to be beyond the capacity of a chicken. It would also be beyond the capacity of a human infant and yet it has recently been demonstrated that 6- to 8-week-old infants manifest constancy in their perception of size.

Underconstancy and Overconstancy

When an object is very far away—such as a house in a valley seen from a mountaintop miles away—it clearly looks tiny. This fact suggests a falling off of constancy as the distance to the object increases, called underconstancy. In some experiments performed out-of-doors when a standard object was placed at a great distance, the subjects typically matched it with a nearby comparison object that was objectively smaller, and the further away the standard the smaller was the comparison object selected. Thus, experiments confirmed the fact of underconstancy (see Figs. 2-8 and 2-21).

On the other hand, in many other experiments, when the standard was very far away, observers typically matched it with a nearby object that was larger. See Fig. 2-18, uppermost curve.[13] This finding was labeled overconstancy. How can we explain the contradictory results, and what is the meaning of underconstancy and overconstancy?

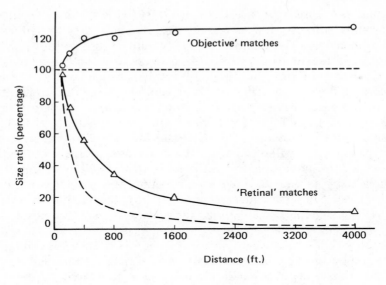

Figure 2-18

Let us first consider underconstancy. As previously noted, that things look small at great distances is an observable fact in daily life, so that when observers in experiments match in this way it is precisely what we should expect. But why do objects appear small at great distances? The traditional answer has been that there is an underestimation of perceived distance. If an object is at 400 yards but the perceptual system records the distance as only 300 yards, then according to the formula on p. 33, perceived size will necessarily be less than when the object is nearby and distance is correctly perceived.

There are reasons for believing that the distance of a very distant object is not correctly registered. We know that accommodation of the lens does not change appreciably beyond several feet and change of convergence of the eyes is slight beyond 30 or 40 feet, so that little *additional* information from these sources is available once an object is well beyond these limits. Also, there are situations where information about distance is severely restricted, as, for example, in viewing an airplane in the sky. Many of the known cues to distance are not present in this case. Therefore, the argument is logically defensible that the falling off of size constancy is based on an underestimation of distance. Yet in the more typical situation of viewing objects on the ground, many of the cues continue to provide information about distance even for objects that are far away.

There is another way of explaining underconstancy. When an object is very far away, its visual angle is extremely small. The reader will recall that it was maintained (p. 38) that we are capable of responding to visual angle per se. Now when an object is far away, so that its visual angle is perhaps 1/100th of the angle subtended by that object when it is near, the difference in extent of field subtended is clearly present in our awareness. Therefore, in this sense of perceived extensity, we say the distant object looks small. Yet at the same time, we also experience the size of the object veridically, based on taking distance into account. According to this interpretation, therefore, constancy of size does *not* fall off (and distance is not necessarily registered incorrectly) but we come to notice more and more the extreme differences in visual angle.

Why then, it may be asked, do judgments of size in constancy experiments often reflect what appears to be a compromise between perfect constancy and visual angle matching, as is indicated in Fig. 2-8. It is data of this kind that have been taken as evidence of underconstancy. There are two possible explanations of such compromise data. The first is that results of experiments generally summarize the judgments of all subjects employed. If, for objects at great distances, some should respond in terms of perfect constancy (thereby emphasizing their experience of objective size) and others should respond in terms approaching visual angle matching (thereby emphasizing the extensity aspect of size perception) the resulting averages might look like those in Fig. 2-8. The second possible explanation is that a given observer might be unsure about which aspect of his own size perception to emphasize in his response. He might, therefore, select a comparison object somewhere in between the two aspects of his own size experience of the distant object. One can see that what an observer does in the experiment is apt to be a function of what he thinks his task is and, therefore, the specific instructions given become very important.

This leads to a consideration of the other type of experimental finding, namely, overconstancy. As implied earlier, in daily life one never experiences a very distant object as larger than it appears when it is nearby. Therefore, it would seem correct to regard overconstancy as some kind of artifact of the procedure used in these experiments (although psychologists have generally not come to this conclusion). Overconstancy is only obtained when the observer is given instructions to match on the basis of the size he believes the distant object actually *is* (objective-size instructions) rather than on the basis of the way it *looks*. This suggests that the observer, in seeking to give the "right answer," engages in certain judgmental processes along the following lines. "Distant things often look smaller than they actually are.* Therefore, I must take this into account in my judgment so I must select an object as matching the distant standard that looks much bigger than it." If this is indeed a good description of what takes place, overconstancy is clearly an error in judgment and an artifact of a procedure from which we are not obtaining data on perception per se but on perception plus judgmental processes.

Individual Differences

In most experiments in perception and, therefore, in experiments on size constancy as well, individuals differ from one another in the way they respond. There is some evidence that they are consistent in the way they respond if tested at different times or with certain variations in procedure. Therefore, it would appear that the differences obtained are not merely random variations or momentary fluctuations but instead reveal some characteristic or trait of the individual. There are those observers who consistently respond in terms of perfect constancy or close to it, and there are those whose matches reflect comparisons closer to visual angle than to objective size.[16] In the experiments on the moon illusion there were those observers who apparently experienced a strong illusion and others who apparently did not.

What do these differences mean? Psychologists have speculated about this problem and some have suggested that the differences reflect types of intellectual or cognitive styles. Those who respond on the basis of objective size regardless of distance have been thought to be people who spontaneously or naively give themselves over to all the information conveyed to the senses. The relationship between the various aspects of this information (e.g., visual angle and distance cues) governs the reaction. Those who respond on the basis of visual angle on the other hand are considered to be more analytical about the information they receive. They are more capable of or more disposed to abstract a given feature out of the total array of stimulation, in this case isolating visual angle.

---

*It has been suggested that this assumption is based on the experience we have with drawings, paintings, and photographs, in which it is clearly evident that distant objects project a smaller image to the eye.[14] However a different explanation would be that distant things look smaller in the sense of perceived extensity as discussed here. See also reference 15.

There may be something to these speculations, but it must be remembered that the basis for the belief in individual differences stems from the results of experiments. There is no convincing evidence that such differences exist in daily life. To the contrary, in everyday experience there would seem to be good agreement among people as to what they see. When one person is struck by the tremendous size of the moon at the horizon so usually are his companions. This suggests that the differences obtained in experiments may be artifacts of the procedure.

This is the same conclusion we arrived at in discussing the findings of under- and overconstancy. There are the two aspects of size perception, extensity and objective size. Which of these is emphasized in an experimental task may be a function of the instructions and, more important in the present context, the individual interpretation of the instructions. When presented with a very distant object and asked to match its size with a nearby comparison object, the observer is faced with a dilemma. If he matches in terms of objective size he may still be aware of the difference in extensity; if he matches in terms of extensity, he may still be aware of the difference in objective size. His response may therefore be based on a decision, as to which aspect to emphasize and, further, he may not even be clearly aware he is making such a decision. Nevertheless, having done so, the observer may consistently abide by this decision if tested again. In conclusion, perhaps there are no true individual differences in the way the size of objects is *perceived* at varying distances but only differences in the way observers decide what to emphasize in the task imposed on them with certain built-in ambiguities concerning what is required.

Another Possible Explanation of Size Constancy: Relational Determination

It will become clear in subsequent chapters that there are many instances in which a perceived quality is determined by the relationship of one thing to another. Whether a surface appears light gray or almost black depends in part upon the intensity of light reflected by its surroundings; whether a line appears vertical or tilted depends in part upon the orientation of the background in which it is seen. Suppose perceived size were a function of the context in which the object is seen. Consider a man in front of a house as depicted in Fig. 2–19*a*. The image of the man stands in a certain relation to the image of the

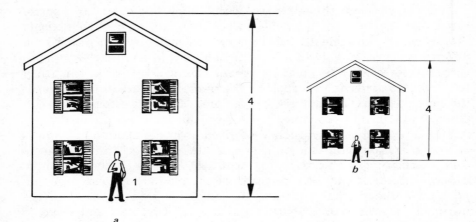

Figure 2-19

house, let us say a proportion of 1 to 4. Perhaps it is this proportion that gives rise to the impression of the man's size. This means he would look bigger if the house were smaller and smaller if the house were bigger.

If now the observer views the man from a much greater distance, the image of man and house will be much smaller, as shown in Fig. 2-19*b*. However the ratio of the man's image to the image of the house remains the same, namely, 1 to 4. Therefore if the relative size of images determines perceived size, the man should appear to be the same size at the far distance as at the near distance. Size constancy would then be based on the fact that image *relationships* do not vary when the distance of objects from the observer varies. It would in no way depend upon taking distance into account.

To test this hypothesis it is necessary to demonstrate that size does indeed depend on such stimulus relationships. The following experiment has been performed.[17]   On one side of an otherwise dark room the observer sees a luminous line inside a luminous rectangle as shown in Fig. 2-20*a*.   By turning around to face the opposite side of the room he sees a second luminous rectangle, which is much larger than the first. The two rectangles are equidistant from the observer. Inside this second rectangle, *b*, is a luminous line that can be made longer or shorter.   The task for the observer is to indicate when this line appears to be the same length as the line in the other rectangle. The experiment is conducted in the dark since otherwise the wall of the room would serve as a frame of reference that would be common to both rectangles and to the lines within the rectangles.   Such a *common* background

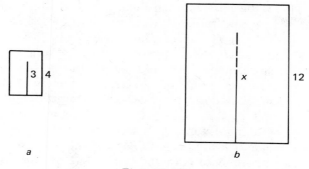

Figure 2-20

would oppose the proportionality effect since the latter clearly depends on *different* frames of reference.

From the values shown in Fig. 2-20, it can be seen that the observer should set the comparison line at 3 inches if size is judged solely in terms of absolute size of the retinal image, since the standard line is 3 inches long and since both lines are the same distance away. He should set the comparison line at 9 inches if size is judged solely in terms of the ratio or proportion of the line to its background, since the standard line is 3/4 of the length of its rectangle and the large rectangle is 12 inches. On the average, observers set the comparison line at between 6½ and 7 inches. Thus there is a very strong proportionality effect.*

Having established the fact of relational determination in an experiment that itself does not fall under the constancy paradigm—since the objects compared are here *equidistant*—we can now apply the findings to the constancy situation. Imagine two sheets of cardboard of the same size, about 20 inches wide and 40 inches high. Down the center of one sheet is a line 30 inches high. This cardboard is placed 60 feet away. The other cardboard is placed at a distance of 20 feet but in a different direction. The observer is to judge when a variable line in this nearer cardboard is the same length as the line in the more distant cardboard. If the reader considers the values in this example, he will realize that the retinal images cast by the two cardboards are completely analogous to those yielded by the rectangles of the previous experiment as shown in

---

*A possible criticism of this experiment is that the observer perceived the larger rectangle as nearer than the smaller one. Relative size (or size perspective) is in fact a cue to depth (see Chapter 3, p. 83). If this occurred, the line in the small rectangle would have appeared larger than an equal-size line in the large rectangle and this would explain the tendency to select a larger line in the large rectangle. However, the investigators were able to prove in control experiments that this explanation of the obtained effect is not correct.

Fig. 2–20. This is because one cardboard is three times farther than the other. Based on the findings of the previous experiment, we must predict that the observer will select a line about 22 inches long. If there were no constancy, he would select a line 10 inches long (1/3 of 30); if there were perfect constancy, he would select a line 30 inches long.

Therefore a considerable part of the results typically obtained in the constancy experiment is derivable from the proportionality principle, and this means that to that extent it is not necessary to explain constancy in terms of taking distance into account. In the study cited here, the investigators demonstrated the efficacy of the proportionality principle in further experiments entailing placement of the objects being compared at different distances from one another.

Does this mean that the assumption made throughout this chapter, namely, that size perception entails the taking into account of distance, is wrong? There are various reasons for thinking it is not wrong, for there are several limitations of the proportionality principle. First, size constancy is manifested in situations where the proportionality principle cannot be operating, such as in a dark room with no frames of reference present, i.e., with only the objects being compared visible. Indeed the proportionality effect depends upon the object being seen within or adjacent to a larger object serving as frame of reference, and this is by no means always the case in daily life or even the most typical case. A man alone in the desert or a boat on the water has no surrounding frame of reference and yet constancy prevails. Second, perceived size is often perfectly constant at varying distances whereas the results of the proportionality experiment allow us to predict only a compromise outcome. Still another limitation of the proportionality principle is that it can only determine the apparent size of one object *relative* to another, i.e., one object in one frame of reference may appear to be equal to, larger than, or smaller than another object in a different frame of reference. But this says nothing about the specific or absolute size of an object, e.g., how large one might say it was in measurable units such as inches or feet. On the other hand, when distance is taken into account in assessing the size of a retinal image, we do end up with an impression of a specific size. (For a further discussion of the meaning of specific size, see the section on p. 71, Perceived Size in Relation to the Size of the Retinal Image.)

Therefore, the most plausible conclusion is that perceived size is primarily determined by taking account of distance. There is also a proportionality effect that often plays a role in size perception in daily life but it is not a necessary determinant of the tendency toward constancy. Undoubtedly the two factors often cooperate in yielding perfect constancy but situations exist where they may oppose one another.

Feature Detector Mechanisms and Size Perception

As the reader will discover in subsequent chapters, evidence has been accumulating that there are individual neurons in the brain of various animals (and probably in man) which respond when the appropriate region of the retina is stimulated by certain kinds of patterns (see p. 219; p. 283; p. 315; p. 490). Such neural units have been referred to as feature-detector mechanisms. One such feature is the size of the retinal image of an object (its visual angle).[18] Perhaps, therefore, a mechanism of this kind accounts for the perception of extensity rather than the collective firing of all central neurons responding to excitation of all the retinal cells stimulated by the image of the object.

But more recently the claim has been made that there are central neurons in the brain which discharge in response to an object of a given size in the environment, regardless of its distance, and therefore despite changes in the size of its retinal image.[19] Such a mechanism would require that information about the distance of the object in some way changes the size of the retinal image to which the central neuron responds.[20] The evidence for this claim is thus far only fragmentary and in fact recent findings suggests that in the human visual cortex, neurons which *detect* size respond to visual angle rather than object size.[21] However some sensory physiologists expect that sooner or later they will find such size-constancy detector neurons somewhere in the brain and that then size constancy will be explained. The writer, while agreeing that all perceptual phenomena can ultimately be explained in terms of neurophysiological events, finds it difficult to believe that the kind of mechanism proposed here, namely the discharging of some individual neuron in the brain, can do justice to the phenomenon of size constancy.

As we have seen, the latter seems to be based on a process of taking account of distance wherein the observer is generally aware of the distance and also to some extent aware of the extensity of the object based on its visual angle. Out of these components the perceptual system constructs the appropriate object size and that is why the process has the character of unconscious reasoning. The discharging of a single cell in the brain does not seem to be an adequate physiological basis of such a process nor does it account for the various components of the total experience. Moreover various kinds of information about distance can affect size perception. Where it is at least conceivable that oculomotor changes of accommodation of the lens and convergence of the eyes could affect the size of the retinal image to which a central detector neuron responds, it is difficult to imagine that such a mechanism would be triggered by the so-called pictoral cues to depth (perspective, shading, and the like). Yet these pictorial cues to depth also affect phenomenal size.

In subsequent chapters, where relevant, the findings concerning feature-detectors and the possible relevance to the perceptual problems under discussion are briefly considered. In each case it is argued, as here, that these mechanisms cannot adequately account for perception, with the single exception of a phenomenon known as the after-effect of movement (pp 219–223).

Is Size Constancy Innate or Learned?

It is not possible on purely logical grounds to decide whether size constancy is the result of an innately given mode of functioning of the brain or is the result of a learning process. The issue is whether the taking-into-account of distance in the evaluation of visual angle is learned. This question should not be confused with the one discussed in Chapter 3, namely, whether the perception of distance and depth is learned. It is possible that an animal capable of perceiving the distance of an object at birth may still perceive the size of that object in terms of its visual angle, and, therefore, will not demonstrate size constancy. Conversely, it is possible to imagine that size is perceived correctly at birth while a particular cue to depth is not yet effective because it is based on learning. Once that cue is learned, it would have an effect on size. For example, the effect that taking distance into account has on the perceived size of the pennants shown in Fig. 2–17 may well be based on a learned pictorial cue.

As to the evidence, until just recently there were no studies that could be considered definitive. As noted previously, experiments have shown that animals of various species behaved on the basis of constancy of size, but these were mature rather than newly born animals. Therefore, all that one could conclude is that size constancy was not a higher mental or intellectual process restricted to human functioning. A study conducted many years ago in Germany that revealed constancy in an 11-month-old infant was perhaps more relevant.[22] The infant, who was first trained to select the larger of two boxes presented side by side, continued to select the larger one when it was placed much further away and the image it cast was now smaller than that of the objectively smaller box.

Evidence of appreciable size constancy in infants under a year of age rules out certain kinds of empiricist theories—for example, that the learning process is gradual entailing years of experience walking around in the environment—but the evidence cannot rule out the possibility of learning early in the infant's life. It also does not rule out some degree of further learning as the child matures. In fact, some investigators have presented what they take to be evidence of the development of constancy as a function of age. That is to say, they have tested children of different ages and plotted a curve of the degree of size constancy against age. According to their findings, the older the child, the greater is the tendency toward complete constancy. The results of one experiment comparing size perception in children from 6 to 12 years of age with adults is shown in Fig. 2-21.[23]

However, there are reasons for skepticism about these findings. We now know that different instructions will produce different results in studies of constancy. Instructions to match on the basis of the size the distant object is believed to be (objective-size match) will yield complete constancy;* instructions to match in terms of perceived size will yield less than complete constancy; whereas instructions to match

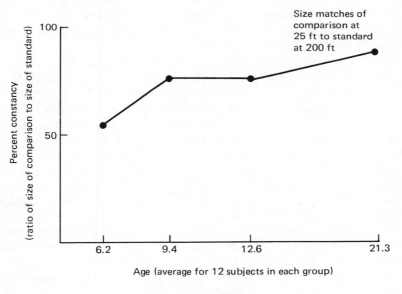

Figure 2-21

*In fact, at great distances it will yield overconstancy, as was discussed previously.

in terms of visual angle will yield still less complete constancy. (See Fig. 2–18, which illustrates results of one study employing two of these instructions.)[24] The effect of instructions depends upon how they are understood and whether they are carried out. If, therefore, a child did not fully understand the instructions or interpreted them differently than did an adult or had difficulty in complying with them, we would have to predict a difference in his judgments. For example, when an object at a great distance does look small, the adult might tend to react to the instructions to match objective size by ignoring the diminutive appearance and judge on the basis of what he believes to be a valid rule, namely, "things at a distance which look small are actually larger than they appear." The child would perhaps be less able to do this. Therefore, the results obtained may be more a function of differences in interpreting or carrying out instructions than of differences in perception.

This brings us to one of the more definitive recent investigations, which, in fact, suggests that when a method is employed that does not depend upon instructions, the perception of a 6 to 8-week-old infant is very much in accord with objective size regardless of distance. The technique employed made use of a method devised by Skinner in conditioning animals.[25] The infant is first conditioned to turn its head to one side in order to obtain a reward (the reward or reinforcement consists of the experimenter suddenly appearing above a table saying "peek a boo"). When the infant turns his head even slightly he closes a microswitch that operates a recording device.

The stimulus to which this head-turning response is conditioned is a white cube 30 centimeters on a side placed 1 meter away (Fig. 2–22a). Following this, the test object is changed, the reward is no longer given, and the frequency of head turning is recorded. This method presumes that the infant will respond in about the same way to any stimulus object that appears identical or very similar to the one used in training (a fact discovered years ago by Pavlov in his work with dogs and other animals); he will respond to a lesser degree or not at all to an object that appears very different. When the 30 centimeter cube is presented at 3 *meters* (Fig. 2–22b), the infant typically turns his head quite frequently (though not as frequently as when the cube remains at 1 meter); when a 90 centimeter cube is placed at 3 meters, the infant turns his head much less frequently (Fig. 2–22c). Thus the infant apparently sees the 30 centimeter cube at the greater distance as quite similar to the conditioned cube, despite the decrease in the size of its visual angle; conversely he must see the 90 centimeter cube as quite different (larger) despite the fact that at 3 meters it yields a visual angle identical to that subtended by the conditioned cube at 1 meter. Therefore, it is clear that the infant is more responsive to a cube that remains constant

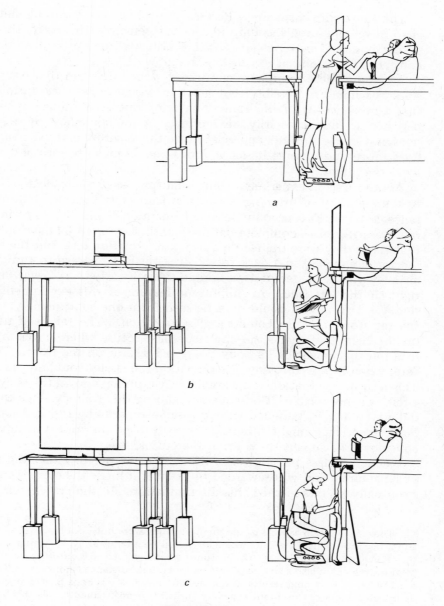

a

b

c

Figure 2-22

in size than to one that remains constant in visual angle. The 6- to 8-week old infant apparently manifests size constancy.

The results are surprising. Because they are and because the method is so novel and entails assumptions about perceived similarity, this experiment should be repeated (possibly utilizing some other measure of constancy) before final conclusions are drawn.*

Assuming these results are confirmed, does this mean that size constancy is innate? Possibly, but a role of visual experience during the first several weeks of life cannot be ruled out even though such experience would necessarily be limited. A human infant of this age does not move around appreciably in the environment, although it does move and observe its hand. Also people move toward and away from the infant.

Another recent experiment using infant rats as subjects clearly points to the necessity of prior experiences, at least in that species, before distance is taken into account in size perception.[26] In this experiment, rats were reared in complete darkness until they were 34 days old. At that time, they were trained on a size discrimination task, but the training was conducted in a dark room. The rat had to learn to run down an alley to the larger of two luminous circles whether it was on the right or the left side. An important feature of this experiment was that the two circles could only be seen from one spot, namely, when the rat stood directly behind a glass partition. The rat itself turned on the light that made the circles visible because when it was in that location the weight of its body depressed a lever on the floor. Therefore, when it moved to any other position the circles could not be seen. This also means that once the animal began running down the alley, the circle was not visible. Consequently, during this training stage the rat did not obtain experience with the same object at varying distances. Such experience might otherwise be said to be the source of any size constancy that might show up in the critical test.

When the glass partition was lifted, the rat ran to either the small or large circle and was rewarded by food if it made the correct choice. Eventually all rats learned this discrimination. In the critical test, also

---

*There are certain aspects of the method which were not ideal in the experiment and a few aspects of the results which are not altogether clear. Concerning method, the choice of head-turning as an indicator of what is perceived is unfortunate because head movement is also a source of information about distance (motion parallax, see pp. 114ff). Concerning results, when the 90 centimeter cube is placed at the near distance of 1 meter the infant typically turns his head frequently. Is this because the distance of the cube remains the same as in training despite the change in size? One might have expected size to be a more salient aspect of the situation in training and the responsiveness to the 30 centimeter cube at 3 meters does support this expectation.

conducted in the dark, the larger circle was moved back along the alley until it subtended a visual angle equal to that of the small circle. Presumably, cues to distance such as accommodation, convergence, and motion parallax could be thought to be available to the rat. In this situation, the animals chose randomly, indicating an absence of size constancy. In a variation of this procedure, the large circle was moved so far away in the critical test that its visual angle was now smaller than that of the small circle. As a result, the rats now selected the small circle since its visual angle was now greater. Therefore, it is clear that these rats reacted solely on the basis of visual angle. A control group of rats reared normally in daylight given the same training chose the larger circle in the critical test. Therefore, it is evident that dark-rearing has in some way eliminated perception in terms of size constancy. However, these dark-reared rats do react to depth per se since when placed on a narrow ledge with a deep drop to one side and a shallow drop to the other they avoid the deep side (see description of the visual cliff in chapter 3). When the same experimental animals we placed in cages and left in a laboratory room for a week with the lights on and again given the critical test, they then displayed size constancy.

It therefore seems clear that some visual experience is necessary for the appearance of size constancy—in rats at least—and it is plausible to suppose that the essence of such experience is the approach to and withdrawal from objects in the environment. In this way the animal learns to take distance into account in assessing visual angle. In other words although the rat can perceive distance innately, it cannot make use of it in size perception without experience. But the learning process is very rapid; even *less* than a week may be adequate.

However, a different problem must be borne in mind. By approaching and withdrawing from objects—or seeing moving things approaching and receding—the organism can learn that objects at a distance *are* larger than they appear. But why does such knowledge affect the way the objects *look*? There are countless examples in perception where knowledge concerning the actual state of affairs has no influence on what is perceived—for example, most optical illusions are unaffected by knowing that they are illusions. Therefore, if past experience is to play a role in bringing about changes in the appearance of things, a theory is required that can explain how such experience can affect the processing of the stimulus in a way that leads to a change in appearance.

One idea that merits attention is the following. When a change is produced in the retinal image by virtue of the organism's own movements, there is reason to believe that the change is not perceived as an event in the environment. For example, the change in location of the image of things as we move about in a stationary environment does not lead to the experience of things moving. This has been called position constancy and is discussed at length in Chapter 5. Apparently the retinal change is discounted because information reaches the brain that the change was produced by the observer's movement. That is, the retinal change is attributed to the observer's movement rather than to the object's movement. In the same way, the enlargement or reduction in size of the image of objects when we approach them or withdraw from them might be discounted because information is available that it is *our* movement that led to this retinal change.* If the retinal change is discounted, the object will not appear to change in size. Such a discounting principle may be innate.

In the situation where the observer is stationary and the object approaches or recedes from him, it is also possible that size constancy is innately determined. The expansion and contraction of the object's image is ambiguous in that it could either represent an object changing its size or an object of constant size changing its distance from the observer. It has now been demonstrated that very young infants react to this kind of stimulus change as if they perceive the object changing its distance (see the discussion of the "looming" effect on p. 128). Therefore, it is plausible to suppose that these infants perceive the object as constant in size under such movement conditions because the stimulus change is accounted for by the perception of change of distance.   If so, size constancy would have to be understood as the manifestation of a preference on the part of the perceptual system for this outcome.

These facts suggest that constancy of size in situations where the observer or object is in forward or backward *motion* would not have to be learned.   But then the problem remains of explaining size constancy when the observer is stationary as in the experiments on human infants and rats described previously. It is possible to argue that through experiences when the organism or object is in motion and constancy prevails, a process of learning occurs that later is carried over to situations when the organism or object is stationary. If so, the nature of this learning process remains to be clarified. The main point of this analysis is that size constancy as a fact of perception is held to be innately determined for these conditions of motion so that the problem of explaining constancy under static conditions reduces to explaining how it comes to be transferred. Whereas if constancy is entirely a matter of learning,

---

*This idea was first suggested by von Holst.[27]

the problem is how perception can change simply because knowledge about the unchanging size of objects is acquired.*

Shape Constancy

Only in the special case where an object is in a plane perpendicular to the line of sight does the image cast on the retina have the same shape as the object.† For example, a rectangle in such a plane will yield an image that is rectangular (see Fig. 2–23). In the more general case, the object is in a plane slanted with respect to the line of sight.

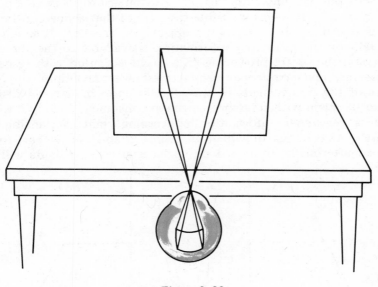

Figure 2–23

*The entire discussion here of whether size constancy is innately determined or learned is predicated on the assumption that perceived size is based upon a process of taking distance into account. If, however, perceived size were relationally determined (as considered in the discussion on pp. 57–60), it would seem plausible to believe that learning is not necessary. Phenomenal size would simply be a direct function of the size of the retinal image of the object *relative* to the size of the image of the frame of reference for that object. However, as noted at the conclusion of that discussion it is unlikely that this basis of perceived size is the primary one.

†We are restricting the discussion to two-dimensional objects such as shapes cut out of cardboard.

As a result, the shape of the image is no longer the same as that of the object. In the case of the rectangle, the image will be that of a trapezoid (see Fig. 2-24). This can easily be understood by considering only the two vertical sides of the rectangle. They are equal in size, but one side is nearer the observer. Consequently, the nearer side will project a longer image than the farther side and the result is a trapezoidally shaped image.

Yet it seems to be the case in daily life—and laboratory experiments confirm this—that we perceive shape veridically. Hence the term *shape constancy* has been applied to this phenomenon. In general, whenever perception is more in accord with the external object than with the proximal stimulus (or retinal image in the case of vision) or, to state it another way, whenever perception remains more or less the same despite changes of the proximal stimulus, it is customary to speak of a perceptual constancy. It seems plausible to suppose that shape constancy is based upon taking the slant of the object into account. If an elliptical image falls on the retina but information is available to the perceptual system that the object producing that image is slanted with respect to the observer, then a circle may be perceived rather an ellipse.

Most of the points made in this chapter concerning size constancy can also be made with reference to shape constancy, namely: what is crucial is *registered* information concerning slant; an analogue of Emmert's law obtains in which the *same* shaped image, as, for example an afterimage, projected on surfaces at *varying* slants will look

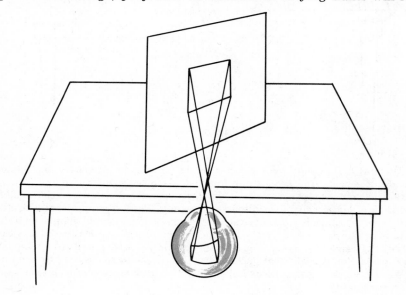

Figure 2-24

different in shape in each case; in the absence of information concerning slant, the perceived shape might be thought to be ambiguous (however, there is reason for believing that under such conditions the assumption is made that the object is in a plane perpendicular to the line of sight and the shape is perceived accordingly); shape constancy is perceptual and not judgmental although at times judgment may play a role; shape constancy is found in various animal species and in human infants 6 to 8 weeks old;[28] underconstancy is often obtained in experiments, particularly when an object is seen at a very appreciable slant, i.e., the subject matches the standard object at a slant to a comparison object that is a compromise between the standard object's true shape and the shape of the distorted retinal image.

It is possible to derive shape constancy from size constancy. Instead of speaking about the slant of the object, one can think of the different distances of the various sides of the shape. The example in Fig. 2–24 of the rectangle at a slant will serve to illustrate this point. If the distance of the side that is further away is taken into account, then the size of this side will be perceived veridically; similarly with respect to the nearer side. The result is that both sides are seen to be equal in size. If equal, the object must be a rectangle. However, this is not yet a complete explanation because the rectangle perceived would be foreshortened unless the size of the horizontal axis of the rectangle is also correctly perceived. This size can be correctly perceived by taking into account the slant of the figure.[29]

Perceived Size in Relation to the Size of the Retinal Image*

A second problem concerning the perception of size was alluded to at the beginning of this chapter. At any given distance, an object of a certain size gives rise to a retinal image of a certain size. For example, an apple at arm's length may be represented by an image of about 2 millimeters in diameter. The question to consider is this: How can so small an image represent a perceived object that is so much larger?

Stated in this way, the reader may well feel that the question is absurd and he would be right. It would be foolish to suppose that the

---

*The reader may find this section difficult. If so, it may be advisable to reread it after reading several other chapters in which the problem of perceptual adaptation to distorting optical devices is discussed.

physical size of the image must correspond to the perceived size of the object. Obviously the retinal image must be thought of as encoding information about the environment. The images are small because the eye itself is quite small. The cortical "images" that reach the brain from the retina are also relatively small, but the brain is able to decode the information reaching it and thus subjective impressions of various sizes are achieved.

But it is not absurd to ask what the relationship is between the specific size of a retinal image and the perceived size of the corresponding object. It is innately given that an image of 2 millimeters projected by an object at arm's length will be perceived as the size of an apple? Or is it learned in some way? The answer to this question, the author believes, is based upon a more careful consideration of what it means to say that something appears to be the size of an apple. The size of an apple is characterized by its size in relation to all other things, in particular to the body of the observer, the physical self. It is a size that just fits into the hand and, therefore, one that is small in relation to the body as a whole. It is larger than a grape but smaller than a grapefruit. In short, the meaning of a specific size is given by the set of all possible relationships of that object to other objects.

For objects at any given distance—and it is best that we restrict the discussion of this problem to one distance for the moment—their sizes in relation to one another are perfectly encoded within the image because the image preserves this relative size. The image of the apple will be larger than the image of the grape and smaller than the image of the grapefruit. Furthermore, the image of the apple will be about the same size as the width of the image of the observer's hand. Therefore, it would seem that the absolute size of the retinal image is of no particular consequence. All that matters for the veridical perception of size is that the relative sizes of objects to one another is present in the retinal image of these objects.

There is, however, one difficulty with this view. We can and do perceive size correctly even when only a single isolated object is present as, for example, a luminous object in a dark room. Furthermore, if we view the world through a lens that enlarges or reduces the retinal image, objects do appear to be larger or smaller than they would otherwise. Yet in this case, the relative size of objects to one another is *not* altered. Both examples suggest that the specific size of an object *is* somehow communicated by the absolute size of its image (again bearing in mind that we are referring only to one particular distance.

A possible explanation of this fact is as follows: Throughout life, objects at specific distances do subtend visual angles of specific absolute sizes. Thus it is possible that memories are established that faithfully mirror the size of the visual image of an object. For example, the apple seen at arm's length leaves a memory trace that represents the size of the 2 millimeter image and this trace is associated with the perceived size of the apple. (The term *memory trace* or *trace* is used by psychologists to refer to a more or less enduring record in the brain of a prior mental event.) Given enough experience, the specific visual angle may become a sign of a certain phenomenal size. Thus, after much experience the absolute size of the image itself leads to the impression of a particular size. When this occurs, memory becomes a determinant of perception.

At this point we must reckon with the fact that objects are seen at *all* distances and consequently that the discussion thus far may seem highly artificial. In fact, the main point about size constancy discussed throughout the chapter might be said to be that image size in itself is an ambiguous indicator of phenomenal size. Therefore, the problem is to extend the explanation offered here of how specific image size becomes a sign of specific phenomenal size to the reality that objects are encountered at all distances.

This is not an insurmountable problem. The fact of size constancy is essentially that there is an equivalence of apparent size for an object seen at varying distances. One might say, therefore, that a whole set or family of image-size—registered distance combinations produces the same phenomenal size. If one such combination has acquired the significance of a specific phenomenal size in the manner just suggested, for example, a 2 millimeter image at 2 feet is perceived as the size of an apple—then it would follow that all other combinations in the family acquire the same significance—for example, a 1 millimeter image at 4 feet. Consequently, it is not necessary to maintain that separate learning must occur for every image size-distance combination before image size can become a sign of specific phenomenal size. It is plausible, in fact, to think that objects nearby enjoy a special normative status so that the kind of learning suggested may occur at this distance and then generalize to all other distances. (It is interesting to consider in this connection that size constancy implies taking into account the distance of a far object so as to perceive it the way it should look if it were near. We certainly do not spontaneously do the opposite, namely, take into account the distance of a nearby object so as to perceive it the way it would look if far.)

Perceptual Adaptation

Workers in the field of perception have recently turned their attention to experiments in which the observer is required to view the world through an optical device (prism, lens, or the like) that distorts the retinal image in some way. Examples of this research are discussed in subsequent chapters. There is, however, one type of distortion that is relevant to the present question, namely, magnification or minification of the image. What should be the consequence of viewing the world through a lens that magnifies or reduces the entire retinal image?

On the one hand, based on the reasoning just presented, it might be argued that such a distortion will have no effect at all on perception. There is no change in the size of the image of objects *relative* to one another. All images are magnified (or reduced) equally. On the other hand, based on past experience and the consequent establishment of memory traces, of the kind suggested, the world should appear enlarged (or diminished) at the very outset of the experiment.

The world does appear different when first viewed through lenses that affect the size of the image—although perhaps not as different as one might expect based upon the degree of optical change. However, as the observer continues to view the world through such a device the further question arises, will there be any change over time, any adaptation to the distortion? If the initial reaction to the lenses is based on memory traces of sizes as experienced in daily life, then it follows that the scene should begin to appear increasingly normal by virtue of the acquisition of new memory traces during the period of exposure to the distorted image. Suppose an apple at arm's length seen through a minifying lens subtends a visual angle of about 1 millimeter. At first, the apple looks small because in memory a 1 millimeter image (of a thing at arm's length) is associated with a size approximating that of a golf ball. In time, however, there will be many new traces established reflecting the fact that things the size of an apple at this distance subtend an image of 1 millimeter.

For such adaption to occur, however, the observer must obtain information concerning the true sizes of things he looks at. If, instead, he were to view a single unfamiliar object, he would have no way of ascertaining that it was in fact much larger than it appeared to be. In that event no adaptation is to be expected. If, however, the observer sees familiar objects, or even better, an array of familiar objects in the world including portions of his own body, then he is getting information that the smaller visual angles of all things represent sizes that are larger than at first might appear to be the case. One investigation has demonstrated that, given such information, adaptation to minification does take place.[30] The methodology of this type of research is not discussed here since it proved to be particularly complicated in the case of adaptation to optical distortion of size. It is sufficient to say that research of this kind does support the view stated that it is not necessary for the image to be the size that it is for perception of size to be veridical. The implication is that only through much past experience has it come about that absolute image size signifies specific phenomenal size; otherwise only relative image size would do so. It follows that a newborn infant would see the world much as we do if he started out life wearing a lens that altered the size of the entire image.

Summary

The essential problem about the perception of size is that the perceived size of objects remains more or less constant despite changes in the size of the retinal image (or visual angle) with changes of distance. To explain this fact it is necessary to assume that a process occurs in the perceptual system whereby distance is taken into account in evaluating the size signified by a given visual angle. This process is itself not conscious and at times even the information about distance may not be consciously noted. A corollary of this same process of taking account of distance is Emmert's law, namely, that a retinal image of *constant* size will give rise to *changes* in perceived size as a function of the distance at which that image is located. The moon illusion can be considered to follow from Emmert's law because the terrain provides good cues to distance that the elevated sky does not.

Size constancy is a fact that characterizes *perception*. It is not merely a matter of knowing about or judging size. Among other reasons for this conclusion is the fact that various species of animals and human infants perceive objects as constant in size despite variations in their distance. However, it is not yet known with certainty whether size constancy is present at birth or is based upon experience with the environment. If such experience or learning is required, it is short-ranged, since 6-week-old infants manifest constancy as do dark-reared rats following 1 week of exposure to daylight.

When all information about distance is eliminated, size perception is a function of visual angle. The subjective experience here is that of the extent of the visual field subtended by the image, an experience of pure extensity. Although ordinarily not in focal awareness, differences in extensity also have consequences for size perception in daily life. Thus there are two aspects of perceived size, perceived objective size based on a process of taking distance into account—and that is therefore more or less constant—and perceived extensity that is a function of the visual angle subtended. The interplay of these two aspects explains certain paradoxical experiences such as the way a railroad track appears. It may also explain the so-called falling off of constancy (or underconstancy) with distance: the observer in an experiment tries to compromise between the constant objective size and the ever-diminishing visual angle as the object recedes into the distance. Individual differences in constancy experiments may reflect the emphasis a subject places on one or the other aspect of size perception.

Size relationships also have an effect on perceived size. Since the size of an object relative to a nearby frame of reference remains invariant despite change of distance from the observer, some degree of constancy is to be expected on this basis alone.

Variations in the slant of an object produce variations in the shape of its retinal image but the perceived shape of the object remains more or less constant. This shape constancy as it is called is a phenomenon very much like size constancy and in fact can probably be explained in terms of the constancy of size of the component parts of the object.

A different problem about perceived size, apart from the problem of constancy, is the relationship between the specific size of the retinal image and the perceived size of the corresponding object. An object at a given distance produces a retinal image of a given size, so the question arises, must the image be just that size for the perception to be the size that it is? It is probable that there is no such necessary relationship; rather, the crucial information consists of the size relationships of all objects in the field, including the self, and this is not altered by enlargement or reduction of the entire retinal image. If this is true, adaptation to optically magnified or minified images should be possible and experiments suggest that it is.

References

1. Emmert, E. Grossenverhältnisse der Nachbilder. *Klinische Monatsblätter für Angenheilkunde*, 1881, **19**, 443–450.
2. See Wheatstone, C. One some remarkable and hitherto unobserved phenomena of binocular vision: Part 2. *Philosophical Magazine*, 1852, **4**, 504–523; C. H. Judd, Some facts of binocular vision. *Psychological Review*, 1897, **4**, 374–389.
3. Gruber, H. E. The relation of perceived size to perceived distance. *American Journal of Psychology*, 1954, **67**, 411–426.

4. Rock, I. and W. McDermott, The perception of visual angle. *Acta Psychologica*, 1964, **22**, 119–134; A. R. Hastorf, and K. S. Way. Apparent size with and without distance cues. *Journal of General Psychology*, 1952, **47**, 181–188: W. Epstein, and A. Landauer. Size and distance judgments under reduced conditions of viewing. *Perception & Psychophysics*, 1969, **6**, 269–272.

5. Gogel, W. C. The tendency to see objects as equidistant and its inverse relation to lateral separation. *Psychological Monographs*, 1956, **70**, 1–17; The validity of the size- distance invariance hypothesis with cue reduction. *Perception & Psychophysics*, 1971, **9**, 92–94; The sensing of retinal size. *Vision Research*, 1969, **9**, 1079–1094.

6. For example, see Brunswik, E. *Perception and Representative Design of Psychological Experiments.* University of California Press, 1956; J. J. Gibson. The *Perception of the Visual World*, Chap. 3. Houghton Mifflin Company, 1950.

7. Boring, E. G. The moon illusion. *American Journal of Physics*, 1943, **11**, 55–60.

8. Kaufman, L. and I. Rock, The moon illusion, I. *Science*, June 15, 1962, **136**, 953–961; I. Rock, and L. Kaufman. The moon illusion, II. *Science*, June 22, 1962, **136**, 1023–1031. For a simplified account of this work, see: L. Kaufman, and I. Rock, The moon illusion. *Scientific American*, July 1962.

9. Smith, R. *A Complete System of Optics.* Cambridge, 1738, 1.

10. Miller, A. *Investigations of the Apparent Shape of the Sky.* B. S. thesis, Pennsylvania State College, 1943; H. Neuberger. General Meteorological Optics, in Compendium of Meteorology. *American Meteorological Society*, 1952; McNulty, J. A. and R. St. Claire-Smith. Terrain effects upon perceived distance. *Canadian Journal of Psychology*, 1964, **18**, 175–182.

11. Solhkhah, N. and J. Orbach. Determinants of the magnitude of the moon illusion. *Perceptual and Motor Skills*, 1969, **29**, 87–98.

12. For a summary of this evidence, see Locke, N. M. Perception and intelligence: their phylogenetic relation. *Psychological Review*, 1938, **45**, 335–345.

13. Gilinsky, A. The effect of attitude on the perception of size. *American Journal of Psychology*, 1955, **68**, 173–192.

14. Carlson, V. R. Overestimation in size-constancy judgments. *American Journal of Psychology*, 1960, **73**, 199–213.

15. Epstein. W. Attitude of judgment and the size-distance invariance hypothesis. *Journal of Experimental Psychology*, 1963, **66**, 78–83.

16. Thouless, R. H. Individual differences in phenomenal regression. *British Journal of Psychology*, 1932, **22**, 216–241.

17. Rock, I. and S. Ebenholtz, The relational determination of perceived size. *Psychological Review*, 1959, **66**, 387–401.
18. Blakemore, C. and F. W. Campbell. On the existence of neurons in the human visual system selectively sensitive to the orientation and size of retinal images. *Journal of Physiology*, 1969, **203**, 237–260.
19. Spinelli, D. N. Recognition of visual patterns, Chapter VIII in D. A. Hamburg, K. H. Pribram, and A. J. Stunkard, edit., *Perception and its Disorders*. Williams & Wilkins, 1970; E. Marg, and J. E. Adams, Evidence for a neurological zoom system in vision from angular changes in some receptive fields of single neurons with changes in fixation distance in the human visual cortex. *Experientia*, 1970, **26**, 270–271.
20. Richards, W. Spatial remapping in the primate visual system. *Kybernetik*, 1968, **41**, 146–156; Apparent modifiability of receptive fields during accommodation and convergence and a model for size constancy. *Neuropsychologia*, 1967, **5**, 63–72.
21. Blakemore, C., E. T. Garner, & J. A. Sweet, The site of size constancy. *Perception*, 1972, 1, 111–119.
22. Frank, H. Untersuchungen über Sehrgrössenkonstanz bei Kindern. *Psychologische Forschung*, 1926, **7**, 137–145.
23. Brislin, R. W. and H. W. Leibowitz, The effect of separation between test and comparison objects on size constancy at various ages levels. *American Journal of Psychology*, 1970, **83**, 372–376.
24. Gilinsky, op. cit. 1955.
25. Bower, T. G. R. The visual world of infants. *Scientific American*, 1966, **215**, 80–92.
26. Heller, D. Absence of size constancy in visually deprived rats. *Journal of Comparative and Physiological Psychology*, 1968, **65**, 336–339.
27. Holst, E. von, Relations between the central nervous system and the peripheral organs. *British Journal of Animal Behavior*, 1954, **2**, 89–94.
28. Bower, op. cit., 1966.
29. Wallach, H. and M E. Moore. The role of slant in the perception of shape. *American Journal of Psychology*, 1962, **75**, 289–293.
30. Rock, I. *The Nature of Perceptual Adaptation*, Basic Books Inc., 1966, Chap. 5.

chapter 3

THE PERCEPTION OF
THE THIRD DIMENSION

The problem of the perception of the third dimension arises from the observation that the retina can be considered a two-dimensional surface, so that distance per se is not recorded in the retinal image. If the retina were three-dimensional and a mechanism had evolved whereby the distance of a thing was registered by the location of its image in depth in such a retina, then this location would provide the information about the object's distance. Since such a retina does not exist, the problem is how information is obtained about distance.

The reader may object to this formulation. He may know that the farther away an object is from the eye, the smaller is the image cast on the retina. Therefore, the size of the image might be thought to be the source of information about an object's distance. There is some truth to this argument. Thus, for example, if the image of a person is very small, we might infer that he must be far away. But this principle can only work if each type of object has only one size. Since we perceive the distance of unfamiliar as well as familiar things, the size of the retinal image can hardly be a general explanation of distance perception. However, for familiar objects that typically have a certain size, such as people, books, automobiles, and the like, the size of the image may be a source of information about distance. (Although familiar things come in a range of sizes so that the potential usefulness of familiar-size information is limited.) Whether in point of fact familiar size does operate as a distance cue must be determined by an experiment in which all other possible sources of information are eliminated. We return to this question later in the chapter.

How then do we obtain information about distance? There would seem to be a number of possible answers to this question. It is customary in textbooks on perception to list all the so-called clues or cues that might provide such information. For example, it is known that the thickness of the lens of the eye automatically changes as a function of the distance of the object fixated in order to obtain a maximally sharp image. Such *accommodation* of the lens could provide information that the perceptual system uses in assessing an object's distance. In addition, the angle formed by the direction of gaze of the two eyes in viewing an object changes as a function of the object's distance. If the object is near, the eyes must be turned or converged sharply inward; if it is far, the direction of gaze of both eyes is almost straight ahead. Thus the angle of *convergence* of the eyes could be a source of information about distance.

Then there is the fact that the images in the two eyes are slightly different for a three-dimensional object in the scene. This *binocular disparity* is considered to be a major source of information about distance; the familiar stereo viewers demonstrate the effectiveness of this cue because one achieves depth by viewing two two-dimensional pictures that are drawn or photographed in such a way as to produce disparate retinal images. Movement is also considered to be an important cue. When the observer moves, the separation between the images of objects located at different distances changes. The greater the distance between the objects the greater is the shifting of their images relative to one another with movement. This cue does not require the use of both eyes and thus has been referred to as *monocular parallax*, *head movement parallax*, or simply *motion parallax*.

A word should be said about the use of the word *cue*. As the reader may recall from the brief historical survey in Chapter 1, theorists have argued that vision cannot provide direct access to distance. Berkeley and others who followed him maintained that we only learn about the third dimension from our sense of touch. Since certain sensations from the muscles attached to the lens and the eyeball occur when viewing an object at a certain distance, we associate these sensations with that distance. Hence the sensations become clues about the distance of the object. Terms such as *clue* or *cue* often carry the theoretical implication that they are learned signs of distance. But the term *cue* is also used by modern psychologists in the more neutral sense of an indicator or source of information about distance. It is used this way here and elsewhere in this book. Whether a particular *cue* is or is not a *learned* indicator of the third dimension is a further question, which in most cases is open to empirical investigation.

All the factors referred to in the preceding paragraphs are discussed in more detail in the remainder of the chapter. Are these then to be considered the basis of our veridical perception of the three-dimensional arrangement of the world? Consider the following experiment—which the reader can easily try for himself. Close one eye and look at the scene with the other eye through a tiny pinhole in a piece of cardboard. Hold the head still by placing the chin firmly on a solid object. The impression of depth in the scene will still be vivid. In fact, it may not even be evident that it is any less three-dimensional in appearance than with normal binocular vision. Yet by viewing through the pinhole, all of these cues have been eliminated or made ambiguous. The pinhole makes it unnecessary for the lens to change *accommodation* for objects at different distances. In fact the reader may notice that through the pinhole (or artificial pupil as it is called) objects at all distances are simultaneously in sharp focus. By closing one eye, *convergence* and *binocular disparity* information have been eliminated. (Incidentally, this simple demonstration serves to contradict the widely held belief that depth perception depends upon binocular vision). In holding the head still, *motion parallax* has been eliminated. What remains to account for the continued perception of depth?

A clue to the answer is provided by the finding that if this experiment is done in a dark room where only a few luminous shapes are visible, the correct perception of distance *is* indeed eliminated. The crucial difference seems to be that in the typical daylight scene the array of objects and surfaces is somehow itself a source of information. Another indication that this is so is that a drawing or a picture of a scene generally appears to be three-dimensional and yet all the cues thus far described would in this case contraindicate depth. The surface of the page containing the picture *is* two-dimensional. Therefore, accommodation, convergence, binocular disparity, and motion parallax all attest to the fact that there is no depth within the picture. (Consequently it has been said that there is a kind of dual awareness in viewing pictures: they look three-dimensional but at the same time they look two-dimensional.)

If a picture is viewed through an artificial pupil with one eye, the impression of depth is improved and may be as vivid as in viewing the scene itself. In this case the competition from the other cues is eliminated. Therefore, the picture itself must contain information that is a potent indicator of depth. Presumably it is this same information that is effective in viewing a real scene. Whatever the information derived from the array of objects in the scene, it can be captured in a picture of that scene. A photograph produces the same retinal image that the scene itself produces because the picture is determined by the same laws of optics that determine the nature of the image on the retina. In a drawing the artist deliberately tries to achieve the same end result.

Therefore, it seems plausible to speak of pictorial cues to depth. Whatever can be captured in a picture that will yield a sense of distance

Figure 3-1

to the observer can be considered to be such a cue. The student of art will recognize at this point that such factors have been known for some time. Leonardo da Vinci is generally credited with having enunciated them most clearly. One such factor is *perspective*. Parallel lines in a scene will project a retinal image of lines converging at a point. That point will be on the horizon. Fig. 2-11*a* and 2-17 illustrate this effect, known as *linear perspective*. More generally, objects of the same size that are arranged in a plane receding into the distance, such as the ground or ceiling, will give rise to images that decrease in size as a function of their distance. If the objects are equally spaced, the space between the images of the objects will also decrease in size in a uniform way.* This is referred to as *size perspective* and is illustrated in Fig. 3-1. Da Vinci also described *aerial perspective*, the increasing shift toward the blue end of the spectrum and *detail perspective*, the increasing loss of sharp detail with distance as a result of decreasing visual acuity and impurities in the air.

Another effective pictorial cue is illustrated in Fig. 3-2. The tendency is to perceive two rectangles, one in front of the other. In a typical scene, one thing is often interposed in front of another so that only part of the more distant thing is visible. A convincing illustration of this *interposition* or *overlay* as a cue to depth is illustrated in Fig. 3-3*a* and *b*. By arranging the position of the objects carefully in relation to the position of the observer's eye, an image on the retina is formed as shown in *a*. As a result, the triangle is perceived to lie *behind* the circle and rectangle although the opposite is in fact the case (*b*).

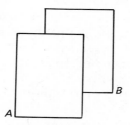

Figure 3-2

---

*These perspective images are nothing mysterious. Given the fact that the size of the retinal image is inversely proportional to the distance of the object (see Chapter 2, pp. 29–30), then it follows that equal sized objects equally spaced will project increasingly smaller retinal images. Thus railroad tracks must produce an image of converging tracks, and so on.

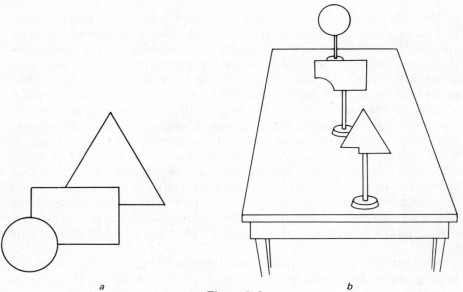

a   *b*

Figure 3-3

Shadow is another important pictorial cue. Differential shading within a three-dimensional object, as shown in Fig. 3-4, is considered to provide information about the object's solidity and depth. Moreover, the location of shadow often is indicative of whether a given region protrudes outward or is indented. Fig. 3-5a is a view of the moon that seems to reveal mounds on the ground. When it is turned upside down as in Fig. 3-5b one correctly sees that they are craters. In Fig. 3-6a and b a similar effect is shown: the cuneiform writing on the tablet appears as intaglio or bas-relief depending upon the orientation of the picture. As a rule, if a region is shadowed at the bottom, Fig. 3-7a, that region appears to be convex, to protrude from the background surface; if it is shadowed at the top, Fig. 3-7b, it appears to be concave, like an indentation in the surface. Since light on the earth generally comes from the sun, from above (or from artificial light, also generally directed downward), convex surfaces or protuberances on a vertical plane will be shaded at the bottom and concave surfaces or indentations will be shaded at the top. Therefore, both the existence of shadow within an object and its location can indicate the presence and direction of depth. However, the location of shadow within protrusions and indentations *on the ground* is not an unequivocal indicator of the direction of depth because there is no top and bottom, although such location is effective in *pictures* of the ground as in Fig. 3-5.

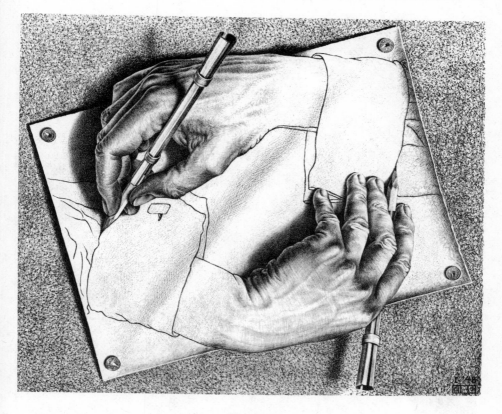

Figure 3-4

What is the clue responsible for the three-dimensional appearance of the objects in Fig. 3-8? It might be thought to be linear perspective because the representations in the drawing of the receding parallel lines in the object converge. But a drawing can be made in what is called parallel (or isometric) projection as shown in Fig. 3-9. Here the same lines now do *not* converge; rather they are parallel. Yet the pictures still look three-dimensional. So it would seem that certain *familiar patterns* are perceived as three-dimensional even in the absence of other pictorial cues.

We have seen that there are various sources of information about the third dimension of space. Many new questions now arise. Can each of the cues we have described actually be demonstrated to work when it is isolated by experiment (or to have an effect when it is varied and all

a

b

Figure 3–5

Figure 3-6

other cues are held constant)? How potent is it in relation to the other cues? Is that cue present at birth (perhaps being attendant upon some necessary state of maturation) *or* is it a learned cue? What is the mechansim underlying the operation of a particular cue?

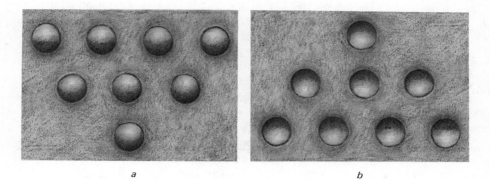

Figure 3-7

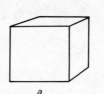

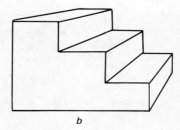

a

b

Figure 3-8

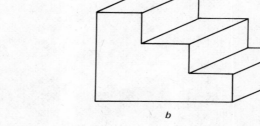

a

b

Figure 3-9

Before considering these questions, a few words should be said about the various attempts to classify the cues. For example, it is obvious that some cues depend upon the use of the two eyes whereas others do not. Convergence and binocular disparity are binocular cues; accommodation, motion parallax, and all the pictorial factors are monocular cues. Or one might wish to distinguish those cues that depend upon some motor act such as the changing of the thickness of the lens (accommodation) or the degree of contraction of the eye muscles (convergence) from those that depend only upon visual information. Whether or not anything is gained by these classifications is not yet clear but there is one distinction that would seem to be important to make.

Some cues inform about the absolute distance of an object from the observer. Accommodation, convergence, and familiar size would be in this category. Other cues can only provide information of how far one object is in relation to other objects but say nothing about how far any one object is from the observer. Binocular disparity, and all the pictorial cues would be in this category. Some psychologists therefore use the term *distance perception* to refer to the first category and the term *depth perception* to refer to the second category.

Since typically we have one unified impression of a scene in which objects are experienced as having definite locations with respect to us as well as to each other, it is plausible to suppose that this results from an interaction of the various cues. To illustrate, suppose there are two objects, A and B, with object B 1 foot behind object A and object A 5 feet from the observer. If one fixates on object A, its absolute distance may be given by accommodation and convergence. But binocular disparity then provides information about the relative location of object B with respect to object A namely, 1 foot behind object A. Therefore, it follows that object B is 6 feet *from the observer* or at least this fact can be "deduced" by the perceptual system by relating the other two facts to one another.

We will now take a somewhat closer look at each cue, examine the available evidence, and consider the questions of effectiveness, importance, and mechanism in each case. The following classification is used. Visual cues are considered separately from oculomotor cues. Two kinds of visual cues are distinguished, those that depend upon movement of either the observer or the object (transforming) and those that do not (static). Finally, two kinds of static visual cues are distinguished, pictorial and binocular.

Static Visual Cues: Pictorial

Perspective

That linear perspective is an effective cue to depth is borne out by the fact that pictures containing only this factor yield a strong impression of three-dimensionality (see Fig. 2–11a). In fact, as noted earlier, there is a conflict in viewing pictures since many other cues indicate no depth. When an experimental conflict between perspective and binocular disparity cues to depth is created by means of a lens over one eye that alters binocular disparity, the effectiveness of disparity is either considerably reduced or entirely eliminated.[1] So the outcome can be considered proof of the great potency of the perspective cue.

During the last 25 years, James Gibson[2] has been arguing that the perception of the world as three-dimensional depends upon the perception of planes receding into depth, particularly the ground plane (rather than depending on perceiving a set of separate objects at differing distances from one another as in the traditional approach to this problem) and that the basis for this perception derives from the fact that planes have textures. Thus, for example, grass on the ground is a texture. But

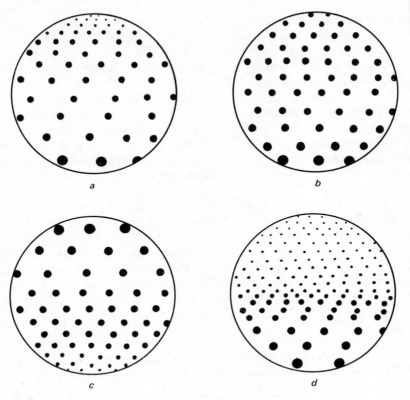

Figure 3-10

because of the way retinal images are formed, i.e., because of the principles of optics, the image of the texture varies in density, giving rise to a gradient. In short, Gibson maintains that the texture gradient is the major source of information about the slope of a plane, at least for the stationary observer. The direction of the gradient would indicate which way the surface recedes from the observer (Fig. 3-10*a* versus *c*); the steepness of the gradient would indicate the extent to which the plane is sloped away from the frontal plane (*a* versus *b*); changes in the gradient would indicate changes in slope (*d*).*

*The claim here is that the texture gradient (or perspective pattern) is, for a stationary observer, the sufficient stimulus for perceiving the slant of a surface. The fact is, however, that a particular pattern of this kind is in itself ambiguous concerning the slant of the surface. The direction of the array with respect to the observer must be taken into account. If the array is localized as "straight ahead," then a retinal image such as that in Fig. 3-10*a* would result from a horizontal plane such as the ground. But if the array were localized as high above the head, this same image would result from a vertical, frontal plane such as the side of a building.

Experiments to test the efficacy of this source of information resulted in findings that the texture gradient *did* create an impression of a sloping surface, but the extent of the perceived slope fell short of the actual slope.[3]   In these experiments, the observer was shown a slide of figures, as illustrated in Fig. 3-10, presented within a circular aperture, and he had to judge the slope by manipulating a comparison surface until it seemed to have the same slope as the surface in the slide.

The texture gradient can be considered to be an instance of size perspective where the elements of the texture are projected in different sizes on the retina.   Gibson deliberately chose size rather than linear perspective as the essential information because it is clearly the more general case.   All surfaces have texture, but unless that texture is regular or ordered there will be no parallel lines explicit or implicit. The fact that the experiments failed to show that irregular size perspective alone is a decisive cue is then quite interesting.   The reader can see for himself that when linear perspective is present the impression of depth is more vivid and more nearly veridical than when size perspective alone is present.*   (Compare Fig. 2-11a or 2-17 with 3-1 or 3-10.)   Fig. 3-11

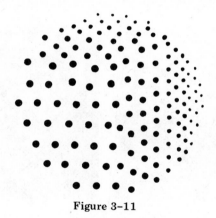

Figure 3-11

*It is possible to examine perspective more analytically.   In the patterns illustrated in Fig. 2-11a or Fig. 2-17, not only does the horizontal extent of objects or horizontal separation between objects diminish with distance but the extents of objects and spaces between them representing the third dimension also diminish with distance.   The latter is called foreshortening.   For example, the separation between the tracks of a railroad diminishes with distance in a picture (or in the retinal image) and the separation between successive wooden ties also diminishes with distance.   Ordinarily, both of these occur together.   The same can be said about irregular patterns such as those shown in Figs. 3-1 and 3-10.   These aspects can be experimentally separated and tested.   There is some evidence that suggests that for regular patterns, perspective (the converging of parallel lines) remains effective but that foreshortening is relatively ineffective.[1]

represents, by texture gradients alone, three planes that meet in a corner. The contours separating these planes were deliberately eliminated. Depth perception is poor; yet contour alone without any texture gradients is a strong indicator of depth (see Fig. 3–8*a*, which represents the same three planes).

As noted earlier, detail perspective and aerial perspective have also been considered pictorial cues to depth. Artists make use of these factors to create the feeling of depth. Yet to claim them as independent cues requires a demonstration of their effectiveness when they are the only factors present. As can be seen in Fig. 3–12, two objects that differ only in clearness of detail do not appear to be at different distances. Of course, one might *infer* that they were at different distances but that does not entitle us to consider aerial and detail perspective as *perceptual* cues. Furthermore, for detail to be a cue presupposes that we know the object and how much detail it should have. It would thus be limited to familiar objects. The most that can be said, therefore, about detail and aerial perspective is that they function as cues provided that other strong cues are already present. But there is no evidence for or against this assertion and it would be difficult to test it.

Figure 3–12

Familiar Size

As noted earlier the size of the retinal image of a familiar object could be a cue to distance provided that the object has only one particular size. For familiar size to work as a distance cue it is necessary that the size of the retinal image for each distance is in some sense "noted" and recorded in memory. This assumption cannot be made lightly because it is generally held that the size of the retinal image is *not* an independent aspect of perceptual experience, but rather is incorporated into the process that takes distance into account and evaluates the objective size of a thing (see the discussion of this issue on pp. 32ff; also see the discussion on p. 73 where it is suggested that memory traces of image sizes are established). However, there is no direct evidence that the size of the retinal image is preserved in memory.

Nevertheless, these assumptions must be correct if familiar size can be shown to be a cue to distance. In a now classic experiment, the observer viewed playing cards of different sizes monocularly in an otherwise dark room.[4] When a card twice the normal size of playing cards was presented, observers tended to judge it to be approximately twice as near as it in fact was; conversely half-sized playing cards were judged to be roughly twice as far from the observer as they actually were. Normal-sized cards were judged to be approximately at their actual distances. Because other cues were eliminated by the method and because errors were a direct function of the size of the retinal image produced, the experiment is an elegant proof of the efficacy of this cue.

However, there are two important qualifications about this conclusion. It has been pointed out that size perspective is a cue to depth, and presumably this does not require familiar objects. What it does require is two or more objects of the same shape that project different sizes to the eye. Thus, if the playing cards of different sizes had been presented to the eye simultaneously or in close succession, one might argue that the effective cue was *relative size*, not familiar size. With this in mind, a number of experiments have been performed aimed at isolating familiar from relative size. The results are still inconclusive.[5] A second, and possibly more fundamental qualification about the playing card experiment, is that it would be plausible to suppose that an observer could *infer* the distance of a familiar object given the size of its retinal image. If the image of a person was very small, one could infer that the person was far away. But this does not necessarily mean that familiar size is a *perceptual cue*, i.e., that it leads to a perceptual impression of distance.

Interposition

There can be little question about the effectiveness of interposition in yielding an impression of one object behind another. All that interposition can do is to give us an impression of relative position in the third dimension; it provides no indication of *how far* behind one object the other object is. That interposition is nevertheless a powerful indicator of such relative position is borne out by a classic experiment in which various cues to depth were opposed to one another in experimentally created conflicts.[6] In one experiment, interposition was set into conflict with binocular disparity, the factor considered by many to be the most effective cue to depth. In a pattern such as that shown in Fig. 3–2, the binocular disparity was such that were it not for interposition, *a* would be perceived to lie well behind *b*. How this can be achieved is explained later. (See footnote on p. 106). The result was that *a* nevertheless appeared to be in front of *b*.

However, it is not clear how one should describe proximal stimulus patterns of the kind we are discussing that lead to an impression of one thing being behind another. Interposition refers to the objective state of affairs, not to the stimulus pattern. That is, in a stimulus pattern such as that of Fig. 3–2 all contours are, of course, in one plane. What is it about such patterns that leads to depth perception in accord with the actual situation? Are they patterns in which one form is incomplete? Obviously that is not a sufficient description since an incomplete square alone will not look like a square behind anything else. Furthermore, how does one define incompleteness unless the figure is very familiar?

The most general description we can give of the kind of stimulus pattern under discussion would be two closed figures that share a common boundary. Fig. 3–13*a* illustrates a pattern that conforms to this description and does not contain familiar figures. It does produce an impression of one figure in front of another, although admittedly the effect is not as strong as in Fig. 3–2. It has been claimed that the basis of the selection of which figure appears in front derives from what happens at the points of intersection, *x* and *y* in Fig. 3–13*a*.*

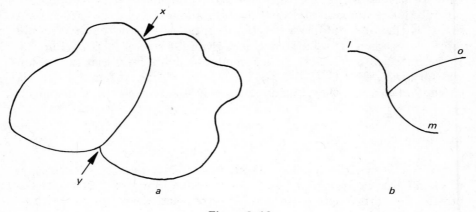

Figure 3–13

*Helmholtz suggested this explanation. For a clear discussion of the problem see reference 7.

As is made clear in the discussion of perceptual organization in Chapter 6, those segments of a line that tend to be smooth continuations of one another tend to be perceived as one unified line; those that entail abrupt changes of direction are perceived as separate lines. Therefore, in considering such a point of intersection, as shown enlarged in Fig. 3–13b, *l*, and *m*, will tend to be perceived as parts of *one* line, whereas *o* will tend to be perceived as a separate line. Since a similar effect will occur at both points of intersection in Fig. 3–13a, the larger contour of which these continuous segments are parts will be perceived as a closed figure. But that means that the portion of this contour that is shared by the other figure will not at the same time be perceived as *belonging* to that figure. The tendency of a shared contour to be perceived as belonging to one region rather than another is the essence of figure-ground organization, which is discussed in detail in Chapter 6. The region to which the shared contour is perceived to belong and give shape to is figure; the other region is perceived as background. Thus, interposition turns out to be a complex factor involving the operation of various principles of perceptual organization.

In cases where two closed figures sharing a common boundary do *not* have points of intersection of the kind just considered other factors may come into play. For example, in Fig. 3–14a, a majority of observers perceive the region at the right to be in front, apparently because part of it at the common boundary juts into and is surrounded by the other figure. This factor is so strong that it may determine the outcome even when what happens at the points of intersection favors the opposite perception (Fig. 3–14b).[8] If no such factor is present, as in Fig. 3–15, one figure may be perceived in front of the other at a given time but it may be either one; in any case the depth effect is weak.*

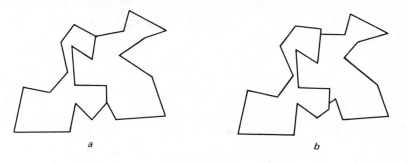

a   b

Figure 3–14

*However the reader is referred to the further discussion of interposition on pp. 137ff where still other factors are shown to determine which region is perceived in front of another region.

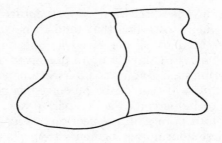

Figure 3-15

Futhermore, such a pattern can also be perceived as two figures in the same plane. At this point it is perhaps no longer meaningful to refer to interposition; rather the drawing illustrates an ambiguous or reversible figure-ground pattern.

Shadow

To judge by the use of shadowing by artists and by experiments described later, shadowing is a very important pictorial cue. It is customary to distinguish *attached shadows*, in which the shadows are the result of the depth within the object itself as in the illustrations in Fig. 3-4 through 3-7, from *cast shadows*, in which one object casts its shadow on a different surface or object. In either case, shadow can provide information about relatively short-range depth relations rather than about the three-dimensional layout of the scene as a whole. That *shadow* does affect perceived depth independently of other cues is attested to by the demonstrations that changing the orientation of the picture completely reverses the perceived-depth relation from convex to concave.

Binocular Disparity

Binocular Depth

Only one static visual cue is nonpictorial (cannot be conveyed by the contents within a single picture), and that is the very important factor of binocular disparity. Information about the location of things in the third dimension is supplied by the location of the two eyes in slightly different positions. A simple illustration of the difference in the images formed in the two eyes resulting from objects at different distances is given in Fig. 3-16a. The reader can easily try this out for himself by holding two objects in the positions indicated and alternately opening and closing each eye. If, however, the two objects are located at the same distance—i.e., in a frontal plane—then the two images are approximately the same (Fig. 3-16b).

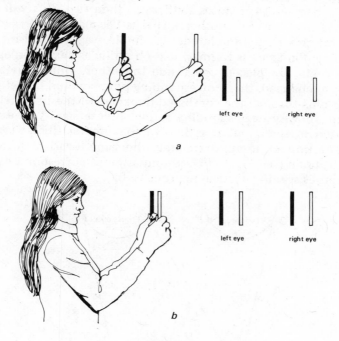

Figure 3-16

But these simple facts of optics raise questions that most people have never thought about. Consider the case in Fig. 3-16b where each eye receives the same image. Why do we perceive only one scene if each eye is transmitting a separate picture to the brain? Why do we not perceive two identical scenes? Apparently the perceptual system correlates the information from the two eyes: if the retinal pictures are identical then what is perceived is the same as would be perceived by either eye alone; if the retinal pictures differ then the different information in each picture will contribute to the percept.

Suppose that the two eyes focus on a single object. By gently displacing one eye with a finger the reader will obtain a double image of the object. What is required for single vision, is that the two images fall in the *same locations* on each retina. For example, if the image of a dot falls on the left retina 3 degrees 14 minutes southwest of the center of the fovea and the image of that dot falls 3 degrees 14 minutes southwest of the center of the fovea on the right retina, then only one dot is perceived. It is as if these corresponding retinal points, as they are called, signify the *same* location in space. If the image of the dot falls, let us say, 2 degrees 30 minutes southwest of the fovea on the right retina instead of 3 degrees 14 minutes southwest, then *two* dots will be perceived, fairly near to one another. That is because *noncorresponding* retinal points are now stimulated. A simple way to envision where corresponding points are is to imagine each retina as half of an egg shell; if the two shells are placed one inside the other, while leaving their orientation unchanged, then corresponding points would be determined by pushing pins through the combined thickness of the two shells. It is not yet known why corresponding retinal points signify one and the same location in space but it is known that neural fibers from these retinal cells terminate in approximately the same location in the visual cortex of the brain (see Fig. 3-17). Stimulation of corresponding retinal locations causes specific cortical neurons to fire.

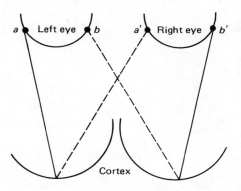

Figure 3-17

To clarify what happens in the binocular disparity situation, consider the situation of Fig. 3-16a, redrawn in Fig. 3-18 as two lines. The two retinal images are similar, but not identical. To eliminate double imagery of the object fixated there is an immediate adjustment of the position of the two eyes such that a particular region in the scene will fall in the center of the fovea of each eye, say the line on the left (*a* and *a'*). Since these are corresponding retinal lines, single vision of that line in the scene

a   b   *a′*   *b′*

Figure 3–18

will occur. But then the line on the right (*b* and *b′*) cannot fall in identical locations.* Therefore, one should predict that this line will appear double because *b* and *b′* falling on noncorresponding regions. If the disparity is great enough one *will* see the line on the right as double. It has been claimed that such double imagery is a cue to depth. But under most circumstances the disparity is not so great and double images are not perceived. Instead one has a vivid impression of depth, in this case of the line on the right behind the one on the left.

An elegant experimental proof of the efficacy of binocular disparity was provided by Charles Wheatstone. He reasoned that if binocular disparity is indeed a cue to depth, as logical analysis suggested it might be, then the proof would consist of artificially synthesizing phenomenal depth by presenting different pictures to the two eyes, pictures that differed in the same way that the retinal images to the two eyes differ in viewing the actual scene.[9] If from two such pictures, both of which are flat, an impression of depth is obtained where none would be obtained from either picture alone (or where the impression of depth is more vivid than would occur from either alone) then one has thereby proven that binocular disparity must be a strong depth cue. Two such views can be combined by deliberately altering the normal convergence of the eyes for objects at the distance presented. In other words, each eye can be made to fixate the same object in its view so that these images will fall in the corresponding foveal region. But this is very difficult to do, at least without considerable practice. It is difficult because they eyes always "want" to look at the same point in space, not two different points, and because accommodation of the lens and convergence of the eyes are generally linked together. Hence, when accommodation is triggered by the actual distance of the two pictures, the convergence called for is one that is normally appropriate for that distance.

---

*For any given distance there is a set of points in the field that fall on corresponding retinal points and the locus of all these points is called the horopter. Single vision occurs for all points in the horopter, and, in theory at least, they should all appear equidistant from the observer.

Therefore, a device is needed to uncouple accommodation and convergence. A simple method is to place a prism in front of one eye. Then that eye can actually be converged with the other eye at the distance of the picture but because prisms deflect the direction of light, what that eye "sees" is its picture, rather than the picture in front of the other eye (Fig. 3-19). The stereoscope invented independently by Wheatstone and Brewster makes use of a half lens placed in front of *each* eye (see Fig. 3-20). The figure shows in cross section how images are formed in the two eyes when the observer views two pictures such as that of Fig. 3-18. Light rays passing through the lenses become parallel, as if emanating from infinitely distant objects. Since the eyes are then accommodated for infinity and are parallel to one another, each can be presented with a separate picture. Another device, also invented by Wheatstone, a mirror stereoscope or haploscope as it was once called, makes use of mirrors to enable the eyes to be converged at the same point in space while still receiving stimulation from separate points in space, the two pictures (Fig. 3-21).

In order to make it possible for the reader to view stereo pictures it is suggested that he hold a blank page or cardboard perpendicular to the page of the book midway between the two pictures as illustrated in Fig. 3-22. The picture on the left is then only visible to the left eye and the one on the right only visible to the right eye. The eyes should be about 8 to 12 inches from the book and the long axis of the head should be parallel to the edges of the book. By imagining one is looking

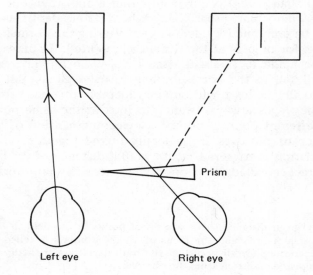

Left eye   Right eye

Prism

Figure 3-19

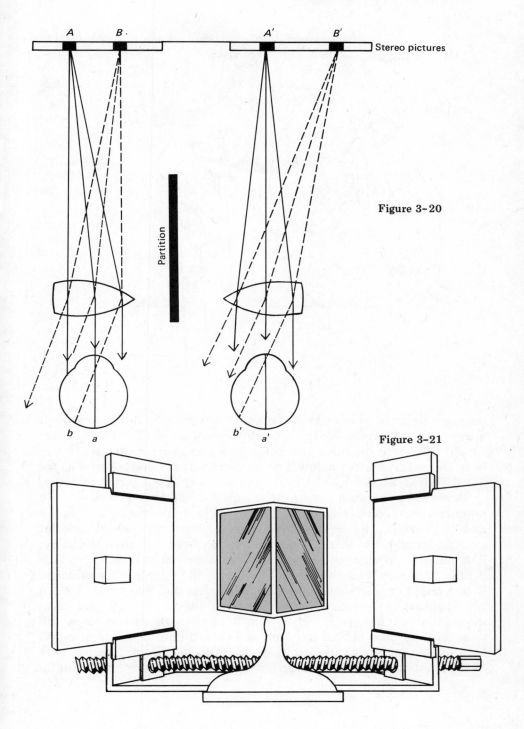

Figure 3-20

Figure 3-21

Figure 3-22

through the book at something far away the eyes will then turn in such a way that each eye is looking at a different picture. The two pictures should then fuse into one combined view and stereoscopic depth will be achieved. A certain amount of trail and error is necessary. Figures 3-18, 3-23, 3-24, 3-25, 3-28, 3-29, and 3-30 can be viewed in this way.

Stereoscopic viewing does produce a vivid impression of depth. In popular stereoscopic viewing of photography many pictorial cues are usually present. The pictures themselves appear three-dimensional; but stereoscopically, the depth is very much enhanced. In the laboratory, it is possible to view patterns that when seen singly do not produce depth. It is easy to make up such patterns; the only guiding principle is to present to each eye approximately what that eye would receive when looking at the actual three-dimensional object. Thus, for example, the double line pattern shown in Fig. 3-18 through a stereoscope will look like one line behind another; the curved lines in Fig. 3-23a will look like a line bowed toward us in the third dimension (the presence of the identical other line in each view serves as a reference for "fusion");

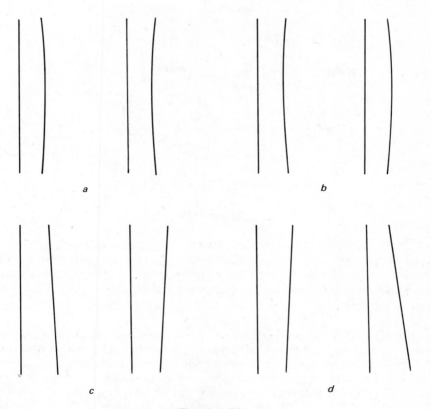

Figure 3-23

the curved lines in Fig. 3-23*b* will look like a line bowed away from us in the third dimension. The reader can imagine how *c* and *d* will look and then try them out. Fig. 3-24 will look like a small rectangle floating behind a larger one; Fig. 3-25 is a familiar object. It should be pointed out, however, that the stereoscopic effect with such simple line patterns is not as easy to achieve as with photographs of scenes, and often it requires quite a few seconds before true depth is realized. For some

Figure 3-24

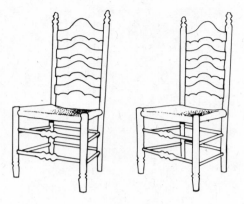

Figure 3-25

observers depth is never achieved from such stereograms.* This has been something of a well-kept laboratory secret for some time. The theoretical significance of it is not fully understood except that it would seem to imply that binocular disparity is most effective when it interacts with other cues.

Another method for achieving fusion and depth from separate pictures is to make use of an anaglyph. Two pictures are presented, one in one color (red) and the other in a different color (green). Each picture represents the stimulus pattern one eye would receive in viewing a particular scene, and the pictures could in fact be photographs taken from slightly separate locations. By viewing each picture with a colored filter only light from the appropriate picture can enter the eye. The red filter permits only the green picture to be seen since it selectively absorbs the complementary green light, thus rendering the green light black: the red line appears faintly red against the background of the white page. The green filter permits only the red picture to be seen. A related technique that makes use of polarized light is called a *vectograph*.

Still another method of creating depth from separate pictures does not require the observer to view through filters or any device in front of his eyes. The optical system that provides a different image for each eye is built into the display card. The card actually contains two pictures, each printed on alternate narrow strips, as shown very much enlarged in Fig. 3-26a. Those marked *l* are seen only by the left eye; those marked *r* only by the right eye. The strips are so narrow that the picture seen by each eye appears continuous. By means of tiny cylindrically (or prismatically) shaped transparent columns directly over the pictures, shown in a cross-sectional view in Fig. 3-26b, light reflected by the strips constituting each picture enters one

---

*There are clear individual differences in the strength and relative dominance of the binocular disparity cue to depth.

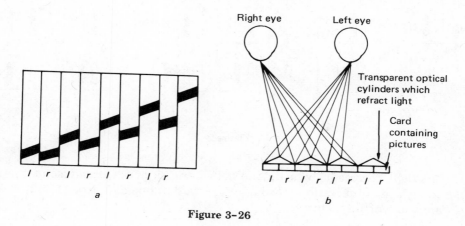

Figure 3-26

eye but not the other. This technique is used in advertisements that the reader has no doubt seen. It provokes curiosity and puzzlement because the impression of depth is vivid at the same time that it is evident that the display card is, in fact, two dimensional. The technique has been referred to as free or parallax stereoscopy and the process of creating the display card is called autostereoscopic photography.

If the patterns presented to the two eyes are reversed, the perceived depth relation is reversed. This is, of course, precisely what one must predict. Thus, for example, if the patterns at the top of Fig. 3-27a presented to the two eyes are reversed (bottom), then it can be "deduced" that the black pencil must be behind the white one.* One can also reverse the patterns revealed to the two eyes by turning each picture upside down (see Fig. 3-27b). Here not only are the left-right and up-down positions of objects reversed but their depth relations are reversed. The object that has appeared in front now appears behind. A less drastic procedure for reversing apparent depth is to reverse each picture only with respect to left and right (see Fig. 3-27c). Wheatstone invented a device that achieves this effect while the observer is viewing the actual scene. By means of mirrors the image each eye receives is

---

*Therefore, it follows that for correct depth perception via binocular disparity, the perceptual system must have the information concerning the eye from which each image originated. This is quite interesting because we are generally not consciously aware of two images at all and, if we are in certain instances when we deliberately try to attend to double images, we still cannot tell from which eye the images originate unless we close each eye alternately. Therefore, here is a case where we must distinguish information known to be registered in the brain from information that is consciously appreciated.

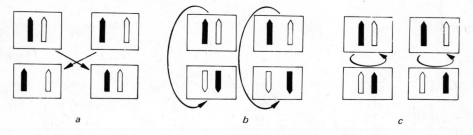

Figure 3-27

left-right reversed.   Wheatstone called the device a *pseudoscope*.   Although his observations through the pseudoscope date from 1852, they are still worth reading.*

> "The natural appearance of the object continues to obtrude itself, when suddenly and at other times gradually, the converse occupies its place.   The reason of this is that the relief and distance of objects is not suggested to the mind solely by the binocular pictures and the convergence of the optic axes, but also by other signs, which are perceived by means of each eye singly; among which the most effective are the distributions of light and shade and the perspective. . . . One idea being therefore suggested to the mind by one set of signs, and another totally incompatible idea by another set, according as the mental attention is directed . . . the normal form or its converse is perceived . . . Some very paradoxical results are obtained when objects in motion are viewed through the pseudoscope.   When an object approaches, the magnitude of its picture on the retina increases as in ordinary vision, but the inclination of the optic axes, instead of increasing, becomes less, as I have already explained.   Now an enlargement of the picture on the retina invariably suggests approach, and a less convergence of the optic axes indicates that the object is at a greater distance; and we have thus two contradictory suggestions."[10]

It has recently been discovered that very complex patterns, which to one eye alone look like a mosaic of light and dark spots, will nevertheless yield depth effects if disparity of a subset of the spots is present.[11]

---

*It is interesting to note that in research on the question of adaptation to inverted or left-right reversed images, with binocular vision one faces the unwanted complication of a pseudoscopic effect.   One investigator, Ewert, seemed unaware that this was the case.   See Chapter 10.   This unawareness was no doubt a function of the fact that other cues continued to indicate the correct depth relations and these cues were dominant.   It is by means of a pseudoscope that an experimental conflict can be created between binocular disparity and other cues, as for example, interposition.

Fig. 3–28 shows two patterns that when viewed through a stereoscope will be perceived as a T floating in front of a background. To produce such stereoscopic pairs, two identical patterns are made, by photocopying one such randomly generated array of spots. Then a piece of one of these patterns is cut out, such as a rectangular piece, and it pasted back again after it is slightly shifted to one side. The empty space is filled with random spots.

Figure 3-28

Even though there is no figure as such presented to either eye, a phenomenal figure does emerge from the binocular viewing in a certain depth relation to the background. This random-dot stereogram technique is particularly useful in eliminating all depth cues but disparity. The achievement of depth under these conditions suggests the working of an extraordinary mechanism whereby identical clusterings of light and dark spots are detected and the disparity between them is interpreted as signifying depth. However, it should be pointed out that here, as with simple line patterns of unfamiliar things, it often takes time to get the depth effect and some observers do not experience depth.

No depth effect is achieved (except under very special conditions) when the disparity is in a vertical retinal direction as is illustrated in Fig. 3–29. Rather one will either perceive both disparate contours as shown in the figure or, if the two images are sufficiently close to one another, one or the other of these contours. This makes sense because vertical disparity cannot occur under natural conditions. It could occur and would indicate depth only if one eye were above the other in

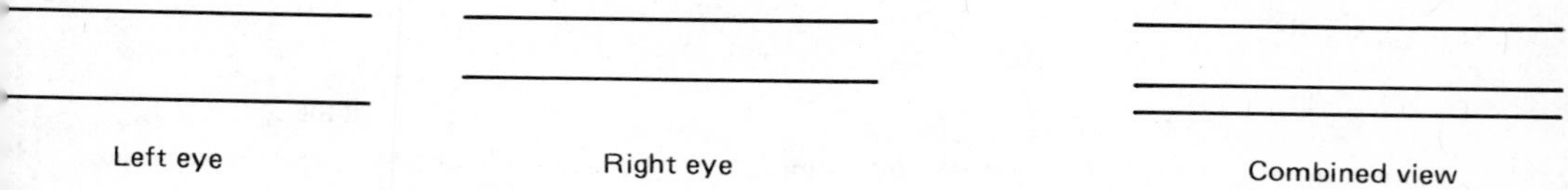

Left eye   Right eye   Combined view

Figure 3-29

the head. Therefore, the perceptual system interprets only horizontal disparity as indicating depth. The absence of disparity explains why it is difficult to tell which rope is behind in a clothesline. Often there are no distinctive marks in the lines that might permit the detection of horizontal disparities. The difficulty is eliminated when clothespins are placed on the lines.

The depth signified by disparity varies with the amount of disparity. In other words the farther apart two objects A and B are the greater is the impression of depth between them. But there is a complication that results from the relationship between the absolute distance of the pair of objects from the observer and the disparity associated with the objective separation in depth between the objects. Suppose object A is 1 foot in front of object B. If object A is 3 feet from the observer this 1-foot separation will produce appreciably disparate images. But suppose object A is 100 feet away. Then the disparity between the A–B images on the retina deriving from the 1-foot separation between objects A and B will be negligible. Does this mean that depth perception based on disparity falls off with an increase in the absolute distance of the set of objects under condiseration?

There is evidence that it does not. The absolute distance of the objects may be taken into account in the assessment by the perceptual system of the depth significance of the disparity. If so, one may speak here of a constancy. Despite variations in the amount of binocular disparity with distance, the depth signified is more or less constant because other information is taken into account. Such a mechanism can be demonstrated by holding disparity constant and manipulating absolute distance cues. In one experiment this was achieved by altering convergence by means of a mirror stereoscope. When the convergence required was doubled (for an object at half the distance) while the degree of disparity and real distance remained constant, the depth impression between objects A and B decreased markedly.* A similar effect can be observed by looking at anaglyph or vectograph figures through appropriate filters. First one notes the depth between the objects in the picture held at arm's length. Then one notes what seems to happen to this depth when moving nearer or farther away from it. Disparity changes with changes in the distance of the picture but not as much as it would for the actual object in depth, and, therefore, the impression of depth varies.

*Physical disparity decreases as the inverse square of distance. Therefore the investigators predicted that as the phenomenal distance was halved, the perceived depth would reduce to one quarter of its former value. This was confirmed by the experiment.[12]

There are certain interesting applications of stereoscopy. One such application is in aerial photography where two pictures taken some distance apart—as far apart on the airplane as possible—reveal topographical features on the terrain that are not visible from a single picture when later viewed in a stereoscope. In fact, camouflage can often be detected in this way because the camouflaged object will appear elevated or depressed much as is the case in the random pattern of spots shown in Fig. 3-28.

Stereoscopic pictures of the moon taken from two distant places on earth yield a depth impression. Stereoscopy has also been employed to determine if printed money is counterfeit. Any slight differences in the location of contours in a genuine and counterfeit bill, too slight to be detected by inspection, will show up in the form of depth differences when the two are viewed stereoscopically.*

Binocular Rivalry and the Mechanisms Underlying Binocular Interaction

In the situation of binocular disparity only slightly different images are involved. It will be helpful now to consider what is perceived when markedly different images are received. We should be able to predict what will be seen on the basis of what has been said about corresponding and noncorresponding points. Thus, for example, suppose the left eye is stimulated by a vertical bar and the right eye by a horizontal bar (see Fig. 3-30a). The reader can try this out by the technique suggested in Fig. 3-22. Since, except for the small region where the bars overlap, noncorresponding points are stimulated by the bars, we should predict that both bars will be perceived. This is more or less what does happen. In Fig. 3-30b examples are shown of combined views resulting from these two half-views.

However, we have not faced up to one important fact. Where, in the example of Fig. 3-30, one eye receives a bar stimulus, the other eye receives some stimulation in the corresponding points. It is stimulated by the white background of the page. Therefore, if point x in one eye is a dark spot and corresponding point x' in the other eye is a light region,

---

*A well-known laboratory illusion, the Pulfrich effect, can be understood in terms of binocular disparity depth information. The observer views an object oscillating back and forth (or a pendulum swinging) in the frontal plane through a filter in front of one eye (the glass in ordinary sunglasses can be used). The object appears to be swinging around an elliptical path toward and away from the observer. The explanation would seem to be that the weaker stimulus reaching the one retina through the filter is transmitted to the brain a brief moment after the stimulus from the other retina. Therefore, in relation to some stationary reference point, the images of the object from the two eyes are, functionally speaking, disparate. Such disparate images would result from an object changing its distance from the observer as it oscillates back and forth and, hence, that is what is perceived.[13]

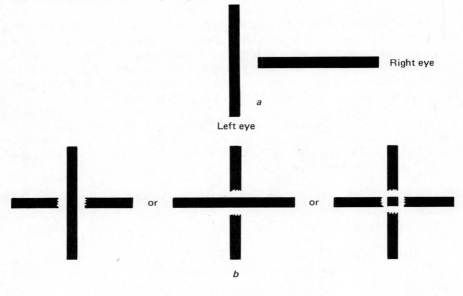

Figure 3-30

how will this conflict be resolved? Both a dark and a light spot should be perceived in the same place in space since corresponding points are involved.

There would seem to be two possible outcomes of this conflict situation and each fits a different theory of binocular vision. Some compromise could occur resulting from a *fusing* by the brain of the two retinal inputs. That would mean perceiving a gray spot resulting from a mixture of a dark and light spot. Or one might perceive one or the other, a dark spot *or* a light spot. In that event one of the retinal inputs is being *suppressed* or inhibited. This is what actually happens; a dark spot is perceived. This means that of the two possibilities, it is the light region that is suppressed. However, if this imaginary experiment had been done with one eye receiving a white spot on an otherwise black background and the other eye receiving a black background only then a white spot would be perceived. Therefore, the black corresponding region would be suppressed. So the rule seems to be that we will perceive whichever of a pair of corresponding retinal locations is a figure or contour and to suppress whichever is a uniform surface or background. Contour predominants over a uniform surface.

But suppose images of different *figures* fall on corresponding points, as at the intersection in Fig. 3-30. What seems to happen is that now one and now the other figure is perceived, the other being alternately suppressed. This alternation is referred to as *rivalry*. Furthermore, a given figure seems to bring part of its background with it. Thus when the horizontal bar is suppressed, one sees a vertical black bar with some white around it in the vicinity of the intersection.

In further support of the suppression theory of singleness of vision is the easily observed fact that the world does not appear dimmer when we close one eye although doing so cuts in *half* the total amount of light energy falling on the retinas. In this case there is no apparent summation of neural excitation stemming from the retinal cells of the two eyes. What is implied by the suppression theory is that for any given pair of corresponding points only the stimulus falling in one of these is perceived; the other is suppressed. This does not necessarily mean that the image to one eye is suppressed in its entirety. In the example shown in Fig. 3-30 suppression occurs for portions of the images in *both* eyes.

At this point we can consider again the situation of binocular disparity. What happens to the double images? If the disparity is great enough, double images *are* perceived. Each contour as figure will prevail in the conflict with the homogenous background region falling on the corresponding place in the other eye. But what happens to the double images when the disparity is not very great? A plausible answer is that the suppression that occurs has a certain range to it, that is, more is suppressed than just what falls precisely in the corresponding retinal regions. The white "ghosts" perceived around the black bars at the intersection in Fig. 3-30 attest to this fact. If this is true it implies that at any moment, while perceiving the depth relation, if one were to examine one's percept carefully, from the standpoint of two-dimensional direction, it would correspond to one or the other of the images presented to the two eyes.

Apart from the question about double imagery there is the further, more fundamental, question of why depth is perceived in the disparity situation. We do not know the answer to this question. Hering proposed that each retinal point not only innately signifies a particular direction in space (local sign), but also a particular depth value.[14] These values are positive in the nasal halves of the retinas, signifying that things are "farther away," and negative in the temporal halves of the retinas, signifying that things are "nearer." Depth values were held to increase (positively or negatively) with increasing distance along the retina from the central fovea. When corresponding points are stimulated, since one is on the nasal side and the other on the temporal side, zero depth is signified because these points are of equal magnitude but of opposite sign. When noncorresponding points are stimulated, the depth perceived is a function of the algebraic sum of the depth values signified by the two points. Although this theory is ingenious, there are many difficulties with it. To mention just one, with one eye closed all points in the field that are actually equidistant from the observer should appear at varying depths, because the depth value signified by their retinal locations are not canceled by depth values of opposing sign from the other eye. Few investigators today take this theory very seriously.

A different theory of stereoscopic depth is based on the notion that the images from the two eyes fuse with one another at some location in the nervous system. If corresponding points are stimulated the fusion occurs at one level in the brain, but if noncorresponding points are stimulated the fusion occurs at a different level. The greater the difference in level, the greater is the perceived depth. The presumption here is that the location of the "level" in the brain of the fusion is the direct correlate of perceived stereoscopic depth. The fusion is also thought to explain the fact of singleness of vision and, as such, is an alternate theory to that of suppression as discussed previously.[15] There are many difficulties with this theory chief among which is the fact that depth from disparity is perceived even when double images are present or rivalry occurs, implying no fusion of the images from the two eyes.*

Very recently it has been found that there are cells in the visual cortex (of the cat) that respond to binocular stimulation by contours in similar orientations in approximately corresponding retinal locations.[19] Some cells discharge with maximum frequency when a specific degree of disparity obtains between the two images, so that one might refer to these

---

*There are certain intriguing problems about binocular disparity that cannot be done justice in this brief discussion. For example, for purposes of simplifying the problem, in all the illustrations it has been assumed that there are only two objects or lines in the field. So when one is fixated, it is clear that the noncorresponding images of the other represent one object in the world. But in reality there are many objects in the field so that, schematically, the two images might look something like this

XXAXXBXX   XXAXXXBX
L eye   R eye

If the observer fixates A, then the B images fall on noncorresponding points. But there is an image of an object X that in the right eye falls on a place corresponding to that of B in the left eye and conversely with regard to the image of an object X in the left eye corresponding to B in the right eye. So for these X–B pairs of corresponding objects there is no disparity. Therefore a "decision" must be made by the perceptual system about which images in the two eyes represent the same thing in the world before disparity differences can be correctly interpreted. It would seem that it is the *similarity* between the images of objects that governs this "decision," for example A with A, B with B and Xs with Xs in the illustration shown. Furthermore, there is evidence that it is not a point by point similarity that governs this decision, but a similarity of the patterns falling on the two eyes. The interested reader is referred to a chapter by Kaufman.[16] For evidence concerning the crucial importance of disparity between *patterns* as the basis of stereoscopic depth, see also Werner[17] and Wallach and Lindauer.[18]

as binocular-disparity detectors. However the finding that such cells exist does not establish what role if any they actually play in the perception of depth. If it can be demonstrated that disparity depth depends upon the discharging of these neural units, then they should be considered to provide a basis for the discrimination by the perceptual system of the presence or absence or degree of binocular disparity rather than to be the direct neural correlate of perceived depth. For if the latter view were to be advanced there would be many facts about disparity that would be difficult to explain. For example, as noted previously, a given degree of disparity can signify more or less depth depending upon absolute distance. Also, as is brought out toward the end of the chapter, the depth signified by a given degree of disparity is subject to change as a result of exposure to conflicting information about depth such as that which results from viewing the world through distorting optical devices. These facts, of course, present difficulties for any theory of depth achieved from binocular disparity including those outlined in the preceding paragraphs.

A different way of looking at the problem of binocular depth is in terms of a reasoning-like process. It is tempting to believe that information deriving from the disparate images is available to the perceptual system and that the perceptual system engages in a process analogous to thinking concerning what spatial arrangement in the outer world has produced these two images. If, as shown in Fig. 3–31*a* the separation between images x and y in the left eye is less than that between x' and y' in the right eye, it "follows" that object Y must be behind X. It "follows" because to receive this wider image $x' -y'$ the right eye must be looking at X-Y from a position that lies closer to the direction that is perpendicular to the plane of X-Y than the left eye; the direction of

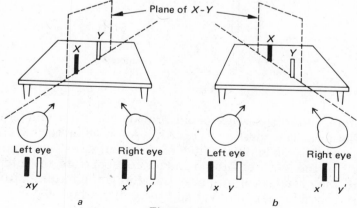

Figure 3–31

gaze of the left eye must be closer to alignment with the plane of X-Y. But, if as shown in Fig. 3–31b, X (on the left) were behind Y (on the right), then the separation between images x and y would have to be greater in the left eye. If a process of this kind occurs, then it would be understandable why the depth signified by a given degree of disparity would be a function of taking into account the absolute distance of the object.

Transforming Visual Cues

When we move or when objects move there is motion within the retinal image. Does this retinal motion contain information about depth relationships? Let us consider first the relatively simple case of two objects at different distances from the eye (see Fig. 3–32). It will simplify matters to assume that only one eye is open. If b is behind a then when the observer is in position 1 there will be a certain separation between the images of a and b. If the observer moves to the right, that separation will increase as shown in 2. The situation is thus quite analogous to binocular disparity. To make the analogy even more complete, position 2 can be considered to be in the same location in space as the other eye. Thus, motion parallax provides the same kind of information that binocular parallax provides. What the latter gives in two simultaneous images, the former gives in successive images.

a b a' b'

Position 1   Position 2

Figure 3-32

Therefore, motion parallax could provide useful information about depth relations. The question is, does it? A few laboratory studies that have isolated this cue imply that it does. In recent years, however, largely as a result of the work of Gibson and his collaborators, the interest has shifted to the examination of image transformation resulting from relative movement between observer and the entire array of points within surfaces of objects. As noted earlier, Gibson believes that the perception of the third dimension depends upon the direct perception of surfaces at various slants and slopes and should not be thought of as a construction based on the locating of isolated objects by virtue of different cues.

When we move relative to a surface, such as the ground, parallax changes result in a differential rate of movement of the images of the texture. Parallax change is based on change of direction. Thus, if an observer moves at right angles to a plane, such as the ground, the nearer a region is to the observer, the more rapidly will its direction change; consequently the more rapidly will its image displace over the retina. In looking out the window of a moving train, one can sense the rapid displacement through one's visual field of the nearby terrain and, by contrast, the relatively slow displacement of the more distant terrain. Thus, there is a gradient in the pattern of flow of the image of the ground (see Fig. 3-33a). Gibson calls this sort of transformation *motion perspective*. If one turns one's eye in order to remain fixated at some specific distance on the ground, then the images of the texture at that distance will, of course, be stationary while that of the terrain in front and in back of that region will flow in opposite directions (see Fig. 3-33b).

Figure 3-33

If we move directly toward a plane, such as a wall, the set of parallax changes of all points is different. Now as the reader can imagine, there is no change in direction of the region that is straight ahead, since it remains straight ahead, but regions off to the side rapidly displace out toward the periphery (see Fig. 3-34). Thus, there is an entirely different parallax cue in this case, an expansion pattern as it is called.

For Gibson, the important information is in the visual transformation. Therefore, it should not matter whether the transformation is produced by the observer's movement or by the movement of the plane or object. Consequently, most of the experimental tests of the efficacy of motion

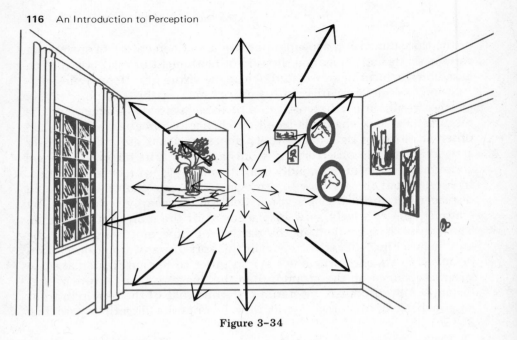

Figure 3-34

perspective as a cue have consisted of creating a flow pattern in the display. Thus, for example, a gradient of retinal velocity can be created by moving luminous spots, which are all in the frontal plane, at different speeds. The spots are moved across the field horizontally with a velocity that decreases from the bottom of the array to the top. This gradient of velocity should, according to Gibson, yield an impression of a surface tilted backward, away from the vertical. Without the movement there would be no reason to perceive the array of spots as a surface sloped backward; rather it should appear to be vertical.

Some experiments of this kind have failed to show the predicted effect.[20] Others have shown some effect but the precise slant of the plane perceived was not in accord with the prediction.[21] The possibility arises that the effectiveness of parallax depends very much on whether it is the observer or the stimulus array that moves. Returning to the two-object situation shown in Fig. 3-32, it would seem quite unlikely that if, instead of the observer moving, a and b were made to move so as to produce the change from 1 to 2, the observer would perceive b behind a. Rather he would undoubtedly perceive a and b in the same plane both moving slightly to the left but a moving more rapidly and, therefore, shifting away from b. The stimulus transformation is ambiguous. However, with no effective information to the contrary the "assumption" that objects are equidistant, in one plane, would probably dominate. Apparently motion parallax per se is not sufficiently effective to overcome this assumption. However, if the observer moves, it becomes plausible to "assume" that the visual stimulus change that is concomitant with the movement is caused by the observer's movement and, therefore, that nothing in the world is moving.* That being the case, the "problem" presented by the changing retinal pattern of Fig. 3-32 can only be solved by perceiving *b* behind *a*.

This is not to maintain that transforming visual patterns seen by a stationary observer will not often result in an impression of depth. Thus, for example, if a sharp shadow of a three-dimensional figure is thrown on a screen and if the figure rotates, then the shadow of the figure will undergo a transformation (see Fig. 3-35).[22] This transforming shadow pattern will often look strikingly three-dimensional even where the object is not at all familiar and its shadow would not look three-dimensional in any of its stationary positions. Logically, the transforming shadow pattern is ambiguous as to what it represents and it could be perceived as a distorting two-dimensional figure. Apparently then, in this case the transformational information is sufficiently potent to overcome the equidistance assumption.† Needless to say, the kinetic depth affect (KDE) can also be presumed to occur when the observer

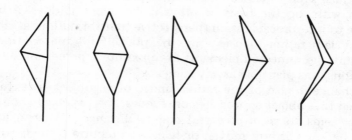

Figure 3-35

---

*The reader is referred to a more extended discussion of position constancy and the distinction between observer-produced stimulus change and externally produced stimulus change on pp. 186-189.

†A very vivid impression of depth is achieved when a pattern such as that shown in Fig. 3-36*a* is drawn on a disk and is rotated (*b* illustrates how the pattern appears following a rotation of 180 degrees). The two-dimensional transformation that results would also be produced by a truncated cone oscillating back and forth about a vertical axis and that is what most observers perceive after a brief interval. The stereokinetic effect, as it has been called, is related to a phenomenon discussed in Chapter 5, concerning the tendency to perceive rotating circular figures as stationary. In the present example, the circles are not seen as rotating and, as a result, one might say that the transformation that occurs can best be "explained" by the perceptual system by inferring a three-dimensional object oscillating back and forth.[23]

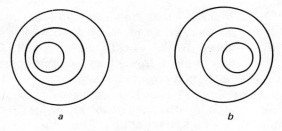

a   *b*

Figure 3-36

changes his position in relation to an object rather than the other way around as described here.

Why this kind of transforming stimulus is effective when some of those employed by Gibson and his co-workers are not is not yet fully clear. In this (KDE) situation, the investigators believe the changing angles and lengths of lines is crucial. But perhaps it is of great importance that the observer is aware to begin with that he is viewing one object. That being the case it becomes a very plausible "hypothesis" that it is a three-dimensional thing rotating. Perhaps the same is true for a surface such as Gibson has studied provided it looks like a surface to begin with, on the basis of other cues. Once it does, it becomes plausible to interpret its various perspective transformations as signifying a certain slant rather than as some inexplicable internal motions. But where only disconnected elements are presented, perceiving such internal motions is as plausible as anything else.*

The change in size of the retinal image of an object or textured surface when that object approaches or recedes, the *expansion-contraction pattern*, seems to be a powerful cue to distance. When a luminous object, shadow pattern, movie, or television picture is made to expand and contract, it will lead to the impression of an object of constant size approaching and receding into the distance. Once again, the stimulus change is ambiguous, but in this case the outcome is unambiguous.†

---

*A KDE effect is obtained for unconnected elements by sophisticated observers instructed to judge figural rigidity, but the impression of such rigidity and coherence is far superior when the elements are connected.[24]

†This statement oversimplifies somewhat. There is no question that the object appears to approach or recede into the distance. There is also no question that it appears more nearly constant in size than its changing image would lead us to predict. However, one is aware of a change in the object's size as well. It is possible that this aspect of the perceptual experience refers to extensity rather than objective size. Conditions are favorable here for noting extensity change because the image is undergoing rapid large changes of size. In fact, it would be surprising if we were not aware of this proximal stimulus change.

It is difficult to assess the overall importance of transforming visual cues for the veridical perception of the third dimension, at least in the human adult. Gibson and his collaborators have now reached the conclusion that this source of information is crucial because static cues or at least monocular static cues are likely to be ambiguous. Since man is a mobile creature this conclusion seems perfectly plausible to them. But the fact remains that in most situations in daily life the perception of distance and depth is excellent without any movement at all on the part of the observer. It is also worth noting that in many animals, survival depends upon adequate distance perception at moments when they are perfectly still, as in amphibia and reptiles that suddenly strike their moving prey or in animals that stalk their prey and remain frozen in position prior to the attack. On the other hand, it is possible that transforming cues do play a crucial role in the early infancy of animals and humans and we return to this matter at the end of the chapter.

Oculomotor Cues

Berkeley was of the opinion that information from accommodation of the lens and convergence of the eyes provided the chief "signs" to the mind about distance. He reasoned that the two-dimensional retinal image could not directly inform about distance so that only by constant association with impressions derived from touch did these muscular adjustments become indicators of distance.

We have already considered the logical possibility of these factors serving as cues. The fact is that normally accommodation and convergence are correlated with changes of distance of the object fixated. The question is whether use is made of such potentially usable information. The question is easily answered, because we can eliminate all but these two cues by requiring the observer to view a *single* luminous object in the dark with the head held stationary. Pictorial cues, binocular disparity, and motion parallax are then all eliminated. When this experiment is done—and the reader can easily try it for himself—distance is still perceived with a fair degree of accuracy. However, if the dark room is very large so that the object can be placed several feet or more away from the observer, then its distance will be underestimated, and increasingly so the greater the actual distance. A better method is to have the observer look at an object through a pair of glasses that simultaneously alters convergence and accommodation so that both cues together now signify a greater (or lesser) distance of the object. The results clearly prove the effectiveness of these two cues combined, but only at distances of less than around 6 feet. [25]

Apparently, the two factors together are effective, at least at short distances. What about each factor taken alone? This is not an easy question to answer because accommodation and convergence changes tend to be linked. It is known that with only one eye open, changes in the thickness of the lens resulting from the automatic focusing with changes of distance of the object lead to changes in the direction of the other, closed eye. In other words, the two eyes are properly converged on the object fixated even though one eye is closed. This is called *accommodative convergence.* (The opposite or *convergent accommodation* apparently also occurs; if convergence of the eyes is manipulated in some way, the appropriate accommodation will be elicited.) To dissociate the two is thus difficult.

However, with only one eye the perception of distance in a dark field is poorer than with two eyes, so apparently the information from accommodative convergence is not quite the same as that from convergence when it is directly triggered by the tendency to eliminate double imagery coming from two eyes. In fact, it had been found that distance perception under such monocular conditions is highly inaccurate for objects beyond a few feet, and even at closer distances it is not too reliable. Hence accommodation is no longer considered to be a really important factor in distance perception. Concerning the mechanism underlying accommodation as a cue, it is known that the ciliary muscle attached to the lens must contract to thicken the lens and must relax to permit it to flatten out. Therefore, it has been thought that the proprioceptive feedback from sensory fibers in this muscle is the source of information, such as it is, about the state of the lens; subjectively stated, the sense of strain to accommodate.* However, it should be noted that there must be some basis for accommodative changes of the lens to be initiated in a particular direction in the first place, i.e., there must be some information that serves as the basis for either a relaxation or contraction of the ciliary muscle. This is usually assumed to be the blurred image. In that case, one might say that the blurred image is a prior cue that already contains the information about distance that shortly will be supplied by the specific accommodation achieved. In other words, it is already known that the object about to

---

*An alternative possibility is that there is some record in the nervous system of the signals *out* to the ciliary muscle and that the record of "instructions" to this muscle is the source of information. See the discussion of the parallel problem concerning the source of information about eye movement, pp. 186–187.

be fixated is at a given distance from the object now being fixated, the exact difference in distance being a function of the degree of blur. One trouble with this idea, however, is that the image can be blurred either because accommodation is too strong or too weak so that unless additional information is contained within the blurred image, blur itself cannot indicate in which direction to change accommodation. The accomodative change is undoubtedly initiated by other cues. Thus, in shifting the eyes to the horizon, accommodation for far vision may begin before the eyes get there.

Convergence can be isolated by the expedient of looking through artificial pupils with both eyes. Here there is no need for accommodative change because a sharp image is present for all distances. However, convergent accommodation may still be present unless drugs are used to prevent change of accommodation.[26] Another method and one used in many classic experiments on this problem is to vary the angle of the mirrors in a mirror stereoscope (see Fig. 3–21). The convergence of the eyes must then change if one is to achieve single vision. Accommodation, however, must remain fixed for the distance of the pictures. Here one does not eliminate accommodation; rather it is held constant.

When experiments are done in this way, a curious result is obtained. (See the discussion on pp. 35 which is briefly summarized here.) The fused stereoscopic "object" consistently appears to get smaller when convergence is increased (the eyes converged at a nearer distance) and larger when convergence is decreased. This effect of distance information on perceived size is what one should expect. However, reports about the distance of the object do not correlate highly with the convergence of the eyes. Therefore it would appear that convergence information is made use of, but it is not revealed by direct reports about distance. It is probable that this paradox results from the secondary effect of the changes in perceived size of the object, which itself is the result of the primary effect of convergence information. Confusion and competition between these two cues then complicate the outcome.

If the reported size changes in experiments of this kind can be taken as proof of the efficacy of convergence, then convergence is indeed a cue. However, the eyes are almost parallel beyond 30 feet so that, logically, further changes of distance cannot be picked up by convergence information and experiments would seem to confirm this analysis. (As noted previously even when *both* convergence and accommodation are available as cues, their combined effectiveness falls off beyond a few feet.) Therefore, this cue is also not considered to be very important, at least in the kind of space perception that occurs out-of-doors. Concerning the mechanism, one can again invoke proprioception, the feedback from sensory fibers in the eye muscles that could transmit information to the brain concerning the degree of contraction of these muscles. One seems to experience a greater strain in looking at a very close object.* Again, however, it can be argued that the relevant information about distance is already present, prior to the convergent change, namely, the double images that seem to trigger the convergence. The greater the separation between the double images the farther must be the object about to be viewed from the one now being viewed.

Do We Learn to See in Three Dimensions or Is It an Inborn Capacity?

Logical Considerations and Evidence

We now consider some of the evidence that bears on the question of the origin of our perception of the world as three-dimensional. Before doing so, it will be helpful to examine more closely what is implied when we assert that three-dimensional perception is either innate or learned. To say that such perception is innate is to say that at birth— or shortly thereafter if an initial period of maturation is necessary—the organism perceives the world as three-dimensional. Objects appear at varying distances from the organism and from one another more or less the way they appear to the adult. The basis of such perception then resides in sensory and neural mechanisms that have evolved to yield this outcome. The designation "innate" should thus not imply that the problem of explanation is solved; on the contrary, the problem is far from solved. But this designation does rule out certain kinds of explanation, namely, those that seek to derive the perception of depth from the history of prior sensory experiences of the organism.

On the other hand, to say that the perception of the third dimension is learned is to imply that at the outset, at birth or soon thereafter, we perceive the world as only two-dimensional. Immediately certain problems arise with this implication. Where does this two-dimensional world appear to be located? If one answers that it appears out "there" at some indeterminate distance from the observer, then this seems to imply acceptance of the fact of three-dimensional perception. Learning would

*However, here too it is possible that it is not afferent information that is crucial but efferent information, namely, some central record of outgoing "instructions" to the eye muscles as to how to contract. In this case there is fairly good evidence in support of the efference theory. See the discussion of this problem on pp. 186–187.

then only give rise to more determinate nuances in an already existing perceptual dimension. If one answers, as some have, that the two-dimensional world does not, at the outset, appear out "there" but rather directly in contact with the eyes, one might ask whether this argument is really plausible. Certainly the world does not appear to be located *inside the head*! Therefore, no matter how close we might wish to argue that the two-dimensional array appears at birth, one might reasonably say that it is from the outset experienced as somewhere outside the observer's head and, therefore, by definition, that the third dimension is implicit.

A further problem with the learning hypothesis is this. Assuming for the moment that the world does appear flat at birth—whatever its absolute distance—how might learning ever be expected to change this mode of perception? An analogous question would arise if it were claimed that initially the world appeared achromatic and only through learning did chromatic color perception emerge. How would that be possible? Learning implies changes that occur through the formation of memories of certain perceptions, through the formation of associations, through the making of new discriminations or through arriving at new understandings of how things or events are related to one another. It does not imply the creation of new qualities of experience out of whole cloth. This is why the philosopher Kant argued that space and time are fundamental categories of mind; that is, they are innate modes of experiencing the world.

Therefore, on the basis of these a priori considerations it does not seem likely that we must learn to perceive the world as three-dimensional. Rather it seems necessary to assume that this perceptual capacity is present at the beginning. However this conclusion does not rule out the possibility that certain stimulus patterns or cues that originally did not produce an impression of depth ultimately do so. It is also possible that the perception of depth becomes more accurate and precise as a result of experience. We first consider experiments that seek the answer to the question of whether or not past experience is necessary for the perception of the third dimension but that are not analytical concerning which cue or cues is operating.

One might think that a definitive experiment on this issue would consist of rearing an animal in darkness or without the opportunity to use vision until it is mature enough to be tested for depth perception. Or one might think that an answer would be forthcoming by questioning people born blind whose sight is ultimately restored. In these cases there would have been no opportunity to learn to perceive the third dimension. Much of the history of research of this kind is considered in Chapter 8, where form perception is the focus of interest.

An early experiment was done with rats reared in darkness for 100 days.[27] In the test that followed the rats were first given a few practice trials in stepping across a short distance from one platform to another. Directly after this practice the platforms were moved further apart and the force of the jump from the starting platform was measured and taken as an index of the accuracy of distance perception. For both the dark-reared and normally reared animals the correspondence between force of jump and actual distance to the second platform was quite good. Hence it would seem that there is an innate basis for the perception of distance in the rat.

However, experiments of this kind are not ideal. For one thing, some learning may occur during the practice period prior to the critical testing. More important, however, is the possibility that rearing an animal in the dark or without pattern vision may prevent a perceptual capacity that is actually innate from being realized or displayed for any number of reasons (see the discussion of this issue on pp. 366–369). Therefore, had the experiment described implied the absence of distance perception it would not have been decisive. The method that is now preferred is to make use of some innate disposition or preference as an index and to test animals or human infants soon after birth.

In one such experiment the index was the pecking response of chickens. It is known that newly hatched chicks will begin pecking at small particles almost immediately after they emerge from the egg. In the experiment, newly hatched chicks were fitted out with prisms over their eyes (see Fig. 3–37).[28] Thus the direction of the light rays to the eyes was altered by the prisms in such a way that the light entered the eye from a particle of grain at the angle it would have for a much nearer object. The result was that the chicks terminated their pecks in mid air. This experiment is perhaps no more than a dramatic demonstration that normal chicks must accurately perceive the distance of the grain on the ground or else they would be unable to regulate correctly the amount of forward movement during the pecking response. In a different experiment with newly hatched chicks it was shown that they preferred to peck at artificial objects that were round and three-dimensional rather than at those that were round and only two-dimensional.[29] This experiment strictly speaking bears on depth perception, whereas the previous one bears on distance perception.

But the most conclusive evidence establishing the innate basis of distance perception in many different species comes from experiments employing what has been called a visual cliff.[30] The basic idea is quite simple. The animal (or infant) is placed on an opaque strip at the center of a large sheet of glass strong enough to support it. On one side the glass is backed by a textured surface; on the other side is a textured surface that is farther away (see Fig. 3–38). Since the glass covers both surfaces, the only basis for an aversion to one side is visual. In other

Figure 3-37

words, any tactual exploration the subject might make with paws, hand, or vibrissae would indicate that both sides are equally firm. Yet typically, the animal avoids the visually "deep" side and eventually walks or crawls over the "shallow" side. Needless to say, this technique makes

Figure 3-38

use of an innate fear of height and only if the height can be visually perceived will there be a tendency to avoid it.*

Using this technique it was found that chicks, infant rats, kittens, lambs, lions, tigers, jaguars, snow leopard cubs, monkeys, and human infants show preference for the shallow over the deep side. So do dark-reared rats. Even 3-day-old infant monkeys are more disturbed when placed directly over the deep side than when placed over the shallow side. This last finding is particularly important because of the similarity of monkeys to humans. Some species, such as aquatic turtles and ducks, show little if any preference for the shallow side but one can assume this indicates no fear of the height in such animals rather than no perception of it.†

As noted, human infants were tested on the visual cliff, but they were 6 months of age or older. Since younger infants do not crawl, it was not possible to find out about a possible aversion to the deep side by the direction in which they left the center strip. However, very young infants were placed directly on the glass and differences in their cardiac responses on the two sides suggest that they did correctly perceive distance.[33] Furthermore, infants as young as 6 weeks of age were the subjects of experiments directed at the question of whether objects appeared to be the same size and shape when viewed at varying distances and slants (see Chapter 2 pp. 64–66).[34] Since it was found that constancy of size and shape did exist for these young infants and since it is quite probable that such constancy depends upon the perception of distance and depth, this work also constitutes evidence for the presence of three-dimensional vision shortly after birth in human beings.‡

This is one issue that has long been debated by philosophers and psychologists that experiment seems to have answered. Perception of the third dimension is given innately; it does not have to be learned. There remains the further question of which cue or cues are innately present and are being utilized in the experiments with infant animals

*Previous investigators had capitalized on the innate fear of height to study the question of distance perception in animals by requiring them to jump down from an elevated platform. In one such study it was found that dark-reared chicks of 1 to 3 days of age were reluctant to jump from a high platform but not from a low one.[31]

†For a summary of experimental work on the visual cliff, see Gibson.[32] See also a recent study of 55- and 106-day-old human infants.[33]

‡In fact, there is direct evidence of distance perception in these experiments because it was shown by the infants' behavior that they could discriminate between situations in which the same object was at different distances.

and humans just described and the related question of whether any of the cues considered in this chapter are learned.

Which Cues Are Innate?

Further research has been directed at the question of which cues are being used by the human and animal infants in these experiments. In work on the visual cliff it has been shown that the animals are probably *not* reacting to a difference in the retinal images of the textured surfaces on the two sides since there is no clear preference when a fine textured surface is placed directly under the glass on one side and a coarse textured surface is placed directly under the other side. Thus, pictorial cues seem to have been ruled out. Nor is binocular vision necessary because avoidance of the deep side of the cliff occurs with the young subjects even when one eye is occluded. Some research on a possible role of inadequate accommodation leading to blurred images for contours on the deep side of the cliff has been taken to rule out accommodation as a relevant cue at least in the chick.[35] Therefore, by a process of elimination it has been concluded that motion parallax is the information which is being used in these experiments.

Motion parallax may well be the major innate cue as these experiments suggest, but one is left with the uncomfortable feeling that the evidence is indirect, i.e., by a process of elimination. It would be desirable to test the hypothesis directly by preventing any head movement. In the experiments on size and shape perception in the young infants, there is the puzzling fact that the infant's head is held in place in a holder that would tend to restrict head movement to a degree. In any case the infants are not bobbing their heads around nor moving around the way animals do on the visual cliff. So one wonders whether adequate movement necessary for parallax information could actually be taking place. Finally it may be worth pointing out that it is not clear whether the motion parallax that is held to be the crucial cue in the experiments on the visual cliff consists of the *relative* displacement of images with respect to one another or the *absolute* rate of displacement of images. For *relative* motion to be effective the animal must perceive the edge of the center strip at the same time he perceives the texture in the surface below. It is not clear whether this edge would be visible when an animal peers down while standing on it. If not, his movements produce a displacement of the image of the textured surface at an absolute rate, which is a joint function of the speed of his own movement and the distance of the surface. The information needed is how far away the surface is, not the slope of these surfaces, so motion perspective would not seem to be germane. It is by no means obvious that parallax in terms of absolute rate of displacement of an image is a cue to distance nor is there any direct evidence to show that it is.*

However, it has been established that one kind of transforming visual cue, namely the expansion pattern generated by an object approaching, *is* an innate indicator of distance. The proof comes from experiments with human infants, some as young as 2 weeks old, in which it was assumed that an object perceived to be rapidly approaching or "looming" as the investigators called it would evoke an instinctual alarm reaction.[37] It had previously been shown that infant monkeys did react with signs of alarm to an expanding shadow pattern but not to a contracting one.[38] This finding was duplicated in the study with human infants. Furthermore, it was shown that the alarm reaction—tensing of muscles, withdrawing the head, raising the arms toward the face—only occurred when the shadow expanded symmetrically. That is, if an object is coming directly toward the observer, its shadow on the screen expands symmetrically in all directions with respect to the observer; if it is on a "miss path," its shadow does not expand in this way. The presence of this reaction in such young infants to only that stimulus transformation, which in fact is correlated with an object about to hit the observer and not to other transformations, and the lack of any age difference among the infants tested, strongly argue in favor of an innate factor at work. Obviously it would be highly adaptive if a symmetrical expansion pattern did elicit a reaction that would have the effect of protecting the organism from an impending collision. Therefore, it is plausible that an alarm reaction to this stimulus would have evolved.

The fact that binocular information was shown not to be necessary for the perception of distance in the visual cliff situation does not, of course, imply that it would not have been sufficient had it been the only source of information available. In fact, the effectiveness of binocular information has now been demonstrated in 7-day-old human infants.[39] The infants looked at a screen containing two shadows of the same ob-

---

*Walk and Gibson suggest that the animal *compares* the rate of image displacement on the two sides of the cliff by looking back and forth.[36] But the question still arises as to whether the information thus obtained would indicate that one side was far enough away in absolute distance to evoke a fear reaction. They also suggest that movement of lowering and raising of the head would produce an expansion and contraction of the retinal image that would be informative about distance. But the fact is that this kind of stimulus change would occur on both sides of the cliff. The animal would have to be able to gauge from the relatively slow rate of expansion of the stimulus pattern on the "deep" side that it was quite far away.

ject each produced by polarized light. Since they viewed these shadows through polarizing filters, singleness of vision of the object could be achieved only if the infants converged their eyes at a distance much nearer than the actual location of the object. Furthermore, only if binocular disparity information was utilized would the object appear solid and three-dimensional. The infants apparently did perceive a solid object and did mislocalize it, because they attempted to grasp it where they perceived it to be, and, in not being able to do so, were distressed, (see p. 381 for a further discussion of this experiment).

Granted that three-dimensional perception is present at birth or soon thereafter and that such perception is mediated by certain cues, such as motion parallax and binocular disparity, the further question arises, do we learn to use *any* of the cues considered in this chapter as indicators or depth? The traditional assumption has been that the pictorial cues are learned so we turn now to a consideration of this issue.

The Origin of Pictorial Cues

As matters now stand, there is evidence supporting three different theories about the perception of two-dimensional patterns as three-dimensional:

1. That pictorial cues are based on past experience.
2. That they are the result of an innate preference to perceive whichever outcome is the simplest.
3. That they are simply innate stimulus indicators of depth.

To demonstrate that past experience can determine such perception, it is necessary to show that a novel pattern, which, without any given experience looks two-dimensional, will look three-dimensional following the relevant experience. Precisely such an experiment has been done.[40] The observers were first shown patterns such as those in Fig. 3–39. They appeared to be two-dimensional just as they no doubt appear to the reader. Following that, a technique was devised whereby these patterns led to a three-dimensional percept. The actual technique was to rotate three-dimensional wire figures behind a translucent screen. At any moment the shadow cast by the figure on the screen would appear two-dimensional were it stationary, but when rotating the ever-changing shadow pattern produces a strong impression of depth, the KDE. (In principle any technique that would have led the observers to perceive the pattern as three dimensional could have served. For example, the three-dimensional wire figure could have been directly pre-

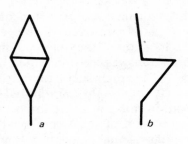

Figure 3-39

sented to the observers. Seen with both eyes at close range it would, of course, have been perceived, veridically, as three-dimensional.) Then in the final stage of the experiment the stationary pattern was again presented. This time most observers perceived it as three-dimensional. Control experiments indicated that the effect was genuinely perceptual (the stationary pattern in the final test *looked* three-dimensional). It was not merely the result of the realization that these patterns *could* represent three-dimensional objects. The effect was specific in that experience with only one rotating pattern, Fig. 3-39*a*, did not produce an impression of depth in the other stationary pattern, Fig. 3-39*b*, and vice versa.

In the light of this finding it becomes plausible to propose that all pictorial cues derive from past experience. The presumption is that at some point in the history of each individual, perhaps in early infancy, perspective patterns, interposition patterns, and the like did not give rise to depth effects. But following a good deal of experience in which these patterns were present and were perceived as three-dimensional *on the basis of other cues*, these patterns themselves in the absence of other cues now evoke an impression of depth.

In other words, it is suggested that an association develops between the type of pattern in question and the perception of that pattern as a three-dimensional array. But in order for such an association to be established, other cues must first serve to create the impression of depth. Since we now know that some cues are innate, the argument made is that these other cues produce the depth perception necessary for the learning to occur. Thus, for example, if an infant looks at a real cube with two eyes or while moving his head, then binocular disparity or motion parallax would result in the perception of the cube as three-dimensional. But while this is happening, the two-dimensional pattern of the cube stimulates the retina. Thus, the conditions for the formation of an association exist. Subsequently the pattern alone as seen in a draw-ing calls to mind the associated impression of depth. There are, however, further problems to be faced in connection with this hypothesis. Why does the coming to mind of the depth association actually affect the subsequent *perception* of the pattern rather than merely lead to the recollection that this was a pattern that had appeared three-dimensional? The memory obtrudes into the perception itself.

As noted earlier, certain two-dimensional patterns will give rise to a strong impression of depth even where it is not evident that these patterns contain any other known pictorial cues. The drawings shown in Fig. 3–9 are cases in point. One would think that, by definition, we are dealing here with the effect of past experience. Yet an attempt has been made to explain the tendency to perceive such patterns three-dimensionally in terms of the prägnanz simplicity principle, namely, that there is a preference to perceive whichever outcome is the simplist.* Objects whose retinal images yield an impression of depth, such as cubes, are often regular. A cube has equal and parallel sides and all its internal angles are right angles; therefore, a three-dimensional percept of the pattern shown in Fig. 3–9a can be said to be simpler than a two-dimen-sional percept of it. It is interesting that it is all but impossible to per-ceive such a pattern two-dimensionally, but the reader can imagine how it might look. It would be an irregular hexagonal shape with three different-sized lines inside. The outer lines and all the angles of such a figure would be different from one another in magnitude.

In a classic experiment designed to test this hypothesis, the figures shown in Fig. 3–40 were used.[41] In each row are shown figures of varying degrees of complexity when perceived two-dimensionally. Thus while *a* in both rows is a complex two-dimensional shape, at the other end, *d*, is a simple, regular two-dimensional shape, namely a regular hexagon in the top row and a diamond in the bottom row. As one goes from *a* to *d*, the two-dimensional complexity decreases. On the other hand, the three-dimensional percept is constant in all cases, namely a cube in the top row and a tetrahedron in the bottom row. Therefore, if simplicity of outcome determines perception, it should be predicted that there will be a strong tendency to perceive *a* and possibly *b* as three-dimensional. In recent years some psychologists have sought objective methods for specifying simplicity.[42]

The results of the experiment and of more recent variations have borne out the prediction based on the prägnanz principle. In short, one tends to perceive both *a* drawings in Fig. 3–40 as three-dimensional

---

*The notion of prägnanz is discussed at length in Chapter 6, pp. 270–275.

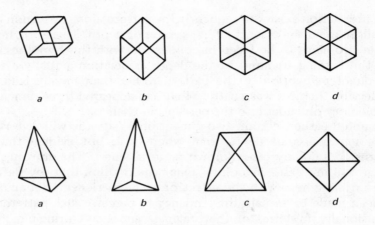

$$a \qquad\qquad b \qquad\qquad c \qquad\qquad d$$

$$a \qquad\qquad b \qquad\qquad c \qquad\qquad d$$

Figure 3-40

and both *d* drawing as two-dimensional, whereas drawings *b* and *c* are somewhat more ambiguous. However, it is possible to explain these results in terms that have nothing to do with simplicity. The patterns in *a* and to some extent in *b* represent the more general cases of the retinal images that would occur in viewing cube-like and pyramid-like objects. Those in *d* are very special cases; such images would occur only in viewing these figures from a unique vantage point. Furthermore, these patterns are familiar two-dimensional configurations, namely a hexagon and diamond. Hence one might invoke past experience as the essential determinant, rather than simplicity of outcome. A further factor is that in *c* and *d* in the cube figure the smooth continuation of the center lines results in perceiving edges, which in fact are in two different planes of the three-dimensional object, as lying in one plane, and this tends to make three-dimensional perception all but impossible. There are patterns for which the two-dimensional percept is quite simple and symmetrical, as in Fig. 3-41, and yet there is a tendency to perceive them as three-dimensional. So the evidence in support of the simplicity principle is

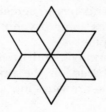

Figure 3-41

not convincing. There are also certain logical difficulties with this principle, and the principle is predicated on a theory of brain action for which there is no evidence (see the discussion of this topic on pp. 281ff).

The distorted-room illusion was thought by its creator, Ames, to demonstrate the effect of past experience on perception.[43] The distorted room is deliberately constructed in such a way that, viewed from one particular vantage point (Fig. 3-42a), it looks normal in every respect. In fact, the back wall of the room slants away from the observer (b), and the more distant side is actually much taller than the nearer side (c). The distances and sizes exactly compensate one another with the result that the back wall, which is in reality trapezoidal in shape, projects to the eye as rectangular. Since the observer views the room with one eye, he has no information that it is anything but normal in shape. The incorrect perception of the slant of the back wall in turn leads to other illusory effects such as an erroneous impression of the sizes of people standing on the left and right sides of the rear wall.

The illusion demonstrates the fact that a particular retinal image can signify many different objects in the world. But the real question is why this image, however it may be produced, is perceived as a normal (or cube-like) room, and the demonstration tells us nothing about this question. The answer could be based either upon the prägnanz principle (since a cube-like percept is highly regular) or upon past experience with rooms. However, another way of looking at this illusion is as follows: One might say that the essence of it is the misperception of the rear wall as rectangular and in the observer's frontal plane rather than as trapezoidal and slanted away from the observer, which in fact it is. But when the room is viewed with one eye from the right position, the rear wall projects a rectangular image. Now with no other information, it is highly plausible that we unconsciously "assume" that objects are in a frontal plane with regard to ourselves.* If this happens in the case of the distorted room, the rectangular image of the rear wall will be interpreted as a rectangular wall. So only this "assumption" is needed by way of explanation.

Contrast this illusion with another one also created by Ames.[45] The observer views monocularly from a distance a two-dimensional trapezoidal representation of a window as shown in Fig. 3-43a and b. The window rotates around a vertical axis. It tends to be perceived as a

---

*This assumption can be considered to be a special case of the tendency to perceive objects that are adjacent to one another as equidistant when there is no other information concerning their distance. See Gogel.[44]

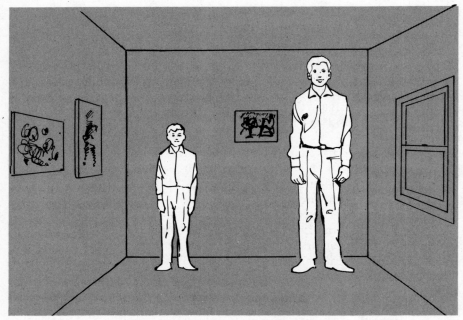

What observer sees from viewing point provided

a

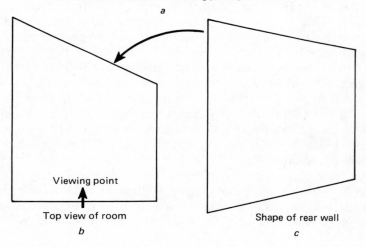

Viewing point

Top view of room

b

Shape of rear wall

c

Figure 3–42

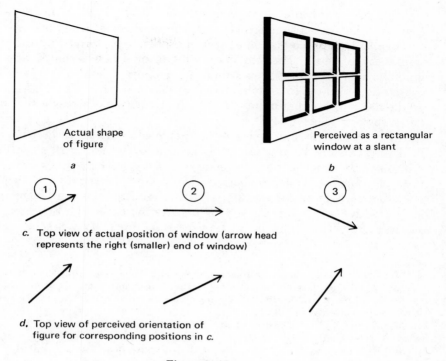

Actual shape
of figure

a

Perceived as a rectangular
window at a slant

b

① ② ③

c. Top view of actual position of window (arrow head
represents the right (smaller) end of window)

d. Top view of perceived orientation of
figure for corresponding positions in *c.*

Figure 3-43

rectangular window and it often appears to oscillate through an angle of less than 180 degrees rather than to rotate through 360 degrees as it actually is doing. The essential factor that leads to the illusory impression of oscillation is that no matter what the actual slant of the window, it is always perceived as slanting away from the observer as shown in Fig. 3-43c and *d*. This, in turn, can be said to result from linear perspective because the shape of the trapezoidal window is such that, given the location of the observer, its image always projects as a trapezoid with the image of its taller side always the longer one. In other words, even when the shorter edge of the trapezoid is nearer the observer, its projected retinal image will still be smaller. Therefore, that side will, in line with perspective, be perceived as farther rather than nearer.

This illusion cannot be the result of a tendency to localize objects in the frontal plane in the absence of definite information. In fact, the opposite is the case. When the window is objectively in the frontal plane, it is not perceived as in this plane. Hence the explanation of the illusion reduces to the explanation of why the object is perceived to be slanting backward into depth when, in fact, it isn't. With the trapezoid figure the cue that produces this illusory impression is linear perspective.*

This leads to the question of why perspective patterns do produce an impression of depth. The implication of Gibson's view is that the texture gradient is an innately given stimulus for depth much as is wavelength for color. Failure to obtain strong evidence for the effect of texture gradients in the experiments cited earlier then constitutes a real difficulty for this view.

An alternative is that we learn that perspective patterns signify planes in depth; this has been assumed to be true over the last two centuries. Although there is no decisive evidence in support of the learning hypothesis, some facts can be better understood if perspective is a learned cue than if it is an innate one. Texture gradient patterns seem to be less effective when the density of texture increases in a downward or sideways direction than in an upward direction. This can be seen in

---

*An illusion of oscillation will occur with any pattern that tends to be perceived as slanting into depth when in fact it isn't. Thus, for example, an ellipse may be seen as a circle, or more circular than it is, slanting backward and, if so, when it is rotated it will be perceived as oscillating.

A more detailed explanation of the impression of oscillation of the trapezoidal window is as follows. In position 1 (see Fig. 3–43c) the window is perceived as slanted back the way it in fact is except that it will appear slanted even more than it is, d (because its image is even more foreshortened than would be that of a rectangle at a lesser slant); in position 2 the window is still perceived as slanted back although it no longer is (because its image is still trapezoidal); in position 3 the window is perceived as going back to where it was a moment before, rather than continuing to rotate, because (a) its image leads to that perceived slant as explained previously and (b) the separation between the images of its two ends is diminishing because the window is turning. In other words to make sense of both a and b the window must be seen at this point as turning the wrong way.

There are other illusions in which we misperceive the direction of movement of objects as a result of a prior misperception of depth relations. For example, when a perspective reversal of a wire cube occurs, so that we perceive the far side as nearer and vice versa, then when the cube rotates in one direction, we perceive it rotating in the opposite direction. A similar effect occurs when we reverse a stationary cube while moving past it. Then the cube appears to be rotating although it is stationary. Furthermore, since depth reversals generally produce size and shape distortions, the cube appears to undergo bewildering transformations of size and shape under such conditions. Illusions of this kind occur despite veridical information from motion parallax. Thus, for example, the image of the near side of the cube is displacing more rapidly than that of the far side, which should serve as information about the true depth relationships. Yet when reversal occurs (despite this information) the parallax changes are interpreted in such a way as to correspond with the reversed depth. This fact suggests that motion parallax information is primarily relative, i.e., the shifts of images relative to one another rather than absolute, i.e., the absolute rate of movement of any component of the image.

Fig. 3-44, where it is questionable if any spontaneous impression of depth occurs at all to naive observers. The direction of the gradient should lead to the perception of a surface whose left side is further away. Photographs and paintings of terrain lose most of their depth when turned upside down. Why should this be so if the gradient is an innate cue? If, however, learning is necessary, then one can understand that only when the orientation of the gradient conforms with the one encountered most of the time, namely that given by texture on the ground plane, is that stimulus pattern an effective cue. Perhaps the observer must first identify what he is looking at. This may account for the initial absence of a depth effect in viewing Fig. 3-44. A negative slide of a plowed field does not produce an impression of depth for most naive observers.[46] It is possible that perspective patterns are associated with planes in depth on the basis of experience. Such learning might occur along lines suggested previously.

The three-dimensional effect of perspective patterns can also be thought of as the result of a preference for the simplest outcome. In the three-dimensional percept the objects that constitute the pattern, whose retinal sizes systematically differ, end up being perceived as equal, or the lines that converge end up being perceived as everywhere equidistant from one another. However, the simplicity hypothesis does not explain why negative or inverted pictures of terrain do not produce good depth perception any more than the texture-gradient hypothesis does.

Figure 3-44

The simplicity and past-experience hypotheses are also relevant to the *interposition* cue. If one thinks about interposition as a cue to depth, the interesting problem arises as to precisely why it works. Logically a pattern such as that in Fig. 3-2 is ambiguous as to the depth relations among its parts. It could represent two figures in the same plane with a rectangle and an L having a common border for part of each figure. It could represent an L in front of another figure that extended under the L. It could also represent one rectangle in front of another (although the figure behind need not necessarily be a rectangle.) Therefore, the spontaneous impression we have of one rectangle in front of another is clearly the result of some process of selection among alternative possibilities in which this perception is "preferred."

The problem then becomes one of explaining the basis of this preference. One hypothesis that has been advanced to explain interposition effects is again,prägnanz. The claim is that the perception of two identically shaped rectangles is simpler than the perception of two different forms, a rectangle and an L-shaped figure. However, an alternative hypothesis is that we have often been stimulated by patterns such as that in Fig. 3-2 and, therefore, via past experience, have come to associate such patterns with the perception of one object in front of another. Since rectangles are familiar figures, we interpret the L-shaped pattern as a rectangle.

However, both hypotheses present difficulties in explaining the interposition effect achieved in viewing a pattern such as that in Fig. 3-13a. The figure perceived when the region on the right is seen to be behind the one on the left is neither simpler nor more similar to the region on the left than when the two regions are seen in the same plane. Nor is either version of the figure on the right familiar. It seems likely that the crucial factor in this case is the tendency to perceive patterns such as this, in which two closed shapes share a common contour, as one figure in front of another that then serves as ground for it. Smooth continuation at the point of intersection then influences which figure appears in front. Therefore, in this possibly most general case of interposition, the explanation does not seem to lie either with simplicity or with past experience.

But there are cases that contradict the influence of smooth continuation at the points of intersection. We have already encountered one such example (see Fig. 3-14b). Fig. 3-45a is perceived by most observers as a square *and* a cross, having a common boundary.[47] This exception to the rule can be explained either in terms of prägnanz (a cross is more regular and symmetrical than the figure that would otherwise have to be perceived at the upper right *if* the square were to be perceived as overlapping it) *or* in terms of past experience (a cross is a very familiar pattern). Fig. 3-45b is perceived as a cross *in front of*

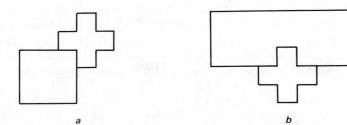

Figure 3-45

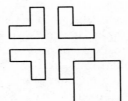

Figure 3-46

a rectangle. Apparently, either on the basis of simplicity or past experience, a cross is seen, although based on smooth continuation at the points of intersection a different figure should be seen, one that lies partially *under* the rectangle. Another exception is shown in Fig. 3-46. Here many observers no longer perceive one square overlapping another in the lower right part of the figure as all observers would if the three other L-shaped figures were not present; rather they see an inverted L and a square in the same plane, sharing a contour.[48] By perceiving a fourth L figure, a symmetry (and, therefore, simplicity) is achieved for the pattern as a whole. Or one might say that given the context of the other L figures, a fourth L figure is a more plausible solution.

Therefore, although some evidence supports the experience hypothesis and many of the facts about pictorial cues fit a simplicity hypothesis, no unequivocal conclusions can be reached about the pictorial cues as a whole. The simplicity hypothesis is predicated on the assumption that the brain functions in such a way as to lead to certain perceptual preferences and, as such, it reduces to the assertion that depth perception is innate. But we can, of course, believe that three-dimensional perception is innate without subscribing to the simplicity hypothesis. Gibson's view that certain higher-order stimulus patterns are direct indicators of depth falls in this category. One striking bit of evidence concerning shadow as an indicator of depth supports such an innate hypothesis.

Since the location of shading on an object is the crucial factor, one might speculate that the effect is the result of the unconscious "assumption" that light comes from above. The obvious question then arises as to the origin of such an assumption. It is plausible to think it is learned. Thus one could argue that we have come to associate patterns in which shadow is underneath with protruding things and those with the shadow on top as indented things. Presumably the basis of such learning could be the fact that other, innate cues are present when we view shadowed objects. In this way the association can be formed. Then, subsequently, the shadow pattern itself can evoke the appropriate depth impression.

A bold experiment was undertaken to test this hypothesis.[49]   Chicks were reared from the time of hatching in a cage environment in which light always came from below.   From day to day the chicks were removed from their cages and placed in a testing box.   They were then tested by placing photographs of widely spaced grains of wheat on the side of the box.   The grains were photographed in such a way that they cast shadows on the background surface.   In one photograph the shadows were at the top and in another the shadows were at the bottom. The question was whether the chicks would prefer to peck at one or the other photograph.   Presumably, if shadow as a depth cue resulted in grains appearing to protrude, then one of these photographs would look like "grains" and the chicks would prefer to peck at them; otherwise not.   For a control group reared normally with light from above, one would expect that the photograph having shadows at the bottom of the grain would elicit more pecking than the other. But for the experimental group one would predict that the photograph having the shadows at the top of the grains would be preferred.

The result was that at first there was no preference, but over a period of a week clear preferences developed and in the predicted directions. This experiment has been widely cited as, first, an unequivocal demonstration of the effect of past experience on perception and, second, a demonstration of the fact that shadow as an indicator of depth is a learned cue.   However, certain objections to the experiment can be made.   Most important is the fact that it is cast shadow rather than attached shadow that is under study, whereas the cue to convexity or concavity is attached shadow.   In the photographs, the grains cast shadows on the background.   It is not the case that the shadow falls on the top or bottom of the grain itself.   To a human observer the grains in *both* photographs appear to protrude so one might well wonder whether they did not do so for the chicks in both groups in the experiment. Since the chicks ultimately did have a preference, it is possible to argue that they came to prefer grains *perceived as protruding in either case*, which had shadows on top or underneath depending upon the group

they were in.   A second question about this experiment is precisely
what shadows during rearing in the cage were instrumental in the learning process.   The cage is wire so that there are no objects on the bottom
of it or on the walls, which would be differentially shaded.

Based on questions of this kind, the experiment was ultimately repeated.[50]   To make sure that it was the perception of convexity or
concavity that the chicks were reacting to in the photographs, they
were first trained to associate either a convex bump or a concave dent
with food reward.   They were presented with both a bump and a dent
and trained to choose one or the other (see Fig. 3-47a).   Depth cues
other than shadow mediated this discrimination learning because pains
were taken to ensure that there were no shadows at the top or bottom

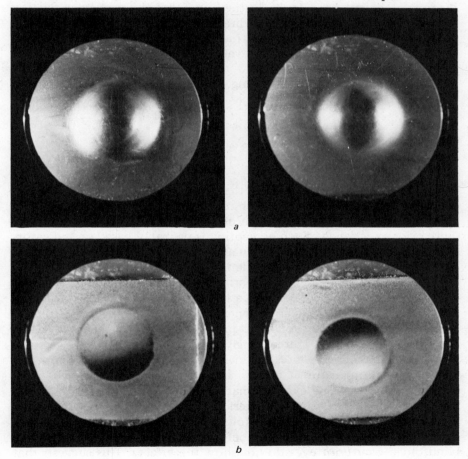

Figure 3-47

of these objects. Following that they were given photographs, which, by virtue of the location of the attached shadow at the top or the bottom, would presumably appear as raised or indented if shadow had the effect for chicks that it has for humans (see Fig. 3-47b). The result was that all chicks tested showed a preference for the photographs with shadow at the top if they had previously been trained to peck at dents and for the photographs with the shadow at the bottom if they had been trained to peck at bumps. Thus it would seem that for these chicks, the location of the shadow creates precisely the same impression of depth that it does for human observers and yet all these chicks were raised with light coming from below. The conclusion seems warranted that the perception of depth in objects as a function of attached shadows does not have to be learned and that the particular relation between location of shadow and direction of depth also does not have to be learned. Presumably, shadow location is a built-in cue that evolved in animals because of its adaptive value. Because light on earth comes from above, the attached shadow underneath a region does reliably signify that something is protruding, and conversely for shadow at the top of a region.

Conclusions

What conclusions can we draw then from all this evidence? We can conclude that perception of the third dimension of space is present in most, possibly all, species at birth or soon thereafter and does not require prior experience. Such perception is probably based on indicators such as motion parallax and binocular disparity, but also on at least one of the pictorial cues, shadow location.

The inclusion of binocular disparity as an unlearned cue is made not only on the basis of some evidence but also on the basis of logical considerations. After all, disparity depends upon specific neuroanatomical arrangements that have evolved to provide us with singleness of vision and depth perception. Interestingly enough, however, there is some evidence suggesting a role of experience in the utilization of binocular disparity as an indicator of depth. In one experiment, adult observers wore a patch over one eye (alternating eyes every few hours) so they had only monocular vision for a period of 24 hours.[51] When they were then tested by stereoscope, it was found that their depth perception was considerably poorer than it was before the experiment; yet observers blindfolded over *both* eyes do not show the effect. This suggests that during vision the continued utilization of disparity information is important for its continued effectiveness.

In other experiments, a conflict was created between binocular disparity and another cue, the kinetic depth effect.[52] This was achieved by the use of a telestereoscope, which has the effect of increasing the magnitude of disparity. Thus, in viewing a transforming shadow pattern, the transformation "said" one thing about the object's depth whereas the increased disparity "said" another, namely that it was deeper than it in fact was. Following a period of exposure to this conflict, depth perception via disparity information alone was tested. It was found that stereo objects now appeared flatter than they would naturally appear. The implication is that the other cue, the kinetic depth effect, was dominant and led to a reassessment of the depth significance of a given amount of disparity. It is as if the perceptual system was being told "this apparently deep object is less deep than it appears—therefore—so and so much disparity does not imply as much depth as it did before."

Other experiments have been done in which the observer wore prisms or other distorting optical devices over his eyes. In one such experiment the observer wore prisms that had the effect of slightly tilting the image in each eye in opposite directions.[53] Consequently an object that was actually vertical appeared at first to be sloping toward (or away from) the observer (see Fig. 3–23c or d for an illustration of this kind of disparity). But following a period of exposure to the prisms, this distorting effect began to wear off and, in fact, on removing the prisms, vertical, nondisparate images in the two eyes now gave rise to an impression of a line sloping toward (or away from) the observer.

An analogous effect is obtained if the observer wears a lens over one eye that has the effect of magnifying the image along the horizontal axis only.[54] Thus the normal correspondence or disparity between the images from the two eyes is altered. It has been shown that the observer adapts to this altered relationship either by walking around in the environment or even by remaining stationary and viewing a perspective pattern such as a rectangle for several minutes.[55] In the latter case the perspective information presumably provides a basis for reassessing the significance of the disparity information. For example, if the rectangle appears to be in the frontal plane because its image is that of a rectangle then the disparity created by the lens over one eye can be reinterpreted to signify "no depth" between the two sides of the rectangle. This type of experiment falls under the category of *prism adaptation* and is discussed in more detail in several other chapters. It is sufficient to note here that some adaptation to altered binocular disparity was achieved. This must mean that corresponding retinal points as defined earlier in the chapter do not necessarily determine the absence of depth and noncorresponding points the presence of depth. However, corresponding points undoubtedly do irrevocably determine singleness of vision.

Some might conclude on the basis of these experiments on disparity that it is a learned cue. But that would be going beyond the evidence. All we are entitled to say is that the depth significance of disparity is subject to change and that with disuse under monocular conditions of viewing, it is subject to reduced effectiveness. But even these are rather striking conclusions about a factor long thought to be a strong innate cue based upon inherited neuroanatomical structures.

We cannot come to any final conclusions about the pictorial cues (other than shadow location). Based on the finding that experience can lead to the perception of a two-dimensional pattern as three-dimensional, one can make out a very plausible case for the assertion that many of the pictorial cues are learned indicators of depth.* The learning of such cues could follow the same course as occurred in the experimental situation. Initially proximal stimulus patterns such as are projected by cubes and rooms, trapezoids, converging lines (linear perspective), and the like would, according to this view, appear flat. But after some amount of experience with such patterns, during which time other cues are rendering the scene three-dimensional, these patterns themselves now acquire the capacity to elicit an impression of depth. Some support for this conclusion comes from scattered findings that pictorial information does not seem to be effective in infant animals or humans, but admittedly this evidence is still quite fragmentary. In any case, it is plausible that such cues are learned whereas it is not plausible, for reasons given earlier, that the perception of three-dimensionality per se is learned. In fact the two propositions, namely, that three-dimensional perception is innately determined and that some depth perception is learned, are highly compatible, the innate cues providing the vehicle for the learning of other cues.

Furthermore it is *not* plausible to believe that certain pictorial cues are innately determined. After all, many of the patterns that elicit a strong impression of depth result from things that are man-made, such as roads, railroad tracks, cubes, and rooms. Therefore, there would have been no reason for the brain to evolve in such a way that such patterns would lead to three-dimensional percepts at a time in evolutionary history when man did not yet exist and his ancestors did not construct objects of this kind. True, the Gestalt psychologists have suggested a reason why many such patterns might produce an impression of three-dimensional objects without recourse to a learning hypothesis, namely, the preference for simple organization, but there are many difficulties with this alternative hypothesis.

*See pp. 129–130, the experiment of Wallach, O'Connell, and Neisser.[40]

Epilogue

Having covered the topic of the perception of the third dimension in the traditional manner—namely, by examining each of the various sources of information separately—a few more speculative thoughts may be in order at this point. The author has the uneasy feeling that the entire approach to the problem of the perception of distance and depth is somehow wide of the mark. One reason for this feeling is that it is possible to eliminate or to imagine eliminating all of the known cues without necessarily eliminating the impression of the scene as three-dimensional. In looking through an artificial pupil with one eye and head stationary, all but the pictorial cues are eliminated or rendered ambiguous. But then we can imagine a scene that contains little in the way of known pictorial cues, namely interposition, perspective, or shadow, and yet one would think the scene will still appear to be three-dimensional. For example, the surface of the moon certainly looks as three-dimensional as that of the earth. (To be sure it would be difficult to eliminate the texture gradient in a real scene, but it can easily be done in pictures as in Fig. 3-48).*

Either of two things must be true.

1. We have as yet failed to uncover certain sources of information about distance.
2. We are looking at the problem in the wrong way when we simply list cues.

Assuming 1 is not correct, what could be wrong with the approach outlined in this chapter? The answer may be that the perceptual system tends to "construct" a three-dimensional scene unless definite cues are present that counterindicate it. It is known that when all texture (or microstructure) is eliminated, as in viewing a completely dark room or in viewing a homogeneously illuminated surface equidistant from the eyes in all directions (as when hemispheres such as halves of Ping-Pong balls are placed over the eyes), this Ganzfeld, as it is called (see p. 503), results in an impression of a foggy *three-dimensional* expanse. Under more typical conditions it is possible that a similar tendency is at work, constructing a three-dimensional scene on the basis of very fragmentary information.

---

*In one published experiment using photographs of a landscape, all texture was deleted by the use of India ink. Nevertheless the observers had an impression of a ground plane and the apparent location of objects within the scene affected their phenomenal size.[56]

Figure 3-48

That some psychologists implicitly accept this interpretation is suggested by the fact that many investigators refer to a factor not yet mentioned here, namely, height in the field. What is meant by this is dramatically illustrated in Fig. 3-49, where the observer misperceives the distance of an object because he tends to locate it at the height where its lower contour falls in the field (assuming other sources of information about its distance are not present). It is implied that this factor, "height in the field," can determine distance in the absence of other information. However "height in the field" presupposes that the observer starts with an impression of the ground plane as extending outward from himself horizontally. Therefore the argument is circular. "Height in the field" means nothing more than the fact that *once we perceive a horizontal plane*, such as the ground, by definition of such a plane, the farther "up" in this plane an object is, the farther away it is. (In fact, the converse would be true of an elevated horizontal plane such as a ceiling. The farther "down" in the plane, the farther away is the object.)[57]

The problem therefore remains, what gives rise in the first place to the impression of the plane as receding into the distance? What psycholo-

a. Physical Arrangement of Rectangle and Triangle

b. What the observer perceives

Figure 3-49

gists may have had in mind when they refer to "height in the field" as a determinant of distance, without explicitly realizing it, is the idea that the perceptual system makes a contribution to what is perceived, namely, it tends spontaneously to construct a three-dimensional mental picture of the scene. Thus in the case of the ground plane, the merest hints that are provided by scattered objects, horizon, and the observer's own known location are incorporated into and help to give body to a mental picture of a plane receding into the distance. Of course, the better the cues available and the more that are available the more vivid is this perception.   It is a process very much like imagining except that here the imagining makes use of whatever stimulus information is given.*

A similar problem arises in connection with the way in which psychologists deal with the pictorial cues, namely, again merely listing all the known sources of information. As noted earlier, some configurations look three-dimensional even though no known cues are present. For example, the figures shown in Fig. 3-9 were deliberately drawn in parallel projection so as to eliminate linear perspective. We were then left to grapple with the problem of why these pictures appeared three-dimensional. However, the problem can be seen in a broader perspective if one considers many other examples usually not included in a discussion of depth perception. Thus, in Fig. 3-50 all objects look three-dimensional. Few would quarrel with the assertion that here

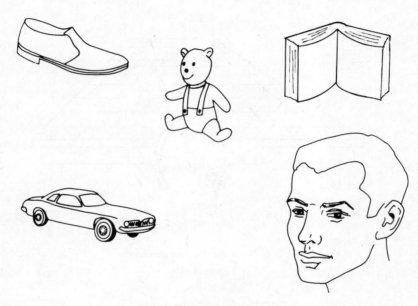

Figure 3-50

*The tendency to imagine a horizontal plane was demonstrated in a laboratory experiment on the moon illusion. Normally the illusion is not present in a totally dark field because there are no distance cues to suggest that the horizon moon is farther away than the elevated moon (see Chapter 2 pp. 39–47). But in one experiment an illusion was obtained in the dark (with only a single luminous line to represent the horizon) provided the observer first saw a luminous ceiling. This prior experience apparently permitted him to imagine the ceiling extending outward from him horizontally.[58]

depth perception is a function of past experience and it would make little sense to try to explain it in terms of a simplicity principle.

In short, pictures of familiar three-dimensional things *look* three-dimensional. Therefore, instead of seeking to isolate specific kinds of information that such pictures contain, it would seem more appropriate to conclude that the process of recognition and identification somehow causes a perceptual change as well. The picture takes on the appearance of the object it represents. Since there is no reason why pictures such as those in Fig. 3-50 should look three-dimensional to observers who have never seen such objects before, the problem becomes one of explaining how past experience can affect perception in this way for those who have had the relevant past experience. By way of speculating about the answer to this question, the author again suggests that a process of imagining or mental construction takes place in which, in this case, the remembered characteristics of the object are subjectively "imposed" upon the stimulus pattern. The reader is referred to a more general discussion of the role of past experience in form perception in Chapter 8, in particular, pp. 347–351.

In any case, if identification can lead to perceptual changes as it seems to do in the pictures in Figs. 3-9 and 3-50, it would seem gratuitous to argue that other processes are the cause of the depth perceived when the so-called pictorial cues are present. Thus it seems plausible to conclude that the depth achieved from the perspective and interposition patterns is generally the end result of recognizing and identifying such patterns. Converging lines are interpreted as a road, sidewall, or, more generally, as an object with parallel sides receding into the distance. Interposition patterns such as that shown in Fig. 3-2 are interpreted as representing one rectangle in front of another. There are problems to be faced here in connection with the question of the generality of what is recognized since we know that interposition patterns consisting of completely unfamiliar objects can nevertheless produce an impression of one thing behind another (Fig. 3-13a). Perhaps in such cases one should *not* consider recognition to be playing a role, but on the other hand it is possible that we can recognize certain isolated features such as the point of intersection in these patterns. But clearly in the case where very familiar objects *are* shown the recognition hypothesis is directly applicable. In fact, on this basis the perceptual outcome in cases such as those in Fig. 3-45a become quite understandable. Once a cross is identified, this perception perseveres, so that this region will not look like an object behind the rectangle, as it otherwise would.

Another problem to which the "cue theory" does not do justice was alluded to earlier in the chapter. Most cues provide information about the relative distance of objects (depth) but not about their absolute distance. Those cues that give absolute distance information are relatively ineffectual beyond several feet (accommodation and convergence). One cue, interposition, only informs about the fact that one thing is in front of another but not about how much in front it is. Yet we generally do have a very clear impression where all objects are in relation to ourselves. Therefore, a process of combining all available information about distance into one coherent picture must occur and this process can also be thought of as one of constructing a three-dimensional picture of the world.

To summarize, it is possible that the so-called cues do not actually operate to *create* the impression of the third dimension but primarily to provide specific support and precision to an already existing predisposition to construct or imagine space as three-dimensional. Without any cues, of course, only the impression of an indeterminate three-dimensional expanse would be present, a world located "out there." The cues then give shape and precision to this three-dimensional expanse indicating the exact shape and slant of planes in depth and the exact absolute and relative distance of things. But in certain cases, the cues themselves depend upon identifying objects (or general features of certain kinds of objects) and, therefore, on a process of imagining how such objects are arranged in the third dimension. Admittedly, however, there is as yet little evidence for this interpretation.

Summary

There are a number of different sources of information about the distance of things from us and from each other. Some of these indicators (cues) are purely visual, i.e., the information is contained in the retinal image, and some are oculomotor, i.e., the information derives from muscular adjustments. Visual cues are either static, i.e., are given by a stationary image, or transforming, i.e., depend upon changes of the image. Static visual cues are either pictorial, i.e., are given by features of the "picture" registered on the retina, or are binocular, i.e., derive from the difference between the two images.

Contrary to the classical view and the opinion of the layman, pictorial cues are not "secondary" but rather are major sources of information about the third dimension of space, at least for mature human observers. The impression of distance is very little diminished when one views an outdoor scene with one eye through an artificial pupil and head stationary, a procedure that eliminates all but the pictorial indicators.

Linear and size perspective, interposition, attached shadow, and certain familiar patterns are the more important of these cues. It is not yet known whether these indicators are learned, are the result of the operation of a simplicity principle, or are simply innate signs of depth. It has been demonstrated that one can learn to perceive a particular pattern as three dimensional provided that other information is available to render the pattern three-dimensional during the learning phase of the experiment and this demonstration could well be considered paradigmatic for all pictorial cues. However, the perceptual outcome of indicators such as perspective and interposition is generally just what one would predict on the basis of a simplicity principle. To add to the difficulty of resolving this question, in one experiment on attached shadow, the findings clearly support the conclusion that this cue is innate.

Binocular disparity is also a major indicator of depth, but the explanation of this is not yet known. A complete understanding of disparity as a cue to depth will require an understanding of certain broader questions concerning the cooperation of the two eyes such as: why and how only one "mental picture" results from two "retinal pictures" when these pictures are identical and fall on corresponding points; why parts of each image are perceived when the two differ and, therefore, conflict with one another; and why this is not the case when the two images differ only slightly as in the disparity situation. There is reason for believing that the answer to these questions is that one of the two images falling on corresponding points is suppressed by the other and that this suppression extends somewhat beyond the locus of the contour. It does seem as if the specific three-dimensional picture constructed on the basis of the two images derives from a rapid-fire unconscious process very much like reasoning. This process makes use of the specific difference between the images to the two eyes (in spite of suppression) and takes account of which eye receives which image. The proof of the effectiveness of binocular disparity is that two-dimensional pictures give rise to a visual impression of depth when each picture is viewed by one eye even when there are no depth indicators in either picture alone.

Transforming retinal patterns stemming from observer movement or object movement is now thought by many to be a major source of information about the third dimension of space. Yet the experimental evidence in support of this belief is not altogether convincing and the three-dimensional impression of a scene is generally quite vivid without any movement at all. Recent work has expanded on the traditional view of movement parallax as the shift of the images of two points relative to one another to the notion of gradients of motion of the entire array of points in surfaces or motion perspective. It was argued that the efficacy of motion perspective as a cue may depend upon it being produced by the observer's own movement. The tendency to discount any retinal change when it is produced by the observer himself may then lead to the proper interpretation of the motion gradient as resulting from the slant or slope of the surface. However, if the object or surface moves instead of the observer and, if further, the "assumption" is made that the object or surface is an interconnected entity, then an impression of a rigid three-dimensional thing moving may also result. There is now evidence that the expansion pattern that typically results from an object approaching is an innate indicator of changing distance.

Accommodation of the lens and convergence of the eyes are the two oculomotor cues to distance. The evidence indicates that both together and each independently provide some information about distance. A question of interest is whether the information derives from the proprioceptive feedback from the contractions of the ciliary or extraocular muscles or from a central record of the "instructions" issued to the muscles. In any case these cues are effective only for relatively near objects. Therefore, contrary to what Berkeley had thought, these are no longer considered to be major indicators of distance.

In considering the question of whether the ability to perceive in three dimensions is learned or is part of our equipment at birth, it was argued that there are logical difficulties with the thesis that such perception is entirely learned. In any case, the evidence from experiments employing the "visual cliff" and other techniques making use of innate preferences and aversions now clearly establishes that in virtually all species of animals the world is perceived as three-dimensional at or close to the time of birth. It is still not certain which cue or cues are responsible for this innate perceptual ability but by a process of elimination, motion parallax is considered likely by many psychologists. However, other experiments have demonstrated the effectiveness of binocular information at a very early stage.

A plausible resolution to the question of origin of three-dimensional perception is that we are born with the ability to perceive the third dimension on the basis of certain cues (probably binocular disparity and motion parallax) and that given such perception, by a process of association, certain stimulus patterns (pictorial cues) can become indicators of the third dimension. But there are difficulties even with this plausible view of the matter.

Finally, on a more speculative level, it was suggested that because none of the cues that have been isolated, nor all of them together, can explain our perceptions of the third dimension under certain conditions, such perception may depend upon an imaginative process of mental construction of the third dimension. Information from the various cues is then incorporated into this imagined space. It was also suggested that many of the pictorial cues to depth depend upon identification and that identification can affect depth perception because the remembered characteristics of the object are (imaginatively) "imposed" upon the stimulus pattern.

References

1. Gillam, B. J. Perception of slant when perspective and stereopsis conflict: experiments with aniseikonic lenses. *Journal of Experimental Psychology*, 1968, 78, 299–305; W. Epstein and C. L. Morgan-Paap. The effect of level of depth processing and degree of informational discrepancy on adaptation to uniocular image magnification. *Journal of Experimental Psychology*, 1974, **102**, 585–594.

2. Gibson, J. J. *The Perception of the Visual World.* Houghton Mifflin Company, 1950.

3. See Gibson, J. J. The perception of visual surfaces. *American Journal of Psychology*, 1950, **63**, 367–384; H. E., Gruber and W. Clark. Perception of slanted surfaces. *Perceptual and Motor Skills*, 1956, **16**, 97–106; W. C. Clark, A. H., Smith, and A. Rabe. The interaction of surface texture, outline gradient, and ground in the perception of slant. *Canadian Journal of Psychology*, 1956, **10**, 1–8.

4. Ittleson, W. H. Size as a cue to distance. *American Journal of Psychology*, 1951, **64**, 54–67.

5. Epstein, W. The known-size apparent-distance hypothesis. *American Journal of Psychology*, 1961, **74**, 333–346.

6. Schriever, W. Experimentelle Studien über stereokopische Sehen. Zeitschrift für Psychologie, 1925, **96**, 113–170.

7. Ratoosh, P. On interposition as a cue for the perception of distance. *Proceedings of the National Academy of Science*, 1949, **35**, 257–259.

8. Chapanis, A. and R. A. McCleary. Interposition as a cue for the perception of relative distance. *The Journal of General Psychology*, 1953, 48, 113–132.

9. Wheatstone, C. Contributions to the physiology of vision: on some remarkable, and hitherto unobserved, phenomena of binocular vision: Part I *Philosophical Transactions*, 1838, 371–394. Reprinted in W. Dennis. *Readings in General Psychology*, pp. 9–20, Prentice-Hall, Inc., 1949; Contributions to the physiology of vision: Part 2. *Philosophical Transactions*, 1852, 1–17.

10. Wheatstone. op. cit. 1852, p. 13–14.

11. Julesz, B. *Foundations of Cyclopean Perception.* University of Chicago Press, 1971.

12. Wallach, H. and C. Zuckerman. The constancy of stereoscopic depth. *American Journal of Psychology*, 1963, **76**, 403–412. See also Gogel, W. C. Perception of depth from binocular disparity. *Journal of Experimental Psychology*, 1964, **67**, 379–386; Scalar perception with binocular cues of distance. *American Journal of Psychology*, 1972, **85**, 477–498.

13. Pulfrich, C. Die Stereoskopie im Dienste der isochromen und heterochromen Photometrie. *Naturwissenschaften*, 1922, **10**, 533–564; 569–601; 714–722; 735–743; 751–761. See also A. Lit. The magnitude of the Pulfrich stereo-phenomenon as a function of binocular differences of intensity at various levels of illumination. *American Journal of Psychology*, 1949, **62**, 159–181.

14. Hering, E. *Beitrage zur Physiologie.* Heft I. W. Englemann, 1861.

15. For a statement of this theory, see E. Boring. *The Physical Dimensions of Consciousness.* Dover Publications, Inc. 1963 (originally published by Appleton-Century-Crofts, 1933). For a clear discussion of this theory and of the suppression theory, see L. Kaufman. *Sight and Mind: An Introduction to Visual Perception.* Chapter 8, Oxford University Press, 1974.

16. Kaufman, L. ibid, 1974. This chapter of Kaufman's provides a much more extended discussion of the entire problem of binocular interaction than is given here.

17. Werner, H. Dynamics in binocular depth perception. *Psychological Monographs*, 1937 (whole no. 218).

18. Wallach, H. and J. Lindauer. On the definition of retinal disparity. *Psychologische Beitrage*, 1962, **6**, 521–530.

19. Barlow, H. B., C. Blakemore, and J. D. Pettigrew. The neural mechanism of binocular depth discrimination. *Journal of Physiology*, 1967, **193**, 327–342. See also J. D. Pettigrew. The neurophysiology of binocular vision. *Scientific American*, 1972, **227**, 84–95.

20. Gibson, J. J. and W. Carel. Does motion perspective independently produce the impression of a receding surface? *Journal of Experimental Psychology*, 1952, 44, 16–18.

21. Gibson, E. J., J. J. Gibson, and O. W. Smith. Motion parallax as a determinant of perceiving depth. *Journal of Experimental Psychology*, 1959, 58, 40–51. For a review of research on this subject, see Epstein, W. and J. Park. Examination of Gibson's psychophysical hypothesis. *Psychological Bulletin*, 1964, **62**, 180–196.

22. Wallach, H. and D. N. O'Connell. The kinetic depth effect. *Journal of Experimental Psychology*, 1953, 45, 205–217.

23. Musatti, C. L. Sui fenomeni stereocinetici. *Archivio Italiano Psicologia*, 1924, 3, 105–120. Musatti attributes the discovery of the effect to Benussi. See also H. Wallach, A. Weisz, and P. A. Adams. Circles and derived figures in rotation. *American Journal of Psychology*, 1956, 69, 48–59.

24. Green, B. F., Jr. Figure coherence in the kinetic depth effect. *Journal of Experimental Psychology*, 1961, 62, 272–282.

25. Leibowitz, H. and D. Moore. Role of changes in accommodation and convergence in the perception of size. *Journal of Optical Society of America*, 1966, 56, 1120–1123; H. Wallach and L. Floor. The use of size matching to demonstrate the effectiveness of accommodation and convergence as cues for distance. *Perception and Psychophysics*, 1971, 10, 423–428.

26. Heinemann, E. G., E. Tulving, and J. Nachmias. The effect of oculomotor adjustments on apparent size. *American Journal of Psychology*, 1959, 72, 32–45.

27. Lashley, K. S. and J. T. Russell. The mechanisms of vision XI. A preliminary test of innate organization. *Journal of Genetic Psychology*, 1934, 45, 136–144.

28. Hess, E. H. Space perception in the chick. *Scientific American*, 1956, 195, 71–80.

29. Fantz, R. L. Form preferences in newly hatched chicks. *Journal of Comparative and Physiological Psychology*, 1957, 50, 422–430. See also R. L. Fantz. The origin of form perception. *Scientific American*, 1961, 204, 66–72.

30. Gibson, E. J. and Walk, R. D. The "visual cliff." *Scientific American*, 1960, 202, 64–71.

31. Kurke, M. I. The role of motor experience in the visual discrimination of depth in the chick. *Journal of Genetic Psychology*, 1955, 86, 191–196.

32. Gibson, E. J. *Principles of Perceptual Learning and Development.* Appleton-Century-Crofts, 1969.

33. Campos, J. J. A. Langer, and A. Krowitz. Cardiac responses on the visual cliff in prelocomotor human infants. *Science*, 1970, 170, 196–197.

34. Bower, T. G. R. The visual world of infants. *Scientific American*, 1966, 215, 80–92.

35. Palen, G. F. Focusing cues in the visual cliff behavior of day-old chicks. *Journal of Comparative and Physiological Psychology*, 1965, 59, 452–454.

36. Walk, R. D. and E. J. Gibson. A comparative and analytical study of visual depth perception. *Psychological Monographs*, 1961, **75**, (Whole no. 519).
37. Ball, W. and E. Tronick. Infant responses to impending collision: optical and real. *Science*, 1971, **171**, 818–820.
38. Schiff, W., J. A. Caviness, and J. J. Gibson. Persistent fear responses in rhesus monkeys in response to the optical stimulus of "looming." *Science*, 1962, **136**, 982–983. See also a prior study with chicks. Fishman, R. and R. B. Tallarico. Studies of visual depth perception: II. Avoidance reaction as an indicator response in chicks. *Perceptual and Motor Skills*, 1961, **12**, 251–257.
39. Bower, T. G. R., J. M. Broughton, and M. K. Moore, The coordination of visual and tactual input in infants. *Perception & Psychophysics*, 1970, 8, 51–53.
40. Wallach, H., D. N. O'Connell, and U. Neisser. The memory effect of visual perception of three-dimensional form. *Journal of Experimental Psychology*, 1953, **45**, 360–368.
41. Kopfermann, H. Psychologische Untersuchungen über die Wirking Zweidimensionaler körperlicher Gebilde. *Psychologische Forschung*, 1930, **13**, 293–364.
42. See Hochberg J. and V. Brooks. The psychophysics of form: reversible-perspective drawings of spatial objects. *American Journal of Psychology*, 1960, **73**, 337–354; F. Attneave. Some informational aspects of visual perception. *Psychological Review*, 1954, **61**, 183–193.
43. See Ittleson, W. H. and F. P. Kilpatrick. Experiments in perception. *Scientific American*, 1951, **185**, 50–55.
44. Gogel, W. The tendency to see objects as equidistant and its inverse relation to lateral separation. *Psychological Monographs*, 1956, **70**, 1–17.
45. Ames, A., Jr. Visual perception and the rotating trapezoidal window. *Psychological Monographs*, 1951, **65**.
46. Wallach, H. Memory effects in perception. Paper read at the *International Congress of Psychology*, Montreal, 1954.
47. Dinnerstein, D. and M. Wertheimer. Some determinants of phenomenal overlapping. *American Journal of Psychology*, 1957, **70**, 21–37.
48. Ibid.
49. Hess, E. H. Development of the chick's responses to light and shade cues to depth. *Journal of Comparative and Physiological Psychology*, 1950, **43**, 112–122.
50. Hershberger, W. Attached shadow orientation perceived as depth by chickens reared in an environment illuminated from below.

Journal of Comparative and Physiological Psychology, 1970, 73, 407–411.

51. Wallach, H. and E. B. Karsh. Why is the modification of stereoscopic depth-perception so rapid? *American Journal of Psychology*, 1963, 76, 413–420.

52. Wallach, H. and E. B. Karsh. The modification of stereoscopic depth-perception and kinetic depth effect. *American Journal of Psychology*, 1963, 76, 429–435.

53. Mack, A. and D. Chitayat. Eye-dependent and disparity adaptation to opposite visual-field rotations. *American Journal of Psychology*, 1970, 83, 352–371.

54. See Epstein, W. and C. L. Morgan. Adaptation to binocular image magnification: modification of the disparity-depth relationship. *American Journal of Psychology*, 1970, 83, 322–329.

55. Epstein and Morgan-Paap, Reference 1.

56. Weinstein, S. The perception of depth in the absence of texture-gradient. *American Journal of Psychology*, 1957, 70, 611–615.

57. See Epstein, W. Perceived depth as a function of relative height under three background conditions. *Journal of Experimental Psychology*, 1966, 72, 335–338.

58. Gruber, H. E., W. L. King, and S. Ling. Moon illusion: an event in imaginary space. *Science*, 1963, 139, 750–752.

chapter 4

THE PERCEPTION OF DIRECTION

We perceive objects as having definite locations with respect to one another and with respect to ourselves. We also perceive objects as having definite orientations—for example, a line is seen as vertical or tilted. Here again, the reader may wonder why the perception of direction or orientation is considered a problem worthy of study by psychologists. One might think that an object—or to be more precise, a single point on an object—would be perceived as "straight ahead" if its image were to fall in the center of the retina, the fovea, and that it would be perceived as "off to the side" if its image were to fall in the periphery of the retina. Or one might think that a line would be perceived as vertical if its image on the retina were vertical, and as tilted if its image were tilted.

It will become clear that this naive formulation contains a measure of truth, but without certain important qualifications, it is essentially false. For example, when the eyes are turned to the side, a point in space that stimulates the center of the retina will not be perceived as "straight ahead." It will appear to be off to the side, where in fact, it is. It might seem to be self-evident that a point stimulating the lower retina would appear to be located below one stimulating the upper retina, but as a matter of fact, the reverse is the case. The retinal image is inverted but we certainly do not perceive the world upside down.

In this chapter we consider the problems of location and direction for points that are equidistant from the eyes as, for example, points that lie in a plane parallel to the forehead (the frontoparallel or, simply, the frontal plane) as shown in Fig. 4-1. In a subsequent chapter we consider the problem of the orientation of objects in this plane. For the most part, we are not concerned with locations and orientations in the third dimension because this reduces to the problem of distance and depth perception that was covered in Chapter 3.

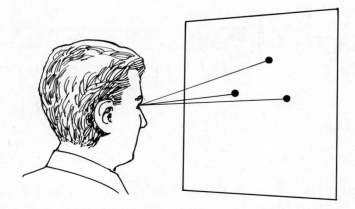

Figure 4-1

Field Location

In order to cope with the complex problems raised by the perception of direction and orientation, it is necessary to make certain distinctions, and to deal with each aspect of the problem separately. As far as the perception of direction is concerned, the major complicating factor in man and certain other species is that the eyes move within the head. Because of this fact, a specific retinal location cannot signify a specific direction in space. As already noted, an image that falls on the fovea will originate from a point located straight ahead of the observer if his eyes are directed straight ahead (X in Fig. 4-2a) but it will originate from a point to the side when his eyes are turned (Y in Fig. 4-2b). Since the direction of the point is correctly perceived in the two instances, it can hardly be true that foveal stimulation always represents the same direction. It would appear that the information concerning the direction of gaze of the eyes must be taken into account in assessing the directional significance of retinal location.

However, suppose for the moment we leave aside the question of direction of gaze and consider only the location of image points on the retina. Is there any sense in which we can say that the stimulation of a particular retinal location will always give rise to a particular phenomenal

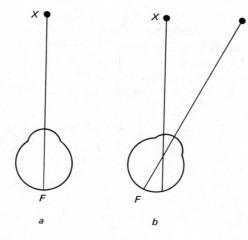

Figure 4-2

location? There is, but it is a subtle one and not easy to grasp. A foveal image will always be experienced as the region at which the observer is looking and this region will appear to be located more or less in the center of the *visual field* at that moment. By visual field is meant the entire visible field at a given moment, extending as far in all directions as it is possible to see. In the same way, a point stimulating the retina at the extreme periphery will always be experienced as far off to the side of the fixated point in a particular direction and as located at the edge of the visual field; a point stimulating the retina between the fovea and the extreme periphery will always be perceived as falling between the center and the edge of the momentary field. These descriptions do not refer to where any point is perceived to lie with respect to the observer— whether straight ahead of him or off to his left or right. A foveal image that is always experienced as the region at which the observer is looking may appear to have any location with respect to the observer.

This aspect of perceived direction is difficult to understand because it is not something we generally attend to. What we do attend to is where things are in relation to ourselves. Since the eyes move constantly and this information is taken into account in assessing where a point is located in relation to ourselves, we do not attend to the fact that an image does signify this invariant property of location. In this sense perceived location in the visual field (or simply "field location") is analogous to the perception of visual angle (or extensity) in the domain of size perception (pp. 37ff). Visual angle or retinal size invariantly signifies perceived extensity in the field but we are generally not aware of this aspect. Furthermore, it is hard to understand what we mean by extensity because information about distance is taken into account with the result that the same retinal size is now perceived as signifying one objective size and now another.

The following example may help to make the meaning clear. Imagine that an observer has formed an afterimage of three points, as shown in Fig. 4-3, with point *b* falling on the fovea. The three points will be

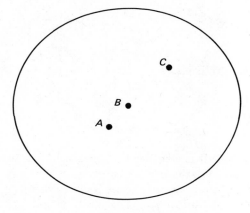

Figure 4-3

located phenomenally as follows: *b* appears to fall in the center of the field; *a* appears to fall below and to the left of *b*; and *c* appears to fall above and to the right of *b*, but farther to the right of *b* than *a* is to the left of *b*.*   Also the three points appear to be aligned, i.e., the three points fall on an imaginary straight line. These descriptions are meant to refer only to location within the momentary field of view, and no reference is made to where the points are with respect to the observer. Now, when the observer moves his eyes, the perceived direction of all three points with respect to the observer will radically change and continue changing as long as the eyes are in motion. (The reader is reminded that in the example under discussion the three points are in the form of an afterimage and that afterimages remain fixed in position on the retina when the eyes move.) Nevertheless, the phenomenal location of the points within the momentary field will not change. Wherever the eyes are pointed, *b* will always be in the center of *that* field of view, *a* will be below *b* and to the left of it, *c* will be above and to the right of *b*, and the points will always appear aligned. Another way of describing

---

*To avoid unnecessary confusion, the inversion and left-right reversal of the retinal image is ignored throughout this chapter.

field location is to say that we experience the location of points relative to each other. In fact, this would seem to be a better way of describing it because we are more aware of this aspect than of the fact that each point has some location with respect to centrality or peripherality in the field. In the example just described, then, we can say that there is no change in the perceived location of the three points relative to one another despite the change in the perceived direction of all of them relative to the observer with change in eye position.

What is the basis of the perception of field location? The answer would seem to be that retinal location provides the necessary information. The retinal image accurately represents the relative location of points in a frontal plane (at least it does for points that are not too far off to one side). Therefore, as long as it is clear that we are concerned here with the perception of field location and not with the perception of where a point is located with respect to the observer—concerning which retinal location per se would be inadequate information—it seems correct to say that the retinal location of points invariantly signifies their phenomenal locations relative to one another. This answer is analogous to the basis of perception of visual angle. That is, the relative size of a retinal image directly provides the necessary information for the perception of extensity; but retinal size alone does not provide the necessary information for the perception of objective size.

In other words, we can subscribe to the formulation of investigators such as Hering that each retinal location is a local sign of phenomenal location in a frontal plane, meaning not only that each retinal location gives rise to a qualitatively unique sensation or neural event but also that each retinal location is a sign of a given location in the visual field.[1] Of course, to say that the location of retinal stimulation is a sufficient basis of perceived field location is to imply that this information is not lost in the transmission into and through the brain. In fact, we now know that the location of points on the retina is represented by corresponding points of excitation in the visual cortex and in another brain center, the superior colliculus. In other words, each region of the retina is connected to a specific location in the brain. Therefore, one might say that there is a central "map" of the retinal image. Neurons having their origin in retinal cells transmit signals to the brain, either directly to the superior colliculus or through a relay station to the visual cortex. As long as the retinal image remains the same, therefore, the pattern of excitation in these central "maps" also remains the same, as, for example, in the case of the afterimage described previously. In this respect, the central "map" is a direct mirror of the retinal image. Eye position itself is not represented within the "map" except insofar as eye position changes the contents of the retinal image. In other words, the basis of perceived field location could well be the location of signals arriving at the superior colliculus or the visual cortex since there is an invariant relationship between retinal location and location in these brain centers. Therefore, one can say that the information about field location present in the retinal image is not lost in transmission into the brain; apparently it is well preserved.* In any event, whatever may be the neurophysiological basis of field location it will be assumed here that the necessary information is provided by retinal location.

A further question is whether the perception of field location on the basis of retinal location is given innately or must be learned. In the last century, several of the great thinkers in the empiricist tradition, Lötze, Helmholtz, and Wundt among others, suggested that we learn the spatial meaning of each retinal location.† According to this view, we start with the fact that each retinal locus is in some way discriminably different from each other locus, i.e., has a different *local sign*, but this difference does not refer to perceived location. That is what must be learned. The learning was said to be achieved in the following way. Consider any retinal point. When stimulated, the eye would have to turn by a specific angle in a specific direction to fixate it, i.e., to bring it into the center of vision. Thus, if it falls 10 degrees below the fovea, the eyes must

---

*At least this statement is correct with respect to gross field location. For more precise localization—of the order of less than 1 degree of visual angle—the terminal location of signals in the brain may not be a sufficient basis and other physiological mechanisms may come into play. Knowledge about the relationship between the locus of retinal stimulation and the locus of projection to these brain centers derives from several kinds of data: a degeneration technique in which the path of atrophy of cells following local destruction of retinal cells is examined; clinical cases where gunshot wounds or other damage to the visual cortex produces blind regions (or scotomata) in specific regions of the visual field; and direct electrical stimulation of the visual cortex during brain surgery in which the patient can localize the "stars" he thus perceives. For a thorough discussion of this issue, see Walls.[2] What has been called field location in this chapter, Walls refers to as oculocentric direction.

There is, however, the problem that the cortical representation of the retinal image is not an exact copy of that image. The cortical representation distorts the retinal image for the following reason. The region of clearest vision, represented by the fovea, subtends a relatively small part of the retina, less than .3 millimeter across or about 1 degree as measured in terms of visual angle. No doubt because this region is so important for vision, a disproportionately large amount of visual cortex is preempted by it. Given this fact, it follows that the cortical representation of any retinal image will be distorted. It also follows that the distortion will vary for different locations in the retina of that same image. It is not known how accurate field location is possible given the distorted nature of the cortical projection. One can only assume that the visual cortex is in some way "calibrated," so that when the cortical representation of the retinal image is "scanned," physically unequal extents are "read off" as psychologically equal and physically equal extents are "read off" as unequal.

†The best reference for a summary of previous ideas on this subject is Walls.[3]

be turned 10 degrees upward to fixate it. This eye movement was said to be the source of learning the spatial significance or field location of that retinal locus. Following such learning, that locus is now the sign of a specific field location even without the necessity of moving the eyes, since stimulation of that locus arouses the *tendency* to move the eyes upward by a specific angle in order to fixate it. (Incidentally, it was thought that this would also explain why the inverted retinal image does not lead to the perception of the world as upside down. The eye moves *upward* to fixate a retinally *downward* image, thus teaching us that the downward retinal direction represents what is spatially upward.) Thus, the argument is that the spatial meaning of all retinal loci are learned in this way from eye movements.

Before learning, according to this view, location cannot be perceived at all. The learning involved would be an amazing achievement given the great number of retina loci. And after the learning, the instantaneous perception of the entire scene as spatially ordered would be an equally amazing feat since it would amount to translating the excitation from each retinal locus into its correct psychological location (as learned) and integrating all these into a unified, ordered array.

Today most experimental psychologists are of the opinion that field location is innately determined and is probably not subject to modification on the basis of learning. The author concurs with this opinion. A number of considerations make that conclusion extremely likely:

1. As already noted, relative retinal location provides the necessary information for field location.
2. We now know (although Helmholtz did not) that this information is preserved in the projection to the superior colliculus and visual cortex. Whenever a neuroanatomical basis for a perceptual function has evolved it is reasonable to suppose that that function is innately determined.
3. An explanation in terms of the learning of the field location of every point such as was outlined in the previous paragraph is unwieldy and farfetched.
4. There is evidence discussed later that indicates that perceived direction in several species and possibly in humans does not have to be learned, and this innately given perception of direction would hardly be possible if field location, which is an essential component of the information necessary for such perceived direction, had to be learned.

Therefore, in the following discussion, it is taken as a working hypothesis that perceived field location is directly given by the location of

points in the retinal image. One might say that the locus of this excitation is an innate directional sign of field location.

Radial Direction

We are now ready to consider the basis of experience of the direction
of a point with respect to ourselves. This has been referred to as *radial
direction* because with the observer as the origin all such directions radi-
ate outward from a center. It has also been called *egocentric localization.* The center of reference or origin for the perceived direction of
points is the eye, but since we typically use both eyes, it has been concluded that the origin is the "Cyclopean eye," the point between the
two eyes.*

Since the eyes assume many different positions and since we nevertheless continue to perceive points in space as lying in a particular constant direction, it is obvious that eye position must be taken into
account. Consider the situation for a point in space that is straight
ahead of the observer. If the eyes are directed straight ahead with respect to the head, that point falls on the fovea. Assuming the perception of radial direction is veridical, as it generally is, this means that the
two items of information, foveal retinal location *and* eyes straight ahead,
together signify a straight ahead radial direction. But suppose now the
eyes are turned to the side. Generally the point, seen out of the "corner
of the eye," will nevertheless still appear to be straight ahead. Therefore, these two items of information, peripheral retinal location *and*
eyes turned to the side, together signify a straight-ahead direction.

Clearly then, there is a constancy of radial direction. As with other
perceptual constancies, the proximal stimulus, in this case retinal location, can vary, but the percept remains constant because other information is taken into account, in this case, eye position. And, as usual, the
corollary also holds that if the proximal stimulus remains the *same*, the
perception will *change* because other information is taken into account.
Thus, an afterimage, the retinal position of which does *not* change when
the eyes change position, will appear in *varying* radial directions when
the eyes move. This effect is analogous to Emmert's law of size percep-

---

*We are, of course, deliberately ignoring here the problem of binocular vision
and the fact that perceived field location and radial direction occur with either eye
alone and for both eyes together. Therefore, it is customary to speak of the "corresponding points" of the two retinas. This problem was discussed on pp. 97–99.

tion where an afterimage appears to change in size when located at different distances from the observer.

There has been only one direct investigation of constancy of radial direction.[4]   In order to eliminate all information other than retinal locus and eye position, the experiments were performed in the dark with luminous points. In one experiment, the subject fixated a luminous mark that was located 30 degrees to the side of his head. While maintaining that fixation, the subject was required to move a second luminous point, which he could see peripherally, until it appeared to be straight ahead of his head. If constancy were perfect, he would set the point objectively straight ahead; if there were no constancy, perceived direction would presumably be a function of retinal location only, in which case a point would appear "straight ahead" when it stimulated the fovea and that would mean moving the spot until it was superimposed on the fixation mark, 30 degrees to the side.

On the average, the subjects set the movable point only a few degrees from the objective median plane of the head (the straight-ahead direction). The direction of the error was toward the fixation mark. From this result we can conclude that a luminous point that remained in the objective median plane would appear to be slightly off to the side opposite that of the fixation mark. Hence the subject compensates by setting the point somewhat to the other side. However, the error is relatively slight, so that one may conclude that even under the more difficult dark-field conditions, there is a high degree of constancy of radial direction. The investigator hypothesized that the small departure from perfect constancy was based on an underestimation of the full extent to which the eyes are turned to the side. If the eyes were erroneously interpreted by the perceptual system to be turned only 28 degrees rather than 30 degrees, then the image of the point would have to fall 28 degrees from the fovea for it to appear straight ahead. That would lead to the prediction that the subjects would set the point toward the side of the fixation mark, on the average 2 degrees from the median plane, which is essentially what they did. Independent evidence was presented attesting to this underestimation of the extent to which the eyes were turned.* Such an explanation of the slight departure from perfect constancy is analogous to explaining the falling off of size constancy in terms of the underestimation of distance.

*In order not to complicate the discussion any more than is necessary at this time, a very important question has not been considered. How is information concerning the position of the eyes provided? One might be inclined to think that such information must derive from the proprioceptive feedback from the specific state of contraction of the extraocular eye muscles, but there is good evidence that this is not true. This problem is discussed in Chapter 5, The Perception of Movement and Events, pp. 186–187.

Radial direction is perceived with greater accuracy and with less variability in the light than in the dark, suggesting that factors other than eye position are relevant. In the dark, even with eyes straight ahead, there is a range of uncertainty of several degrees within which any location may at a given moment appear straight ahead.* In the light, the observer can easily be more *consistent* in his judgments since he can always set a spot in the same place relative to other visible objects. But it is not clear why he should be more accurate, unless it is because he can see a good deal of his own body. Since the task of placing a spot "straight ahead" means by definition setting it in the median plane of the head than, of course, if he could see his head it would be a much easier task than if he could not see it. One can see parts of the head (e.g., nose) and one can see the torso, and the sight of the torso can help as long as one takes into account how the head is oriented with respect to it.†

There are also interesting effects of the structure of the visual field on radial direction. It can be most clearly observed in a dark-room situation. If a luminous rectangle is placed asymmetrically, so that its center is *not* in the observer's median plane, then the radial direction that appears straight ahead to the observer is no longer veridical but instead lies in the direction of the center of the rectangle (see Fig. 4–4a).[5] The slope (or slant) of the plane at which one is looking will also affect radial direction. There is a tendency to perceive as straight ahead whatever point in such a plane is perpendicular to the line of sight (see Fig. 4–4b).[6] In Fig. 4–4, the dotted arrow indicates the objective median plane but the solid arrow indicates the apparent straight-ahead direction.

*The variability of the radial direction of a single point in a dark field (or in any other field that is completely homogeneous) is related to the autokinetic effect (see p. 205). When viewed over a period of time, a single stationary point in such a field will appear to be drifting about.

†For purposes of keeping an already complicated problem as simple as possible, radial direction is discussed with reference to the head as the origin of such direction throughout this chapter. However, it is possible to refer the direction of a point in space to the body of the observer rather than to the head, and a case can be made for doing so for the following reason. When the head is turned it can be claimed that the perceived egocentric direction of a point in the world does not change as it should if such direction is always referred to the head. Thus, one might say that the perceptual system takes into account three factors in assessing an object's direction: retinal locus of its image; eye position; and head position. On the other hand, one can argue that, with respect to the head the object's phenomenal direction does change when the head is turned. Therefore, it is simpler to analyze the problem in this way, but it should be clear that there is no contradiction here and that perceived direction can always be considered in relation to the body simply by including head position in the equation.

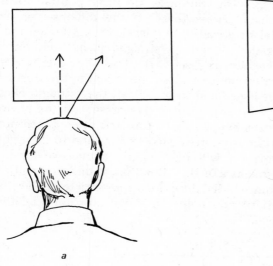
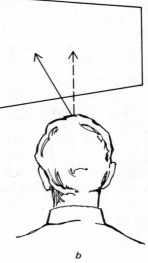

a   *b*

Figure 4-4

The mechanism underlying these effects is not known, but it clearly demonstrates that egocentric direction can be influenced by structural factors in the field, in these cases centrality and perpendicularity. It is as if the perceptual system confuses what is straight ahead and therefore "centered" with respect to the observer with what is centered with respect to the contents of the visual field; or as if the perceptual system confuses what is straight ahead, and therefore in a direction perpendicular to the frontal plane of the observer's body, with what is perpendicular with respect to a plane at which the observer is looking.

We have thus far restricted the discussion to a single point in the field. But, of course, every visible point has a particular radial direction at any given moment. Does this mean that for every retinal locus, eye position is taken into account, with the result that the radial direction of every point in the field is "deduced" separately? This seems unlikely and unnecessary. Given the fact that all points in the field are already located with respect to one another (field location), all it takes is the specification of a radial direction of one point for all other points to acquire simultaneously distinctive radial direction as well. In other words, since for any position of the eyes, the fovea signifies a certain radial direction, other retinal points will necessarily also signify radial directions that are determined by their angular separation from the fovea.

This is illustrated in Fig. 4-5. Suppose the three points shown in Fig. 4-3 stimulate the retina as shown there. If now the observer's eyes happen to be pointed straight ahead at eye level, then *b* which falls in the fovea will have the radial direction "straight ahead" and "at eye level." This much we have already discussed. Since, however, in terms of field location, *a* is located below and to the left of *b*, then, radially, it must appear below "eye level" and to the left of the "straight-ahead" direction. Suppose the same three points are present in the environment but the observer's eyes happen to be directed at *c*. Since now *c* stimulates the fovea, but the eyes are turned upward and to the right in fixating it, its radial direction will be "slightly above eye level and slightly to the right of straight ahead." But then it automatically follows that *a* and *b* will acquire radial directions appropriate to their field locations. Since *b* is left of and below *c*, it will now appear radially "straight ahead, at eye level."

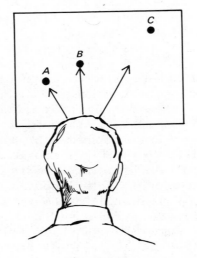

Figure 4-5

The origin of radial direction

How does it come about that we are able to take eye position into account and veridically perceive the direction of objects from the self? In the previous section it was argued that field location does not have to be learned but instead is innately determined by the locus of retinal excitation. Now that it is clear that the perception of radial direction entails the interpretation of field location on the basis of eye position, it is natural to inquire about the origin of this relationship. Is it also innately given?

There is some evidence bearing on egocentric localization in lower animals that suggests that it is present at birth. Newly hatched chicks peck at small objects on the ground with what appears to be a fair degree of accuracy and the pecking becomes even more accurate on succeeding days. This could be taken as evidence of innate visual localization but, on the other hand, it could be argued that it is a case of trial-and-error learning based on the reward of hitting particles of food. However, it has been shown that newly hatched chicks fitted with head masks that contain wedge prisms consistently peck to one side of grain particles offered to them.[7] Such prisms have the effect of displacing the direction in which an object appears to be located (as is explained later, see Fig. 4-6), but this should have no adverse effect if chicks must learn to localize objects. The contrast between these chicks and normal ones strongly supports the assumption of an innate basis of radial direction. The evidence is contradictory as to whether or not the chicks adapt to the prisms. In the initial study, the only change that occurred over time was that the dispersion of pecks around the *perceived* location of the grain particle decreased: this decrease in a normal chick might be considered to be evidence of learning, but in the chicks wearing prisms it cannot represent learning since the food is not obtained. Rather it seems to suggest maturation that permits more precise control over movements. The chick can peck with greater precision at the location where it perceives the food although, in fact, it is not there. However, in a subsequent study, specifically directed at the question of adaptation and using careful measurements, the extent of error of pecking did decrease over the first 8 days of life and errors were made on removal of the prisms.[8]

Experiments have also been performed with salamanders in which the eyes have been twisted around until they are upside down and then set back in place.[9] These animals always swam and snapped in a direction exactly opposite to that of a food lure, up instead of down, or left instead of right. Since the same was true of animals on whom similar surgery was performed during the embryonic stage, it is clear that in this species visual direction is innately determined.[10] There also did not appear to be any adaptation to the altered orientation of the eye.

There are, however, reasons for caution in drawing conclusions from these studies concerning radial direction in man and other higher species.

First, neither chicks nor salamanders have any eye movement to speak of. Therefore, the necessity of a constancy-type of mechanism in which eye position is taken into account is dispensed with. In these species, egocentric localization may be a direct function of the locus of the incoming signal from the retina just as it has been argued here that field location is in man. (In fact, the innateness of direction in these species is good evidence of what was claimed earlier, namely, that the nervous system has evolved in such a way that the location of a visual signal in the neural substrate is an innate sign of direction.) Second, there may be more of a direct reflex-type of link in these species between the incoming sensory signal and the outgoing motor response. Thus, stimulating by a food object of the upper left retina of a salamander may directly result in motor discharges that cause the animal to swim downward and to the right. Whereas in man we presume that between retinal stimulation and response there is a perceptual, cognitive, event that we call awareness of a certain egocentric direction.

Third, we now know that man can learn a new relationship between retinal locus and eye position. The evidence derives from experiments on adaptation to prisms that displace the apparent direction of all objects in the field. Of course, it does not necessarily follow that the amenability to learning in the adult proves that such learning was responsible for the establishment of the ability in the infant. But it is at least a reasonable supposition.* We now turn to the work on adaptation to displacing prisms.

---

*One clinical study suggests that egocentric localization in humans does not have to be learned.[11] Pressure against the eye with a finger or instrument elicits an experience of a spot of light. The pressure stimulates the retinal cells and, since they fire, one experiences light in the corresponding region of the visual field. (This is an interesting example of the doctrine of the specific energy of the nerves originally enunciated by Johannes Muller because it shows that even mechanical stimulation of visual fibers will result in light sensations). If the pressure is at the top of the eye the light spot—or *pressure phosphene* as it is called—is experienced in the lower part of the visual field. This is simply because the upper retina is stimulated and the upper retina represents the lower part of the field. In a rarely cited study, an investigator was able to elicit pressure phosphenes in a few young subjects who had been blind from birth. The subjects were able to localize the phosphenes correctly (although we are not told how they had to respond) despite the fact that they had never before experienced anything more than diffuse light. This study was done many years ago and, if possible, should be repeated with careful control of the manner in which the subject responds to the question "Where is the light?" It is possible that this study is getting at perceived field location (which it is argued here is innately given) rather than perceived radial direction.

Adaption to Optical Transformations
of the Retinal Image

The effect of many different kinds of transformation has been studied in the laboratory. By means of lenses, the retinal image can be enlarged or reduced; by means of prisms, the image can be inverted or rotated, straight lines can be rendered curved, and so forth. Experiments on adaptation to these different kinds of transformation are described in the appropriate places in this book, but since the question of adaptation to a displaced image is relevant to the present topic, the purpose and general methodology of this type of work is now considered.

In first looking through prisms that transform the retinal image in some way, it is not surprising that the world looks different than it normally does. But if after wearing these prisms for a period of time, the world begins to look more nearly normal again or completely normal, this would suggest an adaptability or plasticity that otherwise might never have been suspected. Thus, for example, a lens that reduces the size of the image would initially give rise to the impression that all objects are smaller than they usually are. But suppose after a while things no longer looked small through the lens. This would suggest that in some respect there is no necessary linkage between an image of a given size and a perception of a given size (even with distance held constant). It would also suggest that an adaptation process similar to the one now occurring with lenses, in which retinal images of different sizes had come to signify objects of specific sizes, may have taken place in the infant.

How can we best determine what change if any has taken place? We can, of course, simply ask the subject to tell us how things look from time to time. This yields valuable data but it is limited because the subject grows accustomed to the change and that is not necessarily the same thing as adapting to the change. For adaptation entails a definite change in perception. Another limitation of verbal reports is that they do not provide any quantitative data. A better procedure, therefore, is to take measurements of the relevant aspect of the perception "before" and "after" adaptation. There are two ways of doing this, namely, with prisms on and with prisms off. Consider the case in which measurements are made when the observer is *not* looking through the prisms.* Suppose we are interested in the perception of curvature and straightness, and the prism causes a straight line to appear

---

*This method is considered more trustworthy, if somewhat more conservative, than the one in which measurements are made when the observer *is* looking through the prisms. For a discussion of the methodology and rationale of prism-adaptation research see reference 12.

curved. Before putting on the goggles containing the prisms, the subject is asked to bend a flexible rod until it looks straight. Naturally we would expect him to be correct and set it straight at this time, but the measurements will tell us how precisely he can do this and whether he has any slight bias in one direction. Then after exposure to the prisms, they are removed, and again the subject must set the rod so that it looks straight. It is necessary that this test (before and after) be done with a luminous rod in the dark because otherwise the subject could simply bend the rod until it was parallel to the edges of certain objects in the scene, which he knows to be straight. If adaptation has occurred and is complete and a curved retinal image is now the sign of a straight line, then the subject should bend the rod in such a way that it is convex and gives rise to such a curved image. This is called an aftereffect. The difference between this "after" test and the "before" test measures the adaptation.

Adaptation to displacement

If one looks through a wedge-shaped prism such as shown in Fig. 4–6, objects appear to the right of their true position because the path of a ray of light is deflected toward the base of the prism. Helmholtz was the first to ask whether an observer might adapt to such displacement. He describes the following experiment.

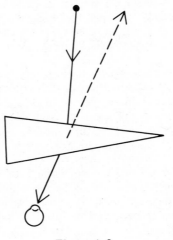

Figure 4-6

"Take two glass prisms with refracting angles of about 16° or 18°, and place them on a spectacle frame, with their edges both turned toward the left. As seen through these glasses, the objects in the field of view will all apparently be shifted to the left of their real positions. At first, without bringing the hand into the field, look closely at some definite object within reach; and then close the eyes, and try to touch the object with the forefinger. The usual result will be to miss it by thrusting the hand too far to the left. But after trying for some little while, or, more quickly still, by inserting the hand in the field, and under the guidance of the eye, touching the objects with it for an instant, then on trying the above experiment again, we shall discover that now we do not miss the objects, but feel for them correctly. It is the same way when new objects are substituted for those with which we have become familiar. Having learned how to do this, suppose now we take off the prisms and remove the hand from the field of view, and then after gazing steadily at some object, close our eyes and try to take hold of it. We find then that the hand will miss the object by being thrust too far to the right; until after several failures, our judgment of the direction of the eyes is rectified again." [13]

This informal little experiment shows an adaptation effect. It includes an "after" test with prisms off (the "before" test without prisms is implicit since it can safely be assumed that there would be no error to speak of in reaching for an object before the experiment began). The observer makes an error afterward in the direction opposite to the one he made with prisms on at the outset. The aftereffect in this case is negative for the following reason. The prisms cause an object to appear to the left of its actual position. Adaptation can be interpreted to imply that the observer learns that "things are to the right of where they appear." With prisms on this learning would mean correct localization. This same learning would, however, result in the error of localization when the prisms are removed and the error would be "to the right."

More recently, the technique for studying adaptation to a displaced image has been improved. Instead of measuring the effect by requiring the subject to close his eyes and point at a target seen a moment before, the subject marks the apparent location of a target under an arrangement where he cannot see his hand. [14] The point of this method—as well as Helmholtz's—is that if the subject could see his hand and the target at the same time, then any tendency to error could be overcome because he would simply correct the initial error by steering his visible hand to the visible target. In the new method, a mirror is used that both reflects the target to the subject's eyes and blocks his view of his hand that has been placed under the mirror (see Fig. 4-7). The subject's accuracy in locating a target is permanently recorded by his markings on a paper placed under the mirror. The subject marks the target before and after exposure to prisms and during the exposure period typically moves his hand back and forth while looking at it through the

Figure 4-7

prisms for a few minutes. A shift in the center of the cluster of target markings takes place.

Do these findings mean that perceived radial direction has been modified merely by looking at the hand through the prisms? Helmholtz thought so because he concludes his description of his experiment with the following comment:

> "Here it is not the muscular feeling of the hand that is at fault or the judgment of its position, but the judgment of the direction of the gaze, as is shown by the fact that, if after having become used to looking through the prisms and finding the visible objects with the right hand, then we close our eyes and try to touch the same objects with the left hand, which has not previously been used, and which was not in the field of view, we find that there will not be any difficulty about touching them with perfect certainty and precision. Accordingly, in a case of this kind the place is determined perfectly correctly, and thereafter it can be found with certainty by another organ of touch." [15]

However, contrary to what Helmholtz reports, recent experiments generally do *not* find that the adaptation effect transfers to the unseen hand. If change in the visually perceived direction of an object has occurred, then of course we would expect that it would be revealed by pointing at it or marking a target with either hand. The fact that the effect occurs only with the hand seen through the prisms suggests that the change has more to do with this hand than with visual perception. There is now a respectable amount of evidence indicating that what has happened is that the subject ultimately reinterprets the felt position of his hand.[16] When he looks at his hand through the prisms, it appears to be displaced from its true position. But the information he has about its true position derives from proprioception, the signals emanating from the joints that indicate where one part of the body is with respect to another part. Suppose, however, in this conflict between visual and proprioceptive information, that vision is dominant. In that case the visual location of the hand would determine its perceived location (in Chapter 8, p. 377 additional evidence is presented to the effect that vision is dominant in such sensory conflict situations).

If the hand is located where it visually is seen to be located, the question arises as to what happens to the proprioceptive information. There is reason to believe that the answer is that it is "captured" by the visual information, i.e., it is made to conform to it. The hand *feels* as if it is located where it is seen to be.[17] In that case, following several minutes during which the hand feels to be, say, to the left of where it in fact is, it is possible that the actual proprioceptive signals from the hand will now, through association, signify a position to the left of where it is. Hence, Helmholtz would, in his "after" test with eyes closed, move his hand to the right of the object, not because, as he thought, the object *visually* appears to be to the right of where it is, but because his hand *feels* to be to the left of where it is. If the hand feels like it is to the left of where it really is, one must position it to the right of a just-seen visual object in order to touch it. Proof that this is what has taken place is provided by the finding that a subject will err in pointing to an unseen sound source with the hand previously seen through prisms but not with the other hand; by the finding that the subject will err in pointing to the "straight ahead" (with eyes closed) with the hand used during exposure but not with the other hand; and so forth.

The fact that visual direction does not change in this type of experiment, where the subject merely looks at his moving hand through the prisms, is not surprising. Why should it? One can only expect a change in visual perception to occur if the observer obtains some kind of potent information that the way things appear through the prisms is not the way they are. Suppose the subject is looking at his hand that is actually

178 An Introduction to Perception

directly in front of him. The prisms will cause the hand to appear off to the side, let us say to the left. Therefore, in order to look directly at it, the eyes must be turned to the left. Since the combination of information "image foveal, eyes turned to the left" has in the past signified the radial direction "to the left" it will do so now. The only reason for any change to occur in this situation comes from proprioceptive information that indicates that the hand is straight ahead. Even if this information about hand position were not overpowered by vision, which it apparently is, it is unlikely that it would be sufficiently potent to produce a change in visual direction of the entire field.

For a visual change to occur, one would think that the observer would have to learn to reinterpret the direction in which his eyes are pointed. In the example given, the eyes are turned left in viewing an object that is straight ahead. If information is available that the object *is* in fact straight ahead, then it would follow that the subject's eyes must be straight ahead, since they are directed at the object. There are several possible sources of such information and research thus far has not clarified which of these is most effective. One such source of information is the sight of the subject's own torso. Since the body can hardly be displaced to the side, the sight of it might conceivably serve as information that the direction in which it appears is straight ahead.

Another potential source of information derives from movement by the subject. Normally, with forward movement, the images of all points in the field displace outward on the retina since the direction of any point in the field from the eye will be increasingly off to the side as it is approached (the expansion pattern discussed in Chapter 3 and illustrated in Fig. 3–34, p. 116). In fact, the farther to the side a given point in the field is, the faster will its retinal image be displaced. The image of the point toward which the observer is moving, however, will not displace at all because it remains straight ahead. Therefore, there is a characteristic "flow pattern" associated with forward movement that may become quite noticeable when the movement is rapid, as in a vehicle. In viewing the world through displacing prisms, the stationary center of the flow pattern will be the spot that is straight ahead of the subject's line of approach. Since that spot is displaced by the prisms, it first appears off to the side. The fact that the stationary center of the flow pattern is located there may be information to the effect that it is actually straight ahead.*

---

*However, for the altered location of the center of the flow pattern to be unambiguous information about radial direction, the perceptual system must also have information that the observer is walking straight ahead.

Whether or not these sources of information are responsible for the change is not yet certain, but visual adaptation to displacing prisms has been obtained. In one study, adaptation was measured by requiring the subject to indicate when the vertical line inside a drum surrounding his head appeared straight ahead.[18] In the exposure period, the subject walked around for two 2-hour sessions, viewing the world through prisms that displaced objects by 11 degrees. The change in the setting of the line amounted to 1.29 degrees. However, if the exposure was continued over a 2-to-4-day period, half of the subjects achieved full adaptation. Since the measure of adaptation in this case is one that directly taps the visual perception of direction and is not ambiguous in its meaning (as is marking a target with the hand), it seems clear that a change in perceived egocentric localization has occurred. Other experiments have shown that head movements alone will lead to adaptation to displacing prisms as will sight of the body even if the subject is stationary.*

There is good evidence that this visual adaptation consists in reinterpreting the direction in which the eyes are pointing (the direction of gaze in Helmholtz's words). In one experiment, the eyes were photographed in the dark, using infrared light, before and after exposure to the prisms.[22] The subject was instructed to look straight ahead. It was found that, following adaptation, the subject tended to turn his eyes to the side when he thought he was looking straight ahead. Since the radial direction of every point in the field is simultaneously determined by the direction in which the eyes are assumed to be pointed, all that is needed for a shift in radial direction to occur is a central reinterpretation of eye position.

The main reason for discussing the work on prism adaptation in this chapter was its possible relevance to the problem of perceived direction. It was explained earlier that the perception of radial direction necessarily entails interpreting field location by taking account of eye position. The further question was raised concerning the origin of this relationship. Do we learn that when the eyes are in a straight-ahead position a foveal stimulus represents an object straight ahead or is this an innately determined relationship? The finding that adaptation is possible and

---

*A controversy has raged over whether or not movement of the observer is a necessary condition for prism adaptation and some evidence supports the belief that the movement must be actively initiated by the observer himself rather than imposed upon him such that he remains passive.[18, 19] But there is now ample evidence that movement is not a necessary condition.[20] For a discussion of this problem and additional evidence bearing on it, see reference 21.

that, further, it is probably based on reinterpreting the directional significance of eye position, clearly supports the interpretation suggested here, that radial direction is based on a constancy-like function in which eye position is taken into account.

By the same token, it is at least possible to believe that the origin of radial direction in the infant is based on this kind of mechanism. The infant could learn that when his eyes are straight ahead, a foveal image represents an object that is straight ahead. On the other hand, it is possible that the relationship between specific eye position and perceived radial direction does not have to be learned in infancy but is given innately. This can be true despite the fact that the relationship is subject to learning. However, even if the relationship is learned in infancy we do not know whether or not the infant learns this on the basis of the same kind of information that the adult makes use of in adapting to a prismatically displaced image. Until the infant begins to move around in the environment, the information based on the flow pattern would not be available. Whatever the information, the set of "rules" by which radial direction is inferred from eye position is stored in memory. For the adult, in adapting to prisms, new "rules" are learned and new memories are established. Adaptation increases as the strength of the new "rules" begins to outweigh that of the old. According to this view of the process, there is no need to think that there is any change in the field location of retinal points or that such location has to be learned in the first place by the infant.

Does this mean that the change that occurs during adaptation is not really visual even in the experiment where the test entails visual direction? There has been some confusion about this issue. By definition, the egocentric location of a visual point *is* a visual experience and, therefore, any change in such perceived location is a visual change. However, if the analysis presented here is correct, that the *mechanism* underlying the change is a reinterpretation of the direction of gaze, then the basis of the change is itself not visual. The basis of the change is concerned with a recalibration of the neural signals that signify the physical position of the eyes.

Summary

The perceived direction of a point with respect to the region between the two eyes as origin—*radial direction* or *egocentric localization*—is based upon the integration by the perceptual system of two sources of information. First the location of the image of the point on the retina must be detected. Retinal location gives rise to the experience of the relative location of a point in the momentary field of view, or *field location*, such that the location of each point relative to all others is given. Since the information concerning relative location in a frontal plane is accurately represented by relative retinal location, and since this information is preserved in the projection of the retinal image to centers in the brain, it is plausible to think that retinal location is an innate directional sign of field location.

However, field location does not in itself signify radial direction, i.e., where a point is with respect to the observer, because in man and certain other species, the eyes move within the head. Therefore, a second, necessary source of information for the perception of radial direction is the direction of gaze of the eyes. Thus, the perceptual system takes into account the position of the eyes in assessing the egocentric location of every retinal stimulus, thereby achieving a constancy of perceived direction. There are, however, certain other factors that may affect perceived radial direction, such as structural aspects of the content of the visual field.

Is the integration of field location and information about the position of the eyes also an innate process or is it learned? Although evidence suggests that radial direction is innately determined in some species—where the eyes move little if at all—experiments on adaptation to prismatically induced displacement in man suggest that the precise relationship between field location and eye position is subject to relearning. Thus, following adaptation, the objectively straight-ahead position of the eyes with respect to the head no longer signifies that a foveal stimulus is "straight ahead"; rather when the eyes are turned to the side by some specific angle an image in this retinal location will appear to have this direction.

The possible sources of information that make such adaptation possible were considered.

References

1. Hering, E. *Spatial Sense and Movements of the Eye.* Trans. by C. A. Radde. American Academy of Optometry, 1942.
2. Walls, G. The problem of visual direction. Part II: the tangible basis for nativism. *American Journal of Optometry and Archives of the American Academy of Optometry*, 1951, Monograph No. 117, pp. 31–32.

3. Walls, G. The problem of visual direction. Part I: the history to 1900. *American Journal of Optometry and Archives of the American Academy of Optometry*, 1951, Monograph No. 117.

4. Hill, A. L. Direction constancy. *Perception & Psychophysics*, 1972, **11**, 175-178.

5. Roelofs, C. O. Optische Lokalisation. *Archiv für Augenheilkunde*, 1935, **109**, 395-415; H. Dietzl. Untersuchungen über die optische Lokalisation der Mediane. *Zeitschrift für Biol.*, 1924, **80**, 289-316.

6. Kleinhans, J. *Perception of Spatial Orientation in Sloped, Slanted and Tilted Visual Fields.* Ph.D. thesis, Rutgers University, 1970. See also I. Rock, J. Goldberg, and A. Mack. Immediate correction and adaptation based on viewing a prismatically displaced scene. *Perception & Psychophysics*, 1966, **1**, 351-354; C. S. Harris, J. R. Harris, and C. W. Karsch. Shifts in pointing "straight ahead" after adaptation to sideways-displacing prisms. Paper delivered at the meeting of the *Eastern Psychological Association*, New York City, 1966.

7. Hess, E. H. Space perception in the chick. *Scientific American*, 1956, **195**, 71-80.

8. Rossi, P. J. Adaptation and negative aftereffect to lateral optical displacement in newly hatched chicks. *Science*, 1968, **160**, 430-432.

9. Sperry, R. W. Effect of 180 degree rotation of the retinal field on visuomotor coordination. *Journal of Experimental Zoology*. 1943, **92**, 263-277.

10. Stone, L. S. Functional polarization in retinal development and its re-establishment in regenerating retinae of rotated grafted eyes. *Proceedings of the Society of Experimental Biology and Medicine*, 1944, **57**, 13-14; Polarization of the retina and development of vision. *Journal of Experimental Zoology*, 1960, **145**, 85-93.

11. Schodtmann, W. Ein Beitrag zur Lehre von der optischen Lokalisation bei Blindgeborenen. *Archiv für Opthalmologie*, 1902, **54**, 256-267.

12. Rock. I. *The Nature of Perceptual Adaptation.* Basic Books, Inc., Publishers, 1966, Chap. 1, in particular, pp. 10-14.

13. Helmholtz, H. von. *Treatise on Physiological Optics* (Trans. from the 3rd. German ed., edit. by J. P. C. Southall), Vol. III. Dover Publications, Inc., 1962, p. 246.

14. Held, R. and N. Gottlieb. Technique for studying adaptation to disarranged hand-eye coordination. *Perceptual and Motor Skills*, 1958, **8**, 83-86; R. Held, and A. Hein. Adaptation of disarranged

hand-eye coordination contingent upon re-afferent stimulation. *Perceptual and Motor Skills*, 1958, **8**, 87–90.

15. Helmholtz, op. cit. 246–247.

16. Harris, C. S.   Adaptation to displaced vision: visual, motor, or proprioceptive change? *Science*, 1963, **140**, 812–813; Perceptual adaptation to inverted, reversed, and displaced vision. *Psychological Review*, 1965, **72**, 419–444.

17. Hay, J., H. L. Pick, Jr., and K. Ikeda. Visual capture produced by prism spectacles. *Psychonomic Science*, 1965, **2**, 215–216.

18. Held, R. and J. Bossom. Neonatal deprivation and adult rearrangement: complementary techniques for analyzing plastic sensory-motor coordinations. *Journal of Comparative and Physiological Psychology*, 1961, **54**, 33–37.

19. Held, R. and A. Hein, op. cit.

20. Wallach, H., J. H. Kravitz, and J. Lindauer. A passive condition for rapid adaptation to displaced visual direction. *American Journal of Psychology*, 1963, **76**, 568–578.

21. Rock, I., 1966, op. cit.

22. Kalil, R. E. and S. J. Freedman. Persistence of ocular rotation following compensation for displaced vision. *Perceptual and Motor Skills*, 1966, **22**, 135–139.

chapter 5

THE PERCEPTION OF MOVEMENT AND EVENTS

Why does the perception of movement present a problem? It would seem plausible to believe that when an object moves, its image will move on the retina and this image movement is interpreted by the perceptual system as movement of the object. If this were the case, movement perception would not present a problem. Indeed, insofar as lower animals are concerned, this account may be correct, but as an explanation of the perceptual experience of human observers, it is grossly inadequate.

The perceptual experience of movement is analogous to other qualities of sensory experience such as color or size—we perceive movement as a property of the object. The ability to perceive movement is clearly very fundamental in animals; it is necessary for survival. Various animals react to movement but not to stationary objects. In man, movement of an object in the periphery of the field can be detected before its exact form is apprehended.

Movement is an "either-or" experience. An object either appears to be moving or it appears to be stationary (although of course its perceived speed may vary). There is no middle ground. If an object is moving too slowly—as in the case of the minute hand of a watch—it will not appear to move at all, although after a while a change in position is detected. Thus, there is a threshold below which a given magnitude of objective displacement per unit time will not lead to perceived movement and above which it will. The task before us is to try to identify the conditions of stimulation or central processes that lead to the perception of movement.

Various kinds of conditions lead to movement perception. When we perceive movement where something actually is moving this is referred to as *real movement perception.* But often we perceive movement where nothing in the real world is in motion. There are several kinds of such illusory impressions of movement, each of which is considered in this chapter: *stroboscobic movement, autokinetic movement,* and the *aftereffect of movement.* Then there is the situation that prevails when the *observer himself is moving,* which may or may not lead to the perception of the environment as moving.

The logical place to begin our inquiry would seem to be with real movement perception. When an object is actually moving, there are several possible explanations of why we see it moving: if the eyes are stationary its image will move over the retina; the eyes move if the observer tracks the object, thus keeping the retinal image stationary; or the image of the object changes its location with respect to that of other visible objects in the field, whether the eyes move or not. In order to separate these various factors and to develop a working hypothesis about the basis of movement perception, we begin with a discussion of the situation that exists when the observer is moving.

Movements of the Observer and Perceived Movement

Our perceptual experience during a period of movement in the stationary environment plainly contradicts the hypothesis that displacement of the retinal image leads to perceived movement of objects. When we move, or move only our eyes or head, the images of all stationary objects displace across the retina but things do not appear to move. This fact has been referred to as *position constancy.*

It would seem plausible to suppose that movement is not perceived under such circumstances because the perceptual system takes into account the fact that the displacement across the retina is simultaneous with and, therefore, caused by the observer's own movement. The image displacement is attributed to movements of the observer rather than to movement of the environment. Of course, for this process to operate, information that the observer has engaged in some movement must be available. Even though the hypothesis does not rest on any one characterization of the information, it is of interest to identify the nature of this information.

One possibility is that it is based on feedback (inflowing signals) from neural receptors embedded in the muscles and joints or the inner ear that fire when the observer moves. There is now good reason to think that this is not correct, at least in the case of eye movements. Helmholtz was the first of many investigators to note that if the eyeball were pushed with a finger, thus moving it and consequently displacing the images of all things in the environment, the entire scene would appear to move.[1] Here there is no position constancy, although we must presume the proprioceptive receptors in the eye muscles would signal that the eye moved. Conversely, if the eye is immobilized and one then tries to move it, information does appear to be registered that it has moved. Ernst Mach achieved this by wedging putty next to the eyes in such a way that when the observer tried to turn his eyes, he could not do so.[2]   At the moment the observer "commanded" his eyes to turn, the entire visual scene appeared to jump. In this case, of course, there was no displacement of the image, since the eyes did not move. Why then did the scene appear to move? Apparently, because the perceptual system received information that the eyes *did* move and if the eyes did move, then a stationary image must signify that the environment moved with the eyes. The same effect occurs in the case of individuals whose eye muscles are paralyzed whenever they attempt to move their eyes.   More recently, the effect has been demonstrated with subjects whose eye muscles were held rigidly by forceps (inserted under the conjunctiva), and who were then instructed to move their eyes.[3]

These examples suggest the surprising conclusion that the intention or "command" to move the eyes is recorded centrally in the brain and treated as information that the eyes *have* moved. Ordinarily, of course, the eyes *do* move a fraction of a second after the command to move them has been issued, so that this kind of eye-movement information normally will lead to the appropriate interpretation of the retinal-image behavior. In the special cases, however, where the eyes do not in fact move, the information leads to illusory effects. The evidence, therefore, supports the conclusion that the crucial information is not *afferent* (proprioceptive) but a copy or record of *efferent* or outflowing signals *to* the muscles. There is further support for this conclusion. It is now known that in the case of limbs of the body, it is receptors in the joints and not in the muscles that provide information about the relative positions of one limb to another. There is no joint in the eye and for this reason alone we should predict that proprioception cannot be the source of information about eye position.

In the case of movement of the head or of the entire body, it is also possible that outflow signals provide information about observer movement although there is no critical evidence available to support this view. However, if an observer is moved by another person—for example, if he is pushed in a wheel chair—he will perceive veridically the environment as stationary and himself as moving. Since he himself does not initiate the action, there can be no registering of efferent signals sent out to his muscles. Rather, changes such as those taking place in the vestibular organ of the inner ear undoubtedly signal the fact of his own movement to the perceptual system, and this is in the family of feedback or proprioceptive sensory data. Given such information, the displacement of the image is discounted and the environment is seen as stationary.

It seems that displacement of the image does not lead to perceived movement if the perceptual system has information that the observer's own movement caused the image displacement. Therefore, movement across the retina clearly is not a condition that necessarily leads to perceived movement. We have also seen an instance of the converse situation, namely, one in which the image does *not* move, but movement of objects *is* perceived. Another example of this is the situation that arises during pursuit movements of the eye when an observer fixates an object and tracks it as it moves across his field. The image of the object will remain more or less fixed in position on the fovea of the retina. Nevertheless, the object will appear to move. Of course, in this situation the image of the stationary background will displace across the retina so someone might argue that the fixated object is seen to move because there is some image displacement on the retina. Or it may be argued that the displacement of the image of the object *relative* to that of the surrounding background is crucial here. However, the same observation can be made when the moving object is a single isolated spot in an otherwise homogeneous environment (such as a luminous point in a darkened room). An even clearer demonstration is based on first forming an afterimage and then noting how it behaves when viewed in a dark room (or with the eyes closed) when the eyes move. The afterimage is imprinted in one location on the retina and yet, when the eyes move, it appears to move.[4] *

Under certain conditions stationary objects appear to move slightly when the eyes move. When the eyes track a moving target, the stationary background appears to move in a direction opposite to that of the moving point, an effect known as the Filehne illusion. But the magnitude of such perceived movement is slight, and often observers do perceive the background as stationary. This finding perhaps can best be understood as a slight departure from complete constancy of position, analogous to similar findings with other of the perceptual constancies. As with such other constancies, there is reason for believing that the result is based on underregistration of the information that must be taken into account by the perceptual system, in this case of the rate at which the eyes are moving.[5]

If displacement of the image is *not* the correlate of perceived movement, what is? From the examples considered thus far, the following principles can be formulated. *When an object is perceived to undergo a change in its location, it will be perceived to move. If the change in the object's location is based on the observer's movement, it will be perceived as stationary.* In the examples thus far considered, location can

---

*With rapid eye movements there is an attenuation or suppression of visual input so that the signals from the retina that produce an afterimage may be so weak that the afterimage disappears. The reader who wishes to try this demonstration is, therefore, alerted to this fact.

be defined as radial direction. The reason that stationary objects do not undergo a change in radial direction when the eyes are in different positions should be clear from the discussion in Chapter 4. Conversely, the reason why a fixated object that moves does undergo a change in its phenomenal location when the eyes change position should also be clear. In the case of movement of the observer, stationary objects do change their radial directions with respect to the observer, but this change is fully accounted for in terms of the observer's movement. Therefore, the objects appear stationary.

The loss and recovery of position constancy

When the observer moves—or just his head or eyes move—the retinal image displaces in a particular direction and at a particular rate. For example, when the head turns 30 degrees to the right (and assuming the eyes remain fixed with respect to the head) the retinal image of the scene shifts 30 degrees to the right. This shifting of the image is discounted and no movement is perceived.* Therefore, we can ask the question, What will happen when the image behaves in a somewhat different fashion when the observer moves? It would seem to follow that if a 30 degree shift of the image to the right following a 30 degree head movement to the right *means* "world is stationary," any other direction or rate of image shifting must mean the world is not stationary. We have already encountered one such case, namely, the situation that exists when the image (or afterimage) is completely stationary and the observer—or just his eyes—moves. In keeping with the prediction, the afterimage appears to move.

It is possible to introduce a more drastic change in the behavior of the image. In a now classic experiment done at the turn of the century, the investigator, George Stratton, wore a lens system that had the effect of inverting the image and reversing it with respect to right and left.[6] He was interested in the question of whether the world would ultimately appear right side up again. However, the lens system changes the direction of movement of the retinal image based on observer movement. Stratton reported that whenever he moved his head or body, the entire scene appeared to move in the direction he was moving and twice as fast. He called this "swinging of the scene," an effect that follows from the account of movement perception presented here.

*The term *discounted* is used here to mean that no movement is perceived in the environment because the image displacement is fully accounted for by the movement of the observer. It has no other theoretical implications.

To make this clear, note that in Fig. 5-1*a* the observer fixates point 2. Because the image is not reversed as it normally is, he sees point 3 off to the left although actually it is to the right. Now if he moves his head to the right, *b*, point 3 stimulates the fovea. Hence point 3 traveled from the apparent left to straight ahead as the head moved to the right. A point changing its location in this manner when the head moves to the right would ordinarily be a moving point. Point 1 is about to move out of the field entirely, but since it has been displacing along the retina to the left, it will shortly be seen moving out of the field to the right, in the direction the head is turning. The observer, therefore, experiences a movement of the entire scene in the direction the head moves. As to the rate of perceived movement: if the image displaced normally, no movement would be experienced; if it were stationary, objects in the scene would seem to move as fast as the head, i.e., to keep pace with it. Because it displaces in the opposite direction by an amount equal to the amount of head displacement, objects in the scene must seem to move through twice the angle the head moves.*

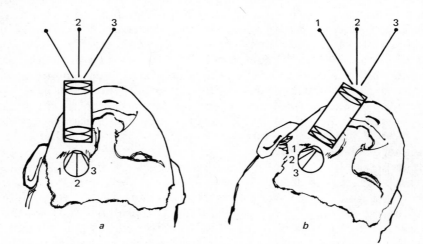

Figure 5-1

*If the observer wearing lenses or prisms in goggles holds his head still and moves only his eyes, the scene does *not* appear to move. For example, if the observer desires to fixate an object that appears to be off to his left, he will turn his eyes to the left. The image of the object will then move toward the fovea just as it normally would. Of course, in doing so the observer will be turning his eyes away from where the object actually is, to his right. Only if prisms were attached directly to the eyes would the scene appear to move during eye movements.

A similar effect seems to occur in animals.[7]   In one experiment the head of a fly was surgically rotated 180 degrees and kept in that position during the experiment.   As a result, the left side of each eye was on the right side of the fly and vice versa.   Consequently, when the fly moved, the images of external objects were displaced in a direction opposite to the customary one, just as in Stratton's experiment.   Before examining the result of this experiment, it is necessary to consider how the fly behaves in the experimental situation under consideration when the head is *not* rotated.   If a fly is placed in the center of a striped drum and the drum is rotated around the fly, then the fly typically begins to turn in the direction of the drum's movement (See Fig. 5–2).   (This is a well-known, virtually universal, reflex referred to as the optokinetic or optomotor response.   In many species, including man, the eyes will turn slowly with the drum until they have gone as far as they can, whereupon they snap back and the process repeats itself.)   If the drum remains stationary and a fly is permitted to move freely around on the platform inside the drum, there is no indication of an optomotor response; yet the image of the drum is sweeping across the fly's retina precisely as in the first situation.   We must, therefore, assume that the drum is not perceived as moving because the brain of the fly receives information that the fly's own movements are producing the displacement of the image.   Discounting occurs.

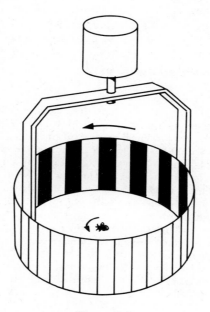

Figure 5–2

When the fly's head is rotated and it is permitted to move freely around on the table, with the drum stationary, a curious thing happens. The fly begins to circle and continues to circle indefinitely. It would seem that the fly circles because the optomotor response has been triggered. This occurs because the direction in which the images of the stationary stripes displace is opposite to the one that would be discounted. Therefore, the drum is "perceived" to turn—although it does not—and a drum "perceived" to be rotating induces the optomotor response.*

But now we must take a closer look at the problem of why the scene appears to move when the retinal image displaces abnormally during movements of an observer. It seems self-evident that if, normally, a certain direction or rate of displacement of the image for a given movement of the observer is discounted, i.e., it leads to perceiving the scene as stationary, then any other behavior of the image must lead to seeing the scene as moving. The question then is whether the normal movement of the image—for example from left to right with rightward head movement—is discounted by virtue of some innate linkage or whether it is perhaps learned.

It was noted earlier that the organism discounts the image displacement because information is available that its own movements have produced that displacement. How does the organism distinguish between instances where it has and instances where it has not produced the image displacement? A plausible answer is that self-produced displacement is perfectly correlated with bodily movement. It begins and ends concomitantly with the observer's movement and its rate is correlated with the observer's rate of movement. If this concomitance is

---

*It is possible that the optomotor response is based on the fact that the stationary animal perceives itself as turning in a direction opposite to that of the rotating drum. (See the discussion of induced movement of the self on p. 217 of this chapter.) If so, the animal would try to "undo" this unwanted effect by rotating in the direction of the moving drum. However, it is unlikely that such an explanation could account for the forced circling of the *moving fly* when the head is rotated because here, to explain the result, it would have to be argued that based on induced movement of the self the fly perceives itself as turning in a direction opposite to the one in which it is actually turning. As noted previously, a human observer looking through reversing prisms or lenses perceives the scene as moving whenever he moves so that no induced movement of the self seems to occur.

The complicating factor in the experiment with the fly is that the drum surrounds the fly, so that conditions exist to generate induced movement of the self. However, the same kinds of effects could in principle be obtained with only a single visual object: when the object moves, it will be perceived to do so; when the fly moves, the object will appear to be stationary; when the eyes are rotated and the fly moves, the object will appear to move and at a rate faster than the fly.

indeed the crucial factor, then it would not seem to be necessary that the image displace in a particular direction or rate in order for the discounting process to take place. If the image were to shift from right to left instead of from left to right with rightward head movement, its displacement would still be perfectly correlated with the observer's movement.

Yet we have seen that under such abnormal conditions, discounting does not take place. The world does appear to move. May it not be the case, at least for human observers, that this effect is the result of a lifetime of experience in which the image always behaves in a particular way for any given movement of the observer? Based on such experience it is possible that we learn the rule that the retinal image moves in the same direction we move and at the same speed. Thus, only the normal displacement of the image comes to signify "world is stationary."

If this reasoning is correct, it should be possible to undo this learning by requiring an observer to view the world for some period of time through an optical device such as the one described earlier. The observer should adapt to the new state of affairs, and this is precisely what happened in the experiment by Stratton referred to previously. The "swinging of the scene" gradually decreased and, after 3 or 4 days, disappeared entirely. Upon removing the lenses Stratton reported that the scene again appeared to move when he moved, i.e., he experienced a negative aftereffect. This means that the abnormal, reversed direction of retinal displacement during observer movement had come to signify that the world was stationary; hence on removing the lenses, the reestablishment of the normal direction of displacement had to lead to an impression of object movement. Other investigators have confirmed Stratton's observations and recently short-range studies with large numbers of subjects and more objective methods of testing have been conducted.[8]   On the basis of this work it is safe to conclude that in man there is no necessary, innately determined, linkage between the specific nature of self-produced image-displacement and constancy of position of objects in the world. Rather, it is clearly the case that position constancy is subject to learning.

Stroboscopic Movement

Everyone, it would seem, knows that moving pictures are made by projecting a series of stationary frames on a screen in rapid succession.

Yet few people seem to be curious about the basis of this effect and those who are seem to be satisfied with an incorrect explanation. The incorrect explanation asserts that the effect is based on the fact that the cells of the retina continue to fire after a given frame is no longer present. Hence there is no experience of a gap or of a dark screen between successive frames. This is true and it explains why, at the optimum projection speed, we do not experience a flicker (although in the early days of moving pictures flickering did occur). But this still leaves unexplained why we experience objects presented in these stationary pictures as *moving*.

The fact of the matter is that we do not know why movement is perceived, but psychologists have reduced the problem to its bare essentials in the laboratory. In a typical experiment, two points of light or two lines are projected alternately on the screen (See Fig. 5-3). First *a* is flashed briefly; then *a* goes off and there is a brief period when nothing is visible; finally *b* goes on for the same duration as *a*; followed by another brief interval; then *a* goes on again and so forth. At very slow speeds of alternation, the observer typically perceives two lines alternating, but no movement; at very fast speeds, he perceives two lines both of which seems to be present simultaneously; at some intermediate speed he sees movement, as if there were only one line moving back and forth.* The illusion of movement is so strong that it cannot be distinguished from real movement. This is clearly the case in modern motion pictures where the basic effect can be analyzed into several different components all of which are changing location simultaneously

Figure 5-3

---

*Since factors such as brightness and distance between *a* and *b* affect the outcome it is not possible to state what these rates are as a general rule. But typically, when *a* and *b* are a few degrees apart and are each on for around 50 milliseconds, the optimum interval or off-period when neither *a* nor *b* is on, is around 50 to 100 milliseconds. If this period is much greater, *a* and *b* will be seen to appear successively; if it is much less, they will appear to be simultaneously on; and in neither case will movement be perceived. However, the period between the onset of *a* and onset of *b* is now thought to be important. If *a* is on for 100 milliseconds or longer, optimum movement will be perceived when there is no off period at all between *a* and *b*.

(see Fig. 5-4). In the figure several actions are depicted as occurring at the same time. The man's arm 1-2 is moving forward and his leg 3-4 is moving upward. Needless to say, filmstrips can be either drawn to simulate such changes of position (animated cartoons) or achieved by moving picture photography. In the latter case, the camera records successive shots taken at brief intervals.

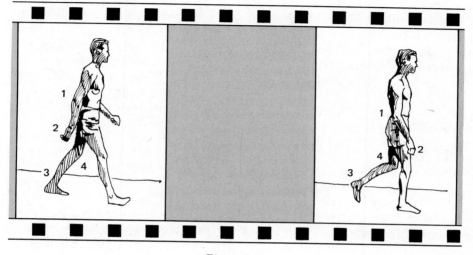

Figure 5-4

A further complication arises in the case of moving pictures that is based on the fact that objects rather than single points or lines are changing location. Suppose we consider a triangle and focus our attention on the three corners as illustrated in Fig. 5-5. If in one frame the triangle is in a given place, *a*, then in the next frame it may be somewhat to the right, *b*. If only point 1 were visible in *a* and only point 3' in *b*, then obviously point 1 would be seen to move to where point 3' is located. This is also true with respect to all other possible changes. But when the entire array 1,2,3 is shown in both *a* and *b*, 1 is seen to move to 1', 2 to 2', and 3 to 3'.

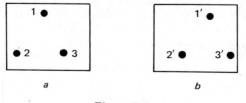

Figure 5-5

Therefore, it would seem that in addition to the basic stroboscopic illusion there is a further principle at work, a tendency to see objects move as-a-whole in such a way as to preserve their overall integrity. This fact has been demonstrated even more dramatically in the following type of experiment. In *a* in Fig. 5-6 three dots are exposed, 1, 2, and 3. In *b* three dots are again exposed, 2′, 3′, and 4. However, the leftmost two dots of *b*, 2′ and 3′, are in the identical place as the two rightmost dots of *a*, 2 and 3 (shown by locating the dots within the rectangular frame of the screen in *a* and *b*). Given these two arrangements, we should predict that only one dot will undergo a stroboscopic effect, namely the leftmost dot in *a*, dot 1, should appear to move to the location of the rightmost dot in *b*, dot 4. Since there is no change of location of the other two dots, they should appear to flash on and off in the same place. Instead, most observers perceive three dots shifting back and forth. The leftmost dot of *a* is seen to move to the place of the leftmost dot in *b*, the middle dot in *a* is seen to move to the middle dot in *b*, and so on. This effect, known as the *Ternus effect* in honor of the discoverer, illustrates the principle that there is a tendency to see an entire configuration move in such a way that each part maintains its role or function in the configuration (e.g., a center spot remains a center spot, and so on). Ternus referred to this tendency as "phenomenal identity."[9] Were it not for this tendency, moving pictures would not be possible, the movement perceived would be utterly chaotic.

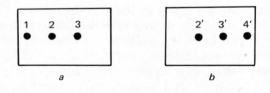

Figure 5-6

An interesting effect that many people have noted in viewing moving pictures is that wheels often appear to be rotating backward, i.e., in a direction opposite to the forward motion of the vehicle. This "wagon-wheel effect" as it has been called, is easily explained. In Fig. 5-7*a*, a wheel is shown as it might appear in one frame of the filmstrip. Suppose the wheel turns approximately 50 degrees between successive frames. Then Fig. 5-7*b* shows how the wheel will look in the next frame. Thus, in actual fact, the spoke marked with an arrow in *a* will have advanced to the position that it is in in *b*. If that spoke in *a* were perceived to move to its position in *b* (and similarly for all other spokes), the wheel as a whole would appear to roll forward. But the spokes are all similar. The spoke marked *x* in *b* is nearer to the place of the spoke marked with an arrow in *a* than is the correct spoke in *b*. It is

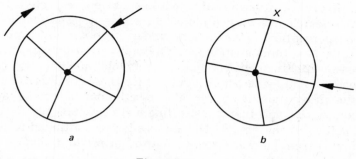

Figure 5-7

known that proximity governs stroboscopic movement, that is, other things being equal, movement will occur between objects that are nearest to one another in *a* and *b*.   Therefore, under these conditions, movement will be perceived toward spokes in *b* that are actually counterclockwise with respect to those in *a*.

Psychologists have been intrigued with this illusion of movement—which has variously been called *stroboscopic movement, apparent movement, Beta movement,* or the *Phi phenomenon*—and the overwhelming bulk of research on movement perception has been concerned with this phenomenon.   It is believed that a full explanation of this illusion would point the way to an overall theory of movement perception and, in general, would unlock some of the secrets of brain function.   There is no movement whatsoever of the retinal image in this situation, thus constituting further evidence against the idea that the perception of movement is based on the movement of the image across the retina.

It was this illusion, among other facts, that led Wertheimer, one of the founders of Gestalt psychology, to conclude that perceptual experience could not be explained on the basis of a one-to-one correspondence between proximal stimulus and sensation.[10]   Rather it would seem that the brain contributes something of its own to the raw sensory input. The component sensations are organized, and this organization then forms the basis or correlate of what we experience.   In fact, Wertheimer went on to postulate a doctrine known as *isomorphism*, which holds that underlying every sensory experience is a brain event that, structurally considered, is similar to that experience.   In the case of stroboscopic movement, since there is no movement in the proximal stimulation to account for the experienced movement, there must be some process taking place in the brain that has the necessary dynamic properties to give rise to such experience.   He postulated that between regions of excitation corresponding to each image (such as *a* and *b* in Fig. 5-3), there is a flow of electrical energy that gives rise to the impression of movement.

This theory (or variations of it) has been widely respected, and a good deal of research has been directed at testing it. The feeling has been that the perception of movement under stroboscopic stimulus conditions reflects a fundamental fact of brain action on a primitive level. One reason for this belief is that lower animals and decorticated guinea pigs react as if they saw movement under these conditions.[11] This has been shown by training an animal to discriminate a moving target from a stationary one and then substituting a stroboscopically flashing stimulus for the moving one.[12] The animals tested continued to respond as if a moving stimulus were present. Another method involved the presentation of an array of vertical columns inside a drum (as in the situation employed to induce the optomotor response).[13] When the columns were flashed in successive positions stroboscopically, the animals reacted precisely as they did when the drum actually rotated. In fact, using the technique that simulates movement in electric signs, it has been possible to show the presence of the illusion in newly born guppies, newly hatched insects, and human infants.[14] Another reason for the belief that the illusion of motion is based on some basic mode of brain function is the fact, already noted, that it requires rather specific stimulus conditions, such as a particular rate of stimulus alternation. Other factors known to be relevant are intensity of light and the distance between a and b.[15]

Some evidence supports Wertheimer's theory or variations of it that holds that there is some interaction in the brain—or in the retina—between the excitations emanating from a and b. This might be called the *spread-of-excitation theory*. For example, it has been found that the illusion of motion occurs more readily if both a and b are placed so as to fall within one hemisphere of the brain rather than, as is more typically the case, when the observer is fixating a point midway between a and b, a is projected to one hemisphere and b to the other.[16] Also the effect is more readily obtained if both a and b fall in one eye as compared with a stimulating one eye and b the other.[17]

One factor contributing to the plausibility of this theory is that some bridging process does seem necessary to explain an apparent motion between two discrete spatially separate retinal-cortical locations. But suppose stroboscopic movement does not require stimulation of separate retinal locations. Perhaps what is crucial is that a and b are perceptually localized in two separate places regardless of where their corresponding images fall on the retina. After all, as noted earlier in this chapter, we know that an object will be seen to move if the observer tracks it with his eyes as it displaces across his field of view despite the fact that the image then remains more or less fixed on the fovea. The experience of movement in this case is based on information from change of eye position that the object fixated is in varying phenomenal locations.

May not the same be true for stroboscopic stimulus conditions? To test this, observers were required to move their eyes back and forth, synchronizing their movements with the flashing of lines *a* and *b*.[18] In other words, as *a* flashed on, the observer's eyes were directed at *a*; as *b* flashed on, his eyes just reached the position where they were directed at *b*, and so forth. Under these conditions, *a* and *b* fell on the *same* retinal locus, not a different one as is usually the case. The majority of observers nevertheless experienced *a* and *b* moving back and forth.* In the converse experiment, it was shown that if only a single point *a* flashes intermittently and the observer is required to move his eyes rapidly back and forth, then no movement is perceived. Yet the eye movement guarantees that *a* falls on separate retinal loci in this procedure. The outcome is predictable in terms of position constancy. Apparently, therefore, spread of excitation is neither a necessary nor a sufficient determinant of stroboscopic movement perception.

From these experiments, one can conclude that what is crucial is the location of *a* and *b* in separate phenomenal places in space. Thus, the stroboscopic illusion fits with the principle suggested earlier, namely, movement will be experienced when an object appears to undergo a change in its location. The only difference between stroboscopic and "real" movement is the fact that in the former case the stimulus is not continuously present.

Why is movement seen in spite of the fact that the stimulus is intermittent? We cannot fully answer this question, but it is relevant to

---

*It is important to make clear that eye movements per se cannot explain the stroboscopic illusion. This was once a popular theory but was disproven by Wertheimer[10] who showed that observers could simultaneously see *a* moving to *b* and *c* moving to *d*, i.e., in opposite directions. The eyes cannot move in opposite directions at the same time. Also, Guilford and Helson[19] showed by photographing the eyes of their subjects that the eyes were often more or less stationary while they nevertheless experienced movement between the two stimuli. The experiment cited here is based on the argument that it is not eye movements that cause the impression of movement but that when the eyes happen to move in the manner indicated, so that only one region of the retina is stimulated, movement is nevertheless perceived.

Recently, however, it has been reported that when this experiment was repeated using pursuit movements of the eyes rather than saccadic movements, flashing lights stimulating the same region of the retina of the moving eye *did not* appear to move. In other words, the very opposite result was obtained.[20] There is a controversy over the question of whether a discounting mechanism occurs during pursuit eye movements which results in position constancy (See p. 188).

point out that the observer tends to identify a and b as the same object. If an object is now here and now there, it is "logical" to assume that it has moved from one place to the other. Experiments have shown that the illusion is facilitated if a and b are identical rather than different in shape or color. Movement can be perceived if a and b are different, but then one has the impression that a is changing into b during the movement.

Movement of a single object would not, however, be a valid "solution" of the problem of what was occurring in the world, if, when b appeared, a appeared with it. In other words, suppose the sequence were a; a and b; a; a and b; instead of a; b; a; b; and so on. Under such conditions it would not be plausible to suppose that a has moved to b for the simple reason that a is again present in the place where it had been a moment ago when b appears. If the procedure is varied slightly so that instead of a appearing with b, an object similar to a appears, a', then it *is* an intelligent solution to perceive a as having moved to b and to perceive a' as some new object that appears and disappears in the place a had occupied. The two variations are illustrated in Fig. 5–8. The result of such an experiment is that it is difficult to perceive movement in the first condition but not in the second.[21]

It would also follow from the hypothesis suggested here, namely, that the perception of movement under stroboscopic stimulus conditions is an intelligent solution of a problem, that information which suggests an alternative solution to the "problem" of the alternate appearance and disappearance of a and b, may eliminate the perception of movement. Suppose, for example, information is available that a and b have not actually disappeared but rather have been momentarily covered over. One way of achieving this is to move an opaque object back and forth, alternately covering and uncovering a and b, as shown

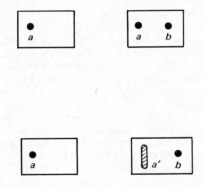

Figure 5–8

in Fig. 5-9. Here *a* and *b* stimulate the retina alternately just as in ordinary stroboscopic movement conditions, but the observer does not
typically perceive movement. Rather, he sees *a* and *b* as continuously
present but as alternately covered and uncovered by the moving
rectangle.[22]

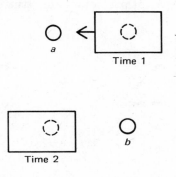

Figure 5-9

One might wish to argue that the introduction of the large moving
rectangle interferes with the perceived movement of the dot, but the
following variation proves this argument wrong. Let the rectangle move
farther than it does in Fig. 5-9 as shown in Fig. 5-10. Now the rectangle is no longer covering the region where *a* or *b* had been seen a
moment before (marked *x* and *x'* in the figure). The rectangle moves
over that region and beyond it, so that it is evident that it is not covering
a or *b*. Therefore, logically, the dot should be visible, but it is not (the
technical method by which *a* and *b* are rendered invisible need not be
discussed here). Consequently, the "solution" to the problem of the
alternate appearance and disappearance of *a* and *b* can no longer be that
they have been covered and uncovered. This leaves little alternative but
to "solve the problem" by perceiving movement of *a* to *b* and this indeed is precisely what happens.

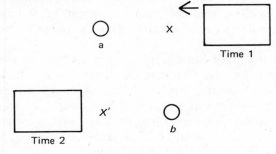

Figure 5-10

An additional fact that fits with the notion of stroboscopic movement perception as an intelligent solution to a problem is that the *kind* of movement perceived is tailored to the orientation of *a* and *b*, as shown in Fig. 5-11. Thus, the configuration seen in *a* will appear to rotate either in the frontal plane or in the third dimension as it moves to *b*. Such effects are not predictable in terms of a spread of excitation theory.

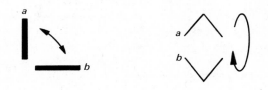

Figure 5-11

Ordinarily, when an object moves very rapidly, its image is little more than a blur across the retina. Perhaps, therefore, even in certain cases in which there is an actually moving object, the more important aspect of the stimulus information is the location of the object in its starting and terminal positions. The intervening stimulation characterized mostly by blur may not contribute much, if anything, to the impression of movement. Precisely this point has now been examined in an ingenious experiment in which the sight of the terminal locations of a moving object was blocked.[23] All the observer could see was the region between the terminal locations through which the object moved. As soon as the speed of the object was quite rapid, on the average beyond 8 degrees per second, it began to appear blurred. At the speed of around 17 degrees per second, a fused blinking line was perceived rather than a moving object. Yet when the terminal locations of the moving object *could* be seen, a sense of movement did occur at and even beyond these rapid speeds. Therefore, this perceived movement must be the result of the sight of the stationary positions of the object. In short, at these rapid speeds, real movement perception is based on the same stimulus information that gives rise to the perception of stroboscopic movement.

In fact, in the same experiment, it was shown that when the intervening space between the terminal locations was blocked from view—the conditions for generating stroboscopic movement—observers only began to perceive movement at a speed of the object, where, had the object been visible in the intervening space, it would have appeared blurred. At too great a speed, around 21 degrees per second, the observers no longer see the object as moving, but rather as simultaneously present in both terminal locations. From these findings the investigators concluded that stroboscopic movement perception has different time constants than real movement perception and that, therefore, the mechanism underlying *it* takes over, as soon as the speed of a moving object is too great for perception to be mediated by the mechanism underlying real movement perception.

The great merit of the notion that the perception of a very rapidly moving object is essentially stroboscopic, i.e., based primarily on the stationary stimulation from its terminal positions, is that it offers an explanation of why a mechanism for perceiving stroboscopic movement evolved. It is difficult to find instances in the natural environment where a moving object gives rise to stroboscopic stimulus conditions. Therefore, one might well ask why such perception evolved if it serves no adaptive purpose. The answer could be that it evolved to mediate the perception of rapid real movement.

Why though, does the perception of stroboscopic movement require just the rate of alternation that it does? One answer, implied by what was stated previously, is that it is based on a separate innate mechanism having its own time constants that is designed to take over when the perception of real movement fails because the movement is too fast. But, based on the hypothesis that stroboscopic movement perception occurs only when such perception is an intelligent solution to the problem presented by the stimulus input, one can argue that at slower rates of alternation, the perceptual system would "expect" to detect the motion from a to b. That is, a truly moving object whose speed was less than about 8 degrees per second would travel from a to b at a rate that should make it clearly visible in its intervening region. Therefore, when in stroboscopic stimulation, a and b flash at a rate compatible with such speed or lower, one ought to perceive the object in the intervening space. Since one does not, it constitutes a contradiction to the solution of movement. Thus, only when the rate of alternation is such that one would not expect to detect movement across this intervening space, is the "solution" of movement a truly good solution.*

---

*There is a phenomenon somewhat similar to stroboscopic movement that occurs at a much slower rate of alternation. If two spots each undergo cyclical variation in intensity, from dim to bright, such that one is dim while the other is bright and vice versa, then the observer will have the impression that a phantom light of constant intensity is moving back and forth behind the plane of the spots, usually in a curved three-dimensional path. The spots then take on the appearance of windows. The motion of such a light source would, of course, "explain" the variation of intensity of each spot, and this perceptual outcome is another example of the preference of the perceptual system for constancy. The optimum rate of alternation for this *wandering phenomenon,* or *w-phenomenon* as its discoverer called it, is between 250 milliseconds and 2.5 seconds. Thus this effect occurs at rates well above those for stroboscopic movement (see footnote on p. 194).[24]

One can also say something sensible about the other end of the range of speeds at which stroboscopic movement ceases, namely, when the alternation is too rapid. At this rapid rate one perceives simultaneity, no doubt because of the persistence of neural discharge even after a is no longer physically present. The point is that it is not plausible to infer movement of a to b if a is still visible. The abolition of movement perception by the perceptual presence of a when b comes on has already been discussed (p. 200).

From this discussion we can readily see that two different theories of stroboscopic movement are possible. One theory claims that the impression of movement is based on an automatic tendency of the nervous system to react to discrete successive stimulation in the same way it would react to continuous movement stimulation because there is some form of spread-of-excitation or neural interaction between the successive stimuli or some other direct sensory mechanism. The other theory maintains that the discrete stimulation lends itself to the cognitive "solution" that movement has occurred and that movement perception occurs only if the stimulus events can best be interpreted in this way.

Although many of the findings seem either to contradict the spread-of-excitation theory or are not compatible with it, and many others support the cognitive theory, a number of other facts support the hypothesis that a direct sensory mechanism is responsible for the perception of movement under stroboscopic conditions. The perception of stroboscopic movement in newly born organisms, such as fish or insects or in decorticated guinea pigs, does not seem to jibe with the notion that a reasoning-like process is responsible for the movement perception although, admittedly, it is possible that the kind of nonconscious, nonverbal, problem-solving postulated could nevertheless occur in these cases.*

---

*A recent discovery also seems to favor the sensory theory. It was found that if a stimulus 2 is a photographic negative of 1, where black and white regions are reversed, and slightly displaced with respect to 1, one perceives movement in a reversed direction, i.e., toward the left if the displacement is to the right, and so on. (see Fig. 5-12a).[25] In the example in the figure, it is not too surprising that the perceived movement should be reversed. The *nearest* unit in 2 of the same shape and lightness as any given unit in 1 is in fact displaced to the left, because all units are the same shape. (This would follow the same explanation as that of the "wagon-wheel effect" described earlier.) Therefore, there is no reason for the perceptual system to "assume" that a differently colored unit in 2 is the one to be identified as the same as a unit of 1 and every reason to "assume" a same-colored unit plays that

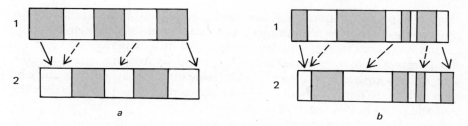

Figure 5-12

Also, as is made clear later in the chapter, there is direct evidence that units in the visual nervous system can "detect" stroboscopic movement because they respond uniquely to a given sequence of discrete stimulation. Therefore, one might conclude that there are two possible bases for the perception of stroboscopic movement, a direct sensory mechanism and a cognitive process of perceptual problem-solving.

The Autokinetic Effect

Another illusion that has intrigued psychologists is one in which a single stationary point of light appears to move. The point must be seen

---

role. But now consider the example in Fig. 5-12b. Here the units are different in shape and size from one another, so that if the perceptual system is guided by similarity of shape and size, normal forward movement will be perceived; if it is guided by color, however, reversed movement will be perceived, in spite of the fact that each unit then must be seen to change its shape as it moves. Since it is the latter that occurs, the investigator concluded that stroboscopic movement perception is based on a sensory mechanism that is triggered by brightness similarity, not form similarity. It is worth noting though that the shift from 1 to its photographic negative 2 generally entails a reversal of figure-ground relations. It seems natural that if a black region is figure in 1 that the perceptual system would identify the most proximal black region in 2 as the same even if it entails a change of shape.

The investigators subsequently reported that the reversed-movement effect occurs under conditions where it is not possible to explain it in terms of an identification by the perceptual system of the nearest region in b equal in brightness to one in a. Even a single region such as a rectangle on a homogeneous ground in a will seem to move in the direction opposite to its displacement in b if b is the negative of a as far as brightness relations are concerned. However, very special conditions are required to produce this effect: a and b must dissolve or fade on and off rather than abruptly appear and disappear and the amount of displacement between a and b must be quite small. The explanation of this effect is not yet known.

against a perfectly homogeneous background and the easiest way to achieve this is to view a luminous point in a completely darkened room. Under such conditions, and following some initial period of viewing, the observer typically experiences the point as drifting, either to one side or upward or downward. So real is the experience that the observer finds it hard to believe the experimenter when he is later told that the point has not moved at all.

This effect is considered to be as yet unexplained although many theories have been proposed to account for it. It has often been suggested that the illusion is based on movements of the observer's eyes. There are at least two things wrong with this notion. First, the observer is usually told to fixate the point and to the extent he succeeds in obeying instructions his eyes are, of course, stationary. Indeed it has been shown by photographing the observer's eyes under infrared illumination that they are in fact stationary at the very moment the point seems to be moving.[26] Second, as the reader should now understand, stationary things do not appear to move when the eyes move. The displacement of the image is discounted; position constancy obtains. Therefore, even if the eyes were in continuous motion there is no reason to consider this as an explanation of what is referred to as autokinetic movement.

However, it is possible to defend the eye movement theory if it is stated in a more sophisticated fashion. If, when the eyes moved, there were *no* centrally registered information to the effect that they had moved, then we would have to predict that the displacement of the image (of a stationary point) *would* give rise to an impression of movement. Ordinarily, the eyes either move in quick jumps from one location to another (saccadic movements) or slowly and smoothly as they track a slowly moving target (pursuit movements). Obviously, pursuit movements are not occurring in the case of a stationary target, and even if saccadic movements do occasionally occur, they would surely be discounted. But even when fixating, minute involuntary movements of the eyes do occur. They tend to drift slowly and to flick saccadically and in addition, to oscillate rapidly back and forth, a kind of continuous tremor. Collectively these involuntary eye movements are referred to as physiological nystagmus. The extent of these movements is extremely small. In all probability, this type of involuntary movement is *not* registered centrally and, therefore, would not lead to discounting of the displacing retinal image. Can eye movement of this kind explain the autokinetic effect?

To test this hypothesis, an experiment was performed that made use of a technique whereby an image on the retina is *prevented* from shifting at all. Various methods to achieve this stabilization of the image have been employed, such as projecting the image onto the retina from a device that is itself mounted on a contact lens placed on the eyeball.[27] Thus, when the eye moves the image moves with it. In the experiment under discussion the technique was modified in such a way that movement of the image was stopped in the horizontal direction only.[28] Therefore, no displacement of the image was caused by slight eye movements only in this direction. The observer, of course, knew nothing about this fact. There were few reports of movements of the target in that direction whereas there were many reports of movement in all other directions.

There is thus evidence to support this modified eye-movement theory.* One difficulty with it, however, is that the excursion of the eyes during these involuntary movements is very small (a few minutes of arc) in relation to the extent of autokinetic movement typically perceived (a few degrees or more). The theory would only be tenable if it were claimed that the cumulative effect of these eye movements over a period of time produced a sizable amount of displacement of the image. But there is a difficulty with this formulation because the target typically does not appear to erratically reverse direction (as do the eyes during nystagmus), but rather seems to drift continuously in one direction. Another difficulty for this theory is that nondiscounted image displacements based on such eye movements also occur under typical conditions in daily life whenever the observer fixates a point in the field. Therefore, the entire scene should appear to drift but, of course, it does not. An explanation is thus required of why such a mechanism only yields an autokinetic effect for a single isolated point in an otherwise homogeneous field.

The author would like to suggest a different approach to the problem of the autokinetic effect. As is brought out in the next section of this chapter, a very important source of information concerning movement is the change of location of one thing relative to other things. Therefore the opposite is also true, that when an object does *not* change its location relative to other objects this is information that the object is *not* moving. But it is precisely this kind of information which is lacking in the autokinetic situation because only a single point is visible. There-

---

*In a subsequent study, an attempt was made to stabilize the retinal image in *all* directions by requiring the observer to view a small afterimage.[29] To prevent eye movements which would lead to an impression of motion of the afterimage for reasons unrelated to autokinetic movement (see p. 188), the observer fixated a small red dot and attempted to maintain the dot in the center of the circular afterimage. Apparently observers were able to do this while nevertheless frequently experiencing autokinetic movement of the afterimage.

fore what one perceives in this situation depends entirely upon the accuracy of the following information: the displacement or nondisplacement of the retinal image and the movement or non-movement of the eyes. Let us assume for the moment that the eyes are stationary because the observer is fixating the point of light (and let us assume that the slight involuntary movement of the eyes is not relevant, contrary to the hypothesis explored in the preceding paragraphs). Then the retinal image does not move. Therefore it would seem that the only basis for perceiving the point moving rather than stationary is some failure of the perceptual system to appreciate that the eyes are indeed stationary. Perhaps, for reasons not yet clear this is the case, so that the system interprets the stationary eyes as slowly drifting. If they were really drifting slowly then a fixated point would have to be interpreted as moving, since the eyes would be tracking it.

There should be no record of eye movement if, with the eyes stationary, no "commands" are issued to the eye muscles to move.* But if for some reason an observer momentarily had the erroneous impression that he was viewing a moving point, then this impression would suffice to induce a feeling that his eyes were tracking it. It is known that effects of this kind occur, as, for example, when one has the illusory impression that an object that one is looking at is moving although it is actually its surroundings that are moving. (See the discussion of induced movement on pp. 210–214.) False impressions of eye movement under such conditions can be thought of as instances of visual capture. Admittedly, it is not clear in the autokinetic situation what triggers the initial "belief" that the point was moving. But once that "belief" took hold it is understandable that the perceptual system could erroneously interpret the eyes as slowly tracking the point.† However, to repeat, this is only possible, because information concerning the point's fixed location with respect to other objects in the field is lacking.

The reader might object that to suffer the illusion that one was tracking a stationary point which was drifting by several degrees implies that the perceptual system would interpret a straight-ahead position of the

---

*One investigator has proposed that "commands" to move the eyes *are* issued in viewing the stationary point. This might result from a state of fatigue of the muscles on one side that would then require abnormal command signals to hold the eyes stationary. These signals are those that ordinarily would signify that the eyes are moving. It was demonstrated that following a period of straining the eye muscles in one direction for 30 seconds, the stationary point subsequently appeared to move in that (or the opposite) direction but not in any other direction.[30]

†It is interesting to note in this connection that the autokinetic effect is highly susceptible to suggestion, and therefore the phenomenon has been studied by social psychologists under conditions where planted "subjects" claim to see the point moving.

eyes as turned to the side. Does this implication do violence to what is known about the precision with which the direction of the eyes is registered? Not necessarily. In studying the perception of radial direction, it was noted in Chapter 4 that observers are neither perfectly accurate nor consistent in setting a target to the straight-ahead position. They can perform this task only within a range of a few degrees of error. This suggests that at any given moment the eyes can deviate a few degrees from the true straight-ahead direction and still be interpreted as straight-ahead: conversely they may be straight ahead and still be interpreted as slightly off to the side. Therefore, if in the autokinetic situation the perceptual system were at a given moment to "interpret" the eyes as slightly turned (although they were not) the observer would have to see the fixated target off to the side.

Relative Displacement and Induced Movement

When an object moves across the field, it changes its location with respect to the observer but it also changes its location relative to all other visible things. What importance, if any, is this relative change? A simple experiment will make clear that relative change plays an important role in the perception of movement.[31]   First, a single luminous point, a, is set to move at so slow a speed that it does not appear to be moving, i.e., it is below the threshold for the detection of movement (see Fig. 5-13). It is the only thing visible. Now a second stationary point b is introduced (see Fig. 5-14). Immediately the observer sees movement. The conclusion is inescapable that the change in relative distance between points a and b leads to perceived movement. We refer to this as object-relative change in contrast to change of position in relation to the observer or subject-relative change. The threshold for object-relative change is lower than that for subject-relative change. Had point a been moving at a speed above the subject-relative threshold, the conclusion about the important role of object-relative change would not be warranted because the perceived movement could be a function either of a's change of location with respect to the observer or with respect to point b. There are thus two separate and independent factors that can lead to the perception of movement: subject-relative change of location and object-relative change of location.

a
● $\longrightarrow$

Figure 5-13

a b
● $\longrightarrow$ ●

Figure 5-14

In fact, in the experiment described, it is not necessarily point *a* that is seen to move when stationary point *b* is introduced; *b* may be seen to move or both *a* and *b* may be seen as moving apart. This ambiguity is precisely what we should expect if the crucial information is relative, i.e., the increasing or decreasing separation between points *a* and *b*.* That information does not specify which point is moving.

Now let us change the experiment in one respect. Let the second object be a luminous rectangular perimeter, *b*, which surrounds *a* rather than a point (see Fig. 5-15). In this situation, all observers will see *a* as moving; the outcome is no longer ambiguous. Moreover the same is true if it is *b* that is made to move and not *a* (see Fig. 5-16). Whether *a* or *b* is actually moving, the observer will see *a* moving. If *b* is moved to the left, *a* will be seen moving to the right. When one objects moves and the observer sees a stationary object near it as moving, the illusory effect is called *induced movement*.

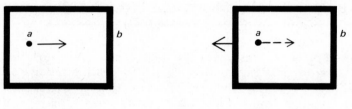

Figure 5-15   Figure 5-16

Apparently a further principle is operating here in addition to the principle that change of relative position is a determinant of movement perception. That object that surrounds the other or otherwise dominates—such as by its greater size—tends to become a frame of reference and, as such, to be seen as stationary. The relative displacement is then interpreted as movement in relation to it. A good example of this effect in daily life occurs when the moon appears to be moving through the clouds (Fig. 5-17). The moon does change its location in the sky relative to us but at such a slow rate as to be far below our movement

*Change of an object's position relative to another can be thought of as a change in configuration or form. That there is merit in this way of looking at object-relative change is borne out by the demonstration that an object moving below the subject-relative threshold and rotating around a stationary point will also be seen to move (or the stationary point will). In other words, although there is no change in the relative distance between the two points in this case, there is a configurational change: the orientation of the imaginary line connecting the two is changing.[32]

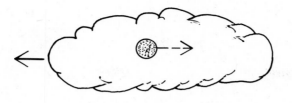

Figure 5-17

threshold. A cloud, however, is changing its position at a faster rate although this too may be below threshold. In any case, the relative
change of position between cloud and moon provides the crucial information; the cloud serves as a frame of reference and it, therefore, induces movement in the moon. Induced movement is one more illustration of the fact that displacement of the image is not a necessary
condition for perceiving movement. The image of the surrounded object is stationary and the object nevertheless appears to move.*

Induced movement can occur even when the object which is actually
moving is displacing at a rate that is above threshold. In other words,
a cloud that is moving so rapidly that when it is seen alone would
clearly be perceived as moving, will nevertheless induce movement in
the moon. This is surprising since the relative displacement between
moon and cloud is now fully accounted for by seeing the cloud move.
Duncker suggested that the surrounded object is seen entirely in terms
of its behavior in relation to its immediate frame of reference. What it
does in relation to more remote reference systems is not relevant. Thus,
although the moon is stationary with respect to a tree or with respect
to the observer, this does not significantly interfere with the induced
movement created by the immediately surrounding cloud. All that
matters is that there is relative displacement between moon and cloud
and that the cloud serves as frame of reference in the moon-cloud
system.

The experience of the cloud on the other hand is a function of its
behavior in relation to its immediate frame of reference, such as the
buildings in Fig. 5-18. Or we may think of the frame of reference in
terms of the subject-relative system of radial direction—straight ahead,

*Other factors that determine which of two or more objects will tend to serve
as frame of reference in addition to that of enclosure are relative size, intensity,
orientation, and constancy. Other things being equal, the larger or more intense,
or vertically oriented, or constant rather than changing object will tend to serve
as frame of reference.[33]

Figure 5-18

left, above, and so on—which is present even when no objects other than the clouds are visible. Duncker, therefore, argued that there is a *separation of systems*: in our example the first is the moon-cloud system, the second is the cloud-building system or cloud-ego system. In this way one can explain why there is more movement perceived than is warranted on the basis of the relative displacement taking place. To repeat, when the cloud moves above threshold, its displacement relative to the moon is fully accounted for by the fact that it is seen to move; yet the moon is seen to move in the opposite direction by an equal amount. There is thus twice as much perceived movement as we might expect.

The concept of separation of system is illustrated by the following laboratory demonstration. A large circle surrounding a black dot is moved up and down. In Fig. 5-19 only the two extreme positions of

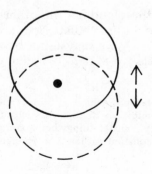

Figure 5-19

the circle are shown. The dot is stationary. Thus, if only the circle and dot were seen, the circle would appear to move up and down and the dot would undergo induced movement up and down in the opposite direction. In addition, however, a small square inside the circle moves sideways (shown in Fig. 5-20 without the large circle). If only the square and dot were seen, the square would appear to move sideways and the dot would be induced to move in the opposite direction, sideways. The entire arrangement is shown in Fig. 5-21. The placement of the objects within the large rectangular frames indicates how they change their locations. As noted, the dot remains in the identical locus on the screen at all times.

What is seen? The square is perceived to move obliquely back and forth from the 7 o'clock to the 1 o'clock positions. This is because at one extreme position, *a*, it is located at 7 o'clock in relation to the large circle; at the other extreme position, *b*, it is in the 1 o'clock position of the larger circle (the change is the result of two relative displacements, large circle downward and square rightward). The dot, however, is seen moving sideways *only*. Thus the change of location of the dot relative to the larger circle (as depicted in Fig. 5-19) has no effect on the perceived direction of movement of the dot. Without the square present, the dot would be seen to move vertically. Thus, the square acting as the immediate frame of reference for the dot insulates the dot from any effect of the outermost frame of reference, the large circle. However, the large circle is the frame of reference for the square. This demonstration can be achieved stroboscopically with two slides of the extreme positions shown in Fig. 5-21.

An interesting application of the concept of separation of system was made by Duncker in relation to the way we perceive movement of points on a wheel.[31]

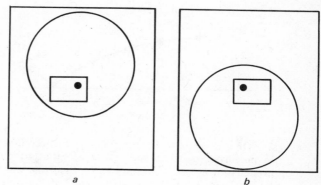

a   b

Figure 5-20   Figure 5-21

Consider a point a on a wheel rolling along the ground (Fig. 5-22). The dotted circles represent successive positions of the wheel and in each the location of point a is shown. In Fig. 5-23 only the path taken by point a is shown. It can be seen that point a describes a path through space that is not circular; a path that mathematicians call a *cycloid*. If only point a were visible—made luminous in a dark room—and the wheel rolled forward the observer would then see this cycloid path.

The fact is, however, that ordinarily when we look at a rolling wheel, although every point on it (except the very center) describes a cycloid, we do not see this. We see points on the wheel turning in a circular path about the hub and we see the entire wheel moving forward along a straight path. Apparently, the hub of the wheel is the reference system for movements of points on the wheel; the background (or possibly the egocentric system of the observer) is the frame of reference for the wheel as a whole. Thus there is a separation of systems.

Returning to the phenomenon of induced movement, the question arises as to why the surrounding moving object is seen as stationary (at least when its movement is below the subject-relative threshold) and thereby serves as frame of reference for the surrounded object. Either could be seen as moving. Duncker attributed this fact to an innate selective principle of organization or preference of the perceptual system. It is also possible to argue that the principle is learned, since ordinarily it is the smaller object within the perceived environment that undergoes displacement.*

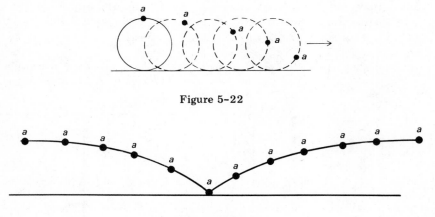

Figure 5-22

Figure 5-23

*One investigator has sought to explain induced movement in terms of changes in perceived radial direction because the latter is known to be affected by the presence of certain structures in the field (see pp. 168-169).[34] There is a tendency for the center of the moving frame of reference to continue to appear to be "straight ahead."[35] If so, the surrounded stationary object must appear to be changing its radial direction.

The importance of object-relative displacement as a determinant of movement perception is made clear in the research of Johansson involving an array of separately moving elements.[24]   In one experiment, two elements are moving at right angles to one another as shown in Fig. 5-24a.   Since the elements both are moving well above the subject-relative threshold, and since there is no frame of reference present to create a separate system, one would think that there is no good reason why the path of each element should not be veridically perceived. But, in fact, what one perceives is shown in Fig. 5-24b: the elements appear to be approaching and receding from one another along an oblique path. This is the dominant impression.   In addition, however, the two elements, as a group, appear to be moving in the opposite oblique direction.

a   b

Figure 5-24

This outcome becomes understandable if one assumes that object-relative displacement exerts a stronger effect on perceived movement that does subject-relative displacement whenever a conflict between the two determinants exists.   Ordinarily, the two are not in conflict but rather lead to the same perception, as when a single object moves in a stationary scene.   But in the case of induced movement or the experiment illustrated in Fig. 5-24, a conflict exists.   What the two elements are doing in relation to each other is not the same as what they are doing in relation to the observer.   The former is apparently dominant, so that one primarily perceives the elements gliding toward and away from each other along the path of shortest distance between them, namely an oblique path.   However, once that is perceived, there remains a component of the motion of the elements not accounted for.[36]   If one analyzes the path of motion in terms of vectors, as Johansson does, then given the perception of motion along the common oblique path, the component not accounted for in this perception is indicated by a vector at right angles to this path (see Fig. 5-25).   In other words, the true motion is dissociated by the perceptual system into two components.

Another example is shown in Fig. 5-26a where one element moves in a vertical path and a second element moves in a circular path. The motions are in phase in the sense that both dots reach the top and bottom

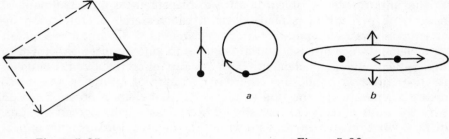

Figure 5-25   Figure 5-26

of their paths simultaneously. What one typically perceives is shown in *b*: the dominant impression is of the element on the right approaching and receding from the one of the left along a horizontal path; secondarily one sees the two elements as a pair moving up and down. One does not perceive the element on the right traveling in a circular path although that in fact is what it is doing; a dissociation of motion occurs.*

The example of the perceived motion of elements on a wheel described earlier can be understood in terms of this analysis. The cycloid paths of the elements of a rolling wheel are perceptually dissociated into two components: an impression of their motions relative to one another, namely rotation about a center and an impression of the residual motion that all elements share, namely a rectilinear translation across the field.

What general conclusions can we reach from the work on relative displacement and induced movement? It would seem that the generalization made earlier remains valid, namely, that whenever an object seems to change its phenomenal location (at a rate above threshold) movement will be perceived. However, it is now necessary to add that phenomenal location may be defined not only egocentrically, in rela-

---

*Johansson's theory about these effects is somewhat different from the one proposed here. He believes that the central factor is the tendency to group elements together and to perceive them as belonging together as a rigid entity on the basis of that vector component of their motion that they share in common. This reduces to the grouping principle of common fate (see pp. 257–258), except that here the perceptual system must first "seek out" and "detect" the common vector and only then can a grouping occur on the basis of it. Once that grouping occurs (for example, two elements moving up and down together in Fig. 5–26) the residue of the motion of the elements is perceived in relation to that moving system as a frame of reference.

tion to the observer as origin of directions, but also *objectively*, in relation to other objects (which may or may not serve as frames of reference). We thus see that change of relative position is a potent source of information in the perception of movement. This fact places the autokinetic effect in a context that makes it somewhat more intelligible: There are no reference objects for the single point of light. Ordinarily, the *absence* of change of relative position is information that objects are *not* moving. Such information is not available in the autokinetic situation.

Induced movement of the self

Among other objects in the visual field is the body of the observer. Parts of the body are, of course, often visible. But even when the body is not seen, it has an inferred location in relation to the scene, that is to say, we are always aware of precisely where in the visual field we ourselves are located. Considering the self, therefore, as an object in the visual field, what should we predict if the observer is surrounded by a moving frame of reference? We should predict that the observer will perceive himself moving although he is stationary; induced movement of the self.

This is precisely what happens. A laboratory technique for studying this effect is shown in Fig. 5-27. The observer is seated on a stool

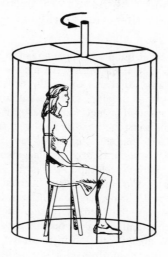

Figure 5-27

in the center of a large drum (the drum can be a lightweight construction somewhat like a lamp shade). The drum is made to rotate around the observer. Ideally, the observer should not be able to see beyond the drum or above or below it. Within 10 or 15 seconds after the rotation begins, the observer typically experiences himself as rotating and the drum as stationary or as turning much slower than it actually is. This effect attests to the efficacy of the frame of reference in governing movement perception and also to the dominance of vision over proprioception. All cues concerning felt position including the vertibular cues from the inner ear are informing the observer that he is stationary. Yet he feels himself turning (still another example of visual capture).

There are examples of this phenomenon in daily life, the best known being that of perceiving one's own train as moving when in fact it is not, as a result of the movement of a train on the adjacent track. This usually occurs when we are seated next to the window facing the other train. That train then fills most of the visual field. Induced movement of the self here includes one's own train. (If, however, we are looking through the window from across the aisle, our own train fills most of the field. In the latter case we might erroneously see a stationary train in the adjacent track as moving when our train is moving. This would be induced movement, but not of the self). Another example is that of experiencing one's own stationary automobile as rolling when we stop for a light as a result of viewing an adjacent car that in fact is rolling. When this happens one is inclined to jam on the brakes. Induced movement of the self also occurs in looking down at a moving current of water, either from a bridge or from a stationary boat.

It is probable, however, that induced movement of the self has applicability to a wider range of phenomena than these occasional instances in daily life would suggest. It is likely that in many situations where the observer is actually moving he would not experience himself as moving—and the environment as stationary—were it not for the induced movement effect. The reason for this deduction is as follows. In discussing position constancy earlier in this chapter (pp. 186ff), we noted that information to the effect that the observer is moving must be centrally registered before we can expect discounting of displacement of the retinal image to occur. One kind of information (relevant at least to active eye movements) is a record of outgoing signals to the musculature. Another is vestibular information that we can assume is present during acceleration and deceleration and in turning movements. Suppose, however, that neither of these is applicable as when the observer is a passenger in a vehicle moving at a constant speed along a straight path.

There would seem to be no information in the latter case. An experiment has confirmed this by showing that if an observer is moved in a wagon at uniform speed in a dark room, he will erroneously see a stationary spot of light on the wall as moving and experience himself as stationary. If, however, a pattern of luminous lines is displayed on the wall instead of the spot, the observer now veridically experiences the lines as stationary and himself as moving.[37]* The only difference would seem to be that in the second situation the observer is surrounded by the displacing pattern, whereas in the first situation he is not. Therefore, the perception in the second situation would seem to be a manifestation of induced movement of the self. From this it follows that in many if not most instances of transportation in a vehicle, perception of one's self and vehicle as moving is a function of the inducing effect of the displacing field that surrounds the observer. This is a paradoxical conclusion—possibly confusing to the reader—because the observer is in fact moving. Yet, as the experiment cited shows, he would not perceive this were it not for the sight of the displacing environment. It is not beyond the realm of plausibility that even in the case where the observer is more actively moving, as in walking, or where he is passively moving but accelerating, the inducing effect of the displacing environment plays a contributory role in the perception of the self as moving and the environment as stationary.†

Can a Movement-Detector Mechanism Explain the Perception of Movement?

Units of the visual nervous system have been discovered in several species that respond to or "detect" movement of a contour over the appropriate region of the retina.[38] These units respond optimally to movement of a contour in a particular direction and not at all to movement in the opposite direction. Can such a detector mechanism explain the perception of movement?

One phenomenon of movement perception that has not yet been mentioned may be explained by this kind of sensory mechanism. If one

---

*It was also shown, in a third situation, that the spot of light was seen as stationary and the self as moving, if the observer were continuously accelerated and decelerated.

†When moving at high speed in a vehicle many observers report that objects such as trees, telephone poles, and the surrounding ground appear to be moving in the opposite direction. This would imply a failure of position constancy. However, it is possible to argue that what one experiences here is the rapid displacement of objects out of the *visual field*, rather than a genuine movement of objects in the world. The term *pseudo-movement* has been used to describe this kind of experience. It may occur at slower speeds too and may even explain the Filehne illusion discussed on p. 188. This experience is analogous to other sensory impressions that are correlated with the proximal stimulus such as extensity in size perception. See pp. 38–39.

observes a pattern, such as stripes, moving in a particular direction for a period of time, and then looks at a stationary pattern, for example the same stripes, the stationary pattern will now appear to move slowly in a direction opposite to the one in which it had previously moved. This effect is known variously as the *aftereffect of movement*, the *waterfall* or *spiral illusion* (because we can easily observe it after first viewing a waterfall or a rotating spiral). It is difficult to explain this kind of effect in terms of any of the principles considered in this chapter. In fact, in this aftereffect, stationary objects appear to be moving but do not seem to change their location, a paradoxical experience and contradictory to the main thesis developed in this chapter that movement perception results from a change in an object's perceived location.

However, it stands to reason that those neural units that are sensitive to a particular direction of movement would become fatigued by the continuous motion of the pattern in one direction. The possible consequences of this effect can best be elucidated by analogy to the negative afterimage that occurs when retinal cells sensitive to a given wavelength are fatigued. As a result, a subsequently viewed gray region takes on a color complementary to the one previously inspected. Hence, one might expect such an aftereffect of motion. In the example of the negative afterimage, the presumption is that cells sensitive to the opposite wavelength are now no longer balanced by equal activity of those sensitive to the color previously inspected. Therefore, they respond more than others and produce the impression of the complementary color. Thus, in the case of movement, it might be assumed that neural units sensitive to a direction opposite to the one just seen now respond more than any other directionally sensitive receptors. There is direct physiological evidence that this is the case. It was shown that the rate of discharge of ganglion cells of the retina of the rabbit decreases when the appropriate region of the retina is exposed to a pattern moving in a particular direction. When the pattern stops moving the rate of discharge from these cells falls below the so-called maintained or resting level of discharge that these cells typically display.[39] Consequently the negative aftereffect of movement may be based on the relatively greater frequency of maintained discharge of those cells that are sensitive to movement stimulation in a direction *opposite* to the one just encountered. There is now an imbalance between units that signal movement in opposite directions. In further support of this conclusion is the finding that after viewing a moving pattern, the threshold for detecting stripes moving in the opposite direction is lower than for stripes moving in the same direction as that of the just seen moving pattern.[40]

It has been found further that the aftereffect of motion depends on the displacement of the image of the moving pattern over the retina rather than on the perception of the motion per se.[41] If during the inspection phase one tracks the moving pattern, no aftereffect occurs, although the movement of the pattern was, of course, perceived. Here there is no image displacement during the inspection period. Conversely, if one moves one's eyes smoothly across a stationary pattern of stripes by tracking a moving fixation mark, the aftereffect *does* occur. Here there is image displacement during inspection phase, but no perceived movement of the stripes. Therefore the phenomenon is misnamed the aftereffect of movement; it is an aftereffect of image displacement. Related to these findings is the fact that the aftereffect is a strictly localized one, i.e., it occurs only in the region of the retinal field stimulated by the moving pattern. Taken together, therefore, there is substantial evidence that movement of contours over specific regions of the retina fatigues the neural units that are sensitive to the direction of displacement occurring, and that as a result units sensitive to movement in the opposite direction dominate for a short period thereafter and give rise to an impression that stationary contours are "sailing" in the opposite direction.*

However, the aftereffect of movement is clearly a very special case of movement perception. It is obviously caused by some changes of the neural medium and belongs in the category of other aftereffects of prior stimulation (see pp. 441 ff). The central question, therefore, is whether the perception of movement in general can be explained in terms of the activity of neural units that are fired by contours moving over the retina. It would seem that the answer to the question is negative. After all, this kind of explanation may be reduced to one based on movement of the image, and virtually all of the evidence covered in this chapter contradicts that thesis. Movement of the image is neither necessary nor sufficient for the perception of movement.

We are left then with the puzzle of accounting for the purpose of these detector mechanisms if they cannot do justice to the perception

---

*The same reasoning can be applied to the perception of a rotating spiral but in some respects this is a special case. Depending on the direction of rotation, the spiral appears either to be moving radially outward from the center or inward toward the center. But no part of the spiral *is* moving in this direction, since it is rotating. Thus, the perception of the direction of movement during rotation is illusory and is an example of a phenomenon described later in the chapter (pp. 231ff). In the aftereffect, the stationary spiral is perceived to be moving in the direction opposite to that experienced during its rotation. Observers often perceive the rotating spiral in depth, turning toward or away from them, and, in that case, the aftereffect also has a three-dimensional character.

of movement. Do they explain movement perception in animals lower in the phylogenetic scale, remaining as vestiges in higher animals? This argument presupposes a perfect correlation between image displacement and perceived movement in such species and it is doubtful this is the case. For example, all animals must discount image motion when they bring it about by their own movement and relevant experiments on the fly were discussed earlier in the chapter.

Perhaps the "detectors" are simply the mechanism which informs the perceptual system that a displacement of an image has occurred without any further implications about movement per se? Some of the investigators who have made these physiological discoveries favor this latter interpretation. According to this view, one could argue that displacement of the image is not necessary for the perception of movement but, if it occurs, it is detected by the neural units in the eye or brain. The information thereby obtained is then assessed by the perceptual system in terms of other information before a decision is reached as to whether or not motion in the environment is occurring. One might think of the discharging of these detector cells as primitive motion signals which then may be cancelled or "vetoed" on the basis of other information (for example if the observer's own movement occurs simultaneous with such signals).

But there are difficulties even with this interpretation. In the case of induced movement it would have to be argued that the motion signal emanating from the displacing image is transferred to the stationary image. Furthermore, the speed of the displacing object may be below threshold, in that with no other object visible no motion is perceived. Yet when the stationary object is introduced, induced movement occurs. Therefore here there is apparently no signal activating detector cells produced by the displacing image which can then be said to be transferred. Rather the information about the displacement is a function of the change of location of the objects relative to one another. Therefore activation of detector cells is apparently not the only source of information about image displacement. A related problem concerns the direction of perceived movement. As noted previously, a dissociation of perceived motion may occur, such that one perceives motion in directions which differ from those of the displacing retinal image.

Stroboscopic movement perception would seem to be another example which cannot be accounted for on the basis of detector units since there is no image displacement over the retina. However, it has been discovered that units of the visual nervous system will respond to discrete successive stimulation of the retina in addition to continuous displacement across it.[42] Can this mechanism then explain stroboscopic movement perception? It can not, for the following reasons:

1. Stroboscopic movement can be perceived across a very wide visual angle, 30 degrees or 40 degrees, and the mechanism discovered does not encompass separations of that magnitude.

2. Stroboscopic movement can be perceived when the identical region of the retina is stimulated successively, provided it "represents" two phenomenal locations in space (so here the activation of this mechanism is not necessary); conversely, when two regions of the retina are successively stimulated that represent only *one* region in space, no movement is perceived (p. 199).   (Here the activation of the mechanism is not sufficient.)

3. One can perceive movement when the image of the first stimulus falls in one eye and is projected to one hemisphere of the brain and the second falls in the other eye and is projected to the other hemisphere (hold up a finger so that it appears slightly left of a fixation spot on a far wall as seen with the right eye only; with the left eye only it then appears to the right of that spot: then open and close the eyes alternately at a rapid rate—the finger will appear to move back and forth. It is not likely that a mechanism of the kind described exists to cover this example).

4. Such a mechanism itself has little bearing on many of the factors that affect the perception of stroboscopic movement such as the similarity of *a* and *b*, the tendency to see the array moving as a whole (Ternus effect), the effect of presenting *a* and *b* by a covering and uncovering procedure, etc.

In conclusion then, the motion-detector mechanism may be sufficient to explain the aftereffect of movement illusion but not the other phenomena of movement perception. The purpose of such neural units, therefore, is not yet clear but perhaps it is to provide information that displacement or rapid change of location of an image is taking place. That information is then interpreted by the perceptual system as signifying movement or not depending upon a variety of other factors. But it does not necessarily follow that the activation of "motion detector" cells is the only source of information concerning image displacement.

The Perception of Velocity

What determines how fast an object appears to be moving? A plausible guess would be the speed at which the image of the object displaces

across the retina.* But now that we know that perceived movement itself does not depend upon the displacement of the image it would be
strange indeed if the perceived rate of movement depending upon the
rate of image displacement.

If phenomenal velocity did depend upon the rate of image displacement, then the farther away an object was from us, the slower it would
seem to move. The reason for this can be understood in relation to the
simple facts of optics discussed on pp. 28–30. As shown in Fig. 5–28, if
an object moves from A to B in 1 second and A-B is nearby, then the
image of the object moves from a to b in 1 second; but if A-B is more
distant, then the image moves a much shorter retinal distance, from a'
to b', in 1 second. Therefore, the nearer the path of movement, other
things remaining equal, the faster is the rate of image displacement.
The rate of image displacement plays some role in determining perceived speed because an automobile seen moving along a road several
miles away seems to be going much slower than in fact it is. But with
objects closer to us, the perceived speed does not change very much
despite the differences in viewing distance. In other words, there is *constancy of perceived velocity*.

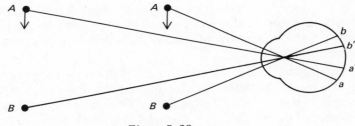

Figure 5-28

An alternative explanation is that perceived speed is a function of
phenomenal extent traversed per unit time. If two objects appear to
move the same distance in the same time they will appear to move at
the same speed. Hence, if a distant object is not too far away so that
the extent or the size of its path is perceived veridically (size constancy), then its perceived speed will also be perceived veridically (speed
constancy).

*There is now some evidence to the effect that the faster the image displaces
across the retina, the greater the frequency of discharge of some neural units.[43]
There thus may be retinal "speed detectors" in some species and possible in man as
well. Nevertheless, as the discussion here brings out, rate of image displacement in
man cannot account for the perception of velocity.

Oddly enough, evidence for this simple deduction has only recently been provided. For many years, a different explanation of speed perception has been favored, one that is discussed shortly, entailing the rate of change of position of an object in relation to its surroundings. To test this deduction, it was necessary to eliminate from view all objects but the moving one so that only subject-relative displacement occurs. This was done by presenting luminous circles that moved downward on a continuous belt in a totally dark room (see Fig. 5–29). One circle, which served as standard, was near the observer whereas the other, the speed of which he could vary, was four times as far away as the standard.[44]

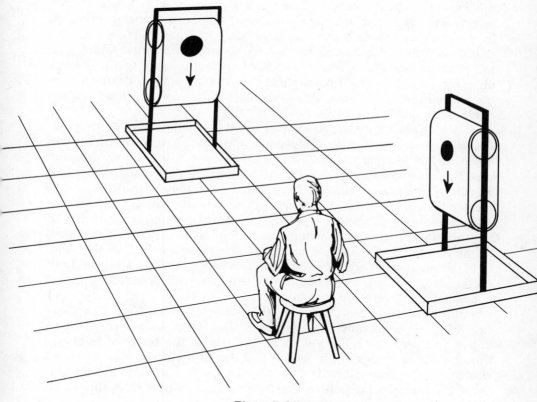

Figure 5-29

When the observer adjusted the speed of the more distant circle so that its speed appeared to be equal to that of the nearer standard, his speed settings were only somewhat higher than the speed of the standard, provided he was permitted to view with both eyes. When, however, the observer performed the same task while viewing the circles through an artificial pupil with one eye, he set the variable to a speed about four times faster than that of the standard.

The artificial pupil had the effect of eliminating information about distance. The observer could, therefore, equate speed only on the basis of speed of displacement of the retinal image.* Hence, the distant circle had to move much faster in order that its image would displace as rapidly as that of the nearer circle. When, however, the difference in distance of the two circles could be appreciated—through binocular cues—speed was a function of phenomenal extent traversed per unit time. The extent traversed by the far circle was perceived almost, but not quite, veridically as was shown in a separate task in which the observers were required to match the size of luminous triangles presented in the dark at the near and far positions. The far triangle was seen slightly smaller and, therefore, had to be made somewhat larger than the nearby standard before it appeared perfectly equal to the average observer. The departure from perfect constancy was no doubt due to the elimination of various cues to distance as a result of presenting the circles in the dark.

It is possible, however, to explain speed constancy in an entirely different way, one that does not depend upon taking account of the distance of the moving object. In fact, for many years the explanation based on size constancy was rejected because in some experiments it was found that the departure from speed constancy with distance was greater than that in size constancy. If perceived speed is a function of rate of *phenomenal extent* traversed per unit time and there is little if any diminution of that phenomenal extent with distance, then there ought not to be any diminution in perceived speed with distance. Yet, in experiments that were conducted, although perceived speed did not decline very much as the distance of the moving object increased, it did not remain perfectly constant.

A discovery was then made that ultimately led to a different explanation of speed constancy. It was found that the perceived speed of an object was very much dependent on the size of the frame of reference through which it moved. In fact, it was shown that the perceived speed was inversely proportional to the size of the surrounding framework. Thus, for example, suppose in Fig. 5-30a a circle moves from the top to

*Thereby indicating that under reduction conditions speed *can* be judged in this way just as can size (see pp. 37-38).

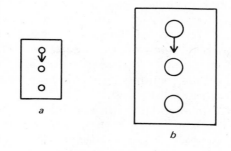

Figure 5-30

the bottom of the rectangle in a given time; then if a circle moves at that objective speed through the rectangle in *b*, which is twice as large as that in *a*, it will appear to be moving at about half the speed as the circle in *a*. To appear to move at the same speed, it must be adjusted to move at about twice the objective speed. This fact was discovered by J. F. Brown and is known as the *velocity transposition effect.*[45] Stated in general terms the principle is as follows: if a frame of reference for a moving object is transposed in its linear dimensions, the velocity of the object must be transposed by a like amount in order that the phenomenal velocity in the two cases be identical. Brown's experiments revealed that this principle is only approximately correct. (It should be noted that the observer sat in a dark room midway between the two rectangles.) For a size transposition of 2 to 1, the speed transposition leading to phenomenal equality was 1.9 to 1; for a size transposition of 3 to 1, the speed transposition was 2.6 to 1; finally, for a size transposition of 10 to 1, the speed transposition was 6.8 to 1. Although the transposition of speed is not complete, it is still very appreciable. Thus, for example, in the case of the 10 to 1 size transposition, an observer perceives two circles equidistant from him as equal in speed when one is moving at approximately seven times the speed of the other.*

It is interesting to relate the transposition effect to the important role that relative displacement plays in the perception of movement. If

---

*There is a possible artifact in Brown's method, namely, as shown in Fig. 5-30 many circles are visible at the same time in any rectangle. Consequently, one will have an impression of a certain number of circles that appear (or disappear) per unit time. Naturally, this kind of "counting" if it occurred would also lead to the transposition result because the size and distance between circles is also transposed. Thus, an equal *number* of circles would move through the two rectangles in the same time only if the objective speed of the field of larger circles was greater.[46] One method for avoiding this possible artifact is to permit only one circle to be visible at a time and to restrict exposure time to one "pass" of the circle. Another method, used by Brown, is to randomize the spacing between circles.

the displacement of an object relative to others or to a frame of reference is a major determinant of movement perception, then it is plausible that the perceived *rate* of the object's movement, its phenomenal velocity, would depend upon the rate of relative displacement.* This is another way of describing the transposition effect: perceived speed depends upon the time required for an object to move from one end of the frame of reference to the other.

The effect of rate of relative displacement on perceived velocity is even more directly demonstrable when two or more objects moving at different speeds or directions are viewed. For example, it is easy to demonstrate that when two objects are moving in opposite directions the apparent speed of each is greater than when either is seen alone or when one object is seen moving with respect to a stationary object.[47]

It is also possible to relate the velocity transposition effect to the similar effect of a frame of reference on the perception of size (see pp. 57-60). The phenomenal length of a line is to some extent a function of its objective length relative to the size of a surrounding frame of reference. If this size transposition effect were complete, one might say that the velocity of a circle in *b* of Fig. 5-30 would then equal that of a circle in *a* when the objective velocities were in the ratio of approximately 2 to 1 *because* the perceived *extent* of the two paths are equal. According to this interpretation, the velocity transposition effect implies that perceived speed is a function of phenomenal extent traversed per unit time. Undoubtedly there is some truth to this explanation, but it cannot be the whole story for the following reason. The velocity transposition effect is much more nearly complete than the size transposition effect. For a size transposition of 2 to 1 the effect on perceived extent is of the order of 1.6 to 1; for a size transposition of 3 to 1 it is of the order of 2.2 to 1; for a size transposition of 8 to 1 it is of the order of 3.4 to 1. Therefore, it would seem necessary to conclude that the velocity transposition effect is to some extent a direct function of the impression of rate of relative displacement rather than of the impression of rate of phenomenal extent traversed.

*However, the precise meaning of the phrase "rate of relative displacement" remains to be clarified. It could mean that the moving object seen within a smaller framework is always nearer to an edge than when seen within a larger framework. The nearer to an edge, the more readily can change of the object's position be detected. An object appears to be moving faster when it is closer to a stationary object than when it is farther away and there is other evidence to support this interpretation of the transposition effect. See Brown,[45] and Wallach.[48] On the other hand, "rate of relative displacement" may be thought of in configurational terms: movement of an object through a given proportion of the total extent of a frame of reference in a given period of time. When the rate of movement of two objects is equal in this relative configurational sense, their velocities may appear about equal. In other words, the movement can be thought of as change of *form*: the changing location of the circle within the rectangle. Perceived speed is then based on rate of change of this form.

It was only several years after Brown published his findings that its relevance to speed constancy was realized.[48]   Consider the situation where two rectangles of *equal* size are viewed but with one being twice as far from the observer as the other (see Fig. 5-31a). Then the retinal images produced by the two rectangles are shown in Fig. 5-31b, since the size of the retinal image of an object is inversely proportional to the object's distance from the observer. Therefore, if we consider the proximal stimulus, the constancy situation as illustrated in Fig. 5-31 gives rise to the same retinal image as does Brown's transposition situation where frames of reference of two different sizes at equal distances are compared.   It should follow that when the image of the far circle in Fig. 5-31a moves from the top to the bottom of its frame in the same

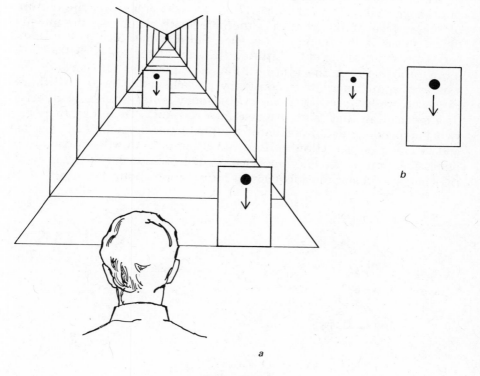

Figure 5-31

approximate time that the image of the near circle moves from the top to the bottom of its frame, that the speed of the two circles will appear about equal.   Since this will happen when the two circles are moving objectively at the same speed, speed constancy is to be expected on the basis of the velocity transposition effect.

However, this conclusion is warranted if and only if the backgrounds serving as frames of reference for the objects under comparison are equal. This will often be true in daily life, as witness the situation shown in Fig. 5–32a and b. Here an automobile moving in front of a row of trees is seen from near, a, or far, b. The rate of displacement of the car with respect to the trees is the same when the car moves at the same speed in the two cases. On the other hand, the situation will often not be of this kind. If, for example, when the car is seen at a distance, the spacing and size of the trees are different, as shown in c, then the car will have to be moving faster to appear equal in velocity to that in a. This would be equivalent to a departure from constancy. A further question is: What of situations where there is no clearly evident frame of reference as, for example, when an object is seen moving across a smooth ground such as the desert? One might argue that the texture of the surface of the ground in the immediate vicinity of the moving object serves as the frame of reference, but it is questionable if this is a very convincing argument. Little in the way of texture is visible. It is more probable that the transposition principle does not account for whatever approximation to constancy prevails under these conditions. However, we have seen that speed constancy is also explicable in terms of a mechanism that takes distance into account. Therefore, there are two independent determinants of the phenomenal velocity of objects, and in any given situation in daily life either or both will contribute to our perception of velocity as a function of factors such as the nature of the background and the adequacy of information about distance.*

a   b   c

Figure 5–32

*However the transposition principle deals only with the impression of the speeds of moving objects relative to one another and says nothing about the absolute (or specific) speed an object appears to have, such as might be stated in inches or feet per unit time. This impression of absolute speed would seem to require taking into account the distance of the moving object. A similar distinction was drawn concerning the perception of size (see p. 60).

The Perception of Events

Some curious effects concerning the direction of movement

Certain perceptual effects stem from the fact that the direction of movement of lines or contours is sometimes ambiguous. Consider first the case of a straight line moving behind an opening as shown in Fig. 5-33a (the dotted section of the line is not visible to the observer). Suppose the direction of the movement of the entire line is downward, as shown by the arrow, so that the line moves from position 1 to position 2. Since all the observer sees is the section of the line through the opening, a little thought will make it clear that the line could have moved from position 1 to 2 in any number of directions. For example, the line could have moved horizontally, as shown in *b*. Note that in *b* the proximal stimulus change of the visible portion of the line is identical with that in *a*.

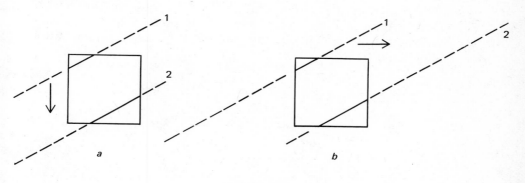

Figure 5-33

With distinctive points such as the ends of the line visible, this ambiguity is no longer present, so that if the entire line were seen, the direction of its movement would be veridically perceived as either that of *a* or *b*. The crucial point, then, about the situation when the ends of lines are not visible, is that any segment of a straight line is equivalent to any other segment, so that no information is received from the proximal stimulus transformation concerning the objective direction of the line's movement. In other words, the segment of the line visible in Fig. 5-33a, position 1, could be moving at right angles to itself, thus remaining in view, and additional segments of the line would come into view; or that segment could be moving downward, as toward position 2, in which case, in position 2, parts of it would no longer be visible and new segments would come into view; or the segment visible in 1 could be moving horizontally toward position 2 as in *b*, in which case none of it would be visible in position 2, and new segments would come into view.

Hans Wallach, who investigated this phenomenon, discovered a number of interesting ramifications of it.[49] Since the stimulus is ambiguous, it might be expected that changes of organization will occur over time and that is indeed the case. As the observer continues to view a pattern such as that in Fig. 5-33, he will at one moment perceive the lines as moving vertically and then, suddenly, he will perceive them as moving horizontally. Consistent with some other data on ambiguous figures, Wallach also found that continued exposure to one alternative (satiation) deliberately made *un*ambiguous will facilitate the perception of the other alternative (see the discussion of this issue in Chapter 6, pp. (263-270).

Wallach also found that there is a preference to perceive the lines moving in a direction parallel to the long axis of an aperture. Thus, if the observer sees the arrangement shown in Fig. 5-34, then regardless of the actual direction of movement of the lines, the observer will tend to perceive the lines moving horizontally. This preference then, makes the outcome far less ambiguous although sudden changes of perception are still possible.

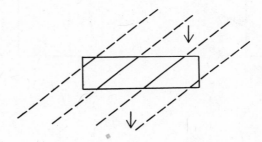

Figure 5-34

The explanation of this effect is probably that when the shape of the aperture is rectangular rather than square, with the exception of lines entering at one corner and leaving the field at the opposite corner, there is no change in length of the segments of all other visible lines. With no information unambiguously indicating that there is any change in the segments of the visible lines, i.e., with no information to the effect that one is perceiving *different* segments of the longer lines of which these segments are parts, it is plausible that we will "assume" that they are the same segments. If so, they must be moving in the direction of the long axis of the aperture. In the case of a square aperture, however, each visible line segment is continuously changing its length. Therefore, the perceptual system is free to "deduce" movement of the line pattern in various directions.

This principle explains the barber-pole illusion. The barber pole is turning around a vertical axis so that any point on the helix is moving horizontally. However, consistent with the fact of ambiguity of such transformations, the parallel lines of the stripes could be moving in any number of directions. In Fig. 5-35b and c, only one stripe is shown to simplify the illustration. The tendency to perceive the movement as vertical is an example of the preference to see the movement parallel to the long axis of the "aperture." Of course, in this case, it is not an aperture but the sides of the pole that limit the observer's view to only parts of the entire array. No doubt, if the observer is very near to the pole, cues will be available as to the actual rotation of the stripes and the illusion will not be seen.

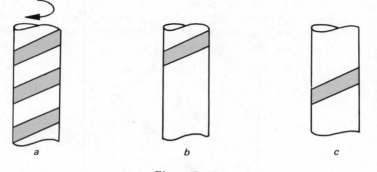

Figure 5-35

Another example of the same effect occurs in daily life when we are moving while looking through a narrow aperture. For example, suppose we can see an oblique rod through partially closed venetian blinds (see Fig. 5-36a). If we were to

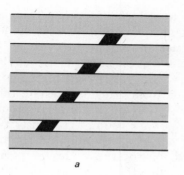
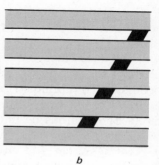

Figure 5-36

move in a downward direction, then the proximal stimulus changes from that in *a* to that in *b*. This change results from movement-produced parallax, and ordinarily there would be no sense of anything moving, only an impression of depth. But in this case, this phenomenon seems to occur; we erroneously perceive movement of the rod in a direction parallel to the openings between the blind slats.

Where the aperture is square and, therefore, where the preference based on the shape of the aperture is not applicable, it has been found that even certain cues that ought to render the stimulus unambiguous may not eliminate perceptual ambiguity. For example, Wallach has shown that the presence of dots in the lines, as in Fig. 5-37, does not guarantee that all observers will always now perceive the direction of movement veridically, although downward movement will, of course, now be preferred; an observer may suddenly see the lines moving horizontally. This, however, is a logical contradiction, since any dot can be seen not to be moving in this direction. The observer solves this "perceptual problem" by perceiving the dots as gliding downward along the lines that themselves are seen as moving horizontally. Other phenomena analogous to this were also discovered.

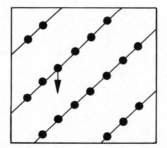

Figure 5-37

Consider now another situation where the information concerning a contour's direction of movement is ambiguous: a homogeneous circle turning about its center produces a proximal stimulus at the eye that is indistinguishable from a stationary circle. Any part of the circle can be superimposed on any other part; no relative displacement occurs. To eliminate all cues that arise from irregularities of the contour or microstructure on the surface, one can rotate a luminous circle or luminous perimeter of a circle in a dark room. The observer will not perceive the circle rotating. Even in an illuminated room, a rotating circle will often not appear to be rotating. However, an interesting question raised by this fact is why the stationary percept is preferred.   Perhaps a simplicity principle must be assumed to be operating; change will only be perceived when the change of stimulus demands it.   In fact, it can be shown that there is a real preference to perceive the circle as stationary, as witness the example illustrated in Fig. 5–38.   If this luminous pattern is rotated, the observer typically perceives the Y pattern rotating inside a *stationary* circle.

Figure 5–38

The preference to perceive the circle as stationary is even stronger than one might imagine on the basis of this last example, because there it can be argued that there is still no information that directly indicates rotation of the circle.   Consider, however, the example illustrated in Fig. 5–39*a*.   When the figure is rotated about the center of the arc, one often perceives a stationary circle that is revealed by a rectangle rotating in front of it.   As can be seen from *b*, the change in the proximal stimulus of the entire configuration is compatible with this perception; the arc now visible could indeed result from a rectangle passing over a complete stationary circle and revealing it; or, of course, it could result from the rotation of the arc that was visible in *a* and that, in fact, is what is actually occurring.   So here it does seem necessary to conclude that there is a strong preference to perceive a stationary circle.   There is a tendency to preserve the identity of the parts of the figure as determined by perceived orientation; the top remains phenomenally the top, the bottom, the bottom, and so on.   The investigator who discovered this effect called it *apparent rest.*[50]

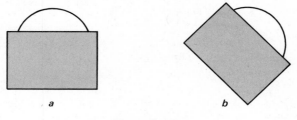

a   b

Figure 5–39

The preference to perceive a curved figure of this kind as maintaining its orientation rather than as rotating is so strong that to achieve this perception one will even perceive the figure as distorting in shape as the following example makes clear.[51] Instead of a circle, a rotating ellipse is viewed. Three successive views are shown in Fig. 5-40 as the figure rotates 90 degrees. Here the stimulus information is adequate to indicate that the figure is rotating about its center, because the long and short axes of the ellipse do in fact rotate. But if one considers a segment of arc of the figure in any spatial position, let us say the segment at the top, information concerning what is taking place remains more or less ambiguous because the transition is a smooth one. The curvature of that uppermost segment changes only slightly. Therefore, the transformation, which is, of course, registered, could result from a rotating ellipse *or* from an elliptical figure that is not rotating but that is distorting, now being an ellipse with its vertical axis longer, now an ellipse with its horizontal axis longer, and so forth. The latter seems to be the preferred mode of perception of most observers.* A simple way to achieve the desired stimulus conditions is to place a drawing of an ellipse on a revolving turntable as shown in Fig. 5-41. The reader can easily try this out for himself.

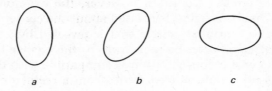

| a | b | c |

Figure 5-40

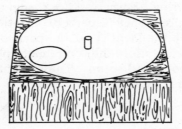

Figure 5-41

*The example of the rotating spiral described on pp. 220-221 is another instance of the phenomenon discussed here. There is a clear preference to see the spiral as moving inward or outward rather than as rotating.

The Perception of Causality

We often have the impression that the behavior of one object causes a certain behavior in another. Thus, for example, when one billiard ball hits another, the movement of the second ball is experienced as having been caused by the movement of the first. If, therefore, perception is to be defined phenomenologically, i.e., on the basis of what we consciously experience, there can be no disputing the fact that we perceive causality. Yet many would be reluctant to consider this kind of experience as perceptual any more than they would regard the awareness of an object's function as perceptual. In a later discussion of this problem (pp. 334–339), it will be argued that the meaningfulness of a familiar object such as a hammer clearly derives from our past experience with that object. Therefore, although familiarity and meaningfulness do enter into our perceptual experience, one might with justice still argue that these should not be thought of as perceptual phenomena. They derive not from the proximal stimulus, nor even from the central events to which the stimulus necessarily gives rise, but rather from an interpretation of the stimulus based on experience.

In the same way, many would argue that the impression of causation, as in the example of the billiard balls, derives from an interpretation of what is happening. They would say that it belongs more in the sphere of knowledge or cognition than perception. All that is given perceptually is that the first sphere moves, until it is contiguous with another; it then stops and the second ball moves in the same direction, and so on. It was to combat precisely this line of argument that the Belgian psychologist Michotte launched his now classic series of experiments.[52]   Although there were many variations of these experiments, the basic idea and method was as follows. The observer sees one square moving at a certain speed and in a certain direction; it then comes into visual contact with a second square that in turn moves at a certain speed and in a certain direction. The simple method Michotte employed to produce this set of stimulus events is shown in Fig. 5–42. Thick lines drawn on a rotating disk appear as small squares and seem to change their location as seen through a slit, *b*. (The impression of these segments of the thick lines moving *along the slit* is an example of the kind of effect described in the preceding section. The lines are, of course, not moving in that direction.) The observer then describes what he perceives.

The main point of Michotte's experiments was to demonstrate that one has the impression of object *A* causing the movement of object *B* if

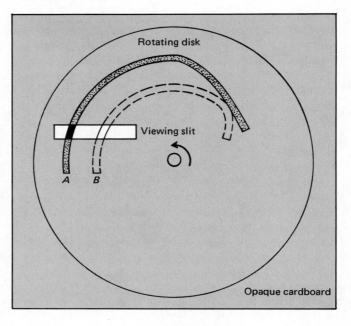

Figure 5-42

and only if certain stimulus conditions prevail: the movement of object
B must occur immediately upon the "impact" of object *A*; the direction
of object *B* must be the same as object *A*'s; the speed of its movement
must either be slower or approximately the same as object *A*'s. If one
of these conditions does not hold, if, for example, there is a delay after
"impact" before object *B* begins to move, then one does not have the
impression of object *A* "launching" object *B*.* Following the argument
the Gestalt psychologists made about stroboscopic movement, Michotte
believed that if a phenomenon depends strictly on certain stimulus conditions, it is likely that it is the result of the spontaneous workings of
the brain rather than of learning and interpretation. Otherwise, he reasoned, why do we not still interpret the event causally when certain
stimulus parameters are changed? Actually, Michotte's argument is not
altogether convincing. An opponent could reply that what one learns

---

*Michotte distinguished various kinds of perceived causality, such as the launch-
ing effect, the releasing or triggering effect, and the entraining effect, and each is
based on certain specific stimulus conditions. In the releasing effect, object *B*
moves away at a speed faster than object *A* so that one has the impression that object *A* triggered object *B*'s movement; in the entraining effect object *A* remains in
contact with object *B* as the latter moves off.

through experience is a set of rules, albeit unconscious ones, about the conditions that obtain when one thing causes another to move.

On the other hand, the interpretation hypothesis is also weak, for a number of reasons. First, it is predicated on the assumption that the perception must be correlated only with the features that can be specified in the proximal stimulus. The argument is that because there can be no representation of cause itself in the retinal image of the moving objects, phenomenal causality cannot be perceptual. However, we have seen countless examples where perception differs from or transcends the proximal stimulus. A good example of this is stroboscopic movement. All the perceptual constancies contradict this assumption as well and it is interesting to note that, historically, the constancies were once also not thought of as perceptual for the very same reason: what is perceived does not correlate with the proximal stimulus, ergo, what is perceived is really not perceived, only judged.

Furthermore, the argument presupposes, but does not establish, that one must learn to perceive causality. In principle, this is an empirical question that experiment can eventually resolve, although it is difficult to see how that might be done at the moment. But there are serious logical considerations that alone must give one pause in glibly asserting that the visual perception of causality is based on prior experience. How could one acquire the experience? At first, according to this view, the young child would only see the movement of the objects but not have the impression that one causes the movement of the other. What then takes place to bring about a change? It is unlikely from all we know about perception that a change would result merely from explanations offered by adults about what is taking place. Therefore, it would seem that the only instrument of change is information from touch perception. But on its face, this hypothesis is not too plausible. It is only in certain situations that we have physical contact with moving visual objects. In these cases, as when the child strikes one object with another, the question arises as to what would be experienced on the basis of touch perception alone. Only the movement and force of impact of the object in hand (or the hand itself striking an object) are tactually felt. The movement of the second object away from the first is only given visually. So the argument would have to be modified to the effect that we learn about mechanical causality by some complex interaction of visual and tactile-proprioceptive experiences. Finally, it is worth noting that in the case of other perceptual properties such as form, size, direction, and depth, the evidence now runs against the claim that visual perception is the result of education by touch (see p. 377ff).

Experiments have been performed with children, although understandably not with infants young enough to test the learning hypothesis decisively. Unless some ingenious technique can be devised whereby the infant can respond in a certain way if and only if it perceives causality, we must be content with studies of older children who can talk (although even here it is a serious problem whether the child clearly understands the distinction the experimenter is making). The results of studies that have been carried out with children—for example with 7-year-olds—suggest that the children perceive causality much as do adults, and perhaps even under stimulus conditions where adults might not.[53]

Before concluding this discussion, it is perhaps in order to comment briefly about the philosophical controversy over the problem of causality. For the philosopher, the central question is what does it mean to say that an event is caused. Does it mean anything more than the fact that whenever B occurs some other event, A, will always occur first? Or does it mean that once A occurs it *must necessarily follow that B will occur.* Here cause is thought of as more than the mere inductive generalization that, given A, B will occur. Cause is of the nature of force or energy that necessarily has certain consequences.

But confusion arose in the history of the analysis of this problem between psychological and philosophical questions. Hume argued that we do not perceive causality but only that one event regularly follows another. However, as a result of much repetition of the sequence of events, A, B, we develop the expectation that B will occur or "must" occur. Others including the empiricist Helmholtz argued that were it not for an innate predisposition to experience events on the basis of a "law of causation," we would not derive very useful knowledge from our experience. Michotte's work is obviously very relevant to this issue and, if he is correct, suggests that Hume was wrong. His experiments seem to indicate that we perceive causality directly as much as we do form, movement, and the like. However, even if Hume was wrong about the psychology of causality, it does not imply that he was necessarily wrong in his philosophical analysis of causality. In other words, even if subjective impressions of causation are innately determined, even if they are perceptual and characterized by a feeling of necessity or force or the like, this in no way implies that cause as a philosophical concept must be understood in this way.

Object Permanence

Implicit in our perception of the world is the assumption that objects are permanent and, therefore, remain present even if they are momentarily not visible. Thus, if we briefly close our eyes or turn away, we expect stationary objects to be where they were when we open our eyes or turn back.

One might think that this is not an aspect of perception comparable to properties such as size, form, direction, and the like, since it would not seem possible to specify the stimulus conditions or central correlates that determine it. Rather, one might be inclined to say that the assumption of the permanent existence of things characterizes perception in the same fundamental way that spatiality and time do. However, Michotte has pointed out that here, as with perception of causality, certain specific stimulus conditions affect the outcome, in this case either producing or not producing the impression that an object, no longer visible, is nevertheless still present.[54] For example, if an object gradually disappears, part at a time, as when a screen moves over it, one has the impression that it is still present behind the screen. But if the object suddenly disappears, all at once, as when the second empty field of a tachistoscope instantaneously replaces the field in which the object was just visible, then one has the impression that the object has vanished and is no longer "there." The first set of conditions support the "inference" that an object is present but momentarily covered, whereas the second set of conditions do not. (Also the second set of conditions will lead to movement perception under stroboscope alternation, but not the first. See pp. 200–201.)

Some experiments have recently been conducted that bear on the question of the origin of the perception of object permanence (also referred to as *existence constancy*). The question is, do infants also make this "assumption" or does the tendency to do so only arise following maturation and learning?

Piaget, who first raised this question, believed that the young child does not make this implicit assumption about the world.[55] In observing his own children he found that they did not always search for objects that he hid. However, this might be more a matter of motivation than of perception or cognition. Other experimental techniques have since been evolved. One method is to monitor an infant's heart rate when a screen first covers and then uncovers an object behind it.[56] During the time the screen is in front, the object can be removed. If the infant does not assume an object's continued existence when it disappears from sight, then it certainly should not be surprised if the object is no longer there when the screen is moved away. But if it does make such an assumption, it should be surprised, and if surprised, its heart rate should accelerate. The result was that children as young as 20 days were startled if the object was not present when the screen moved away, but were not startled when the screen remained over the object for as long as 15 seconds before moving away. The failure to be surprised in the latter case, however, must be a function of limited memory or attention span since if the screen moved again after 1.5 or 3.0 seconds the behavior of the infants made it perfectly clear that they expected the object to still be there.

In another experiment, in addition to removing or not removing the object, conditions were included in which the color or shape of the object or both were changed during the period it was covered. When, for example, a screen glided over a red sphere and then glided off to reveal a green cube, the youngest infants tested, 70 days old, were not startled. Only the complete absence of an object had that effect. Older infants, 98 days of age, *were* startled by this kind of change, but only the 126-day-old infants were surprised by any change, for example, if the red sphere "became" a green sphere. These findings may have more relevance to the question of what an infant attends to or perceives than to the question of object permanence. If the color of the object was not particularly salient in the infant's perception, then obviously changing the color cannot be expected to have any consequences.

The same investigator made use of still other techniques to study aspects of the stimulus transformation that might be relevant to the perception or nonperception of object permanence by infants of different ages.[57] For example, he found that once an infant has been conditioned to suck on a nipple, if it is startled by the disappearance of an object, it will momentarily stop sucking and only continue when the object reappears. Using this method and others, the investigator found that infants seem to assume that an object is present when no longer visible under the same conditions as adults do, namely, if it disappears a part at a time (as when a partition glides in front of it) rather than all at once (as when dimming of the lights gradually causes it to disappear). Where the infants differ is with respect to absolute time intervals. For an older infant or an adult, an object over which a screen moves as fast as 75 centimeters per second is seen as undergoing occlusion, but for an infant it seems to be instantaneously disappearing. Also for the young infant, long delay in the reappearance of the object leads to different behavior than does short delay. For older infants the time interval is not crucial, perhaps because *cognitive understanding* about the permanence of objects has emerged and can affect behavior.

In a recent study, the development of object permanence in the cat was studied.[58] A variety of tests were used over a 2-year span, starting with 6-day old kittens. For example, in one test the animal was first induced to play with an object. Then the object was covered with a cloth and the animal's behavior was observed. Until the animals were about 6 months of age they did not display the immediate and vigorous pawing which one would expect if they were clearly aware that the object was still present behind the cloth. There were, however various intermediate stages. From this, the investigators concluded that object permanence as a characteristic of perception does develop.

However, it is also possible to view this result and some of those with infants, in terms of failure to maintain attention on an object that was no longer visible. It is unlikely that this results from failure of memory, in the light of the fact that only a very brief period of time has elapsed. Perhaps the correct explanation is that young animals, or even mature animals of certain species, and human infants, react more to the present stimulus situation than to anything represented only by memory. That is, ordinarily the present stimulus is salient and therefore dominates behavior. From this point of view, the kitten's failure to maintain interest in the hidden object does not necessarily mean that the assumption of object permanence does not characterize their behavior as much as it does the adults. In fact, the outcome of such tests may depend upon what object is used and how interesting it is to the animal. Very young kittens will continue to watch a hole through which a mouse has run for an appreciable time, and there can be little doubt from their behavior that they are looking for or waiting for the mouse to reappear.

Summary

What conditions of stimulation or what central events lead to the perception of movement? Many facts contradict the hypothesis that movement is perceived as the result of displacement of the image of the moving object over the retina.

When the observer moves, the images of stationary objects in the world shift across the retina, but these objects appear to be stationary (position constancy). Conversely, a stationary image on the retina will give rise to an impression of movement when the eyes move. Therefore, it would seem that the perceptual system takes eye or body movement into account when assessing the significance of the behavior of the retinal image. It was suggested that we perceive movement when an object appears to undergo change in its location in relation to ourselves.

Ordinarily, when the observer moves, the image of stationary objects displaces by an equal amount and in a particular direction. If conditions are such that this image displacement is of a different magnitude or in a different direction, then the world will seem to move when the observer moves. However, experiments have demonstrated that we can adapt to this new state of affairs, so that in time the world will appear stationary once again.   Therefore, it would seem plausible to hypothesize that in principle *any* displacement of the image *concomitant* with observer movement will be discounted by the perceptual system, but that by virtue of past experience, only a particular displacement of the image during observer movement signifies a stationary world.

Stroboscopic movement perception is another fact which contradicts the hypothesis that image displacement underlies the perception of movement.   The fact that it occurs only at certain rates of alternation, and that animals and infants perceive it, has suggested to many that it is based on a primitive tendency of the nervous system to react to a spread of excitation from one locus to another.

But a number of other facts seem to call for a different kind of explanation.   For example, a necessary condition is that the first object suddenly disappear for no apparent reason and that the second object suddenly appear in a different phenomenal location.   Thus the perception of stroboscopic movement can be thought of as a "plausible solution" to the "problem" of a sudden change in an object's location. Stroboscopic movement perception is similar to real movement perception when the object is moving rapidly.   In fact, experimental work suggests that the perception of real movement at fast speeds is based on the same mechanism as stroboscopic movement since it depends only on sight of the object in the beginning and end positions.

A single stationary point of light in an otherwise homogeneous field such as a dark room will generally appear to drift.   Various theories have been advanced to explain this autokinetic effect.   There is some evidence to support the hypothesis that rapid fluttering of the eye that occurs even when the eye is felt to be at rest may be the cause.   However, there are difficulties with this hypothesis.   The central fact about the autokinetic stimulus situation is that there are no other visible objects present that ordinarily would clearly indicate that a change in position of the point has not occurred.   Under these conditions, therefore, the perceptual system might easily be "deceived" into inferring that the point was drifting and that the eyes were slowly tracking it.

The change of location of an object relative to other objects in the field is an important determinant of movement perception.   If the moving object surrounds the stationary one (so that it becomes the frame of reference), it will generally induce a sense of movement in the stationary object.   Induced movement of the self also occurs when we misperceive our own bodies to be in motion as a result of movement of a surrounding reference system.   The importance of change of location relative to other objects is also shown in situations where two or more objects are both moving in relation to one another. The actual path of movement is then often dissociated into two perceptual components, the more salient one being that based on the objects' approach to or separation from one another. Therefore, most of the facts about the perception of movement can be subsumed under the principle that movement is perceived when objects change their phenomenal location (above some threshold rate) where "location" is defined either subject-relatively or object-relatively.

Can the perception of movement be explained in terms of units in the visual nervous system that "detect" the displacement of the image over the retina? Such mechanisms have been discovered in various species. One phenomenon that may be explained along these lines is the aftereffect of movement. However, this phenomenon is a special case. Most of the other facts concerning the perception of movement such as are described in this chapter argue against an explanation along these lines since image displacement is neither a necessary nor a sufficient condition for seeing movement. Therefore, although the role of these so-called neural movement detector mechanisms is to detect the displacement of an image over the retina, information concerning image displacement may or may not lead to movement perception depending upon a variety of other factors.

The apparent velocity of a moving object cannot be a function of the rate at which its image displaces because perceived velocity is more or less constant despite the distance of the object from the observer. Two factors have been isolated. Perceived velocity is a function of the phenomenal extent traversed per unit time; in other words, it is based on size constancy. But perceived velocity is also a function of the *rate* of *relative* displacement per unit time. If a frame of reference is transposed in its linear dimensions, the velocity of the object must be transposed by a like amount in order that the phenomenal velocity in the two cases be identical. Constancy of speed in daily life is most likely a function of both factors.

Several other phenomena concerning moving events were considered: the direction of movement of straight and curved lines or contours is ambiguous under certain conditions. As a result, the perceived direction of movement of such lines may not be perceived veridically. A basic principle that underlies such phenomena is the tendency to perceive the visible part of a contour as representing the same segment of the entire contour rather than as successive segments of it. In the case of circular or curved figures, this principle results in the tendency to perceive these figures as stationary even when they are rotating.

Under certain conditions one has the impression that one object has caused another to move. Various kinds of perceived causality occur and the perception of each depends upon specific stimulus conditions. Although Michotte believed that phenomenal causality is a direct perceptual phenomenon, others believe that it is an interpretation we make of the sequence of movements perceived based on prior experience.

A fundamental characteristic of perceived objects is that they are enduring. It is therefore implicit that if we turn away or close our eyes or another object momentarily blocks our view, the object is still where it was and has not changed. It has been claimed that such object permanence is a perceptual property that depends upon specific stimulus conditions. On the whole, evidence with infant subjects suggests that this characteristic of perception is present from birth, but other evidence with animals suggests that it is based on a process of development.

References

1. Helmholtz, H. von. *Treatise on Physiological Optics.* Vol III. (trans. from the 3rd German ed., edit. by J. P. C. Southall, Dover Publications, Inc., 1962, First pub. in the *Handbuch der physiologischen Optik.* Voss, 1867.

2. Mach, E. *The Analysis of Sensations*, Open Court Publishing Co., 1914 (Republished by Dover Publications, Inc., 1959).

3. Brindley, G. S. and P. A. Merton. The absence of position sense in the human eye. *Journal of Physiology*, 1960, **153**, 127–130.

4. Mack, A. and J. Bachant. Perceived movement of the after-image during eye movement. *Perception & Psychophysics*, 1969, **6**, 379–384.

5. Mack, A. and E. Herman. Position constancy during pursuit eye movements: an investigation of the Filehne illusion. *Quarterly Journal of Experimental Psychology*, 1973, **25**, 71–84. See also A. E. Stoper, Apparent motion of stimuli presented stroboscopically during pursuit movement of the eye. Perception & Psychophysics, 1973, **13**, 210–211.

6. Stratton, G. Some preliminary experiments on vision without inversion of the retinal image. *Psychological Review*, 1896, **3**, 611–617; Upright vision and the retinal image. *Psychological Review*, 1897, 4, 182–187; Vision without inversion of the retinal image. *Psychological Review*, 1897, 4, 341–360, and 463–481.

7. Mittelstaedt, H. Telotaxes und Optomotorik von Eristalis bei Augeninversion, *Naturwissen*, 1944, *36*, 90–91; E. von Holst and H. Mittelstaedt. Das Reafferenz-princip. *Die Naturwissenschaf-*

ten, 1950, **20**, 464–476. See also R. W. Sperry. Neural basis of the spontaneous optokinetic response produced by visual inversion. *Journal of Comparative and Physiological Psychology*, 1950, **43**, 482–489.

8. Wallach, H. and J. H. Kravitz. The measurement of the constancy of visual direction and of its adaptation. *Psychonomic Science*, 1965, **2**, 217–218; Rapid adaptation in the constancy of visual direction with active and passive rotation. *Psychonomic Science*, 1965, **3**, 165–166; Posin, R. Perceptual adaptation to contingent visual-field movement; an experimental investigation of position constancy. Ph. D. dissertation, Yeshiva University, 1966 (Described in I. Rock. *The Nature of Perceptual Adaptation.* Basic Books, Inc., Publishers, 1966, pp. 87–91).

9. Ternus, J. Experimentelle Untersuchungen über phänomenale Identität. *Psychologische Forschung*, 1926, **7**, 71–126 (Trans. and condensed in W. Ellis, *Source Book of Gestalt Psychology*, Selection 11. Humanities Press, Inc., 1950.

10. Wertheimer, M. Experimentelle Studien über das Sehen von Bewegung. *Zeitschrift für Psychologie*, 1912, **61**, 161–265.

11. Smith, K. U. The neural centers concerned in the mediation of apparent-movement vision. *Journal of Experimental Psychology*. 1940, **26**, 443–466.

12. Schiller, P. von. Kinematoskopisches Sehen der Fische. *Zeitschrift für vergl. Physiologie*, 1934, **20**, 454.

13. Gaffron, M. Untersuchungen über das Bewegungssehen bein Libellenlarven, Fliegen and Fischen. *Zeitschrift fur vergl. Physiologie*, 1934, **20**, 299.

14. Rock, I., E. S. Tauber, and D. Heller. Perception of stroboscopic movement: evidence for its innate basis. *Science*, 1965, **147**, 1050–1052; E. S. Tauber and S. Koffler. Optomotor responses in human infants to apparent motion: evidence of innateness. *Science*, 1966, **152**, 382–383.

15. Korte, A. Kinematoskopische Untersuchungen. *Zeitschrift für Psychologie*, 1915, **72**, 193–206.

16. Gengerelli, A. Apparent movement in relation to homogeneous and heterogeneous stimulations of the central hemispheres. *Journal of Experimental Psychology*, 1948, **38**, 592–599.

17. Ammons, C. H. and J. Weitz. Central and peripheral factors in the Phi phenomenon. *Journal of Experimental Psychology*, 1951, **42**, 327–332.

18. Rock, I., and S. Ebenholtz. Stroboscopic movement based on change of phenomenal rather than retinal location. *American Journal of Psychology*, 1962, **75**, 193–207.

19. Guilford, J. P. and H. Helson. Eye movements and the Phi Phe-

nomenon. *American Journal of Psychology*, 1929, 41, 595–606.

20. Stoper, A. E., op. cit., reference 5.
21. Sigman, E. and I. Rock. Unpublished experiment. However, the reader is referred to a recent book in which, contrary to what is claimed above, it is reported that a condition of presentation such as that shown in Fig. 5–8*a does* sometimes lead to an impression of movement. See P. Kolers. *Aspects of Motion Perception*. Pergamon Press, Inc., 1972. Perhaps the difference can be explained by noting that observers can perceive movement under certain conditions where *A* reappears with *B* but naive observers do not tend to do so very much of the time. Another relevant factor is the spatial separation between *A* and *B*.
22. Sigman, E. and I. Rock. Stroboscopic movement based on perceptual intelligence. *Perception*, 1974, 3. A. E. Stoper. The effect of the structure of the phenomenal field on the occurrence of stroboscopic motion. Paper delivered at the 1964 meeting of the Eastern Psychological Association.
23. Kaufman, L., I. Cyrulnik, J. Kaplowitz, G. Melnick, and D. Stoff. The complementarity of apparent and real motion. *Psychologische Forschung*, 1971, 34, 343–348.
24. Johansson, G. *Configurations in Event Perception*. Almkvist and Wiksell, 1950.
25. Anstis, S. Phi movement as a subtraction process. *Vision Research*, 1970, 10, 1411–1430.
26. Guilford, J. P. and K. M. Dallenbach. A study of the autokinetic sensation. *American Journal of Psychology*, 1928, 40, 83–91.
27. Riggs, L. A., F. Ratliff, J. C. Cornsweet, and T. N. Cornsweet. The disappearance of steadily fixated visual test objects. *Journal of the Optical Society of America*, 1953, 43, 495–501. R. W. Ditchburn and B. L. Ginsborg. Vision with a stabilized retinal image. *Nature*, 1952, 170, 36–37; R. M. Pritchard. Stabilized images on the retina. *Scientific American*, 1961, 204, (6).
28. Matin, L. and G. E. MacKinnon. Autokinetic movement: Selective manipulation of directional components by image stabilization. *Science*, 1964, 143, 147–148.
29. Brosgole, L. The autokinesis of an after-image. *Psychonomic Science*, 1968, 12, 233–234.
30. Gregory, R. L. *Eye and Brain*. World University Library, 1966, pp. 99–103.
31. Duncker, K. Über induzierte Bewegung. *Psychologische Forschung*, 1929, 12, 180–259. (Trans. and condensed in W. Ellis. *Source Book of Gestalt Psychology*. Humanities Press, Inc. Selection 12, 1950).

32. Wallach, H. The perception of motion. *Scientific American*, 1959, **201**, 56–60.

33. Oppenheimer, F. Optische Versuche über Ruhe und Bewegung. *Psychologische Forschung*, 1934, **20**, 1–46.

34. Brosgole, L. An analysis of induced motion. *Acta Psychologica*, 1968, **28**, 1–44.

35. Roelofs, C. O. Optische Lokalisation. *Archiv für Augenheilkunde*, 1935, **109**, 395–415.

36. Wallach, H. Informational discrepancy as a basis of perceptual adaptation. Chap. 13 in *The Neuropsychology of Spatially Orientated Behavior* (edit. by S. J. Freedman). Dorsey Press, 1968.

37. Rock, I. The basis of position constancy during passive movement of the observer. *American Journal of Psychology*, 1968, **81**, 262–265.

38. See for example Lettvin, J. Y., H. R. Maturana, W. S. McCulloch, and W. H. Pitts. What the frog's eye tells the frog's brain. *Proceedings of the Institute of Radio Engineering*, 1959, **47**, 1940–1951; D. H. Hubel and T. N. Wiesel. Receptive fields, binocular interaction and functional architecture in the cat's visual cortex. *Journal of Physiology*. 1962, **160**, 106–154. Barlow, H. B., R. M. Hill and W. R. Levick. Retinal ganglion cells responding selectively to direction and speed of image motion in the rabbit. *Journal of Physiology*, 1964, **173**, 377–407.

39. Barlow, H. B. and R. M. Hill. Evidence for a physiological explanation of the waterfall phenomenon and figural after-effects. *Nature*, 1963, **200**, 1345–1347.

40. Sekuler, R. W. and L. Ganz. After-effect of seen motion with a stabilized retinal image. *Science*, 1963, **139**, 419–420.

41. Anstis, S. M. and R. L. Gregory. The after-effect of seen motion: The role of retinal stimulation and of eye movements. *Quarterly Journal of Experimental Psychology*, 1965, **17**, 173–175.

42. Grüsser-Cornehls, W., O. J. Grüsser, and T. H. Bullock. Unit responses in the frog's tectum to moving and nonmoving visual stimuli. *Science*, 1963, **141**, 820–822; H. B. Barlow and W. R. Levick. The mechanism of directionally sensitive units in rabbit's retina. *Journal of Physiology*, 1965, **178**, 477–504.

43. Barlow, Hill, and Levick, op. cit; Maturana, H. R., J. Y. Lettvin, W. S. McCulloch, and W. B. Pitts. Anatomy and physiology of vision in the frog, Rana Pipiens. *Journal of General Physiology*, 1960, **43**, 129–175; D. Finkelstein and O. J. Grusser, Frog retina: detection of movement. *Science*, 1965, **150**, 1050–1051.

44. Rock, I., A. L. Hill and M. Fineman. Speed constancy as a function of size constancy. *Perception & Psychophysics*, 1968, 4, 37–40.

45. Brown, J. F. The visual perception of velocity. *Psychologische*

Forschung, 1931, 14, 199–232. (Reprinted in I. M. Spigel, ed. *Visually Perceived Movement*, Harper & Row, Publishers, Inc., 1965).

46. Smith, O. W. and C. Sherlock. A new explanation of the velocity transposition phenomenon. *American Journal of Psychology*, 1957, **70**, 102–105.

47. Johannson, G. Configurations in the perception of velocity. *Acta Psychologica*, 1950, 7, 25–79.

48. Wallach, H. On constancy of visual speed. *Psychological Review*, 139, 46, 541–552.

49. Wallach, H. Über Visuell Wahrgenommene Bewegungsrichtung. *Psychologische Forschung*, 1935, **20**, 325–380.

50. Metelli, F. Zur Theorie optischen Bewegungswahrnehmung. *Ber icht über der 24. Kongress der Deutschen Gesellschaft für Psychologie. Im auftrage der Deutschen Gesellschaft für Psychologie herausgegeben, von Prof. Dr. H. Heckhausen. Eischeinungsjahr, 1965. Verlag für Psychologic Dr. C. D. Hogrefe-Göttinger.

51. Musatti, C. L. Sui fenomeni stereocinetici. Archivio Italiano Psicologia, 1924, **3**, 105–120; H. Wallach, A. Weisz, and P. A. Adams. Circles and derived figures in rotation. *American Journal of Psychology*, 1956, **69**, 48–59.

52. Michotte, A. *The Perception of Causality*. Basic Books, Inc., Publishers, 1963. Originally published under the title *La Perception de la Causalité* ed. de L'Institute Supérior de Philosophie (Etudes de Psychologie), III, 1946.

53. Olum, V. Developmental differences in the perception of causality. *American Journal of Psychology*, 1956, **69**, 417–423; Developmental differences in the perception of causality under conditions of specific instructions. *Vita Humana*, 1958, 1, 191–203.

54. Michotte, A. Perception and cognition. *Acta Psychologica*, 1955, 11, 69–91.

55. Piaget, J. *The Construction of Reality in the Child*. Basic Books, Inc., Publishers, 1954.

56. Bower, T. G. R. Object permanence and short-term memory in the human infant. Unpublished manuscript, 1966.

57. Bower, T. G. R. The development of object permanence: Some studies of existence constancy. *Perception & Psychophysics*, 1967, 2, 411–418.

58. Gruber, H. E., J. S. Girgus, and A. Banuazizi. The development of object permanence in the cat. *Developmental Psychology*, 1971, 41, 9–15.

chapter 6

THE PERCEPTION OF FORM I: ORGANIZATION

Why should there be a problem about the perception of form? If an object has a certain shape, it will produce a retinal image of that shape. The neural impulses arising from the image presumably are transmitted to the brain and lead to the perception of a shape corresponding to the object.

There is some truth in this statement but it overlooks many problems. However, the problems are not so easy to grasp. The problem we consider in this chapter is illustrated in Figure 6-1a. Undoubtedly, the reader will see a design that resembles the letter "H." Yet the letters "W" and "M" are physically present in the pattern of lines, and therefore, images of "W" and "M" are present on the retina. They can be seen clearly in b where the two letters have deliberately been separated. The question, therefore, arises as to why they are not perceived in a. (Of course, now that their presence has been noted it is possible

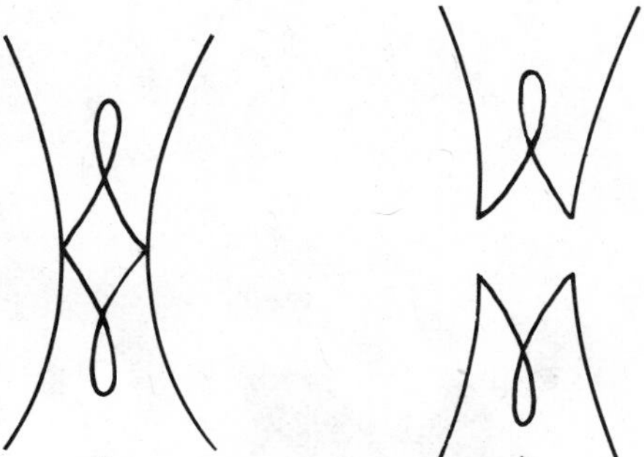

Figure 6-1

to perceive them even in *a*, but we still need to explain why they are not spontaneously seen.) If the reader responds, "because the "W" and "M" are hidden or camouflaged in *a*" then we must ask what determines or makes possible the camouflage. Another example of failure to perceive something despite its representation by a retinal image is shown in Fig. 6-2. When the bottom half of the figure is covered over, the top half will be perceived as $\sqrt{16}$.

A different kind of example will be helpful. Fig. 6-3 may at first be seen as a silhouette of a meaningless object, something like a chess piece. Yet the contour on the right side is also that of a profile of a face looking to the left. Although the face is not perceived at first, the reader can now perceive it and, in fact, it may now be difficult to look at the pattern without becoming aware of it. In Fig. 6-4 the reader may discover a word (of white letters) that at first is not perceived. These examples illustrate the point that the same retinal image can lead to different possible form percepts. Logically, one can say that the retinal image is ambiguous as to what it represents in the world. Before it can lead to a specific perception, the image must be *organized* in a particular way. Therefore, the reader can now understand one reason why it is an oversimplification to say that form perception can be explained on the basis of the retinal stimulation. More generally, the retinal image can be considered to be a pattern of varying brightnesses and colors, so we have the problem of explaining how the perceptual system carves

Figure 6-2

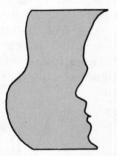

Figure 6-3

Figure 6-4

specific shapes out of this mosaic. In this chapter the concept of organization as a necessary determinant of perceived form is discussed in detail.

Perceptual Organization

In Figs. 6-1 and 6-2 the problem is to explain why particular parts—in these cases lines—are or are not perceived as belonging together. This aspect of organization is referred to as grouping. The problem here is to explain why certain units are perceived as distinct and segregated from other units, in other words, to account for what goes with what. In Figs. 6-3 and 6-4 the problem is to explain why a contour is perceived as belonging to and giving shape to a region on one of its sides rather than a region on the other side. This aspect of organization is referred to as *figure-ground perception*. We consider both of these problems in this section, starting with the problem of grouping.

What are the principles or laws that govern the manner in which various elements of the proximal stimulus for vision, the retinal image, are grouped? Fig. 6-1 illustrates a principle that Max Wertheimer named "good continuation." When a straight line or curve continues from any point in a manner that does not abruptly depart from the curvature prior to that point, one might say it has a smooth continuation. Thus, for example, in Fig. 6-5a all the dotted lines exemplify smooth continuations of the solid line, whereas in Fig. 6-5b they are discontinuous, i.e., the lines change direction abruptly. The Gestalt psychologist used the charmingly subjective term *good* continuation to stand for smooth transitions of a curve whereas *bad* continuation referred to abrupt changes of curvature.

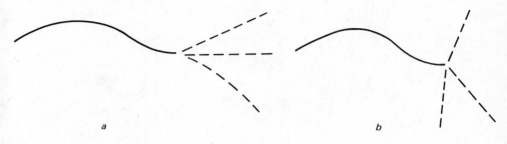

a   *b*

Figure 6-5

Good continuation, as a principle of organization, implies that there is a "preference" to perceive segments of lines that in some sense are smooth continuations of one another, as one line or form. Therefore, in Fig. 6-1a the "W" and "M" tend not to be perceived spontaneously because there is a preference to see the sides of the "W" and "M" as long lines. If, however, the continuation at the junction point is not as smooth, as in Fig. 6-6, then the "W" and "M" are more readily perceived. Another example of this principle is shown in Fig. 6-7. This will spontaneously be seen as two lines crossing each other, *A B* and *C D*. Yet this is by no means the only way the pattern can be perceived. It can be perceived as two horizontally oriented angles touching, *A C* and *B D*, or as two vertically oriented angles touching, *A D* and *B C*.

These illustrations bring out a very important point. We assume that what we experience is given by the stimulus; these examples, however, make clear that the stimulus is ambiguous and can lead to more than one perceptual outcome. Therefore, what we perceive is based partly on the stimulus and partly on a selection made by the perceptual system. Wolfgang Köhler, the Gestalt psychologist, referred to the belief that the percept was nothing more than a copy of the proximal stimulus (which in turn is a copy of the outer object), as the "experience error."[1] It is a natural error because we are unaware that such a process of selection is occurring and because we localize visual things that we experience as "outside" in the environment. We are unaware of the basis of selection, i.e., we are unaware of the principle of organization that governs the selection in any given situation.

A number of principles govern the grouping of the stimulus array in addition to good continuation. Another is proximity. Other things being equal, units that are closer together will tend to be perceived as part of a single entity. Thus, Fig. 6-8 is seen as a series of columns although there is no logical reason why it cannot be seen as a series of

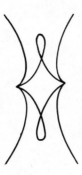

Figure 6-6

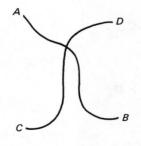

Figure 6-7

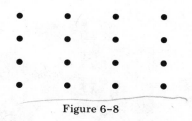

Figure 6-8

rows (in fact, with effort, it can be seen in this way). It is *relative* proximity that matters here, because the perception can be changed by making the dots closer together horizontally while preserving the absolute distance between them vertically, as shown in Fig. 6–9. Now rows are seen.*

Similarity is another principle of grouping. In Fig. 6–10 the distance between dots is equal in both directions so that proximity does not favor either organization. But the dots in columns are similar to one another whereas those in rows are not. It is not yet certain what *kinds* of similarity affect grouping, but it is clear that color (achromatic and chromatic) and size are two effective dimensions. In fact, a well-known pseudoisochromatic test for color vision is predicated on the tendency for areas of similar color to cluster together into a unit. Fig. 6–11 illustrates this test using achromatic color differences rather than chromatic differences. The very dark units are similar to one another and form a larger unit, in this case the letter G. In the color test, the similarity is one of chromatic hue so that only if the observer can discriminate colors does he perceive the larger unit. Similarity of line orientation

Figure 6-9   Figure 6-10

*It is possible that another principle of grouping has been overlooked. When units are connected, particularly at their ends, there is a strong tendency to perceive such units as parts of one entity. However, it is impossible to separate the factor of connectedness from proximity since anything connected is ipso facto contiguous. Therefore, it is not easy to prove that connectedness is a principle of grouping, but the author believes that it is.

Figure 6-11

determines grouping but similarity of form, with the orientation of the line components of the forms held constant, does not.[2]   Thus in Fig. 6-12 *a* and *b*, one quadrant immediately is perceived as different from the remainder of the array because the similarly oriented lines are grouped together.   But in *c* one does not immediately perceive one quadrant as distinct.

The factors that affect organization can either oppose one another or cooperate with one another.   Fig. 6-13*a* illustrates the opposition of proximity and similarity, whereas Fig. 6-13*b* illustrates their coopera-

a   b   c

Figure 6-12

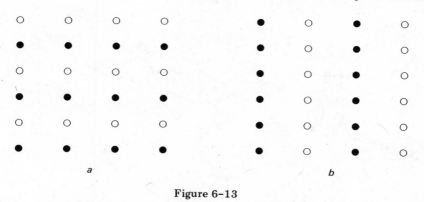

Figure 6-13

tion. Where such factors are in opposition, the grouping is likely to be unstable and ambiguous; where they cooperate, the grouping is extremely stable and unambiguous.

Although several of these principles were known earlier, the credit for describing them as determinants of organized perception in daily life should go to Wertheimer, the Gestalt psychologist.[3] * In addition to good continuation, proximity, and similarity, Wertheimer listed closure as another "law" of perceptual organization. By closure is meant that, other things being equal, units that together form a closed figure or whole will be organized together and perceived as such. As with all these principles, it is necessary to demonstrate it under conditions where no other factors can be responsible for the grouping achieved. Fig. 6-7 shows a pattern that illustrates good continuation: *AB* and *CD* are perceived crossing each other. But in Fig. 6-14*a*, by virtue of closing *AC* and *BD*, an entirely different organization is achieved. In Fig. 6-14*b* the word written in the top half is not detected at first because of the tendency to perceive the entire closed figure as one entity.

Wertheimer listed three other grouping principles, common fate, objective set, and past experience. The role of past experience in perceptual organization is discussed at length in a subsequent chapter; objective set is a special kind of past experience. Common fate refers to situations

---

*A considerable amount of space in this chapter is devoted to a discussion of the Gestalt point of view. Not only did the Gestaltists make clear the necessity of perceptual organization for form perception but they suggested an answer to the question of how it was achieved. Thus over a period of many years Gestalt psychology offered the only systematic theory about form perception. The most relevant references are Köhler,[1] Wertheimer,[3] and Koffka.[4] There were, however, some precursors and contemporaries of the Gestaltists who also dealt with the problem of perceptual organization.[5]

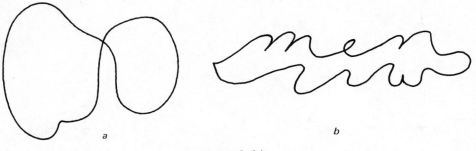

a   b

Figure 6-14

where units move in the same direction at the same speed. Without such movement, one organization of the array occurs; with movement, the units moving together tend to form a group. An illustration of this factor in operation is shown in Fig. 6-15. Each spot moves up and down in simple harmonic motion. The first and third spots are in phase and the second and fourth spots are in phase. The moment the spots are set in motion, the first and third spots and the second and fourth spots form strong subgroupings, as if they were rigidly connected in some unexplained fashion.*

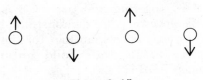

Figure 6-15

In grouping, the entire arrangement must be taken into account. Thus, for example, on the basis of good continuation, one tends to group *i* with *ii* and *iii* with *iv* in Fig. 6-16a. However, when this pattern is embedded in the larger one of Fig. 6-16b, then one groups *ii* and *iii* together as a straight line crossing a continuous line wave pattern. In Fig. 6-17a proximity results in a grouping containing pairs of dots. But in Fig. 6-17b proximity does not necessarily win out, although no other principle of grouping is present. If proximity governed the outcome here, one would perceive an extra dot at each end. An alterna-

*This example is one given by Johansson.[6] In the previous chapter Johansson's research on the effect of grouping on movement perception was briefly described (pp. 215-216).

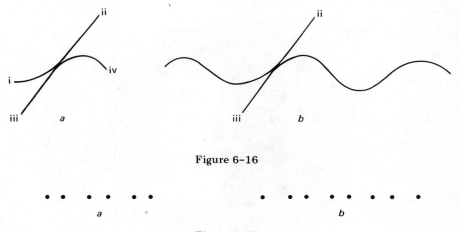

Figure 6-16

Figure 6-17

tive grouping that does better justice to these end dots is to perceive those dots as pairs that are in fact farther apart from one another. Fig. 3-46 in Chapter 3 illustrates still another example of the effect of the entire arrangement on perceptual organization.

Grouping also occurs in sense modalities other than the visual. Thus, for example, in audition, one will organize a rhythmic succession of sounds on the basis of proximity, experiencing as clusters those sounds that are, relatively speaking, closer together in time. Similarity, good continuation, and closure are no doubt also effective, although the precise meaning of good continuation and closure in the realm of audition remains to be established. Such grouping effects undoubtedly play a major role in music and musicians have intuitively been making use of them throughout history.

So much for a brief discussion of the problem of grouping. A principle of selection (or organization) that is operating all the time in the perception of form is illustrated in Fig. 6-18. Either the black region on the left or the white region on the right can be seen as the figure. The other region then becomes the background. The same central contour thus either "belongs" to the black region or to the white region, and the shape of these two regions is completely different. This can best be seen in Fig. 6-19 where the two alternative percepts have been separated from one another. Fig. 6-19*a* can be described as a sharp, claw-like structure protruding outward and Fig. 6-19*b* as a gently curving figure with "fingers." The shapes in Fig. 6-19*a* and *b* are identical with those seen alternately in Fig. 6-18. That the two shapes are thoroughly different from each other was demonstrated in a famous experiment by

Figure 6-18

Figure 6-19

Edgar Rubin in which these kinds of ambiguous patterns were shown twice. If the first time the patterns appeared, the observer saw one region as figure and the second time he saw the other region as figure, there was no recognition, i.e., no feeling that this second figure had ever been seen before.[7] Although the two regions share the same physical contour, that contour results in an entirely different phenomenal shape depending upon which region it "belongs" to psychologically.

Rubin is to be credited with the realization that either of two adjacent regions can be figure or background; he referred to this fact as *figure-ground perception*. Not only is the figure "thing like," but it is said to appear to lie on top or in front of the background, which is shapeless and seems to extend under the figure. Even the typical situation in daily life of a single closed contour (such as in Fig. 6–19a or b) can be considered to be ambiguous because it is possible to perceive the surrounding region as figure and the inner, surrounded region as ground. In that case, the inner region looks like a hole and it is the surrounding area that has a shape.

Although a logical possibility, this kind of figure-ground organization is rare. There must, therefore, be some further principle that leads to the preference to see the inner region as figure and the surrounding region as ground. That principle is surroundedness. The inner or surrounded region tends to be seen as figure. There are other principles at work in figure-ground perception. For example, Fig. 6–20a can be seen as either a black or white propeller-like figure. There may be a slight preference for the black figure but the pattern nevertheless is ambiguous enough to be seen either way. However, the same pattern oriented so that the white propeller blades are vertical and horizontal (Fig. 6–20b) is no longer as ambiguous. The white figure is favored.

The special character of the vertical and horizontal orientation seems to give added weight to the regions that are in these orientations. That the black in Fig. 6–20a tends to be perceived as figure reflects a general preference for black over white. This may result from a greater contrast between black and the surrounding gray than between white and that gray. It was to minimize such a difference in contrast that Figs. 6–18, 6–19, and 6–20 were shown on a gray background, since other-

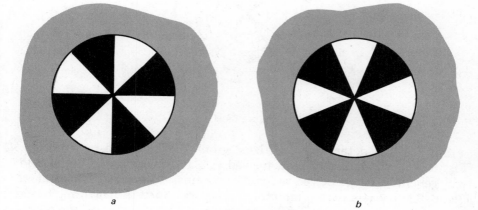

a   b

Figure 6–20

wise the white regions would not have contrasted at all with the white page surrounding them. Obviously, if it is difficult to differentiate a region from the background of the page, it is less likely to stand out as figure. It is possible that the gray used in these figures was too light, and, therefore, still provides greater contrast for the black regions, but it is also possible that there is another reason for a preference for black as figure. In literate societies, written and printed material is almost always black on white paper. Thus black may be favored because of past experience.

Another factor is size. In Fig. 6–21 one tends to perceive the cross containing straight lines as figure despite the fact that the other cross ought to be favored as figure because its arms are horizontal and vertical. Other things being equal, the smaller region will be seen as figure. An interesting aspect of this drawing is that when the regions with circular arcs are perceived as ground, there is a strong impression that the smaller cross as figure lies on top of a background containing complete circles. This clearly illustrates Rubin's point that "ground" has the phenomenal character of lying under or behind "figure." The circular arcs thus show a tendency toward closure into complete circles. If one can succeed in reversing this figure, so that now the cross with circular arcs becomes figure, then the closure effect is not present. Thus there is a kind of logic operating here. If the arcs are part of ground then they may continue under the cross figure and join up to form circles; if they are part of figure, then they must end at the borders of each segment of the cross figure.

Figure 6–21

Still another determinant of figure-ground organization is symmetry. Fig. 6–22a will generally be perceived as black columns and Fig. 6–22b will generally be perceived as white columns. The effect is clearer in Fig. 6–22a because here symmetry and color cooperate in favoring black columns whereas in Fig. 6–22b they are opposed. In spite of the opposition, however, white columns are still favored in Fig. 6–22b. Thus,

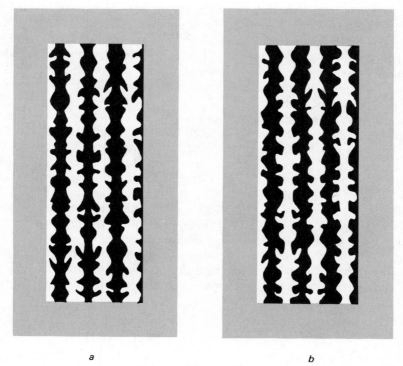

a   b

Figure 6-22

factors such as surroundedness, orientation, specific color (or degree of contrast), size, and symmetry influence the selection of figure.*

Change of Perceptual Organization

It has already been noted that various perceptual organizations of the same retinal image are possible. Usually in daily life only one particular

---

*Gestalt psychologists and others have described a number of *consequences* of perceptual organization. By and large, these refer to differences in perceived chromatic or achromatic color depending upon how the stimulus array is organized. Thus, for example, it has been claimed that when a given chromatic area is figure it appears to be more brightly colored than when it is ground. Several such effects are discussed in Chapter 11 pp. 544-547. For a summary of other effects of this kind in figure-ground perception, see Koffka[4] pp. 187-190.

organization is realized, but there are times when a change occurs despite the fact that the retinal image is constant. Needless to say, this fact is of great theoretical significance because change in perception with no change in stimulation contradicts theories that claim that what we perceive is directly explicable in terms of the proximal stimulus. This fact seems to demand a theory that explains perception in terms of more central neural events.

To study such change in the laboratory, psychologists make use of so-called ambiguous or reversible figures. An ambiguous figure is one for which no one perceptual organization is strongly favored on the basis of principles of organization. The reversible or Necker cube illustrated on p. 8 of Chapter 1 (Fig. 1-2) is such a figure as are those reversible drawings shown in Fig. 3-40 and 3-41 of Chapter 3. Figs. 6-18, Fig. 6-20, Fig. 6-21, and Fig. 6-22 in this chapter were deliberately made to be ambiguous. Figs. 6-23 through 6-26 are examples of reversible figures in which familiar objects are represented.

Fig. 6-23 looks either like the head of a duck facing left or of a rabbit facing right. Fig. 6-24 looks like the profile of a chef tilted 45 degrees counterclockwise or a cartoon outline of a dog tilted 45 degrees

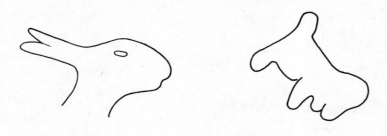

Figure 6-23   Figure 6-24

clockwise. Fig. 6-25 can be seen as a three-quarter profile of a young woman or as a profile of an older woman with a large nose. Fig. 6-26 can be organized as black or white figures of various familiar shapes. With figures such as these, shifts in perceptual organization occur as the observer continues to view them. The question is, why do such shifts occur?

Before answering this question, another question must be considered. What determines the initial perceptual organization of such figures for a given observer? One answer is that although neither organization is so strongly favored in some of these figures that it alone remains dominant, still in each case there may be some factor that tips the balance in

Figure 6-25

its favor. Thus, as already noted, the black regions may be favored in
Figs. 6-18 and 6-20*a* and the symmetrical regions are favored in Fig.
6-22. In the case of the reversible cube, the version illustrated in *b* of
Fig. 1-2 (Chapter 1) seems to be favored, possibly because it represents
a case more frequently encountered in daily life than does *c*, namely a
cube resting on a horizontal surface below eye level. But if there are indeed figures where neither organization is favored on the basis of any
general principle, then it would seem likely that the initial perception is
based on random factors, such as where the observer happens to be fixating. In fact, such random factors undoubtedly play a role even in
cases where general principles are relevant, since it is not the case that
the initial perception of ambiguous figures always conforms to these
principles.

   The more interesting question, however, is what determines the
change in organization after the observer has been perceiving the figure
in a particular way? Why should a change occur at all? The answer that
has been suggested—indeed the only answer given currency in the literature—is that figure perception entails an underlying process of neural
events which is self-satiating. Just as continued stimulation in a given

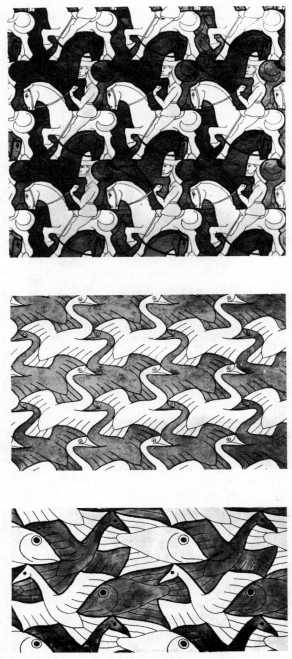

Figure 6-26

region of the retina leads to achromatic and chromatic adaptation effects based on neural fatigue, (see pp. 220 and 534) so it is held that continued stimulation by a pattern of contours may lead to a satiation effect that ultimately blocks the neural process necessary for the continued experience of the form that is perceived. Köhler derived this explanation from a specific theory of form perception in which it was held that the cortical projection of a contour in the retinal image is associated with a flow of direct current in the cortical medium.[8] This current flow eventually alters the condition of the neural medium in such a way as to increase its resistance to the continued flow of that current. As a result, the current is forced to flow in a different direction. The theory is discussed in Chapter 9, pp. 441–445. Although this specific theory does not have many adherents, there is general acceptance of the hypothesis that figure reversal is based on a process of neural fatigue, inhibition, or satiation resulting in a change in the firing of cortical cells. The firing of one set of cells, which leads to one perceptual outcome, ceases and the firing of another set of cells, which leads to another perceptual outcome, begins.

There is some evidence in support of this kind of theory. Prior viewing for a period of time of *one* of the two forms that are present in the ambiguous pattern will facilitate reversal when that ambiguous pattern is later presented.* More subjects then begin by perceiving the other alternative and that alternative is seen for longer intervals of time than the one corresponding to the figure presented for prior viewing.[9] It has also been demonstrated repeatedly that the time to reverse from one organization to the other and back again declines progressively as the observer continues to view an ambiguous figure.[10] This would follow if the satiation that has built up during the perception of one organization is not dissipated completely during the period when the other organization is perceived. Moreover, this increased rate of reversal over time is considerably reduced if the exposures are very brief, or are separated by intervals, or if rest periods are introduced.[11] Under these conditions it would seem that the satiation is dissipated. On the other hand, some evidence does not follow from the satiation theory. Rate of reversal as a function of duration of observation increases even if fixation on one point in the figure is not required or if another figure of a

---

*It is interesting to realize that an experiment following this design can also be thought of as testing the role of past experience in the perception of an ambiguous figure. Thus a conflict between two potential determinants can be said to exist, past experience facilitating the organization that has just been presented and satiation facilitating the other organization.

different size is substituted for the original during the period of viewing.[12] Under such conditions, satiation cannot be understood in terms of a localized change of the regions of the neural tissue in the visual cortex to which the retinal image of the figure projects.

There are certain other problems with this kind of theory. If a process of satiation occurs as a result of continued inspection of a figure, then some difficulty in perceiving it should accompany inspection even if it is *not* ambiguous. Why is satiation or fatigue only prominent with ambiguous figures?* As a matter of fact certain figures that are, in terms of structure, *not* ambiguous can reverse. Figs. 6-3 and 6-4 are cases in point. But these reversal perceptions can often occur very quickly (they can sometimes even occur first) so that satiation does not seem applicable. More important, it is clear that the only reason that these figures are reversible is that the contour is also the outline of very familiar shapes, letters in Fig. 6-4 and a profile of a face in Fig. 6-3. Therefore, we see that past experience is a determinant of reversal and this is a fact that seems to be alien to the kind of mechanism postulated by the satiation theory.

It is not clear precisely how satiation would lead to figure reversal. Consider figures such as those shown in Fig. 6-20 or 6-21. A satiation or fatigue effect would presumably occur for all the contours of the pattern, those that are part of the figure and those that are part of the ground. So it would have to be argued that there is a distinct flow of current (or discharging of cells) that represents the particular perceptual *organization* initially achieved, different from the flow of current or firing of cells stimulated by the individual contours per se, and it is this neural process that is fatigued.[13] But such a theory of perceptual organization has never been developed, so it is difficult to apply it to the problem of *change* of perceptual organization. In any event, not all reversible figures are of the figure-ground variety. For figures that reverse in perspective, such as the cube, it is all the less clear how this kind of theory would apply. In such cases, the perceptual change is one of depth relations. As for the kind of reversible figure shown in Figs. 6-23 and 6-24, the same outer contour signifies two different familiar objects. In Fig. 6-25 the change concerns the role that specific parts of the drawing play in the object perceived, for example, whether a given contour is the side of a young woman's face or the nose of an

---

*To be sure, there are certain effects of continued fixation of any figure. For example, the contours seem dimmer after a while. There are also certain interesting aftereffects (see pp. 441ff). But the figure continues to be perceived as the same figure. There is no loss or change in organization.

older woman. What is being satiated in these cases that would lead to such changes?

Furthermore one can often—although not always—succeed in changing perceptual organization by intending to do so. Or one can often succeed in maintaining a percept rather than changing it.* In one study it was found that no increase in the rate of reversal occurred over time if the observer was instructed to "hold" a given perception rather than to switch as often as possible.[15] The satiation theory has no way of dealing with facts of this kind. Although it is true that *no* perceptual theory to date can account for the effects of intention on perception, the satiation theory is a kind of theory that does not seem to be compatible with it. Satiation is automatic and is unrelated to cognition, motivation, and the like.

Similar to the effects of intention is the effect of knowledge about the ambiguity of the figure. First of all, once the observer becomes aware of the two possible organizations of an ambiguous figure, reversal becomes almost inevitable. In most experiments the observer is told in advance that he will be shown an ambiguous figure and sometimes the two perceptual organizations are pointed out to him. He is also usually told that the figure will reverse. In the absence of such awareness it is entirely possible that reversal will not occur at all. This is certainly true for a figure such as the old-and-young woman (Fig. 6-25) and may be true for other kinds of ambiguous figures as well (for example, Figs. 6-3, 6-4, 6-23, and 6-24). Once the possibility of the other organization is known, this knowledge may lead to the intention of perceiving it. Yet reversal should have nothing to do with such knowledge according to the satiation theory. It is possible that the accelerated rate of reversal over time can be explained in terms of the increasing familiarity with the alternative organizations although the evidence cited concerning the effect of intervals or rest periods cannot easily be accommodated by such a theory.[16]

Perhaps for many ambiguous figures, reversal will occur spontaneously, without prior knowledge about the possibility of the other organization, and without conscious intent to reverse. But if at all possible, it would obviously be desirable to so revise the method of studying the

---

*When one deliberately tries to shift from one organization to another, one often fixates in the center of the region one is trying to perceive as figure. Although fixation is, therefore, a factor in reversal—and, as noted earlier, probably in the *initial* perception of reversible figures—change of fixation is by no means necessary for reversal. An afterimage of a reversible figure will reverse after a while and yet in this case one cannot change one's fixation. It is also probable that eye movements are often caused by rather than the cause of figure reversal.[14]

reversal problem that the subject is naive about the very existence of the different alternatives in the figure. Of course, if repeated reversal of a figure over a period of time is under study the subject cannot remain naive after the first reversal. But naive subjects can be used in studying the problem of *initial* reversal of an ambiguous figure. In that way it should be possible to determine the spontaneous perception of such figures without knowledge of reversibility and intention to reverse entering into the process. Given these contaminating factors, it would seem that virtually all the research on the subject thus far conducted is inconclusive. In any event, if the satiation theory is incorrect, the problem remains, why does reversal occur? A possible answer is suggested in the last section of this chapter.

Prägnanz

Wertheimer and the Gestalt psychologists believed that all of the principles of grouping were manifestations of a tendency of perceptual organization to be "good," "simple," "stable," "internally consistent," "regular," "symmetrical," or to use the German word that the Gestaltists employed to include all of these notions, *prägnant*. *Prägnanz* means significant, pithy, conveying the essence of something, but this is not exactly the meaning intended by the Gestalt psychologists.

The trouble with the use of this concept is that several unrelated concepts are covered by it. One idea is that there is a preference for that perceptual organization that is the simplest. Unfortunately, it is by no means always clear what is simple, although often there is an intuitive appreciation of what is meant. For example, one might say with some justification that it is a simple outcome to perceive Fig. 3-2 in Chapter 3 as two rectangles, one overlapping the other. This ambiguous pattern could also lead to other perceptual outcomes, for example, a rectangle (above) nestled against a reversed L-shaped figure (below). This percept consists of two different figures whereas the first consists of two identical figures. Therefore, "two rectangles" may be considered to be a simpler perception. Another sense in which this is simpler is that a regular rectangle is seen below instead of above an L-shaped figure. At this point, "simple" takes on the meaning of "good," "regular," or "symmetrical." Clearly, a rectangle is more regular and symmetrical than an L-shaped figure; it has fewer sides and angles and its angles are all the same and its opposite sides are equal.* The preference for the symmetrical columns as figure in Fig. 6–22 can be considered to be an example of this aspect of prägnanz with prägnanz defined in terms of regularity or symmetry.

The notion of internal consistency comes closest to the distionary meaning of prägnanz. The idea is that a figure may express a principle or mathematical relation of some kind. For example, Fig. 6–27a is a sine curve the amplitude of which decreases in a regular manner from left to right. Fig. 6–27b is a negatively accelerating curve. The principles that govern the generation of these two figures can be grasped from exposure to only part of what is shown in Fig. 6–27. Thus, if only the left half of either a or b is seen, the observer could infer how the remainder ought to look. The remainder can, therefore, be said to be

---

*Julian Hochberg has argued that prägnanz can be reduced to a simplicity principle and has suggested an objective method for predicting what is simplest in any given stimulus array.[17] He believes that there is a tendency to prefer that organization which requires a minimum number of components (lines, angles, and the like) to specify it. Thus, for example, according to this view one will perceive the patterns shown in Fig. 3–40 of Chapter 3 as two-dimensional or three-dimensional depending upon whether in each case the two or three-dimensional object can be described on the basis of fewer components. In other words, that perceptual organization will be preferred that requires the minimum amount of information to specify it. This idea, therefore, relates perceptual organization to the modern discipline known as information theory. Attneave has similarly argued that one can describe simpler, "good" forms on the basis of less information because such forms tend to be redundant.[18] Thus, for example, a symmetrical figure is redundant since we can predict the shape of the entire figure if we know only half of it. Good continuation can also be thought of as an organization that is redundant, namely, to an extent the entire line is predictable in terms of only a portion of the line. These investigators imply that the principles of grouping described by the Gestalt psychologists govern how we organize the stimulus array because of a preference on the part of the perceptual system for an efficient, economical description of that array.

One problem with this approach is that it must be presupposed that the perceptual system samples the alternative organizations before a decision can be made as to which is the simplest. Only after the symmetry, or regularity of one alternative and the asymmetry or irregularity of another alternative are in some sense "perceived," can the perceptual system "decide" in favor of the organization that can be "described" on the basis of less information. It is also not clear what the relationship is between an economy principle such as is suggested here and the achievement of veridical perception. What organization must serve to achieve is the veridical perception of objects in the world whether this can be achieved economically or not. It should also be noted that an information-theory approach to perceptual organization tells us nothing about the mechanism of organization. Some of the limitations and difficulties with the concept of prägnanz as discussed in this section apply to the information theory approach as well.

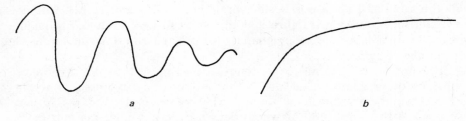

a b

Figure 6-27

required, to be *necessary*, *fitting* with, or *coherent* with the part that is seen. From the standpoint of this last definition, the principle of good continuation can be seen to be an example of prägnanz. Only a part that fits in with the lawful development of the beginning of a figure can be a good continuation.

Prägnanz has been used in another sense, namely to refer to singular or distinctive values of a variable stimulus factor. For example, of all possible orientations of a line, the horizontal and vertical are distinctive. Of all possible curvatures of a line, straightness is distinctive. Of all possible angles, a right angle is distinctive. The presence or absence of distinctive features such as these is important for the appearance of a figure. Thus, for example, if a figure has a horizontal base, then we will immediately be aware of a change if that figure is tilted slightly, whereas if it has no horizontal or vertical lines in it, we may not be aware of a change if it is slightly tilted. Under marginal perceptual conditions, such as poor illumination or tachistoscopic presentation, a slightly curved line will presumably be perceived as straight and two lines not quite perpendicular to each other will be seen as forming a right angle. These effects are not directly related to the problem of grouping, but Wertheimer gives an example of an effect that is. Suppose an array of dots such as that shown in Fig. 6-28 is presented. The separation between a–b, c–d, e–f, and g–h is the same and less than that between b–c, d–e, f–g, and h–i. But the difference is slight. Therefore, the observer will either tend to see the dots as equally spaced, so that no subgroupings occur, or he will tend to exaggerate the difference and see the pairs a–b, c–d, e–f, and so on. A homogeneous spacing is distinctive, but if the observer notes the lack of homogeneity and groups on the basis of proximity, a better grouping is achieved if in his perception he exaggerates the difference in proximity. Either of these alternatives is a prägnant step according to Wertheimer. It is possible that the preference for the horizontal and vertical regions as figure in Fig. 6-20b also illustrates prägnanz as thus defined.

The Gestalt psychologists suggested a model of brain function to ex-

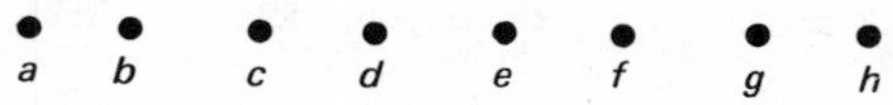

● ● ● ● ● ● ● ●
a   b   c   d   e   f   g   h

Figure 6-28

plain prägnanz. The model derives from the tendency of physical systems to move toward equilibrium, or otherwise expressed, toward a minimum of energy, when they are not constrained from doing so by mechanical arrangements. The clearest example in the natural world is that of the soap bubble. The molecules of the soap solution attract each other such that they tend to take up a minimum of space. However, the air trapped inside keeps the solution in the form of a surface membrane. The shape of the membrane that takes up a minimum of surface is a sphere and so by forming a sphere, the thickness of the membrane can be maximum. The potential energy of a spherical membrane is at a minimum. Here is a case in nature where an object becomes perfectly symmetrical simply as a result of the interplay of physical forces. A crystal is another example. The solar system and spiral galaxies can also be considered to be examples of the interplay of physical forces resulting in regular configurations.

According to Köhler, the brain also works in this way. Thus if the structure of brain events is similar to the structure of perceptual experience—a doctrine the Gestaltists called *isomorphism*—then there would have to be symmetry in the neural processes underlying a perceptual object that had symmetry. The brain process underlying the perception of a circle is a symmetrical one. Furthermore, just as with the soap bubble, if the proximal stimulus departed somewhat from perfect circularity—for example an ellipse—then there would be a tendency for the brain event to move toward perfect symmetry. That would imply a strong tendency to see the ellipse as circular. More generally, it would imply a tendency to favor that percept that was the most regular whenever alternative modes of perceiving existed.

By way of critical analysis of the concept of prägnanz, the following points seem important. First, the different usages of the term should be clearly distinguished and different names given to them since it is not obvious that they share any common meaning. Thus we could have (a) a *simplicity-regularity principle* of preference in ambiguous stimulus constellations; (b) an *internal consistency* principle that results in a preference in ambiguous stimulus constellations such as the preference for "good" over "bad" continuations (and also predicts how certain figures would be completed); (c) a *distinctive value* principle that is of importance in characterizing figures and that may occasionally exert a preference for a particular perceptual organization (for example, the preference for the white cross in Fig. 6–20*b*).

Second, not all of the laws of grouping considered here can be said to be manifestations of a law of prägnanz. Good continuation can be included under aspect (b); symmetry as a determinant of figure-ground organization can be subsumed under (a), and perhaps under certain conditions so can closure, although not in the example shown in Fig. 6–14*a* (because the two closed regions are not simple or regular). But it is not clear why proximity and similarity or figure-ground organization in general should be thought to be principles that relate to prägnanz.

Third, it must be borne in mind that perception of form is generally veridical. That means that regardless of how complex, irregular, asymmetrical, and internally inconsistent a figure may be, our perception of it will usually correspond to its objective shape. Therefore, prägnanz in any of these meanings has essentially no effect in situations where the stimulus is relatively unambiguous or is not marginal or attenuated.* This is an important qualification of the possible efficacy of the prägnanz principle.

Fourth, referring to the simplicity-regularity principle, it is by no means always clear what perceptual outcome *is* the simplest. For example, "two rectangles" does seem simpler than "a rectangle and an L-shaped figure," but when two rectangles are seen, one is behind the other whereas when the two different shapes are seen they are in the same plane. Isn't one plane simpler than two?

Fifth, what might be considered the prägnant outcome in either the (a) or (b) meaning may be preferred on the basis of past experience. It is, of course, implicit in the Gestalt approach to perception that the organization achieved is the result of the spontaneous workings of the brain and, therefore, is not for the most part, determined by past experience. The question of whether or not past experience plays a role in perceptual organization or perhaps completely accounts for it is discussed in more detail in a later chapter. Suffice it to say here that many man-made objects and many geometrical patterns are regular and symmetrical, so that, of necessity, we have a good deal of experience with such forms. Thus, for example, we have often seen one rectangle be-

---

*The Gestaltists argued that the presence of the proximal stimulus representing a figure acts as a constraint opposing prägnant tendencies. Therefore, they predicted that with the stimulus removed, the memory trace would now be free to change in a prägnant direction. Hence studies were conducted to determine whether memory for form would reflect a tendency toward regularity, symmetry, or a singular value. The classical experiment was by Wulf in 1922.[19] However that experiment had many methodological flaws. In research since then eliminating these flaws, little evidence of such memory change has been obtained but perhaps the appropriate figures have not been used.[20]

hind another, and surely, have rarely seen a rectangle abutting and co-
planar with an L-shaped figure. Therefore, a past-experience hypothesis will often predict the same outcome as a prägnanz hypothesis. (See
also the discussion of the Gestalt interpretation of the perceived depth
of certain figures on pp. 131ff.)

Sixth, a demonstration that the law of prägnanz does govern perceptual organization in particular cases would not imply that the brain
model proposed by Gestalt psychologists is valid.

Do the Gestalt Principles of Grouping Explain Perceptual Organization in Daily Life?

If two branches are seen one over the other, then generally our perception of which parts belong with which other parts will be correct. It
would seem, therefore, that the principle of good continuation is responsible for this outcome. By the same token, if the branches are bent
in the manner shown in Fig. 6–29a and if a tree occludes the central region as shown in Fig. 6–29b, then we will misperceive which part goes
with which because of the operation of the same principle of organization. Far more often than not, however, this principle will lead to veridical perception.

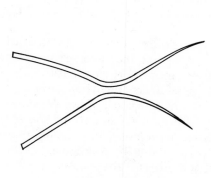
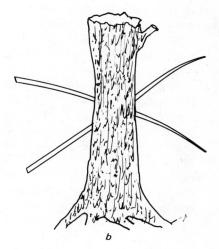

a

b

Figure 6-29

Often, the environment contains three-dimensional things that are seen in front of a more-or-less homogeneous background such as the sky, ground, floor, or wall. Things are often homogeneous in color. Therefore, abstracting from three-dimensionality, Fig. 6–30 represents a typical stimulus situation that we meet in daily life. Are any of the principles of perceptual organization that have been considered relevant to our ability to organize this pattern veridically, namely as a compact thing on a homogeneous background?

Figure 6–30

We would be guilty of the experience error if we presupposed that the organized percept is simply given by the retinal image. Logically speaking, this stimulus is as ambiguous as any of the others we have considered. It is possible to imagine that either (a) no organized percept at all occurs, in which case we would experience a chaotic mosaic of varying brightness and color; or (b) an organized percept occurs that is not veridical, as would be the case if we grouped part of the darker figure with part of the background. That we do organize this stimulus array veridically, therefore, is an achievement that must be based on processes in the nervous system.

A case can be made to support the assertion that three principles of grouping are operating here, proximity, similarity, and figure-ground organization. The difficulty in applying proximity and similarity in this instance is that the object does not consist of distinguishable units as in the earlier examples. However, the following illustration indicates that it is possible to think of the units as infinitesimal segments of the object. In Fig. 6–31a, proximity leads to a grouping of three sets of three lines. In Fig. 6–31b the grouping is improved by the even greater relative proximity of the lines; Fig. 6–31c, therefore, is the logical extreme in the progression of increasingly greater relative proximity. Each of the subgroups in Fig. 6–31c is a perceptual unit or thing exactly like that of Fig. 6–30. The same argument can be made concerning simi-

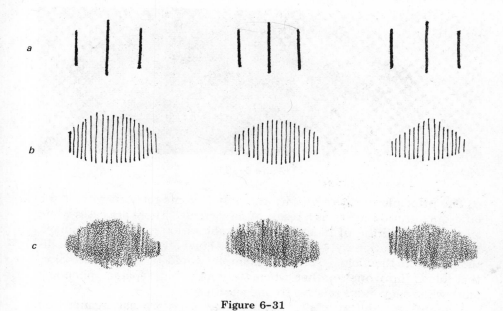

Figure 6-31

larity.   Every region inside the boundary of an object like that shown in Fig. 6-30 is similar in color (or lightness) to every other such region and different in color from regions outside the boundary. The latter regions are similar to one another. Therefore grouping by similarity would also lead to the perception of the entire object as separate and distinct from its background. Fig. 6-32 is a useful illustration of how an object could be thought of as consisting of infinitesimally small units that then are grouped together on the basis of proximity and similarity.

Figure-ground organization enters in because it is logically possible to perceive the homogeneous outer light gray region of Fig. 6-30 as figure and the inner dark gray region as ground. The dark gray region would then look like a hole cut out of the surface of the light gray region surrounding it. Therefore, the perception of the dark gray region as figure must be considered to be the end result of a process of figure-ground organization based on the principle of surroundedness referred to earlier.[21]

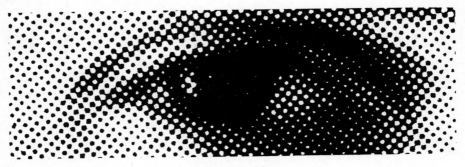

Figure 6-32

The principle of common fate can only become relevant when a specific organization arises as a result of movement. There are cases where an animal by virtue of its camouflaging coloration is all but invisible as long as it is stationary. When it moves, however, it emerges as a distinct unit in the field. Another example would be cloud formations that blend into one another when stationary but separate phenomenally when they move relative to one another.

Camouflage itself attests to the presence of perceptual organization, but here the organization achieved is not veridical. In natural camouflage, similarity is clearly the most important principle at work (Fig. 6-33). Countershading in fish refers to the fact that viewed from above the dorsal surface has a dark color similar to the dark appearance of the ocean or river bottom (b); viewed from below the ventral surface of the same fish is a light color, one that closely matches the appearance of the surface of the water and sky viewed from below (c). Thus, by virtue of similarity, the fish all but disappears as a visual object. Another principle, "disruptive coloration," entails breaking up the surface color of an animal into different regions, each of a different color (d). Thus, similarity can no longer operate to unify all regions of the animal into one thing and, in fact, some parts of the animal may now be grouped with regions of the background. These same principles of camouflage are used by man in warfare.

Although we occasionally misperceive, as in the case of camouflage, the units that we perceive generally exist as units in the environment. How does this remarkable achievement come about merely on the basis of certain principles of organization that are operating inside the head? Why, for example, does grouping by similarity generally result in the perception of units that are, in fact, units? One answer to this question is to say that the laws of organization are learned and naturally we learn on the basis of principles that will yield correct perception. The

a

b

c

d

Figure 6–33

difficulties with this answer and the evidence bearing on it are discussed in detail at a later point, so no more will be said about it here.

The answer given by Gestalt psychologists is twofold. First, regarding the perception of the natural environment, evolutionary change has guaranteed that the brain will operate on the basis of laws that work, that is, that generally yield veridical perception. Objects in the natural environment are generally compact and often are of a color different than the background. Therefore, perceptual organization via proximity and similarity will typically result in the perception of things that actually are present as distinct entities. In other words, proximity and similarity evolved as laws of neural organization because of the nature of the environment in which animals evolved. In some other environment, different laws of organization would have evolved. Second, regarding man-made objects, the answer is simply that we make objects that we will be able to see. Therefore, we typically color an object uniformly. Only if we want to camouflage it do we do otherwise.

Difficulties and Limitations of the Gestalt Approach to Organization

One difficulty with the Gestalt approach to perceptual organization in daily life was already mentioned, namely, most objects do not consist of units that can then be said to combine according to this or that principle. Rather many objects are uniform and indivisible, so we have first to analyze it into artificial units and then to explain how these units combine to give us the object. Of course, the principles of grouping refer to the proximal stimulus rather than to the object in the world. Therefore, one can ask whether there are specifiable units in the retinal image of a uniformly colored object that can then be said to form groupings on the basis of proximity and similarity. The answer is that it would be artificial to think of the image of such an object, considered from the standpoint of a picture focused on the retina, as consisting of separate units, since it is a distribution of light intensities. However, considering the retina physiologically, it consists of separate cells and functionally related clusters of cells so that from this point of view one might plausibly say that such separate units exist.

A further difficulty arises when we try to deal with real objects in the environment rather than with line and dot drawings. For certain reasons real objects contain stimulus information that renders them somewhat less ambiguous than was implied by the description given in the preceding sections. Consider the problem of figure and ground. Normally, an object is perceived to be in front of the background by virtue of various cues to depth. If the very meaning of figure is that it is a shaped entity *in front of* a background, then it is difficult to imagine that the background in the real environment could even spontaneously be organized as figure. It is literally perceived to lie behind the object. Therefore, we might say that the situation is not ambiguous in the typical case encountered in daily life. If not ambiguous, then no special processes of figure-ground organization need be assumed to be operative.* In fact, if this reasoning is sound, it could be argued that the figure-ground organization achieved in line drawings that *are* ambiguous results from transferring modes of perception from daily life to such drawings; this is an effect of learning. For example, the principle of surroundedness that operates in viewing line drawings would then be a learned principle, because objects are ordinarily closed figures that are "surrounded" by a background.

A further limitation of the Gestalt approach to perceptual organization is that the principles discussed are not explanatory. That is, they do not tell us why proximity or similarity results in grouping. This in itself is not a criticism since many important laws in the natural sciences are not explanatory, as, for example, Boyle's law or Newton's laws of motion. Descriptive laws enable us to account for specific phenomena in a systematic way and often lead ultimately to real explanation. But in the case of perceptual grouping, without an understanding of the underlying mechanism that leads to grouping by similarity, good continuation, and the like, we are left with a set of more or less unrelated principles.

Of course, the Gestaltists did think of the laws of organization as manifestations of the fundamental law of prägnanz and they did have a physiological theory of prägnanz. But it has been argued here that not all the principles of organization exemplify prägnanz, that the law of prägnanz is not clear and has not been verified, and, in any case, there is no evidence that the brain events underlying perception are analogous to equilibrium processes that occur elsewhere in nature. Gestalt psychologists also tended to refer to forces of attraction between the neural representations of the perceptual units. Thus, in the case of proximity, the closer together the projected "images" in the visual cortex are

---

*It is still the case that grouping must occur if all the parts of the figure are to be perceived as belonging together so that the figure is segregated from the background. Such grouping then remains as a contribution of the nervous system. It is not given in the proximal stimulus.

of units in the visual field, the stronger are the forces of attraction. In the case of similarity, it was implied that similar neural representations attract each other more than dissimilar ones. Thus, forces of attraction were thought to *explain* the grouping.

The thinking here is predicated on an assumption that at least superficially seems plausible, namely, that a factor such as proximity refers to the relative nearness of the retinal (and therefore cortical) representations of the figural units in the field. Ordinarily, of course, when an array of dots such as those in Figs. 6-8 or 6-9 are viewed, the retinal images of the dots that are objectively closer together will also be closer together. However, it is possible to create a situation in which this is not the case. When an equally spaced array of dots is viewed at a slant, the distance between the retinal images of dots in the horizontal direction will be compressed relative to the distance between images of dots in the vertical direction. This is illustrated in Fig. 6-34*b*. The question then arises as to what grouping we should predict the observer will see in looking at an array such as the one illustrated. Based on the retinal image, we should predict he will see rows because proximity (in the retinal image) is greater within rows than within columns. But if the observer is aware that he is viewing a slanted surface and if constancy of size and shape prevail, then he will experience the distances between dots in all directions as about equal.

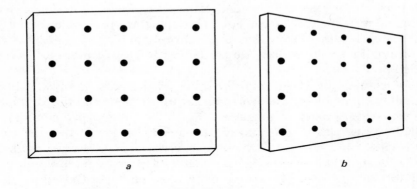

a   b

Figure 6-34

This question was put to an experimental test. The dots consisted of luminous beads strung on strings and viewed from a distance in a dark room. It was found that with binocular vision, the observer (viewing an arrangement such as that of Fig. 6-34*b*) perceives equal spacing; with monocular vision he sees rows. In other words, as long as the observer viewed the array with two eyes, grouping was determined not by proximity in the retinal image but by perceived proximity. When the observer viewed with only one eye, there was no information available that the array of beads was rotated into the third dimension, so that constancy for the distances along the horizontal axis could not occur.[22] This finding means that the law of proximity cannot be understood as the result of stronger attractive forces between the more proximal neural representatives of stimuli in the brain. Before proximity can regulate perceptual organization, a certain amount of processing of information concerning spacing must first occur. The objective distance between units in space must first be perceived and only then does relative proximity among such units determine grouping.

A similar analysis can be made of other principles of grouping. For example, in the case of similarity as a grouping principle, is it the similarity of the retinal images of units that matters or is it the perceived similarity of the units that produce the retinal images? In one recent study the investigators asked whether grouping on the basis of similarity of line orientation is a function of the orientation of the retinal images of the lines or of the perceived orientation of the lines. The experiment was based on the finding that grouping is superior when some of the lines are vertical and some horizontal than when some lines are clockwise oblique and others are counterclockwise oblique (see Fig. 6–12a vs. Fig. 6–12b). What will be the case if the observer views such figures with his head tilted 45 degrees so that the vertical and horizontal lines in a produce oblique retinal images and the oblique lines in b produce horizontal and vertical retinal images? Apparently the grouping is now improved for the oblique lines, suggesting that the retinal state of affairs is quite important in this case. But grouping of the horizontal and vertical lines remains better with the head tilted than it is for the oblique lines with the head held upright, thereby indicating that the perceived orientation of the lines plays a role as well.[23] Therefore, in this study, both retinally and phenomenally defined similarity is relevant for grouping.

Alternative Approaches to the Problem of Organization

The feature-detector explanation

It is now known that the information conveyed by the light energy stimulating individual receptor cells of the retina depends upon the combined action of a large cluster of these cells. Many neighboring receptor cells must all be active before a neural impulse can be transmitted to the next level of the visual nervous system, that is, two or more impulses must *summate* before a neuron on which they converge will discharge. Furthermore, impulses from one neuron will block or *inhibit* the firing of a neighboring neuron. In fact, before certain cells at higher levels in the retina or deeper in the brain will discharge, a certain state of affairs must first obtain in an entire set of retinal cells. A set of such cells that behaves as if it were a unit is called a *receptive field*.[24] For many of these receptive fields, a neural unit at some higher level in the visual nervous system will discharge (or to be more accurate, discharge at a frequency higher than some very low resting or maintained level) only if the cells in the central region are all strongly stimulated by light and at the same time the remaining cells in the peripheral regions are not stimulated at all (or stimulated only weakly). For other receptive fields, the converse is the case, namely, a higher neural cell will respond when the peripheral regions of the receptive are stimulated by light and the central region is not. Therefore, one might say that such neural units serve to detect the presence of small spots, and this has been found to be the case in the frog and the other species when such spots are moving.[25] That is, only if small convex forms are imaged over the appropriate receptive field will a higher-level neuron discharge.

The output from a set of neural units that respond to small spots may converge on still higher neural units such that these higher units will then serve to detect that state of affairs. For example, if the image of an edge or line stimulates the retina in a particular orientation, it will fall across several receptive fields. As a result, several higher neural units will fire, each in response to the distribution of light and dark within a particular receptive field. A still higher neural unit may then respond as a result of the simultaneous discharging of these units and this may be said to detect the presence of the contour or edge. Such slit, edge, or line detector mechanisms have been discovered in a few species.[26] Even more complex detector units have been found which receive their inputs from a set of line detector units. This kind of mechanism has been thought capable of accounting for the discrimination of certain other attributes of form such as angle, specific size, and the like.*

Therefore, one might say with justification that some degree of perceptual organization is innately "wired into" the nervous system. Be-

---

*This is obviously a very condensed summary of much recent research in sensory physiology. In addition to the references given a very useful introduction to this work and its possible implications is available in a recent text.[27]

fore we knew about such feature-detector mechanisms, we had to argue that even a single line stimulus could not be expected to lead to a unified percept of one thing unless the separate neural signals triggered by the various separate retinal cells stimulated by the image of the line were organized into such a unit on the basis of principles such as proximity or similarity. Now that we know about these mechanisms, however, we might say that we have a basis for explaining organization: The discharging of a cortical neuron *signifies* that a line stimulus is present and affords a basis for the perceptual discrimination of a short line in a specific orientation from one in a different orientation.*

However, this kind of mechanism can hardly be considered an adequate explanation of the facts of perceptual organizations, although it may well play an important role in the process. There is first of all the fact that the receptive fields cover relatively small areas of the retina, varying from a few minutes to several degrees of visual angle. The problem, therefore, remains of explaining how objects that cover more of the visual field are organized. Perhaps the more complex or higher-order cells that have been discovered, that discharge only as a result of the combined response of various lower-order detector cells, can signify a more extended visual object.

---

*A neurophysiological theory concerning perceptual organization that has been quite influential was proposed by Hebb 25 years ago.[28] The basic idea was that although at the outset (in infancy) a single perceptual unit such as a line or corner would *not* be perceived as a unit, as a result of repeated stimulation in any specific locus of the retina, changes occur in the cortical neurons fired by the receptor neurons. Connections between cortical neurons allegedly become strengthened when they fire together, with the result that the whole network (or cell assembly) can be set off by the firing of only some of the receptor neurons. Presumably it is the growing tendency of the cortical cell assembly to function as an integral unit that explains the eventual tendency to perceive a line or corner as *one* unit.

This theory has now been supplanted by the discoveries of feature-detector neural units described here. While there seems to be some evidence that these mechanisms are to an extent innate there is also growing evidence that exposure to typical features of the environment (e.g., contours in various orientations) at an early stage of development plays a central role in the kind of detector units which emerge. (See the discussion of this recent work in Chapter 8, p. 367). Therefore, although Hebb's specific theory was not correct, some of his general ideas concerning physiological changes based on prior stimulation were sound. But the further question of the role these neural units play in perception remains to be clarified. Recent evidence suggests that the presence of edge-detector units in the brain which respond to specific orientations of contour images on the retina is not necessary for the perception of contours in that orientation. Furthermore the research with animals on the origin of form perception suggests that perceptual organization is innately determined in various species and certainly does not require a long period of learning as Hebb implied. (See pp. 361–371.)

But a more fundamental limitation of this kind of explanation of perceptual organization, at least at the present stage of our knowledge, is that it tells us nothing about the basis of selection of one or another organization such as are discussed throughout this chapter. Thus we still want to know why similarity, proximity, closure, good continuation, and common fate determine grouping. (And it might be added, why perceived rather than retinally varied proximity and similarity are relevant here.) We still want to know why figure-ground organization occurs, giving shape to one side of a contour but not the other, and is determined by principles such as surroundedness, relative size, or symmetry. To explain how a contour is perceived is not to explain why that contour yields a particular shape depending upon which region adjacent to it becomes "figure" and why the shapes thereby achieved are so different from one another for one and the same contour. To repeat a point made earlier, even a figure not ordinarily considered to be ambiguous is, from this point of view, ambiguous in that its contour could be organized in such a way that the central region would appear as "ground" (a hole) and the surrounding region as figure. We still want to know what determines change of perceptual organization, and it is obvious that this would constitute a special problem for any theory of perception based on the reaction of the nervous system to the proximal stimulus alone since the change occurs with no change in the proximal stimulus. Also, it is obvious that factors that can affect organization and change of organization, such as intention, knowledge, and past experience are not accounted for by such a theory.

A cognitive decision explanation

The author would like to suggest a kind of explanation of perceptual organization that borrows heavily from the Gestalt approach but pictures the central mechanism in a rather different way. The essence of the Gestalt theory is that proximity, similarity, good continuation, and the like result in perceptual groupings because forces of attraction or equilibrium tendencies among the neural representations of the stimulus objects lead spontaneously to such outcomes. But suppose instead that the stimulus constellation, as yet unorganized, or perhaps only partially organized, is first registered centrally. At that point, the stimulus information is cognitively evaluated, albeit unconsciously and nonverbally, on the basis of the question "what entity or entities in the objective world are most likely producing this stimulus distribution?"

Thus, in the case of a pattern such as that shown in Fig. 6-19 or 6-30, the alternative organizations are rapidly "tried" and the decision is made that the center, surrounded region is figure rather than the surrounding region. This selection is therefore made and is based on the principle of surroundedness just as Rubin and the Gestaltists argued. But the selection or preference is viewed here as a decision rather than as based on a spontaneous brain process entailing the interplay of physical forces. The selection is a plausible solution to the problem of what is most probably present in the environment that would produce this pattern of stimulation. The selection might be based on past experience in which information about distance generally indicates that compact things lie in front of a background extending on all sides around it or the selection might be based on as yet unknown innate principles.*

The decision as to which region is to be considered figure leads to a process of description of the shape of the region so regarded. It is neither a conscious nor a verbal description. Thus, for example, in Fig. 6–18, if the black region is taken to be figure, then the shape enclosed by its borders is the one "described." That means that the central contour makes a sharp protruding figure. If, conversely, white is taken to be figure, then the shape "described" is one containing gentle curves and a gap. This is why the same contour can lead to different shapes depending upon the region to which it belongs, and this is why only one figure at a time can be perceived in such ambiguous patterns (although the switching can be very rapid). That black is favored may simply mean that a set has developed for this decision based on experience with written and printed material.

Grouping on the basis of either proximity or similarity can be viewed as a plausible inference as to what units in the environment probably belong with what other units. The "decision" makes use of information concerning objective distances of units from one another rather than merely the projected retinal-cortical distances between the images of such units. The fact that the entire stimulus arrangement is "taken into account" in the grouping achieved very much fits the notion that perceptual organization is more in the nature of an act of problem solving than of the automatic workings of specific laws of grouping. Thus, in order to "explain" the presence of the end dots in Fig. 6–17b a grouping may occur that runs counter to the law of proximity.

In the case of compact, homogeneously colored objects, such as the one pictured in Fig. 6–30, it is not necessary to invoke proximity and similarity of artificially created subparts to explain the resulting organi-

---

*A theory of perceptual organization similar to the one outlined here, but based exclusively on past experiences of various kinds, was developed by Brunswik.[29]

zation. Rather one can say that the existence of a compact region of the field of uniform color is registered centrally and that the decision is made that that region is a unified thing whose shape is given by its outer contour. Therefore, that shape is implicitly described. The perception of a line as a segregated thing in the environment is based on a similar process. The uniformity of color of this "thin" region of the field is detected and the decision is made that this thin region is a thing. In that event, its shape is "described" in itself rather than the shape of a region adjoining the line which, in the latter case, serves as contour.

Why is a decision reached that lines that are good continuations of one another belong together as one unit rather than lines that are not good continuations? First, it must be understood that, apart from the question of organization, we are capable of detecting good continuations from abrupt or bad continuations. How we do this is a separate problem, but it would seem that we can discriminate abrupt transitions from smooth transitions and that we can discriminate patterns which consistently carry out some principle of progression from those that do not. Given that ability, the question then is why there is a preference for the good continuation when several alternative modes of organization are possible. A possible answer is that it is a plausible inference for the "decision-maker" to draw that the good continuation represents what is present in the environment. Were that not true, the aesthetically striking good continuation would be pure coincidence. For example, to perceive Fig. 6-1a as an "M" and "W" spontaneously would mean that the beautifully good continuation of the sides of the figure—which, as noted, is certainly detected—is pure coincidence. Perhaps, then, good continuation works because the perceptual system rejects the possibility of such coincidence. Even the touching of the ends of two lines—without good continuation—is a coincidence we are apt to reject and that is why the spontaneous perception of Fig. 6-6 as an "M" and "W" still may not occur for all naive observers. But it is less of a coincidence than that shown in Fig. 6-1a. Separating the end points as in Fig. 6-1b eliminates this factor. (See the footnote on p. 255.)

This line of reasoning may also explain other effects of organization that have been subsumed under prägnanz. Thus, for example, the favoring of the symmetrical regions as figures in Fig. 6-22 may be based on the same principle of rejection of coincidence. That is, to "decide" that the asymmetrical regions are figures is to accept the coincidence that there happens to be a striking degree of symmetry between these figures about the vertical axes of these ground spaces. It thus seems far more plausible to the "decision-maker" that the symmetry resides in the *things* that are in the environment. In order to consider the two alternatives, however, it might be argued that they each must be "tried out" in turn.

If perceptual organization is indeed the outcome of a decision process, then the fact of perceptual change, of reversal of ambiguous figures, rather than being anomalous, becomes far more understandable. One has only to make the further assumption that the effort on the part of the perceptual system to solve the problem of what the proximal stimulus represents is continuous and does not come to a halt once a particular organization is selected. From the moment the stimulus is registered there is a constant process of trial and error, of oscillation from one possible "solution" to another.

Where each organization is equally "good" or "plausible" as in a truly ambiguous figure, it is then understandable why conscious reversals occur. Where, however, an organization is achieved that has a high probability of being the correct "solution," a stabilization occurs. That is why unambiguous figures rarely reverse and certain ambiguous figures cease reversing if they contain one organization that is recognized as familiar and meaningful. Thus it becomes difficult to perceive Fig. 6-4 as a set of black forms once the white regions are seen to represent a word. Stabilization means that one organization is now preferred, so that conscious reversal is not experienced, although the trial and error process may continue below the level of awareness.

The fact that drawings such as Fig. 6-3 and 6-4 spontaneously reverse in the first place, so that the familiar organizations occur despite the fact that they are not ambiguous in the structural sense of the term, seems to suggest a process of continuous trial and error on the part of the perceptual system. Otherwise, why doesn't the observer continue indefinitely to perceive these figures the way he does at the outset? If recognition can only *follow* perception and perception presupposes organization, then the organization of Fig. 6-3 as a white face must occur *before* recognition. (See the discussion in Chapter 8, pp. 342-343 on this argument). But why should this organization be achieved before it is recognized? The implication is that unconscious shifts in organization are occurring all the time for all figures but only become stabilized and enter conscious awareness when one organization becomes the more "plausible," either because recognition occurs or for structural reasons.

The kind of theory outlined here is, therefore, compatible with past-experience effects on reversal rather than incompatible, as is the satiation theory. It also can deal with effects on reversal of conscious intention mentioned earlier in this chapter. If reversal is generally based on an unconscious "decision" to try a new way of organizing the proximal stimulus, then it is plausible that a conscious decision can have a similar effect. That knowledge about the possibility of organizing a figure differently can affect reversal is also a fact that is compatible with this theory.

Summary

The phenomenal world consists of distinct, segregated entities of particular shapes but perception is not merely a copy of the retinal image. The retinal image is an ambiguous indicator of what is present in the world. Therefore, an explanation is required of why an organization is achieved that is generally, but by no means always, veridical. The Gestalt psychologists suggested various principles to account for the fact that units in the field are grouped with one another and that certain regions of the field become figure and others ground. They believed that a basic principle of such perceptual organization was the preference for the simplest (or prägnant) outcome and that underlying this preference was a tendency for forces in the brain to distribute themselves in such a way as to achieve equilibrium, to minimize potential energy.

When the retinal image is ambiguous in the sense that no one principle of organization is dominant (as with reversible figures), perceptual organization often changes from moment to moment. The currently preferred explanation is that a process of neural fatigue, satiation, or inhibition blocks the brain events that underlie one percept, thus making conditions favorable for the alternate percept to occur. Despite some fragmentary evidence in support of this explanation of reversal, there are many difficulties with it. Familiarity with the alternative organizations, knowledge of the ambiguity of the figure, and intention to reverse are all relevant factors with which this explanation does not deal.

The prägnanz hypothesis was criticized on the grounds that the concept covers several unrelated notions which should be considered separately, that not all the laws of grouping and organization are manifestations of prägnanz, that it is by no means always obvious what perceptual outcome is simplest, that form perception is generally veridical despite alleged forces in the brain "striving" toward equilibrium, that the perceptual outcome predicted on the basis of prägnanz is often the same outcome predictable on the basis of past experience, and, finally, that verification of this law does not necessarily imply that the Gestalt model of brain events is correct.

A reasonable good case can be made out for believing that, apart from prägnanz, the Gestalt principles of organization can account for both veridical perceptual organization in daily life *and* instances of nonveridical perception such as in the case of camouflage. Difficulties with this approach are the necessity of first reducing objects to artificial units, the fact that information is sometimes available (such as cues to depth) that renders the stimulus less ambiguous than it has been thought to be, the fact that at present there is no good explanation available that unifies all the principles of organization and makes them intelligible, and the fact that the laws of grouping refer to the physical characteristics of the proximal stimulus (such as the proximity of one unit to another) whereas experiment has shown that in certain cases it is the perceived characteristics that are relevant.

An alternative approach derives from recent discoveries that indicate that units of the visual nervous system respond if and only if certain contours stimulate particular regions of the retina. Therefore, a mechanism can be said to exist that detects various features of the proximal stimulus. That being the case, organization can be said to be innately built into the nervous system. However, it is questionable if such mechanisms, as far as they are now understood, can do justice to the perceptual organization of the field of objects as they are typically encountered in daily life or to most of the phenomena described in this chapter, where selective principles of preference for one organization over another are generally operating.

By way of speculating, the author suggested that perceptual organization may be the result of a rapid-fire, nonconscious, process of problem-solving. The proximal stimulus is analyzed by the perceptual system in terms of the question "What entities in the world does this array most probably represent?" The Gestalt laws are applicable because it is "plausible" that units that are similar belong together or that a region that is surrounded is more likely to be a "thing" in the world, or figure, than a region that surrounds. Good continuations, symmetrical regions, and the like are perceived because the perceptual system rejects the presence of such arrangements in the retinal image as mere coincidence. Since, according to this view, perceptual organization results from a "decision," reversals of ambiguous figures can be understood if one assumes that the process of decision is a continuous one, entailing constant trial and error or oscillation from one possibility to another.

References

1. Köhler, W. *Gestalt Psychology.* Liveright Publishing Corp., 1947, p. 162.
2. Beck, J. Perceptual grouping produced by line figures. *Perception & Psychophysics*, 1967, 2, 491–495; R. R. Olson and F. Attneave. What variables produce similarity grouping? *American Journal of Psychology*, 1970, 83, 1–21.

3. Wertheimer, M. Untersuchungen zur Lehre von der Gestalt, II. *Psychologische Forschung*, 1923, 4, 301–350. See a condensed translation in W. Ellis. *A Source Book of Gestalt Psychology*, Selection 5. Humanities Press, Inc., 1950; also see the condensed translation in D. C. Beardslee and M. Wertheimer. *Readings in Perception*, Selection 8. Van Nostrand Reinhold Company, 1958.

4. Koffka, K. *Principles of Gestalt Psychology.* Harcourt Brace Jovanovich, 1935.

5. Schumann, F. Beiträge zur Analyse der Gesichtswahrnehmungen, I-IV. *Zeitschrift für Psychologie*, 1900, 1902, 1904, 23, 24, 30, 36; M. J. Zigler. An experimental study of visual form. *American Journal of Psychology*, 1920, 31, 273–300; E. Rubin. Die Psychophysik der Geradheit. *Zeitschrift für Psychologie*, 1922, 90, 67ff.

6. Johannson, G. *Configurations in Event Perception.* Almkvist and Wiksell, 1950.

7. Rubin E. *Visuell Wahrgenommene Figuren.* Glydendalske, 1921.

8. Köhler, W. *Dynamics in Psychology.* Liveright Publishing Corp., 1940; W. Köhler and H. Wallach. Figural aftereffects, an investigation of visual processes. *Proceedings of the American Philosophical Society*, 1944, 88, 269–357.

9. Hochberg, J. Figure-ground reversal as a function of visual satiation. *Journal of Experimental Psychology*, 1950, 40, 682–686; V. R. Carlson. Satiation in a reversible figure. *Journal of Experimental Psychology*, 1953, 45, 442–448.

10. Köhler, op. cit. 1940, pp 67–82; K. T. Brown. Rate of apparent change in a dynamic ambiguous figure as a function of observation-time. *American Journal of Psychology*, 1955, 68, 358–371; L. Cohen. Rate of apparent change of a Necker cube as a function of prior stimulation. *American Journal of Psychology*, 1959, 72, 327–344.

11. Spitz, H. H. and R. S. Lipman. Some factors affecting Necker cube reversal rate. *Perceptual and Motor Skills*, 1962, 15, 611–625; P. E. Thetford. Influence of massing and spacing on Necker cube reversals. *Perceptual and Motor Skills*, 1963, 16, 215–222; J. Orbach, D. Ehrlich and H. A. Heath. Reversibility of the Necker cube: I. An examination of the concept of "satiation" of orientation. *Perceptual and Motor Skills*, 1963, 17, 439–458; J. Orbach, D. Erlich, and E. Vainstein. Reversibility of the Necker cube: III. Effects of interpolation on reversal rate of the cube presented repetitively. *Perceptual and Motor Skills*, 1963, 17, 571–582.

12. Spitz and Lipman, op. cit; Cohen, op. cit.
13. See Orbach, Ehrlich, and Heath, op. cit. and Orbach, Ehrlich and Vainstein, op. cit.
14. Woodworth, R. S. *Experimental Psychology.* Holt, Rinehart & Winston, Inc., 1938, pp 648–649; C. H. Pheiffer, S. B. Eure, and C. B. Hamilton. Reversible figures and eye-movements. *American Journal of Psychology*, 1956, 69, 452–455.
15. Pelton, L. H. and C. M. Solley. Acceleration of reversals of a Necker cube. *American Journal of Psychology*, 1968, 81, 585–588.
16. An attempt to explain reversal in terms of learning processes and strategies has been made by Ammons and his co-workers. See, for example, R. B. Ammons, P. Ulrich, and C. H. Ammons. Voluntary control of perception of depth in a two-dimensional drawing. *Proceedings of the Montana Academy of Sciences*, 1959, 19, 160–168.
17. Hochberg, J. and E. McAlister. A quantitative approach to figural "goodness." *Journal of Experimental Psychology*, 1953, 46, 361–364; J. Hochberg and V. Brooks. The psychophysics of form: reversible perspective drawings of spatial objects. *American Journal of Psychology*, 1960, 73, 337–354.
18. Attneave, F. Some informational aspects of visual perception. *Psychological Review*, 1954, 61, 183–193.
19. Wulf, F. Tendencies in figural variation. Translated and condensed as Selection 10 in W. Ellis. *A Source Book of Gestalt Psychology.* Humanities Press, Inc., 1950.
20. Hebb, D. O. and E. N. Foord. Errors of visual recognition and the nature of the trace. *Journal of Experimental Psychology*, 1945, 35, 335–348; I. Rock and P. Engelstein. A study of memory for visual form. *American Journal of Psychology*, 1959, 72, 221–229. But see E. Goldmeier. *The Fate of the Trace.* Manuscript in preparation.
21. The argument outlined here is stated in more detail in a paper by C. B. Zuckerman and I. Rock. A reappraisal of the roles of past experience and innate organizing processes in visual perception. *Psychological Bulletin*, 1957, 54, 269–296.
22. Rock, I. and L. Brosgole. Grouping based on phenomenal proximity. *Journal of Experimental Psychology*, 1964, 67, 531–538. See also H. H. Corbin. The perception of grouping and apparent movement in visual depth. *Archives of Psychology*, 1942, No. 273.
23. Olson and Attneave, Reference 2.
24. Hartline, H. K. The receptive fields of optic neural fibers. *American Journal of Physiology*, 1940, 130, 690–699. Barlow, H. B.

Summation and inhibition in the frog's retina. *Journal of Physiology*, 1953, **119**, 69–88.

25. Lettvin, J. Y., H. R. Maturana, W. S. McCulloch and W. H. Pitts. What the frog's eye tells the frog's brain. *Proceedings of the Institute of Radio Engineering*, 1959, 47, 1940–1951; H. B. Barlow, R. M. Hill, and W. R. Levick. Retinal ganglion cells responding selectively to direction and speed of image motion in the rabbit. *Journal of Physiology*, 1964, **173**, 377–407.

26. Hubel, D. H. The visual cortex of the brain. *Scientific American*, 1963, **209** (11); See also D. H. Hubel and T. N. Wiesel. Receptive fields, binocular interaction and functional architecture in the cat's visual cortex. *Journal of Physiology*, 1962, **160**, 106–154; Receptive fields and functional architecture of monkey striate cortex. *Journal of Physiology*, 1968, **195**, 215–243.

27. Lindsay, P. H. and D. A. Norman. *Human Information Processing*. Academic Press, Inc., 1972, Chap. 2.

28. Hebb, D. O. *The Organization of Behavior*. John Wiley & Sons, Inc., 1949.

29. Brunswik, E. and J. Kamiya. Ecological cue-validity of "proximity" and of other Gestalt factors. *American Journal of Psychology*, 1953, **66**, 20–32.

chapter 7

THE PERCEPTION OF
FORM II: SPECIFIC SHAPE

At the beginning of the previous chapter it was pointed out that an explanation of perceived shape that relies exclusively on the shape of the retinal image is not adequate. The stimulus array first must be organized. However, even when the appropriate organization is assumed, we are far from an adequate statement of the relevant stimulus conditions and central processes underlying the experience of specific shape. By specific shape we mean the shape that makes one figure appear similar to or different from other figures. Thus, for example, a circle and a triangle appear different but a circle and an ellipse appear similar. Reference to perceptual organization cannot explain the differences among perceived shapes since the identical principles of grouping may account for the perception of a circle or a triangle as a distinct unit.

It is obvious that to extract information about shape from the retinal image of an object, the perceptual system must focus on the *geometrical relationships* among the parts of the image of the figure. It has long been known that recognition of a form is not impaired when changes of various kinds are made—a figure can be presented in various colors, sizes, retinal positions, and the like and yet be experienced as the same form. This fact is called transposition and it is true for other perceptual modalities as well. An auditory form—a melody—can be transposed to a different key and be heard as the same melody. That even a novel figure looks the same regardless of size is clear from Fig. 7-1, and if the reader fixates any point on either contour or the dot in the middle he will note that either figure looks about the same regardless of its retinal location, that is, when seen "out of the corner of his eyes" (peripherally) or when seen centrally. Therefore, the impression of a particular shape does not depend upon the discharging of a specific group of neurons.

Figure 7-1

In order for a transposed melody to be recognized it is necessary to assume that the nervous system detects primarily the intervals between notes and the rhythmical relationships between notes. The experience of a melody cannot be based on the sum total of the specific tone sensations that make it up, because when the melody is transposed, none of these components is the same. In the same way, visual form must be based not on the sum of specific component lines or contours that constitute it but on the manner in which these components are related. For example, in a square, the opposite sides are parallel, the sides are all equal, and the angles are all right angles. In a triangle, there are three sides, the sides converge toward each other, and so on. These geometrical relationships remain unchanged with transposition.

The capacity to extract information about figural relationships is not restricted to human beings. Many species of animals react to forms in the same way humans do. Thus, for example, if a rat is first trained to go to a triangle instead of a cross, it will continue to do so even when smaller or larger figures are substituted for the original ones; or if line figures are substituted for the original solid figures. (Fig. 7-2).[1] Infant monkeys perceive in much the same way.[2]

Training figures

Test figures

Figure 7-2

How is information obtained about these geometrical relationships? Such relationships reduce to the perception of the relative locations of points that constitute a figure. In Chapter 4 it was concluded that the awareness of the location of points relative to one another (or field location) is given by the relative location of their corresponding retinal images. Therefore, one might say that when several points are seen, their perceived locations relative to one another define a specific shape (always assuming that the appropriate organization is achieved so that the points in question are grouped together as one entity).

The idea that perception of form is synonymous with the perception of the location of the points that constitute the form relative to one another was current among theorists of the last century and earlier, but little is heard about it today. Perhaps the main reason for this change is that the Gestalt psychologists not only stressed the necessity of organization but they were critical of elementarism, the belief that any percept can be explained as the sum of the perceptions of its parts. Rather, they stressed the fact that forms have whole-qualities or Gestalt-qualities, i.e., phenomenal qualities relevant to the whole configuration. A phenomenal square clearly is not merely the sum of four straight lines or four right angles.* Although this is true, perceived form does depend upon the set of relative locations of the parts of the form, or, to state it more carefully, the entire set of spatial relationships of the parts of a figure to one another. The reality of a phenomenal whole quality does not preclude analysis.

But whatever the reason, the fact is that little is said today about phenomenal location in relation to the problem of form perception. One does, however, find a good deal of emphasis on the perception of contour, so much so that one has the impression that contemporary psychologists have assumed that contour perception and form percep-

---

*Credit for first emphasizing the phenomenal reality of whole qualities in perception and for pointing out that such qualities, as, for example, a melody, cannot be explained as the sum of all the perceived parts goes to von Ehrenfels.[3] In the early Gestalt literature, therefore, one finds reference to "Ehrenfels qualities." This concept should not be confused with the notion of expressive or physiognomic qualities that it is said perceived forms often have. By an expressive quality is meant the experience of an object or event as expressing feeling or emotion. Thus a given visual figure or melody may be immediately experienced as "sad" or "ominous" or "gay." Little is known about the basis of these phenomenal properties, but they are by no means restricted to forms. Thus, for example, a color is experienced as "warm" or a sound as "frightening."

tion are synonymous.* This emphasis mistakes the building blocks of form for the building itself. Contours are simply markers of locations. Normally, of course, the locations of the points constituting a figure are given by contours, but it is possible to indicate these locations without contours. Figures consisting only of dots certainly lead to an impression of the forms that they would represent if the dots were connected (as in Fig. 7–3).

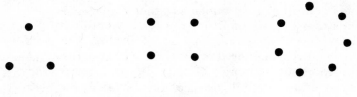

Figure 7–3

Even more to the point is the phenomenon of subjective contour. Under certain conditions, we perceive contours where none exist physically. Fig. 7–4 shows several examples (a similar effect can be noted along the tops and bottoms of the letters in the word illustrated in Fig. 6–4). The exact conditions that lead to subjective contour and the mechanism underlying it are still under investigation.[7] However, it seems likely that it results from a process of imagining a contour to be present because the stimulus array can be most plausibly interpreted as a surface of a given shape lying over certain components of the array. This phenomenon illustrates that perceived forms should not be thought of as deriving from a set of contours since here the contour is not only absent as a stimulus but it only becomes a psychological reality at the moment the form as a whole is imagined. Other evidence along this line is given in the following sections.

Visual Form Perception Without a Retinal Image

If phenomenal form reduces to the perception of a set of relative locations, it should be possible to induce an experience of a form solely

---

*Thus the work of Hebb[4] on cell assemblies (see footnote, p. 285), of Hubel and Wiesel[5] on orientation-specific detectors (see p. 284 and pp. 315ff of this chapter), and of Köhler and Wallach[6] on figural aftereffects (see pp. 441ff) illustrates the emphasis on theories largely concerning the perception of contours.

Figure 7-4

on the basis of generating a set of such perceived locations. In Chapter 4 it was explained that the position of the eyes is one determinant of perceived location (or direction). A point whose image falls on a given location on the retina—for example the fovea—will be experienced in varying directions in relation to the observer (radial direction) depending on where the eyes are directed. Suppose an observer were to track a moving point with his eyes as the point described a path of a given shape. In that case there would be no image of the path's shape extended over the retina because only the same small region of the fovea would be stimulated by the point. Yet information about eye position would be available. That is, the relative locations of the moving point would presumably be experienced on the basis of the changing position of the eyes. Perhaps this information would also produce an impression of shape.

To investigate this question an experiment was performed in which a narrow slit in an opaque rectangle was moved back and forth in front of a luminous line drawing as shown in Fig. 7-5.[8] By using a luminous figure in a dark room, only a small spot of light stimulated the eye at

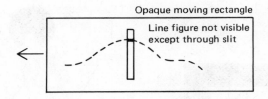

Figure 7-5

any one moment, and thus this procedure is equivalent to one in which a point of light traces out a pattern. The observer sees a small "spot" that appears to be moving. In one condition, the observer tracked the luminous spot.* In a second condition, the observer fixated a small luminous mark that remained stationary while the slit revealed the "moving" spot going back and forth on both sides of the stationary spot. In this condition, therefore, the moving spot traces out an extended image of the figure over the retina. As a test of what the observers perceived, they were required to select the correct figure from among similar alternatives on a recognition chart. Correct recognition was frequent in *both* conditions but it was no more frequent in the second condition, where the spot traced out a retinal image, than in the first condition where it did not.

The main point then has been established, namely, that the crucial information for form perception is relative location and that this information can be obtained without an extended retinal image. However, some further considerations about the perception of form under these conditions are worth discussing. It can be argued that this experiment only proves that it is possible to have an idea about the *path* traversed by a moving spot under the conditions employed. The observer does not perceive a *figure* as he does when viewing a continuous line drawing under normal conditions. This is true. But it was found that with one change in the procedure, the impression the observer gets *is* generally that of an extended figure rather than of a moving point. The change consists of performing the experiment with lights on. Under these conditions, of course, the observer sees the opaque surface with the slit in it moving back and forth and he sees the line element revealed through the slit moving up and down within the slit.

This stimulus situation is ambiguous, because there are different ways in which it can be perceived. The dark element can be seen as moving up and down the slit as the slit moves back and forth, and some observers do see it this way. Therefore, the "selection" of the percept of a stationary line being uncovered by a slit is an

---

*Recordings of eye movements were taken to substantiate that the observer actually did track the spot.

achievement of perceptual organization. Why this latter perception is favored under these conditions is not known. It might be considered to be an outcome favored by simplicity because it is simpler than the perception of an element moving up and down within a slit moving sideways. Some weight would seem to be given to this interpretation by the fact that it makes a difference whether the region of the figure seen through the slit does or does not change its slope.* If it changes its slope, the figure-percept organization is much more likely to occur. Since an element moving up and down while simultaneously tilting clockwise and counterclockwise within a slit moving sideways is even more complex, the increased favoring of the line figure organization can be said to be based on its relative simplicity.

In a further experiment, however, it was demonstrated that the importance of change of slope is not so much that its presence is a factor in eliciting the perception of a line figure as it is that its absence interferes with this perception. When the slit is made so narrow that the absence of slope change can no longer be detected, a line figure is perceived *more* often than when the slit is the normal width; if, however, the same change in slit width is made when slope change is present, then there is no effect on what is perceived. This finding suggests that slope change does not enter in as a factor affecting simplicity but rather as a factor affecting the "intelligent solution" to the problem posed by this unusual stimulus situation. A figure successively exposed through a slit *must* be seen to change its slope from moment to moment if the slit is wide enough to reveal such change. Therefore, if the slope is seen not to change, this information is incompatible with the "solution" of a line figure revealed by a moving slit.[9]

We must now return to the question of why presenting the figure with the room lights on generally leads to the perception of a figure, whereas uncovering a luminous drawing in the dark never does. The investigators believe that stimulus information that an aperture in an opaque surface is uncovering a figure is crucial. In the dark, there is no reason for such an impression because nothing is visible but an isolated spot of light. With the room lights on, however, the observer sees the

---

*In order to reveal the figure in such a way that the element visible through the slit does *not* change its slope, an entirely different method of presentation was devised in which there is no line figure behind the opaque surface. Instead, an impression of a line figure is *simulated* by moving up and down a small dark element that completely fills the slit. This is achieved by means of a wire the bottom of which rides on a cutout cam of the figure (not visible to the observer) and the top of which contains the element (see Fig. 7-6). As the opaque surface containing the slit moves sideways, the element moves up and down. Except for the fact that the slope of the element does not change, the stimulus impinging on the retina is the same under these simulated conditions as under the condition described in Fig. 7-5. In a variation of this method it is also possible to simulate a line figure *with* change of slope. This simulated presentation also leads to a vivid impression of a line figure being uncovered under certain conditions (see text).

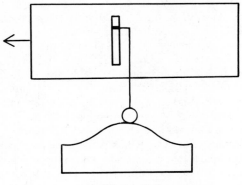

Figure 7-6

element completely filling the slit as the slit moves sideways and he sees that an opaque surface surrounds the slit. It thus becomes a plausible hypothesis, unconscious to be sure, that a line figure is being uncovered.

In summary, this research demonstrates that an experience similar to form perception can occur under conditions where there is no extended image of the form on the retina. There is, however, visual information about the locations of the parts of the figure relative to one another as well as other kinds of information that support the "hypothesis" that a line figure is actually present in the environment and that parts of it are being successively revealed.

Shape Constancy Revisited

These findings contradict the thesis that form perception is based on a retinal image of the shape. A retinal image is not a *necessary* condition. There are several other reasons for rejecting that formulation, all of which tend to show that the retinal image is far from being a *sufficient* basis of form perception. One such reason is that the retinal image of a figure changes radically as the figure is viewed from different vantage points and yet, within certain limits, the perceived shape remains the same (see p. 69). Shape constancy implies that perceived shape is not a direct function of the shape of the retinal image but rather is a function of that image in conjunction with information about the slant of the object in question.

Therefore, if the relative location of the parts of a figure with respect to one another must be apprehended before the shape of the figure can be correctly perceived, changes in slant introduce a further complication. Consider a rectangle at a slant that projects a trapezoidal retinal image. If only the relative locations within that *image* were to be analyzed we would perceive a trapezoid. Therefore, after the mechanism that yields constancy has done its work, taking into account the slant of the figure, the relative locations within the corrected percept must be analyzed if the true shape is to be veridically perceived. For example, the end points of the small side of the trapezoidal image (*b* in Fig. 7–7) must be "described" as being as far apart from each other as the end points of the large side of the image (*a*). This can only be expected to occur if the information is available that the smaller side is farther away than the larger side; if farther away—by just the right amount—it will be perceived as a line the same size as that of the "larger" side.

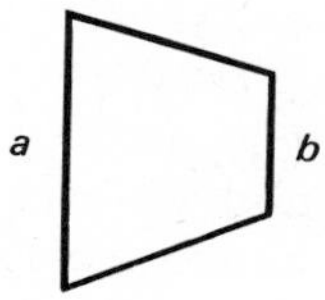

Figure 7–7

Orientation

Fig. 7–8 undoubtedly will seem unfamiliar to most people. However, if the page is rotated 90 degrees clockwise, the figure may be recognized as an outline map of the continent of Africa. This simple example demonstrates that orientation is an important aspect of specific shape and, therefore, that change of orientation results in a change of such shape. Consequently, even very familiar things may be difficult to recognize if disoriented, such as pictures of human faces or printed words when seen upside down. Handwriting is virtually impossible to recognize in this orientation.

This fact may seem to contradict certain earlier conclusions. Based on the transposability of size and position, it was concluded that what matters for form perception is the set of internal spatial relations that constitute a figure, the position of the parts relative *to one another.* If so, a change of orientation should have little effect on perceived

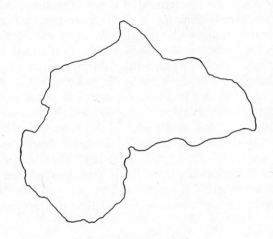

Figure 7-8

shape—that is, forms should also be transposable in orientation—since the *internal* spatial relationships are not altered when the orientation of the figure is changed. But is it true that the orientation of the retinal image of a figure cannot be changed without altering the way the figure looks? When we disorient a figure, several things happen at once. The figure's retinal image changes its orientation and, in addition, the figure changes its orientation in relation to the up and down of the environment. In Fig. 7-8, a region different from the usual one is now at the top of the page.

A simple experiment provides an answer to the question. If the reader holds the book vertically so that the figure of Africa in Fig. 7-8 is right side up and then tilts his head 90 degrees clockwise, he will observe that there is essentially no change in the appearance of the figure; it continues to look like Africa. Yet the retinal image has been transformed and in fact is in the position indicated in Fig. 7-8. Therefore, changing the orientation of the image alone—without changing the orientation of the figure in the environment—apparently does *not* affect shape, at least for a figure such as the one used. This means that forms *are* transposable in orientation.

Another way of separating the two factors—orientation of the retinal image and orientation of the figure in the environment—is to tilt both the figure and the observer by the same amount. This could be achieved if the reader examines Fig. 7-8 with his head tilted 90 degrees counterclockwise with the book remaining upright. Now the retinal image of Africa is in its customary orientation, but the figure is nevertheless tilted with respect to the vertical axis in the environment. There is, however, one serious difficulty with this simple experiment, namely, that the reader knows the figure is tilted. As a result he can reorganize his perception on the basis of his knowledge of the true top and bottom of the African continent. Therefore, the reader is not perceiving as top of this figure that part of it that is uppermost on the page but rather that part he "knows" to be top. In order to carry out this experiment properly, naive observers must be required to view nonfamiliar or novel figures.[10]

In one such experiment, the observer is first shown a series of figures similar to the one in Fig. 7-9a in a training series. The observer himself is upright. Following this, a test series is shown containing the figures already seen in training plus some new figures. The observer is to say whether or not any of the test figures had been seen in the training series. In the test, however, the observer is tilted. As shown in the illustration in Fig. 7-9b, the observer tilts his head 90 degrees. Each training figure is shown twice at different points in the test series, once in the same orientation on the screen it had in training (change of retinal orientation alone) and once when it is tilted 90 degrees, the same way the observer's head is tilted (change of orientation in the environment alone). Since no mention is made of the possibility of tilting the figures, it is assumed that the observer will consider the top of any figure to lie in the uppermost direction on the screen.

The result is that recognition is quite good for the upright test figures, which confirms what was said earlier, that disorientation of the

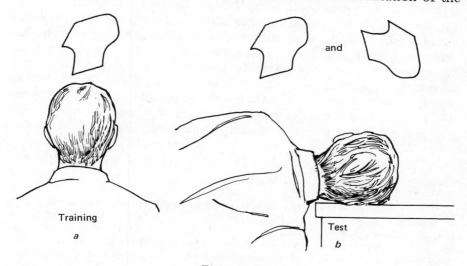

Figure 7-9

retinal image alone generally does *not* lead to a change in the way a figure appears. On the other hand, there is a marked decline in the recognition of the test figures that are tilted 90 degrees in comparison to the recognition of untilted figures, despite the fact that the retinal image is in the same orientation in the test as in training.

This result and others along the same lines suggest that what matters most about orientation is assigning the directions top, bottom, left, and right to a figure. Ordinarily, we assign these directions unconsciously on the basis of which region of the figure is at the top in the environment. But we can also assign these directions differently if instructed to do so or if a part is a clue as to how the entire figure is actually oriented—for example, the features in an inverted face immediately lead us to recognize it as a face and thus to assign "top" to the hair and "bottom" to the chin. This assignment of directions is a crucial aspect of form perception, at least in older children and adults.* With a different assignment of directions, a novel figure can look as different or more different from the way it looked before as two figures that are, geometrically speaking, totally different forms.

Why is this the case? The answer that suggests itself is that from the standpoint of *description*, different orientations of a given geometrical pattern are entirely different. Since we are not aware of engaging in such a process of description we must assume that it occurs unconsciously and is not verbal in nature. Thus, for example, Fig. 7–10*a* looks like, and would be "described" as, an asymmetrical irregular quadrilateral resting on a side whereas Fig. 7–10*b* appears as, and would be "described" as, a symmetrical, diamond-like figure standing on one end. Fig. 7–11*a*, a square, would be "described" as having opposite sides that are parallel and equal, four right angles, and as resting in stable equilibrium on a side. Fig. 7–11*b*, a diamond, on the other hand, might be "described" as having opposite sides that are equal and parallel, but not necessarily as having right angles. That an angle is exactly 90 degrees is only apparent when its sides are horizontal and vertical.[11] Another difference is that the diamond rests unstably on a point. Finally, as far as symmetry about the vertical axis is concerned, the opposite sides of

*Very young children seem indifferent to orientation to judge by their tendency to identify pictures of objects and letters in any orientation with no effort to orient the pictures correctly. But laboratory evidence on this question by and large has not confirmed this observation. Rather it has established that for young children, as for adults, upright figures are recognized more frequently than disoriented figures.

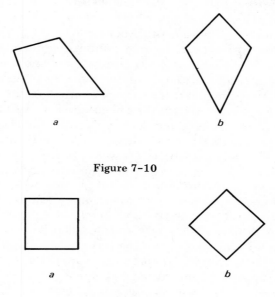

a   b

Figure 7-10

a   b

Figure 7-11

the square are seen to be symmetrical, whereas for the diamond it is the adjacent sides and opposite angles that appear symmetrical.*

Therefore, the analysis that underlies our experience of specific shape entails more than just the apprehension of the location of its constituent points relative to one another. It includes reference to the location of the parts of the figure relative to up-down, left-right coordinates.

One problem about orientation remains. The evidence cited in the preceding pages suggests that the orientation of the retinal image of a figure *per se* has no effect on the way it appears. Yet it is perfectly obvious that it is difficult to identify printed or written words or pictures of faces if these figures remain upright and are viewed with the head inverted. Since presumably the observer is well aware that the figures are upright, there is no change in the assignment of directions and yet recognition is very much impaired. Apparently, with complex material of this kind, there is a new factor to consider.

*The fact that a square looks different when tilted 45 degrees into its "diamond" orientation was first pointed out by the great physicist and philosopher Ernst Mach.[12]

The explanation may be as follows. When simple figures, such as those already considered, are viewed with the head tilted, they are easily recognized because there is no change in their assigned directions. But underlying this outcome is a process of psychological correction, analogous to what occurs in perceptual constancy. On a primitive level of processing, the perceptual system begins with the orientation of the retinal image. There is an egocentric sense of up and down and left and right that is correlated with orientation in the retinal image (see pp. 458ff). Therefore, the first thing to happen when an upright figure such as that of Africa is viewed with the head tilted is that the region lowermost on the retina is perceived as egocentrically uppermost (keeping in mind the inversion of the retinal image), the region uppermost on the retina is perceived as egocentrically lowermost, and correspondingly with respect to the left and right regions of the image and the right and left egocentric "sides" of the figure. If the process were to end here, the figure would not be recognized because there would be a misassignment of directions. However, almost immediately, the correction process begins. Information is available (from the felt position of the head and from visual cues) that the top of the figure is elsewhere. So we correct the retinally based percept accordingly, suppressing the initial assignment of directions and substituting new ones.

If the figure is very complex, as are words, the correction required overtaxes the capacity of the system. We may correct one or two letters at a time, but the other uncorrected ones look strange. The uncorrected letters are perceived on the basis of the assignment of directions arising from the orientation of the retinal image. As a result, many letters are unidentified and others are misidentified, because many letters become different letters when inverted (*b* and *q*, *d* and *p*, *u* and *n*).

Other Psychological Factors in Form Perception

The effect of orientation on perceived shape demonstrates that we cannot understand form perception merely on the basis of the retinal image, even if we think about the image in terms of its geometrical *relationships*. The retinal and cortical "picture" is psychologically elaborated by the assignment of directions to it and by the "description" of it in terms of these assigned directions. If the perception of form does entail a process somewhat like analysis or description, then it is possible that certain features of a figure are emphasized more than others or that certain features characterize a figure in a particular way. In order to get at this question, one investigator introduced certain changes in a figure and then asked observers to indicate how similar the altered figure was to the original.[11] If the features that were altered were not central to the phenomenal character of the figure, the new figure ought to look very much like the original; whereas if the features were central, the new figure ought to look quite different.

The technique used was to present one figure, the standard, and two altered comparison figures. The observer selected that comparison figure that appeared more similar to the standard. An example is shown in Fig. 7-12: *a* is the standard and *b* and *c* are the comparison figures. As the reader will agree, *c* is more similar to *a* than is *b*, and nine observers out of ten selected it as such. The outer contour is the same in *a*, *b*, and *c* so that the only difference is in the placement of the horizontal lines. In *c* the horizontal lines are both moved down but the separation between them is the same as in *a*; in *b*, the bottom line is moved down in relation to the upper one. From the standpoint of extent of change, considered quantitatively, *b* and *c* are about equal. From the standpoint of internal figural relationships, again, the changes in *b* and *c* are about equal.

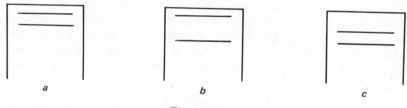

Figure 7-12

Clearly, therefore, some other principle is needed to explain the preference. The investigator believed that it was a matter of perceptual grouping. In *a* the two lines are grouped with one another and apart from the upper contour. Comparison figure *c* preserves that grouping whereas *b* destroys it. If this reasoning is correct, it suggests that in perceiving *a*, the separation between the two internal lines was, psychologically speaking, more important than was the exact separation of both lines from the upper contour. This experiment demonstrates that perceptual organization enters into and characterizes phenomenal shape even after the basic units have been formed.

In Fig. 7-13, virtually all observers selected *b* as being more similar to *a* than *c*. This is surprising because *c* is actually a complete transposition in size of *a*. In *b*, the size of the dots and the spacing between

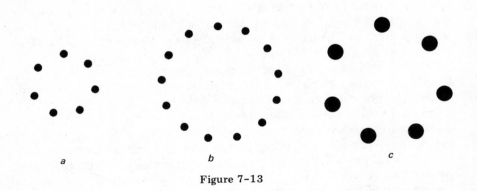

Figure 7–13

them are *not* transposed. Therefore, *b* introduces *changes* of certain figural relationships whereas *c* does not. What seems to be happening here is this: One can think of the *form* of a configuration and one can think of the *material* that makes it up. In this case, the form of *a* is a circle and the material consists of dots. In Fig. 7–12 the material consists of thin lines. Apparently in a figure such as Fig. 7–13*a*, we do *not* apprehend the material *per se* as entering into the form relations. Therefore, if we enlarge the figure, as in *b*, it is best to keep the material unchanged. If we change the material, then the observer is struck by this change and this leads to an overall impression of difference. However, if the figure is small, so that the size of the material is appreciable in relation to the size of the figure, then the material ceases to be mere material. It becomes part of the form. Thus, Fig. 7–14*c* is more similar to *a* than *b* for most observers.

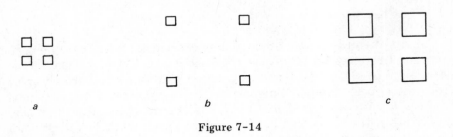

Figure 7–14

Symmetry is a particularly important feature of form. If one figure is symmetrical and another is constructed in such a way as to be objectively similar to the first but lacking in symmetry, then the two will probably look quite different. But it turns out that for symmetry to emerge psychologically, it must be symmetry about a vertical axis. This was demonstrated in an experiment illustrated in Fig. 7–15. Fig.

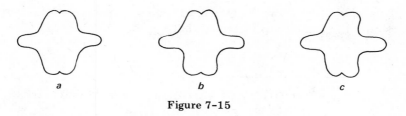

Figure 7-15

7-15*a* is symmetrical about both vertical and horizontal axes; Fig. 7-15*b* is symmetrical only about the vertical axis; and Fig. 7-15*c* is symmetrical only about the horizontal axis. The overwhelming majority of observers chose *b* as more similar to *a* than *c* was to *a*. The experiment can be repeated by turning the page 90 degrees. Now—as the reader will appreciate—*c* appears more similar to *a*. Since *b* and *c* entail the same degree of change, the outcome cannot be understood either in terms of degree of change quantitatively considered, or degree of change of figural relations. That the powerful effect of vertical symmetry on the appearance of a figure is of a psychological nature is brought out by a subsequent study in which it was shown that *b* in Fig. 7-15 will look more like *a* than *c* even if the observer's head is tilted 45 degrees or 90 degrees in viewing the three figures.[13] Therefore, it is symmetry about the perceived vertical direction in the environment that matters, rather than symmetry about the vertical retinal-cortical axis.

One final example. In Fig. 7-16, *b* looks quite different from *a*; however *d* looks fairly similar to *c*. Yet *c* is *a* turned 45 degrees and *d* is *b* turned 45 degrees. Therefore, physically speaking, *c* and *d* are as similar to (or different from) one another as are *a* and *b*. The reason *b* looks different from *a* is that we immediately detect that its angles are not right angles, because the sides in *a* and *b* are at or close to the horizontal and vertical directions. Since this is not true for *c* and *d*, we fail to be struck by the difference in angles and, therefore, the two figures do not look particularly different.

Both this last example and the previous one on symmetry can be said to illustrate prägnanz at least in one sense of that term as discussed in Chapter 6 (pp. 00). The vertical and horizontal directions are unique

Figure 7-16

or distinctive. Therefore, how a figure relates to these axes is very important in the overall impression of that figure.

The Perception of Complex Forms and the Role of Attention

In order to explain why disoriented figures look different it has been suggested here that form perception is based upon a process very much like description in which the orientation of the figure affects how it is "described." But since we are not aware of describing a figure, since form perception seems to be more or less immediate, and since it can safely be assumed that infants and animals perceive form, such a process of description would have to be rapid-fire, unconscious, and nonverbal. Some of the findings just reported on the effect of symmetry or unique orientations of parts of figures can also be understood if we assume that a figure is unconsciously described, and that certain features very much affect how a figure is described. Transposition of form lends itself to this kind of explanation. What remains the same about a figure that is enlarged or reduced in size is the way the perceptual system would describe the shape based upon the relative location of its parts.

This way of looking at form perception implies that the process is not merely one of automatic registration of the image as occurs in photography. Rather, operations of a cognitive nature, that is, somewhat analogous to thought processes, must be performed upon the registered stimulus. If that is true, it suggests that there may be certain limitations in what can be perceived in any given brief encounter. Suppose a form is very complex, as, for example, as shown in Fig. 7-17. This figure is complex because of the many minor fluctuations in the curvature of its sides. Are all these nuances perceived?

We are, of course, capable of perceiving these nuances simply by directing our attention to each in turn, but the question of interest here is what typically happens when a person looks at such a figure the first

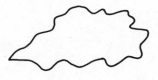

Figure 7-17

time without any special set to attend to any one region. An experiment to answer this question has been done.[14] The subject was told to look at the figure for a few seconds. He was then immediately given Fig. 7-18 as a recognition test and was asked to select the correct one.

Figure 7-18

Performance was no better than chance. As the reader can see, the two figures are essentially alike in overall shape, differing only with respect to the nuances of the contour in one region. Apparently these nuances did not enter into the spontaneous "description" of the figure and, therefore, memories of them were not established. As a result, there was no basis for discriminating between the two alternatives on the test. Needless to say, if a subject is shown only the small section of contour (Fig. 7-19) he has no difficulty in selecting the correct one in a recognition test (Fig. 7-20). What had been an inessential detail as part of a more complex figure is the essential shape of this figure.

Failure to perceive every nuance of a complex figure when there is no special reason for doing so can undoubtedly be attributed to failure to attend to such nuances. Very little is known about the process of

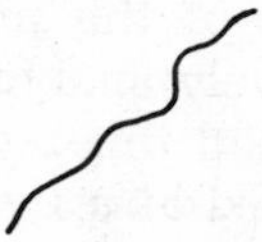

Figure 7-19

Figure 7-20

attention, but in this case it would seem that without a special set to attend to a given detail, the overall or global shape of the figure receives the subject's attention. Apparently such attention is vital for the process of figural description that constitutes form perception. Ordinarily, no special set to attend to the overall shape is required; it occurs spontaneously.

But suppose conditions are such that there is no reason to attend to a figure at all, although we are looking directly at it. This often happens in daily life, as, for example, when we glance at wall paper with a certain pattern or look at a tie that contains a given design. In an experiment designed to induce this inattentive state of mind, subjects were told that the purpose of the experiment was to study afterimagery.[15] After viewing a triangle, the subjects were shown a series of sheets of different colors and containing various line patterns. They were to report if they saw an afterimage of the triangle on each such sheet. Thus, whatever pattern was present on the sheet was not itself anything to be attended to but only a part of the "screen" on which the afterimage did or did not appear. The last sheet shown to the subject contained a relatively simple figure (see Fig. 7–21). By that time all afterimagery of the triangle had disappeared but the subject was still attending to this rather than to the figure on the sheet. Immediately following exposure to this sheet, the subject was given a recognition test in which he had to select this figure from among two (or more) alternatives. Performance on this test by these subjects was very poor. By way of comparison, subjects who saw Fig. 7–21 under more typical conditions, where they did attend to it, did very well in the recognition test.

From this we can conclude that perception of form requires more than mere passive registration of the retinal image. Even a relatively simple figure must be cognitively analyzed, or "described," if genuine form perception is to occur, and this requires attention. Furthermore, even where attention is directed at a figure, specific nuances of it will not be "described" if it is sufficiently complex and if attention is not specifically directed at these features. The necessity of attending to certain features of complex forms before they can be adequately perceived

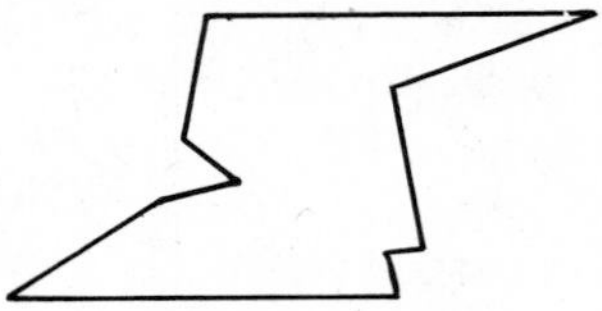

Figure 7–21

may explain why we often have difficulty discriminating among similar instances of certain kinds of objects, as, for example, faces of animals or members of races different from our own, or the like. The reader is referred to a discussion of this problem on pp. 371ff of Chapter 8.

Is Specific Shape Determined by Shape-Detector Mechanisms?

Is there an alternative to the theory of form perception presented here? Can the perception of form be determined by the discharging of cells which respond to specific features of the shape of the retinal image? These mechanisms were briefly described in the previous chapter in connection with the question of perceptual organization. There is evidence that for certain species a higher-level neuron in the visual system will discharge if and only if a small round (moving) spot stimulates the appropriate receptive field of the retina.[16] Also, as noted in the previous chapter, a mechanism exists in certain species for "detecting" contours in varying orientations.[17]

There are many reasons why mechanisms of this kind do not adequately explain the perception of form such as characterizes human and much of animal perception. There are an infinite number of possible shapes. Therefore it seems clear that form perception cannot be explained by assuming that for every possible shape—in any possible retinal location—there are specific built-in detector cells which will respond only to that shape. Rather, to maintain the theory that the detector mechanisms explain form perception, it would have to be claimed that we perceive a particular shape because there are cells which respond to the various *parts* of the figure, so that the perception of the overall shape of the figure results from the collective discharging of these cells. Thus, for example, one might maintain that we perceive a square when two vertical and two horizontal orientation-specific contour "detectors" are actively discharging.

The reader will readily see the difficulties with this kind of theory. A square is not merely the sum of vertical and horizontal component contours. Many other figures can consist of these same parts. The essence of form, as was pointed out earlier in this chapter, is the relative locations of the parts of a figure to one another. What gives specific shape, what makes a figure similar to or different from another figure is primarily a matter of the overall geometry, that is, the whole set of spatial relations constituting a figure. This cannot be reduced to the sum of parts such as contours considered as isolated units, so that whether or not two figures appear similar or different with respect to one another can hardly be a function of the number of identical edge detector units triggered by the two figures. In the case of a square, what matters is that the sides are equal and parallel and that the corners are right angles. The contours simply mark the location of the sides. What the discharging of the neural units responding to the four edges conveys is presumably that there are four edges in certain orientations. But what tells us that the edges are parallel and that the separation between vertical edges is about the same as that between the horizontal edges? That can only be provided by information about *relative* position. While some edge-detector units only discharge if the contour stimulates a specific region of the retina and to that extent may be said to convey information about retinal location, this still does not explain how the crucial information is extracted about the location of the contour *in relation to all others.* Moreover, if the location of the contour is indeed what is important then it is *not* so much the detection of the presence of an edge or contour per se that is central, although it is the latter that the investigators who have made these discoveries have stressed. The information about location can probably be obtained without the activation of edge detector units simply on the basis of locus of retinal stimulation, a point emphasized in Chapter 4 in discussing the perception of field location.

To follow up this point one might ask the more general question, are the contour detector mechanisms necessary for the perception of form? This question can be reduced to the question whether extended retinal images of contours are *necessary* for form perception. We have already seen that they are not, as witness forms consisting of subjective contours and forms derived from successive exposure through a narrow slit.

Moreover very recent findings concerning the relationship between detector units in the brain and perception bear directly on this question. Evidence has been accumulating that exposure to certain restricted environments during the development of animals such as the cat results in a restriction of the kind of neural units which are subsequently present in the brain. For example, if the kitten is exposed only to vertical contours during rearing, only units responsive to image contours in that retinal orientation can be found to be present in the visual cortex.[18] Given this fact, one investigator has asked what the consequences are for perception in such animals.[19] He found that rather than being blind to contours in orientations for which they have been shown to have no detector units—as one should predict if these units are indeed the basis of discriminating one contour from another—they can discriminate them from one another almost as well as contours in orientations for which they do have the appropriate units. (This evidence is very recent and at least one report suggests the opposite conclusion on the basis of a few observations.[20]) Research in this area is now developing at a very rapid pace and almost any finding is apt to be soon outdated. Nevertheless the study in question was thorough and does lead to the startling conclusion that the so-called contour-detector units in the cortex are not necessary for the perception of contours.

Apart from the question of the necessary role of such neural mechanisms in form perception is the question of whether or not their operation would provide a sufficient explanation. The answer to this question also is clearly in the negative. First of all there is the fact of perceptual organization. It was noted in Chapter 6 (pp. 283ff) that while the form-detector units can be held to explain certain aspects of organization—for example why a line is perceived as a unified entity—by and large they do not do justice to most of the problems concerning the organization of the perceptual field. Then there is the fact that if perceived form were directly determined by the collective discharging of those higher neural units which react to stimulation by a figure's contours, when the orientation of the retinal image of a figure changes, the perceived form would have to change, because an entirely different set of detector cells would now be responding. Yet the fact is that as long as there is no change in the assignment of directions to a figure, as when an observer tilts his head in viewing a stationary figure, there is no change in phenomenal shape despite the changed orientation of the image. Conversely, phenomenal shape does change when there is no change in the orientation of the retinal image, provided there is a shift in the assignment of directions.* Moreover many of the facts referred to in this chapter suggest a role of cognitive processes in form perception. The special role of salient features of a form, the role of attention, the failure to perceive every nuance of a complex figure and the like, suggest that form perception cannot be fully explained merely on the basis of the extraction of information concerning contours.

Therefore at the present stage of our knowledge, it is difficult to know what role to assign to these neural mechanisms. It does not even seem to be correct to infer that their role is that of providing a basis for

---

*However there is now evidence that the orientation of the retinal image of a contour which causes some cortical units to discharge changes as a function of a change in the orientation of the animal. Therefore it might be claimed that such an *orientation-constancy* detector mechanism explains these facts concerning the effect of orientation in form perception. See pp. 490–492 for a more complete discussion of this kind of mechanism.

discriminating various features of the proximal stimulus from one another. The evidence cited here suggesting the presence of form perception in animals lacking the relevant detector units argues against even this modest interpretation of their function. Yet these units exist and must serve a purpose. A few investigators have begun to speculate about the possibility that they are concerned with memory rather than perception.[21]

The Problem of the Straight Line

The features that distinguish the appearance of one figure from another can easily be described. Thus, height and width are equal in a square but are unequal in a rectangle; opposite sides are parallel in a rectangle but diverge in a trapezoid and so on. The description refers to the internal geometry and also takes into account the directions top, bottom, and sides. The internal geometry consists of certain *relationships* of parts to one another.

But how would we describe a straight line? It is not obvious what the relationships are to which to refer. What makes a straight line look different from a curved line? One is inclined to answer that it "looks straight," but of course that is no answer at all. It might be thought that a straight line can be described as the line that appears to be the shortest distance between two points, but, in the author's opinion, it is probably the other way around, namely, once perceiving a line as straight, we have the impression that that straight path is the shortest distance between the line's terminal points. The only factor that can be specified would seem to be the parallelism of the various contiguous segments of a line to one another. This can be made clear by imagining a curved line to consist of a number of straight segments, as shown in Fig. 7–22. It is evident that these segments are not parallel to each other. Therefore, the line looks curved rather than straight. Presumably the difference in the slope of the retinal image of the component segments is the basis of our ability to discriminate straight from curved lines. If so, it would seem to follow that the retinal image must be straight for the perception to be that of a straight line. From this one might infer that the perception of straightness or curvature is innately determined.

However, it is also possible to think about curvature of a line in relation to the observer. One might say that the reason why the line in Fig. 7–23 looks curved is that the two ends are located off to the ob-

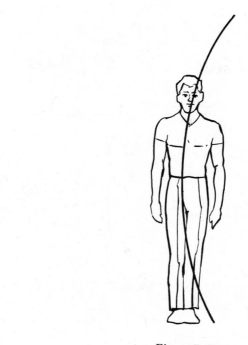

Figure 7-22   Figure 7-23

server's side, whereas the center part is located straight ahead of him. If the line were straight—and vertically oriented—then all points on it would be located straight ahead. From this way of looking at line curvature, one might define it in terms of the set of radial directions of all points that constitute the line.

We have seen in Chapter 4 that radial direction is subject to adaptation when an observer views the world through prisms. A wedge prism has the effect of curving the retinal image of all straight lines that are parallel to the base of the prism, as shown in Fig. 7-24. The reason for this is that the angle of incidence of the rays of light from the ends of the line to the prism is greater than the angle of incidence of the rays of light from the center of the line. The greater the angle of incidence, the greater is the refractory displacement effect of the prism. Reducing a line to only three points, its ends and center, the question arises whether an observer might adapt *differentially* to displacement. That is, will the adaptive shift for the end points be greater than for the center point? In discussing adaptation to displacement (altered radial direction) in Chapter 4, pp. 174ff, we concluded that the basis of such adaptation consisted of a reinterpretation of the significance of eye position

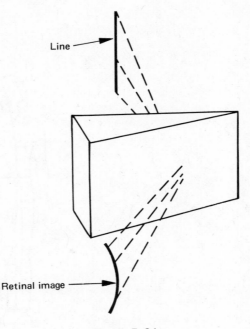

Figure 7-24

in the central interpretation of retinal location. Thus, to fixate a point straight ahead, the observer had to turn his eyes to the side. If this turned position of the eyes comes to signify that an image falling on the fovea is straight ahead, then perceptual adaptation is achieved.

Because of the greater displacement by the prism of an object that is straight ahead *and* far above eye level or far below eye level, an even greater turning of the eyes is necessary to fixate it than when it is *at* eye level. Suppose, therefore, the perceptual system in time takes this into account so that for objects above or below eye level a foveal stimulus only appears straight ahead when the eyes are turned more to the side than for objects at eye level. In that event, the end points and center of the line will all once again appear to be straight ahead. If so, by this way of defining line curvature, the line ought to appear straight. In Chapter 4 we discussed the probable basis of adaptation to displacement, namely, information available to the subject concerning the true location of objects seen through the prism that enables him to form new associations between eye position and perceived direction of gaze. To explain adaptation to curvature, therefore, we have only to make a further assumption, that different associations are formed for objects seen *above* or *below* eye level on the one hand and objects seen *at* eye level on the other hand.* The same kind of information can lead to this differential adaptation to displacement as was discussed in Chapter 4.

However, in addition to the fact that lines can be described as a set of points each having a given radial direction, there are other essential characteristics of lines. When we move around in the environment, a curved line, or let us say, a curved rod, will project a somewhat differently shaped image to the eye depending upon our vantage point. See Fig. 7–25. If the rod is in a plane perpendicular to the line of sight, then the shape of the image will be the same as the shape of the rod. But if we move around and view the rod from the side, then it will project a straight-line image. In between these extreme positions the image will transform as we move, i.e., its degree of curvature will change. The more curved the rod, the more its image changes during movement. But the shape of the image of a straight line never changes. When a straight line is seen through a prism, its retinal image is curved, but the curvature of this image never changes as we change our position in relation to the line. That is so because the line, which is always straight, is always transformed by the prism in exactly the same way. The situation becomes somewhat more dramatic if we imagine what happens when the observer moves 180 degrees from one side of the rod to the

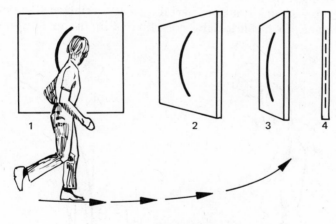

Figure 7–25

*Of course, if the prism is turned in such a way that its base is up or down, then horizontal lines will appear curved. In that event, for adaptation to occur, different associations will have to be formed between left, right, and straight-ahead eye positions and perceived elevation of gaze.

other. If the rod is really curved, then normally the curvature changes from convex left to convex right when we get to the other side. But through prisms, a straight rod continues to appear convex to one side regardless of the direction of viewing. So the fact that the image does not transform as we move around a rod is potential information that the rod is a straight one. We do not know if the perceptual system makes use of such information.

Another potential source of information is the way the image of a prismatically viewed straight line behaves when we move in a direction parallel to the line. Imagine an observer wearing prisms bending over and looking down at a line in the floor as he moves along the line (Fig. 7-26a). What he sees is shown in Fig. 7-26b. If an observer not wearing prisms walked along a straight path as he looked down at a curved line, he would soon veer off the curved line to the left or right (dotted path in Fig. 7-26b). But the observer wearing prisms walking along a straight line will not veer off the path so that the line will continue to remain directly underneath. Only a straight line will remain directly underneath an observer walking a straight path. Therefore, the behavior of the prismatically perceived line is potential information that it is straight and not curved as it first appears to be, as long as independent information is available to the perceptual system that the observer is walking in a straight path.

These sources of information pertain to the relationship between line and observer, to his left-right coordinates in the examples given.

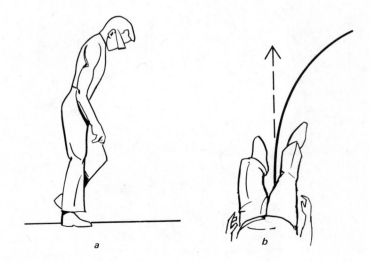

a   b

Figure 7-26

To the extent they are effective, they may tend to offset the information present within a curved image that indicates it is curved, namely, the fact referred to earlier that the different segments of a curved line are not parallel to one another. However, the information derived from walking in a direction parallel to a straight line seen through prisms can also be thought of as indicating that its various segments are parallel to one another. The reason is as follows. Normally when we move, the images of all points sweep across the retina in a direction parallel *to one another.* If we happen to move in a direction parallel to a straight line, the image of all points on that line will sweep along the same path, one behind the other. If the line is curved, then, as shown in Fig. 7–27a, the path of the images of its constituent points would be in parallel paths but not along a single path. However, if it is a straight line viewed through a prism, then the behavior of the points in its image will be as shown in Fig. 7–27b. Therefore, the moving observer is receiving potential information that the various segments of the line must be parallel to one another.

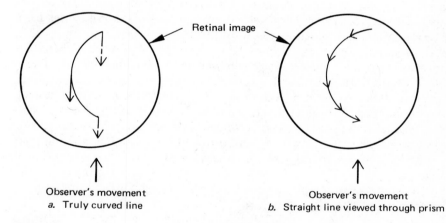

Retinal image

a. Observer's movement
Truly curved line

b. Observer's movement
Straight line viewed through prism

Figure 7-27

This brings us to the question of whether adaptation to curvature does occur in viewing the world through prisms. Before we can try to answer this question, however, a related phenomenon must first be considered.

The Gibson effect

Some years ago Gibson began research on the problem of adaptation to prismatic displacement.[22] However, he was sidetracked by his subjects' reports that the curved appearance of straight lines seen through the prism seemed to lessen in time. The subjects also reported that on removing the prisms, straight lines and edges appeared to be curved in a direction opposite to the one they appeared to have with prisms on. As a result of these observations, Gibson began to study adaptation to curvature. His subjects sat and looked at a straight line through prisms for a few minutes, and measurements were taken of how curved the line appeared to be. Then the prisms were removed and the curvature of a line was varied until it appeared to be straight. The extent to which the line had to be curved in order to look straight, to compensate for the fact that otherwise it looked curved in the opposite direction, was a measure of the aftereffect, which Gibson called a negative aftereffect.

At this point, Gibson made a change in the method that quite probably had an important effect on the nature of research in perception over the subsequent 30 years. He reasoned that since the retinal image or proximal stimulus is what matters for perception and since, further, a straight line viewed through prisms yields a curved retinal image, the process of adaptation could be just as easily studied if a truly curved line were viewed without prisms. That would also produce a curved image. His subjects were required to sit and look at curved lines for a few minutes and adaptation was found to occur in this situation just as it had when using prisms. Therefore, it seemed to follow that the adaptation had nothing to do with prisms *per se* or information the subject might gather about the world. Rather, the effect is of a different kind, more analogous to adaptation to color, in which continued viewing leads to changes of neutral or chromatic color and to negative aftereffects. And such effects are *nonveridical*, whereas adaptation to prisms is generally veridical. In other words, if a curved line begins to appear *less* curved than it is merely by continued fixation, this is a nonveridical change and is a very different kind of effect, one would think, than the veridical one in which a prismatically viewed straight line comes to look increasingly straight.

In fact, certain findings at the time supported the view that Gibson's effect was similar to other classical kinds of adaptation, namely, the effect was restricted to only that part of the retina that the line had stimulated. This means that the subject must fixate a point on the line so that its image will fall in one place on the retina. The same is, of course, true for classical color adaptation. We thus seem to have an effect here in which continued exposure leads to some change in a localized area of the neural substrate. Gibson regarded it as representative of a tendency toward what he called *normalization*, in which a persistent quality tends to become the neutral or normal quality, as when a chromatic hue begins to look gray with continued fixation. The neutral curvature in the family of convex left and convex right curves is the straight line. Gibson discovered that a similar adaptation effect occurs with tilted lines—that is, a tilted line looks less tilted with continued viewing and a vertical line seen subsequently appears tilted in the opposite direction—and this too he regarded as a tendency toward normalization. Subsequently, many other effects of continued exposure of line figures were discovered—the so-called figural aftereffects—and Gibson's findings were then considered to be special cases of this kind. We discuss these aftereffects in the chapter on illusions.

Prism adaptation to curvature

In the light of Gibson's effect, we must expect that in viewing the world through prisms there will be some adaptation that has nothing to do with perceptual learning, that is, with forming new associations based on sensory information. Of course, subjects in prism experiments are free to move their eyes around so that one might think conditions are not right to obtain the Gibson effect. But there is some evidence that an effect of this kind can occur with freely moving eyes and is not necessarily based on a localized change of the neural substrate.

One might inquire about the magnitude of the Gibson effect. It seems that the effect is small. A curved line viewed for about 2 minutes (without prisms) appears only very slightly less curved, and a straight line viewed afterward appears only very slightly curved. Fig. 7-28 shows a line curved by an amount equal to the average effect one usually obtains in an experiment of this kind, namely the equivalent of 3 or 4 diopters.* The reader will see that it is just a bit above the difference threshold between straight and curved (but this experiment is usually performed with a single isolated line on a very large cardboard or a luminous line in the dark where we cannot use nearby straight edges as a basis of comparison as the reader can use the edges of lines of text or edges of the page). As far as is now known, the effect does not increase with viewing beyond a few minutes.

What then is the magnitude of adaptation to curvature in experiments with prisms? The answer is that the effect progressively increases

---

*A diopter is a unit used to express the refractory power of a lens or a prism. Light passing through a 1 diopter prism will be displaced by 1 centimeter at a distance of 1 meter. Fig. 7-28 approximates the image curvature produced by viewing a straight line about 1 meter long at a distance of 1 meter through a 3 or 4 diopter prism.

Figure 7-28

over time, more sharply over the first few days and then levels off. This in itself seems to be different from the way the Gibson effect behaves. At the end of 42 days the average effect is about 5 or 6 diopters as illustrated in Fig. 7-29.[23] * One can draw two opposite conclusions from this result. On the one hand, the change would seem to be greater than the Gibson effect so that the consequence of prolonged viewing of the world through prisms cannot simply be reduced to the Gibson effect. But, on the other hand, the change is disappointingly small if perceptual adaptation to prismatic distortion is expected to occur and if it is to be viewed as the result of learning.

Figure 7-29

*In this experiment, as in many of the others done on adaptation to curvature, the prisms were of a 20 diopter strength. Hence the 6 diopter change means that adaptation was 30 percent of what would have constituted complete adaptation.

One might argue that the observer has to overcome a lifetime of prior experience in the relatively short period of time he wears the prisms. If *normal* perception is also viewed as the end result of a process of learning, very strong associations indeed must exist between a straight retinal image and a straight phenomenal line, and who is to say just how much new exposure of a different kind is required to offset this.

There are other reasons for believing that genuine adaptation to prisms occurs. In one investigation, the observer was required to remain within the confines of a cylindrical room that contained only irregular luminous spots on the surface of the walls arranged in a random pattern.[24] Hence, there were no straight edges that would result in retinal images of curved lines, so there was no reason for a Gibson-type effect to occur. On the other hand, by moving around the room, information was available of the kind discussed concerning the location of the spots with respect to the observer. For subjects who actively walked around the room for 30 minutes, a change of 3.35 prism diopters occurred in the curvature of a line judged to be straight. Another investigator demonstrated that prism adaptation occurred for subjects who viewed a *curved* line. The line was curved by just such an amount and in a direction that appeared straight through the prisms at the outset, because its retinal image was straight.[25] Therefore, there could be no reason to expect a normalization effect to take place. But the line is curved, and information is available concerning this because the subjects are permitted to move their heads. Hence, the subjects could learn that the straight image signified a curved line and apparently they did, because adaptation did occur.

We are, therefore, left with several unanswered questions. Is the perception of the curvature or straightness of a single line or edge innately determined? If so, it could be argued that we should not expect any change as a result of prism adaptation, no matter how long or effective the exposure. But then what is the meaning of the small effect that *is* obtained, an effect that does *not* seem to be entirely reducible to normalization? On the other hand, one might think that the perception of line curvature is to a large extent learned early in life. In that case, why is prism adaptation, even after 42 days of continuous exposure, so modest? Perhaps we have not yet hit on the most crucial information and the ideal method of conducting experiments on adaptation to prisms. Or, perhaps, the explanation of the limited degree of adaptation is that there are two determinants of perceived line curvature, an innate one, based on the perceived orientation of the segments of the line with respect to one another, and a learned one, based on the perceived location of points on the line with respect to the observer. The result is that the observer in an adaptation experiment is in a conflict situation in which one determinant does not permit adaptation and the other does. The former may, therefore, operate as a constraint on the possible effectiveness of the latter.*

Summary

The fact that phenomenal shape is constant despite the transposition of the retinal image of a figure in size or position suggests that the essential information, which distinguishes one form from another, is the set of geometrical *relationships* of the parts of a figure to one another. Ordinarily, the contours of the extended retinal image of a figure delineate these relative locations, but the contours should be thought of as markers of location rather than as essential factors in form perception. If the essential information about relative location can be conveyed without the presence of an extended image, as in tracking a moving point, shape can nevertheless be experienced.

However, a number of facts indicate that such information about the location of the parts of a figure relative to one another is a necessary but not a sufficient basis of form perception. A cognitive process very much like description must occur based to a large extent on the information about relative location of the parts of the figure but including other features as well. This act of description is not consciously experienced and it is not verbal in nature. It takes into account the slant of the figure in the third dimension and the orientation of the figure with respect to the up-down, left-right coordinates. It is very much influenced by salient features of a figure such as symmetry. It requires attention, and if a figure is very complex such description will often not do justice to all its nuances.

The veridical perception of the curvature or straightness of a single line presents a special problem. One might explain it in terms of the perceived locations of the points that constitute it relative to one another by thinking of a line as consisting of a set of contiguous segments. From this standpoint, a straight line is one whose contiguous

---

*Richard Held has suggested an explanation along these lines of the limited amount of adaptation to prismatically created curvature.[26] For Held, the innate determinant is based on detector mechanisms that discriminate straight from curved contours.

segments are parallel to one another and the perception of line curvature could well be innately determined. But one can also refer to the perceived location of the points of a line relative to the observer, i.e., the set of radial directions of the points constituting a line. A straight line according to this analysis is one for which all points are perceived as straight ahead (when it is vertical) or at the same height (when it is horizontal). Since it is known that we can adapt to prismatic displacement—by a process of reinterpretation of the direction of gaze of the eyes—the possibility arises that adaptation to prismatic curvature of lines may occur. It would be based upon a *differential adaptation* to the displacement of the ends versus the middle of such lines. Evidence indicates that although such adaptation occurs and is greater than a related phenomenon of normalization of curved lines, the Gibson effect, it is nevertheless relatively slight. The reason for the limited extent of such adaptation is not known, but it was suggested that the innate basis of the perception of line curvature may operate as a constraint.

References

1. Lashley, K. S. The mechanism of vision: XV. Preliminary studies of the rat's capacity for detailed vision. *Journal of General Psychology*, 1938, 18, 123–193.
2. Zimmermann, R. R. and C. C. Torrey. Ontogeny of learning, Chap. 11 in *Behavior of Nonhuman Primates*, II, edit. by A. M. Schrier, H. F. Harlow, and F. Stollnitz. Academic Press, Inc., 1965.
3. Ehrenfels, C. von. Über Gestalt qualitäten. *Vierteljahresschrift für wissenschaftliche Philosophie*, 1890, 14, 249–292.
4. Hebb, D. O. *Organization of Behavior*. John Wiley & Sons, Inc., 1949.
5. Hubel, D. H. and T. N. Wiesel. Receptive fields, binocular interaction and functional architecture in the cat's visual cortex. *Journal of Physiology*, 1962, 160, 106–154; Receptive fields and functional architecture of monkey striate cortex. *Journal of Physiology*, 1968, 195, 215–243. D. H. Hubel. The visual cortex of the brain. *Scientific American*, 1963, 209(11).
6. Köhler, W. and H. Wallach. Figural aftereffects: an investigation of visual processes. *Proceedings of the American Philosophical Society*, 1944, 88, 269–357.
7. See Kanizsa, G. Margini quasi-percettivi in campi con stimolazione omogenea. *Rivista di Psicologia*, 1955, 49, 7–30; S. Coren. Subjective contours and apparent depth. *Psychological Re-*

view, 1972, **79**, 359–367; R. L. Gregory. Cognitive contours. *Nature*, 1972, **238**, 51–52.

8. Rock, I. and F. Halper. Form perception without a retinal image. *American Journal of Psychology*, 1969, **82**, 425–440.

9. Rock, I. and E. Sigman. Intelligence factors in the perception of form through a moving slit. *Perception*, 1973, **2**, 357–369.

10. See Rock, I. *Orientation and Form*. Academic Press, Inc., 1973; also I. Rock. The perception of disoriented figures. *Scientific American*, 1974, **230**, (1), 78–85.

11. Goldmeier, E. Similarity in visually perceived forms. *Psychological Issues*, 1972, **8** (No. 1) 1–135.

12. Mach, E. *The Analysis of Sensations*. Open Court Publishing Corp., 1914 (Republished by Dover Publications, Inc., 1959).

13. Rock, I. and R. Leaman. An experimental analysis of visual symmetry. *Acta Psychologica*, 1963, **21**, 171–183.

14. Rock, I., F. Halper, and T. Clayton. The perception and recognition of complex figures. *Cognitive Psychology*, 1972, **3**, 655–673.

15. Rock, I. and F. Halper. Unpublished experiment.

16. Barlow, H. B. Summation and inhibition in the frog's retina. *Journal of Physiology*, 1953, **119**, 69–88; Lettvin, J. Y., H. R. Maturana, W. S. McCulloch, and W. H. Pitts. What the frog's eye tells the frog's brain. *Proceedings of the Institute of Radio Engineering*, 1959, **47**, 1940–1951; Barlow, H. B., R. M. Hill and W. R. Levick. Retinal ganglion cells responding selectively to direction and speed of image motion in the rabbit. *Journal of Physiology*, 1964, **173**, 377–407.

17. Hubel, D. H. and T. N. Wiesel. op. cit.

18. Hirsch, H. V. B. and D. N. Spinelli. Visual experience modifies distribution of horizontally and vertically oriented receptive fields in the cat. *Science*, 1970, **168**, 869–871; Modification of the distribution of receptive field orientation in cats by selective visual experience during development. *Experimental Brain Research*, 1971, **13**, 509–527; Blakemore, C. and G. F. Cooper. Development of the brain depends on the visual environment. *Nature*, 1970, **228**, 477–478; Blakemore, C. and D. E. Mitchell, Environmental modification of the visual cortex and the neural basis of learning and memory. *Nature*, 1973, **241**, 467–468.

19. Hirsch, H. V. B. Visual perception in cats after environmental surgery. *Experimental Brain Research*, 1972, **15**, 405–423.

20. Blakemore & Cooper, op. cit.

21. Spinelli, D. N., H. V. B. Hirsch, R. W. Phelps, and J. Metzler. Visual experience as a determinant of the response characteristics of cortical receptive fields in cats. *Experimental Brain Research*, 1972, **15**, 289–304; Blakemore and Mitchell, op. cit.

22. Gibson, J. J. Adaptation, after-effect and contrast in the perception of curved lines. *Journal of Experimental Psychology*, 1933, **16**, 1–31.

23. Pick, H. L., Jr. and J. C. Hay. Adaptation to prismatic distortion. *Psychonomic Science*, 1964, 1, 199–200.

24. Held, R. and J. Rekosh. Motor-sensory feedback and the geometry of visual space. *Science*, 1963, 141, 722–723.

25. Cohen, M. Visual curvature and feedback factors in the production of prismatically induced curved line after effects. Paper read at *Eastern Psychological Association* meeting, New York, April 1963.

26. Held, R. Dissociation of visual functions by deprivation and rearrangement. *Psychologische Forschung*, 1968, 31, 338–348.

chapter 8

THE PERCEPTION OF FORM III: INNATE OR LEARNED?

Since Bishop Berkeley wrote his famous treatise, *An Essay Towards a New Theory of Vision* in 1709, the idea that visual perception is learned has been widely held and deeply entrenched. The basis for this view stems in part from the fact that the retinal image seems to be an inadequate determinant of perception. Berkeley was particularly concerned with the perception of the third dimension. Since the retinal image is two dimensional, he concluded that it itself cannot account for three-dimensional perception. He argued that the visual experience of spatial properties derives from touch. We return to a discussion of this question later in the chapter.

As we have seen, the retinal image does not provide us with a sufficient explanation of perceptual experience: retinal stimulation changes as a function of distance, vantage point, illumination, and so on, yet perception generally remains constant. Furthermore, the image is ambiguous with respect to the object or event in the external world that produces it. Thus, for example, the same image may be projected by a small, near object or a large far object. Berkeley implied and others have reasserted again and again that such inadequacy or ambiguity can only be overcome by a good deal of prior experience in which we learn how to interpret the image.

There are, of course, alternatives to this conclusion and some would say that the proximal stimulus is *not* as ambiguous or inadequate as it has been thought to be. In this chapter we discuss the legitimacy of the empiricists' claim both in terms of logical and empirical considerations.

Perception, Recognition, and Identification

Before proceeding, it is necessary to draw attention to a distinction that is often overlooked, thereby creating a great deal of confusion. When we look at an object, such as a hammer, several aspects of our perceptual experience should be distinguished from one another. First, we perceive a certain shape (see Fig. 8-1). The first time we ever saw a hammer we presumably perceived it to have the same shape it has for us now. Second, the hammer looks familiar—we recognize it as something we have seen before. Even if we have never seen a hammer being used and were ignorant of its function, it would now look familiar. Finally, it also appears to us as a thing that is used in a certain way. That is, we identify it, and seem to perceive its function or meaning as well.*

All of these aspects are present in our awareness immediately and simultaneously the moment the hammer is encountered. Nevertheless,

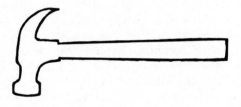

Figure 8-1

*The term *meaning* is generally reserved for words, either written or spoken, since clearly words are meaningless except for those who have learned what they represent. A visual form, on the other hand, is not merely a symbol that arbitrarily can be made to stand for this or that object. Still the fact is that at some stage in development, the function or use of objects in the world is not known, whereas later on it is. Therefore, in this sense one might legitimately apply the term *meaning* to visual forms analogously to the way it is used for words.

one must distinguish between the content of phenomenal experience and the functional events that give rise to such experience. Therefore, although we simultaneously perceive a familiar and meaningful object of a given shape, still as regards the origin of these several components of our experience, logical considerations compel us to make certain distinctions. The familiarity of an object, i.e., whether we recognize it or not, is by definition a matter of past experience. Similarly, identification is an outcome of prior learning. But the phenomenal shape of an object is not necessarily based on past experience.

When the empiricist says that perception is determined by past experience, he is presumably talking about a quality such as form and not about the qualities of familiarity and meaningfulness. We will shortly consider the justification for his claim, but for the moment it is useful to examine further the distinction we have made. If past experiences are to have any effect on subsequent perception (or behavior, for that matter) they must leave behind some enduring representation in the nervous system; namely, memory traces. Each perceptual experience may be thought to leave a memory trace that in some as yet unknown manner can represent the properties and characteristics of the object or event perceived. Therefore, if recognition implies an experience of familiarity, of having seen the object before, it seems reasonable to suppose that it is caused by some communication between the present percept and these prior memory traces.

This raises an intriguing problem, namely, how are only the correct traces—those representing the object now being perceived—communicated with? After all, a great number of traces are stored in the nervous system of the different objects and events perceived over a lifetime, assuming that traces endure for a long period of time. Yet to recognize something implies that the *relevant* traces, those of that object, are aroused. We have no understanding of how this amazing selectivity comes about, and almost instantaneously at that, but we do know that similarity between present percept and memory trace is a crucial factor in the process. Some believe that all memory traces are rapidly searched out or scanned and when one is reached that is similar to the organized stimulus, the search ends. However, the enormity of the task and the rapidity of recognition has suggested to others that there is not time for such a search to occur. An alternative suggestion is that the correct trace is selected on the basis of a resonance principle analogous to sympathetic sound vibrations—singing a particular tone, for example middle C, will set the C strings on the piano into vibration. In the same way a trace is selectively aroused because it is similar to the current percept. However it occurs, recognition seems to require that the current percept be identified as being similar to a given memory or set of memories.

That it is similarity and not identity that is crucial is evidenced by the fact that the identical object need not be present for recognition to occur. The observer may or may not realize that the object is somewhat different. When he does not realize it, we have an instance of faulty recognition, as when a person approaching us is misperceived as someone we know. When he does realize it, we have an experience of familiarity-with-a-difference as when we see a friend who has grown a moustache. Therefore, whether or not memory traces are selected depends upon factors that govern similarity. Several of these factors were discussed in Chapter 7. Wherever the internal geometry, orientation, and salient features of a figure are not changed or not changed very much—as in transposition of size—recognition will generally occur.

We must also assume that meaning is carried by memory traces. In the example of the hammer, we can imagine that the child sees his father using it. Memories of the hammer moving up and down, striking a nail embedded in wood, and making a certain noise are established and are associated with the memory trace of the hammer's shape. If these memories are aroused when the hammer is seen again, they could provide the basis for the experience of identifying the hammer, of knowing what it is and how it is used. But these traces—i.e., traces of movement, of banging down on a nail, and so on—are not themselves directly similar to the shape of the hammer, so that they cannot be directly evoked on the basis of similarity by the stimulus of the hammer when encountered again. Only the trace of the shape of the hammer is similar to the hammer seen now. Therefore, the process must occur in three steps, namely:

1. The perception of the shape of the hammer when it is seen again, (A' in Fig. 8-2).
2. The trace of the shape of the hammer (A) is selected on the basis of similarity to the perception of hammer now occurring (A').
3. Once A is aroused, it in turn arouses or redintegrates the whole network of traces representing the related objects and events that were experienced at the earlier time (B).

The latter (B) represents the meaning of the object. B was associated with A originally and is now evoked because part of the association (A) is evoked. The entire sequence of events presupposes that the first thing to happen is the perception of the shape of the hammer, so that perception—or to be more precise, the neurophysiological events that underlie the perception—must occur *before* any of the relevant traces

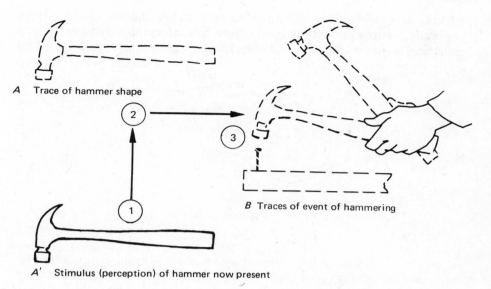

A   Trace of hammer shape

B   Traces of event of hammering

A'   Stimulus (perception) of hammer now present

Figure 8-2

can begin to exert an influence.*   We return to this important point later.

As noted earlier, recognition and identification are by definition matters of past experience.   Therefore, whether or not recognition and meaningfulness are determined by past experience could hardly constitute the subject matter of debate between nativists and empiricists. In fact, some would argue that these are not topics of perception but of cognition.   Nevertheless, a good deal of confusion has arisen because of a failure to distinguish recognition and identification from other aspects of perception such as form per se. For example, some projective techniques used by clinicians, such as the Rorschach inkblot test, are sometimes considered to be tests of individual differences in perception. These individual differences are, of course, thought to reflect differences in past experience. But what actually is involved in this test? To some slight extent there may be differences in the form perceived—as when one individual organizes the white region between the darker blot

---

*This point, that associative recall of B can only occur after percept A communicates with the memory trace of A was originally made by Höffding and is discussed by Köhler.[1]

regions as figure rather than ground—but this is the exception. More generally, people perceive the same form but interpret it differently. To illustrate, suppose Fig. 8-3 is shown to many people and they are asked

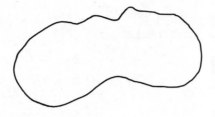

Figure 8-3

to describe what they see. Obviously, there will be many different responses from "artist's palette" to "amoeba" but that does not imply any differences in the perceived shape of the figure. What it does imply is that the same shape can remind people of different things, particularly when it is not a good likeness of anything in particular. As far as the clinical or projective aspect of the Rorschach test is concerned, it is not unreasonable that differences in personality and in motives and attitudes would play a role in the particular interpretation that comes to mind, but this is not to say that motives determine the form that is perceived.

Another example of possible confusion between perception and interpretation is a well-known experiment on the effect of need state. Both hungry and nonhungry subjects were shown blurred pictures of various objects to see whether the hungry subjects would identify more of them as food or objects related to food.[2] The hungry subjects gave more food-related responses than the nonhungry subjects. Does this mean that need affects perception? Probably not. Naturally the hungry subjects had food on their minds. Therefore, it is not surprising that they would tend to interpret a poorly defined shape as representing a food object. But the shape *per se* of what they perceived might very well have been identical to the shape the nonhungry subjects perceived.

The distinction between perception, recognition, and identification is relevant to the work of theorists who are seeking to explain cognitive processes on the basis of an analogy to computers. In discussing what they call pattern recognition, they actually have in mind pattern identification and it is not clear if they admit a prior step of perception. According to these investigators, pattern recognition of a letter of the alphabet consists in identifying the letter, in other words, in classifying it. One line of thought about how this process occurs is that the proximal stimulus is analyzed in terms of various features. For example, does it have a vertical line, a closed loop, asymmetry, and so on? If it does contain a certain cluster of such features it is "identified" as, say, the letter *P*. It is not clear, then, according to this view, if prior to this "identification" there is a stage of perception of the form per se. How does the *P* look the first time it is seen by a child, before it can be recognized? Or to bring out this point in another way, all the items in Fig. 8-4 will be identified as examples of the letter *A*, but surely their

Figure 8-4

shapes differ, and without specific learning that they are different kinds of *A*'s, they would not be perceived as having anything in common. Furthermore, suppose a child who had learned his letters forgot the name of one. Still he would recognize it as very familiar. Identifying the letter is a further step, based on the fact that this form is associated with a name. In the case of letters the name constitutes the meaning of the form. It is probable that some of this confusion stems from the desire to build a theory explaining the behavior of a computer capable of "reading" rather than a theory that would do justice to cognitive processes in animals and men.

The interpretation or identification of a form as representing a particular familiar object is not to be confused with the notion of "description" of a form discussed in Chapters 6 and 7. It was suggested there that a nonconscious process of "describing" the geometrical and other features of a figure may occur that governs our experience of its *shape*. Identification as discussed here implies a further step concerning the meaning or function of the figure following the perception of its shape. Presumably the arousal of the appropriate memory trace on the basis of similarity of form, which accounts for identification, requires that this process of "description" of the form occur first. However, under certain circumstances it is possible that, as a result of a particular identification of a figure, its shape may be perceived differently (see the discussion on pp. 348-351).

Logical Considerations

Possible kinds of experience effects

Apart from producing an experience of recognition and meaning in previously seen objects, what other kinds of effects on the perception of form might past experience be expected to have?

1. The most all-embracing possibility would be that the visual direction of retinal location is entirely a matter of learning. This was the position taken by Wundt and others and was discussed critically in Chapter 4. If it were true, the perception of specific shape would then only be possible after such learning of visual direction had taken place.

2. An alternative possibility would be that certain aspects of form perception bearing on specific shape depend upon past experience or, if innately given, are nevertheless modifiable by past experience. Line curvature would be a good example of this kind of effect. The evidence presented in Chapter 7 indicates that adaptation effects do occur but only to a limited extent. Another possible example of this category of effect would be that experience is responsible for the tendency to assign the directions top, bottom, and sides to forms and for perceived shape to be a function of such assigned directions. There is at present no decisive evidence for or against this possibility.

3. A widespread form of empiricism is that which claims that the perception of segregated units, the organization of the visual field, such as was discussed in Chapter 6, is the end result of learning. A good deal of the research on the role of experience in form perception has been concerned with this claim. A variation of this hypothesis would be that perceptual organization *can* be determined by or modified by experience, but more generally, is not learned. It has been claimed that the effect of experience in perceptual organization is particularly evident in situations where a set or expectation is created.

4. Still another possible role of experience in form perception is in permitting perceptual discriminations to be made that otherwise would not be made. A good example in the adult would be learning to distinguish the faces of chimpanzees from one another or, in the child, learning to distinguish one printed word from another.

Investigators have not always been clear about which of these possible effects of experience their experiment was designed to examine. A number of experiments were explicitly directed at the question of whether past experience determines perceptual organization. These experiments are discussed later under the category of indirect evidence, pp. 343ff. Some work has also been directed at the possible role of experience in permitting difficult perceptual discriminations to develop; this is discussed under the appropriate heading later in the chapter, pp. 371ff. But the greatest amount of research and undoubtedly the most crucial research has not been analytical with respect to these theoretical possibilities. Rather, the question has simply been: Is or is not form perception present in animals or humans when the possibility of its having been learned is ruled out? The answer has been sought by experiments in which the subjects are required to discriminate forms from one another; this is discussed later under the category of direct evidence, pp. 361ff. Since the capacity to perceive forms as different from one another depends upon the presence of perceptual organization *and* of specific shape, one might justifiably say that all of the research in this category is aimed at investigating simultaneously both of these hypotheses.*

How can we learn to see if we must see to learn?

If perceptual organization is entirely a matter of learning, then the infant or adult who sees for the first time would experience an utterly chaotic mosaic of light, dark, and colored spots. It is difficult to imagine what this might be like. Assuming for the moment that this is what is experienced, the question that arises is How can this experience be transformed into an organized array of objects? What principle of learning could lead to such a change? Suppose one were to believe that we learn to perceive visual form by touching and grasping things. Such actions could not, of course, be initially guided by what is seen because presumably organized things are not seen. They would have to be blind gropings. But apart from this problem, since the hands themselves would not be perceived as distinct visual entities, there is the more fundamental problem of how anything useful could come out of such encounters. At the moment of grasping an object, the visual experience would continue to be that of an unorganized mosaic and accompanying

*The recent findings discussed in Chapter 7 (p. 316) and later in this chapter (p. 367) suggest another possible hypothesis about the role of past experience in form perception. Young animals raised in an environment which provides very restricted kinds of visual stimulation subsequently are found to have correspondingly limited kinds of cortical feature-detector units. Thus it might be argued that early experience plays a crucial role in shaping the structures in the brain which are important for form perception.

this would be a tactile-proprioceptive experience. (Would the latter experience be organized, so that we would be aware of a distinct object? If so, is *it* innately given? If not, how is *it* learned? This problem is generally overlooked by the advocates of this hypothesis.)

In any case, even assuming that touch—or any other source of information one might want to invoke—informs that there is a distinct object of such and such size and shape, visually no such object would be present in experience. What useful memory of such a chaotic visual array could possibly be established that would in any way prove useful for subsequent visual experience? In short, it is difficult to imagine how we can learn to see if, to begin with, we see nothing. Whereas, conversely, if, to begin with, we do experience an organized field of objects, then all kinds of other learning would be possible.

How can the trace determine the percept?

The learning hypothesis can take different forms. It might be argued that what is learned are principles of organization. But in the light of the questions raised in the preceding paragraphs, it is not clear how this would come about. Or it might be argued that we can learn to organize specific forms on the basis of prior experience with those forms. Many of the experiments that have been performed to demonstrate an effect of experience are based on this form of the argument. The subject is first given an experience with a particular form and is then shown an ambiguous pattern that contains the form. The question is whether the subject will tend to organize that pattern in such a way as to perceive the now familiar form.

Suppose we grant that in some way the perceptual field is organized at a particular time so that, as a result, a memory trace that represents this organized experience is established. The hypothesis that specific past experience determines perceptual organization can be translated into the more concrete proposition that memory traces determine such organization at a subsequent time. The question now to be faced is this. Prior to the moment at which the memory trace determines the perceptual organization, what does the observer perceive? The stimulus is present but is not yet organized or is organized differently from the way it will be in a moment after the trace does its work. How is the relevant trace selected in advance from among all those in the central nervous system so that this trace and no other will be the one that will play a role in organizing the ambiguous stimulus array?

Ordinarily, we would think, a trace is activated *after* the organized percept occurs. It is selected on the basis of *similarity to that percept* and it results in recognition and identification. But to say the trace *determines* the percept is to imply that it is selected before the percept is achieved. On logical grounds, how could this be possible?[3] We will consider experiments that are clearly predicated on the assumption that such a process can occur, and we will discuss possible answers to the question of how it could occur.

Experimental Evidence

It will be helpful if we separate into two categories the evidence on the question of whether or not experience is necessary or beneficial for perception of form. In one type of experiment, the question is raised whether past experience effects can be demonstrated in a person who already has had normal visual experience. Since it is so difficult to work with animals or humans who have had no prior visual experience, this *indirect* approach for many years was favored. The question posed is the necessarily more limited one of whether past experiences can be shown to affect perceptual organization (not whether it is the necessary determinant of it) and, if so, what kind of effect it can have. In another type of investigation, the question whether form perception is present in a subject that has had no prior visual experience is *directly* tested.

Indirect evidence

The design of this kind of experiment is as follows. In the training period, a stimulus pattern is first presented that is either unambiguous or conditions are such that it is always organized in a particular way. Then, in the test period, a stimulus array is presented in which the pattern seen in training is physically present so that it can be perceived if the subject organizes the array in the same way he did in training. The array, however, can also be organized in another way. What is presented in the test may be physically identical with what was presented in training. Examples will make this clear. The crucial question is whether for subjects given the training, the test pattern will tend to be organized in such a way that what was perceived in training is again perceived.

The classic experiment in this group was performed by Gottschaldt some years ago.[4] The logic of the experiment was that if form perception is determined primarily by experiential factors, a complex figure *b*, containing a simple form *a*, which has been seen many times in the past, should be perceived as the familiar unit *a* plus other parts. (See Fig. 8-5.) Simple outline figures were, therefore, presented repeatedly to subjects. Later, complex figures that contained the *a* figures were shown and the subjects were instructed to describe them. It was found that the complex *b* figures were rarely described as the *a* figure with additional lines.

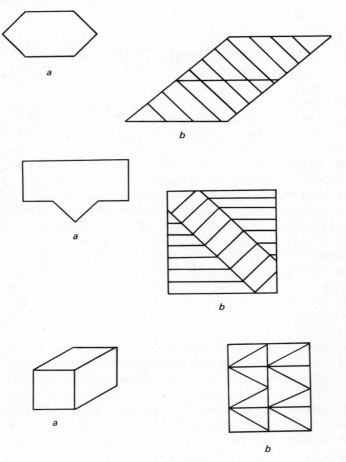

Figure 8-5

The experiment has been criticized on the ground that it only shows that familiar units can be camouflaged if they are embedded in larger contexts. But this criticism misses the point completely. It is still necessary to explain why the physically present figure is phenomenally absent. The camouflage occurs because grouping factors determine what is perceived rather than past experience. Only those additional lines will successfully camouflage the *a* figure, which, because of the laws of grouping, yield different organizations. A few lines in certain locations will achieve this effect, whereas a whole network of other lines may not. Good continuation is undoubtedly the major factor operating in Gottschaldt's figures.*

Gottschaldt also found that if his subjects were instructed to look for the simple figure in the complex one, they generally could find it, although this was sometimes difficult even with these instructions. This is, of course, an entirely different issue. The crucial question is whether or not past experience *spontaneously* gives rise to particular perceptual organizations and the answer to that in Gottschaldt's experiment is no. Whether it is possible to change an organization intentionally is another question that is not necessarily related to the effect of experience. One can achieve a perceptual organization intentionally that is completely new. When one succeeds in organizing the complex figure in such a way that the simple figure emerges as a distinct unit, then, of course, it is recognized. So the role of experience in this case may be only that of permitting recognition. The more interesting question is how intention can affect perceptual grouping and to this at present we have no answer.†

A classic experiment by Rubin investigated the question of whether or not past experience influenced figure-ground organization.[8] The plan of Rubin's experiment was as follows. In the training session, the subject was shown patterns such as that illustrated in Fig. 8-6. As each pattern was presented, the subject was instructed either to organize the central region (which was green) as figure *or* the surrounding black region as figure. The patterns were shown repeatedly, and every time a given figure appeared it was to be organized by the subject in the same way. Then, in the test, the figures were shown briefly and without any advance instructions.

The question at issue was whether a figure would be organized in the test in the way it had been organized in training. The result was that

---

*It is often claimed that a subsequent experiment by Djang[5] invalidated Gottschaldt's findings. However, the present writer does not believe that this conclusion is correct. For a full discussion of other evidence of this indirect kind see Zuckerman and Rock.[6]

†The technique of requiring an observer to find a simple figure in a complex one has been developed by Witkin as a personality test, the so-called Embedded Figures Test. See Witkin.[7]

Figure 8-6

about 60 percent of the time the figures in the test were so organized and 40 percent of the time they were not. In itself, this is not a very strong showing on behalf of past experience. However, several features of this experiment are in need of revision. First, although the figures used by Rubin were strictly speaking, ambiguous, since it is *possible* to see either region as figure, in fact, the figures are strongly biased toward the inner region (principle of surroundedness in figure-ground organization). Thus, for a figure that the subject during training is instructed to organize in this way, perceiving the inner region as figure in the test is to be expected without any prior experience. Conversely, for a figure in which the surrounding black is to be perceived, the question can legitimately be raised whether such a report in the test truly reflects what the observer perceived. It is difficult to see the black region as figure. Finally, there is the question of how much time is allowed during the test exposure. Obviously, if unlimited time is allowed, the subject can shift his organization one or more times. When he organizes it the same way he had in training, the subject will, of course, recognize the figure and, as a result, may report this as his perception.* Rubin did not control this aspect of the experiment.

On logical grounds a good case can be made for the assertion that past experience *cannot* be expected to determine the perceptual organization in an experiment such as Rubin's. The argument was presented on p. 342. The difficulty with Rubin's experiment is that for a particular test figure to be organized in terms of past experience with that figure, the memory trace of the earlier perceptual organization must be activated and begin its work when the test figure appears. At this moment in time, the test figure is not yet organized one way or the other.

---

*The reader may recall that in Chapter 6, p. 260 a related experiment by Rubin was described on the *recognition* of previously perceived figure-ground patterns. Only if the pattern was organized in the same way on two different occasions was it recognized. But here the issue under discussion is whether prior experience will *determine* the way it subsequently is organized.

Therefore, the memory trace cannot be selected on the basis of similarity to the perceived figure. Why then would just that trace and no other influence the perceptual organization? Of course, once a given perceptual organization occurs in the test, for whatever reason, then if it is the right one, the relevant trace will be activated and recognition will occur. But in that event the trace did not in any way cause the perception; its activation followed the perception.

With this reasoning in mind, other investigators repeated Rubin's experiment many years later, incorporating a number of changes designed to eliminate some of the possible flaws in Rubin's method.[9] They predicted that there would be no effect of experience and the results tended to substantiate that prediction. The procedure consisted of presenting in training only half of the ambiguous figures later to be shown in the test (see Fig. 6–19 for an illustration of the type of figure used). Thus, there would be no question of what was perceived. The test figures were prepared in such a way as to be genuinely ambiguous (see Fig. 6–18) so that it was equally likely that a naive person would see the black or the white region as figure. A subject was repeatedly shown a number of training half-figures, some black, some white, some on the left, some on the right. In the test, the critical figures were presented one at a time with new figures of the same general style, for 1 second. The result was that the number of instances where critical test figures were organized in accord with the training experience was not significantly greater than the number organized in the other way. However, in a few repetitions of this experiment, a significant experience effect was obtained.* Somewhat different procedures were employed in these later experiments so that we are not yet in a position to know what conditions are crucial.

There is, however, at least one experiment in this category where there is no disagreement about the fact of a past-experience effect on perception. In this experiment, fragmented figures of the kind illustrated in Fig. 8–7 were first shown to subjects in a training period.[11] As the reader will note, identification of such figures is not always immediate and it is often necessary to give the observer hints. The footnote identifies the figures and may help the reader to recognize some of them.† Typically, these figures at first look like meaningless arrays of fragments and then suddenly they are reorganized and look like the ob-

---

*Gottschaldt, in repeating Rubin's experiment, obtained his effect, but he attributed it to an expectation and effort on the part of the subject to recognize the familiar figures. When he repeated the experiment so as to minimize this possibility, he failed to obtain the effect. See the other references given.[10]

†Top row: man, sailboat; rabbit. Middle row: dog; stove; locomotive. Bottom row: cat; horse and rider; child on tricycle.

Figure 8–7

jects they represent. In the training period, by allowing ample time and giving hints, all subjects were able to organize the figures into meaningful units. The crucial question was whether, as a result of this prior experience, these subjects would be able to identify the figures when presented again some weeks later for 1 second. Subjects in a control group who had never seen the figures before identified very few in the test, whereas identification in the experimental group was very high.

The use of the term *identification* here should not be taken to mean that this experiment demonstrates an effect of experience on recognition and associated meaning but not on perception. If novel (nonsense) figures of the same fragmented style had been used instead of fragmented figures of objects, then, of course, only subjects who had seen them in training would be able to recognize them in a test. But there is a genuine perceptual change when in viewing potentially familiar figures one goes from an initial "nonsense" organization to a subsequent "meaningful" organization. The figure looks different when it is recognized. Regions, which prior to recognition had no particular relationship to one another, now belong together and vice versa; various parts of the figure now appear as three-dimensional whereas initially they did not, and so on. Thus, the perceptual change can best be characterized saying that the figure now looks like the object it is recognized to represent. The term *recognition-perception* might be useful. It is safe to assume that the experimental subjects in the test achieved this meaningful perceptual organization and that is why they identified the figures. If they did not do so it would be hard to understand how they could identify each figure. The conclusion thus seems inescapable that prior experience enables the subjects later to quickly achieve a perceptual organization that otherwise would not occur.

How then is this possible on logical grounds if it means that the traces established in training are influencing the perceptual organization in the test? A possible explanation is that in the test the first thing to happen when a figure is exposed is that it is organized as a meaningless array, a "nonsense" organization, just as it was at the beginning of the training exposure (see Fig. 8–8). This is plausible because at this point

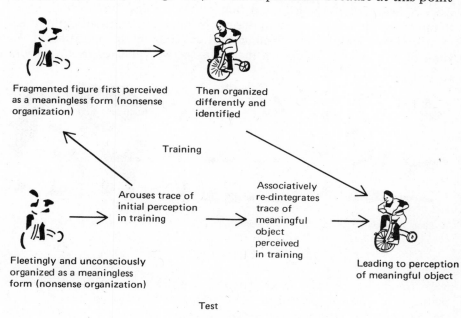

Fragmented figure first perceived as a meaningless form (nonsense organization)

Then organized differently and identified

Training

Arouses trace of initial perception in training

Associatively re-dintegrates trace of meaningful object perceived in training

Fleetingly and unconsciously organized as a meaningless form (nonsense organization)

Leading to perception of meaningful object

Test

Figure 8–8

we are assuming that there is no contact with memory traces. Therefore, perception should be the same as it would be for someone who had never seen the figure before. However, this perceptual event takes place immediately and is not consciously experienced, perhaps because it is so fleeting. The "nonsense" organization is similar to the trace of the "nonsense" organization left behind from the early stage of the training exposure. Therefore, this trace is activated and the subject recognizes the figure as one seen in training. That trace is associated with a trace representing the "meaningful" organization and it is this latter trace that facilitates the correct perceptual organization in the test. Stating the matter in more cognitive terms, a "decision" is made by the perceptual system that the nonsense pattern seen in the test most probably represents the meaningful object that that same nonsense pattern had been found to represent when it had been seen before.

Central to this explanation is the hypothesis that activation of the relevant trace can occur on the basis of an initial organization in the test that is not the same organization as the one the observer consciously perceives. Once again it is necessary to clearly separate phenomenal facts from the functional events one must assume are taking place. It is the similarity of that initial organization to the initial organization from the training period that permits access to the right trace. Support for this interpretation derives from an unpublished experiment in which the "nonsense" organization is deliberately modified at the time of the test.[12] As shown in Fig. 8-9, two types of modifications

Original fragmented figure   Reduced test figure   Supplemented test figure

Figure 8-9

were prepared for each figure used in training. One type is drawn in such a way that the overall pattern is even more reduced than the original fragmented figure (an elephant in the illustration). Parts of each fragment are eliminated. However, the pattern is still similar to the original nonsense figure since each fragment remains intact. The other type is drawn in such a way that it is a better representation of the object than the original figure. Supplementary material is added. However, it is no longer very similar to the original nonsense figure because the component fragments are joined together or otherwise no longer retain their identities. Proof that the desired changes were successfully achieved comes from a control experiment in which these modified figures were shown to naive subjects. Identification of what the figure represents was much better for the second or supplemental type of modification than for the reduced type.

But the prediction was precisely the opposite in the main experiment, namely, that having seen the regular fragmented figures in training, subjects who were now briefly shown the modified, reduced variations in the test would identify them more often than those who were shown the modified supplemented figures in the test. The reason for this prediction is that only the reduced test figures are similar as "nonsense" organizations to the initial organization in the training session. Therefore, only in the case of these test figures is the necessary bridge to the relevant memory trace provided. The result fully supported the prediction in spite of the fact that the supplemented test figures are better representations of the familiar objects as shown by the control experiment.*

The argument here is essentially the same as was made in Chapter 3 in connection with the role of past experience as the basis of various pictorial cues to depth. When an interposition or perspective stimulus pattern is encountered, prior to contact with memory traces, it is fleetingly organized as two-dimensional. But this perceptual organization is similar to those that occurred in the past with such patterns, at which time an impression of depth was produced by other unlearned cues. Therefore, by a process of recognition based on similarity of the two-dimensional organization of percept and trace, memories of the pattern representing depth are associatively aroused and affect the present perceptual organization.

---

*A central problem that is not considered here is how one achieves the organization in the initial exposure to the fragmented figure that leads to recognition and identification. What is it that takes place that produces the shift from the initial meaningless "nonsense" organization? A possible answer to this question is that we identify a part of the figure (for example, a wheel in the lower right figure in Fig. 8-7) and this part evokes a trace of the entire object, which in turn leads to the perceptual reorganization. Evidence for this hypothesis was obtained by Barbara Sang and the author in an unpublished study in which the "part" thought to be the possible basis of recognition in each figure was altered, either favorably to make it more noticeable or a better representation of that part, or unfavorably, to make it a poorer representation of that part. Such alteration had a profound effect in the predicted direction on the ability of subjects to identify the fragmented figures.

Set

A special case of experience determining perceptual organization is where the relevant experience immediately precedes the critical stimulus pattern. It has been assumed that under such conditions an expectation is created of what that pattern will be. This state of affairs is referred to as *experimental* or *objective set*. Often a whole series of prior items is presented first and the organization encouraged by the series is thought to create the expectation. Thus, for example, suppose an observer is shown in sequence the various dot patterns of Fig. 8-10. He starts out by perceiving in (1) the first two dots, second two dots, and so on, as paired and continues with this organization even in (4) where, in fact, proximity no longer favors this organization.

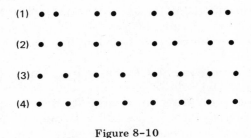

Figure 8-10

In one of the earliest experiments of this kind, subjects were first shown briefly a series of inkblot figures that had a faint resemblance to animals and they were told this.[13] At the end of the series was the critical figure at the top in Fig. 8-11. The subjects were to describe and sketch each figure. A new series of figures was then shown, which faintly resembled mountain scenes, and the subjects were also told this. At the end of this series, the critical figure was again shown. Subjects in a control group were shown both sets of figures in random order (except for the placement of the critical figure that appeared twice near the beginning and at the end of the series). The subjects were given the information that the figures represented either animals or mountain scenes.

As expected, subjects in the control group generally described the critical figure in the same way on the second exposure and recognized it. Subjects in the experimental group, however, described, sketched, and presumably perceived the critical figure very differently in its second exposure than in its first. Typical examples of drawings are shown in the illustration; those on the left for when it appeared at the end of the "animal series," those on the right for when it appeared at the end

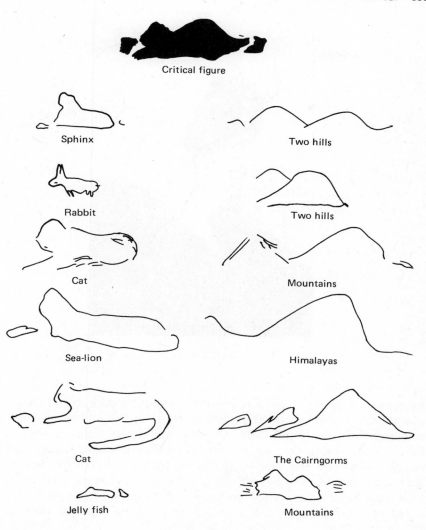

Critical figure

Sphinx

Two hills

Rabbit

Two hills

Cat

Mountains

Sea-lion

Himalayas

Cat

The Cairngorms

Jelly fish

Mountains

Figure 8-11

of the "mountain series." That perception was different on the two occasions is indicated by the failure of recognition for the majority of
subjects.

A different example is shown in Figs. 8-12 and 8-13. If an observer
first views Fig. 8-12, he will see the face of a young woman. He will
then also see a young woman's face in the more ambiguous Fig. 6-25
of Chapter 6. However, if a different observer had seen Fig. 8-13 first,

Figure 8-12

he would then have perceived the ambiguous figure as the face of an old woman.*   This kind of experiment should be conducted with naive observers who have not first seen the ambiguous figure, as the reader has.   (These examples can be thought of as instances, where the perception achieved can best be described by referring to the figural and spatial properties of the object the figure represents, for which the term *recognition-perception* had been previously suggested.)   Still another example is shown in Fig. 8-14a and b.   After having looked at Fig. 8-14a, most observers will perceive Fig. 8-14b as that of the profile seen in a, although it is also possible to perceive it as a different profile, the one facing to the left.[15]

It would thus seem to be relatively easy to demonstrate effects on perception of prior experience under these particular conditions, where-

---

*Leeper performed an experiment of this kind but used a modification of the figure shown.[11]   The original comes from a drawing in *Puck* and was described by Boring.[14]

Figure 8-13

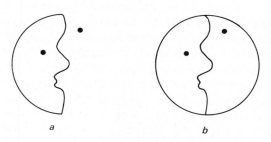

Figure 8-14

as it is not easy to find evidence for a role of experience under other conditions. What then is the essential factor in these conditions? Clearly, it is not necessary to present a sequence of preparatory items as in the first examples, because in the subsequent examples only one prior item was shown. Nor does it follow that a state of expectation must develop from that prior item because all that is involved is exposure to that item. The single factor remaining, therefore, that seems to distinguish experiments of this kind from the previous ones we discussed, is the recency of the past experience.*

In fact, an investigation was undertaken to find out if the crucial factor in these experiments is the expectation that develops of what is to be presented or merely the recent exposure of the relevant stimulus.[16] In one experiment in the study, subjects were shown the following series: 1. The picture of the young woman, Y, (Fig. 8-12). 2. The picture of the old woman, or O (Fig. 8-13). 3. Y 4. O 5. Y 6. O 7. Y. The eighth figure shown was an ambiguous drawing that could be perceived in either way. The subjects were told at the outset that the pictures of the young woman and the old woman would alternate and that they were to call out their identification as quickly as possible. As a result of these instructions and the alternating series, there can be no question that the subjects expected the eighth figure to be the old woman. (Another group of subjects had the series 1. O 2. Y 3. O 4. Y 5. O 6. Y 7. O 8. ambiguous, so that they would have the expectation of the young woman in position 8.) However, if it is the most *recent* experience that influences the perception of the ambiguous figure, then the ambiguous drawing should tend to be perceived as the young woman by the subjects in the first group and as the old woman by the subjects in the second group.

Therefore, the two possible determinants, expectancy and recency, oppose one another. The result was that 73 percent of the time the ambiguous drawing was identified as the same face as the immediately preceding figure, in spite of an expectation to see the other figure. In none of the other experiments in the study was any evidence found to indicate that expectancy per se has any effect on perception. Unfortunately, others who have repeated this experiment or conducted a similar experiment have not obtained the same result. The importance of the study described here, therefore, is in illustrating how it is possible to separate expectation from other possible determinants such as recency. The question must remain open whether experience that occurs immediately before an ambiguous stimulus is presented has a strong effect on how that stimulus is perceived (in contrast with the effect of experience that occurs at an earlier time). One would not be too surprised if recent experience is ultimately shown to have a strong effect. We know

---

*This argument does not strictly apply to the experiment with inkblots, because the recent past experiences provided by the series do not represent the same object as the critical figure, but only objects from the same categories (animals or mountain scenes). Therefore, to explain that finding in terms of recency rather than expectancy, one would have to argue that the prior exposures of these items serves to mobilize the trace of the critical object.

that successively presented stimuli are organized into temporal patterns as in the rhythmical beating of a drum, in melodies, or in visual sequences such as the kinetic depth effect. To understand such temporal patterning one must assume that all but the momentary stimulus is represented in the form of memory traces and that the traces interact with one another and with the momentary stimulus. Since these traces are so recent, they are still active, so that it would not be necessary to raise the question about how they are selected.

However, the organization of an ambiguous figure as a result of a recently established trace is not quite the same thing as the organization of a sequence of stimuli such as tones into a melody. Even if the recent trace can be said to be still active, the question still arises as to how it actually determines the organization of the ambiguous figure. An hypothesis relevant to this question was suggested in Chapter 6, p. 289. It was proposed that what typically happens on exposure to an ambiguous figure is that the alternative modes of organization are "tried out" and that oscillation from one to the other takes place, very rapidly and unconsciously. When the organization that is "preferred" for any reason occurs, it is stabilized and the observer has the conscious experience of that percept. One reason for "preferring" a particular organization is that it is very familiar; another might be that it is congruent with a recent perception.*

If the oscillation hypothesis should prove to be correct, it would provide an answer to the logical dilemma posed earlier in this chapter concerning the influence of a memory trace on subsequent perception. The answer would be that the memory trace is selected *after* the perception occurs, and the effect of the trace is one of stabilizing or fixing that perception. Thus, the problem of how the trace could be selected in advance of the perception is avoided. It is possible that this same mechanism explains other past-experience effects and not only those based on recency. For example, there is little question that most observers perceive Fig. 8-15 as a face in spite of the fact that no face is presented immediately before it, and in spite of the fact that the face is deliberately made white, which is the nonpreferred color. True, this demonstration does not properly control for exposure time, and it is possible that in very brief exposures the face would not be perceived as figure any more than the other region. It can also be argued that the face region is preferred for structural reasons, because it juts into the black region, and not becuase it represents a familiar object. But the author believes on the basis of preliminary research that this *is* a genuine

---

*Some evidence exists in support of this hypothesis.[17]

Figure 8-15

experience effect that can be confirmed even with brief exposures. As such it contradicts the negative results of the repetition of Rubin's experiment described earlier since it too is concerned with the effect of experience on subsequent figure-ground organization. Perhaps the crucial difference is in the *degree* of experience provided.

Many other more recent experiments have been performed on the effect of set on perception, but they have not generally been directed at the question of how the proximal stimulus is organized. Rather the question at issue has been whether or not the identification of a briefly exposed stimulus pattern is facilitated if the observer knows in advance what to expect. Such experiments are more relevant to the role of selective attention or selective "tuning" in perception than to the role of past experience, which is the focus of concern in this chapter. Although this research is not strictly relevant to the present topic, it is briefly considered.

When confronted by a very complex stimulus pattern or an array consisting of many components, selective attention will play a decisive role.* In experiments

*We have already considered the possible effect of selective attention in the perception of complex figures (pp. 312ff), but the research described employed novel material and, therefore, was not directed at the question of identification of familiar figures as in the research now under discussion. Also in the research now under discussion exposure is typically very brief. The role of selective attention is considered again later in this chapter in connection with the problem of learning to make discriminations (pp. 371ff).

done many years ago, the question was investigated of how much can be perceived in a single glance. If an array of letters is presented briefly, the subject typically can correctly report no more than four or five. But in more recent research, an array of letters was presented arranged in rows of three and the subject's attention was directed to a particular row. If a fraction of a second after the array was exposed, a signal was given to report a particular row, the subject was able to report all of these letters correctly.[18]   If, however, the signal was delayed, performance dropped off sharply. This suggests that in some sense of the term perception, all items in the array are perceived. Some sensory representation of each item endures for a fraction of a second. Perception during that brief period is based on the persistence in the visual system of the neural discharging triggered by the retinal image of the letters even after the letter display is turned off. Unless the items are further processed, however, these sensory representations will quickly fade away. The processing must occur within the period when the sensory representation of all items is still present, a matter of milliseconds.

Precisely what this processing consists of is not yet clear but it is plausible to suppose that it involves the kind of figural "description," which, in the last chapter, was suggested as a necessary basis of perceiving specific shape. In the case of letters, such "description" would then lead to identification and the identified letters could then be stored in memory. Attention in this kind of experiment, therefore, results in transforming the sensory registration of stimulus items into identified perceptions that establish more enduring memory traces. The limited performance in the earlier studies resulted from the fact that by the time four or five letters were processed and reported by the subject, sensory memory of the remaining items was no longer available.

Other studies have examined the effect of attention on the identification of attributes of a briefly exposed stimulus. For example, if figures that differ in several dimensions such as color, shape, and the like are presented tachistoscopically, will instructions that direct the subject to attend to one attribute affect the accuracy of report? As might be expected, attention does influence performance, but the further question then arises as to precisely why it does. Is perception facilitated by selective attention in this kind of task? It seems unlikely that we would perceive an object's color less well merely because we are attending to its shape. It is more probable that attended-to and unattended-to attributes are perceived equally well, but that the latter attributes are not as accurately reported because the former are noted (and usually also reported) first. Further research was directed at the question of whether the effects of selective attention in studies of this kind are perceptual or memorial.*

In some studies a figure was exposed tachistoscopically and the effect of selective set on identification was investigated. This kind of experiment may bear on the effect of expectation on reading since the eyes move rapidly during reading and remain stationary for only brief periods. Thus, correct identification and errors of identification may, to some extent, be said to be governed by the set that develops from the context of the preceding words and sentences. In experiments on figure identification the subject was told that the figure is one of a number of alternatives

---

*For a review of the literature on the effect of selective attention, see Egeth.[19]

and the question at issue was whether this information improves performance. If performance is improved, is it because the information affects perception or only facilitates identification by delimiting the possible alternatives before the visual memory fades? By presenting the alternatives before the figure was exposed to some subjects and only after the figure was exposed to other subjects, the attempt has been made to control for such nonperceptual factors. Presumably, only alternatives presented before exposure could affect perceptual processing when the figure is present so that superior performance in the before condition relative to the after condition would seem to imply that perception has been affected. But this technique has been criticized on the grounds that perception of the alternatives afterward may interfere with the processing of the figure, thus retarding performance relative to the before condition. Although new techniques have been evolved to cope with this problem, the evidence is not yet decisive.

Even if these problems are resolved, so that it is established that the effect under study in this kind of experiment is perceptual, the problem still remains of understanding what kind of perceptual effect it is. Does selective attention determine or modify perceptual organization in these situations? These experiments are different from those considered earlier where an ambiguous figure is presented that can be organized in different ways. The focus here is on identification of a form so that the question at issue is how expectation might facilitate the processing of the figure in order to facilitate such identification. Is it possible that the effect is one of improving or sharpening the articulation of the perceived figure? The subject may be better able to look for and find certain features of the figure if he knows what to expect than if he does not. Perhaps the expectation facilitates the correct figural "description," one that conforms more closely to the shape of the object that the figure represents, rather than to some other object. If this were the case, such effects could be considered as instances of recognition-perception (see pp. 349 and 354). However, it is also possible that the selectivity may improve the process of recognizing and identifying the figure while leaving its phenomenal form unchanged. Identification may be genuinely facilitated by information in advance because the subject can compare the perceived figure with the alternatives; whereas when he is given the information only afterward he must compare the less adequate memory trace with the alternatives.*

---

*There is one area of research not discussed at all in this book in which the typical experiment is similar to those discussed here, namely, one in which a figure or word is very briefly exposed. The question at issue is not whether selective attention or expectancy affects identification but whether, prior to the conscious awareness of what is being presented, there is a below-threshold stage of non-conscious perception. Such processes have been variously referred to as subliminal perception, or subception, or perceptual defense. To a great extent this research was inspired by the writings of Sigmund Freud and seeks to establish the presence of unconscious motivational processes in cognition. Since the concern is not with attributes of perception such as size, form, movement and the like—central to this book—but rather with the identification (the meaningful content) of the stimulus, this research will not be considered here. Suffice it to say that the evidence has not been convincing and many of the better known experimental effects have either been shown to be artifacts of uncontrolled factors or to be explicable in other ways. For thoughtful appraisals of much of the research in this area see Allport[20] and Dixon.[21]

In summary, the results of the experiments that indirectly seek to assess the role of past experience on the perception of form seem to warrant the following conclusions:

1. Where principles of organization favor a particular perception of a proximal stimulus pattern, past experience will not spontaneously lead to a different perception.

2. Where the proximal stimulus is ambiguous in the sense that the principles of organization can lead to different perceptions, past experience may or may not influence its organization.

3. Where the proximal stimulus can be identified as a familiar object or as one of several possible familiar objects, past experience leading to recognition and identification will often affect subsequent perception. The stimulus pattern will then be organized in such a way as to conform to the characteristics of the previously identified object.

If experience is to have an effect, there nevertheless must first be a perception of the pattern that is itself *not* a function of experience, and through that perception the relevant memory traces can be activated on the basis of similarity. The trace can then play a role in reorganizing the percept or in stabilizing it. It is also probable that the trace in question must be quite strong or otherwise potent if it is to affect perception since a trace of a very familiar or recently encountered object will have an effect where a relatively unfamiliar one will not.

Direct Evidence

The most frequently cited evidence allegedly supporting the hypothesis that form perception is learned is that dealing with the restoration of sight to those born blind because of congenital cataracts. A cataract is an opacity of the lens; vision is restored by removing the entire lens or the opaque region of it. In principle, this is an ideal natural experiment because we have as a subject an articulate person who has had no prior visual experience and who can tell us about what he perceives. If this subject now perceives in much the same way that normal people do, then clearly past experience as a determinant is ruled out. If his perception is essentially unorganized or organized very differently from the normally sighted, then it would seem to imply that we must learn to perceive. Much of the evidence about these medical cases of congenital blindness, seems to many to support the empiricist hypothesis.[22]   It has been claimed that these patients could not immediately distinguish forms from one another once their vision was restored; a long process of learning was necessary before this was possible.

"There are, however, serious deficiencies in this evidence. . . . The conditions and the exact time after the operation of the observations were not adequately described; the extent of vision present before operation varied from case to case; some of the cases were young children whose reports are difficult to evaluate; [the adequacy of the corrective lens provided, or if any was provided, is not known.] Moreover, the patients, after operation, were faced with a strange new world and often the investigator (usually the surgeon) did not know what questions to ask, or what tests to perform, in order to elicit the subject's experience. In one case, for example, the patient "had great difficulty in describing her sensations in such a way as to convey any clear conception of them to another." Much of this evidence, therefore, is inconclusive. . . . it appears that no distinction was made in these studies between perceptual and interpretative processes. In the eighteenth and nineteenth centuries (when most of the cases studied . . . occurred) the problem was posed by investigators in the following way: Would a blind person, who can distinguish a sphere from a cube by means of touch, be able to identify these forms visually when seen for the first time? Observations of these newly sighted patients seemed to show that they could not. There is, however, no reason to expect such a result. The patient might see the sphere and cube as different forms but would not know their appropriate names until permitted the use of touch. Moreover, even if told which was which, he would have to remember this information, so that further learning would be required for correct identification, although not for perceptual discrimination.

It is clear from some of these cases that the visual field of the patient was not an undifferentiated blur but did consist of forms and shapes which could be perceived but, of course, not named. Frequently, the case report describes the patient looking at something and asking "what is that?" One intelligent patient, as a matter of fact, was able to identify a ball as round and a toy brick as square upon first presentation. In a more recent case, the report also suggests that the patient could see objects but was not able to identify them. The observations on newly sighted patients, therefore, in no way lend support to an empiricist theory of form perception."[23]

Another direct approach to the problem of the role of experience in form perception is to experiment with infants or animals, either by inquiring into the nature of their perception at birth or soon thereafter, or by depriving them of vision from birth until the time of testing. Since animals and infants do not talk, it is necessary to infer what they perceive from their behavior. In the case of animals, the technique that has been preferred required the animal to learn to discriminate two forms, by always rewarding one. Since such learning would not take place if the difference between the forms could not be perceived, successful learning presupposes form perception. Because, further, it has been assumed that in many species the ability to learn such a problem and to perform adequately requires a certain level of development, the experiment was not performed until the animal was sufficiently mature.

Therefore, the animal was reared without vision until the time of the experiment. Unfortunately, this leads to certain difficulties in the interpretation of the results.

However, another possibility is that an animal may have certain innate preferences or aversions in response to visual stimuli and that the behavior involved may well be present at birth. If such behaviors are elicited, then form perception must be present. We have already considered examples of this kind of evidence although not in connection with form perception. Thus, the innate capacity to perceive distance by many species of animal could be demonstrated using the visual cliff because of innate fear of falling from a height.

In research on the properties of the stimulus that will elicit various instinctual reactions, it has been found that one such property is form. Thus, for example, herring-gull chicks on the morning after hatching will peck more at artificially constructed models of the bill of the parent if these models are elongated, point down, and have a protrusion near the end.[24]

With this same approach in mind, one investigator reasoned that newly hatched chicks may very well have a preference for certain shapes because they begin to peck at small particles on the ground shortly after hatching.[25] The chicks were left in a lightproof room from 1 to 3 days after hatching until the moment of the experiment. At that time they were placed in test boxes that contained various small solid figures of various shapes set into the wall and covered with transparent plastic (see Fig. 8–16). When the chick pecked at a figure, a sensitive microswitch was depressed and thus recorded the peck. In one experiment, there were four figures available, a sphere, an ellipsoid, a pyramid, and a star. The total number of pecks at these figures by 100 chicks were 24,346 for the sphere, 28,122 for the ellipsoid, 2,492 for the pyramid, and 2,076 for the star. Another experiment established that the chicks were not preferring the round and elliptical figures on the basis of a possible difference in size between them and the other figures. Therefore, it is clear that the preference for rounded shapes is strong. There seems little alternative to the conclusion that chicks soon after hatching and with no prior experience perceive form.*

The preference technique has also been used with primate and human infants. Some years ago a method was devised to study the question of whether infants perceived color, which consisted of noting on which colored region placed overhead the infant tended to fixate most often. This method has now been used to find out whether infants prefer to

---

*The chicks also preferred a three-dimensional sphere to a flat round disk, thus indicating innate depth perception as well.

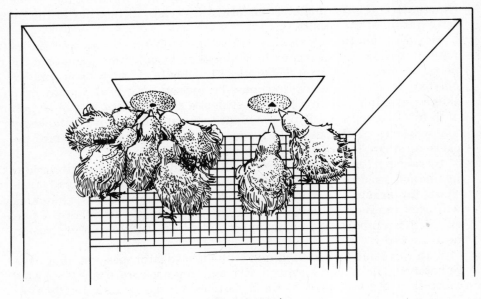

Figure 8-16

look at one pattern rather than another.[26]   If they do, the implication is that they must perceive a difference and that presumably implies form perception. The observer views the infant's eyes through a peephole as shown in Fig. 8-17 and records where the infant is looking. The direction of the gaze is revealed by what is reflected from the central pupillary area of the surface of the eye. Motion pictures can also be taken through the peephole and the films examined later.

Preferences clearly do exist for infants even during the first week of life and these preferences change over time. The infant generally looks at more complex patterns in preference to less complex ones. However, these studies provide little evidence for *form* preference, i.e., that one shape is preferred over another. Thus, for example, Fig. 8-18*a* is preferred over *b*, but there is no preference between *c* and *d*. The outer shape of *a* and *b* is the same; only the internal pattern differs. This technique has been used with newborn infants and with more detailed analyses of precisely where in a given pattern the infant prefers to look.[27]   Thus, a newborn infant will prefer to look at a triangle rather than a homogeneous field, and in doing so will show less variation in eye position. There also appears to be a tendency to look at certain parts of figures, such as the vertices. Nevertheless, it is not clear what these findings mean. The preference for complex figures or even for

Figure 8–17

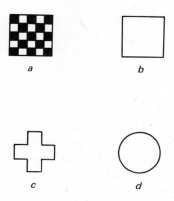

a   *b*

c   *d*

Figure 8–18

certain parts of figures does not necessarily prove that organized form perception is present or that the forms look the same to infants as they do to us. It is possible that the eye movements are guided by maximal differences in *stimulation* rather than in the perceptual organization of that stimulation. Only clear preference among forms of equal complexity and equality of other physical attributes, such as luminance, would indicate the presence of form perception.

The experiment briefly referred to in Chapter 2, p. 71 on the origin of constancy of shape—although directed at the problem of constancy rather than of form perception—does indicate the presence of form perception, at least in the 2-month-old infant.[28]   The plan of this experiment followed the one on size perception (p. 64). The infants were able to discriminate between a rectangle and a trapezoid of about the same size. The data derived not from what the infant preferred to look at but from the extent to which the infant continued responding with slight turning movements of the head that had been conditioned to a particular shape when that shape was changed in the test.

Much of the evidence gathered from experiments on animals reared to maturity in darkness, or without the possibility of patterned vision, seems to indicate a deficit in form perception. This result was taken as supporting the empiricist position. In the earliest experiments of this type, the animals were reared in complete darkness. For example, in one study, chimpanzees were kept in the dark from 7 to 16 months before testing began.[29] It was evident that the visual perception of these animals was poor; they gave little evidence of discriminating objects from one another, and a number of typical visual reflexes were absent. Subsequently, however, careful examination indicated cellular changes in the visual system of these animals, a condition known as *optic atrophy*. Apparently, exposure to light is necessary for the normal maturation and continued viability of the visual nervous system. In subsequent experiments, therefore, animals were reared not in darkness but without patterned vision. This can easily be accomplished by either rearing animals from birth with plastic head covers or eye covers that are translucent but not transparent, *or* by rearing them in darkness but providing a certain amount of exposure to light each day at which time such covers are used.

Several experiments of this kind have been conducted with various species.[30]   Generally, the results of these experiments indicate some deficit in form perception since the experimentally reared animals require a greater number of trials to learn a form discrimination than do normally reared animals. However, there are a number of reasons why this evidence may be misleading. First, it still seems to be the case that the normal maturation of the visual system is prevented, even with some exposure to light each day. There is evidence that in kittens, forced disuse of an eye by suturing the eyelids closed or through the use of light-diffusing occluders results in the impairment of the visual system's capacity to respond to stimulation by contours and edges.[31] There is also evidence that rearing in diffuse light adversely affects visual acuity in monkeys.[32] *

Very recently a new line of research has been initiated in which animals are reared during their first weeks or months under conditions where they are exposed only to certain restricted kinds of stimulation. For example kittens were raised in a chamber where only vertical lines or only horizontal lines were present.[34] In one study one eye was exposed to contours in one orientation and alternately the other eye was exposed to contours in another orientation.[35] What all these experiments reveal is that subsequent to the restricted visual experience the animals do not have the kinds of neural "detector" units in the cortex which normal animals of the same age have. Typically only those units can be found which are responsive to the kind of patterns which were present in the restricted environment. These findings challenge the earlier belief that the detector mechanisms are present in very young kittens independent of any visual experience and are therefore innately determined.[36]

But what is not yet entirely clear is the consequence for perception of such restricted exposure. A few observations cited in one study imply that the animals are "blind" to contours in orientations not encountered during the earlier period.[37] However in another study specifically designed to answer this question, in which the animals were given several form discrimination problems, a very different conclusion was reached.[38] Whereas there was some slight superiority in learning to discriminate between contours in orientations for which the cats had had prior exposure over those between which they had not had prior exposure, the fact is the cats could learn to make the latter discrimination relatively easily. Other research also suggests that the deficit is primarily one of reduction in acuity rather than the inability to perceive contours in certain orientations.[39] Therefore although it is premature to draw any final conclusions the evidence thus far suggests that the edge-detector units are not necessary for the perception of contours although they seem to play some role in mediating visual acuity. As stated previously (pp. 317–318) this leaves unexplained what the precise function is of these neural mechanisms.

In any event, whatever the role may prove to be of exposure to the environment in the determination of the structure of the visual nervous system, it is important to understand that the necessity for such exposure does not imply that form perception is the result of prior learning. The empiricist hypothesis as explored in this chapter is that we learn to perceive form on the basis of past experience, and this is quite different than the assertion that the neural mechanisms which must mediate

---

*In the rat, however, a species that has evolved to live in darkness, dark-rearing for 90 days even without diffuse light exposure, does *not* result in poorer learning of a form discrimination.[33]

perception require certain conditions for their growth and maturation. In the context of the discussion here, what matters is that the elimination of these necessary conditions by rearing animals in the dark, in diffuse light, or other restricted conditions of stimulation, seems to result in an abnormal visual nervous system. Therefore experiments employing this method become very difficult to interpret with respect to the issue of learning to perceive form.

A second reason why evidence based on rearing animals without pattern vision may be misleading is that in some studies, where ability to discriminate dimensions other than form have been tested, visual deficits have also been found. Thus, for example, chimpanzees reared without patterned vision take longer to learn a size discrimination than the normal controls. Since few would argue that size perception must be learned (where the objects compared are both at the same distance), this finding casts doubt on the meaning of the form discrimination data.

Third, it is possible that the difficulty in discrimination learning is based on some fundamental visual impairment other than form perception per se. For example, the chimpanzees studied had difficulty in coordinating their eye movements both in binocular fixation and the pursuit of moving objects, and suffered from spontaneous nystagmus, i.e., involuntary oscillations of the eyes. It is possible too that if position constancy is learned, it may not have been achieved during the abnormal conditions of rearing, so that now, in the testing, the world appears to move whenever the animal moves. All of these things would obviously interfere seriously with learning a visual discrimination of any kind. Furthermore, there is the possibility that animals reared without pattern vision may be deficient not in form perception but in visual-motor coordination. Thus, if the discrimination training requires the animal to run or fly from a starting position to the place where the figures are located, a deficit may occur for experimental animals that actually is not based on difficulty in form perception. There is evidence that the development of visual-motor coordination is adversely affected by rearing animals in the dark or without pattern vision.

Fourth, one can consider the meaning of the *absolute* number of learning trials for the experimental animals and the *absolute difference* between experimental and control animals rather than simply the fact of statistically significant group differences. For example, in one study with ring doves, after 8 to 12 weeks of wearing plastic hoods over the eyes, the doves required an average of 126.8 trials to learn to discriminate a triangle from a circle.[40] The control group averaged 77.7 trials. Since there were 30 trials per day, it took about 4 days or less than 2 additional days for the experimental animals to learn. If form perception was completely absent in these animals, it ought to take a long time indeed before they could begin to learn a problem that required form perception as a precondition.

Fifth, it is entirely reasonable that a perceptual ability present at birth would fail to appear if prevented from being used over the long critical period of earliest development. There is evidence to support this statement. For example, chickens reared until 10 weeks of age in the dark or with translucent hoods manifested a number of anomolous behaviors, such as random pecking in the air, slowness in developing recognition of food, pecking inaccuracy, and retardation or complete failure in learning to discriminate a circle from a triangle.[41]   Yet we know that newly hatched chicks display none of these difficulties and are able to discriminate form. Or, to cite another example, rats reared for 10 months in darkness no longer avoid the deep side of the visual cliff, whereas after 1 month of dark-rearing they do.[42]   So the premise on which these experiments is based is false, namely, that if following the experimental rearing, the ability is not displayed at the time of testing, then it was not present at birth.

Sixth, learning a discrimination entails more than just perception; cognitive factors are also involved. An animal might perceptually distinguish a triangle and circle from the start, but nevertheless requires training to learn that a response to one stimulus is followed by reward whereas response to the other stimulus is not. A human subject might require several trials before realizing that a triangle is always rewarded and a circle is not. But no one would argue from this fact that on these first few trials the subject did not perceive the forms veridically. It is plausible that an animal deprived of visual form experience since birth would be somewhat retarded in its ability to solve a discrimination problem. There is evidence that intelligence is to some extent a function of the richness and variety of stimulation in the environment in which a human or animal infant is raised, and that an impoverished environment has a serious effect on cognitive and emotional growth. Clearly the dark-field or homogeneous-light environments used in the experiments under discussion would be in the category of "impoverished." (Many of the points made here are also applicable to the data on human subjects whose sight is restored.)

The most direct approach to the problem under consideration would be to find out if an animal can learn to discriminate between different shapes soon after birth. It had been thought that in primates, discrimination learning would not be possible until the animal was mature and, by that time, an experiment would no longer be crucial. But now it has been found that by making use of the right techniques, infant monkeys can begin to learn discriminations of achromatic or chromatic color, size, and form from the first day of life.[43]

In one experiment, 11-day-old rhesus monkeys had to learn to discriminate a triangle from a circle (see Fig. 8–19). On the average, it

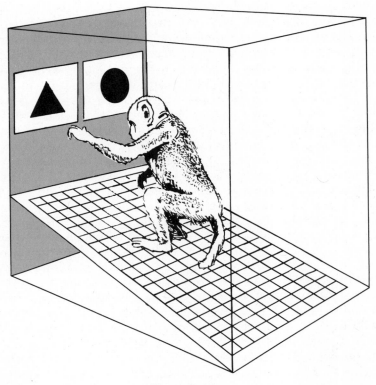

Figure 8–19

took them 10 days (25 trials per day) to reach the criteria of being correct on 21 or more of the 25 trials per day for 2 consecutive days. However, it seems clear that they were performing at a beyond-chance level long before that. In a comparable experiment the investigators found that, on the average, it took about as long for 11-day-old monkeys to learn to discriminate two equal-size rectangles that differed only in neutral color. And it required an average of 24 days for another group of 27-day-old monkeys to learn a size discrimination problem. Since few would think that learning is necessary for the discrimination of neutral colors or sizes (when the objects compared are under the same illumination and at the same distance) it is probable that the length of time required to learn these problems, including that of form discrimination, has to do with cognitive factors such as those discussed previously. In fact, the equivalence of the results for form and neutral color problems would seem to be very strong evidence that form perception is present at birth in the monkey.

Following the learning of the form discrimination problem, that is, in this instance, to choose a black triangle rather than a black circle, the monkeys were tested on pairs of figures that differed in certain respects from the original ones. It was found that the animals preferred an outline triangle over an outline circle, a broken-line outline triangle over a broken-line outline circle, a white triangle over a white circle, and so forth, but that they did not have a preference when given a black diamond and a black square or other pairs where both test figures differed too markedly from the originals. These tests provide further evidence that the original discrimination was made on the basis of *form* perception and suggest that the chimpanzees' perception of these forms is very much like, if not identical to, that of humans.

Thus, it appears that whereas there is no unimpeachable data supporting the empiricist hypothesis, there is some data indicating the presence of form perception at birth in some species or soon thereafter in other species and in human infants.*

Learning to Make Discriminations

Figure 8-20

---

*In a different line of research, one investigator has asked the question whether the various Gestalt laws of grouping are innate or based on experience.[44] Although these experiments are bold and ingenious, in the present author's opinion it is not certain that they succeed in their intent of isolating the laws of grouping under study.

Everyone agrees on the existence of one kind of effect of experience on perception, although there is little understanding of exactly what is learned or how the learning takes place. Clearly, we learn to discriminate objects from one another that are quite similar, often members of a class, which at the outset we were unable to differentiate. There are countless examples. The child learns that printed or spoken words differ from one another; the adult learns that identical twins are, after a while, distinguishable from each other; he learns that members of other races actually look quite different from one another; the specialist learns to discriminate animal faces, birds, trees, X-ray pictures, and so forth.

Is this kind of effect of experience perceptual in nature? Is it really true that identical twins, or monkeys of the same species, or sheep, for example, look identical at first, but eventually come to look different? Compare Fig. 8–20 with Fig. 8–21. Since there is a stimulus basis for the slight difference in the appearance of twins, the question arises as to why this stimulus difference did not initially lead to a perceptual difference. One answer is that generally only one member of a class is seen at a time. When another member is seen, the similarities far outweigh the differences so that we are struck by the essentially identical appearance of the two. Furthermore, the question of memory enters into the problem. If not every subtle nuance of the initial member is recorded (or preserved) in memory, then clearly there will be no basis for making the necessary discrimination when the second member is encountered. Placed side by side, however, the reliance on memory is obviated and the two members can be discriminated immediately.

Or can they? The trouble with the "thought experiment" posed here is that when the two members are placed side by side and examined, the observer is now in a different state of mind; he is comparing the two and *looking for differences*. Although it may even then be difficult to find the difference, generally it will be noted. This simply confirms the fact that the members of the class differ enough from one another that the difference is perceptible under the right conditions. What would be the effect of presenting the members together but under conditions where the observer is not looking for differences? This is a difficult experiment to do because at some point we have to ask the observer whether or not the figures appear identical. If we ask him while the figures are still present, we immediately evoke the special attitude of looking for differences; if we ask him after removing the figures, we get into problems concerning memory.

Still the fact remains that once discriminations are learned, the members of a class will look quite different from one another even if they are seen one at a time. Therefore, there must be some basis in memory for the discrimination that did not exist before. A plausible explana-

Figure 8-21

tion of what is involved here may run as follows. During the initial encounter with a member of a new class, not every nuance is noted, attended to, implicitly "described," or in short, perceived. (The complex figure shown in Fig. 7-17 of Chapter 7 is another good example.) The stimulus features of every such nuance are registered, but we have repeatedly seen that one must distinguish between the proximal stimulus as a physical entity and the psychological organization to which it gives rise. Therefore, there are no memory traces or adequate traces established for every facet of the figure. A good working rule about memory and learning is that only that which is perceived is encoded in memory.

That being the case, it is not surprising that when another member of the class is encountered later it will appear identical to the previously seen member. There simply is no basis for discrimination between them, but it would be misleading to lay the blame merely on a failure of memory. That failure reflects a more fundamental fact, namely, an inadequate or incomplete perception in the first place. Hence, when discriminations are finally made, they imply that the relevant nuances of the figure are perceived, and are, therefore, recorded in memory.

How does the change come about? One obvious answer is that often it is necessary to discriminate members of a class from one another, so we begin looking for features that will enable us to discriminate them. This involves attending to different aspects of the figure and the important psychological process of attention is one that we know very little about. Thus, for example, if we want to be able to discriminate one automobile make or model from another, we soon realize that we must notice subtle differences in overall shape to which we initially paid no attention (see Fig. 8-22).

However, more often than not, the ability to discriminate develops unconsciously, without any deliberate effort on our part, and with no awareness of the feature that enables us to make the discrimination. We do not know how this happens, but it is possible that mere repeated

Figure 8-22

exposure to the members of the class in question will be sufficient. The reason may be that the memory trace (or trace complex that represents all prior encounters with the same and similar objects) becomes increasingly differentiated with repeated exposure to the members. Perhaps on each exposure, a feature is "noted" that had not been on prior exposures. Thus, a trace of *that* feature is established, and so on. With the development of an increasingly "enriched" trace, there is a basis for comparison between the present figure and previously seen figures that heretofore did not exist.

Laboratory research on this problem is still at an early stage. Experiments have been conducted to demonstrate that discrimination among novel figures not initially made will be made with repeated exposure. In one such experiment, it was shown that children took much longer than adults to arrive at such discrimination.[45] Experiments have also been performed to test two hypotheses concerning the basis of discrimination learning, hypotheses that have been hinted at in the preceding paragraphs.[46] One hypothesis, which the investigator refers to as "the learning of prototypes" and others have called the *trace enrichment hypothesis*, is that a detailed memory trace is acquired of each object more or less along the lines suggested here. The other hypothesis, referred to as the *differentiation hypothesis*, is that the subject learns which dimensions of difference between the objects to be discriminated are relevant. For example, a child might learn that orientation is a dimension that is relevant in distinguishing certain letters from one another.

The plan of the experiment was as follows. First the subjects, kindergarten children, had to learn to discriminate standard figures from certain transformations of these figures (see Fig. 8–23). Each child learned some figures and some of the transformations of the kind shown. Following that, two experimental groups were formed. One group, the Differentiation Group, now had to learn to discriminate new figures from one another but with the same kinds of transformation they were given in the first part of the experiment. For example, if the children had learned to discriminate standard figure *A* in Fig. 8–23 from those with different line curvature (1 and 2), they now had to learn to dis-

Standard   Transformations

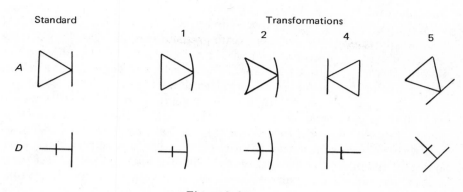

Figure 8-23

criminate standard figure D from those with different line curvatures (1 and 2). The other group, the Prototype Group, now learned to discriminate the same figures as before but with new transformations. For example, if the children had learned to discriminate standard figure A from 1 and 2, they now had to learn to discriminate standard figure A from 4 and 5.

The children in the Differentiation Group who were tested with new figures and previously learned transformations did best on the new task. This is taken as evidence for the differentiation hypothesis, namely, that what is important is learning what aspects or dimensions of the form are relevant for the proper identification. Of course, it is not surprising that this group did well, since training on the first task is tantamount to telling the children that such aspects as curvature of lines or left-right orientation are important. It is probable that a set would develop to look for such features in the second task. The children in the Prototype Group who were given the old figures but with new transformations were significantly poorer than the Differentiation Group, but were significantly better than a control group that received new figures *and* new transformations in the second task. This is taken to mean that a prototype or enriched trace may develop and may be useful in discrimination learning under certain conditions, but that it is less of a factor than the learning of the relevant dimensions.* However, it is

*Further research on tactual form discrimination in children suggested that the superiority of the Prototype Group over the Control Group disappears under conditions of testing in which the figures compared are *simultaneously* presented. When the subject must rely on memory of the standard he is apparently aided by the presence of a trace that represents the standard more faithfully.

possible that for the children in this group, the Prototype Group, the very set to look for certain dimensions that would develop in the first task would operate to depress learning in the second. The subject may be attending to dimensions that would not help him to discriminate.

Even granting that the conclusion drawn by the experimenter is correct, and the crucial factor in form discrimination is that of becoming attuned to the relevant features of the object, the question still remains as to how this knowledge is acquired, how it is stored, and how it is applied. Is it in the form of a conscious, verbal principle: for example, "to discriminate one sheep from another, note the width of the nose and the distance between the eyes?" This seems unlikely. But what would it mean to say that we have learned the dimensions that are relevant for discrimination but we are not aware of what they are? A further problem is how this knowledge is stored. Must it not be stored in the form of memory traces of some kind? In that event, the hypothesis comes closer to the trace-enrichment hypothesis. Finally, there is the question of how the learning is applied at the time a discrimination is made. After we have learned to distinguish twins and are looking at one of them and perceive him as distinct from the other, we may not be able to pinpoint the respect in which he looks different. So it would appear that the learning is applied unconsciously as well.

Before concluding this discussion, a brief comment is warranted about the question of when it is and when it is not necessary to learn to discriminate forms from one another. To the extent that form perception is innately determined—and much of the evidence and argument in this chapter is in support of this conclusion—it is not necessary to learn to discriminate most forms from one another. They look different to begin with. It takes a number of trials for animals to learn a form discrimination for the same reason it does to learn a color or size discrimination problem, and not because the form differences are not perceived: the animal must solve a problem, i.e., that form is the relevant feature and that one of the two forms is always rewarded.

The necessity for perceptual learning arises only when the difference between forms is very slight or when complex forms must be discriminated that are globally similar but differ in nuances. This occurs primarily for members of a class of objects. However, there undoubtedly are species differences and developmental differences concerning what degree of similarity and difference among figures requires such perceptual learning. The adult easily discriminates one face from another (at least for individuals of his own race), whereas the infant probably finds it difficult to do so; the adult would not confuse different kinds of triangles whereas the young child probably would, and so on.

Vision and Touch

Reference was made at the beginning of the chapter to the hypothesis suggested by Berkeley concerning how visual perception is learned, which was that we learn to interpret the retinal image on the basis of information supplied through touch perception.* Berkeley's thesis has never really lost its appeal as evidenced by the following quotation from John Dewey two centuries later: "Ultimately visual perception rests on tactual . . . Spatial relations are not originally perceived by the eye, but are the result of the association of visual sensations, with previous muscular and tactual experiences."[47] Although the modern-day empiricist emphasizes the role of prior *visual* experience on the development of perception, the Berkeleyan hypothesis still crops up from time to time and is still held by many optometrists and ophthalmologists who are concerned with training children to overcome perceptual deficiencies of one kind or another.

If one thinks about the matter carefully, however, the logic of the thesis is not at all clear. Why should the set of discrete sensations emanating from, say, the fingers be considered to be a direct source of veridical information about the nature of object properties, or so much a better source than vision? This problem was briefly discussed earlier in the chapter (pp. 341–342). And what sense would this claim make for various species of animals? Can a bird learn about visual form through touch perception? Furthermore, one may ask if the sense of touch is sufficiently precise to be the source of the great accuracy in form and space perception that obtains in vision. To get at this issue experimentally, a sensory conflict can be created in which the eye receives information concerning the nature of an object that is different from the information the hand receives if the object is simultaneously grasped. For example, suppose that a 1-inch square is viewed through a reducing lens so that it looks like a ½ inch square.[48] If now the observer grasps the square—ideally grasping it from behind, through a thin cloth so that he does not see his hand—in principle, touch perception should inform

---

*"Touch perception" or "tactual perception" is used here to mean perception resulting from feeling an object with some part of the body, generally the hands. Although sensations triggered by the deformation of the skin of the fingers is a source of information that there is contact with an object, the perception of shape and size through touch is undoubtedly based on the proprioceptive information deriving from the position of the fingers or other parts of the body relative to one another.

him that it is a 1-inch square. Therefore, a conflict of information exists. If touch educates vision, one would think that the observer would rely on it and, therefore, judge the square to be larger than it appears to be visually.

But that is not what happens. Rather, observers judge the square to be roughly the same size as when, in a control experiment, they view it through the lens without touching it. They are generally unaware that there is a contradiction and, further, they believe that the square *feels* to be the size that it appears to be. In other words, not only is vision the dominant sense but it "captures" touch, so that the latter is perceived as conforming to the former. More relevant to the problem of form perception is the observation that when an observer runs his hand along a straight rod viewed through a prism, which causes it to appear curved, the rod actually feels curved as well.[49] Experiments on form perception analogous to the one described on size perception have been performed.[48] Instead of a reducing lens, a cylindrical optical device was used which had the effect of making objects appear narrower than they actually were. Thus, a square looked like a narrow rectangle, but through touch, of course, it should feel like a square. The result was again that vision completely dominated the experience and the shape experienced by the fingers was felt to conform to the visual impression (see Fig. 8-24).

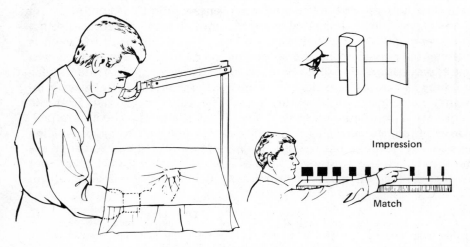

Figure 8-24

These experiments show that when vision and touch provide conflicting information, we perceive on the basis of the visual information.

However, this is an immediate effect. The belief that vision is origin-ally educated by touch is based upon the fact that the infant has a long period of continuous experience with the two senses. Perhaps, there-fore, the experiments described on what happens at the moment of ex-posure to a conflict situation are not crucial to the argument. One might want to argue that a more relevant question is: "What is the ef-fect of a period of exposure to such a sensory conflict that is long enough to allow a change in perception to take place?"

In the experiments cited it is possible that vision suppresses touch only during the period of exposure to the conflict, and that as soon as a person no longer sees the object his touch perceptions return to nor-mal. It is even possible that although vision is at first dominant, it eventually undergoes a change so as to conform with touch. But the converse could also occur. Given sufficient exposure to the conflict, what is experienced by touch may be altered so that misperceptions by touch persist even after vision is eliminated. With this question in mind, experiments were undertaken to determine whether changes in percep-tion would occur as a result of exposure to the conflict that is contin-ued over a period of time.[50]

In one such experiment, the subject handled squares of various sizes while looking at them through a reducing lens over a period of 30 min-utes. Thus, there was some basis for expecting that perception through vision or touch would undergo a change. Without entering into a dis-cussion of all the problems connected with measuring the effect, suffice it to say that tests after the exposure period established that it was touch perception not visual perception that had changed. When, after the exposure period, the subjects selected by touch alone squares that they felt were the same size as previously experienced squares, the great majority chose a larger square than they had before the exposure pe-riod. Thus, vision had educated touch; the subjects had learned that the size value of the felt square was smaller than before because it was as-sociated with a smaller visual percept during the exposure period. Therefore, afterward, the square experienced by touch alone had to be larger before it would seem to signify a particular size.

Experiments on the effect of a left-right reversal of the retinal image were also performed.* The subject looks through reversing prisms while viewing his hand moving back and forth. If the hand moves in one di-rection, and, therefore, is felt to be moving in that direction, but ap-

---

*Although such research, including that on the perception of size just described, is not directly concerned with form perception, it is discussed here because it is di-rectly relevant to the Berkeleyan thesis and dramatically demonstrates the domi-nance of vision over touch.

pears visually to be moving in the opposite direction, what will be experienced? The result indicates that even in this radical conflict situation, vision "captures" touch and the observer ultimately feels his hand moving in the direction in which it is seen to move.[51]

The subject looked through a right-angle prism that, in the manner of a mirror, reverses the visual field right for left (see Fig. 8–25). The subject viewed his hand through the prism, while drawing and doodling, but he was not allowed to write and, therefore, he did not see any letters or numbers while looking through the prism. Although most subjects at first felt their hand move in one direction while simultaneously seeing it going in the opposite direction, so that the felt hand and the seen hand seemed to be separate things, within minutes the subjects no longer experienced any contradiction between how they saw their hand move and how they felt it move. Consequently, they no longer had the trouble drawing or doodling that they had at the outset.

Was there an aftereffect of this visual "capture?" To find out, at the end of each prism-exposure period the subject's view through the prism was blocked. Various letters or numbers were then read to him and he was asked to write them quickly. The subjects were also requested to report whenever they thought they had written a letter backward. The result was that errors occurred for about 30 per cent of the letters. Either the subjects wrote the letters backward or they believed that they had written them backward when, in fact, they had not. Every

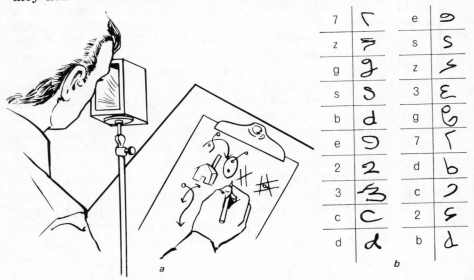

Figure 8–25

subject made at least one such error. Fig. 8-25*b* shows the figures written by two subjects. It is quite surprising that a short period of exposure to left-right reversal could lead to errors in writing letters and numbers that are so familiar and that have been written correctly so many times in the past.

One might wish to argue that none of these experiments is relevant to Berkeley's thesis because they do not tell us about the relationship between vision and touch in the infant. Perhaps, vision is initially educated by touch, but later, as a result of years of independent visual experience, the relationship reverses itself, and vision becomes dominant. This question was recently investigated in infants 7 days old and older.[52] In one condition, a visual object was presented and the tendency to grasp it and the nature of the grasping behavior was carefully observed. It was found that all the infants studied shaped their hands appropriately in anticipation of grasping the object. In another condition, an object was placed in the infant's hand while it and his hand were out of sight. It was found that there were no instances of appropriate shaping of the hand in response to the physical contact, nor did this contact ever lead to an attempt to look at the object, at least in the youngest infants. In a third condition, the infants viewed two polarized shadows cast by an object through polarized filters with the result that they perceived a stereoscopically produced object located in front of the shadow screen that, in fact, was not there at all. The infants sought to grasp this "object" and were upset when they could not. In another experiment, the stereoscopic percept was such that it looked like a flowing entity without definite surfaces rather than a solid object. This led to a different type of hand behavior, namely, the infant moved his hand to the object but stopped short with his hands open and did not close his hands over it.

This investigation establishes that very young infants are guided in their earliest exploratory actions by pure visual perceptions so that even the experience of an object as a solid tangible thing would seem *not* to be the result of the education of vision by touch as so many have believed. The appropriate shaping of the hand in advance of contact suggests veridical form perception by vision alone. Conversely, the infant's early behavior does not seem to be guided by pure tactual perceptions.

From these several investigations one can draw the conclusion that not only was Berkeley incorrect but the opposite of his hypothesis is true, namely, that the child learns about the tactual size and shape of objects by obtaining visual experience of them simultaneously. In other words, when the child grasps an object, the position of the fingers with respect to one another and to the hand as a whole transmits proprioceptive signals to the brain. The size or shape that comes to be signified by this complex of signals may well be, by virtue of association, the result of simultaneously seeing the object. This is, of course, the meaning of the adaptation experiments described previously. It suggests that the apprehension of size and shape by touch is accomplished by a process of *visualizing*, at least in those who are not born blind.

Summary

Logical considerations suggest that we could not learn to perceive form in infancy and the experimental evidence indicates that indeed it is not necessary to do so. Rather the evidence shows that perceptual organization leading to distinct and segregated specific shapes is present at birth or shortly thereafter in various species. This conclusion is based on an analysis of the direct evidence that reveals the presence of form perception at or shortly after birth when appropriate methods are employed: either making use of innate preferences of a given species or training an animal to respond to form at a very early stage of development. Other methods, in which subjects are deprived of vision from the time of birth and then tested, were shown to be inadequate and misleading.

The widely venerated classical hypothesis that visual perception is learned early in life on the basis of touch perception was put to experimental test by creating a sensory conflict between vision and touch. The results indicate that vision is dominant, and, in fact, that what is experienced by touch in such a conflict situation conforms to or is "captured" by what is experienced by vision. Further research demonstrated that continued exposure to such conflict situations results in an adaptive change of touch perception, not of visual perception as the classical hypothesis would predict. Experiments have also shown that vision is dominant over touch even for the 1-week-old human infant.

But the conclusion about the innate basis of visual form perception does not necessarily preclude effects of past experience on perception. In this regard it is important not to confuse perception of form per se with the recognition and identification of previously seen forms. The latter events are by definition a function of prior experience. Normally, recognition must be assumed to be based on events that occur *after* form is perceived—despite the immediacy of recognition in one's experience—and to depend upon the similarity of the perceived form to memory traces of that form seen in the past. This raises the question of how it would be possible for specific traces of previous perceptions to determine the form that is perceived since that implies that the appropriate trace is influencing the perceptual organization before the form is perceived.

An analysis of the indirect evidence, in which a possible effect on form perception of specific experience given to sighted subjects is investigated, indicates that past experience has little effect on what is spontaneously perceived when various principles of organization lead to a perceptual outcome different from one that would be determined by such experience. Even when the proximal stimulus is ambiguous, perception is not necessarily governed by past experience. In certain cases, however, where a configuration is potentially recognizable as a familiar object, it will often be perceived in this way—particularly after it has been so recognized—rather than as a novel configuration. There is reason for believing that the kind of experience that comes immediately before perception of the critical figures, as in experiments on set, is especially effective, but there is no clear direct evidence that this is based on an expectation; alternatively, whether such effects are based on the recency of the experience is not yet known with certainty. But whenever past experience does affect the form that is perceived, it is probable that the perception depends upon a prior step in which the configuration is first organized as it would be without such experience. Once that occurs, the arousal of the appropriate trace leading to recognition makes possible a perceptual reorganization of the configuration.

Learning to discriminate one complex figure from others that are quite similar is clearly another kind of effect of past experience on form perception. The necessity for such experience arises because the global features of certain classes of figures, as, for example, faces of animals or humans, are at first attended to rather than the more subtle nuances that distinguish one figure of the class from others. Thus, repeated experience provides the opportunity of attending to and forming adequate memories of such subtle features.

In conclusion, therefore, although form perception is for the most part innately determined, there are the following effects of past experience:

1. The establishment of memories that lead subsequently to the recognition and identification of forms.
2. The reorganization of certain potentially familiar configurations once contact with the appropriate memory traces has been made.

3. The discrimination of members of certain classes of complex forms. To these one might add effects discussed in other chapter, as follows.
4. The modification of specific shape, such as line curvature, on the basis of adaptation to optical distortion.
5. The modification of the neural substrate on the basis of prior exposure to certain patterns of stimulation.

References

1. Köhler, W. *Dynamics in Psychology.* Liveright Publishing Corp., 1940, pp. 125–144.
2. Levine, R., I. Chein, and G. Murphy. The relation of the intensity of a need to the amount of perceptual distortion: a preliminary report. *Journal of Psychology*, 1942, **13**, 283–293.
3. See Wallach, H. Some considerations concerning the relation between perception and cognition. *Journal of Personality*, 1949, **18**, 6–13.
4. Gottschaldt, K. Über den Einfluss der Ehrfahrung auf die Wahrnehmung von Figuren, I. *Psychologische Forschung*, 1926, **8**, 261–317.
5. Djang, S. The role of past experience in the visual apprehension of masked forms. *Journal of Experimental Psychology*, 1937, **20**, 29–59.
6. Zuckerman, C. B. and I. Rock. A reappraisal of the roles of past experience and innate organizing processes in visual perception, *Psychological Bulletin*, 1957, **54**, 269–296.
7. Witkin, H. A. Individual differences in ease of perception of embedded figures. *Journal of Personality*, 1950, **19**, 1–15.
8. Rubin, E. *Visuell Wahrgenomenne Figuren.* Gyldendalske, 1921.
9. Rock, I. and I. Kremen. A re-examination of Rubin's figural aftereffect. *Journal of Experimental Psychology*, 1957, **53**, 23–30.
10. Gottschaldt, K. Über den Einfluss der Erfahrung auf die Wahrnehmung von Figuren, II. *Psychologische Forschung*, 1929, **12**, 1–87. See also M. B. Dutton and P. M. Traill. A repetition of Rubin's figure-ground experiment. *British Journal of Psychology*. 1933, **23**, 389–400; H. G. Cornwell. Prior experience as a determinant of figure-ground organization. *Journal of Experimental Psychology*, 1964, **68**, 108–109; E. Botha. Past experience and figure-ground perception. *Perceptual and Motor Skills*, 1963, **16**, 183–288; R. J. Vetter. Perception of ambiguous figure-ground patterns as a function of past experience. *Perceptual and Motor Skills*, 1965, **20**, 183–188. In a recently completed unpublished study by Irvin Rock and Joel Girgus, re-

producing the conditions of the Rock and Kremen experiment, but increasing the amount of experience in the training phase fourfold, again no effect of such experience was evidenced.

11. Leeper, R. A study of a neglected portion of the field of learning: The development of sensory organization. *Journal of Genetic Psychology*, 1935, 46, 41–75.

12. Vogel, A. The role of past experience in the perception of fragmented figures. M. A. thesis, New School for Social Research, 1954.

13. Zangwill, O. L. A study of the significance of attitude in recognition. *British Journal of Psychology*, 1938, **28**, 12–17; See also J. S. Bruner and A. L. Minturn. Perceptual identification and perceptual organization. *Journal of General Psychology*, 1955, **53**, 21–28; B. R. Bugelski and D. A. Alampay. The role of frequency in developing perceptual sets. *Canadian Journal of Psychology*, 1961, **15**, 205–211; G. J. Steinfeld. Concepts of set and availability and their relation to the reorganization of ambiguous pictorial stimuli. *Psychological Review*, 1967, 74, 505–522.

14. Boring, E. G. A new ambiguous figure. *American Journal of Psychology*, 1930, 42, 444–445.

15. Schafer, R. and G. Murphy. The role of autism in a visual figure-ground relationship. *Journal of Experimental Psychology*, 1943, 32, 335–343.

16. Epstein, W. and I. Rock. Perceptual set as an artifact of recency. *American Journal of Psychology*, 1960, 73, 314–228.

17. Epstein, W. and D. DeShazo. Recency as a function of perceptual oscillation. *American Journal of Psychology*, 1961, 74, 215–223.

18. Sperling, G. The information available in brief visual presentations. *Psychological Monographs*, 1960, 74, No. 11, Whole No. 498: See also E. Averbach and G. Sperling. Short-term storage of information in vision. In *Symposium on Information Theory*. edit. by C. Cherry, Thornton Butterworth, Ltd., 1961, pp. 196–211. A similar experiment on novel visual forms was conducted by C. W. Eriksen and J. S. Lappin. Selective attention and very short-term recognition memory for nonsense forms. *Journal of Experimental Psychology*, 1967, 73, 358–364.

19. Egeth, H. Selective attention. *Psychological Bulletin*, 1967, 67, 41–57.

20. Allport, F. H. *Theories of Perception and the Concept of Structure*. John Wiley & Sons, Inc., 1955.

21. Dixon, N. F. *Subliminal Perception: The Nature of a Controversy*. McGraw-Hill Publishing Co., 1971.

22. Senden, M. von. *Space and Sight: The Perception of Space and Shape in the Congenitally Blind Before and After Operation.* Trans. by P. Heath, Methuen & Co., Ltd., 1960.

23. Zuckerman, and Rock, op. cit. 1957, pp. 286–287.

24. Tinbergen, N. and A. C. Perdeck. On the stimulus situation releasing the begging response in the newly hatched Herring Gull chick (Larus a. argentatus). *Behavior*, 1950, 3, 1–39.

25. Fantz, R. L. Form preferences in newly hatched chicks. *Journal of Comparative and Physiological Psychology*, 1957, **50**, 422–430. See also R. L. Fantz. The origin of form perception. *Scientific American*, 1961, **204**, 66–72.

26. Fantz, R. L. Ontogeny of perception. Chap. 10 in *Behavior of Nonhuman Primates*, Vol. II (edit. by A. M. Schrier, H. F. Harlow and F. Stollnitz, Academic Press, Inc., 1965.

27. Hershenson, M. Visual discrimination in the human newborn. *Journal of Comparative and Physiological Psychology*, 1964, **58**, 270–276; P. Salapatek, and W. Kessen. Visual scanning of triangles by the human newborn. *Journal of Experimental Child Psychology*, 1966, 3, 155–167; P. Salapatek. Visual scanning of geometric figures by the human newborn. *Journal of Comparative and Physiological Psychology*, 1968, **66**, 247–258.

28. Bower, T. G. R. The visual world of infants. *Scientific American*, 1966, **215**, 80–92.

29. Riesen, A. H. Arrested vision. *Scientific American*, 1950, **183**, 16–19.

30. Riesen, A. H. Plasticity of behavior: psychological aspects. In *Biological and Biochemical Bases of Behavior* (H. F. Harlow and C. N. Woolsey, eds.). University of Wisconsin Press, 1958; Stimulation as a requirement for growth and function in behavioral development. In *Functions of Varied Experience* (D. W. Fiske, and S. R. Maddi, eds.). Dorsey Press, 1961; A. I. Siegel. Deprivation of visual form definition in the ring dove: I. Discriminatory learning. *Journal of Comparative and Physiological Psychology*, 1953, **46**, 115–119; B. Meyers and R. A. McCleary. Interocular transfer of a pattern discrimination in pattern-deprived cats. *Journal of Comparative and Physiological Psychology*, 1964, **57**, 16–21.

31. Wiesel, T. N. and D. H. Hubel. Single cell responses in striate cortex of kittens deprived of vision in one eye. *Journal of Neurophysiology*, 1963, **26**, 1004–1017; Comparison of the effects of unilateral and bilateral eye closure on cortical unit responses in kittens. *Journal of Neurophysiology*, 1965, **28**, 1029–1040; Extent of recovery from the effects of visual deprivation in kit-

tens. *Journal of Neurophysiology*, 1965, **28**, 1060-1072; L. Ganz and M. Fitch. The effect of visual deprivation on perceptual behavior. *Experimental Neurology*, 1968, **22**, 638-660; Ganz, L., M. Fitch and J. A. Satterberg. The selective effect of visual deprivation on receptive field shape determined neurophysiologically. *Experimental Neurology*, 1968, **22**, 614-637.

32. Riesen, A. H. and R. L. Ramsey and P. D. Wilson. Development of visual acuity in rhesus monkeys deprived of patterned light during early infancy. *Psychonomic Science*, 1964, 1, 33-34.

33. Gibson, E., R. D. Walk and T. J. Tighe. Enhancement and deprivation of visual stimulation during rearing as factors in visual discrimination learning. *Journal of Comparative and Physiological Psychology*, 1959, **52**, 74-81; D. O. Hebb. The innate organization of visual activity: I. Perception of figures by rats reared in total darkness. *Journal of Genetic Psychology*, 1937, **51**, 101-126.

34. Blakemore, C. and G. F. Cooper. Development of the brain depends on the visual environment. *Nature*, 1970, **228**, 477-478; Blakemore, C. and Mitchell, E. D. Environmental modification of the visual cortex and the neural basis of learning and memory. *Nature*, 1973, 241, 467-468.

35. Hirsch, H. V. B. and D. N. Spinelli. Visual experience modifies distribution of horizontally and vertically oriented receptive fields in cats. *Science*, 1970, **168**, 869-871; Modification of the distribution of receptive field orientations in cats by selective visual exposure during development. *Experimental Brain Research*, 1971, **13**, 509-527.

36. Hubel, D. H. and T. N. Wiesel. Receptive fields of cells in striate cortex of very young, visually inexperienced kittens. *Journal of Neurophysiology*, 1963, **26**, 994-1002.

37. Blakemore and Cooper, op. cit.; See also Ganz and Fitch, op. cit.

38. Hirsch, H. V. B. Visual perception in cats after environmental surgery. *Experimental Brain Research*, 1972, **15**, 405-423.

39. Muir, D. W. and D. E. Mitchell. Visual resolution and experience: acuity deficits in cats following early selective visual deprivation. *Science*, 1973, **180**, 420-422; Freeman, R. D., D. E. Mitchell, and M. Millodot. A neural effect of partial visual deprivation in humans. *Science*, 1972, **175**, 1384-1386.

40. See Siegel, in reference 30.

41. Tucker, N. F. The effect of early light and form deprivation on the visual behavior of the chicken. Unpublished Ph. D. dissertation, University of Chicago, 1957.

42. Nealy, S. M. and D. A. Riley. Loss and recovery of discrimination of visual depth in dark-reared rats. *American Journal of Psychology*, 1963, **76**, 329–332.

43. Zimmermann, R. R. and C. C. Torrey. Ontogeny of learning. Chap. 11 in *Behavior of Nonhuman Primates*, Vol. II, (edit. by A. M. Schrier, H. F. Harlow and F. Stollnitz). Academic Press, Inc., 1965.

44. Bower, T. G. R. The determinants of perceptual units in infancy. *Psychonomic Science*, 1965, **3**, 323–324; Phenomenal identity and form perception in an infant. *Perception & Psychophysics*, 1967, **2**, 74–76.

45. Gibson, J. J. and E. J. Gibson. Perceptual learning: differentiation or enrichment? *Psychological Review*, 1955, **62**, 32–41.

46. Pick, A. D. Improvement of visual and tactual form discrimination. *Journal of Experimental Psychology*, 1965, **69**, 331–339.

47. Dewey, J. *Psychology*, Harper & Bros., 1899.

48. Rock, I. and J. Victor. Vision and touch: an experimentally created conflict between the senses. *Science*, 1964, **143**, 594–596; I. Rock and C. S. Harris. Vision and touch. *Scientific American*, 1967, **216**, 96–104.

49. Gibson, J. J. Adaptation, after-effect and contrast in the perception of curved lines. *Journal of Experimental Psychology*, 1933, **16**, 1–31.

50. Rock, I., A. Mack, L. Adams, and A. L. Hill. Adaptation to contradictory information from vision and touch. *Psychonomic Science*, 1965, **3**, 435–436.

51. Harris, C. S. Perceptual adaptation to inverted, reversed and displaced vision. *Psychological Review*, 1965, **72**, 419–444; I. Rock and C. S. Harris, op. cit.

52. Bower, T. G. R., J. M. Broughton, and M. K. Moore. The coordination of visual and tactual input in infants. *Perception & Psychophysics*, 1970, **8**, 51–53.

chapter 9

ILLUSIONS

The one area in perception where it is obvious that there is a problem requiring explanation is that of the so-called geometrical illusions. Why do two lines of equal length, near enough to one another so that comparison is easy, appear so different in length when they are embedded in a context of other lines? Why does a perfectly straight line appear curved when presented among a set of other lines? Despite a hundred years of investigation, the explanation for most of the illusions is still not known. It is interesting to speculate on why so much effort has been expended in an attempt to explain illusions. One reason is surely that we become very curious about what it is about an illusory pattern that makes us subject to such a perceptual error. Perhaps another reason is that historically it was always apparent that an illusion poses a problem, whereas it was not so apparent that veridical perception poses just as much of a problem. Today, some psychologists believe that the geometric illusions do not warrant too much attention because they are not representative of perception in everyday life.[1]

We have already encountered a number of illusions. Stroboscopic movement, induced movement, the perception of certain two-dimensional patterns as three-dimensional, and, of course, the moon illusion are cases in point. It was appropriate to discuss each of these effects and others in their proper contexts rather than to leave them for this chapter. Illusory perceptions are so frequent that usually an investigator does not even ask whether or not the phenomena under study are illusory or veridical. Wherever general principles of perception are at work, as in the constancies or in movement perception, it is easy to find or to invent illusions. Thus, for example, when it has been established that distance is taken into account in the assessment of retinal-image size, then we can predict that if the image size remains *constant* (as with the moon), an illusory change of size will be perceived if distance information is now varied. Thus, some illusions can be explained as outcomes of certain basic laws of perception.

But, by and large, illusions stemming from geometrical patterns of various kinds do not seem to be of this type or at least it remains to be proved that they are. Therefore, it is desirable to treat them separately. Before going further, it will be helpful to define the term *illusion*. An illusion is a sensory impression or perception that is false or incorrect. By "incorrect" is meant that what we see (or hear or feel) does not correspond with the objective situation that can be determined by other means, e.g., measurement.   In the well-known Müller-Lyer illusion shown in Fig. 9–1, the two horizontal lines (or shafts) are of equal length, but the one with the outward-going arrowheads (*a*) appears to be appreciably longer than the other. If we accept this definition, then there are two types of illusions, those that are based on certain physical conditions (and can, therefore, be explained in terms of the proximal stimulus to which such conditions gives rise), and those that are psychologically determined. Examples of the first kind are mirages and distorted perceptions based on viewing objects in water or through prisms and the like. We do not discuss illusions of this type since their explanation lies outside of psychology. Only the second type of illusion concerns us in this chapter.

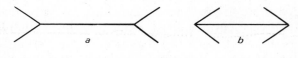

a   *b*

Figure 9–1

It is inadvisable to define illusion as a perception that does not correspond with the proximal stimulus although in many cases this would seem to be a plausible way to define it. For example, in the case of the Müller-Lyer illusion, the retinal images of the two shafts, are *equal* and yet these lines do not look equal. In this case, reference to the lack of correspondence between retinal image and perception points up the illusion all the more clearly. But the fact is that perception is often not in correspondence with the relevant feature of the stimulus reaching the sense organ although the perceptual experience is nevertheless veridical. For example, it would obviously be inappropriate to call the veridical perception of size (at varying distances) an illusion.

As the reader now knows, the proximal stimulus is often an ambiguous sign of what is present in the scene. This is clearly brought out by the various demonstrations devised by Ames.[2] The best known of these is the distorted room illusion illustrated in Fig. 3–42, Chapter 3. The distorted room and other Ames demonstrations illustrate dramatically that the same retinal image can be generated by various external objects (a rectangle in a plane perpendicular to the line of sight and a particular trapezoid in a plane slanted away from the perpendicular both produce a rectangular retinal-image shape). The observer, however, will usually have a definite perception of one object that may or may not correspond to what is actually in the world. If it does correspond, his perception is correct or veridical; if it does not, his perception is illusory. Thus, the only useful definition is the one suggested in terms of noncorrespondence between the perception and the objective situation.*

The Geometrical Illusions

There is no universally accepted method of classifying geometrical illusions. However, most of the well-known illusions can be considered to be either perceptual distortions of magnitude (length or size) or perceptual distortions of direction of line. Many of those illustrated here will already be familiar to the reader.

Illusions of magnitude

The best-known example is the one reported by Müller-Lyer in 1889: two equal-length lines having either inward or outward-turning arrowheads at their ends (see Fig. 9–1).[3] The illusory effect is appreciable although the exact magnitude of this effect depends upon the particular conditions of presentation. Illusions can be measured by arranging the stimulus pattern so that one of the components being compared can be varied. The observer then equates the variable component subjectively with the other component. The extent to which he must alter it to achieve a subjective match is a measure of the illusion. For the present writer, the shaft at the right, *b*, must be made as long as shown in Fig. 9–2 to achieve a sense of equality with the shaft at the left, *a*. As the reader can determine with a ruler, the shaft in *b* is 1¼ inches, whereas in *a* it is 1 inch. Thus, for one subject at least, the illusion of length is 25 percent.

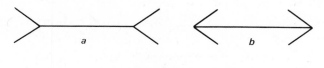

a   *b*

Figure 9–2

*Another reason why it is not wise to define illusion in terms of the proximal stimulus is that in the case of illusions based on physical conditions there *is* agreement between retinal image and percept. Yet what is immediately perceived in these cases is surely illusory.

Hundreds of experiments have been performed on this illusion and many facts have been established. Thus, for example, the greatest illusion occurs when the angle of the arrowheads with respect to the shaft is small and when the length of the arrowheads is neither too small nor too large in proportion to the length of the shaft. It is also known that it is not necessary for the shaft to be present as such and that other elements can be substituted for the arrowheads. Some of these variations are shown in Fig. 9–3.

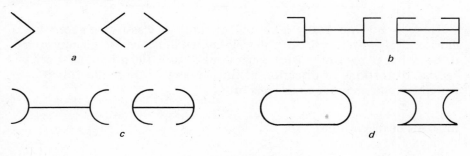

Figure 9–3

Another well-known illusion is known as the Sander parallelogram and is shown in Fig. 9–4.[4] The two diagonals shown in dotted lines are equal in length but appear to be unequal. This illusion is constructed by locating the point on the bottom line that is directly under the middle of the top line. This point is the origin of the diagonals. Many experiments have been conducted on this illusion in which the conditions of presentation have been varied. Thus, for example, it is now known that the illusion is even greater if many of the line components are eliminated and if the observer has to imagine the diagonals.[5] (See Fig. 9–5.)

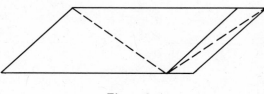

Figure 9–4

It has been proposed that the Sander illusion can be reduced to a special case of the Müller-Lyer illusion. (The attempt at reducing various illusions to a few fundamental ones is certainly desirable since we would then only need to explain these fundamental illusions to explain

Figure 9-5

them all.)   The diagonals in the Sander parallelogram terminate at intersections that can be thought of as arrowheads; the diagonals can be thought of as the shafts. The diagonal on the right in Fig. 9-4 ends in inward-going arrowheads that form acute angles, but the one on the left ends in inward-going arrowheads that form obtuse angles. Therefore, the illusion can at least be considered similar to the Müller-Lyer figure. However, the proper test of this hypothesis requires that the two lines under comparison be alike in all respects except for the one thought to be crucial, namely, the angles formed by the arrowheads. We can, therefore, separate the two halves of the figure and create a new figure in which each "diagonal" terminates at arrowheads that have the same obtuse and acute angles as in Fig. 9-4 but where the two "diagonals" are now in the same orientation (see Fig. 9-6). There is not much difference in the apparent length of the two horizontal shafts as there should be if the hypothesis were correct.

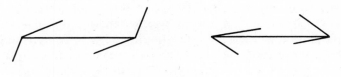

Figure 9-6

Still another well-known illusion of length was first described by Ponzo.[6]   It consists of two equal lines placed inside two converging lines, as shown in Fig. 9-7a, or as the top and bottom of a rectangle embedded in a set of converging lines as shown in Fig. 9-7b. The upper line appears longer. Experiments have established the conditions for obtaining a maximum effect, such as the exact angles of the converging lines and the size and placement of the two critical lines.

The vertical-horizontal illusion, first presented by Oppel, is also well known: a vertical line looks somewhat longer than a horizontal line of equal length.[7] For many years, the standard demonstration of this illusion was the one shown in Fig. 9-8a. There is, however, an error of ex-

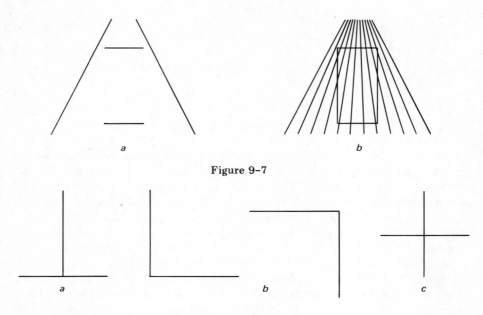

Figure 9-7

Figure 9-8

perimental method present in this demonstration. The two lines are *not* the same in every respect except orientation; they should be the same to test the hypothesis that the illusion is a function of their orientation. Another difference is that one line is bisected by the other. Since a bisected line will appear shorter than a nonbisected line (as shown in Fig. 9-9), there is a confounding of two illusions in Fig. 9-8*a*. To isolate orientation it is necessary to present the lines in the form of an L or a cross as shown in Figs. 9-8*b* and *c*. When these modes of presentation are used, it is found that a vertical line appears to be 5 to 10 per cent longer than an objectively equal horizontal line.[8]

Figure 9-9

But as the reader is aware by now, *vertical* and *horizontal* are ambiguous terms. Is this illusion the result of the different orientations of the retinal images of these lines or is it the result of the difference in the perceived orientations of the lines in the environment? (See pp. 303ff and p. 457). It is easy enough to separate these factors by requiring the observer to view the lines from a tilted position. Thus, for example, if the observer is tilted by 45 degrees, the lines now yield oblique images on the retina although they continue to be perceived as vertical and horizontal in the environment. In this condition the illusion is eliminated. Conversely, if the lines are themselves presented in an oblique orientation, as shown in Fig. 9–10, *and* observer is also tilted 45 degrees, then neither line is perceived to be vertical or horizontal, but one yields a vertical image and the other yields a horizontal image. The former line now appears to be longer.[9] A direct confrontation between perceived orientation and retinal orientation can be arranged by presenting the lines in the customary positions as in Fig. 9–8*b* but tilting the observer by 90 degrees.[10] The environmentally horizontal but retinally "vertical" line now appears longer. Therefore, it is clear that the orientation of the image of the lines on the retina is the crucial factor.

Figure 9–10

It would seem probable that illusory experiences of this kind must be occurring often in daily life. Lines in the environment that produce vertical retinal images should look longer than those of the same length that project horizontal images. But since we do not subject our perceptions to measurement, we take them to be veridical and we are not aware that they are, at times, nonveridical or illusory. This fact must be true also for the patterns that produce other illusions, although these are encountered less frequently. Of course, artists, architects, fashion designers, and others are well aware of such illusory effects and take them into account in their work.

An illusion discovered in the last century by Delboeuf is shown in Fig. 9–11.[11] Here we are dealing with size or area rather than length. The inner circle on the left looks larger than the equal-size circle on the right. A variation of the illusion is shown in Fig. 9–12. The outer circle on the left looks smaller than the equal-size circle on the right.

Interrupted or divided lines generally look longer than uninterrupted ones as shown in Fig. 9–13*a*. A similar effect occurs for extents or spaces as shown by the apparent distance between the end points on the left and right of Fig. 9–13*b*. These examples illustrate what is referred to as the filled-space or Oppel-Kundt illusion, filled space usually appearing greater in magnitude than unfilled space.[12] (It is this effect

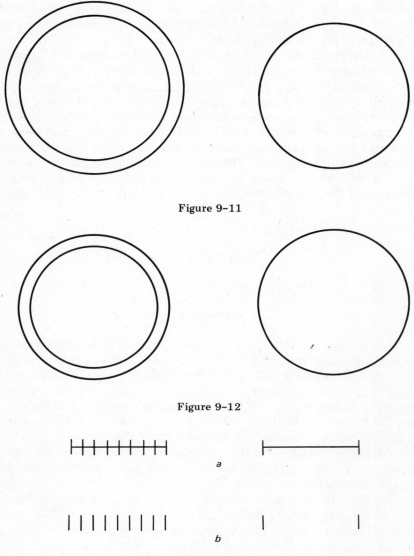

Figure 9–11

Figure 9–12

a

b

Figure 9–13

that has been thought to be relevant to the moon illusion, since the horizontal moon is seen across the "filled" terrain whereas the zenith moon is seen across empty space). But there are often contradictory outcomes in illusions of this kind depending upon the specific pattern employed. Thus, the divided line in Fig. 9-9 does not appear longer than its comparison line, but shorter. Therefore, one division—or perhaps even a few divisions—has an effect opposite to that of many divisions.

Fig. 9-14 illustrates the Jastrow illusion.[13] The two figures are identical, but the size of the lower one seems to be much greater than that of the upper one.

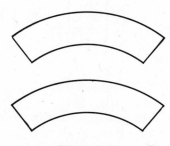

Figure 9-14

One other illusion of magnitude was first described by Ebbinghaus.[14] The equal-size center circles in the two configurations shown in Fig. 9-15 appear unequal; the one on the left appears larger.

 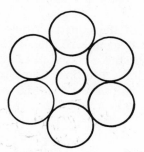

Figure 9-15

Illusions of direction of line

There are many striking illusions of this kind. In the Poggendorff illusion shown in Fig. 9-16 the two solid, oblique lines do not appear to be continuations of one another although they are.[15] This illusion can be measured by requiring the observer to position one of the oblique lines until it seems to be a continuation of the other one. The dotted

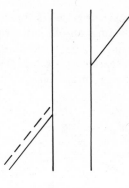

Figure 9-16

line in Fig. 9–16 shows that position for the writer. It could be argued that this effect is one of line displacement rather than of line direction since the two oblique lines appear parallel but not aligned with each other, as if one line is simply displaced at right angles to itself. However, the same end result could be the outcome of a change in the perceived direction of each line, the top one pivoting clockwise about its lower end, the bottom one pivoting clockwise about its upper end (see Fig. 9–46). Many investigators believe that this is the nature of the effect.

Variation of the construction of the array of lines affects the magnitude of the Poggendorff illusion. For example, it is known that the orientation of the oblique lines in relation to the parallel lines is important. The closer the lines come to a perpendicular direction, the less is the illusion (compare Fig. 9–16 with Fig. 9–17). The *absolute* orienta-

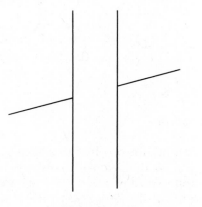

Figure 9-17

tion of the oblique lines is also important. The illusion is considerably
lessened if a figure, which otherwise yields a strong illusion, is so
oriented that the oblique lines are vertical or horizontal (see Fig. 9–18).

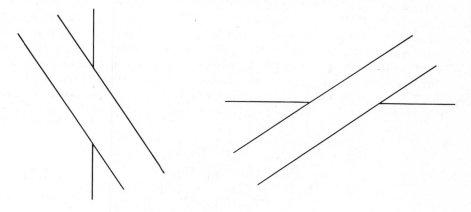

Figure 9–18

It is also known that a similar illusion occurs even if the central figure
does not have parallel lines or is not regular (see Fig. 9–19*a* and *b*).[16]

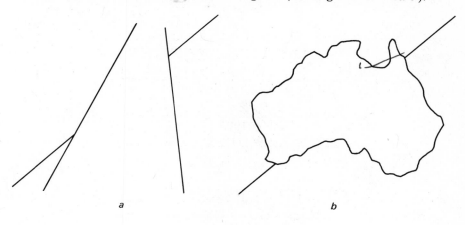

a   b

Figure 9–19

A number of illusions seem to illustrate a similar effect, namely, the
subjective impression of bending or curvature resulting from lines crossing or intersecting one another. Famous examples of this kind are the

Zöllner illusion shown in Fig. 9-20, the Hering illusion shown in Fig. 9-21, and the Wundt illusion shown in Fig. 9-22.[17] The oblique lines in Fig. 9-20 appear bent away from one another rather than parallel; the horizontal lines in Figs. 9-21 and 22 appear curved, away from each other in Fig. 9-21 and toward each other in Fig. 9-22. The Hering and Wundt illusions are really one and the same: the horizontal lines in both cases are curved away from the vertex of the oblique lines but the vertex is at the center in Fig. 9-21 and at the top and bottom in Fig. 9-22. Furthermore, if one views only the left or right half of Figs. 9-21 and 9-22, the horizontal lines may appear bent away from one another rather than curved, and if these half figures are rotated 45 degrees and

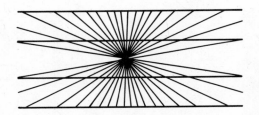

Figure 9-20

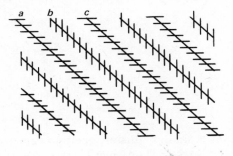

Figure 9-21

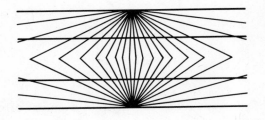

Figure 9-22

compared with Fig. 9-20, the essential similarity will readily be grasped. In all three figures, the straight lines are crossed by a number of oblique lines and the straight lines appear to be bent in the direction opposite to the oblique lines.

Many other illusions are constructed on the basis of this principle in that they would seem to be reducible to an apparent tilting of certain lines away from other lines that cross them. The distortion of the square in Fig. 9-23 (the Ehrenstein illusion) and of the circle in Fig. 9-24 (the Orbison illusion) are cases in point.[18]   The version of the

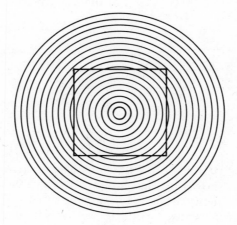

Figure 9-23

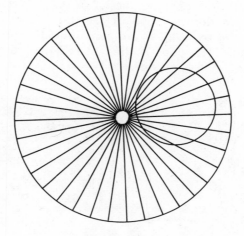

Figure 9-24

Ponzo illusion shown in Fig. 9–7*b* is also of this type. The converging lines that cross over the left and right sides of the rectangle would cause these sides to appear to be bent away from the vertical. Therefore, two illusory effects may be confounded in this figure since the top of the rectangle would appear smaller than the bottom even without the intersecting lines, as is shown by the effect in Fig. 9–7*a*.

A different kind of example of an illusion of direction, in which apparent curvature is affected, is shown in Fig. 9–25. The two center curves are identical, but appear different (less curvature in the figure on the right). This illusion seems to be different from those discussed previously because no intersection of lines is involved.

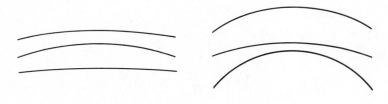

Figure 9–25

The so-called "twisted-cord" illusions also entail a perceptual change of direction as is shown in Figs. 9–26, 9–27, and 9–28.[19] In Fig. 9–26, the letters are perfectly straight but appear tilted. In Fig. 9–27, the circles appear as an inwardly turning spiral. In Fig. 9–28, the straight vertical and parallel lines appear curved and not parallel to one another. These illusions are so strong that it is necessary to use a straight edge or to trace the circles to convince oneself of the true state of affairs. The name *twisted cord* derives from the fact that we can imagine creating these illusion figures by using a cord constructed by intertwining a white and black strand. The cord is then placed over the checkered background shown in the illustrations.

Figure 9–26

Figure 9-27

There would seem to be several factors common to the patterns in the three illustrations. The components that make up the lines or circles consist of black-line segments ending in black triangles as shown in Fig. 9-29. (These are also white line segments ending in white triangles, but in the interest of simplicity we ignore these in the analysis.) These line segments are slanted away from the direction of the entire line that they constitute. Then there is the checkered background pattern. Fig. 9-30a and b shows that the illusions are still present when the background pattern is removed, and, conversely, Fig. 9-31 shows that with the slanted segments eliminated the background pattern does not create an illusion.

Therefore, the essence of these illusions seems to be the fact that there is a tendency to perceive the direction of an entire line on the

Figure 9-28

Figure 9-29

a

b

Figure 9-30

basis of the direction of the component line segments that constitute it.[20] In Fig. 9-32*a* and *b*, the triangles are eliminated so that the only factor remaining is the slope of the line segments. The illusions persist. That they are not as strong here as in Fig. 9-30 is probably based on the fact that the triangles exaggerate the slope of the line segments; an imaginary line connecting the centers of the two triangles is even more tilted than the line segment. If this analysis is correct, the prob-

Figure 9-31

lem remains of explaining why an entire line takes on the apparent direction of its component parts.

The factors underlying illusions can be added to or subtracted from one another, thus leading to stronger or weaker illusions, respectively. Thus, for example, in Fig. 9–33 three factors cooperate to produce the impression that the vertical extent between arrowheads in *a* is much greater than the horizontal extent between them in *b*, namely, vertical versus horizontal orientation, the Müller-Lyer effect, and filled versus unfilled space. Conversely in Fig. 9–34 two factors oppose one another, the vertical orientation favoring the extent on the left and "filled" space favoring the extent on the right, with the result that the two equal extents look about equal.

Theories

A number of theories have been proposed to explain these illusions. In the following discussions of these theories, some additional facts about the illusions are brought out where relevant.

Gestalt theory

Since the Gestalt school more than any other has stressed the importance of stimulus relationships in determining what we perceive and has exposed the fallacy of the constancy hypothesis (p. 19), this theory as a

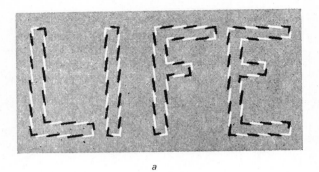

a

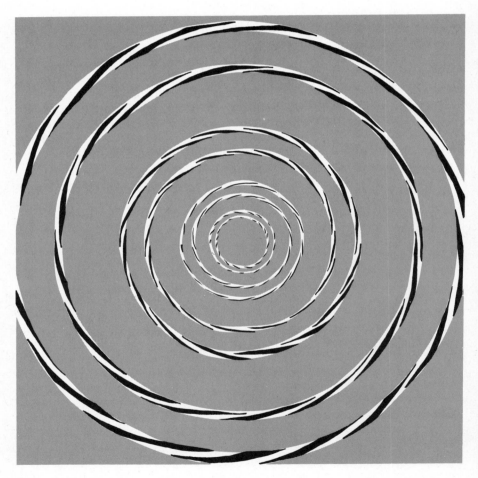

b

Figure 9-32

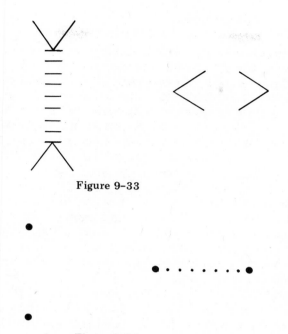

Figure 9–33

Figure 9–34

general doctrine is well suited to deal with illusions. If what we perceive is, generally speaking, not merely a function of the circumscribed stimulus under examination but of other stimuli in the field as well, then illusions are no longer anomalous or surprising but exactly what we should expect. For example, if neutral color is based on the ratio of intensities of neighboring regions, then contrast, although illusory, is exactly what we must predict (see Chapter 11). Or if perceived speed is a function of rate of displacement relative to a frame of reference, rather than absolute speed of displacement of the retinal image, then changes in the size of such a reference frame can produce powerful illusions of speed as exemplified by the transposition effect (see p. 227).

By the same reasoning, one might say that it is not surprising that the apparent length of the shafts in the Müller-Lyer illusion would be affected by the context of the arrowheads at the ends. But it is at this point that Gestalt theory becomes too general to provide the specific explanation required for most of the geometric illusions illustrated in this chapter. We want to know *why* the outward-going arrowheads make a line appear longer or *why* the oblique line components in the Poggendorff illusion do not appear to be aligned.

Ultimately, a more specific physiological theory of illusions was proposed by Köhler; this is described in the final part of the chapter.

The eye-movement theory

The impression of length is thought to be based on scanning a figure by moving the eyes from one end to the other. In the case of the Müller-Lyer illusion, the outward-going arrowheads lead to scanning movements of greater extent than the inward-turning arrowheads because the observer includes these parts in his scan, thereby erroneously creating the impression that the shafts are of different lengths. There is, in fact, some evidence that eye movements are affected by the presence of the arrowheads.[21] Or it might be claimed that the effort of making vertical eye movements is greater than that of making horizontal movements in scanning the vertical-horizontal illusion, and that one's impression of extent is based in part on the effort expended in moving the eyes. But it is now known that impressions of size and shape are not dependent on eye movements. The Müller-Lyer illusion and the vertical-horizontal illusion are still very much present even if the patterns in Fig. 9–1 and Fig. 9–8 are viewed for only a fraction of a second, too brief to permit scanning.

Even if this difficulty is disregarded, other difficulties remain. It is not clear in the case of many of the illusions why the scanning movements of the eyes would be greater for the extent that looks larger. So the argument becomes circular: the claim is that the extent or effort of eye movement is greater for whatever region of a figure looks larger, but there is often no independent explanation of why such differences in eye movement should occur. Perhaps the differences in eye movements which have been found are effect rather than cause. We tend to move our eyes further because the extent in question already looks longer. If the eye-movement theory were to be applied to illusions of direction, it would have to be maintained that we scan a straight line in a curved path or a curved line in a straight path. But again the question would be, why do we do this? It seems to presuppose the illusion.

A somewhat more sophisticated, modern version of this theory would be that it is the intention or neural command to the eye muscles to move in a particular (and incorrect) direction or extent that produces the illusion, not the actual eye movement. This version of the theory is not contradicted by facts such as the presence of illusions in brief exposures. No actual eye movements occur.

Some psychologists believe that perceived location, extent, and shape are actually determined by those movements of the eyes that would have to be executed in order to fixate each region of a stimulus array. Therefore, according to this view, the intention (or efferent readiness) to move the eyes through the greater overall distance of the shaft with outward-going arrowheads in the Müller-Lyer illusion produces the impression of a greater extent than the intention to move the eyes through the lesser overall distance of the shaft with inward-going arrowheads. (See the discussion of efferent commands as information about eye position in Chapter 5, p. 187.) In the case of the Müller-Lyer illusion the argument is not necessarily circular because the overall length of the two half figures of the illusion *are* in fact different. In one experiment, the deduction was tested that, with ample opportunity to scan the figures saccadically, the observer would learn that his initial efferent commands to the eyes were inappropriate and thus he would learn to equate the extent of intended movements for the two components making up the illusion figure.[22] This would result in a decrement in the illusion. Such a decrement occurred as others have found in the past, and furthermore, it occurred only if scanning movements were allowed, not if fixation was required. Furthermore, recordings of eye movements revealed a difference in extent for the two halves of the illusion figure at the outset and a diminution in this difference as a result of the practice.

However, as these investigators admit, this change in eye-movement behavior could very well be the result of, rather than the cause of, the decrease in the illusion as a result of the prolonged exposure to it, whatever might be the cause of that decrease. The question is still left unanswered for many of the other illusions: why are these intended eye movements incorrect in the first place? This version of the theory, therefore, also generally presupposes the prior existence of the very illusions it seeks to explain. It is also debatable, if not farfetched, to claim that intended oculomotor movements can actually explain the perception of visual direction, size, and shape.

The apparent-distance, perspective, or misapplied constancy theory

Certain visual patterns create the impression of depth. (See the illustrations of the pictorial cues to depth in Chapter 3.) For example, a railroad track produces a retinal image like that shown in Fig. 2–17, and this image in itself, without any other cues to depth, yields a strong three-dimensional impression. Such images are perspective transformations of equal-size objects at equal spacing in the third dimension. Even drawings or photographs of scenes of this kind are seen in depth, despite the presence of other information that the pictures are two-dimensional, and here the perception is illusory.

In addition to the depth effect of pictures of this kind, however, there is also an awareness that the objects depicted at different distances are the same objective size (for example, the telegraph poles or railroad ties). In that case, it follows that if two objects at different distances were drawn in the *same* size they would look different. The pennants in the figure illustrates this effect. An analogous case for shape as a function of the slant of the surface is shown in Fig. 9-35. By virtue of taking slant into account, acute and obtuse angles look like right angles and two right angles in this figure look like obtuse angles. These effects follow from the general principle that we take distance and slant into account in assessing size and shape (see Chapter 2).

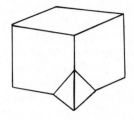

Figure 9-35

The explanation outlined here of these illusory effects of pictures of scenes in depth may be correct, but it has also been applied to many of the geometrical illusions where its applicability is not always obvious.* For example, it could be claimed that in the Ponzo illusion shown in Fig. 9-7, the top line looks longer than the bottom one because the con-

---

*There is, however, a puzzling problem connected with illustrations such as that of Fig. 2-17. The pennants, which in the drawings are objectively equal, certainly look unequal in size. This is to be expected if distance is taken into account (Emmert's law, p. 33). But the telegraph poles or the ties of the railroad track, which in the drawing are objectively unequal, do not appear to be equal. That is, constancy does not seem to obtain or even much of a tendency toward constancy. If distance is taken into account in the case of the pennants, why is it not in the case of the ties? The absence of constancy might be attributed to the fact that in a drawing such as this we tend to perceive more in accord with visual angle or extensity (see p. 38) perhaps because other cues indicate that the picture is flat and also because each tie is adjacent to its neighbors and the tracks clearly converge. But then why don't we perceive the pennants veridically in terms of their visual angles, which are equal? There are three possible kinds of answers to this dilemma: 1. Some tendency toward constancy *is* present for the ties but it is not obvious without measuring it. 2. The pictorial distance information is taken into account, but for reasons that are not yet fully clear, extensity relations dominate for the unequal ties but not for the equal pennants *or* 3. The illusion of the pennants has nothing to do with depth perception. The pennants can be thought of as the test objects of the Ponzo illusion, as is brought out later, and it is possible that the Ponzo illusion is not based on depth processing.

verging lines are seen in depth (as a perspective representation of actually parallel lines such as a road). Fig. 9–36 illustrates the illusion within a familiar scene. It has also been claimed that the Müller-Lyer illusion is based upon a tendency to see the line patterns as three-dimensional representations of the junction of several surfaces, as illustrated in Fig. 9–37.* The vertical line of the *a* pattern would then appear farther away than the "arrowheads" because the wall surfaces in *a* open toward the viewer; conversely, the arrowheads in *b* appear farther than the vertical line because the wall surfaces are bent away from the viewer. Accordingly, the vertical line in *a* would appear larger than that in *b*, because it appears farther, following this logic.

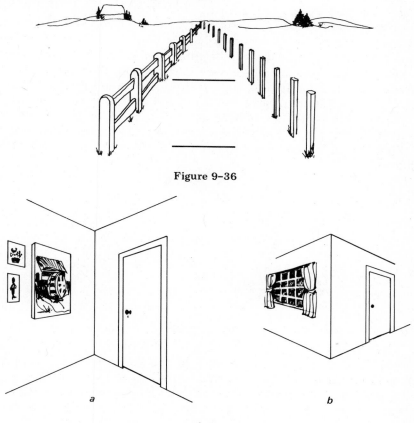

Figure 9–36

a   *b*

Figure 9–37

*The perspective theory of illusions is far from new, having been proposed by several investigators over a considerable span of time.[23]

There are many difficulties with this theory even in the instances where a plausible case can be made out for it. In the Ponzo illusion, the two lines under comparison presumably appear at different distances within the overall pattern because of linear perspective. But in the Müller-Lyer illusion all that can reasonably be claimed is that *within each figure*, the shaft appears in front of or behind the arrowheads. For the illusion to occur, however, the two shafts must appear at different distances *from one another*. There is no reason why this should be expected to be the case, particularly if the two figures are spatially separated or seen one after the other.

Another difficulty with the theory is that illusions, such as the Müller-Lyer and Ponzo, remain just as strong even when the observer has no impression of depth whatsoever. The Müller-Lyer illusion is generally not seen as three-dimensional. The depth effect in the Ponzo illusion (if the reader has any) can be eliminated or at least much reduced by turning Fig. 9–7a 90 degrees or 180 degrees, whereas the illusion persists. In reversible figures, such as those shown in Fig. 9–38, one can perceive a as a tunnel or as a truncated pyramid; one can see b as part of an open box with the two front sides missing or as a closed box standing on an edge. Yet such perceptual reversals have no effect on the Ponzo illusion; the upper of the two horizontal lines appears larger at all times.[24]

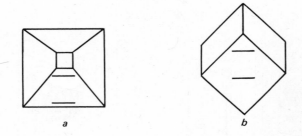

a   b

Figure 9–38

In other experiments, stereograms of the Ponzo illusion figure were prepared in which the lines to be compared (hereafter to be referred to as the test lines) were seen as lying in the same plane as each other and in front of (or behind) the remaining lines of the pattern (to be referred to as the inducing lines), which were seen in depth. Thus, the rectangle in Fig. 9–7b was seen in a vertical plane, in front of the converging lines, which, via stereoscopy, were made to appear as receding into the distance. This illusion should be eliminated under these conditions if the basis for it is the location of the horizontal lines of the rectangle at different distances from one another. Yet the illusion persists. The rectangle looks like a trapezoid with its top larger than its bottom. On the other hand, an illusion that presumably *is* based on an impression of depth, such as that shown in Fig. 2–17, *can* be eliminated by stereoscopically presenting the pennants in one plane in front of the background. Stereograms of the Müller-Lyer pattern, which had the effect of elevating or lowering the shafts with respect to the arrowheads (as suggested in Fig. 9–37), failed to enhance the illusion and reversing these depth impressions failed to eliminate the illusion.[25]

It has been argued that the perspective cues that induce the illusion need not lead to conscious awareness of differences in depth. It is sufficient if the depth cue is registered.[26] (See the discussion of this issue in Chapter 2, pp. 34ff.) After all, the illusions under discussion are presented as line drawings on a page and as such are two-dimensional, so that the veridical cues to the two-dimensionality of the drawing may overpower the linear perspective cues within the drawing, which nevertheless may have certain effects.

It is not clear whether this argument should be taken to mean that none of the evidence just cited is relevant, i.e., the presence of illusions when there is either no difference in perceived depth between test lines or when there is a difference in depth opposite to that required by the misapplied constancy hypothesis or when the perceived depth called for by the theory is present but the illusion is not enhanced. The hypothesis implies that a given perspective pattern leads to an inappropriate constancy effect regardless of any or all conflicting cues to depth and, therefore, regardless of the depth or lack thereof that is consciously perceived. In that event such a hypothesis would be essentially untestable. However, illusions, such as the Müller-Lyer, do occur under conditions in which there is no *a priori* reason whatsoever to predict a perspective effect, for example, see Fig. 9–3, *b, c, d*. This illusion is also known to reverse when the test lines are smaller than the distance between intersecting arrowheads (see Fig. 9–39) and it is difficult to reconcile this fact with the hypothesis under discussion.[27] Finally, it is not clear how the hypothesis could be sensibly applied to the version of the Müller-Lyer illusion illustrated in Fig. 9–3a. The center arrowhead cannot simultaneously be part of a depth cue to the effect that something is both nearer and farther away.

Figure 9–39

Despite these criticisms, an impressive case has been made in support of a perspective interpretation of the Poggendorff illusion.[28] The argument is as follows: The oblique lines are "processed" as horizontal lines receding in depth whether or not the observer is consciously aware of it. However, the parallel lines tend to define a frontal plane having edges equidistant from the observer. Since the oblique lines are attached to the parallel lines, with one being above the other, they cannot both belong to the same horizontal plane and, therefore, are not colinear (aligned) in three-dimensional space. The oblique lines, therefore, do not appear aligned. Fig. 9–40 illustrates this reasoning by deliberately introducing a strong impression of depth of the kind implied by the theory.

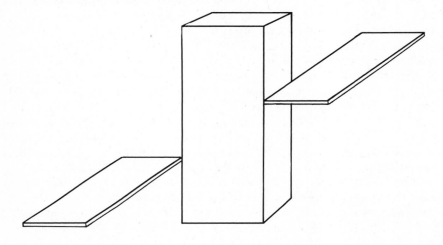

Figure 9–40

A number of predictions follow from this theory. The illusory effect should be greater for a greater separation between the parallel lines and for a more acute angle of the oblique lines since these variations would increase the vertical separation of the horizontal planes in three-dimensional space. The truth of these predictions has been demonstrated.[29] The effect should tend to disappear or be reduced when the oblique lines are horizontally or vertically oriented because in either of these orientations the lines would not tend to be "processed" as receding in depth; they would appear instead to lie in a frontal plane. We have already seen that the effect *is* significantly reduced under these conditions of presentation. The effect should be eliminated or much reduced if the parallel lines do not define a frontal plane but rather one that has the same slant as that of the oblique lines. Under these conditions, the oblique lines on both sides *would* both belong to the same horizontal plane in three-dimensional space as illustrated in Fig. 9–41. The reader can see that the illusion is greatly reduced. This deduction has been tested experimentally and supported.[30] The illusion should be eliminated or reduced if the oblique lines appear behind the plane of the parallel lines because then there would be no tendency to "process" them as attached to that plane at their inner ends.

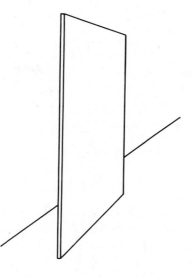

Figure 9-41

This has been achieved by stereoscopic presentation and the prediction has been substantiated.*

It is critical to the theory that there be a tendency to perceive the inner ends of the oblique lines as being attached to the parallel lines, but it is not clear why they should be perceived in this way. Each oblique segment if "processed" as receding in depth could be perceived as going behind the plane of the parallel lines at the point of intersection. In any event, further tests of the theory must be made in which figures are used that eliminate any tendency toward depth processing or which reverse the depth called for by the theory in a manner similar to the tests of the Müller-Lyer and Ponzo illusions described previously. For example, in the illustration shown in Fig. 9-42, there is no reason to expect any depth impression or depth processing. The oblique lines are here part of a narrow rectangle whose sides are parallel so that the absence of perspective is information that the rectangle is in a frontal plane. The illusion, however, is still present. This raises the further question of whether or not the perspective theory, even if correct, explains the entire Poggendorff effect. In all the tests of the theory described previously, some residual illusion effect remains under circumstances where no illusion at all should be predicted.

In summary, it seems clear that, by and large, the illusions cannot be explained by the misapplied constancy theory.† At most, some illusions

---

*See the discussion on pp. 429–430 and the illustration in the book by Julesz,[43] pp. 3.55–356.

†Needless to say, the moon illusion can be explained in terms of a constancy mechanism, but that is a somewhat different application of such a mechanism than the one being considered here in relation to two-dimensional line drawings.

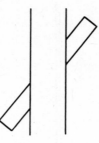

Figure 9–42

may be based in part on such a constancy mechanism. The Poggendorff illusion may be one. The Ponzo illusion of Fig. 9–7a may be affected to some extent by the tendency to see the test lines at different distances, particularly if the viewer is aware of this possibility, but apparently this is not the major factor. Or, to give still another example, there seems to be a tendency to perceive the long lines in the Zöllner illusion shown in Fig. 9–20 as going into depth (because the intersecting short lines can be seen as vertical fence posts or horizontal railroad ties, respectively). If so, it is plausible to say that lines b and c appear to diverge from one another at the top as they do because they appear farther away at the top. But then lines a and b should also appear to diverge from one another at the top for the same reason, but, on the contrary, they appear to converge. Therefore, it is not clear that the perspective hypothesis applies at all in this example, and even if it does, it can hardly be the whole story.

The neural-displacement theory

A process in one place in the nervous system can inhibit (or block) a process in a neighboring place. The illusion of contrast shown in Fig. 11–8 of Chapter 11 has been explained in terms of the strong inhibitory effect of the bright surrounding region on the inner square in a. Inhibition by one contour might conceivably also have the effect of causing another contour to appear displaced from its actual location.* How this could come about requires some further discussion.

It has already been explained that an image falling in a particular locus on the retina leads to the firing of cells in a particular locus in the visual cortex. It needs

---

*There is some evidence that contours exert an inhibiting effect on the perception of other contours.[31]

now to be added that there is some dispersion in this pattern of cortical firing; the transmission of the retinal signal diverges somewhat as it goes through the visual pathways. Since, however, a sharp retinal image leads to a sharp percept, it seems plausible to assume that the visual stimulus is located phenomenally on the basis of the center of the distribution of cortical firing, as illustrated in Fig. 9–43. Now if as

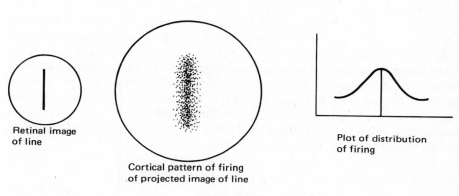

Retinal image
of line

Cortical pattern of firing
of projected image of line

Plot of distribution
of firing

Figure 9–43

a result of the presence nearby of another contour, the firing of some of the cells triggered by the original contour were to be inhibited, the distribution would no longer be symmetrical as shown in Fig. 9–43 but rather would look skewed, as shown in Fig. 9–44. The center of this pattern would, therefore, be shifted away from the locus of the second contour as would be the perceived location of that

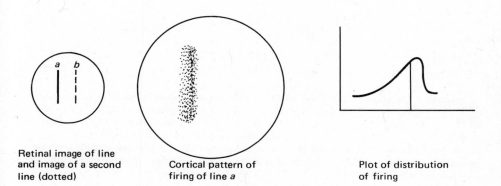

Retinal image of line
and image of a second
line (dotted)

Cortical pattern of
firing of line *a*

Plot of distribution
of firing

Figure 9–44

contour. This phenomenon of contour displacement would thus be the result of lateral inhibition.*

It is obvious that this kind of theory could explain certain illusory effects. For many years it has been held that some illusions stem from a tendency to perceive acute angles as being greater than they actually are. For example, the Poggendorff illusion (see Fig. 9–16) can be attributed to such a tendency. It was natural, therefore, for contemporary theorists to speculate that this tendency might be the result of lateral inhibition as outlined here. Presumably, the inhibition would result in each line of the angle appearing displaced outward from where it would appear to be were the other line not present (the dotted lines in Fig. 9–45). In the case of the Poggendorff illusion, therefore, the oblique lines would be displaced clockwise at the points where they form acute angles with the vertical lines, as shown in Fig. 9–46, so that they no longer appear to be continuations of one another.

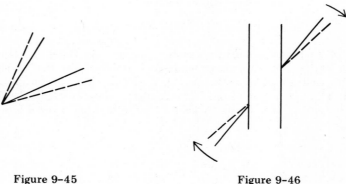

Figure 9–45   Figure 9–46

*Another version of the lateral-inhibition theory applies only to orientation. According to this view, the retinal image of a contour in a given orientation gives rise to the discharging of neural units that "detect" that orientation (see the discussion on p. 284 and pp. 315ff, but it is held that the contour would produce a distribution of activity among the population of cortical orientation detectors, exciting those tuned for that orientation or close to it and inhibiting others. A nearly contour in a different orientation will, therefore, inhibit some of these units from firing, thus shifting the peak of activity much as in the version outlined in the preceding paragraph.[32]

According to this theory, the *vertical* sides of these angles must *also* be displaced, counterclockwise, and since this does not seem to be evident, some further explanation of this fact is required. Another problem is that the amount of inhibitory displacement of contour would be a function of distance, the effect being greater for greater proximity of contours. Therefore, when two lines meet at an angle, the amount of displacement ought to result in the lines appearing to curve away from one another as shown by the dotted lines in Fig. 9-47. Thus, the perceived increase in angle should occur but it should be curvilinear rather than rectilinear, gradually tapering off. This certainly is not what is observed.

Figure 9-47

Apart from these difficulties, it cannot simply be assumed that the lines forming acute angles appear displaced from one another; it must be proved. One method employed was to determine whether the location of a point that seems to lie along the path that continues the direction of a line differs depending upon whether a second line intersects the first. This is illustrated in Fig. 9-48a and b. In a, the dot appears to lie along the path of line *l* when in fact it is, as shown by the dashed line; in b with line *m* present, it may only appear to lie along the path of line *l* when it actually is not in that position. The displacement is exaggerated in the figure. In the experiment the dashed line is not present. It was found that such an effect occurs.[33]

Unfortunately, this carefully done study is, for a number of reasons, still inconclusive concerning the question of whether or not and in what manner one line causes another to appear tilted away from its actual position:

1. It was not possible to distinguish between an effect of overestimation of acute angles or underestimation of obtuse angles since, in the study as shown in Fig. 9-48, *l* forms both an acute and obtuse angle with *m*. One can only say that the findings suggest that a line appears more inclined toward the perpendicular to another line than it actually is.

2. Occasionally the induced effect on line orientation was in the opposite direction to the one just stated.

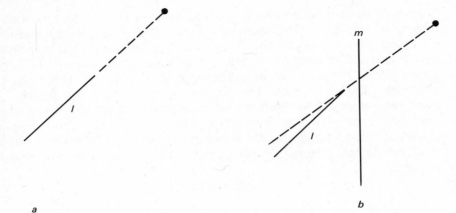

Figure 9-48

3. There was very little effect for small angles, those less than 25 degrees where the inhibitory effect would be expected to be large (and in some illusion figures just such small angles are employed).

4. The absolute orientation of the test line and of the inducing line also has an important influence on the outcome (apart from the relative orientation of the lines to one another). For example, if the inducing line is at 45 degrees with respect to the vertical of the environment, there is very little effect. Thus, it is difficult to separate such effects of absolute orientation from the main effect under study.

5. Finally, these investigators obtained virtually the same effect on perceived orientation if the test "line" consisted of two dots at either end rather than a continuous line. This finding throws doubt on the meaning of the study since there are no longer two contours that can be said to displace from one another because of lateral inhibition.

Another method of testing whether or not lines forming angles are phenomenally displaced from one another is to require the observer to set a comparison line parallel to one side of an angle as shown in Fig. 9-49: the line c is varied in orientation by the observer until it appears parallel to the standard line b.[32] The extent to which the orientation of c departs from objective parallelism with b measures the inhibitory displacing effect of a. This is determined for various angles of line a to b. The investigators found a maximum displacement effect for very small angles, around 10 degrees, leveling off to no effect at 90 degrees, but then increasing again at very obtuse angles, around 170 degrees.

It would have been desirable to include a control condition in which line a was not present (as in the previously described study) but in any case, the fact that the average setting of c varied as a function of the

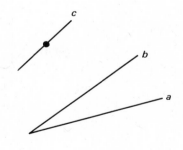

Figure 9-49

angle of line *a* to *b* does suggest that a genuine displacement effect occurs. But this does not prove that such an effect is based on a contour-
inhibition mechanism. Perhaps the same effect would be obtained if
dots at the terminal locations were used and the observer had to imagine the lines connecting them. In that event, some factor other than
contour inhibition would have to be inferred. There is also the puzzling
finding of a marked effect when lines *a* and *b* form an angle close to 180
degrees, i.e., puzzling from the standpoint of a theory of lateral inhibition. The investigators believe that this is to be expected because, in
their theoretical view, orientation, not position, is the major factor (see
footnote on p. 418) and line *a* at 170 degrees to *b* is in the same orientation as when it is 10 degrees from *b*. But if position were indeed a secondary factor, the applicability of lateral inhibition to geometrical
illusions would be all but meaningless since multiple lines in many
orientations are present.

When put to a direct test in an actual illusion pattern, the evidence
is against the hypothesis that the Poggendorff illusion results from an
overestimation of the acute angles formed by the oblique line with the
parallel lines. Investigators have modified the illusion figure as shown in
Fig. 9-50.[34] Here there are no acute angles, but as much of an illusion
was obtained as in the original figure. Conversely, in another modified
figure (Fig. 9-51), the acute angles were present but portions of the
parallel lines were eliminated. Now the reverse illusion was found. The
imagined continuation of the lower oblique line seems to be *above* the
upper oblique line, not below it.

It is by no means certain that the illusions of line direction result
from a tendency to misperceive the angles formed by intersecting lines.
But if there is such a tendency, the just described experiment is interesting because it analyzes the two possible reasons why intersecting
lines might appear somewhat displaced in the direction of the perpen-

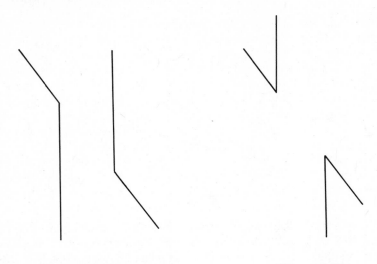

Figure 9-50
Figure 9-51

dicular to one another: The tendency for acute angles to appear greater than they are or the tendency for obtuse angles to appear smaller than they are. Since the result with Fig. 9-50 favors the second reason, it would seem to rule against the lateral-inhibition theory. It is difficult to see why obtuse angles should appear less obtuse than they are in terms of displacement of one line from the other. The effect is in the opposite direction since the lines of an obtuse angle must appear displaced *toward* one another if the angle becomes less obtuse. Therefore, we are left with a hypothesis about intersecting lines that might explain various illusions, that such lines tend to appear displaced in the direction of the perpendicular to one another, but it is no longer a contour-displacement hypothesis based on lateral inhibition.*

In fact the outcome with Fig. 9-51 seems to directly refute the hypothesis of an overestimation of acute angles (and to be in direct contradiction of the findings of the experiment described in Fig. 9-49): the obvious interpretation of the reverse illusion obtained is that acute angles are here *underestimated*. However, it is possible in the case of

---

*However these effects can be explained by the perspective theory of this illusion as discussed on p. 414. In Fig. 9-50, one can perceive the parallel lines as defining a plane receding in depth at a slant opposite to that of the oblique lines. The oblique lines would then not be in the same horizontal planes. But it is unlikely that the parallel lines of Fig. 9-51 would create an impression of a frontal plane because they are quite removed from one another.

this experiment that another confounding factor is at work. We may be inclined to judge the orientation of the sides of these angles somewhat in terms of the direction in which the angles as such are pointing. If so, this result would follow from the so-called confusion theory of illusions, to be discussed shortly.

Even more convincing evidence against the lateral-inhibition explanation of the Poggendorff illusion is the fact that the illusion occurs when the contours of the parallel lines are created subjectively (see Fig. 9–52).[35] Here there are no angles formed at all, at least by physically present contours. Essentially the same implication derives from the result of a study in which it was found that a modest Poggendorff illusion occurs without any lines at all. Each line component of the illusion is replaced by dots at its ends and the observer is required to imagine lines connecting these dots. However, the illusion obtained in this case is significantly less than the traditional one.[36] Therefore, if this illusion does result from a misperception of the angle formed by the intersecting lines, imagined or real, such a misperception is not caused by an inhibitory displacement effect.

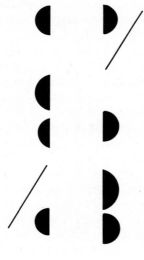

Figure 9-52

An explanation based on a misperception of the angles formed by intersecting lines has been made of most of the illusions entailing change of line direction, such as are shown in Figs. 9–20 through 9–24. At each point of intersection of the test line with an inducing line, the test line can be said to be displaced away from the inducing line toward the perpendicular of the inducing line, and the overall effect is cumulative. This is illustrated for one of the lines in the Zöllner illusion in Fig. 9-53. In the vicinity of each intersection, the test line would appear tilted as shown in *b*. Strictly speaking this should produce an overall impression of a jagged but untilted line rather than the smoothly tilted line one does see, so the hypothesis as such does not do complete justice to the facts. Perhaps a necessary supplemental assumption is that the overall effect is based on the same principle illustrated in Fig. 9-32*a*, namely, that a line as a whole will appear to slope in the direction of the slope of its components. Another illusion that might be explicable in terms of displacement of lines from one another is the Ponzo illusion, providing that the pattern used is the one shown in Fig. 9-7*b*. The vertical sides of the rectangle appear sloped inward toward the bottom; this can be thought to result from the intersection of these lines with the inducing lines, in other words, the tendency for the test lines to appear more nearly perpendicular to the inducing lines than they are. If the sides appear sloped inward, then the figure is no longer a rectangle; it becomes a trapezoid (therefore, the top and bottom must appear different in length). It should be recalled that the stereoscopic presentation of Fig. 9-7*b* still leads to the illusion since that is what is to be expected if this illusion is based on the intersection of lines. The lines still cross each other despite the difference in perceived depth. But without the sides drawn in and without the large array of inducing lines, as in Ponzo's original figure shown in Fig. 9-7*a*, this kind of explanation is no longer applicable because there are no intersecting lines. Therefore, the Ponzo illusion in Fig. 9-7*a* must have an entirely different basis.

A recent finding, which once again severely challenges the applicability of the lateral-inhibition contour-displacement hypothesis of these illusions, is that a similar effect occurs when, instead of a horizontal line, a series of dots is substituted in the Wundt-Hering type of illusion (see Fig. 9-54). The "line," which the observer imagines to connect these dots, appears just as curved as the actual line.[37] As noted earlier, a good case can be made for assuming that the Wundt and Hering illusions are special cases of the Zöllner illusion. The finding that the former illusions do not require intersecting lines, therefore, suggests that the Zöllner illusion does not require them either. The Zöllner illusion, in turn, reduces to the effect of a set of small parallel oblique lines on a straight test line drawn through them. Presumably, the only purpose of presenting many test lines in the Zöllner figure is that when each is caused to appear tilted in opposite directions, the illusory impression of its tilt is easily seen. Therefore, it is reasonable to assume that the fundamental problem for all the illusions shown in Fig. 9-7*b*, 9-20, 9-21, 9-22, 9-23 and 9-24 is why a set of tilted inducing lines produces an impression of opposite tilt in a test line.

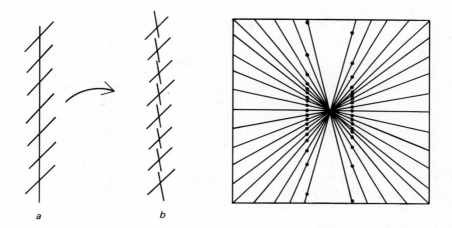

Figure 9-53   Figure 9-54

That this effect is not one of angular contour displacement is suggested in the informal demonstration shown in Fig. 9-55*a*. Here the test line is replaced by dots and the illusion is obtained; conversely in Fig. 9-55*b*, the intersections are preserved but only a weak illusion is obtained. One might even argue that a very strong illusion should occur in *b* because the presence of the continuous straight test line in the traditional illusion figure ought to act as a constraint against the illusory tilt effect (because, as already suggested, if the illusion is based on angular displacement at each intersection, the line as-a-whole should appear jagged or disjointed).

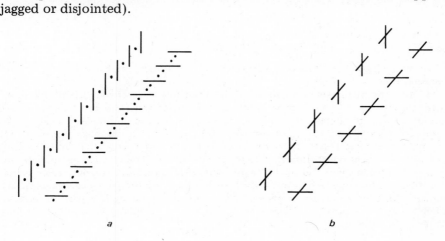

Figure 9-55

These findings and observations suggest the possibility that psychologists have been viewing the illusions of line direction in the wrong light when they assume that they are caused by phenomenal changes in the angles of intersecting contours. Perhaps the illusions that seem to suggest this kind of explanation can be described more aptly in terms of apparent shifts in the phenomenal *locations* of the points of intersection or in the phenomenal *orientation* of the locus of a set of such points.* For example, perhaps the proper way to describe the Poggendorff illusion is to say that the point of intersection of the oblique lines with the parallel lines appears too low on one side and too high on the other; perhaps the points of intersection in the Zöllner, Wundt, and Hering illusions collectively yield the impression of a line that is tilted away from the tilt of the inducing lines. If this way of viewing these illusions is correct, the problem, of course, remains of accounting for these phenomenal shifts.†

If lateral inhibition results in a displacement of contours from one another, certain other kinds of illusions should occur in addition to those entailing intersecting lines. For example the two small lines in Fig. 9-56 should not appear to be aligned since the one on the left should be displaced upward by the large line below it, and the one on the right should be displaced downward by the large line above it. Although an effect of this kind has been reported when the observer fixates the *X*, it is certainly not obvious if one views the figure under

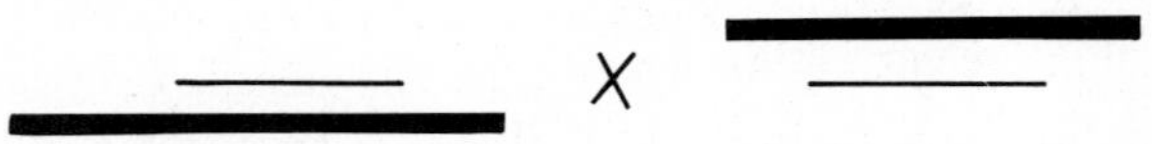

Figure 9-56

*For a brief discussion of a similar view, see Pressey and den Heyer, cited in reference 34.

†These comments are consistent with the conclusions reached in Chapter 7 about form perception. There it was proposed that perceived form can best be understood in terms of the set of phenomenal locations of the points that constitute it, rather than in terms of a set of retinal-image contours. It was also proposed that the perceived form results from an act of description of a figure that takes account not only the location of its parts relative to one another (its internal geometry), but its orientation in space and salient features, as well. From this it would seem to follow that illusions are based on faulty "descriptions" by the perceptual system. Although the problem remains of explaining why the inducing line pattern leads to such faulty "description" in each case, this way of thinking about illusions may prove to be valuable.

more natural conditions.[38] By the same token, certain illusions of magnitude should occur. The inner circle on the left in the Delboeuf illusion shown in Fig. 9–11 ought to appear smaller than the circle on the right since the outer circle ought to have the effect of displacing the contour of the inner circle inward in all directions. But, in fact, the inner circle on the left appears larger than the one on the right. The outer circle on the left in Fig. 9–12 ought to appear larger than the circle on the right since the inner circle ought to have the effect of displacing the outer circle outward in all directions. The opposite is the case.

In summary, the neural-displacement theory would seem at first to have the potential of explaining a number of well-known illusions. It has the additional virtue of being compatible with a different class of illusory phenomena showing the effect of the prior exposure of a pattern on subsequently seen patterns, the figural aftereffects discussed in the last section of the chapter. But when this theory is considered carefully, one finds a number of difficulties and contradictory facts. Moreover, the neural-displacement theory is not relevant to many illusions, including the Delboeuf illusion, the Ebbinghaus illusion, the Müller-Lyer illusion, the Sander parallelogram illusion, the vertical-horizontal illusion, the Jastrow illusion, and the various "twisted cord" illusions. So as is true of every theory that has been proposed, the neural-displacement theory cannot be considered an adequate explanation of geometrical illusions.*

---

*With certain modifications, it has been claimed that the neural-displacement theory is applicable to the Müller-Lyer illusion. The argument is that the neural representatives of the contours of the angle forming each arrowhead affect one another in such a way that the apparent vertex is displaced inwardly. As a result the apparent separation between vertices is decreased between inward-turning arrowheads and increased between outward-turning arrowheads.

Another contour-displacement theory of illusions with very similar implications that is currently receiving a good deal of attention is based on the fact that optical distortions of the eye tend to blur the image. Assuming that the perceived location of a contour corresponds to the peak of distribution of energy on the retina, it is proposed that because of the blurred images, such a peak shifts inwardly from the vertex of intersecting lines, thus explaining the Müller-Lyer illusion and with the further implication that acute angles would appear greater than is warranted by their actual angle.[39] However, such theories are vulnerable for all the reasons discussed previously (and others to be brought out later in the chapter concerning illusions achieved by binocular fusion) since they are also predicated on the idea that acute angles formed by retinal contours are overestimated.

Contrast and assimilation theory

Although contrast itself can be considered an unexplained phenomenon, many psychologists have thought that certain illusions can be reduced to contrast effects. A good example is the Ebbinghaus illusion shown in Fig. 9-15. In contrast with the small inducing circles in the figure on the left, the center, or test, circle appears large, whereas in contrast with the larger inducing circles in the figure at the right, the center circle appears small. Thus, the two center circles look unequal in size. Or to take another example, the apparent curvatures of the center lines in Fig. 9-25 can be said to be a function of contrast with the curvature of the inducing lines. In the figure on the left, the curvature of the center line is greater than the inducing lines; in the figure on the right, the curvature of the center line is less than that of the inducing surrounding lines. Therefore, the two center lines do not appear to have the same curvature.

The Ponzo illusion of Fig. 9-7a might be explained along the same lines. The top line fills most of the space between the converging lines whereas the bottom line does not. Therefore, the top line in relation to its frame of reference, the space in which it is perceived, appears large; the bottom line in relation to its frame of reference appears small. It has been demonstrated that an effect similar to that in the Ponzo illusion occurs in a pattern such as Fig. 9-57a.[40] From this, it is but a simple step to the variation in Fig. 9-57b. None of the other theories considered does justice to this illusion: the perspective theory fails to account for several variations (see Fig. 9-38a and b), and a theory based on intersecting lines is only applicable to variations such as that illustrated in Fig. 9-7b.

a   b

Figure 9-57

The Jastrow illusion (see Fig. 9–14) can be thought of as resulting from the contrast of the top line of the bottom figure with the bottom line of the top figure. Illusions of line direction can be considered to be instances of contrast. Thus, the apparent direction of each vertical line in the Zöllner illusion (see Fig. 9–20) is opposite to that of the short oblique lines that intersect them.

This theory, if it can be considered a theory, is obviously not applicable to many other illusions and, in fact, some illusions seem to call for the very opposite kind of explanation. Thus, for example, if the arrowheads in the Müller-Lyer illusion are thought of as frame of reference, then the shaft embedded in the outward-going arrowheads ought to appear smaller than the one embedded in the inward-going arrowheads. The former provide a larger frame of reference than the latter and, by contrast, ought to lead to a diminishing effect on its enclosed line and vice versa with respect to the latter. (But if test lines shorter than the separation between angle vertices are used (see Fig. 9–39), precisely such an effect is obtained. This suggests that another factor comes into play for the entire separation that is strong and opposes this contrast, or relational, effect.) In the case of the Sander parallelogram, the larger frame of reference of the subdivision on the left in Fig. 9–4 ought to bring about a reduction rather than an increase in the apparent size of the oblique line within it and vice versa concerning the smaller subdivision on the right. In one study it was shown that these differences in size of the two inner subdivisions are crucial; the larger the subdivision, the larger the oblique line within it appears.[41] (But again it has been demonstrated that the illusion reverses if test lines shorter than the separation between opposite angles are used.)[42] So these effects may call for an *assimilation* or *confluence theory* of illusions according to which the component being judged partakes of or is assimilated into its background rather than contrasts with it. The Delboeuf illusion (see Fig. 9–11 and 9–12) can also be understood in terms of assimilation.*

It is relevant to this discussion that there is an effect on some illusions of separating the test lines from the plane of the inducing lines in three-dimensional space. This can be achieved by drawing either set of lines on a transparent sheet and viewing the other set, placed behind, through that sheet. Or it can be achieved by stereoscopic presentation. It has been found that various illusions, such as the Ebbinghaus and Ponzo illusions, are substantially weakened if not entirely eliminated

---

*Some contrast and assimilation effects in color perception are analogous to those in pattern perception. Sometimes one region contrasts in color with adjacent regions and sometimes it assimilates to or partakes of the color of the adjacent region. See Fig. 11–8 and 11–9 of Chapter 11 for examples of such effects.

under such conditions.[43]   It is plausible that contrast would be lessened by such a perceptual separation of planes and there is independent evidence that this is so even in the case of neutral color interaction (see the discussion in Chapter 11, p. 527). The Müller-Lyer illusion is also weakened by this method of presentation. This suggests that the tendency of the shaft to be assimilated to or confused with the arrowheads is lessened by such separation in depth.*

The notion of contrast can be thought of in connection with the stress placed on relational determination by Gestalt theory. Thus, it will be recalled that evidence exists attesting to a relational basis of perceived size (see pp. 57ff). There it was pointed out that the tendency for size to be determined by the relationship to the frame of reference is offset by the fact that under typical conditions in daily life, there are usually frames of reference that are *common* to the objects being compared. This has the effect of attenuating the relational effect. The author has little doubt that if the two configurations of circles making up the Ebbinghaus illusion (see Fig. 9–15) were separated and seen as luminous patterns in a dark field, the size illusion would be greatly increased.

When seen as a drawing in a book, not only can the inducing circles affect the center circle in the *other* as well as in the same figure but the page serves as a frame of reference that is the *same* for the two inner circles. Therefore, there is only a slight difference in the apparent size of the two inner circles in Fig. 9–15. The same reasoning would apply to the variation of the Ponzo illusion shown in Fig. 9–57b. (Analogously, neutral color contrast can be thought of as an attenuated version of the determination of neutral color by ratios of adjacent regions of luminance. See pp. 512–513.)

In the same way, perceived curvature can be thought of as a function of the relationship of one curvature to another rather than the absolute curvature of a line. Thus, the crucial question is whether a line is more or less curved than neighboring lines. From this point of view, the effect in Fig. 9–25 becomes understandable. Therefore, when the notion of contrast is considered in terms of a theory that stresses determination of perceptual phenomena by stimulus relationships, it becomes more meaningful as a theory of illusions. Once again, however, it is clear that many illusions cannot be explained in this way.

---

*These findings seem to be at variance with one or two experiments described earlier testing the perspective theory (pp. 412–413) where certain illusions were *not* eliminated by three-dimensional presentation. The rule seems to be this: Whenever test and inducing lines are separated in depth and where an array of inducing lines does not cross over the test lines, then illusions will be weakened or eliminated.

Confusion or incorrect comparison theory

Some illusions seem to have resisted explanation by any of the theories that have been outlined. One of these is the Müller-Lyer illusion. A common-sense explanation of this illusion is that the observer is not making the right comparison, namely, instead of comparing the two inner lines as instructed, the observer compares the two whole figures with one another. Even if the observer tries to do so, he will be unable to isolate the inner lines. A recent demonstration lends support to this interpretation. When the pattern shown in Fig. 9–58 is viewed, the shaft on the right appears to be lower than that on the left.[44]   There is no illusion of length because each line has one inward and one outward-going arrowhead. The illusion of location is presumably the result of the inability to separate the line from the arrowheads, so that the upper arrowhead on the left that extends upward causes the end of the line to appear higher, whereas the upper arrowhead on the right, which extends downward, causes the end of that line to appear lower and similarly for the bottom end of both lines.

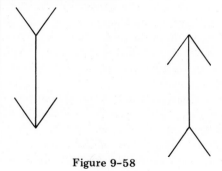

Figure 9–58

In this connection, although the whole figure of the shaft with the outward-going arrowheads is longer in the Müller-Lyer illusion than the shaft alone, the figure with the inward-going arrowheads is not shorter than the shaft alone. Therefore one might think that the explanation suggested here should predict an asymmetrical effect, i.e., the illusion is more the result of the elongating effect of the outward-going arrowheads than it is of the compression effect of the inward-going arrowheads. This has shown to be true by comparing each of these with a line without arrowheads.*

*See Binet.[45]   Some investigators now believe that there are two different illusions constituting the Müller-Lyer effect because factors such as the angle and length of the arrowheads have somewhat different effects on the apparent size of the two shafts.[46]

But there is still some illusory effect produced by the inward-going arrowheads. Perhaps this results from a tendency to confuse the length of the shaft with the distance separating the ends of the arrowheads, which, in this case, is less than the length of the shaft. To test this hypothesis, investigators varied the distance separating the inward-going arrowheads.[47] When they did so by holding the length of the oblique lines of the arrowheads constant and varying the angle they formed with the shafts, the illusion was found to be greater for smaller angles; when the investigators varied the angle but also varied the length of the oblique lines so as to hold constant the distance separating the ends of the arrowheads, the illusion remained constant; when they held the angle size constant and varied the distance separating the ends of the arrowheads by varying the length of the oblique lines, the illusion increased as the inter-end distance decreased. Therefore, there would certainly seem to be a confusion of the length of the shaft with the distance between the ends of the arrowheads. (This finding thus makes sense of the previously known facts about the angle and length of the arrowheads referred to on p. 392.)

In further support of this theory is the finding that differentiation of the shaft from the arrowheads, such as by the use of different colors or by the introduction of small gaps between the ends of the shafts and the arrowhead oblique lines, results in a smaller illusion. Also instructions to observers to attend only to the shafts and to ignore the arrowheads decreases the illusion.[48]

It has also been demonstrated that the apparent midpoint of the shaft of a figure such as that in Fig. 9–59 is displaced in the direction of the outward-going arrowhead (the dot in the figure that appears to be in about the center of the shaft is in fact nearer to the right end of it). One can understand this effect as resulting from the unintentional inclusion of the outward-going arrowhead in the extent to be bisected.[49]

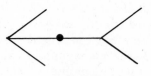

Figure 9–59

Still another indication that the Müller-Lyer illusion is based on a psychological process in which the arrowheads are included in the assessment of the length of the shafts is illustrated in Fig. 9–60. One can attend to the dashed-line figure in *a* and compare it to the solid-line figure in *b*; in that event the shaft in *a* appears longer. Or one can attend to the solid-line figure in *a* and compare it to the dashed-line figure in *b*; in that event the shaft in *b* appears longer. Thus, the illusion is not a function of the mere presence of one or the other set of arrowheads but rather of a perceptual act. Otherwise there could be no illusory effect since *a* and *b* are identical figures.*

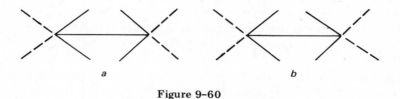

Figure 9-60

Another good example of this kind of effect is one illustrated in Woodworth's classic book *Experimental Psychology*.[51]   In Fig. 9-61, the distance between the left side of circle *a* and the right side of circle *b* is the same as that between the right side of *b* and the left side of *c*. However, one apparently cannot avoid comparing the distances between *circles* rather than between points (as instructed) so that the first distance appears shorter than the second distance. Woodworth called this the confusion theory since it is held that we confuse what it is we are to compare. A better name might be the incorrect comparison theory. The Delboeuf illusion (Figs. 9–11*a* and 9–12) can be encompassed by this kind of explanation since it can be argued that we cannot avoid comparing the entire double figure with the single circle. In the Sander parallelogram it can be claimed that we confuse the areas of the two inner parallelograms with the diagonals, comparing the former rather than the latter.

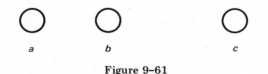

Figure 9-61

There is a similarity between the confusion theory and the explanation offered of various illusions in terms of assimilation (or confluence). The test line is assimilated to the inducing lines or surrounding space

*A demonstration somewhat like that in Fig. 9-60 was given by Köhler to illustrate that the perceived midpoint of the shaft was determined by which set of arrowheads one attended to.[50]

and, therefore, it itself is not perceived independently but is confused with the inducing lines.

However many of the other illusions do not seem to be amenable to this kind of explanation; almost the very opposite of confusion occurs in illusions that are explicable in terms of contrast.

Further Facts about Illusions

A number of experimental findings concerning illusions not yet mentioned must be taken into account by any proposed theory. Some of these findings are sufficiently decisive to rule out one or more of the theories that have been considered, at least to rule them out as the necessary basis of all illusions.

Binocular separation of test and inducing lines

It is possible by means of a stereoscope to present the test line or lines of an illusory pattern to one eye and the inducing lines to the other eye.[52] The two parts are then perceptually fused so that the observer sees the overall illusion pattern. Fig. 9-62 illustrates this for the Poggendorff illusion.

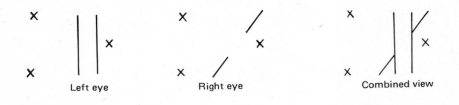

Left eye   Right eye   Combined view

Figure 9-62

If, under these conditions, no illusion were perceived it would establish that processes in the retina are responsible for illusions; or, to put it differently, it would establish that more central events in the brain are *not* the cause of illusions. Since the observer perceives the same illusion pattern, by this method of presentation as he does by the normal presentation, he should experience the illusion unless for some reason it is crucial that the entire pattern stimulate one retina. Thus, for example, in the Ponzo illusion, since the fused images will give rise to the perception of a perspective pattern, the abolition of an illusion via such binocular presentation would rule against the apparent distance theory. Conversely, it might be held to support the neural-displacement theory because it could be claimed that the relevant contour displacement would not take place if the contours that inhibit each other are no longer both registered on one retina.

Although the last word has probably not yet been said on this subject, it now appears that most illusions do occur under this method of viewing and they are of about the same order of magnitude. For a while it had appeared that illusions were appreciably reduced or eliminated with this technique, but there is now evidence that this may have resulted from the problem of binocular rivalry that can occur under conditions of stereoscopic observation. As noted in Chapter 3, when disparate or different patterns are presented to the two eyes, either depth perception or a state of binocular rivalry may result. If rivalry were to occur with the illusion figures, it would be difficult for the observer to achieve the fused pattern, which, of course, is a necessary condition for observing whether or not the illusion is present.

In order to achieve the desired result of binocular fusion of the two patterns (such as those illustrated in Fig. 9-62) the patterns must be brought into proper registry. In other words, images of the line components must fall in just the appropriate regions of each retina such that the desired combined view will be obtained (the combined view must be that of *a* in Fig. 9-63 rather than that of *b* or *c*.) For fusion to occur in this example, the images of the inner ends of the two oblique lines for one eye must fall on points of one retina that correspond to the images of the vertical lines on the other retina. It will be recalled that only corresponding retinal points are located in the same phenomenal direction of space. Such proper registry is not easy to achieve when each eye is presented with a different pattern. It can be facilitated by presenting some components which are identical for the two eyes, as the *x*'s shown in Fig. 9-62. One such mark is to be fixated. When these marks are properly fused the two patterns are in correct registration. However, movements of the eyes will throw the patterns out of registry and this in turn will lead to binocular rivalry. Therefore, this kind of experiment is difficult to do properly. Great pains must be taken to achieve the desired fusion before observations about the illusory effects are made. One method recently employed was to flash the two stereoscopically presented patterns briefly, so as to minimize eye movements. Fusion is then achieved.

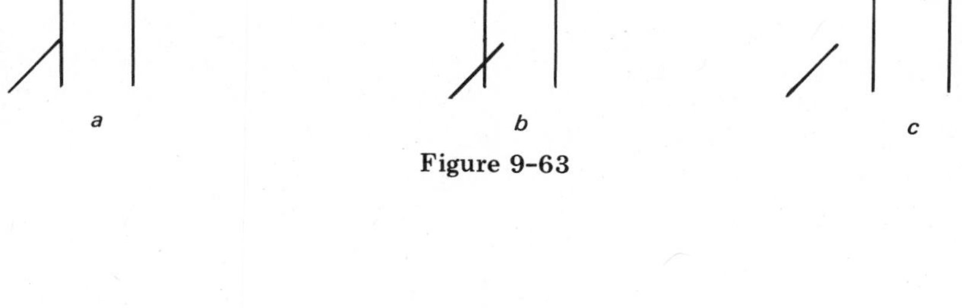

Figure 9-63

When such precautions are taken, it appears that most of the illusions occur under these conditions of presentation as they more or less normally do or only very slightly reduced in magnitude.[53] Therefore, central theories of illusions are not ruled out. Conversely, the achievement of illusions under these conditions seems to challenge peripheralistic theories, such as that of lateral inhibition, at least if such inhibition is thought to occur within the retina.

However, not all investigators have studied the same illusions and the particular half views presented for binocular combination have differed from study to study. The conclusions that can be drawn very much depend upon the illusion tested. For example, in many investigations the vertical-horizontal illusion was included. Yet it would seem obvious that this is one illusion that, logically speaking, ought not to require the presence of the vertical and horizontal images in one eye. The illusion would not seem to be caused by the effect of one of these lines *upon* the other, but by the very difference in their orientation. The choice of half views is important because neither pattern should contain all the elements sufficient to produce the illusion. If it does, it is gratuitous to attribute the achievement of the illusion via binocular fusion to central events. For example, if one eye receives an image of all the arrowheads of the Müller-Lyer illusion and the other eye only the two shafts, then the occurrence of the illusion for the fused images proves nothing. The illusion is present without the shafts, as is evident in Fig. 9–3a.

Illusions without contours

It is possible to achieve a state of affairs in which the overall pattern of an illusion is perceived without any line contours being present at all. By means of two identical random patterns of black and white dots or the like, in which disparity of certain regions is introduced, stereoscopic viewing will lead to the perception of illusion patterns. (See the discussion of the so-called Julesz patterns in Chapter 3.) Under these conditions no contours are presented to either eye (this has the added advantage of eliminating the problem of binocular rivalry).*

This technique nevertheless does produce many of the classical illusions, including the Müller-Lyer, the Ponzo, the Poggendorff, the vertical-horizontal, and the Ebbinghaus illusions. Some difficulty in achieving illusions such as that of Wundt and Zöllner have been reported using this method, although a weak Zöllner illusion has been obtained. (There

---

*This method was first used by Papert.[54] It was further extended by Hochberg.[55] Recently, Julesz[43] has demonstrated such effects in a book where the reader can experience them for himself.

are, however, technical difficulties in achieving the conditions necessary for producing the fused image in these cases). The conclusion, therefore, seems warranted that many illusions are of central origin and that lateral inhibition based on the retinal proximity of contours cannot be a necessary basis of the illusions.

Stationary image

Illusions occur even if the retinal image of the pattern cannot move. Thus, if an afterimage is first formed of the illusion pattern, the observer can then inspect his afterimage, and when this is done, the illusions still persist. Or, even better, a stabilized image can be achieved by other means and this too does not eliminate or reduce illusions.[56] This is an interesting fact, but the only theory that has been considered here that is challenged by this finding is the eye-movement theory. Obviously, one cannot scan an object if its retinal image remains fixed. However, the more sophisticated, intended eye-movement theory is not contradicted by this finding.

Illusions via touch perception

It has been reported that many of the classical illusions are experienced in about the same way when they are constructed as raised outlines and felt with the fingers by blindfolded or blind observers. If the same explanation is to cover vision and touch perception, some theories fall by the wayside, namely, the eye-movement theory (all versions) and the apparent-distance theory.

The import of this fact for the neural-displacement theory requires more careful consideration. If touch perception is achieved by moving the tip of a finger over the pattern so that only one point of the pattern at a time stimulates it and only this one region of the skin is stimulated, it would seem difficult to defend the lateral inhibition theory of contour displacement. There would be no analogue of two simultaneous (or even successive) contours stimulating adjacent regions of the sensory surface as occurs in vision. The spatial arrangement of the pattern is only apprehended by an appreciation of the changing phenomenal positions of the finger somewhat analogous to the form perception achieved when a figure is exposed successively through a narrow slit, since then there is no extended retinal image of the figure (Chapter 7, pp. 298ff). By contrast, if the entire relief pattern were pressed on the surface of the skin, then contours would be present, and since it is known that lateral inhibition occurs in the tactile modality, such an outcome would *not* challenge this theory.[57]

The actual experimental findings are still rather meager. A few experiments have been done using the method of pressing a raised figure onto the skin.[58] Although illusions were experienced, they were not very great. In the case of one particular figure, the filled-space illusion, the results suggest an *under* rather than an overestimation of the divided (or "filled") extent in the tactile modality.[59] More data are available using active manual exploration and, by and large, many illusions have been found to occur under these conditions. Furthermore, it has been shown that certain conditions have a similar effect on visually and optically experienced illusions, for example, the angle of the arrowheads with respect to the shaft in the Müller-Lyer illusion.[60] But since the subjects freely move their fingers and can simultaneously touch the figure in several places at once, the theoretical picture is not as clear as it would be if only the tip of one finger moved over the figure as suggested. Therefore, the precise meaning of these findings is not yet clear.

It should also be borne in mind that in sighted individuals touch perception, having been educated by vision over a lifetime, may consist of a visualizing of the touched object. (See the discussion of this relationship in Chapter 8, pp. 377ff). Therefore, the finding that the illusions are experienced through touch perception is not altogether surprising, particularly if illusions result from a process such as is suggested by the contrast, assimilation, or confusion theories. However, it has been reported that those born blind also experience the illusions through touch perception; if this is true the theoretical import of tactually experienced illusions is quite considerable.[61]

Cultural and Age Differences in the Perception of Illusions

There is evidence that children and adults differ in the perception of illusions and that peoples of different cultures also differ from one another in this respect. In one study, four illusion figures, the Müller-Lyer, the Sander parallelogram, and two versions of the vertical-horizontal illusion, were presented to people of several different African cultures and a few groups of Americans.[62] Various precautions were taken to make sure that subjects understood the task. For example, the test lines to be compared were colored differently from the inducing lines. Subjects whose overall performances were highly inconsistent were not included in the final analysis of the data. The result was that the African subjects were much less susceptible to the Müller-Lyer and Sander illusions but more susceptible to the vertical-horizontal illusion than the American subjects. The differences were rather striking. For example, some groups of Africans, the Bete, Suku, and Bushmen, perceived the test lines in the Müller-Lyer figure almost veridically compared to a 20 per cent illusory difference for people of Evanston, Illinois; conversely, the Toro and Banyankole of Africa perceived a vertical line as about 20 per cent longer than an equal-length horizontal line compared to hardly any difference at all among the Bete and a 7 per cent difference among people from Evanston.

The investigators took these results as evidence of "cross-cultural differences in visual inference systems learned in response to different ecological and cultural factors in the visual environment."[63] They speculated that the lesser susceptibility to the Müller-Lyer and Sander illusion among Africans may result from little exposure to rectangular objects in three-dimensional space such as occurs in more carpentered, technologically advanced, environments. As a result, there is less tendency to interpret dihedral angles in line drawings as perspective representations of rectangular objects. These investigators suggest a similar explanation of the opposite differences in the vertical-horizontal illusion, namely, the tendency to interpret vertical lines as extensions away from the observer in the horizontal plane. Presumably such a tendency would be more inclined to develop among those living in open, flat terrain. In other words, the investigators invoked the misapplied constancy theory of illusions, assumed that the pictoral cues to depth are based on learning, and thus applied this theory to their findings of cultural differences.

If these differences among cultural groups are not merely artifacts of difficulties of communication and understanding of the task, then it is understandable that psychologists would conclude that the crucial difference between these peoples is based on learning. However, even accepting for the moment the conclusion that learning plays a central role in the perception of illusions, it does not necessarily follow from this that it is the difference in the physical environment leading to differences in responsiveness to pictoral cues to depth that is responsible. Other as yet unknown factors may be implicated. There are certainly major differences among cultural groups in the amount of exposure to pictures and drawings, and we are not yet in a position to assess the effect that such exposure might have on the perception of illusion figures.

In any case, one should be cautious about applying the perspective-learning theory to these findings. First, societies that do not create a carpentered environment have some exposure to perspective-type patterns. These societies are no longer isolated and many products of industrialized societies find their way to these peoples. Also, within the natural environment there are objects such as trees that have parallel sides that project to the eye as converging lines. Conversely, people living in technologically more advanced societies are not deprived of experience with open terrain. Moreover, the serious difficulties with the perspective theory of illusions have already been discussed. If a case for this theory can be made at all it would be in connection with illusions such as the Ponzo rather than the Müller-Lyer, vertical-horizontal, and Sander illusions employed in this study.[64]

A further problem for the past-experience hypothesis is that the investigators themselves confirmed what many others have found, namely, that children are *more* susceptible to many illusions, not less.[65] Why should this be true if illusions result from habits of perception learned on the basis of certain features in the environment? Adults are, of course, more sophisticated, know about illusions, and, therefore, consciously or unconsciously may try to respond "objectively" by being more analytical. Adults are certainly better able to attend to the test lines than children, and it is known that attention is a relevant factor. The incorrect comparison theory would seem to be applicable here. Children may be even more prone to compare the wrong things than adults. If true, the data from children is a better measure of the spontaneous character of illusions than data from adults. In support of this interpretation is the fact, not yet mentioned, that very brief presentations of illusions (1/10 or 1/20 of a second) *increases* illusory effects in adults.[66] With more time, the opportunity to be analytical, to try to discount the effect of the inducing lines, increases. In any event, the data from children argue against the theory that the illusions result from a process of prior learning. From this point of view, the *decreased* susceptibility to certain illusions in primitive societies is all the more puzzling, since such peoples, if anything, would be quite unsophisticated about them.

Some illusions are apparently perceived by animals to judge by the way in which they transfer learned discriminations of size to illusion patterns.[67] Thus, birds and monkeys apparently are subject to the vertical-horizontal illusion. The results for illusions such as the Müller-Lyer are difficult to interpret because convincing techniques have yet to be utilized which assure that the animal is responding only to the test lines rather than to the whole pattern. In any event the finding of illusions in these mature animals does not of course rule against past experience as a determinant of illusions. While unequivocal evidence that various animals experience the geometric illusions would cast doubt on the perspective theory it would not seem to discriminate among the various other theories.

Illusory Aftereffects

All of the illusions discussed thus far appear at first glance at the figures. However, it has been known for some time that illusory effects occur as a consequence of what has been viewed previously. Thus, for example, in color vision, the phenomenon of successive contrast refers to the fact that following the inspection of a colored region, a gray region will take on the color complementary to the one just seen. Another example is the waterfall illusion (or spiral) illusion discussed in Chapter 5, p. 220.

Figural aftereffects

In Chapter 7 we considered the aftereffects of inspecting a curved line (pp. 323ff) and in Chapter 10 we describe a similar aftereffect of inspecting a tilted line (p. 477). Subsequent to these discoveries by Gibson, the Gestalt psychologist Köhler and his associate Wallach published the results of a study of other kinds of aftereffects that follow upon prior inspection of line patterns.[68] The kind of effect discovered by these investigators is illustrated in Fig. 9–64. The observer first fixates the mark shown by an X. At that time, only the black rectangles (I for inspection figures) are visible. Following a period of about 60 seconds, the I

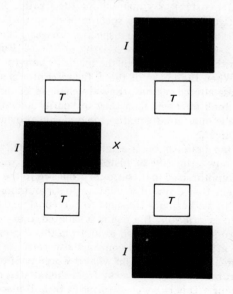

Figure 9–64

figures are quickly removed and the outline rectangles (*T* for test figures) are substituted. The main effect in this particular figure is that the two *T* rectangles at the left appear farther apart vertically than the two at the right, although they are in fact placed so as to form the four corners of a large imaginary rectangle. Another example is shown in Fig. 9–65. Following the inspection of the *I* circle, the *T* circle on the right appears smaller than the one at the left.

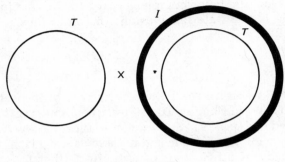

Figure 9–65

The purpose of fixation is to ensure that the image of the inspection figure will fall in a particular locus on the retina (and, therefore, its projection will fall in a particular locus in the visual cortex). By maintaining the fixation in the test period, the images of the test figures will fall in a specific position on the retina (and cortex) in relation to the prior position of the inspection images. The composite drawings in Figs. 9–64 and 9–65 illustrate these relative positions. Köhler believed that something happened in the visual cortex in the regions where the contours of the *I* figure had projected. When the image of the *T* figure contours are then projected to an area close to these altered regions, they are changed or distorted by the affected region and thus look different than they ordinarily would. The *T* figure on the left of Fig. 9–65 falls in an unaffected region and thus provides a basis of comparison for the other *T* figure.

What happened to the brain in these affected regions? The theory is complicated, and since it is now primarily of historical interest it will only be briefly outlined here. Köhler hypothesized that contours projected to the visual cortex generate an electrical current that flows from contour to surrounding region and back. As a result, the neural tissue becomes resistant to the continued flow of current, a phenomenon referred to as *satiation*. If a region is satiated, there will be a tendency for the path of the current to be deflected away from this region. When a test figure is projected to the affected region its contours also generate a current, but the path taken by this current is different from what it would be if it did not fall in an affected region. The current is deflected away from the satiated region on one side of the test figure contour. This is believed to result in a displacement in the perceived location of the test contour away from the satiated region. The aftereffects typically can be reduced to such changes in the perceived location of contours or, otherwise expressed, can be reduced to changes in the perceived distance of one contour from another. Thus, in Fig. 9-64, the distance between the two T figures on the left is increased and the distance between the two on the right is decreased (because satiation displaces the apparent location of the T figures away from the regions where the I figures had projected); in Fig. 9-65, the distance from one side of the T circle on the right to the other is decreased and, therefore, its overall size is decreased.

In Chapter 4 it was suggested that the apparent separation of contours from one another is determined by the locus of points in the retinal (and cortical) image. Köhler believed that this answer was inadequate and that an answer in terms of *process*, not merely physical location in the brain, was called for. Therefore, he postulated that the basis of perceived separation of contours is the strength of interaction between their respective figure currents. Ordinarily, the nearer the contours, the stronger is this interaction. Physical proximity of contour-representations in the visual cortex will, to a great extent, correlate with perceived proximity. But an additional factor determining the strength of figure-current interaction is the state of the neural medium. With physical proximity held constant but resistance of the medium varied, two contours will vary in their apparent distance from one another. This is why satiation can have the effect it has. Satiation decreases the interaction of figure currents on one side of a contour with adjacent contours. As a result, a contour will appear displaced away from a satiated region. The reader can now understand how the effects in Figs. 9-64 and 9-65 would be accounted for. It is important to understand that Köhler is presenting a general theory of form perception, not merely a theory to explain illusory aftereffects.

This ingenious theory has played an important role in the field of perception over a period of many years. Gibson's aftereffects can be derived from the theory on the assumption that a straight (or vertical) T figure will be displaced away from the pattern of satiation left by a curved (or tilted) I figure so that it will then look curved (or tilted).*

---

*The explanation is oversimplified here. It must be further assumed that there is a stronger displacement effect at the ends of these lines where the I and T lines are separated than in the middle where they coincide. This theoretically important fact is referred to as the distance paradox by Köhler and Wallach, and they offer an explanation of it in their monograph. However, one aspect of Gibson's findings is not accounted for by the theory, namely, the normalization of the I line itself. In other words, where the theory can explain the aftereffect on a test line, it cannot easily explain the change in the inspection line.

For further discussion of this problem, the reader is referred to Prentice and Beardslee.[69]   A very different interpretation of one of the Gibson effects has recently been suggested by Coren and Festinger.[70]   These investigators believe (and present supporting evidence) that a curved line is initially perceived as more curved than its physical dimensions warrant. What a period of inspection achieves, therefore, is a correction of this illusory initial perception much in the way that other illusions have been shown to decrease with continued viewing. The basis of the correction is held to be based on the information obtained from erroneous eye movements in viewing the curved line that leads to more nearly correct intended eye movements (see the discussion of the eye movement theory on p. 00 where various difficulties with it were considered). An important limitation of this interpretation is the very opposite of the limitation of the satiation theory, namely, it fails to do justice to the aftereffect in which a straight test line appears curved.

The theory of figural aftereffects was brought to bear on a fact concerning illusions mentioned briefly earlier in this chapter. It had been found at around the turn of the century that continued practice with illusions, such as that of Müller-Lyer, tended to decrease the illusory impression.[71] This was interpreted to mean that the perception of illusions has much to do with attitudes, sets, attention, and so forth, such that practice was able to alter the outcome. Köhler argued that the change in magnitude of the illusion with "practice" was not a learning effect at all but a progressive buildup of greater satiation in the more enclosed region between the *inward*-going arrowheads. As a result, the end points on this side of the figure were displaced from one another more than were the end points on the other side of the figure. Here the *I* figure affects itself, rather than a *T* figure; this has been called *self-satiation*. Various predictions based on this interpretation were confirmed.[72]

An attempt has also been made to explain reversals of perceptual organization in terms of the satiation theory. The reader is referred to the discussion of this problem in Chapter 6, pp. 265–270.*

There are a number of difficulties with the satiation theory, and it has been challenged by various experimental findings. Figural aftereffects of certain kinds can be obtained without fixation, i.e., with freely moving gaze.[73] A related fact is that aftereffects, such as those discovered by Gibson, can be obtained if the *T* figure falls in a region of the field that is *not* satiated. It now seems probable that there are two distinct effects of inspecting a curved or tilted line, namely, (a) a nonlocalized normalization effect with consequent aftereffects along the lines Gibson had in mind, and (b) a localized figural aftereffect.[74] A further relevant fact is that several repetitions of the experiment on the effect of repeated exposure to the Müller-Lyer illusion have failed to obtain a decrement in the illusion when the observer fixates; the decrement is found only when he is free to move his eyes.[75] This is the very opposite to what should occur according to Köhler's theory.

---

*Another application of this theory was the attempt to explain the absence of any distortion in perceived spatial relations despite the known fact that the cortical projection of the retinal image *is* distorted (see footnote, pp. 164). The idea is that for any uniform distribution of contours—as, for example, in a checkerboard pattern—the distribution of the cortical representations of such contours will be more dense in the region projected from the periphery of the retina as compared with those projected from the fovea. But the denser the distribution of the contours in the cortex, the greater is the satiation. It was suggested that as a result of a lifetime of experience with such uneven satiation and assuming that cumulative exposure can lead to a quasipermanent state of satiation of the neural tissue, then differences within the cortex of such permanent satiation could explain the absence of perceived distortion. The unequal permanent satiation will compensate for the unequal spatial representation of retinal extents in the visual cortex.

Köhler himself discovered two kinds of figural aftereffects that are not easily explained by his own theory, namely, what he called a kinesthetic aftereffect and an aftereffect in the third dimension.[76]   In the former, the blindfolded observer first inspects a cylinder of a certain diameter by feeling it with his hand. Following that, a somewhat larger or smaller test cylinder grasped by the same hand will no longer feel like it is the same size as an objectively equal-sized cylinder grasped by the other hand. The point is that it is difficult to conceptualize this effect in terms of a localized projection in the brain geometrically isomorphic with the proximal stimulus pattern as in the case of visual aftereffects. The same point can be made about the second discovery, namely, an aftereffect in depth. Here the inspection of a figure at a given distance will lead to an illusory localization in depth of a test pattern placed slightly in front of or behind where the I pattern had been. The theory would be directly applicable to a finding such as this only if the cortical representation of objects perceived at different distances were isomorphically projected at appropriate cortical "depths."*

Aftereffects as simultaneous illusions

It is possible to explain the figural aftereffects as special cases of simultaneous illusions. The idea is quite simple, namely, if the I figure gives rise to an afterimage, then that afterimage may be present when the T figure is present.[38]   It is presupposed that a displacement effect would be present if I and T figures were seen simultaneously and this turns out to be true. The reader can try this out by fixating the X in Fig. 9–64 since in this figure the I and T patterns are both present. The mechanism underlying this displacement effect could be the lateral inhibitory effect of one contour on another, as discussed earlier in the chapter. This theory also requires strict localization of the I and T patterns because only in this way would the T figure fall in the proper location with respect to the afterimage.

What is attractive about this theory is that the same mechanism, lateral inhibition, is held to be the cause of illusions and aftereffects. In fact, once the parallel is drawn between inducing lines in illusions with the inspection lines in aftereffect experiments and with the affected or

---

*Köhler was able to demonstrate by electrical recording that direct currents *are* generated by contours.[77]   But other experiments have been performed in which steps were taken to disrupt the flow of such direct currents that the theory considers crucial for form perception per se. This was achieved either by inserting metal conductors into the visual area of the brain of animals or by inserting insulating material, but the procedures did not seem to interfere with their perception of patterns, inasmuch as they continued to discriminate one form from another.[78]   There are, however, certain questions that can be raised concerning these experiments.

test lines in illusions with test lines in aftereffect experiments, the similarity becomes quite striking. Thus, for example, in the Zöllner *illusion*, if one considers a single line and the oblique inducing lines that intersect it, the apparent tilt of the test line is said to be the result of its angular displacement at each intersection with an inducing line. Correspondingly, the Gibson tilted-line *aftereffect* is said to be the result of the angular displacement of the test line away from the afterimage of the tilted inspection line. Or the apparent curvature of the straight lines in the illusion of Fig. 9–23 and the Gibson curvature aftereffect on a straight line of the prior inspection of a curved line can both be said to result from the angular displacement of the test line from the inducing line or lines.

Unfortunately, there are many difficulties with this theory, both in accounting for the figural aftereffects and in accounting for simultaneous illusions. As to figural aftereffects, since this theory has in common with Köhler's theory the central notion of displacement of test contours from inspection contours that, in turn, presupposes strict retinal localization of these contours, it runs into most of the difficulties described previously which, therefore, need not be repeated here. As to illusions, the theory is vulnerable for all the reasons cited earlier because it is a lateral-inhibition theory of contour displacement, and many of these reasons are quite formidable. Some illusions, such as that of Delboeuf, are in precisely the opposite direction to the presumably analogous aftereffect generated by corresponding inspection and test contours (compare Fig. 9–11 with Fig. 9–65).

Perhaps the conclusion to be drawn is that those figural aftereffects that depend on strict retinal localization can be explained most economically in terms of a displacement of test contour away from an afterimage of a prior inspection contour. (The theory should be qualified to say that it is the persisting neural events initiated by the inspection contour that matters, which normally produce an afterimage, but that can have similar effects regardless of whether an afterimage is phenomenally experienced.) Whether or not any of the classical illusions considered in this chapter can be explained by such a neural-displacement mechanism seems doubtful or, at any rate, remains to be demonstrated. At best, perhaps for some illusions, some portion of the illusory effect is based on this kind of mechanism.

Summary [79]

Illusions are nonveridical perceptions. Although illusions often occur in the perception of space, color, and movement, these can generally be understood in terms of the same general principles that explain veridi-cal perception.   Therefore, they do not constitute special problems. Since the geometrical illusions are not in any obvious way of this kind, they are considered separately.

The better-known classical illusions and certain experimentally de-rived facts concerning these illusions were described. They were classi-fied as either illusions of magnitude or of direction of line. Various theories were considered.

Gestalt theory stresses the importance of stimulus relationships for perception. Although this point of view may be well suited to deal with illusions in a very general way, with certain exceptions it fails to come to grips with the specific effects of the various illusions. One such ex-ception concerns illusions that can best be explained in terms of con-trast, since here perception can be regarded as being determined by stimulus relationships, proportions, or ratios. Another exception con-cerns the theory developed to explain the figural aftereffects.

The eye-movement theory maintains that illusions of extent or direc-tion are based on faulty scanning movements of the eyes of extent or direction, the error presumably being generated by the inducing line pat-tern.   In this version of the theory, perceived extent and directions are presumed to be a function of eye movements. Such a view is no longer tenable. According to a more sophisticated version of the theory, it is the intention to move the eyes a certain distance or in a certain direc-tion that determines phenomenal extent or direction and in illusion fig-ures faulty efferent intentions come into play. There is some evidence in support of this view, but as a general theory it tends to be circular. The intended or actual scanning movements are probably caused by rather than the cause of the illusion. The fact that many of the classical illusions are experienced tactually obviously cannot be encompassed by the theory.

The apparent-distance, perspective, or misapplied constancy theory maintains that the illusion figures contain pictorial cues to depth, bring-ing into play inappropriate constancy mechanisms. Although such an explanation may well be correct with regard to the illusory experience of depth and constancy in drawings of three-dimensional scenes, it is very questionable if it is applicable to any of the classical illusion fig-ures. Illusions are experienced when depth is not or when it is the re-verse of that required by the theory. Although a more sophisticated version of the theory holds that the pictorial cues may have conse-quences for perceived extent and direction even if the depth itself is not consciously perceived, the very nature of several illusions does not fit this theory or is logically incompatible with it. Even those illusions that do seem explicable in terms of the theory can be accounted for by other theories.

Quantitative differences in measures of illusions obtained from people of different cultures have seemed to many to support the perspective theory. But it is far from established that such differences result from past experience with very different physical environments and the illusions that have been tested are difficult to explain in terms of misapplied constancy. Furthermore, the fact that young children are more rather than less susceptible to many illusions than adults flatly contradicts the hypothesis. Also, the existence of the tactually experienced analogues of many of the classical illusions cannot be encompassed by the theory.

The neural-displacement theory holds that by a process of lateral inhibition, one contour leads to the phenomenal displacement of another nearby contour. Consequently, the angle of intersecting lines will be misperceived. Presumably, such a theory could explain many of the classical illusions of line direction. There is now some direct evidence that an intersecting line will alter the perceived orientation of a test line but more research is needed before the precise meaning of this finding will be clear. However, certain deductions from the theory as applied to illusions do not seem to be substantiated by observation or experiment. In particular, experiments have failed to indicate that illusions of line direction are a function of a tendency to overestimate acute angles. One well-known illusion may even be the result of a tendency to underestimate obtuse angles. It is not evident how this would follow from the lateral-inhibition theory of contour displacement. Most damaging, however, to this theory—or any theory that reduces certain illusions to an effect of contour displacement—is the finding that the perceived shift in line direction occurs when the contours are not physically present, such as when dot figures are used instead of lines. This suggests the possibility that some illusions, which for a century had been thought to be based on the misperception of *angles*, in fact are based on the misperception of the *location* of intersections or of the orientation of a set of such locations.

Apart from these considerations, the neural-displacement theory, logically, is not at all applicable to certain illusions. It is also difficult to reconcile this theory with the finding that the illusions occur via stereoscopic fusion wherein the images of the allegedly inhibiting and inhibited lines are not both stimulating the same retina. Moreover, under certain conditions of manual exploration the presence of tactually experienced illusions would be hard to explain by such a theory.

The contrast theory maintains that a large inducing object or surrounding space will make a test line appear small and a small inducing object will make a test line appear large; a set of tilted inducing lines will make a test line appear tilted in the opposite direction, and so forth. This kind of theory can explain several illusions. It can be made more rigorous by subsuming contrast under the category of relational determination as described under the "Gestalt theory." On the other hand, certain illusions seem to require the very opposite kind of explanation. Instead of contrasting with a surrounding object, a test line seems to assimilate to it, to partake of it, so to speak. This has been referred to as the *assimilation theory*. The contrast and assimilation theories together can account for a number of illusions and of experimental variations of them that have been tested. On the other hand, some illusions do not seem to fit under either of these theories.

The confusion or incorrect comparison theory is similar to the assimilation theory in holding that we compare the wrong figures with one another because it is difficult to separate test lines from inducing lines. There is now a substantial body of experimental data in support of this theory, particularly in the case of the Müller-Lyer figure. Although this theory is not contradicted by any known facts about illusions and is compatible with many such facts (e.g., binocular fusion; tactual illusions; larger illusory effects in children) it is not now obvious how it would apply to most of the illusions of line direction.

Illusory aftereffects occur when a test pattern is viewed following a prior viewing of a different (or inspection) pattern. One major category of aftereffect requires that the inspection and test patterns be localized in the same approximate region of the retina. The test pattern usually appears displaced in a direction away from the region where the inspection pattern had been located. Gestalt psychologists developed a theory to explain this displacement based on a satiation of the cortical tissue by the flow of direct current generated by the contours of the figures. They applied this theory not only to their own findings on displacement but to the Gibson aftereffects of tilt and curvature, the geometrical illusions, the decrement of such illusions with prolonged exposure, the general problem of perceived form and the absence of distortion in form perception despite the "distorted" cortical projection of the retinal image, and the perceptual reversal of ambiguous figures. Analogous aftereffects were discovered concerning the third dimension of space and tactual perception of size and form. Various difficulties with the theory were considered.

A recent proposal was examined that the figural aftereffects result from the persistence of the inspection figure as an afterimage. The test contour is held to be displaced from the afterimage contour by lateral inhibition. There is evidence to support this interpretation and it would seem to have the potential virtue of explaining many of the classical illusions and the figural aftereffects by the same principle. But as a theory of figural aftereffects it runs into several of the difficulties encountered by the satiation theory, and as a theory of illusions it runs into all of the difficulties encountered by the neural-displacement theory.

References

1. Gibson, J. J. *The Senses Considered As Perceptual Systems.* Houghton Mifflin Company, 1966.
2. Ittelson, W. H. and F. P. Kilpatrick. Experiments in perception. *Scientific American*, 1951, 185, 50–55; W. H. Ittelson. The *Ames Demonstrations in Perception.* Princeton University Press, 1952; F. P. Kilpatrick (ed.). *Explorations in Transactional Psychology*, New York University Press, 1961.
3. Müller-Lyer, F. C. Optische Urteilstäuschungen. *Dubois-Reymonds Archiv für Anatomie und Physiologie*, 1889, Suppl. Vol., 263–270.
4. Sander, F. Optische Täuschungen und Psychologie, *Neue Psychologische Studien*, 1926, 1, 159–166.
5. Runyon, R. A. and M. R. Cooper. Enhancement of the Sander illusion in minimal form. *Perception & Psychophysics*, 1970, 8, 110–111.
6. Ponzo, M. Rapports de contraste angulaire et l'appréciation de grandeur des astres à l'horizon. *Archives Italiennes de Biologie*, 1912, 58, 327–329. The variation in Fig. 9–7b is one of Ehrenstein's illusions. See Reference 18.
7. Oppel, J. J. Über geometrisch-optische Täuschungen. *Jahresbericht des physikalischen Vereins zu Frankfurt am Main*, 1854–1855, 37–47.
8. Finger, F. W. and D. K. Spelt. The illustration of the horizontal-vertical illusion. *Journal of Experimental Psychology*, 1947, 37, 243–250.
9. Rock, I. and J. Simon. Unpublished experiment.
10. Künnapas T. M. Influence of head inclination on the vertical-horizontal illusion. *Journal of Psychology*, 1958, 46, 179–185; G. C. Avery and R. H. Day. Basis of the horizontal-vertical illusion. *Journal of Experimental Psychology*, 1969, 81, 376–380.
11. Delboeuf, J. L. R. Sur une nouvelle illusion d'optique. *Revue Scientifique.* 1893, 51, 237–241.
12. Oppel, J. J., Über geometrisch-optische Täuschungen. (Zweite Nachles) *Jahresbericht des Physikalischen Vereins Zu Frankfurt am Main*, 1860–1861, 26–37.

13. Jastrow, J. A study of Zöllner's figures and other related illusions. *American Journal of Psychology*, 1891, 4, 381–398.

14. Ebbinghaus, H. *Grundzüge der Psychologie.* von Veit and Co., 1902.

15. J. C. Poggendorff attributed the illusion to Zöllner who reported it in 1860. It was named for Poggendorff by E. Burmester. Beitrage zur experimentellen Bestimmung geometrisch-optischen Täuschungen. *Zeitschrift für Psychologie*, 1896, 12, 355–394.

16. Hotopf, W. H. N. The size-constancy theory of visual illusions. *British Journal of Psychology*, 1966, 57, 307–318.

17. Zöllner, F. Über eine neue Art von Pseudoskopie von ihre Beziehungen zu den von Plateau und Oppel Beschriebenen Bewegungsphänomenen. *Poggendorff's Annalen der Physik und Chemie*, 1860, 110, 500–523; E. Hering. *Beitrage zur Physiologie* I. Englemann, 1861; W. Wundt. Die geometrisch-optischen Täuschugen. *Abhandlungen der Sachsischen Gesellschaft der Wissenschaften. Mathematisch-physikalische Klasse*, 1898, 24, 53–178.

18. Ehrenstein, W. Versuche über die Beziehungen zwischen Bewegungs und Gestalt-Wahrnehmung. *Zeitschrift für Psychologie*, 1924, 95, 305–352; W. D. Orbison. Shape as a function of the vector field. *American Journal of Psychology*, 1939, 52, 31–45.

19. Fraser, J. A new visual illusion of direction. *British Journal of Psychology*, 1908, 2, 307–320.

20. Cowan, T. M. Some variations of the twisted cord illusion and their analyses. *Perception & Psychophysics*, 1973, 14, 553–564.

21. Judd, C. H. The Müller-Lyer illusion. *Psychological Review Monograph Supplement*, 1905, 7. Whole No. 29, 55–81; A. L. Yarbus. *Eye Movement and Vision.* Trans. by B. Haigh. Plenum Publishing Corporation, 1967.

22. Festinger, L., C. W. White, and M. R. Allyn. Eye movements and decrement in the Müller-Lyer illusion. *Perception & Psychophysics*, 1968, 3, 376–382. See also S. Coren and P. Hoenig. Eye movements and decrement in the Oppel-Kundt illusion. *Perception & Psychophysics*, 1972, 12, 224–225.

23. See Thiéry, A. Uber geometrisch-optischen Täuschungen. *Philosophische Studien*, 1896, 12, 67–126; R. Tausch. Optische Täuschungen als artifizielle Effekte der Gestaltung Prozesse von Grossen-und Formenkonstanz in der natürlichen Raumwahrnehmung. *Psychologische Forschung*, 1954, 24, 299–348. More recently, it has been advanced by R. Gregory. Visual Illusions. *Scientific American*, 1968, 219, 66–76.

24. Fisher, G. H.   An experimental and theoretical appraisal of the perspective and size-constancy theories of illusions. *Quarterly Journal of Experimental Psychology*, 1970, **22**, 631–652.

25. Pitblado, C. B. and L. Kaufman.   On classifying the visual illusions. Unpublished paper, 1967, described in Kaufman, L. *Sight and Mind*. Oxford University Press, 1974, pp. 359–362; M. A. Georgeson and C. Blakemore.   Apparent depth and the Müller-Lyer illusion. *Perception*, 1973, **2**, 225–234.

26. Gregory, R. L.   Distortions of visual space as inappropriate constancy scaling. *Nature*, 1962, **199**, 678–680; Visual illusions, op. cit. *Scientific American*, reference 23.

27. Fellows, B. J.   Reversal of the Müller-Lyer illusion with changes in the length of the inter-fin lines. *Quarterly Journal of Experimental Psychology*, 1967, **19**, 208–214.

28. Gillam, B.   A depth processing theory of the Poggendorff illusion. *Perception & Psychophysics*, 1971, **10**, 211–216.   The theory was originally propounded by W. Filehne. Die geometrisch-optischen Täuschungen als Nachwirkungen der im korperlichen Sehen erworbenen Ehrfahrung. *Zeitschrift fur Psychologie und Physiologie der Sinnesorgane*, 1898, **17**, 15–61 and later by R. T. Green and E. M. Hoyle. The Poggendorff illusion as a constancy phenomena. *Nature*, 1963, **200**, 611–612; The influence of spatial orientation on the Poggendorff illusion. *Acta Psychologica*, 1964, **22**, 348–366.

29. Weintraub, D. J. and D. H. Krantz. The Poggendorff illusion: amputations, rotations, and other perturbations. *Perception & Psychophysics*, 1971, **10**, 257–264.

30. Gillam, op. cit., 1971.

31. See Fry, G. A. and S. H. Bartley.   The effect of border in the visual field upon the threshold of another. *American Journal of Physiology*, 1935, **112**, 414–421.   G. von Békésy. *Sensory Inhibition*.   Princeton University Press, 1967; for a summary of the evidence, see L. Ganz. Mechanism of the figural after-effect. *Psychological Review*, 1966, **73**, 128–150.

32. See C. Blakemore, R. H. S. Carpenter, and M. A. Georgeson. Lateral inhibition between orientation detectors in the human visual system. *Nature*, 1970, **228**, 37–39; C. Blakemore and E. A. Tobin.   Lateral inhibition between orientation detectors in the cat's visual cortex. *Experimental Brain Research*, 1972, **15**, 439–440.

33. Bouma, H. and J. J. Andriessen.   Induced changes in the perceived orientation of line segments. *Vision Research*, 1970, **10**, 333–349.   A subsequent study employing the same method revealed a maximum displacement effect at an angle of 15° much

as was found by the investigators cited in the previous reference. S. J. Tatz, W. I. Heimer, and R. P. Runyon. Visual displacement effects under conditions of minimal stimulation. Unpublished paper.

34. These observations were first made by C. H. Judd. A study of geometrical illusions. *Psychological Review*, 1899, **6**, 241–262. They were subsequently tested by Green and Hoyle, op. cit, reference 28, and by F. Restle. Illusions of bent line. *Perception & Psychophysics*, 1969, **5**, 273–274. See also Weintraub and Krantz, op. cit., reference 29; A. W. Pressey and K. den Heyer. Observations on Chiang's "new" theory of geometrical illusions. *Perception & Psychophysics*, 1968, 4, 313–314.

35. This effect was first noted by M. Farnè. On the Poggendorff illusion: a note to Cumming's criticism of Chung Chiang's theory. *Perception & Psychophysics*, 1970, 8, 112. However, the illustration in Fig. 9–53 is derived from R. Gregory. Cognitive contours. *Nature*, 1972, **238**, 51–52.

36. Coren, S. Lateral inhibition and geometric illusions. *Quarterly Journal of Experimental Psychology*, 1970, **22**, 274–278.

37. Coren, S. Lateral inhibition and the Wundt-Hering illusion. *Psychonomic Science*, 1970, 18, 341. A similar effect in this type of illusion using subjective contours instead of dots is illustrated in N. Pastore. *Selective History of Theories of Visual Perception: 1650–1950*. Oxford University Press, 1971, p. 277.

38. Ganz, L., op. cit., reference 31.

39. Concerning the neural-displacement theory of the Müller-Lyer illusion, see von Békésy, op. cit., reference 31, p. 228; B. D. Burns and R. Pritchard. Geometrical illusions and the response of neurons in the cat's visual cortex to angle patterns. *Journal of Physiology*, 1971, **213**, 599–616. Concerning the optical-distortion theory, see C. Chiang. A new theory to explain geometrical illusions produced by crossing lines. *Perception & Psychophysics*, 1968, 3, 174–176.

40. Fisher, G. H. Towards a new explanation for the geometrical illusion. *British Journal of Psychology*, 1969, **60**, 179–185.

41. Cooper, M. R., R. P. Runyon, S. J. Tatz, and W. I. Heimer. The Sander illusion as a function of relative space and component lines. *Perception & Psychophysics*, 1972, **11**, 102–104.

42. Litchford, G. Reversal of the Sander illusion. Unpublished M. A. thesis. C. W. Post College of Long Island University, 1970.

43. See Julesz, B. *Foundations of Cyclopean Perception.* University of Chicago Press, 1971.

44. Holding, D. H. A line illusion with irrelevant depth cues. *American Journal of Psychology*, 1970, **83**, 280–282.

45. Binet, A. La Mesure des illusions visueles chez les enfants. *Revue Philosophique*, 1895, **40**, 11-25.

46. See Sekuler, R. and A. Erlebacher. The two illusions of Müller-Lyer: confusion theory re-examined. *American Journal of Psychology*, 1971, 84, 477-486.

47. Erlebacher, A. and R. Sekuler. Explanation of the Müller-Lyer illusion: confusion theory examined. *Journal of Experimental Psychology*, 1969, **80**, 462-467.

48. Benussi, V. Zur Psychologie des Gestalterfassens (die Müller-Lyersche Figur). In A. Meinong (ed.). *Untersuchungen zur Gegenstandstheorie und Psychologie*. Barth, 1904; S. Coren and J. S. Girgus. Differentiation and decrement in the Müller-Lyer illusion. *Perception & Psychophysics*, 1972, **12**, 446-470.

49. Morgan, M. J. Estimates of length in a modified Müller-Lyer figure. *American Journal of Psychology*, 1969, 82, 380-384.

50. Köhler, W. *Gestalt Psychology*. Liveright Publishing Corp., 1947, p. 170.

51. Woodworth, R. S. *Experimental Psychology*. Holt, Rinehart and Winston, Inc., 1938, p. 645.

52. Witasek, S. Über die Natur des geometrisch-optischen Täuschungen. *Zeitschrift für Psychologie*, 1899, **19**, 81-187; S. Ohwaki. On the destruction of geometrical illusions in stereoscopic observation. *Tohoku Psychologica Folia*, 1960, **19**, 29-36; R. H. Day. *Perceptual and Motor Skills*, 1961, **13**, 247-258.

53. Schiller, P. and M. Wiener. Binocular and steroscopic viewing of geometric illusions. *Perceptual and Motor Skills*, 1962, **15**, 739-747; G. H. Fisher and A. Lucas. Geometrical illusions and figural after-effects. The distorting and distorted components of illusions. *Vision Research*, 1970, **10**, 393-404.

54. Papert, S. Centrally produced geometrical illusions. *Nature*, 1961, **191**, 733.

55. Hochberg, J. Illusions and figural reversals without lines. Paper delivered at the 1963 Meeting of the Psychonomic Society, Bryn Mawr, Pennsylvania.

56. Pritchard, R. M. Visual illusions viewed as stabilized retinal images. *Quarterly Journal of Experimental Psychology*, 1958, **10**, 77-81.

57. von Békésy, op. cit., reference 31.

58. Révész, G. System der optischen und haptischen Raumtäuschungen. *Zeitschrift für Psychologie*, 1934, **131**, 296-375; von Békésy, op. cit., reference 31, p. 228.

59. Craig, F. E. Variations in the illusions of filled and unfilled tactual space. *American Journal of Psychology*, 1931, 43, 112-

114; C. S. Parrish. The cutaneous estimation of open and filled space. *American Journal of Psychology*, 1895, 6, 514–520.

60. Over, R. A comparison of haptic and visual judgments of some illusions. *American Journal of Psychology*, 1966, **79**, 590–595; R. Rudel and H.-L. Teuber. Decrement of visual and haptic Müller-Lyer illusion on repeated trials: A study of crossmodal transfer. *Quarterly Journal of Experimental Psychology*, 1963, **15**, 125–131.

61. Révész. op. cit., 1934; C. H. Bean. The blind have "optical illusions." *Journal of Experimental Psychology*, 1938, **22**, 283–289; Y. Hatwell. Étude de quelques illusions géométrique tactiles chez les aveugles. *L'Anee Psychologique*, 1960, **60**, 11–27.

62. Segall, M. H., D. T. Campbell, and M. J. Herskovitz. Cultural differences in the perception of geometric illusions. *Science*, 1963, **139**, 769–771; There were also previous studies such as one by W. H. R. Rivers. Observations on the senses of the Todas. *British Journal of Psychology*, 1905, **1**, 321–396.

63. Segall et al., op. cit., p. 771.

64. Leibowitz, H., R. Brislin, L. Perlmutter and R. Hennessy. Ponzo perspective illusion as a manifestation of space perception. *Science*, 1969, **166**, 1174–1176.

65. Piaget, J. *The Mechanisms of Perception* (G. N. Seagrim, Trans.). Basic Books, Inc., Publishers, 1969; J. F. Wohlwill. Developmental studies of perception. *Psychological Bulletin*, 1960, **57**, 249–290.

66. Piaget, J., V. Bang and B. Matalon. Note on the law of the temporal maximum of some optico-geometric illusions. *American Journal of Psychology*, 1958, **71**, 277–282; Schiller and Wiener, op. cit., 1962.

67. Révész, G. Experiments on animal space perception. *British Journal of Psychology*, 1924, **14**, 386–414; C. N. Winslow. Visual illusions in the chick. *Archives of Psychology*, 1933, No. 153; K. E. Dominguez. A study of visual illusions in the monkey. *Journal of Genetic Psychology*, 1954, **85**, 105–127.

68. Köhler, W. and H. Wallach. Figural after-effects: an investigation of visual processes. *Proceedings of the American Philosophical Association*, 1944, **88**, 269–357.

69. Prentice, W. C. H. and D. C. Beardslee. Visual "normalization" near the vertical and horizontal. *Journal of Experimental Psychology*, 1950, **40**, 355–364.

70. Coren, S. and L. Festinger. An alternative view of the "Gibson normalization effect." *Perception & Psychophysics*, 1967, **2**, 621–626.

71. Judd, C. H. Practice and its effects on the perception of illusions. *Psychological Review*, 1902, 9, 27–39; E. O. Lewis. The effect of practice on the perception of the Müller-Lyer illusion. *British Journal of Psychology*, 1908, 2, 294–306.

72. Köhler, W. and J. Fishback. The destruction of the Müller-Lyer illusion in repeated trials, I and II. *Journal of Experimental Psychology*, 1950, 40, 267–281 and 389–410.

73. Held, R. Adaptation to rearrangement and visual-spatial aftereffects. *Psychologische Beiträge*, 1962, 6, 439–450.

74. Morant, R. B. and J. R. Harris. Two different after-effects of exposure to visual tilts. *American Journal of Psychology*, 1965, 78, 218–226.

75. See Festinger, White, and Allyn, op. cit., 1968, and the discussion of their experiment on p. 409.

76. Köhler, W. and D. Dinnerstein. Figural after-effects in kinesthesis. *Miscellanea Psychologia, Albert Michotte*, Libraire Philosophique, Joseph Vrin, 1947, 196–220; W. Köhler and D. A. Emery. Figural after-effects in the third dimension of visual space. *American Journal of Psychology*, 1947, 60, 159–201.

77. Köhler, W. and R. Held. The cortical correlate of pattern vision. *Science*, 1949, 110, 414–419.

78. Lashley, K. S., K. L. Chow and J. Semmes. An examination of the electrical field theory of cerebral integration. *Psychological Review*, 1951, 58, 123–136; Sperry, R. W. and N. Miner. Pattern perception following insertion of mica plates into visual cortex. *Journal of Comparative and Physiological Psychology*, 1955, 48, 463–469; R. W. Sperry, N. Miner and R. E. Meyers. Visual pattern perception following subpial slicing and tantalum wire implantations in the visual cortex. *Journal of Comparative and Physiological Psychology*, 1955, 48, 50–58.

79. Three books on illusions may prove useful to the interested student. One by M. Luckiesh. *Visual Illusions.* Dover Publications, Inc, 1965 was originally published in 1922. A second is by the physicist S. Tolansky. *Optical Illusions.* Pergamon International Popular Science, 1967. Most recent is a book by J. O. Robinson. *The Psychology of Visual Illusion.* Hutchinson University Library, 1972.

chapter 10

ORIENTATION

Orientation in perception refers to seeing objects as vertical, horizontal, tilted, right side up, upside down, and the like. Two aspects of phenomenal orientation should be distinguished: the orientation of an object with respect to the observer and the orientation of an object with respect to the environment. Fig. 10-1 shows a tilted line in the subject's frontal plane. This line is tilted in both senses—with respect to the subject himself and with respect to the environmental vertical. These two meanings can be separated by placing the observer in a tilted position as shown in Fig. 10-2. A truly vertical line (a) is not parallel to the vertical axis of the body; conversely, a line (b) that is upright with respect to the body is environmentally tilted. We refer to the first aspect as "egocentric" orientation and to the second as "environmental" orientation.

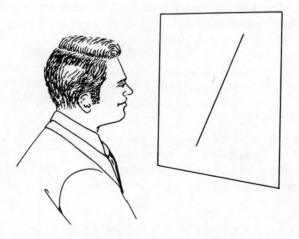

Figure 10-1

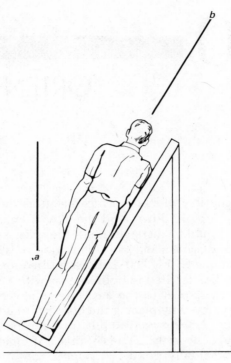

Figure 10-2

Although the two kinds of perceived orientations are related in a number of ways, it is desirable to consider them separately.*

Egocentric Orientation

If an observer were floating in space, where there no longer is any visible world or gravitational force, we could still talk meaningfully about egocentric, observer-centered orientation. What determines perception of the orientation of an object with respect to the self? One

---

*Since various terms are used in this chapter the meanings of which may become confused, they are redefined in the summary on p. 494. The reader may, therefore, wish to consult these italicized definitions in the summary from time to time.

possibility would be the orientation of the retinal image of the object. If a line is retinally vertical, it ought to appear to be egocentrically vertical; if the image is tilted on the retina, the line ought to appear to be egocentrically tilted. As usual, there is some truth in the common sense answer but it leaves many questions unanswered.

The inversion of the retinal image

The first question to consider is one that did not come into focus in the example given of the tilted line. The retinal image is inverted and left-right directions are reversed with respect to the scene represented by it. (For the sake of simplicity, just the word inverted is used here.) The image is inverted because the lens system of the eye refracts light, so that the rays cross over one another inside the eye as shown in Fig. 2–4. Therefore, it seems sensible to ask why the scene appears upright and not inverted.

This question implies an assumption that is unwarranted. The image on the retina is transmitted to the visual cortex, and it is now known that the cortical representation is in the same orientation as the retinal image; it too is inverted (and, therefore, the question could be rephrased as: why is vision upright if the cortical "image" is inverted?)* The assumption is that the upper region of the visual cortex ought to signify an "up" egocentric direction and vice versa, or that a left region of the cortex ought to signify a "left" egocentric direction and vice versa. But there is absolutely no reason to think that this should be the case. Events in the brain underlying perception encode information about events in the environment, but they are not copies of the environmental events. We do not expect the perceived *size* of an object to equal the physical size of its retinal image or its cortical representation. Nor do we expect that underlying the experience of a hue such as red or a neutral shade of gray are events in the brain that are themselves red or gray. Rather it is obvious that the events causing these experiences are neural processes of some kind. (To clarify this point, let us suppose that the visual cortex was located on the top of the brain where the sensory-motor area is, instead of where it actually is, at the back of the brain. In that case, the cortical representation of the retinal image

---

*The philosopher Descartes had speculated that the cortical "image" was ultimately re-erected when the nerve fibers from the brain reached the pineal body. This would mean that the fibers from the visual center of the brain to the pineal body crossed from top to bottom and left to right, and vice versa. This was his answer to the question of how upright vision was possible with an inverted image.

would lie in a horizontal plane. Then it would no longer make any sense to say that the cortical "image" was upright or inverted with respect to the scene represented. Yet, if through evolution, the visual cortex had that location there would be no reason to think that the visual perception of orientation would be any different. Therefore, the question of how vision can be upright with an inverted retinal image is a pseudo-problem that does not require a solution.

Is an Inverted Image Necessary for Upright Vision?

Having laid to rest the question of how upright vision could result from an inverted image, the following problem arises. Because the image is inverted and vision is upright, either the lower retina innately signifies an "up" egocentric direction (and vice versa), and the left retina innately signifies a "right" egocentric direction (and vice versa), *or* it does not matter at all what the orientation of the image is. The lens inverts the image and an inverted image is as good as any other image orientation insofar as yielding veridical perception of orientation is concerned.

The reason why any orientation of the image-as-a-whole might suffice is that it is quite plausible that what matters for uprightness of vision is the *relative* orientation of images to each other and to that of the body of the observer. An analogy from the perception of size may be helpful. It was pointed out previously that it would make little sense to expect a direct equality between size of retinal image and size of object perceived. But we *can* assume a correspondence between *relative* image size and *relative* perceived size (assuming for the sake of argument that all objects are at one distance). In other words, if one object is perceived as larger than another it is because its image (and cortical representation) is larger than that of the smaller object.

Therefore, as far as orientation is concerned, it can be argued that the absolute physical location of a signal arriving in the cortex of the brain is not what matters, but what does matter is the relative location of such signals with respect to one another. Since by perceived egocentric orientation we mean the orientation that an object is perceived to have relative to the self, then what matters for uprightness is that an object be perceived in its correct orientation in relation to the body of the observer. Since the body, or parts of it, is an object in the visual field, then its retinal image is also inverted. Therefore, the image of any object is not inverted with respect to the image of the body. In short, relative orientation of object to self, or of object to all other objects for that matter, is not affected by the fact that the entire image, absolutely speaking, is inverted. This point is illustrated in Fig. 10-3.

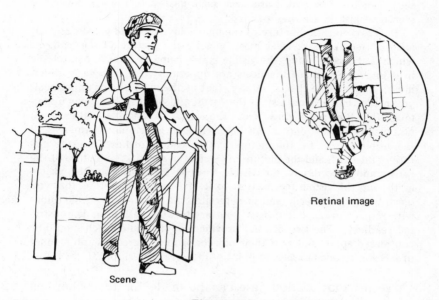

Scene

Retinal image

Figure 10-3

The reader may be inclined to argue that this analysis leaves out any consideration of where we *feel* the parts of our bodies to be located. Therefore, we cannot deal with the problem merely by pointing to the relativity of visual direction. It might be thought that a particular orientation of the retinal image is necessary in order for vision and proprioception to be in agreement. But does it really make sense to compare directions across two sense modalities in this way and to say that one is upright or inverted with respect to another? The feet *feel* like they are at one end of the body and the head *feels* like it is at the other end. That is all one can say about location apprehended through tactile-proprioceptive "feel" and it in no way can be said either to agree with or to be at odds with perceived visual orientation. Writing in 1709 the philosopher Berkeley analyzed the problem in these terms:

> "If we confine our thoughts to the proper objects of sight, the whole is plain and easy. The head is painted furthest from, and the feet nearest to the visible earth [by "painted" Berkeley means imaged on the

retina]; and so they appear to be. What is there strange or unaccountable in this? Let us suppose the pictures in the fund [retina] of the eye to be the immediate objects of the sight. The consequence is that things should appear in the same posture they are painted in; and is it not so? The head which is seen seems furthest from the earth which is seen; and the feet which are seen, seem nearest to the earth which is seen; and just so are they painted.

But, say you, the picture of the man is inverted, and yet the appearance is erect: I ask, what mean you by the picture of the man, or, which is the same thing, the visible man's being inverted? You tell me it is inverted, because the heels are uppermost, and the head undermost? Explain me this. You say, that by the head's being undermost, you mean that it is nearest to the earth; and by the heels being uppermost, that they are furthest from the earth. I ask again, what earth do you mean? You cannot mean the earth that is painted on the eye, or the visible earth: for the picture of the head is furthest from the picture of the earth and the picture of the feet nearest to the picture of the earth; and accordingly the visible head is furthest from the visible earth, and the visible feet nearest to it. It remains, therefore, that you mean the tangible earth, and so determine the situation of visible things with respect to tangible things: contrary to what hath been demonstrated [earlier]. The two distinct provinces of sight and touch should be considered apart, and as if their objects had no intercourse, no manner of relation to one another, in point of distance or position."[1]

So it seems that a good case can be made for the belief that upright vision could result from *any* orientation of the image-as-a-whole. However, it is also possible that there is an innate basis of perceived orientation and, in that event, of course, upright vision would be linked with an inverted image. In fact, the reader may be wondering how it could be the case that perceived orientation is not innately determined by retinal locus if, as was argued in Chapter 4, field location is considered to be innately determined. This requires some explanation. Consider the case of two lines crossing one another as shown in Fig. 10–4*a*.

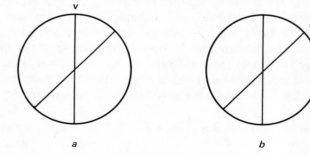

Figure 10–4

Based on the relative location of the points constituting these lines to one another, it would follow from what was said in Chapter 4, that, without any need for learning, these lines would be perceived veridically as crossing each other and as diverging from one another by some particular angle. That perception is based on the geometrical relationship of the retinal images of the lines. However, this does not say anything about the absolute orientation of these lines. Unless the vertical direction along the retina is innately tagged as "vertical," there is no reason to assume that the vertical line in Fig. 10–4a would be perceived as vertical. Suppose a different direction along the retina were to be tagged "vertical." In that event, the line marked v in Fig. 10–4b might be perceived as vertical, the other line would then be perceived as tilted, and *this would in no way change the perceived relationship of the two lines to one another*; they would still appear to cross one another and to diverge from one another by a specific angle.

Therefore, there is no contradiction in asserting that field location is innately determined by retinal locus whereas egocentric orientation is not necessarily innately determined. Assuming for the moment that *any* orientation of the retinal image can in principle lead to upright vision for the reason given previously, the fact remains that in the adult, upright vision *is* linked with a specific orientation of the image. The following experiment makes this clear. In order to isolate egocentric from environmental orientation, the observer is required to judge the orientation of an object in a horizontal plane such as the floor or ceiling. Fig. 10–5 illustrates an experimental technique for studying the perception of the egocentric orientation of a line.[2] The observer must indicate when the luminous line seen in the dark appears to be parallel to the long axis of his head (egocentric vertical) or parallel to a line connecting his eyes (egocentric horizontal). Subjects can perform this task with a fair degree of accuracy, generally setting the line to within 5 degrees of these directions. Since the line was presented in an otherwise dark room where only the line was visible, and since, further, the line was exposed for only a fraction of a second at a time so that its direction could not be gauged by eye movements, it would seem that egocentric orientation is determined by retinal-image orientation, at least in adults.

In this situation, the subject cannot perform the task simply by aligning the line with his own visible body, since only the line is visible. Therefore, the relativity hypothesis outlined in the preceding paragraphs cannot explain the outcome. Another fact that indicates that a particular retinal orientation does determine a particular egocentric orientation derives from experiments on adaptation to optically produced changes of the orientation of the image. If an observer looks at the world through a prism or lens system that inverts or rotates the entire retinal image, the scene initially always looks upside down or tilted. One might say

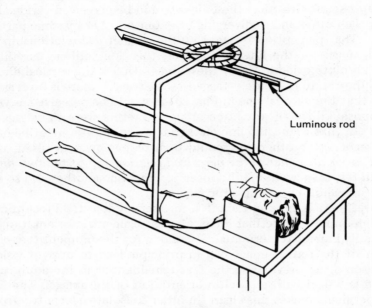

Luminous rod

Figure 10-5

that this is precisely what is to be expected prior to any adaptation, but it is only to be expected if we assume a prior linkage between specific orientation of the image and perceived orientation. From the standpoint of the hypothesis that perceived egocentric orientation is relative, it should not matter at all how the optical system alters image orientation. The image of the observer's body is also disoriented by the optical system. In fact, one could ask the question With respect to *what* is the visual scene as a whole perceived to be inverted or tilted when viewed through such a device?

The most plausible answer to this question is that in the adult only a vertically oriented retinal image will appear egocentrically upright. It is with respect to these retinal coordinates that an optically altered image will appear tilted or upside down. But if these coordinates do not innately determine egocentric orientation, the only conclusion to be reached is that a process of learning has resulted in this linkage. If so, it should be possible to unlearn it and to form new linkages; that is precisely the question posed by the experiments on adaptation to an optically disoriented image that we consider shortly.

Apart from such research on adaptation, there is very little in the way of direct evidence bearing on the question of whether egocentric orientation is innately determined or is learned. In Chapter 4, experiments were cited that seemed to indicate that *radial direction* is innately determined in a few lower species and possibly also in man (see p. 171). Although radial direction and egocentric orientation are not the same, they are related, and if it could be shown beyond doubt that higher species such as man can discriminate radial up from down or left from right without prior experience, then it would follow that egocentric orientation also does not depend on such experience. Direct evidence bearing on egocentric orientation would entail a demonstration that the orientation of an *extended object* or *a line* is veridically perceived. Furthermore, steps would have to be taken to isolate egocentric orientation from environmental orientation as in the procedure illustrated in Fig. 10–5.*

Adaptation to a disoriented image

Many experiments have been performed to find out if we can adapt to an image whose orientation has been altered by an optical system of some kind. The classic study was done by George Stratton around the turn of the century, using a lens system that re-erected the retinal image so that it was actually upright rather than inverted.[3] This experiment has been repeated several times with certain variations. More recently, other experiments have been done on adaptation to a tilted image.

Before describing these experiments, it would be helpful first to consider on what basis adaptation might be expected to occur. There would seem to be two requirements. First, sensory information must be available to the subject that the seemingly tilted or inverted scene is in fact upright. Second, an association must be established between the new retinal coordinates and this sensory information. For example, if a prism that causes the retinal image to be tilted by 30 degrees clockwise

---

*In considering the question of the innate or learned basis of egocentric orientation, the phenomenal meaning of such perception should be borne in mind. By definition, egocentric orientation refers to the orientation an object appears to have, not in the environment, with respect to the ground or to gravity, but with respect to the observer's own head (or body). *Vertical* here means an object that looks like it is aligned with one's head, *upward* means a direction that is from chin toward forehead, and *downward* is in the opposite direction. Therefore, in order to experience the egocentric orientation of an object, one must first have a mental image of one's own head. It is plausible (although by no means absolutely necessary) to assume that such imagery or awareness of the head as a phenomenal object is the product of experience.

is worn, then the 30 degrees clockwise oblique orientation on the retina must ultimately signify the egocentric vertical orientation for adaptation to occur. This association would replace the one that existed prior to the experiment. The problem is to isolate the kinds of sensory information that could lead to such a change.

Obviously, if a stationary observer views an isolated line that is parallel to the vertical axis of the body through a set of prisms (so that the retinal image of the line is tilted) and he does not see his own body, there is no information that the line is oriented differently with respect to him than a tilted line without the prisms. If, however, (1) he does see part or all of his own body, or (2) he moves, or (3) he looks at familiar things whose orientation is known, he will get information as to the line's true orientation with respect to himself. To best illustrate the process, we consider the situation for a prismatically tilted field, rather than an inverted one. Adaptation could begin if information becomes available that an object that appears to be tilted is actually parallel to the vertical axis of the head. Consider first information based on sight of the body. Parts of the body are visible. Any part of the body seen through the prism will at first appear tilted. Therefore, objects in that tilted orientation will be perceived to be parallel to the seen body. As shown in Fig. 10-6, if a seated observer looks down at a line on the floor parallel to the vertical axis of his body, he will see it as aligned with his body. Hence, the observer is receiving information that a particular oblique retinal orientation is aligned with the egocentric vertical. One might say that he is learning that an orientation that appears egocentrically tilted is not tilted because he can literally see that it is aligned with his body. (Given an awareness through proprioception that the head is not tilted with respect to the rest of the body, the orientation of objects with respect to the head can be arrived at by sight of the

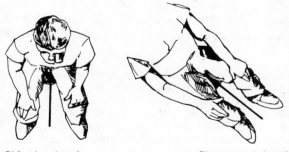

Objective situation   Phenomenal situation

Figure 10-6

body). A memory trace of the image of the line in the tilted orientation could be established, and this could become associated with a trace representing the fact that the line is aligned with the vertical axis of the body. Ultimately, the tilted image of the line alone will signify a direction aligned with the head.

However, one does not always see parts of one's own body and some species of animals very rarely or never do so. This brings us to the second source of information mentioned previously, namely, movement of the observer. To illustrate how this could lead to adaptation, consider an observer wearing prisms viewing a vertical rod from a sitting position (Fig. 10-7a). The part of the rod that is at eye level will appear straight ahead, but the rod will appear tilted. Therefore, when the observer is about to get up, he should expect that the upper region of the rod will not appear straight ahead because, for an actually tilted rod, the upper region would then be off to his right. However, the upper part of the rod, which is now at eye level, remains straight ahead when the observer stands up. Therefore, his head must have been gliding along a direction congruent with the rod (Fig. 10-7b). This happens because the rod *is* parallel to the head. When the observer moves, the displacement of the image is always in a direction congruent with the direction of displace-

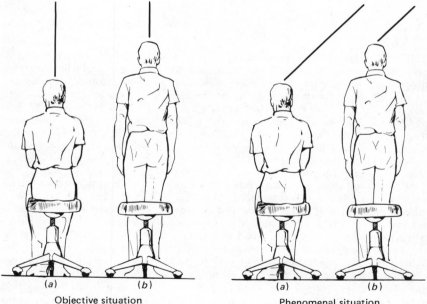

| (a) | (b) | (a) | (b) |
| Objective situation | | Phenomenal situation | |

Figure 10-7

ment of the head. Therefore, if information is available as to the actual direction in which the observer is moving (either through a central record of "commands" issued to the muscles or through proprioceptive feedback) then an oblique direction on the retina can become the stimulus for (or sign of) an egocentrically vertical phenomenal direction. Another example of this process is that of an animal walking in a forward direction. A line on the ground parallel to the direction of its movement would at first appear oblique with respect to the path of movement. But the line would remain directly below the animal's head and the image of the line would flow in a direction congruent with that of the line; therefore, its orientation must be one of alignment with the head-body axis.*

Finally, familiarity with the orientation of various objects in the environment might conceivably play a role in adaptation (the third possible source of information mentioned previously). Various objects (trees, houses, people, or the like) are known from past experience to be upright in space. If so, then given that the observer feels himself to be vertical in space through gravitational information, one might say that information is provided that such objects are parallel, not tilted or inverted, with respect to himself. This possible source of information requires neither sight of the body nor movement.†

*There is a real problem here, however, that must be faced. For movement of the observer to provide unequivocal information about the egocentric orientation of objects, the actual direction of such movement must be "known." Presumably the source of this information is either proprioceptive or a central copy of efferent signals, but the question then arises, why isn't such information "captured" by vision? (See the discussion of visual capture on p. 378.) If it were to be affected by vision in such a way, the subject would then misperceive the direction of his own movements and no adaptation would be possible. A similar problem arises in connection with the argument that movement of the observer provides the necessary information for adaptation to prismatically induced curvature (see pp. 322–323 of Chapter 7).

†There is good reason to be skeptical of this source of information since it depends upon knowledge. As the reader by now is well aware, what we know about an object or event will rarely affect how it is perceived. Therefore, although we might know that a tree is not tilted, it could very well continue to look tilted when seen through prisms. However, a factor described later in the chapter, concerning the role of major structures in the environment such as rooms, may serve as a source of information for adaptation to an optically disoriented retinal image. The coordinate directions of a structure that serves as a visual *frame of reference* tend to define which directions in the neighborhood of that structure are horizontal and vertical (see pp. 483ff). Therefore, sight of such structures might serve as information for prism adaptation.

We are now in a position to examine the experimental evidence beginning with Stratton's experiment.* Stratton viewed the world monocularly through a lens system that necessarily restricted his field of vision because the lenses were set into a tube. The restricted field may be detrimental to adaptation because very little of the body of the observer would be visible at any one time. Throughout each day Stratton wore the lenses over his right eye while the left eye remained covered. At night, both eyes were covered. Therefore, during the period of the experiment, he either saw through the lenses or did not see at all. Stratton wore lenses for 3 successive days in a preliminary experiment and for 8 days in the main experiment a few months later. During this period, he performed the various routine activities of daily life as best he could, reading, writing, eating, walking, sitting, and so forth, much as he would have done under normal conditions. He recorded all his experiences and observations, noting any changes that occurred.

In summarizing Stratton's findings, it is best to distinguish between motor adjustment and perception. As to motor adjustment, there is no question that adaptation was successful. At first, as is to be expected, movements guided by vision were in the wrong direction. For example, to grasp an object to his left, which, of course, appeared to be to his right, Stratton reached to his right. Therefore, such movements had to be reversed. Gradually, however, this initial difficulty was overcome. By the end of the eighth day of the main experiment, Stratton's motor coordination was quite good.

The perceptual changes are not so easy to describe and, in fact, there is still disagreement about the results. For the most part it would seem that Stratton continued to experience the scene as upside down *in relation to himself*, but on many occasions the scene appeared upright. These occasions increased in frequency as the experiment progressed. Thus, during the preliminary experiment Stratton noted:

> "(If) full attention was given to outer objects, these frequently seemed to be in a normal position, and whatever there was of abnormality seemed to lie in myself, as if head and shoulders were inverted and I were viewing objects from that position, as boys sometimes do from between their legs. At other times the inversion seemed confined to the face or eyes alone." [5]

*Stratton's purpose in conducting his experiment was to demonstrate that two widely held theories of vision of that period were incorrect, namely, the projection theory and the eye-movement theory, since both theories presupposed that an inverted retinal image was necessary for upright vision. [4]

During the fourth day of the main experiment Stratton reported:

> "The feeling of the inversion or uprightness of things was found to vary considerably with the strength and character of the representation of my body. When I looked at my legs and arms or even when I reinforced by effort of attention their new visual representation, then what I saw seemed upright rather than inverted. But if I looked away from my body and gave exclusive force to its pre-experimental image, then everything in sight seemed upside down. Especially was it noticeable that during active movements of the body, as in brisk walking or in coping with objects whose arrangement was relatively unfamiliar, the feeling of the uprightness of the scene was much more vivid than when the body was quiet."[6]

Finally, on the eighth day Stratton said:

> "As long as the new localization of my body was vivid, the general experience was harmonious, and *everything was right side up.* But when, for any of the reasons already given—an involuntary lapse into the older forms—the pre-experimental localization of my body was prominently in mind, then as I looked out on the scene before me, the scene was *involuntarily taken as the standard* of right directions, and my body was felt to be in an inharmonious position with reference to the rest. I seemed *to be viewing the scene from an inverted body.*"[7]

Stratton concluded that in time the experience of inversion would have permanently disappeared.

When Stratton finally removed the lenses at the end of the eighth day, he was surprised and bewildered by the appearance of the world for several hours—*although it did not appear that things were upside down.* As far as motor coordination was concerned, Stratton did frequently make incorrect movements and bumped into things for quite a while. There were also distinct signs of vertigo while walking and moving about, such as occurred during the early stages of adaptation.

Several conclusions can be drawn from Stratton's report:

1. Perceptual adaptation and motor adaptation should not be confused. One can learn to correct one's movements without necessarily perceiving the world any differently. Stratton clearly adapted insofar as sensory-motor coordination is concerned, as did every other investigator who repeated this experiment. But whether Stratton—or the later investigators—adapted perceptually is not fully clear.

2. In the opinion of this author, Stratton did not adapt perceptually to the re-erected image. The main reason for this conclusion is that the scene did not appear inverted on removing the lenses, that is, there was

no negative aftereffect. (By contrast, there was such an aftereffect concerning apparent movement of the scene based on Stratton's movements,
which confirms that adaptation to the "swinging of the scene" discussed
in Chapter 5 occurred.) As noted in Chapter 4 (footnote, p. 173), the
more conservative test of adaptation is the presence of an aftereffect.
Furthermore, even the descriptions of how the world looked during
adaptation do not indicate that it appeared to be *egocentrically* upright (except for fleeting moments on certain days when Stratton was
actively moving or attending to his visible body).

3. What did seem to have taken place for the most part, and there
were many statements to this effect, is that the scene appeared right
side up but not egocentrically right side up. This calls for some clarifica-
tion. Stratton's experiment was concerned with egocentric orientation.
Thus, if the entire experiment had taken place with the observer bent
over and looking down at the floor, the question at issue would be
whether an object on the floor that at the outset would appear egocentrically upside down would ultimately appear egocentrically right side
up. This is illustrated in Fig. 10-8. At the beginning, an arrow on the
floor pointing in the direction shown in *a* would appear to be pointing
in the opposite direction, toward the subject, and so would his own feet
if seen, as shown in *b*. If adaptation occurred, the arrow and feet would

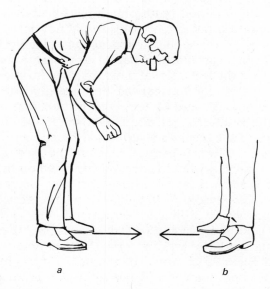
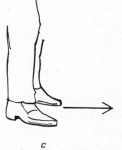

a   b   c

Figure 10-8

appear veridically to be pointed in the observer's forward, egocentrically "up" direction, as shown in *c*.

When, however, one does the experiment as Stratton and others have done, with the observer walking around in an upright position, confusion arises between egocentric and environmental orientation. Consider first the situation (without lenses) when we bend over and, with head inverted, look at the world through our legs. Then the sky is egocentrically in the downward direction and the ground is in the egocentric upward direction. But we are aware that the sky is *environmentally* up and the ground down. We realize that this state of affairs results from the inversion of our head. Similarly, standing upright but wearing inverting lenses, the sky also appears to be in an egocentric downward direction and the ground appears to be in an egocentric upward direction. But we are aware that the sky is up *in the environment* and the ground is down, and as is brought out in the latter part of this chapter, a strong tendency may exist to perceive the sky as up and the ground as down, even through inverting lenses. The only way to reconcile perceiving the sky as up but still as egocentrically down is to imagine the sky as being viewed from an inverted posture; this is precisely what Stratton seems to have done on and off throughout his experiment. The important point then is that the perceptual experience of egocentric inversion (i.e., sky as "down" in relation to the observer) apparently remained in force throughout most of the exposure period (with only a few exceptions). Had genuine egocentric adaptation taken place, this would not have remained true. The scene would have come to appear right side up in every sense of the term, and there would have been a clear negative aftereffect on removing the lenses; the scene would have appeared inverted.

4. At the beginning, a sensory conflict existed between objects or parts of the body seen visually and heard or felt. This is, of course, to be expected since only vision is altered. Stratton went so far as to believe that the very experience of the scene as inverted was based on such intersensory disharmony, as he called it, because he could not see any other reason why the field-as-a-whole should appear disoriented on first looking through the lenses. Since Stratton reports that the apparent conflict between modalities disappeared as the experiment progressed, one can conclude either that vision ultimately conformed with touch and audition or that touch and audition conformed with vision. There are two reasons for believing the latter was the case. First, it does not seem that visual adaptation occurred as would be required for the former explanation to hold. Second, there is evidence (discussed in Chapter 8, p. 378) that vision dominates other modalities in conflict situations (visual capture) so that what is experienced through such modalities conforms to that visual perception. There is also direct evidence

that it is touch perception that undergoes change. In Stratton's experiment, this dominance was not immediate but seems to have required a certain amount of exposure to the lenses.[8]

By and large, others who repeated Stratton's experiment also failed to obtain a perceptual change to the inverted image, although in some of these studies the emphasis was more on motor than on perceptual adaptation.[9] Motor adaptation is so successful that subjects have ultimately been able to ride bicycles and to ski while wearing the inverting optical device.[10]   Only in one study—the most recent of all—was it claimed that visual adaptation took place.[11]   The subject viewed the scene through a mirror placed under the visor of his cap and direct vision of the scene was blocked. This technique results in an inverted, but not left-right reversed field.   Also the mirror allows a much wider field of view than any of the lens systems used by the earlier investigators. Unfortunately, the reports of the subjects are not as clear as one might wish, although it is alleged that occasionally they did experience the scene as upright in every respect. However, certain clever tests were introduced in this study that do suggest a perceptual change. For example, a letter was presented that ought to look different depending on which part is perceived as the top ("W" or "M"), and the subject was to say which letter he perceived.   The subject's spontaneous reactions to these tests both during and after the exposure period indicated that perceptual adaptation had taken place.[12]   Since the results of this study stand in contrast with all the others on complete re-erection of the retinal image, it is best to withhold final judgment about whether or not upright vision from a re-erected image is ever possible in adults.

Several studies with animals have been conducted in which the orientation of the retinal image has been altered.   In these studies, the direct question raised is not whether the scene appears right side up or upside down in relation to an observer, as in the adaptation research with human observers, but rather whether the optical alteration permanently disturbs the animal's visual-motor coordination.   As noted previously, the problem of motor adjustment should not be confused with the problem of the perception of orientation.   It is at least possible that, as was true for Stratton and others, an animal viewing the world through prisms might learn to make the appropriate movements again in the absence of any change in perception. However, this is not too likely, because in animals, motor coordination is even more closely linked to perception than it is in humans.   Even in human subjects, a very deliberate effort is required to correct one's movements when first looking through the distorting optical device.   Only after a good deal of conscious effort of this kind is it possible for visual-motor coordination to become reestablished on an automatic basis. In animals, it would seem probable that as long as an object continued to appear to be located in a particular radial direction, its spontaneous movements toward that object would continue to be aimed in that direction. Therefore, the question of adaptation in animals seems to be whether or not perceptual change is possible.

If we can view these studies as bearing on perception, it would seem that it is radial direction rather than egocentric orientation that is under study, even though the change introduced entails the altered orientation of the retinal image. The test employed in this research with animals concerns the apparent direction of a goal object; for example, does the animal swim or peck or reach toward the upper left direction where the object in fact is, or toward the lower right direction where the optical device ought to cause it to appear to be? However, as noted earlier in the chapter, radial direction is related to egocentric orientation. Thus, for example, in man, an object stimulating a region of the retina directly below the fovea will appear to be in an egocentrically upward direction with respect to the point fixated in the frontal plane, and, ipso facto, will, depending upon eye position, appear to have a radial direction directly above the point of fixation. If adaptation to an optically re-erected image were to occur, the same retinal stimulus would now appear in an egocentrically downward direction and, also, therefore, in a radial direction *below* the point of fixation. Therefore, if and only if this entire reasoning is correct, can we consider the research with animals on altered orientation of the retinal image as directly relevant to the problem of perceived egocentric orientation.

One investigator used left-right reversing prisms on adult hens; they failed to show any adjustment after 3 months.[13] Other investigators fitted inverting prisms on fish, and in another study, the head of the fly was rotated 180 degrees.[14] The behavioral evidence in both cases was that no adaptation occurred.

But studies with kittens and a monkey gave somewhat different results. One investigator fit a binocular inverting lens system on a rhesus monkey.[15] The monkey was obviously very disturbed by the optical change. At first, it tended to remain frozen in position much of the time, to occasionally back away from objects, and to invert its head and view the world from between its legs.* However, during the last few days of the 8-day experiment the animal was clearly able to negotiate the environment successfully and could reach for objects correctly.

---

*This investigator used a binocular apparatus similar to that used by Ewert[9] on humans. A binocular system that inverts the retinal images in the two eyes is essentially a pseudoscope and has the effect of reversing the depth information provided by binocular disparity. See the discussion and footnote on p. 106, Chapter 3. Some of the effects in this study of a monkey may result from this fact.

It is possible, though, in an animal as advanced as a monkey, that, as with man, motor adaptation could occur without any real change in perception.

In a well-designed and carefully done experiment, it has been shown that kittens who first view the world through an inverting prism did not seem to have great difficulty in getting about in the environment.[16] The experimental animals were reared in the dark until they were 2 months old. They were then fitted out with prisms that inverted the retinal image but did not reverse left and right. Their performance was compared to control kittens treated in the same way except for the absence of the prisms. Although the control kittens improved *more* than the kittens wearing prisms over a period of 4 weeks on a series of tasks given each day, the experimental kittens did not behave very differently in their initial exposure to the visual world than the control kittens, and they did improve substantially as the experiment progressed. A most important feature of the procedure was that the arrangement of the obstacles in each spatial task was varied from day to day so that the kittens could not learn a particular path. Therefore, improvement would reflect the adequacy of perception or visual-motor coordination in general, rather than acquisition of specific habits. When the kittens of the two groups were then transferred to the opposite condition (i.e., nonprism to prism and vice versa) all of them were disturbed by the change, although perhaps not so much as one might expect. However, the prism to nonprism transition was not so disruptive as the nonprism to prism transition. The kittens of both groups improved substantially in subsequent days.

From this study one can conclude that although there may be certain reasons why the normally inverted image leads to less difficulty in visual-motor coordination, an inverted image is not necessary for such coordination in mammals. This fact, in turn, implies that the inverted image is not necessary for the veridical *perception* of egocentric orientation, because, as noted earlier, it is difficult to imagine that a kitten could perceive the world as upside down but nevertheless learn to *behave* appropriately (as a human being is apparently able to do). In this study, the kittens that wore the prisms did not have prior normal visual experience as is the case in the studies cited previously on humans. This may be the crucial difference and makes sense if one assumes that the lifetime of experience with a normally oriented image creates such a strong association between that image orientation and upright vision that it becomes all but irreversible.

It is understandable why Stratton chose to study the question of adaptation to a *re-inverted* image. Much of the controversy in the past had centered around the question of how upright vision was related to inverted image. But from a theoretical point of view, it would be just as significant if one could demonstrate that adaptation is possible to a tilted retinal image. If it is, then it would follow that it is not necessary for the image to be in its normal orientation in order to achieve the veridical perception of egocentric orientation.

There is much to gain from working with a tilted image rather than a reinverted one. First, it makes possible a more objective and quantifiable test of adaptation than could be obtained with complete inversion. The subject can be asked to indicate when a luminous rod seen in the dark appears "vertical." The change in the average inclination of the rod from "before" to "after" would measure the adaptation. With complete inversion no such test is possible—and this brings out a second important difference—because adaptation here would seem to be an all-or-none affair. One would not expect adaptation to a reinverted image to progress by degrees from 0 degrees to 180 degrees such that at some stage the scene appeared tilted sideways. With a tilted image, partial adaptation can be expected to occur and one can measure progressive change. One of the weaknesses in Stratton's experiment and those that followed was the uncertainty about the outcome because of total reliance on introspective report. Although this might be satisfactory in some situations, in the adaptation situation it is not, because there is so much ambiguity about the meaning of *upright* vision or *normalcy* of vision. There is a confusion between two possible outcomes, namely, becoming increasingly accustomed to the inversion (so that although the scene does appear upside down, after a while one grows quite used to it and pays little attention to it), and genuine perceptual change. Therefore, an objective test is much to be desired.

Several studies have been completed using a system of prisms that tilt the retinal image. In general, it is clear that adaptation to the tilt occurs although there is still room for disagreement about the nature of the perceptual change. In an early study, the investigator himself wore prisms for one week that produced a tilted image of 75 degrees. Objective tests were not included, but the subject's report does suggest a perceptual "righting" of the initially tilted scene.[17] More recently, adaptation to prismatic tilts of various angles was studied using objective tests of rod orientation and a good number of subjects.[18] In one experiment the prism tilted the image by 20 degrees. The average change in setting a rod to the vertical after one hour of walking up and down a hallway was 6.8 degrees. Since subjects ordinarily can judge when a line is vertical with great accuracy, even in an otherwise totally dark room, the impression that a line tilted by roughly 7 degrees is vertical is evidence of significant perceptual change. Others have confirmed that a perceptual change does occur although the magnitude of the change obtained depends upon specific conditions such as degree of optical tilt, duration of exposure, and the like. Presumably, if the exposure to prisms continued, adaptation would be complete and there is some evidence to support this supposition.

Do these findings provide evidence that the normal orientation of the retinal image is not necessary for upright vision, that given adequate opportunity for new learning, a different orientation of the image can also serve? Unfortunately, there is a problem concerning the meaning of the adaptive change obtained in studies of this type. Setting a rod to the vertical is not necessarily a test of perceived egocentric orientation; in fact, one would imagine that a subject would be responding in terms of the perceived orientation of the line in the environment when told to indicate when it appeared to be vertical. It is possible that adaptation to the prisms consists of a growing acceptance of the prismatically tilted scene as one that is environmentally upright, i.e., as not tilted with respect to gravity. In fact, a tilted scene often appears less tilted than it is, even on first exposure. (See pp. 483ff.) It is possible that this tendency toward a "righting" of the scene increases over time and that the magnitude of an aftereffect of such righting also increases over time. This could happen without necessarily implying adaptation to egocentric orientation. The subject could reconcile acceptance of the prismatically tilted scene as upright and still as *not* aligned with his own vertical axis by sensing himself to be somewhat tilted in the environment.

To complicate matters further, there is another kind of adaptation to tilt that must be taken into account. As was discussed in Chapter 7, Gibson discovered a tendency for a curved line inspected for a short period of time to appear less curved, and consequently for a straight line seen directly afterward to appear curved in the opposite direction (see pp. 323ff). Gibson also discovered a similar tendency for a tilted line to appear less tilted following inspection and a vertical line seen afterward to appear tilted in the opposite direction.[19] As with curvature, this so-called normalization tendency of tilted lines occurs with truly tilted lines—i.e., it is not dependent on the use of prisms—and, therefore, it cannot be thought of as a process of learning about how the line is actually oriented. Gibson also found the effect to be restricted to the region of the retina stimulated by the tilted line.

There are similarities as well as differences between adaptation to a prismatically tilted image and the effect of inspecting a tilted line. In both cases the observer is exposed to tilted retinal images for a period of time. One could argue, therefore, that adaptation to a prismatically tilted image is nothing more than the cumulative effect of normalization of all tilted images of vertical lines in the environment. There is now good reason for rejecting this interpretation. The magnitude of the normalization effect is of the order of 1 or 2 degrees, whereas adaptation to tilting prisms has been found to be greater. Also adaptation to prisms has been found in experiments in which no vertical lines are present, only randomly placed luminous spheres in an otherwise dark room.[18] Finally, prism adaptation occurs for familiar scenes, the image of which is tilted by 45 degrees, whereas there is no normalization effect at all at inclinations of 45 degrees.[20]

A further point about the normalization effect to consider is whether the normalization is toward the vertical in the environment or toward the egocentric vertical? If it is the former, as experimental results suggest, then this is one more reason why normalization and adaptation to prism tilt should not be considered as being similar.[21]

In an effort to isolate egocentric orientation, an experiment was performed in which the subject looked through tilting prisms, but in both the exposure and testing phases, he bent over looking down at the floor as shown in Fig. 10–8a.[22] In the test conducted in the dark before and after the prism-wearing phase, the subject indicated when a luminous spot that rotated about a stationary luminous mark in a horizontal plane on the floor appeared to be at the "12 o'clock" position as in a clock. The only basis for this judgment is egocentric, i.e., when the rotating spot seems to be exactly "above" the stationary mark. In other words, since the rotating spot always remains the same distance from the stationary mark and since both are in the plane of the floor, the only possible basis for perceiving a change in the location of one with respect to the other is with respect to the observer's left-right, up-down egocentric coordinates. In the prism-exposure phase, with the lights on, the subject either remained stationary looking down at his feet and torso or he walked along a path on the corridor floor bent over and looking down at his feet and floor. The latter condition but not the former resulted in a significant shift of about 5 degrees in the setting of the spot to the "12 o'clock" position. An effect of about the same magnitude was obtained in another variation when the observer in walking around could not see his own feet because he wore a semicircular collar around his waist. All he could see was the floor. These findings suggest that the crucial information leading to the adaptation is based on movement of the observer.

By way of conclusion, the evidence suggests that adaptation to optically altered orientation of the scene is possible and, therefore, that egocentrically upright vision does not require that the image be in the particular (inverted) orientation it happens to have normally. However, the evidence is still meager and, to that extent, the question raised by Stratton should perhaps continue to be considered an open one.

Environmental Orientation

What determines how an object appears to be oriented in the environment, i.e., whether it appears to be horizontal, vertical, or tilted in relation to the plane of the ground or to the direction of the pull of gravity? One might be inclined to answer that a line will appear to be horizontal if it is seen to be parallel to the ground, vertical if it is seen to be perpendicular to the plane of the ground, and tilted if it is somewhere in between. There is a good deal of truth to this answer, but that it oversimplifies the problem is borne out by considering what happens when the ground is itself tilted, as along the side of a hill. We do have sensory information concerning the direction of gravity so that we are not completely dependent on the visual scene for judgments about environmental orientation.

The role of gravity

Experiments with luminous lines have been conducted in dark rooms, in order to determine how an object appears to be oriented when information is supplied solely by gravity. An upright observer can judge the vertical and horizontal in a dark field with great accuracy. This might be thought to be based on the fact that a line will look vertical when its image falls in a vertical retinal orientation, that is, one might think that this orientation of the retinal image is the stimulus correlate of the perceived vertical. Perhaps in some species of animals this is true, but in man and many other animals whose head and body are themselves often in tilted positions, it cannot be true. The observer can still judge with fair accuracy when a luminous line in a dark room is vertical or horizontal in space even if he himself or just his head is tilted. Since, the orientation of the image of the line can vary without greatly affecting the direction perceived as vertical, it is clear that the stimulus correlate of perceived environmental orientation is not the orientation of the retinal image.

The independence of perceived orientation in the environment and retinal orientation provides another example of constancy. As with other constancies, it is plausible to believe that the significance of the feature of the retinal image that is relevant, in this case its orientation, is assessed on the basis of other information, in this case information concerning the direction of gravity. There are various sources of this information, but undoubtedly the most important source is derived from the vestibular apparatus (or otolith organs) in the inner ear. Hair cells in two structures, the utricle and saccule, are embedded in a gelatinous substance and are bent by the pull of gravity on tiny granular crystals. This bending or shearing force causes nerve fibers attached to the hair cells to discharge as a function of degree of head tilt. It is of interest that we are completely unaware of this source of information, i.e., there are no conscious sensations from the inner ear. In addition, information concerning the direction of gravity derives from pressure against the skin and from the different reaction of the neck and other muscles when the head or entire body is tilted.

The constancy mechanism, which permits more or less veridical perception of the vertical and horizontal of the environment when the observer is tilted, may operate in the following way. Suppose the observer is tilted 30 degree clockwise as shown in Fig. 10-9. Then the eyes are also tilted by roughly this angle.* Therefore, correct judgment of the

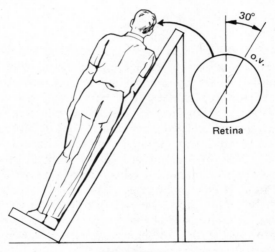

Figure 10-9

*The eyes tend to rotate back in the direction of the true upright orientation but can only do so to a slight extent. Thus when the observer or just his head is tilted 30 degrees, his eyes may only be tilted by 26 degrees. The magnitude of this countertorsion or counterrolling of the eyes, as it is called, increases with increasing tilt of the body and reaches approximately 6 degrees at 90 degrees body tilt. However, in order not to complicate the discussion unnecessarily, it is assumed that the eyes do not tilt with respect to the head.

vertical direction of space requires that the image of the line being judged stimulate the retina at an angle 30 degrees counterclockwise (dotted line in figure) from the objectively vertical direction on the retina (solid line *O.V.* in figure). Presumably this 30 degrees counterclockwise retinal orientation is centrally assessed by the perceptual system as signifying the vertical of space because other nonvisual information is available that the body is tilted 30 degrees clockwise in relation to gravity.

As with other constancies, compensation is not complete. When the observer is tilted by a very large angle, for example, 90 degrees, in a dark room, judgment of the vertical and horizontal is inaccurate. There is a constant error in one direction; an objectively vertical line will look tilted by 8 degrees or more in the direction opposite to that of the observer. In order to appear vertical, the line must be turned by that amount in the same direction as the observer. This effect was first noted by Aubert and is now known as the Aubert or A effect.[23] It can be explained on the basis of an underestimation in the magnitude of tilt of the body (or just the head). Thus if the observer is tilted 90 degrees clockwise, but the information concerning body tilt received by the perceptual system is that he is tilted only 80 degrees, then a retinal direction 80 degrees counterclockwise from the objective retinal vertical rather than 90 degrees is the one that will be assessed to signify the vertical of space. Therefore, a truly vertical line that stimulates the 90 degrees counterclockwise retinal direction will give rise to a perceived line that seems to be tilted away from the vertical in the direction opposite to that of the observer's tilt.

It is not easy to establish that this explanation is correct. To be sure, one can directly determine the observer's perception of the inclination of his body when it is tilted and this has been done. However, analogous to the problem of the role of distance perception in size perception (pp. 34ff), an observer's conscious judgment of the inclination of his body may not correspond exactly with the information concerning such inclination that is registered and utilized by his perceptual system. For example, the observer may be aware that his body is tilted 90 degrees because he is told to lie down on his side on a table or because he makes use of cues such as the pressure he feels on his skin or his muscular adjustments. Therefore, if the subject is asked to judge his body position he may do so accurately. At the same time, as far as the direct perception of the inclination of objects is concerned, the perceptual system may primarily make use of information from the vestibular apparatus of the inner ear.   This information may not be accurate, as suggested here.*†

Another line of research has been pursued to demonstrate that information about gravity, in providing information about the observer's orientation, can affect the perception of the environmental orientation of objects. If a person moves rapidly in a circular path, a centrifugal force acts on him in a direction outward from the center of rotation. Thus, if an observer is in a small enclosure running along a circular track, the force of gravity and the centrifugal force conjointly produce a resultant force as shown in Fig. 10-10. It can be predicted that if the enclosure is dark, the person will set a luminous rod in more or less the direction of the resultant force

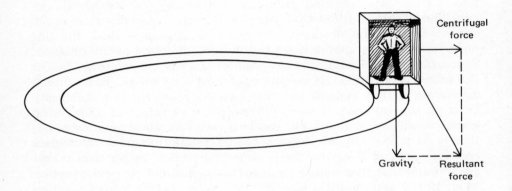

Figure 10-10

*Aubert studied this question and subsequently Ebenholtz found that observers do underestimate the lateral tilt of their bodies when they are tilted 90 degrees.[24] However, they apparently overestimate its tilt when it is rotated backward (in the median plane) and yet they make errors in judging when a line is vertical analogous to the Aubert effect. Ebenholtz draws the same conclusion as the one suggested here, namely, that the information used by the perceptual system in achieving constancy may not be identical with that used in achieving body perception.[24]

†Some have thought that the Aubert effect is explicable in terms of the countertorsion of the eyes referred to in a previous footnote. But a little thought will convince the reader that this countertorsion is in the wrong direction to explain the Aubert effect, and in any case the magnitude is too small to explain it. However, another constant error has been found to occur in judging the vertical in a dark field, namely, a tendency to perceive an objectively vertical line as slightly tilted in the *same* direction as the observer when he is tilted by only a moderate amount. This effect, discovered by G. E. Müller and known as the E-effect, is in the right direction and of about the right order of magnitude to be explicable in terms of countertorsion of the eyes.[25]   For a more detailed discussion of the A- and E-effect and of other topics relevant to this chapter, see Howard and Templeton.[26]

when asked to indicate the direction that appears vertical to him. It has been demonstrated that this is indeed the case.[27]   Although this seems like an impressive demonstration, it really only makes the same theoretical point as can be made with far less expensive apparatus simply by tilting the subject in a dark room. In that situation, too, as we have seen, the subject will align the rod in the direction of the pull of gravity. This is really all the centrifuge experiment shows because as far as the subject is concerned he feels he is tilted in the environment. The effect follows from the laws of physics. In other words, both methods result in a change in the direction of the force acting on the subject with respect to the vertical axis of his body.

The visual frame of reference

In any event, it is perfectly clear that gravity information alone, within certain limits of accuracy, enables us to perceive those orientations in the environment which are vertical, horizontal, or tilted. But as noted at the beginning of this section, what appears to be horizontal or vertical in the environment certainly also ought to be a function of how the object is oriented with respect to the perceived ground plane or to objects such as trees and houses that can be considered to define these directions as much as gravity does. Experiments have demonstrated that such visual information does exert a powerful effect on the perception of environmental orientation.

To begin with a modest observation, error tendencies, such as that of the Aubert effect, are never observed when the judgments are made with the room lights on. Thus, judgments of the vertical axis made from any tilted position of the head or body will be essentially perfect when the entire scene is visible. This is not merely a matter of knowing what the "right answer" is. The rod *looks* vertical to the tilted subject when it is vertical. Yet one has only to turn out the room lights for the same rod to look tilted. Therefore, it is obvious that the visual coordinates of the room themselves serve as determinants of the vertical and horizontal and, in doing so, tend to offset whatever error is generated by inadequate gravitational information.

More impressive evidence comes from creating a conflict between gravitational and visual information. This can be achieved either by tilting the room (or other visual "surrogates" of the vertical-horizontal coordinates of space) or by a centrifuge that changes the direction of the visual scene in relation to the resultant force acting on the body. Max Wertheimer[28] is generally credited with the observation that in such a conflict orientation determined by the visual field is dominant.[28] He looked through a tilted mirror at the reflection of the room and after a short while reported that the room "righted" itself and things no longer appeared tilted.

A controversy then developed between those who thought gravitational information was more important and those who thought that visual information was more important.[29] Various experimental techniques were developed. Either the subject looked at a room that was actually tilted or at a scene through prisms that caused it to appear tilted or at a large luminous perimeter of a rectangle that could be tilted. The technique of placing an adjustable rod in the tilted scene was developed to make measurement possible. The subject had to indicate when the rod appeared vertical (see Fig. 10-11). If he aligned it with gravity as in *a*, it would signify that the surrounding visual field (or frame of reference as it has been called) has no effect; if he aligned it with the sides of the frame of reference closest to the vertical, *b*, it would signify the complete dominance of the visual information and no effect at all of gravity. Most subjects seem to compromise in this situation, as shown in *c*, which implies that both factors play a role. There are, however, marked individual differences. Thus, one might conclude that there is a tendency toward "righting" of the field as Wertheimer claimed, but that it is not complete as he implied.

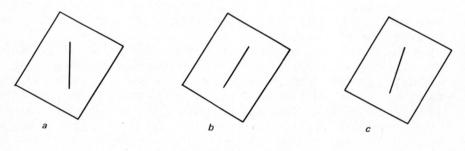

Figure 10-11

There is, however, some reason for caution in drawing any conclusions from this kind of experiment. The subject is in a situation where no single setting of the rod is entirely satisfactory to him. If he perceives the tilt of the frame of reference veridically, he ought to align the rod with the direction of gravity. However, if he does that, the rod will "look wrong" as shown in Fig. 10-11*a*, because the immediately surrounding frame of reference has a particularly strong impact on the enclosed object.* One can view this situation as an instance of a "separa-tion of system." Thus, in the case of movement perception, it is the behavior of a frame of reference immediately surrounding an object that has the greatest effect on how that object will be perceived. Even where the movement of the frame of reference is veridically perceived, it will tend to induce an impression of movement in the enclosed stationary object (see pp. 211ff).

If, on the other hand, to make the rod "look right," the subject sim-ply aligns it with the tilted frame of reference, as in Fig. 10-11b, this is also unsatisfactory because the subject is aware the frame is tilted. Consequently he compromises.† In any event, the orientation of the rod that the subject selects cannot be taken as evidence about the per-ceived orientation of the frame of reference. It is quite probable, in the light of a separation of systems effect, that there is little if any "right-ing" of the frame of reference itself, although the latter does have a great effect on the perceived orientation of the rod within it.

In one situation there is no question about the "righting" of the frame of reference. Experiments have been performed in which the subject is *inside* a tilted room[31] (Fig. 10-12). In this situation, the "vertical" axis of the room is perceived as vertical regardless of the room's physical orientation. Not only does the observer tend to align the rod with this direction but he also aligns his own body with it when the chair on which he is seated is tilted and he is asked to bring himself to the upright position. This same effect occurs in specially constructed tilted houses at amusement parks, in listing ocean liners, or in airplanes that are banking or even flying upside down in the clouds. For exam-ple, a passenger in a banking plane often experiences himself in an up-right position. There is evidence that some animal species react in the same way when placed in a tilted room. In one experiment, rats had to run into a tilted box on a dowel that ran through the box.[32] The rats

---

*Evidence from an entirely different quarter attests to the powerful effect of the visual frame of reference on how an enclosed object appears to be oriented. As noted in Chapter 7, pp. 303ff, the phenomenal shape of a figure is governed by the ten-dency to assign the directions "top," "bottom," and "sides" in accordance with the visual up, down, and horizontal defined by the scene. In some experiments the test figures were presented within a *tilted* scene. Recognition was adversely affected unless the critical figures were tilted so as to be aligned with the tilted scene.

†The individual differences obtained in these situations may, therefore, not so much represent differences in perception as differences in decisions about how to deal with an essentially unsolvable problem. Much work has been done investigating the possible implications about personality of the alleged perceptual differences be-tween people in these experimental situations.[30]

Figure 10-12

tended to shift their posture toward the vertical direction of the box. In other experiments, pigeons were first trained to peck at a key with a vertical line and were later tested when the experimental chamber was tilted. The pigeons responded more to a line tilted parallel to the walls of the chamber than they did to a gravitationally vertical line.[33]

The difference between this situation and those where the observer himself is not *in* the room may be that when the observer looks into the room from the outside, he uses gravitational information about his own orientation in space to assess the significance of the orientation of the image of the frame of reference. The observer has information that he is upright so that consequently the tilted frame is perceived as tilted.* But if the observer is himself in the room, then he not only experiences himself as tilted in the relation to it but by virtue of "visual capture," he feels tilted as well. Once that happens, the information he obtains from gravity concerning his own position is superseded by information from vision. Or to state it differently, the observer's perceptual system

---

*Experiments using a tilted frame, viewed from the outside, produce a substantially greater effect when the observer himself is tilted. If tilted, the observer is less sure on the basis of gravity which direction is vertical, so that he gives more weight to the visual information.

receives the *wrong* information about his own position, namely, that he is tilted, and if it uses that information, the observer will judge the room to be upright.

There is some similarity between the tendency of a tilted frame to "right itself" and the tendency of tilted lines to "normalize." As was pointed out earlier in the chapter, we do not know for sure whether normalization is toward the vertical in the environment or toward the egocentric vertical. If it is the former, then it too is a type of "righting." However, it is also clear that normalization is different in important respects from the tendency toward righting of a frame of reference. For one thing, normalization at most is a matter of 1 or 2 degrees, whereas righting of a frame can entail a shift of 30 to 40 degrees. Also, normalization has been thought to be restricted to the region of the retina stimulated and, therefore, to require the eye to be stationary during the exposure phase; righting of the frame is not localized in this way. Finally, normalization is a process that presumably changes the state of the neural substrate in a particular region as a result of the continued presence of the contours of the line, whereas "righting" of the frame is essentially instantaneous.*

Since it is clear that both gravitational *and* visual information are determinants of the perception of orientation in the environment, one might conclude that the controversy between advocates of each factor is a meaningless one. That is not necessarily the correct conclusion. Under certain conditions each factor could be shown to be sufficient— as, for example, gravitational cues are in the dark field—and yet under conditions of a conflict between the two, one could be completely dominant. In research on the relationship between vision and touch, vision has been repeatedly shown to be the dominant factor. Since the information concerning gravity is concerned with the position of all or of parts of the body and is, therefore, similar in kind to information derived from proprioception (or touch), one might expect vision to be dominant.

In the situation where the observer is *in* the tilted room, this is indeed the case. Here the conflict is a direct one: gravitational information implies one orientation of the observer's body and visual information implies another. In experiments where the observer is *not* in the room, but rather views a tilted room or frame from the outside, the conflict is indirect: gravitational information relates directly to the orientation

---

*Wertheimer had noted that the righting of the mirrored scene took place only after a few moments had elapsed because, he believed, the immediate memory of the nonmirrored scene had first to wear off. Although there is some evidence that a delay in testing increases the effect slightly, it is still correct to say that the tendency toward righting is instantaneous.[34]

of the observer's body and, through that information, it relates indirectly to the orientation of visual objects. Since the observer is not in the room, there is no good reason why gravitational information about body position should be captured by visual information. Therefore, one might say that the conflict here is between two different visual determinants of orientation, one in which gravitational information about body position plays a fundamental role (and that is veridical) and one that is governed by the visual frame of reference. Therefore, it is not necessarily to be expected that one of these determinants will be dominant. Even so, in many of the experiments, the compromise setting by subjects is on the average closer to the vertical defined by the visual frame than that defined gravitationally; but, as noted previously, this does not necessarily mean that the tilted frame looks upright.

The advocates of each position also seem to have in mind the question of the *genesis* of the perception of environmental orientation. This question should be kept separate from that of the relative potency of the two determinants in the adult. Which factor, they ask, is primary? Of course, the very meaning of environmental orientation would seem to be based upon the fact of gravity. If we lived in a very different sort of environment where no such force existed, there would be no "vertical" or "horizontal" orientation of space (although the egocentric orientations would still obtain). Therefore, from an evolutionary point of view one might justifiably say that gravity was the primary factor. But that does not necessarily imply anything about ontogenetic primacy, the order in which the two types of information become effective in the developmental history of the individual.

We do not know which factor is primary in development and, logically, a good case can be made for both factors. Thus, one could say that the ability to use gravitational information and to take the position of one's own body into account in judging the vertical is given innately. If so, one could learn to make use of the visual framework because the vertical of the framework will generally coincide with the direction perceived as the gravitational vertical. An association between the two could develop, and when the adult encounters the unusual situation where the visual framework is actually tilted, there can be a strong tendency to rely on that visual information even though it now conflicts with gravitational information.

Not all visual arrays are equally effective. Thus, for example, a specially constructed room built to look like a real room has a much greater impact on judgments of the vertical than a luminous rectangular perimeter. Some believe that this is simply because a room has many more vertical and horizontal lines within it than a mere rectangle, i.e., the reason for the difference is purely structural. The room is also three-dimensional whereas the luminous perimeter is usually not. However, it is entirely possible that the room is more effective precisely because it is a room and the vertical axis of a room has, through past experience, become clearly identified with the vertical of space. This question can be settled experimentally. For example, one could present a luminous pattern that was highly structured, as in Fig. 10–13a. It is unlikely that such a frame of reference would exert a stronger influence than one without the inner lines. It has been shown that a pattern such as that shown in Fig. 10–13b has only a very slight effect on judgments of the vertical and the introduction of such a set of tilted lines to the back wall of a tilted room does not increase the effect.[35] A related fact that provides support for the "experience hypothesis" is that a frame tilted by 45 degrees is ambiguous. Which direction is vertical and which is horizontal? In fact, the frame may be perceived as a large diamond and, if so, the direction that appears vertical may remain aligned with gravity. *However*, if a *room* is tilted 45 degrees the directions are not ambiguous. This is clearly a past experience effect.

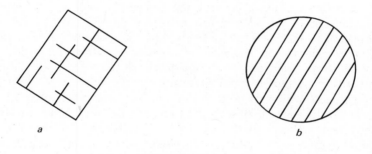

a   b

Figure 10–13

A case can also be made for the opposite hypothesis, namely, that it is by virtue of the innate tendency for the main coordinates of a visual framework to define the vertical and horizontal of space that we as infants learn to make use of gravitational information. The constancy of the perceived vertical and horizontal that is found when a tilted observer judges these directions in a dark field could be learned. In a normally illuminated environment, for each tilted position of the observer, the retinal images of the vertical and horizontal coordinates of the visual framework fall in specific orientations. Since, according to this argument, these environmental orientations are veridically perceived in the normal scene, associations can be formed linking each set of retinal orientations with each position of the body so that later on, in the dark, gravity information alone suffices. There is, at the moment, no evidence to support this interpretation.

Of course, it is also possible that neither factor is primary and that both factors are present soon after birth. Conversely, it is possible that a good deal of past experience is necessary to make proper use of gravity information *and* visual information.

Feature Detector Mechanisms
and Perceived Orientation

It seems natural to inquire whether the sensory mechanisms that allegedly detect the orientation of contours can be considered to account for the perception of orientation as discussed in this chapter. Since these cortical units discharge actively when an edge or contour is in the appropriate orientation within the *retinal receptive field*, one would think that they could only be considered to provide a direct basis for the perception of *egocentric orientation*. It is doubtful, however, if the activity in such units can be regarded as a sufficient account of the perceived orientation of an object with respect to the self because (1) we discriminate up from down and left from right as well as various tilts. (2) Some degree of adaptation to prismatically tilted images occurs. This means that a retinally vertical contour will no longer be perceived as egocentrically "vertical" and correspondingly for other orientations. (3) Certain structures in the visual field affect egocentric orientation (see p. 493 and Fig. 10–14). That the discharging of such units is not necessary for the perception of egocentric orientation is suggested by the fact that we can perceive the orientation of the imaginary line connecting two dots or of subjective contours (see p. 298) or of a single moving point that we track. There is also the very recent finding referred to in previous chapters (pp. 316 and 367) that the cat can discriminate between contours in orientation for which, as a result of restricted conditions of exposure during development, it has no edge-detector units.[36]

In any case, such units cannot account for the perception of *environmental orientation* since the latter is not directly correlated with the orientation of the retinal image of the object. The perceived orientation of objects is relatively constant despite altered head position. Now, however, neural units have been found in the cat the discharging of which is more closely correlated with the orientation of the object rather than the orientation of its image.[37] Vestibular information concerning body position presumably alters the "tuning" of these units in some way. However, there are relatively few such cells in comparison to those which continue to respond to a specific orientation of the retinal image of a contour regardless of body position.

Can the active discharging of these cortical cells account for the veridical perception of environmental orientation despite changes of body orientation, that is, the fact of orientation constancy? The reasons given above why a contour-detector mechanism is not necessary and does not do justice to the perception of egocentric orientation are equally applicable to the perception of environmental orientation. Moreover the visual frame of reference exerts a powerful effect on the perception of an object's orientation in the environment and, therefore, on constancy, but it is difficult to see how this factor can be relevant to the operation of the detector mechanism.

Therefore once again we are faced with the problem of uncovering the purpose served by these mechanisms if they do not mediate the perception of egocentric or environmental orientation. Those neural units which continue to respond to a given orientation of a contour in the environment for varying tilts of the subject certainly seem to be the kind of mechanism which is designed to achieve constancy. Therefore if they are neither necessary nor sufficient for orientation constancy, their existence is all the more puzzling.

The Relationship Between Egocentric and Environmental Orientation*

What relationship is there, if any, between the perception of egocentric orientation and the perception of environmental orientation? It would seem most likely that the presence of the egocentric coordinate directions in the visual field plays a crucial role in determining the perception of environmental directions. The process would be somewhat as follows. Imagine first an observer in a dark room who is tilted and is judging which direction is vertical in the environment. As shown in

*The reader may find this section difficult and it may be advisable either to omit it entirely or to come back to it only if further study and research on this topic is contemplated.

Fig. 10-9, correct judgment calls for selecting an orientation of a line whose image falls as many degrees away from the objective retinal vertical orientation in one direction as the observer is tilted in the opposite direction. But in discussing this process earlier (p. 480), we glossed over the question of how the observer knows what orientation coincides with the retinal vertical. The answer that seems probable is that this orientation is the one that appears to be aligned with his own body axis (or just his head axis if only the head is tilted), i.e., perceived egocentric orientation is a direct function of retinal orientation. In other words, the process may be as follows: (1) There is a certain orientation in the visual field that seems to be parallel to the body, namely, one that is determined by the vertical retinal orientation. (2) The observer has information concerning how far from the vertical of space he is tilted. (3) It follows that the direction that is vertical in space must be at an angle of so many degrees away from the direction that appears parallel to the body.*

The presence in the visual field of the egocentric vertical and horizontal also plays an important role in situations where the visual framework has been tilted.

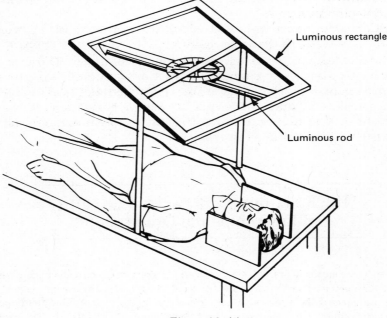

Luminous rectangle

Luminous rod

Figure 10-14

*Certain problems arise in connection with this interpretation, chief among which is that perception of the vertical is more accurate and less variable when the observer is upright than the perception of egocentric orientation is known to be, based on experiments that have isolated egocentric orientation (see p. 463). How is this possible if the former is derived from the latter?

Since the axis of the frame that stands for the vertical is now not aligned with the egocentric vertical of the upright observer, either of two things must happen: (1) The observer, feeling sure he himself is upright, must perceive the frame to be tilted, or (2) the observer in taking the frame to define the vertical and horizontal of space must perceive himself to be tilted. The results of the experiments cited earlier suggest that (1) occurs when the observer is not *in* a tilted room and that (2) occurs when he is.

In the preceding paragraphs, the implication is clear that the directions that appear egocentrically vertical and horizontal are directly determined by retinal orientation and that they are not themselves affected by the structure of the visual field. However, this is an oversimplification. "Field effects" exist for egocentric orientation as well. In one experiment, an observer lying in a supine position in a dark room had to judge when a luminous rod was aligned with his head. Surrounding the rod was the luminous perimeter of a rectangle as shown in Fig. 10-14. When the rectangle was tilted 15 degrees from the subject's median plane, his settings of the rod deviated by around 9 degrees in that direction. If the rectangle was placed so as to be parallel to the body and not tilted, the settings of the rod to the egocentric vertical were now more or less *perfect and consistent.* Yet without the rectangle present, as described earlier, judgments are variable and not precisely accurate.*

There has been some confusion between experiments on adaptation to tilting prisms and experiments on exposure to a tilted room. Superficially, they are similar experimental paradigms; both produce a tilted retinal image. But the issue in the prism paradigm is whether egocentric orientation can change and, as such, this problem need have nothing to do with the effect of a tilted scene on the perception of the environmental vertical. As noted earlier, one could imagine such a prism experiment taking place in outer space where there are no environmental directions, or the experiment can be done—indeed has been done—with the observer bent over and looking down at the floor. On the other hand, the tilted-room paradigm need have nothing to do with egocentric change. An observer inside a tilted room will probably perceive it as upright but he will also probably have veridical (or almost veridical) perception of his own orientation relative to the room. Furthermore, this effect does not require adaptation; it is more or less immediate. In fact, one would imagine that with prolonged exposure to a tilted room, with the opportunity to move around and to see one's own body, there would be no adaptation of the kind that could be expected to occur in prism experiments for the simple reason that in the former situation all available information continues to indicate that self

*An unpublished experiment performed by Sheila Hafter.[38] This kind of field effect is analogous to those that occur in the perception of radial direction (see pp. 168-169). It is possible that effects of this kind occur when the observer is upright as well. In other words, when an upright observer views a tilted rectangle, perhaps he no longer veridically perceives egocentric orientation. Instead, the orientation that appears egocentrically vertical may be one that is somewhat inclined toward the vertical of the frame. If so, this may lead to a slight tendency of the frame to "right" itself because the discrepancy between framework and perceived egocentric coordinates would not be as great as it is objectively.

and room are *not* aligned. Whereas in the prism experiment, self and room *are* aligned and all available information indicates that they are aligned.*

However, there are at least some respects in which there is a relationship between the two experimental paradigms. The tendency for the main coordinates of the visual framework to define the vertical and horizontal of the environment can serve as information to the prism wearer to the effect that the scene is upright. This probably explains the effect described repeatedly by Stratton in which the scene appeared upright but he himself then seemed to be viewing it from an inverted position. In other words, the contents of the visual field—sky, ground, and the like—exerted a strong influence on the directions seen to be up and down in the environment. The discrepancy between environmental up and down and egocentric up and down left no alternative but to imagine (or "feel") the self to be inverted in the environment.

There is some evidence that, in the absence of movement, a tilted scene can contain information that will lead to adaptation. If an observer wearing prisms remains absolutely stationary while viewing an indoor scene, he will adapt, as is indicated by a significant shift in his settings of a luminous line to the vertical before and after the exposure period.[39] If he sees only luminous lines during the exposure period, he will show either no change or only a very slight one. When the experiment is done in this way, it is clearly one on adaptation to tilting prisms. But the same experiment can be done without prisms by requiring an observer to view a tilted room for a period of time and this too produces adaptation.[40] If, in the prism experiment, the observer does not move and does not see his own body, then the retinal image is essentially the same in both cases. It thus seems clear that the visual information that determines perception of the vertical and horizontal in the environment is also a source of information that can lead to perceptual adaptation. Whether this adaptation is egocentric in nature is not yet clear.

Summary

Two aspects of the perception of the orientation of an object in a frontal plane must be distinguished, namely, egocentric and environmental orientation.

Egocentric orientation refers to the perceived orientation of an object in relation to the self: environmental orientation refers to the perceived orientation of an object in the environment.

---

*Of course, one can use a prism as a simple, inexpensive method of studying the perception of the vertical when the framework is tilted rather than a tilted room or the like. The prism is inserted through an opening in a box and the observer can only see the room through the prism. However, this is not to be thought of as an experiment on adaptation to a prism.

Egocentric orientation

There is no real problem about the fact that the world appears egocentrically right side up although the retinal image is upside down. It *is* a legitimate question, however, to ask whether an inverted image is necessary for upright vision. Since *upright* here means the perceived orientation of things in relation to the self (or body) and since the image of the body as an object in the field suffers the same fate as do all other visible objects, it can be argued that upright vision ought to be possible regardless of the absolute orientation of the entire image. But when the world is viewed through an optical system, which alters the orientation of the retinal image, it no longer appears to be upright. This suggests that specific orientations of the retinal image do signify specific egocentric orientations. The same fact has also been demonstrated by experiment, in which the observer is able to judge the egocentric orientation of a line in a horizontal plane when nothing else, including his own body, is visible. This technique isolates egocentric from environmental orientation. Whether the linkage between retinal and perceived egocentric orientation is innately determined or learned early in life is a further question.

In either case, it is at least possible that a new linkage could be learned and experiments on adaptation to a reoriented retinal image address this question. With some few exceptions, the evidence based on adaptation to a *reinverted* image by Stratton and others suggests no fundamental change in egocentric orientation, i.e., the world continues to look upside down *in relation to the self.* Other changes, such as motor adaptation, do occur. Data from analogous experiments with animals are contradictory: lower species do not adapt, whereas higher species may. However, it is interesting that the best evidence for upright vision from an optically reinverted image comes from the study of kittens who never saw the world in a normal way.

Research on exposure to a prismatically *tilted* image has also been conducted. A major advantage of this kind of research is that objective measurement of change is possible. The results indicate that adaptation occurs, although in most of this research it is not clear if the adaptation is to environmental or egocentric "tilt." However, it has been demonstrated that the perceptual change that occurs in these experiments is not merely one of normalization. *Normalization refers to the tendency of tilted lines to appear somewhat less tilted after a short period of exposure.* Experiments have also been directed at the question of the nature of the information that leads to the adaptation obtained. Three possible sources have been investigated, namely, sight of the observer's body, movement of the observer, and sight of structures such as rooms that, because they serve as frames of reference, tend to be perceived as upright in the environment.

Environmental orientation

There are two sources of information about the visual orientation of objects in the environment. That gravity alone is effective can be shown by the ability of an observer to perceive whether a luminous line is vertical, horizontal, or tilted in space in an otherwise dark field. Since such perception is possible—with some degree of error—even when the observer is tilted, it can be thought of as another example of perceptual constancy. The position of the body is apparently taken into account by the perceptual system in assessing the orientation signified by a given retinal image.

Another source of information is derived from the orientation of major components of the visual field itself, such as the ground plane, trees, buildings and rooms, which can serve as frames of reference to "define" what is vertical and horizontal in the environment. When, in experiment, such a frame of reference is itself tilted, so that it conflicts with information about the direction of gravity, objects now appear upright only when, on the average, they are tilted in the direction of the frame. However, the strong effect that the frame exerts on the perceived orientation of objects within it does not mean that a "righting" of the frame itself occurs. *By "righting" is meant the re-establishment of a tilted frame of reference as phenomenally upright.* Rather, there is undoubtedly a separation of systems effect operating here, in which the frame affects the phenomenal orientation of objects within it, but the perceived orientation of the frame is determined either by other frames of reference external to it or by gravity information. Only when the observer is actually inside a tilted room does "righting" occur. Since the felt position of the observer's body is now misperceived—another example of visual capture—gravity information in this situation, as centrally interpreted by the perceptual system, is now congruent with the information provided by the frame of reference. "Righting" of the frame of reference is not to be confused with normalization. "Righting" is more or less immediate and is much greater in magnitude than normalization.

Little is known about the ontogenesis of the perception of environmental orientation or whether either or both sources of information are effective soon after birth, without the necessity of learning.

Although considered separately in the chapter, the perception of egocentric orientation and environmental orientation are related in various ways. For example, the successful operation of a constancy mechanism, in which the perceived orientation of an object in the environment is assessed on the basis of the registered tilt of the observer's body, may depend upon the capability of perceiving which orientation in the field is egocentrically vertical. Furthermore, the perception of egocentric orientation is itself subject to field (or framework) effects such as affect the perception of environmental orientation. Finally, it was noted that experiments on prism adaptation are concerned with possible change of egocentric orientation and should not be confused with experiments employing tilted rooms and the like that are concerned with the immediate effect of the frame of reference on the perception of environmental orientation. Nevertheless, there is some theoretical overlap between the two experimental paradigms.

References

1. Berkeley, G. *An Essay Towards a New Theory of Vision.* E. P. Dutton & Co., Inc., 1910, pp. 65–66 (words in brackets added). First published in 1709.
2. Rock, I. The perception of the egocentric orientation of a line. *Journal of Experimental Psychology*, 1954, 48, 367–374.
3. Stratton, G. Some preliminary experiments on vision without inversion of the retinal image. *Psychological Review*, 1896, 3, 611–617; Upright vision and the retinal image. *Psychological Review*, 1897, 4, 182–187; Vision without inversion of the retinal image. *Psychological Review*, 1897, 4, 341–360 and 463–481.
4. See Stratton. op. cit., 1897, pp. 182–187.
5. Stratton, op. cit., 1896, p. 616.
6. Stratton, op. cit., 1897, p. 354.
7. Ibid., p. 469.
8. For a more complete discussion of this issue, see C. S. Harris. Perceptual adaptation to inverted, reversed and displaced vision. *Psychological Review*, 1965, 72, 419–444; and I. Rock, *The Nature of Perceptual Adaptation.* Basic Books, Inc., Publishers, 1966, pp. 21–25 and 222–244.
9. Ewert, P. H. A study of the effect of inverted retinal stimulation upon spatially coordinated behavior. *Genetic Psychology Monographs*, 1930, I, no. 3 and 4.

10. Snyder, F. W. and N. H. Pronko. *Vision with Spatial Inversion.* University of Wichita Press, 1952; I. Kohler. *The Formation and Transformation of the Perceptual World.* Transl. by H. Fiss. *Psychological Issues,* 1964, 3, no. 4, 1-173.

11. Kohler, I. op. cit., reference 10.

12. See also Kottenhoff, H. Situational and personal influences on space perception with experimental spectacles, Part I: Prolonged experiments with inverting glasses. *Acta Psychologica,* 1957, 13, 79-97.

13. Pfister, H. Über das Werhalten der Hühner beim Tragen von Prismen. Ph. D. dissertation, University of Innsbruck, 1955.

14. Mittelstaedt, H. Telotaxis und Optomotorik von Eristalis bei Augeninversion. *Naturwissen,* 1944, 36, 90-91; E. von Holst and H. Mittelstaedt. Das Reafferenz-prinzip. *Die Naturwissenschaften,* 1950, 20, 464-467.

15. Foley, J. P., Jr. An experimental investigation of the effect of prolonged inversion of the visual field in the rhesus monkey. *Journal of Genetic Psychology,* 1940, 56, 21-51.

16. Bishop, H. E. Innateness and learning in the visual perception of direction. Ph. D. dissertation, University of Chicago, 1959.

17. Brown, G. G. Perception of depth with disoriented vision. *British Journal of Psychology,* 1928, 19, 135.

18. Mikaelian, H. and R. Held. Two types of adaptation to an optically rotated visual field. *American Journal of Psychology,* 1964, 77, 257-263; S. M. Ebenholtz. Adaptation to a rotated visual field as a function of degree of optical tilt and exposure time. *Journal of Experimental Psychology,* 1966, 72, 629-634.

19. Gibson, J. J. and M. Radner. Adaptation, after-effect, and contrast in the perception of tilted lines, I and II. *Journal of Experimental Psychology,* 20, 453-467 and 553-569.

20. Morant, R. B. and H. K. Beller. Adaptation to prismatically rotated visual fields. *Science,* 1965, 148, 530-531.

21. Prentice, W. C. H. and D. C. Beardslee. Visual "normalization" near the vertical and horizontal. *Journal of Experimental Psychology,* 1950, 40, 355-364; R. H. Day and N. J. Wade. Visual spatial aftereffect from prolonged head tilt. *Science,* 1966, 154, 1201-1202. But a different conclusion was drawn by M. Coltheart and C. M. Cooper. The retinal reference of the tilt aftereffect. *Perception & Psychophysics,* 1972, 11, 321-324.

22. Mack, A. and I. Rock. A re-examination of the Stratton effect: Egocentric adaptation to a rotated visual image. *Perception & Psychophysics,* 1968, 4, 57-62.

23. Aubert, H. Eine scheinbare bedeutende Drehung von Objekten bei Neigung des Koppes nach rechts odor links. *Virchows Archives*, 1861, **20**, 381-393; G. E. Müller. Über das Aubertsche Phanomenon. *Zeitschrift für Psychologie und Physiologie der Sinnesorgane*, 1916, 49, 109-244.

24. Ebenholtz, S. E. Perception of the vertical with body tilt in the median plane. *Journal of Experimental Psychology*, 1970, **83**, 1-6; The constancy of object orientation: Effects of target inclination. *Psychologische Forschung*, 1972, **35**, 178-186.

25. G. E. Müller, op. cit., reference 23.

26. Howard, I. P. and W. B. Templeton. *Human Spatial Orientation.* John Wiley & Sons, Inc., 1966. See also an article by R. H. Day and N. J. Wade, Mechanisms involved in visual orientation constancy. *Psychological Bulletin*, 1969, **71**, 33-42.

27. Mach, E. *Grundlinien der Lehre von den Bewegungsempfindungen.* W. Englemann, 1875; C. E. Nobel. The perception of the vertical: III. The visual vertical as a function of centrifugal and gravitational forces. *Journal of Experimental Psychology*, 1949, **39**, 839-850; B. Clark and A. Graybiel. Visual perception of the horizontal following exposure to radial acceleration on a centrifuge. *Journal of Comparative and Physiological Psychology*, 1951, 44, 525-534; H. A. Witkin. Perception of the upright when the direction of the force acting on the body is changed. *Journal of Experimental Psychology*, 1950, 40, 93-106.

28. Wertheimer, M. Experimentelle Studien über das Sehen von Bewegung. *Zeitschrift für Psychologie*, 1912, **61**, 161-265.

29. Gibson, J. J. and O. H. Mowrer. Determinants of the perceived vertical and horizontal. *Psychological Review*, 1938, **45**, 300-323; S. E. Asch and H. A. Witkin. Studies in space orientation I and II. *Journal of Experimental Psychology*, 1948, **38**, 325-337 and 455-477; H. A. Witkin and S. E. Asch. Studies in space orientation IV. *Journal of Experimental Psychology*, 1948, **38**, 762-782.

30. See Witkin, H. A., H. B. Lewis, M. Hertzman, K. Machover, P. B. Meissner, and S. Wapner. *Personality Through Perception.* Harper & Row, Publishers, Inc., 1954.

31. Witkin, H. A. Perception of body position and the position of the visual field. *Psychological Monographs*, 1949, **63**, No. 7.

32. Reiss, B. F., H. Kratka and A. Dinnerstein. The relationship between the tilt of the visual field and the deviation of the body position from the vertical in the white rat. *Journal of Experimental Psychology*, 1951, **40**, 531-537.

33. Thomas, D. R. and J. Lyons. Visual field dependency in pigeons. *Animal Behavior*, 1968, **16**, 213–218; see also J. Lyons and D. R. Thomas. The influence of postural distortion on the perception of the visual vertical in pigeons. *Journal of Experimental Psychology*, 1968, **76**, 120–124; R. L. Fantz. Response to horizontality by bantam chickens in level and tilted rooms. *The Psychological Record*, 1959, **6**, 61–66.

34. See Asch and Witkin. Studies in space orientation II, reference 29.

35. Singer, G., A. T. Purcell and M. Austin. The effect of structure and degree of tilt on the tilted room illusion. *Perception & Psychophysics*, 1970, **7**, 250–252.

36. Hirsch, H. V. B. Visual perception in cats after environmental surgery. *Experimental Brain Research*, 1972, **15**, 405–423.

37. Horn, G. and R. M. Hill. Modifications of receptive fields in the visual cortex occurring spontaneously and associated with bodily tilt. *Nature*, 1969, **221**, 186–188; D. N. Spinelli. Recognition of visual patterns. Chap. 8, in D. A. Hamburg, K. H. Pribram and A. J. Stunkard, (ed.). *Perception and Its Disorders*. The Williams & Wilkins Co., 1970; D. Denney and C. Adorjani. Orientation specificity of visual cortical neurons after head tilt. *Experimental Brain Research*, 1972, **14**, 312–317. However, see the further research on human subjects by J. M. Findlay and D. M. Parker. An investigation of visual orientation constancy using orientation specific properties of acuity and adaptation. *Perception*, 1972, **1**, 305–313; D. E. Mitchell and C. Blakemore. The site of orientation constancy. *Perception*, 1972, **1**, 315–320.

38. See Rock, I. *The Nature of Perceptual Adaptation*. Basic Books, Inc., Publishers, 1966, pp. 71–72.

39. Morant and Beller, op. cit.; A. Mack. The role of movement in the perceptual adaptation to a tilted retinal image. *Perception & Psychophysics*, 1967, **2**, 65–68.

40. Austin, M., G. Singer and R. H. Day. Visual orientation illusion following judgments with a tilted visual field. *Nature*, 1969, **221**, 583–584.

chapter 11
THE PERCEPTION OF
NEUTRAL COLOR

We again start with a problem that may not strike the reader as a problem at all. What determines the perception of objects as white or gray or black? Colors in the white-gray-black continuum are sometimes referred to as achromatic or neutral in contrast to chromatic hues such as red, green, and blue. An object will appear neutrally colored when it does not selectively absorb some wavelengths of light and reflect only other wavelengths. Thus, if "white light," which is comprised of light of all wavelengths, falls upon the object it will appear neutrally colored, since the object reflects all wavelengths equally.

The basis for the perception of a chromatic surface is selective absorption and reflection. A surface looks red, for example, when it reflects predominantly one band of wavelengths of light to the eyes. Since there are cells in the retina that are selectively sensitive to light of certain wavelengths, we have some understanding of the basis of chromatic color perception. To state it simply, the stimulus correlate for chromatic color is the wavelength of light. What is the stimulus for neutral color? To this question the reader may be inclined to answer "the intensity of light." A white object reflects far more of the light striking it than does a black object. In fact, a white surface is defined as one that reflects about 80 percent of the light illuminating it, a medium gray surface as one that reflects about 40 percent, and a black surface as one that reflects about 3 percent of the light striking it.

It may prove helpful before proceeding further to define carefully some of the terms that are used here. In referring to the *objective conditions in the environment*, the term *reflectance* is used to describe the physical characteristic of a surface that results in its reflecting a particular proportion of the light it receives. Reflectance is the ratio of reflected light intensity to illuminating intensity. The term *illumination* is used to describe the intensity of light falling on a surface from some source. In referring to the *proximal stimulus*, i.e., the retinal image of a particular surface, the terms *luminance* or *intensity of the retinal image* are used. Luminance equals reflectance times illumination since the intensity of light reaching the retina from the surface depends upon the illumination falling on the surface *and* on the reflectance characteristic of that surface. (Luminance can also be measured by instruments.) Finally, in referring to *what is experienced*, terms such as *perceived neutral* (or *achromatic*) *color, lightness, black, gray,* and *white* are used to describe impressions of the color of a surface. The term *brightness* is used to refer not to the perceived neutral color of a surface but to an impression of how dim or intense it appears to be.

To resume the argument, one might think it is plausible that an object is perceived as white rather than black because the light reflected to the eye is much more intense than the light reflected by a gray or black object. Retinal cells discharge with greater frequency for an increased intensity of stimulating light, which seems to provide the physiological basis of the perception of different neutrally colored objects.

Nevertheless, the stimulus correlate for neutral color *cannot* be the intensity of light (or luminance) because the amount of light reflected from an object is not determined exclusively by the reflectance of the surface but also by the illumination falling on the object. If the illumination is high, as in bright sunlight, a white surface reflects very intense light to the eye; but if the illumination is low, as in a dimly lit room, the same surface will reflect very weak light to the eye. Yet the surface will appear more or less the same color, namely, white, in both cases. We have here another constancy, referred to by terms such as *brightness constancy, lightness constancy, neutral* or *achromatic color constancy.*

Were it not for variations in illumination, there would be a high correlation between the intensity of light reflected to the eye by a surface and the perceived neutral color of that surface.* But, as shown in Fig. 11-1, many different combinations of illumination and reflectance can transmit *the same* intensity of light to the eye. Conversely, variation in the strength of illumination will *alter* the intensity of light reaching the eye from a single surface. Therefore, the problem is to explain how, despite the *single* source of information reaching the eye from a given surface, namely, intensity of light (or luminance), the observer nevertheless can have an unambiguous impression of each of the two factors that contribute to that single source, namely reflectance and illumina-

---

*Another relevant factor is the slant of the surface with respect to the source of light. This factor is discussed later in the chapter.

tion. Referring to Fig. 11-1, the problem is how the observer can discriminate situations *a, b,* and *c,* if in all three cases the same stimulus reaches the eye from the object.

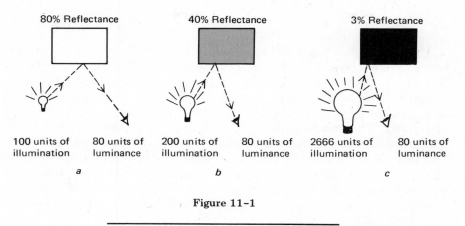

Figure 11-1

Lightness versus Brightness

Before proceeding, an important distinction must be made. Superficially there are similarities between the continuum of perceived colors from black to white, or degree of lightness on the one hand, and the continuum of perceived brightnesses, from dim to very bright, on the other hand. For example, one might be inclined to call a dark room "black." Or one might be inclined to regard a white object as "brighter" than a gray object. But for various reasons, it is important not to confuse these two aspects of perception, both of which derive from neutral light.

Some examples may help. Consider a source of light such as an incandescent bulb. It may appear to be dim or bright, but in neither case would we refer to it as having a color such as white or gray. Rather it appears to be emitting light, to be shining or luminous. (The term *white light* is, therefore, unfortunate; rather we should speak of *neutral light.*) The same is true about the sky when it is thoroughly overcast. Poetically it may be called gray, but to the author it does not look like a gray *surface.* Rather it looks luminous and has a particular brightness. Another example is a situation that provides uniform stimulation throughout the entire field, a Ganzfeld (see p. 145), in which no contours whatsoever are visible. The observer has the impression of looking into a diffuse, three-dimensional fog. No "things" are perceived, and regardless of the intensity of light, the field never looks like a

shade of gray.* Rather, it looks either dim or bright. A completely
dark room can be considered to be a special case of a Ganzfeld, and a
dark room looks dark, not black. Darkness is the experience correlated
with the absence of light, but this is not true of blackness. For the color
black to be experienced, certain specific conditions of contrasting luminances must obtain.

These examples suggest that when conditions give rise to the perception of a surface, the surface will be seen as a particular shade of gray.
But when conditions are such that an object surface is not perceived, as
in the case of the sky, the Ganzfeld, or the dark room, no nuance of
gray will be perceived, but there will be an impression of a particular
brightness. The psychologist David Katz described various modes in the
appearance of colors, such as *surface color, luminosity, transparency*,
and the like.[1] He noted that a region seen through a small opening
often no longer looks like a hard surface of a definite shade but rather
like a disembodied patch of light of a certain brightness (or hue),
and for this he suggested the term *film color* (sometimes called
aperture color).

In contrast to other modes of appearance, such as luminosity or
film color, a white piece of paper looks white and a black piece of coal
looks black. This is essentially true regardless of the intensity of light
falling on the object. However, if the white paper is in bright sunlight
it looks quite different in one respect from the way it looks in an indoor
unlit closet; it looks brighter in sunlight, not whiter. The same is true
of the coal; it looks brighter in sunlight, but not lighter in color. Therefore, in the following discussion we employ the term lightness (or neutral color) constancy in preference to the traditional "brightness constancy."†

*Instead of the cumbersome phrase *white-gray-black continuum*, the word *gray*
will be used in the remainder of the chapter to refer to the entire range of neutral
colors.

†The distinction between lightness of color and brightness has been deliberately
drawn sharply here, because it is important that the difference between these two
modes of appearance is understood. By and large, the difference is clear enough in
daily life as many of these examples illustrate. Nevertheless, there are borderline
situations when the distinction is more difficult to make and where, therefore, observers might disagree. An example might be the appearance of the sky when overcast but with clouds visible. Some might say that the sky looks gray. Similarly,
some might think it correct to describe a completely darkened room as black.

Two Theories of Neutral Color and Neutral Color Constancy

The classical explanation of the constancy of neutral color (despite varying illumination) is that the level of illumination is taken into account in assessing the light an object reflects to the eye. Helmholtz suggested a process of this kind.[2] Thus, for example, although a white object in dim illumination reflects little light, it is perceived to be receiving little illumination. Therefore, the low intensity of its retinal image may still be "thought" to emanate from an object of high reflectance. Conversely, the high intensity image from a black object in strong light is assessed as resulting not from a high-reflectance or whitish object but rather from a low-reflectance object receiving strong light.

The most telling criticism of this theory was first pointed out by Hering.[3] To make his criticism clear, imagine that the only object visible in a room is a single cardboard. A beam of light from a hidden projector illuminates only the cardboard. As a result, an image of the cardboard of a certain intensity is focused on the retina. Now the problem is how the observer could possibly know the strength of the illumination falling on the cardboard, in order properly to take it into account, if all he has available as information is an image of a given intensity. That same image could result from a black surface receiving strong light, a white surface receiving much less light, or any number of combinations of reflectance and illumination. (In the example under discussion, constancy does *not* prevail, in that the cardboard tends to look white or light gray regardless of what color it is.)

Admittedly this is a rather artificial situation since only one surface is visible. However, Hering's argument is just as valid in the more typical situation where many objects are visible simultaneously. If one argues that we are able to assess how much light is falling on object 1 (in order to "deduce" its reflectance) by virtue of information deriving from objects 2 and 3, the problem still arises as to how the latter information is unambiguously given. We cannot know if objects 2 and 3 are in intense or weak light until we first know their reflectance, but we cannot know that unless we know whether these objects are in intense or weak light. Of course, there are other "cues" to strength of illumination such as the direct sight of the source of light, shadows, dust particles in the air, highlights, and the like, but it is very questionable if these are actually useful and important indicators of illumination. In any case, these cues have been eliminated in experiments and constancy nevertheless prevailed; they have been retained in other experiments and contancy did not prevail.

A different kind of theory dating back at least to Hering that was put forth recently with certain important differences by Hans Wallach is that the specific neutral color perceived is determined by the relationship or interaction of light intensities of neighboring regions.[4] In other words, Wallach suggested that it is not the absolute intensity of light reaching the retina from one region in the field that determines its apparent neutral color, but rather the ratio of intensity of one region to that of a neighboring region.* When illumination changes, as, for example, when the sun goes behind a cloud, neighboring regions in the scene are usually affected equally, or when the light in a room is turned off, an object on the wall and the wall surrounding it both undergo the same decrement in illumination. Therefore, as is shown in Fig. 11–2, the ratio of light intensities of the white surface and the surrounding gray wall remains unchanged : in the example given, it remains 2 to 1.

If ratios of luminance are indeed the basis of the perception of the varying nuances of neutral color, it should be possible to create subjective impressions of specific colors in the absence of surfaces of the appropriate reflectances. In one experiment, Wallach made use of two identical slide projectors one of which projected only a disk of light on a white screen and the other of which projected only a ring of light that fit closely around the disk. The room was otherwise dark. The intensity of light that reached the screen was independently varied by placing a neutral density filter, which transmits only a certain percentage of the light, in front of each projector. The density of the filter was varied to permit more or less light to pass through.

---

*This idea suggested by Wallach, that perceived neutral color is a function of the ratio of light intensities, is different from the theory of Hering and others that color is a function of contrast. A contrast type of theory based on the role of both excitatory and inhibitory neural events has more recently been advanced by Jameson and Hurvich.[5] They believe that the ratio hypothesis is oversimplified because in daily life perceived neutral colors do not remain perfectly constant with changes in illumination and because some laboratory experiments reveal changes in perceived brightness with changes in absolute luminance while the luminance ratios remain invariant.

Both kinds of theories have in common the belief that cognitive operations, such as taking illumination into account, are not necessary but rather that sensory mechanisms suffice to explain constancy. They also share the belief that the perceived color of one region is profoundly affected by the light reaching the eye from adjacent regions. To the extent that these various theories agree that what matters is relative luminance, they are similar enough to be considered together, as a very different approach from that of the classical theory. But in this chapter, the classical theory is compared with the ratio formulation rather than the contrast formulation. The reader is referred to p. 537 for an elaboration of the differences between these formulations.

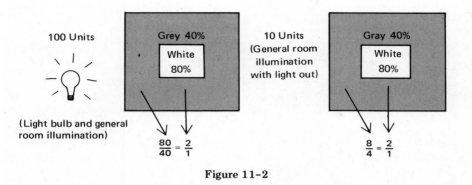

100 Units

(Light bulb and general room illumination)

Grey 40%

White
80%

10 Units
(General room
illumination
with light out)

Gray 40%

White
80%

$$\frac{80}{40} = \frac{2}{1}$$

$$\frac{8}{4} = \frac{2}{1}$$

Figure 11-2

If the intensity of light in the disk was kept constant, the variation of the intensity of light in the ring resulted in a change in the appearance of the disk from black to white. If, for example, the intensity of the ring was half or a little less than half of that of the disk, the disk looked white. When the intensity of the ring became slightly greater than that of the disk, the disk looked light gray. The disk became an even darker gray as the intensity of the ring increased still further until eventually when the ring was 27 times more intense than the disk, the disk appeared quite black. Since the screen on which the projected ring and disk appeared was white (or, more precisely, had a reflectance of 80 percent), the perceived neutral color of the disk was clearly not being determined by the actual physical reflectance character of the screen, but by the ratio of light intensities. It is remarkable that the disk could even be made to appear black merely by changes in the surrounding ring, despite the fact that it always was reflecting light in this experiment, and if seen without the ring would have looked luminous. Fig. 11-3 illustrates this experiment.

A further experiment makes it clear that a specific ratio determines a specific neutral color. Here two pairs of projectors were used so that two ring-and-disk arrangements can be seen (see Fig. 11-4). Although the absolute intensity of one ring and disk pair was much greater than that of the other pair, the two disks appeared to be the same gray to the observer when the ratios of intensities of ring to disk were about the same in each pair. In Wallach's experiment, the intensity of the ring and disk of one pair was set at a fixed value, the ring of the other pair was set at an intensity value much higher than the ring of the first pair, and the observer had the task of varying the intensity of the disk until its apparent color matched that of the other disk.

The room must otherwise be totally dark and the two ring and disk pairs must be separated from one another. If these precautions are not

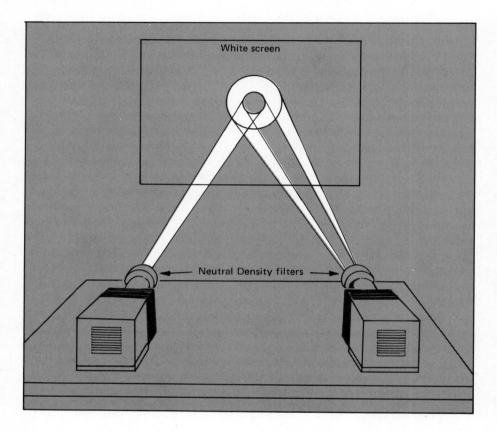

Figure 11-3

taken, other ratio effects enter into the equation and change the outcome. For example, the ring of one pair may affect the perceived color
of the disk of the other pair. If the room were not dark, the bright region of the screen or wall surrounding each pair would also affect the
outcome, and since the luminance of the wall is equal for both pairs it
would tend to have the effect of requiring the *same* absolute luminance
in each disk for the perception of equal neutral colors. This explains
why the two disks do not appear to be the same gray in the illustration
in Fig. 11-4 although the ratios of intensities of disk to ring are approxi-

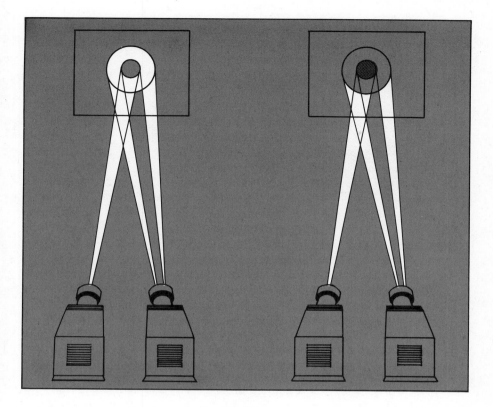

Figure 11-4

mately the same in these two pairs. The dark-room conditions of the experiment cannot be duplicated in such an illustration.*

It is implied in this argument that the ratio that matters most is that between adjacent regions, but it is also implied that regions that are not directly adjacent can have some effect upon each other. This can be shown in the following demonstration. If a disk is surrounded by a ring whose intensity is greater, the disk will look gray (Fig. 11-5a). If the disk and ring is surrounded by another ring of still greater intensity (Fig. 11-5b), the inner disk will look somewhat darker than the first disk.

---

*However, it should be noted that even under the ideal conditions of Wallach's experiment, deviations from a strict ratio prediction occurred. When the ring-disk ratios in the two pairs are equal, the disk in the pair of lower luminances appears somewhat darker than the other disk. Therefore, its luminance must be increased slightly before a subjective match is attained.

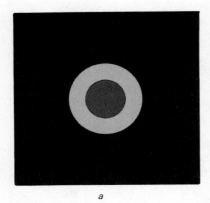

a   b

Figure 11-5

According to the ratio hypothesis, we can specify the ratio that will give rise to a particular neutral color, just as we can specify the wavelength that will give rise to a particular hue. The ratio is the proximal stimulus determinant or correlate of neutral color. Thus—under pure dark-field conditions at least—a 1 to 2 ratio, where the second value refers to the disk, leads to the perception of white, a 2 to 1 ratio is the stimulus for the perception of a light gray, and a 27 to 1 ratio or more produces an impression of black in the disk. If this conclusion is correct, then the reason why a particular surface typically looks white and another surface looks gray in daily life is not that they are "really" white or gray—or to speak more rigorously, not because they have fixed reflectances—but rather because given their reflectances they typically will reflect more or less light than other surfaces. In other words, a white object will reflect much more of the light incident upon it than will any other object in the field. Consequently this object will lead to a more intense image than that of objects adjacent to it and it is this ratio, not the reflectance property of the white surface per se, that determines the color perceived.

Therefore, any number of factors can alter the perceived lightness of an object. For example, if light falls on one object but *not* on adjacent surfaces, that object will look different from the way it usually does. A demonstration by the psychologist Gelb is of this kind (see Fig. 11-6).[6] A black surface illuminated by a beam of light that does not illuminate the surrounding regions will appear whitish or light gray. The normal ratio in which a black object will reflect *less* light to the eye than its surroundings has been altered. Now the black object reflects more light to the eye than its surroundings.

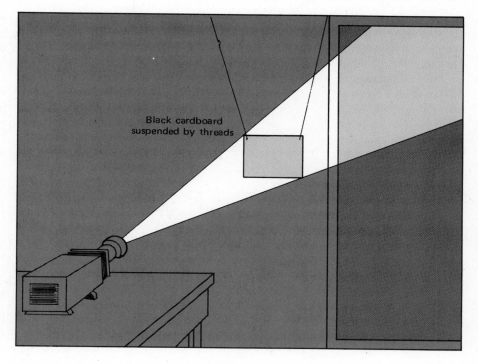

Black cardboard
suspended by threads

Figure 11-6

Another example is that of the hidden shadow (see Fig. 11-7).[7] A shadow is cast upon a white card by an object in front of a light hidden from view. The shadow falls exactly at the edges of the white card, none of it falling on the wall behind. Under these conditions, the white card looks dark gray. The white card no longer reflects more light to the eye than its surrounding area. Therefore, the ratio of the luminance of the white card to that of the surrounding area is drastically altered. The crucial fact in both this and the Gelb demonstration is that illumination is no longer the same for the object and its background as it is normally.

Both demonstrations illustrate a fact that is typical of all perception, namely, that knowledge about the actual state of affairs has no effect on what is perceived. The Gelb effect is just as striking if the observer first sees the arrangement with the room lights on. The observer then *knows* that the surface is black, but when the room lights are turned off—and only the single beam of light remains on—he nevertheless perceives it as white. Therefore, if the classical theory is to be maintained that a process of correction occurs in interpreting color stimulation, the

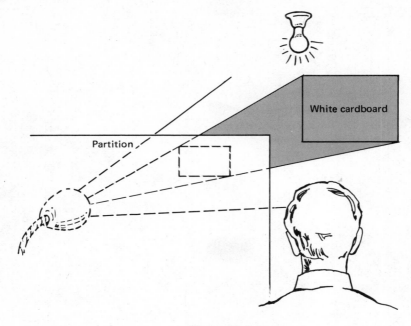

Figure 11-7

correction cannot be held to be based upon what is known about the situation. It would have to be based upon the immediately given stimulus information.

But other factors may be operating to bring about changes in the perceived neutral color of an object. The fact of simultaneous brightness contrast is a case in point. In Fig. 11-8 two regions of equal reflectances are shown, one surrounded by black, the other by white. It is obvious that these regions do not appear the same. Constancy of color does not obtain, yet the difference is precisely what we must predict on the basis of the ratio hypothesis. One might think that the

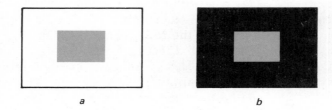

a   *b*

Figure 11-8

difference ought to be much greater than it appears here if neutral color is exclusively determined by ratio. In *a*, a ratio of about 2 to 1 obtains (the "1" refers to the inner rectangle), whereas in *b* a ratio of about 1 to 8 obtains. Therefore, the inner rectangle in *a* should look middle gray, which it does, but the rectangle in *b* should look luminous, which it does not. The answer to this seeming violation of the ratio principle is, of course, that the inner rectangle in *b* is also influenced by the white page surrounding the outer rectangle (or the white surrounding the inner rectangle in *a*) and this has the effect of darkening it. If *a* and *b* were to be cut out and placed far apart in a dark room, and each was illuminated by equal-strength floodlights so that no light fell beyond the outer rectangle, then the inner rectangle in *b would* look luminous and, therefore, would look drastically different from that in *a*, not merely slightly different as in Fig. 11–8.* So the classical fact of simultaneous brightness contrast (better called simultaneous lightness contrast) can be considered to be an instance of neutral color determined by ratio but where several ratios must be taken into account.

An effect that seems to be the very opposite of contrast is illustrated in Fig. 11–9. The gray regions in *a* appear to be lighter than those in *b*, although one would think that the white and black stripes would, if anything, by contrast, have the opposite effect. This kind of effect was called a *spreading effect* by von Bezold and now is referred to as *brightness assimilation.*[9] A similar effect has been observed for hues. Although this phenomenon is not yet satisfactorily explained, it is possible that it results from a tendency to react to the achromatic or chromatic color impression of the entire array, even if the observer is presumably comparing only isolated regions within the array. Thus, the overall impression of Fig. 11–9a is lighter than that of *b* because white stripes and gray is a lighter configuration than black stripes and gray. In one investigation it was shown that if steps are taken to force the observer to attend *only* to the gray regions, that the gray areas in *a* look

*The inner rectangle in *a* would not look very different under such dark-room conditions than it does in Fig. 11–8. For both *a* and *b* the change introduced by viewing them in a dark room is to eliminate the white regions of the page surrounding the outer rectangles and to replace it by darker regions. The black rectangle in *b* separates the inner gray rectangle from the darkening effect of the white page but not entirely so. Therefore, in a dark room there would be no such darkening effect at all. The white rectangle in *a* only separates the inner gray rectangle from a possibly lightening effect of the outer black rectangle in *b* but it seems that there is no such effect. Hence the absence of light surrounding the outer white rectangle in *a* in a dark room has no effect to speak of. It has been shown in an experiment that increasing the size of a black region surrounding a gray test region on an otherwise white background makes the gray region appear lighter; whereas the size of the area of a white region surrounding a gray test region on an otherwise black background has little, if any, effect on the appearance of the gray region.[8]

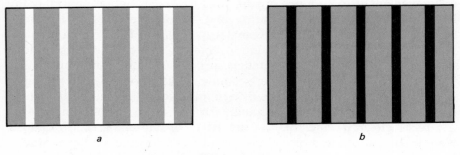

a   *b*

Figure 11-9

darker than those in *b*.[10]   If this explanation is correct, assimilation effects need not be considered to contradict the ratio hypothesis of neutral color perception.*

As noted previously, when the ratio moves beyond 1 to 4 the disk no longer looks white, it looks luminous. So at this point we are no longer talking about the perception of neutrally colored surfaces of varying shades. Further increases in the ratio will simply increase the apparent brightness of the luminously appearing disk. Since the ring in all the examples cited is surrounded by the dark field, it is infinitely more intense than its outer surroundings, so that it would follow that the ring would tend to appear luminous (this is, of course, true of any single region seen in an otherwise dark field; the Gelb demonstration is of this kind when the room is made totally dark). However, the disk on the inside of the ring does tend to offset this tendency to some extent. Therefore, the ring will appear to be more or less luminous. It is thus clearly not to be expected that the ring will reveal the effect of ratio in the same unambiguous way the disk will.

Other experiments aimed at testing the ratio hypothesis of perceived neutral color have not always confirmed it but the conditions of testing were not always appropriate. For example, in some experiments, the observer was required to compare a standard test area of a given intensity (surrounded by a region of a different intensity) with a comparison area that was seen against a completely dark background. Under such conditions, the comparison area will look luminous: it will not appear to be any nuance of gray. The test area, however, will appear to be a particular gray. When the luminance of the test area and its background is now increased, the perceived gray of the test area may remain con-

---

*The explanation of these assimilation effects offered here is quite similar to the confusion or incorrect comparison theory of certain geometric illusions (p. 431).

stant (as the ratio-hypothesis predicts) although the apparent "bright-ness" of the test area will undoubtedly change. Since the comparison area, appearing luminous, can never be matched in shade of gray to the test area, it is not surprising that observers would tend to select weaker or stronger intensities to match the test area depending upon the "bright-ness" of the test area. The opposite error has also been made, namely, the test area itself is isolated or partially isolated, i.e., surrounded on some or all sides by darkness.

In other experiments this inappropriate method was avoided, but one has the impression that the observers were not clearly instructed about the nature of the match they were supposed to make. Thus, they are either told simply to match the test and comparison areas without fur-ther elaboration or to match the brightness of test and comparison areas. What they should be instructed to do if the test is to be unam-biguous is to match the particular *shade of gray* and to ignore differ-ences in "brightness." Even with proper instructions, there may be a tendency to confuse brightness and lightness so that the observer tends to select a somewhat less intense disk in the brighter pair (since other-wise it looks too "bright") to match the disk in the dimmer pair than is predicted by the ratio hypothesis.

In still other experiments, including a now classic study first done in 1894, the test and comparison areas are adjacent (or, to be more pre-cise, the regions surrounding these areas are adjacent) instead of being separated as in Wallach's method.[11] As a result, when the intensity of test area and its surrounding field is varied while keeping the ratio be-tween them constant, the ratio of test area to the comparison field is not held constant.*

Nevertheless, the data of several experiments seem to indicate that what is perceived is not always the precise function of ratio that the ratio hypothesis demands. When the intensity of the test area is greater than that of its surrounding—as, for example, a light gray disk on a dark gray or black background—variations in absolute luminance result in slight changes in the matches that subjects make to the test area. This is particularly true for extreme changes in luminance. This change may result from the fact that if the luminance of the test area is greater than that of the surround, the test area may appear luminous rather than any neutral color. If so, changes in the absolute luminance of the two re-

*However, in fairness it should be stated that some subsequent investigators adopted a different method of avoiding a direct effect of the two fields on one an-other, namely, one field was viewed with one eye only and the other field was viewed with the other eye only. This interocular method presumably avoids an ef-fect of one field on the other.

gions can only affect apparent brightness and should be expected to do so.   More generally, however, the ratio principle is not symmetrical: it strictly governs the outcome for regions of lower intensity but not for regions of higher intensity.   Therefore, absolute luminance changes in situations where the test region is of an intensity greater than its background will lead to changes of perceived color.   On the other hand, constancy tends to be maintained when the intensity of the test area is less than that of its surroundings, as, for example, a medium gray on a white background.   In this case the ratio principle holds.   The writer and another observer have obtained constancy under these conditions with a change in luminance from one value to 1/10,000 of that value.*

A Laboratory Experiment on the Constancy of Neutral Color

The standard laboratory experiment on neutral-color constancy devised some years ago by Katz is illustrated in Fig. 11–10.[15]   Two samples of gray are affixed to a white background.   A partition divides the white background so that light from a lamp on one side illuminates the background unequally.   One side is in the shadow of the partition.   The gray sample on one side, the side on the right in the figure, serves as the

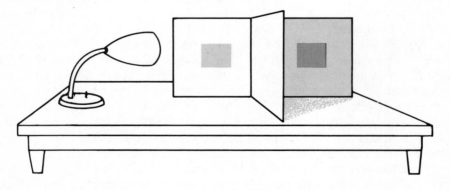

Figure 11–10

*Among the most frequently cited tests of the ratio hypothesis (or contrast theory as many call it) besides that of Hess and Pretori are those of Heinemann[12] and Jameson and Hurvich.[13]   For a review of work in this area, see Freeman.[14]

standard. The task for the observer is to select a gray sample on the other side, the one near the lamp, that appears to be the same gray as the standard. (Standardized samples of all shades of gray are commercially available for this kind of experiment. The reflectance of each sample is specified.) Another way of doing the experiment is to use a color wheel. White and black cardboard disks are interlaced as shown in Fig. 11-11. When the pair of disks is spun rapidly by means of a motor, the observer sees a gray whose shade is determined by the amount of black and white in the mixture. The standard can then be one such spinning disk pair of a certain perceived shade of gray and the comparison can be another in which the ratio of black to white is changeable. Color wheels have the effect of eliminating perception of irregularities in the grain or texture of the surface, or microstructure as it is called.

If the arrangement in Fig. 11-10 were such that the two samples reflected the same absolute intensity of light, then a low-reflectance surface would have to be selected on the left side to compensate for the extra amount of light reaching it. If, on the other hand, complete constancy of color obtained, an observer would select a gray equal in reflectance to that of the standard. Observers typically select a gray sample that is somewhat darker than the standard, but not too different from it. Thus, a strong tendency toward constancy is the rule in this kind of experiment and it is widely agreed that this outcome is a good representation of what typically happens in daily life.

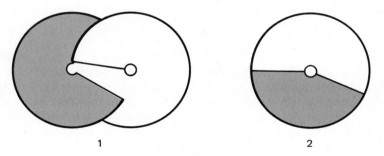

Figure 11-11

The departure of the typical match from a match that would be based on equality of the retinal images of the two samples is dramatically brought out when the samples are viewed through small apertures such that only the samples are visible, not the surrounding regions. Such an arrangement is referred to as a reduction screen and is illustrated in Fig. 11-12. The sample typically selected as matching the standard under these conditions is drastically different in color from the stand-

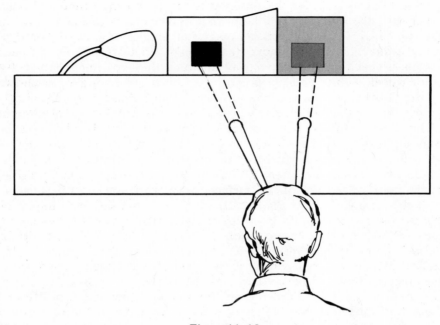

Figure 11-12

ard, in the example here, generally close to black. Following a match by an observer, if the screen is suddenly lifted, he is usually astonished to learn that he has just judged these two samples to be equal. Here would seem to be an instance in which perception is governed by physical equality of the retinal images of the samples. The results obtained with a reduction screen can be considered matches of the reflected light intensities, and this can serve as a useful measure when no instrument for measuring luminance is available. The reasoning here is as follows. Assuming the observer is matching on the basis of physical intensity of the two retinal images, then he must compensate for the difference in illumination by the difference in reflectance. If, for example, he selects a reflectance value in the region near the lamp that is three times darker than that of the standard in shadow, it would imply that the standard must be receiving one third as much light.

It is possible to express in quantitative terms the extent of the tendency toward constancy of an observer or group of observers (see Fig. 11-13). If an observer matches on the basis of absolute intensity by selecting a reflectance value of the comparison object that will compensate for the difference in illumination, he displays no tendency to-

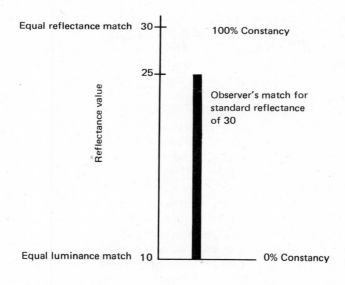

Figure 11–13

ward constancy; if he matches by selecting a reflectance value equal to the standard he displays total constancy. If he matches by selecting a reflectance value somewhere in between these two extremes, as is typically the case, then the degree of constancy can be expressed in terms of the value of this matching reflectance relative to the 0 and 100 percent constancy reflectance values.

To illustrate, suppose the standard (on the right in Fig. 11–10) has a reflectance value of 30 and receives one third the light that the comparison sample receives. Then the point in Fig. 11–13 representing 0 constancy would require a match of 1/3 of 30 or 10 (to compensate for the difference in illumination). The point representing total constancy would require a match of 30. Therefore, the total interval between no constancy and total constancy would be 30 minus 10 or 20. If the subject selects a value of 25 to match the standard then the interval between this match and no constancy would be 25 minus 10 or 15. The ratio would then be 15 to 20 or 75 percent. This method of expressing the degree of constancy was introduced by Egon Brunswik[16].* It can be generalized to apply to other perceptual constancies by thinking of one point as the proximal stimulus match, another as the constancy match, and a third as the obtained match.

How can the results of the experiment described be best explained? Both theories outlined here have offered explanations of the strong tendency toward constancy in the main part of the experiment. The classical theory would expect constancy to be present because it would be evident to the observer that the right side of the screen was in shadow. This would be particularly true if the edge of the shadow of the partition is visible. The edge of a shadowed region or penumbra has been considered to be a strong clue to the presence of a shadow; this issue comes up again later in the chapter. But now we come to a further question. Why according to the classical theory is constancy not complete in this situation? Of course, it is a general fact that perceptual constancies are almost never complete, the perception typically being a compromise between complete constancy and a match based on the proximal stimulus, but in each case the question arises why this is so. In the case of neutral color constancy it might be held that the information concerning the difference in illumination is underestimated. Not all of the diminution in intensity of light on the shadowed side is attributed by the perceptual system to the fact that one side is in shadow. This incorrect estimation of illumination differences might be thought to result from inadequate cues.

It is doubtful if this kind of explanation can do justice to the facts. If the edge of the shadow of the partition is not visible, cues to the difference in illumination are either eliminated entirely or very much reduced. This would probably not alter the outcome very much if at all. If so, the question raised by Hering arises, how does the observer get the information concerning illumination if all he has to go on is the intensity of light reflected by each surface? That intensity depends upon the illumination received *and* upon the reflectance of the survace.

---

*A modified ratio making use of logarithms was subsequently introduced by Thouless.[17] A ratio measure of constancy is very much a function of the *difference* in viewing conditions. In the example given, if the standard received one tenth the light of the comparison sample instead of one third, then even if the subject departed further from constancy by matching the standard to a reflectance value of 24, the Brunswik ratio would be higher than 75 percent. This may explain the paradoxical fact that many experiments on size, shape, and achromatic color constancy seem to reveal an increased tendency toward constancy the *greater* the difference in distance, orientation, or illumination between standard and comparison object. Generally the matches increasingly depart from constancy as a function of such differences in viewing conditions but at a much slower rate than what would be a proximal stimulus match. Therefore, the constancy ratio often goes up.

When the reduction screen is present, the observer is deprived of all information on the two sides. Since the reduction screen itself is uniform in color and more or less uniform in illumination (it is in *front of* the lamp and not differentially illuminated by it as is the background of the samples), according to the classical theory it is plausible for the observer to "assume" that illumination is equal for the two samples being compared through the openings. That being the case, the absolute intensity of light from the two samples must be equal for them to look equal. The very word *reduction* derives from the theoretical idea that the main effect of such a screen is to *reduce* or eliminate cues concerning the true state of affairs.

The ratio hypothesis can also deal with all these findings, quite elegantly in fact, and without the necessity of accounting for how differences in illumination can be registered. First of all, since the gray sample on the right *and* its background are both in the shadow of the partition, constancy is to be expected on the basis of ratio of light intensity. That is, the ratios of background to sample for both pairs remain equal. Since, however, the two "pairs" of sample-and-background are not isolated from one another, other ratios must be taken into account in the prediction. In particular, the bright white screen on the side of the lamp would have the effect of darkening somewhat the gray sample on the side in shadow. (The kind of effect demonstrated in Fig. 11-5*b* of a nonadjacent area). To compensate for this effect the observer would have to select a somewhat darker shade of gray in the sample on the left than that of the standard on the right and that, in fact, is what he typically does.*

It should be emphasized that this experiment on constancy duplicates most of the complex conditions that exist in daily life, whereas the ratio hypothesis can make precise predictions only under artificial lab-

---

*However, another explanation of the departure from complete constancy is possible, different from that of the classical or ratio theories. Suppose constancy is actually complete. Nevertheless, were the observer to select a gray that is the same as the standard, he might well be struck by the fact that the two surfaces look different, the one in strong light appearing "bright" the one in weak light appearing "dim." Since the instructions to the subject in the typical experiment do not always make it clear that he is to match on the basis of shade of color and not on the basis of brightness, he may feel that he has not succeeded in properly matching the comparison to the standard. He may, therefore, try to compensate for the perceived difference and to do so he may select a darker gray on the brightly illuminated side. Similar reasoning can be applied to the outcome of experiments on size perception, shape perception, and the like, where it is generally also found that although there is a strong tendency toward constancy, the average comparison setting falls short of complete constancy. The reader is referred to the discussion in Chapter 2, pp. 53-55 of the analogous finding in experiments on size perception.

oratory conditions. Thus, for example, in the typical situation in daily life many regions of different intensities are simultaneously present, the regions being compared may not be surrounded by or adjacent to regions of equal reflectances, the illumination may not be identical for the critical region and its surroundings, and so forth. As is true when applying any scientific hypothesis to a complex real-life situation, it is often difficult or impossible to make a precise prediction.

When the reduction screen is present, the intensity of light reflected by the screen is the same throughout and hence the light reflected by the samples is surrounded by equal intensities. Therefore, a match based on ratio now requires the samples to be physically equal in intensity. The only way that can be achieved, given the inequality of illumination on the samples, is to match on the basis of unequal reflectances, and that is precisely what happens. The student seeking to understand the outcome with the reduction screen in terms of the ratio hypothesis often incorrectly assumes that the screen eliminates the surround of the samples much as in the case of a sample seen alone in a dark room. If that were true, the samples would appear luminous. This is not so. The screen does eliminate the formerly visible surround but it substitutes a new one, in this case one that is equal on the two sides (see Fig. 11–12). Thus, the two apertures can appear to be the same shade of gray only if they stand in the same ratio to the *common* background. That can only be achieved if the samples reflect equal intensities of light to the eyes. That, in turn, could not be achieved if the two shades were made objectively equal, because one sample is receiving much more light than the other.

Thus, it appears that both theories can account for the findings in the classical laboratory experiment on neutral-color constancy (although not equally well) and this seems to be true for most of the other known facts about the perception of neutral color. Thus, for example, the Gelb effect (see Fig. 11–6) can be explained by the classical theory as the result of depriving the observer of information about illumination. (But then we may ask why the observer always "assumes" the cardboard is light in color and in dim light.) When a white cardboard surrounds the black one, the black one now is perceived as black. Thus, it could be said that the introduction of the white cardboard supplies the information about illumination that, until its introduction, was lacking. (However, it is not really clear why the introduction of a second surface should have this effect given the problem described by Hering.) On the other hand, according to the ratio hypothesis, as explained earlier, the black cardboard alone should look light gray or white (if the background is dimly illuminated by indirect light from the projector), or possibly luminous (if the rest of the field is really dark). The conditions for constancy no longer exist. When, however, the white card-board is placed behind the black one, the ratio is now around 27 to 1 and thus we must predict that the black cardboard should appear to be black. The reader can see that the two theories can similarly be applied to the hidden-shadow paradigm illustrated in Fig. 11-7.

Given this state of affairs, psychologists have tried to design critical experiments that would allow a decision between the two theories. For example, instead of placing a large white cardboard behind the black one a small piece of white paper has been used. This should be adequate as information about illumination in line with the classical theory but not adequate from the standpoint of the ratio hypothesis. In other words, if the role of the white object in this experiment is to provide information about illumination, its size should not matter; if its role is to provide a particular ratio of luminances, it is not fully adequate because it is only adjacent to the black cardboard in one small region. The result seems to be that the black cardboard no longer looks white or luminous but, on the other hand, it does not look black either. It looks gray and somewhat lighter in the regions not adjacent to the white paper. This finding is thus not easily explained by the classical theory.[18]

Further Evidence Bearing on the Two Theories

Apparent spatial position

The location or orientation of a surface will affect the intensity of illumination falling on it. For example, in Fig. 11-14 some parts of the room do not receive as much light as others and as a result some surfaces reflect less light to the eye than adjacent surfaces of the wall. The reader can observe this fact in any room. In Chapter 3 attached shadow was discussed as a cue to three-dimensionality. What is the appearance of such shadowed surfaces? The consensus is that they appear to be about the same color as the adjacent surfaces, that is, constancy obtains, although they also appear to be less "bright." Yet from the standpoint of the ratio hypothesis this should not occur. Thus, for example, the narrow shaded region of the rear wall in Fig. 11-14 where it recedes should appear to be some particular gray darker than the surrounding regions because it reflects less light to the eye than these regions.

Figure 11-14

On the other hand, we would predict constancy from the standpoint of the classical theory. It seems perfectly obvious that the surface in question is not receiving the same amount of light as the surrounding surfaces. In fact, in this kind of situation, unlike those discussed earlier in the chapter, there *is* a basis for differentiating reflectance from the illumination falling on a surface, namely, the slant of the surface as compared to that of neighboring surfaces. Although it remains true that the specific reflectance value of any single surface cannot be "deduced" without unambiguous information about illumination, the reflectances *relative to one another* of two surfaces slanted with respect to one another can be "deduced" if one perceives the two surfaces as receiving relatively different illuminations. Therefore, it makes sense that an observer could "infer" that the region of lower luminance in Fig. 11-14 was the same color as those surrounding it and he could account for the weaker intensity of light reaching his eye on the basis of the relative shadowing of this region. One might say that the shadowing plays the role of a cue to depth and, therefore, does not lead to an impression of a different gray. However, it should perhaps be noted that if there are no other visible clues to indicate that one surface is in shadow, then the tendency to perceive that surface and those adjacent to it as equal in shade of color represents a preference of the perceptual system. After all, one of these surfaces could be a darker shade of gray than the others.

That the perception of the slant of the surface can affect perceived neutral color is brought out dramatically by eliminating or altering the perception of the slant. There are various ways of doing this, such as by closing one eye or by blocking off from view the contours at the edges of the surface (for example, where the region on the back wall of Fig. 11–14 meets the ceiling and floor). When this is done, the surface is "flattened out," appearing to be in the same plane as the neighboring surfaces, and a marked change in its apparent color occurs. In the example illustrated in the figure, the surface now appears dark gray, not at all the same color as the walls on either side. Since the observer now does *not* have the impression that the surface is receiving less light than the surrounding surfaces but rather can infer that all these surfaces are receiving the *same* amount of light (since they are all in the same plane), the only way to make sense of the difference in luminance is to perceive the center surface as darker than the surrounding ones.*†

In these examples, one surface simply does not receive any direct light at all from a particular source and thus is essentially shadowed. But a similar effect occurs when a surface, while receiving light from the same source as a comparison surface, is differently slanted with respect to that source. If a surface is perpendicular to the direction of light rays from a source of light, it receives the maximum of light from it; if it is slanted with respect to this direction, then less of the light from the source is distributed over the entire surface so that the density of light per unit area, the luminance, is less (see Fig. 11–15). Therefore, if an observer had information about the location of the source of

---

*A similar effect was first noted by Mach.[19] See also Katona[20] and Beck.[21].

†The implication of the argument here is that in all situations where two or more surfaces are perceived to be in the same plane, the perceptual system may operate on the basis of an "assumption" that they are receiving equal illumination. That being the case, luminance differences must represent neutral color differences. This argument is relevant to the problem raised by Hering of the impossibility of determining the illumination falling on a surface in order to deduce its reflectance. It remains true that we cannot determine the absolute illumination but if we tend to assume that neighboring regions receive the same illumination then we can at least deduce that surfaces which differ in luminance *differ* in their reflectance properties and the more so the greater the difference in their luminances. However this deduction still would not tell us what shade of gray a surface was, only that it was lighter or darker gray than some other surface. Therefore the ratio formulation is still required, that is that a given nuance of gray is a function of a specific ratio. Nevertheless if such an assumption of equal illumination is made by the perceptual system, the perception of neutral color based on luminance ratios may entail more of a cognitive operation than has been implied in this chapter.

Figure 11-15

light, the perceived slant of the surface ought to play a role in the perception of its reflectance. If a surface reflecting a given intensity of light to the eye is perceived to be in position *a* in the figure, it ought to appear to be darker than if it is perceived to be in position *b*. It would have to have a much higher reflectance value in position *b* to yield as intense an image as a lesser reflectance value would in position *a*.

Experiments have been done investigating this question. For example, the trapezoidal pattern shown in Fig. 11-16*a* will, when viewed with one eye from a particular position (*b*), look like a rectangle resting on the table.[22] But the moment the observer is permitted to perceive its true orientation by using both eyes, namely, standing upright on the table, its apparent color has been found to change. Of course, in such experiments the observer must be given information about the direction

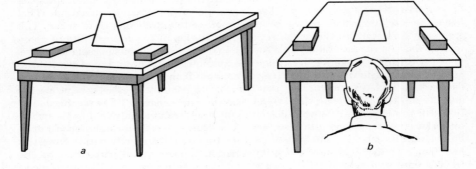

Figure 11-16

of the source of light. In the illustration this is indicated by the location of the shadows on the cubes. However, it should be noted that the change in apparent color is modest, much less than is to be expected if the difference in illumination suggested by the 90 degree difference in slant were fully taken into account by the perceptual system. In one recent study introducing certain careful controls, no effect at all was obtained.[23]

The failure to obtain the effect—or to obtain a strong effect—may result from the fact that it depends upon inferring the direction of illumination from other objects in the scene, the shaded cubes, and then applying this information to the perception of the color of the critical object, the trapezoid. This is not too far removed from acquiring knowledge about illumination such as might be supplied verbally, and information of this kind rarely if ever affects perception. Perhaps the experiment should be done with two figures of the same reflectance seen *simultaneously*, an upright trapezoid and a horizontal rectangle. When viewed monocularly, they both would appear as rectangles resting on the table and the observer would, therefore, incorrectly perceive the two figures as having the *same* orientation with respect to the source of light. The perceptual system could then infer that the unequal luminances of the two surfaces cannot signify equal reflectance values. But when viewed binocularly the two figures would be correctly perceived to have different orientations from one another and, therefore, with respect to the source of light. In that event the difference in luminance between the figures could be attributed to this difference in orientation. The kind of effect illustrated in Fig. 11-14 *is* easily observed as the reader can verify for himself. The effect of "flattening out" the adjacent surfaces is substantial, and in this case the simultaneous perception of the slants of the surfaces relative to one another would seem to be crucial.*

Very recently the role of the apparent distance of a surface from its background has been investigated.[24] According to the ratio hypothesis, all that matters is the intensity of one region in relation to that of an adjacent region. *Adjacent* here presumably means regions whose retinal

---

*In the kind of situation illustrated in Fig. 11-14 it is particularly difficult to distinguish between lightness of color and brightness. Many observers report that the shadowed surface does indeed look darker than the non-shadowed surfaces adjacent to it. However when they succeed in "flattening out" the surfaces so that they all appear to be in one plane there is a dramatic change since now the shadowed surface definitely looks like a very dark gray region. The comparison between the appearance of that surface before and after the shift from three to two dimensions helps to clarify for the observer that the "darker" appearance at the outset was one of lower brightness rather than of lower lightness of surface color. In any event the subtlety of the phenomenological impression in such situations may also explain the difficulty in obtaining clear cut experimental results.

images are alongside one another. If so, the nuance of gray perceived should not be different if a disk is lying directly on a background surface or if it is suspended by a thread so as to lie some distance in front of that background. Yet it has been shown that the position of the disk in depth does matter. When it is not perceived to lie in the plane of the background, the background has less of an effect on its color. From the standpoint of the classical theory, it could be argued that when the two surfaces are in different planes it need not be "assumed" that they are receiving the same illumination.

Cast shadows and the role of the penumbra

In Fig. 11–17, a shadow cast on a flat surface is shown. Does it look like a shadow on a surface of a given color or does it look like a gray spot? To some extent, it does look like a darker gray region in the figure but much that is present in the actual scene is lost in the photograph. Therefore, the reader should examine an actual shadow of this kind and observe what he perceives. Most observers agree that they perceive a shadow on a region that is the same apparent color as that surrounding it rather than a region of a darker gray. From what has been said thus far, one would think that the ratio hypothesis must predict no constancy in this case. Unlike other instances where an entire region is shadowed, including both object and surround, (where, therefore, the ratio between object and surround can be said to remain constant), here there is only one homogeneously colored surface and the shadow introduces a difference of intensity between the shadowed region and the region surrounding it. Hence the shadowed region should now look like a dark gray spot.

The classical theory would hold that since it is evident that we are viewing a shadow, we take that into account in assessing the meaning of the lower intensity of light reaching the eye from that region. How is it evident that it is a shadow? A shadowed region is typically ringed by a gradual transition from dark to light, a penumbra. The penumbra is caused by the fact that most sources of light are somewhat extended rather than a single point. In a famous experiment, Hering outlined a shadow with a thick dark line (see Fig. 11–18) thus eliminating the penumbra.[25] The result was that the shadowed region then looked like a gray spot. So one might think that the fact of constancy in the case of shadowed regions of this type represents a clear victory for the classical theory. Unfortunately, it is not that conclusive because advocates of the ratio hypothesis can argue that the gradual transition of the penumbra has the effect of interfering with the interaction between the repre-

Figure 11-17   Figure 11-18

sentations of the shadowed and unshadowed regions in the visual nervous system and such interaction is the basis of the ratio effect. Other methods of introducing such a gradual transition between adjacent regions—as, for example, rotating a gray disk with a scalloped edge on a white background—produces a similar outcome.[26]

Constancy in transparency situations

Suppose we look through smoked glass or a neutral density filter that only permits a portion of the light striking it to pass through (Fig. 11-19a). Objects then ought simply to look darker through such glass,

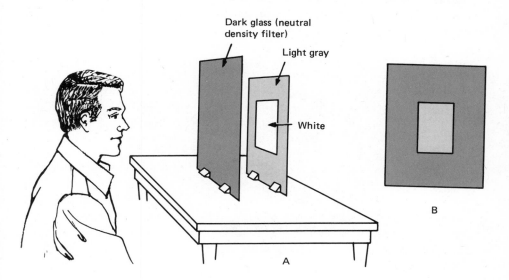

Dark glass (neutral density filter)

Light gray

White

B

A

Figure 11-19

but do they? What we see is shown in Fig. 11-19*b*. The inner white rectangle looks almost white.

If the observer were to take into account that he was looking through dark glass he might "conclude" that the object behind was a lighter color. However, such a tendency toward constancy only seems to occur when more than a single object or region is visible and this fact opens up the possibility of explaining the tendency toward veridical perception of the object's color in noncognitive terms.

In laboratory experiments on this phenomenon a rapidly rotating propeller (an episcotister) is often used. The size of the openings between the blades of the rotating propeller determines how much of the light from objects behind it gets through. At one moment the eye is stimulated by the light from the object seen through the opening; at the next moment it is stimulated by the light from the blade of the episcotister when it moves in front of the object. At fast speeds the effective stimulation at the eye is the weighted average of the two shades, taking into account the angular size of the blades in relation to the openings. Consider the situation illustrated in Fig. 11-20. The intensity of light reaching the eye from the white disk is attenuated by the rotating black episcotister so that we might think it will look gray. But generally in such experiments the observers perceive the color with a strong tendency toward constancy, i.e., as white, and at the same time they have the impression they are looking through a darker surface in front. Does this mean the observer is taking into account the fact that he is looking through a surface that is occluding some of the light from the object?

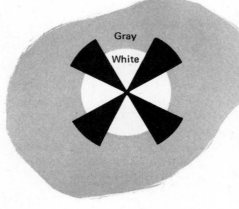

Figure 11-20

The ratio hypothesis can also explain the tendency toward constancy. Since the episcotister is in front of the background too, the light reaching the eye from that region is also attenuated. Therefore, the ratio of light intensity of white disk to gray background is not altered by the interposition of the episcotister. (The ratio is also maintained in the example illustrated in Fig. 11–19.) The stimulation the eye receives when the episcotister rotates is shown in Fig. 11–21. In fact, the same stimulation results if the drawing shown in Fig. 11–20 is itself rotated rapidly and in this case there is no reason to speak of transparency. Furthermore, if the episcotister is exactly the size of the white disk so that its blades do not cover the background at all, the ratio of the disk to background then *is* altered and the disk no longer looks white.

Constancy in children and animals

The implication that is drawn from the classical theory is that the achievement of constancy is a process somewhat like reasoning. A judgment is made (albeit unconsciously) about surface color by the taking account of illumination. Presumably, the ability to make such judgments is the result of a good deal of past experience. It then would seem to follow that in infancy neutral color is perceived on the basis of absolute intensity of light reflected by an object and only later does the child learn to correct for illumination. However, it has never been made explicitly clear how such a process of learning could be expected to occur (keeping in mind the paradox posed by Hering) or how learning could alter the perception of color. On the other hand, the implica-

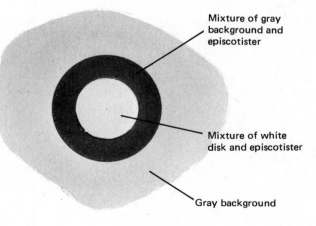

Mixture of gray
background and
episcotister

Mixture of white
disk and episcotister

Gray background

Figure 11–21

tion one draws from the ratio hypothesis is that intellectual processes are not involved and learning seems to be unnecessary. The ratio of intensities would be the stimulus correlate of neutral color just as wavelength is considered to be the stimulus correlate of chromatic color.

The behavior of various species of animals indicates that they perceive on the basis of constancy. Thus, for example, in one well-known experiment, young hens were first trained to peck at grain only from the darker of two sheets of paper.[27] Then the darker paper was placed in direct sunlight while the lighter one was left in weaker illumination. The hens still went to the darker paper despite the fact that it now reflected much more light than the lighter paper. With similar techniques it has also been shown that monkeys and fish react on the basis of constancy.* A good case can be made from the evidence for the assertion that animals spontaneously perceive neutral color (and other perceptual properties such as size and shape as well) in terms of constancy in much the same way as do human adults. In fact, the ability to perceive or to be aware of the difference in "brightness" when surfaces of the same reflectance values are viewed under different illuminations may well be the more difficult achievement.

It is now also established that children as young as four years of age perceive neutral color in terms of constancy although the particular conditions of the experiment seem to affect the outcome. On the other hand, there is some evidence that suggests that the index of constancy (e.g., Brunswik ratio) increases as a function of the age of the child. Therefore, some investigators have concluded that even if a tendency to perceive in terms of constancy is present at birth or in very early infancy it is also influenced by learning.

None of this evidence is crucial with respect to the question of whether neutral color constancy is innately determined because the animals and children were not tested at birth or were not deprived of the opportunity of visual experience prior to the experiment. Nevertheless, these findings have been considered to contradict the implication of the classical theory that constancy is based on an intellectual process of judgment. A fish may possibly have learned in some way to perceive in terms of constancy but it is doubtful if, in now doing so, it is using judgment.

However, there is now evidence that at least in the case of the chicken, constancy is present soon after hatching and without the possibility

---

*For a summary of work on constancy with animals, see Locke[28]

of learning. Chicks kept in total darkness from the time they were hatched displayed the same preference that all chicks have for lighter grain even when the lighter grain was placed in low illumination and the darker grain was placed in strong illumination.[29]

Sensory Mechanisms

Those who believe that there must be a direct sensory basis of the perception of neutral color—such as the response of the nervous system to intensity of light—have sought to explain constancy in terms of various physiological mechanisms. Hering suggested three such mechanisms, namely, the automatic adjustment of the size of the pupillary opening controlling the amount of light that enters the eye, the adaptation of the eye to light of varying intensity, and what he called a "reciprocal interaction" between adjacent regions of the retina.[3]

Pupillary adjustments

The pupil automatically adjusts to the amount of light in the scene, contracting to increased illumination and dilating to decreased illumination. Therefore, more light does not necessarily reach the retina whenever the illumination increases, nor less light whenever the illumination decreases. The change in size of the pupil might compensate for such changes of illumination. Hence one might think that the existence of this mechanism might make it possible to argue that the absolute intensity of light, leading to a specific rate of discharging of the visual neurons, is, after all, the basis of the perception of neutral color.

There are several reasons why this argument is incorrect. First, although the variation in pupil size is considerable, the area of the pupil changing by as much as a factor of 17, variations in illumination can be as great as a factor of hundreds of thousands. Therefore, the intensity of light reaching the retina from a given object can and does vary appreciably, in spite of pupillary adjustments, and yet the apparent gray of that object may remain more or less the same. Second, one can eliminate an effect of changes of pupil size by viewing the scene through a tiny opening, an artificial pupil. Yet constancy nevertheless prevails as one looks through this small opening at objects in different illuminations. Finally, and most important, the logic of the argument holds for only the case of an object of a given reflectance viewed under different illuminations. Here, the change in the size of the pupil as a function of change in illumination would tend to lead toward equalization of intensity on the retina. But suppose we compare a white object in dim light with a black one in strong light. The pupillary adjustment is triggered by the light reaching the eye so that no discrimination can be made between the contribution of intensity of illumination on the object and the contribution of the object's reflectance. Therefore, the pupillary adjustment would be the same in the two cases, resulting in images of equal intensity from the white and black object. However, one will look black and the other white.

Adaptation

This mechanism also works toward the end of compensating for variations in illumination. The sensitivity of the retina changes as a result of continued exposure to light of a given intensity. Therefore, by virtue of such adaptation effects, the rate of firing is not necessarily increased or decreased by corresponding increases and decreases in the level of illumination. On the basis of such adaptation, the sensitivity of the eye to light can change by a very appreciable amount, by a factor of 100,000 so that the limitation referred to concerning pupillary change is not applicable here.

But the other argument, namely, that the retina adapts on the basis of the intensity of the light that reaches it remains applicable. Therefore, objects of low reflectance in strong light should lead to the same adaptation tendencies as objects of high reflectance in weak light. If adaptation maintains a constancy in the perception of identical neutral colors under conditions of varying illumination, then adaptation must *equalize* the perception of different neutral colors that are in different illuminations. There is no evidence that the latter tendency occurs.

Therefore, it is not clear exactly what the role is, if any, of adaptation insofar as the perception of neutral color is concerned. When one opens one's eyes—or comes out of a dark room—everything appears to be very "bright." As one continues to view the scene this impression of brightness disappears and no doubt this is based on light adaptation. But white objects do not thereby begin to look gray. So perhaps it is plausible to think that the diminution in the rate of firing of cells based on adaptation does lead to a change in the impression of "brightness" but not in the shades of white, gray, and black of objects. (A similar statement might well apply to the effect of pupillary change.)

Since the eyes are constantly moving, the images of different objects in the scene are changing their locations on the retina from moment to moment. Inasmuch as adaptation is a function of specific locus on the retina, a region that at one moment is stimulated by a strong light, and is adapting accordingly, at another moment is stimulated by weak light, and vice versa. It is doubtful, for the reasons outlined, that such fluctuations alter the apparent neutral colors of objects, but it is at least conceivable that they might have effects in carefully controlled laboratory experiments where fixation is required, at least in cases where the instructions do not clearly distinguish surface color from brightness perception.*

Lateral inhibition

By "reciprocal interaction" Hering meant that a bright region of the field would have a darkening effect on an adjacent region and a dark region would have a brightening effect on an adjacent region. (He also believed that chromatic colors affected adjacent regions by inducing the complementary color.) What was theory for Hering is now known to be factually true. From experiments on the horseshoe crab, Limulus, where the nerve fibers from the retina are large and easily accessible, Hartline and his associates demonstrated that the rate of discharging in one fiber is attenuated when a fiber from an adjacent region of the retina is stimulated by light.[31] This inhibitory effect of adjacent fibers upon one another is now known to be a very general phenomenon of the nervous system of virtually all species.

Therefore, it seems plausible that lateral inhibition, as it is called, ex-

---

*A somewhat different approach to adaptation has been taken by the psychologist Harry Helson.[30] Rather than thinking of it in specific, localized, physiological terms, Helson views adaptation as a psychological adjustment in which we tend to evaluate or gauge objects on the basis of how they compare to the prevailing level of stimulation. That level tends to be perceived as neutral. Thus, for example, if the entire scene, consisting of objects of varying nuances of gray, is illuminated by red light, then most objects will appear to be neutral or achromatic rather than red despite the fact that they reflect predominantly "red light" to the eye. That being the case, only very intense light of that wavelength, reflected by white or light gray objects, will look red and a dark object takes on the complementary hue.

Applying this reasoning to the perception of neutrally colored objects receiving neutral light, it can be argued that whatever the illumination in a given scene, there is an adaptation to it, so that objects of middle reflectance values will look medium gray and objects of high reflectance value will, therefore, in relation to the prevailing level of adaptation, look white, and so forth. This theory is, of course, similar to the ratio hypothesis because the perceived neutral color of an object is a function of its intensity relative to the intensity of all other objects in the field. However, it is a more complicated theory because a multiplicity of factors are held to affect the level of adaptation.

The description of Helson's theory given here is necessarily condensed and oversimplified. Helson holds that the adaptation level is a function of all potentially relevant stimuli each of which is weighted in terms of its probable contribution to the outcome. Prior stimulation is among the factors that influence adaptation level. The theory has been applied to various phenomena in perception, not merely to the one under discussion here.

plains contrast and constancy effects. If the intensity of light on a ring surrounding a disk is increased or if the reflectance of the ring is increased such changes should have the effect of lessening the rate of discharging of neurons stimulated by light from the disk. This should lead to a diminution of the disk's perceived lightness. Conversely, decreasing the intensity of stimulating light in the ring should have the effect of releasing the disk from such inhibitory influences, thereby increasing the perceived lightness. Therefore, lateral inhibition would seem to explain simultaneous contrast.

To explain constancy, one must keep in mind the *direct* effect of changes of light intensity stimulating the inhibited area, in this case the disk. Suppose the intensities of the disk and ring are increased. Then the ring will have an increased inhibitory effect on the disk, but the disk will also have an increased excitatory effect from the increased light falling directly on it. Therefore, one might suppose that the direct excitatory effect and the indirect inhibitory effect of the surrounding area will more or less cancel one another out. This then might be the physiological mechanism that explains why ratio determines perceived neutral color, i.e., the reason why such perceived color remains approximately constant as long as the ratio remains constant, despite variations in absolute intensity of light.*

It is likely that lateral inhibition affects neutral color perception under certain conditions. Thus, for example, in the pattern shown in Fig. 11-22, the so-called Hermann-Hering grid, the intersections of white stripes look somewhat darker than the remainder of the stripes (at least those intersections seen in peripheral vision). The white intersections are surrounded on four sides by white, whereas regions elsewhere on the stripes are surrounded only on two sides by white. Therefore, there is more inhibition on the intersections by the high intensity of the white surround than there is on the other white regions. Hence the intersections appear darker. The implication is that when one views any extended region of uniform color, such as a white page, it would everywhere look much lighter were it not for the inhibiting effect of each point on adjacent points. Hence it is only under special conditions,

---

*Of course, it is not necessary to suppose that the excitatory and inhibitory effects of changing illumination would always exactly cancel one another. The specific outcome would depend upon a variety of factors such as the areas of the adjacent regions, their spatial positions relative to one another, their absolute luminances, the background or maintained level of spontaneous discharging that is present even in the absence of stimulation by light, and so on. Therefore, departures from constancy and certain variations in perceived neutral color as a function of ratio can also be encompassed by this theory.

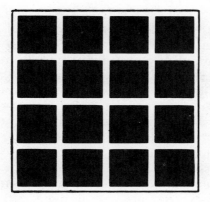

Figure 11-22

where the inhibition is reduced or increased in one region, that this fact of inhibition is revealed.*

If lateral inhibition is the basis of constancy, the rate of discharging in a given region of the field is presumed to remain more or less constant despite variations in illumination, because increases or decreases in direct excitation are balanced by increases or decreases in inhibition from adjacent regions. Underlying this explanation is the notion that the correlate of neutral color is the effective intensity of stimulation or rate of discharging of the fibers in question.

It is thus clear that the lateral inhibition hypothesis of contrast and constancy is different from the ratio hypothesis. The lateral inhibition hypothesis asserts that the absolute rate of discharging of fibers in a given region determines the color of gray perceived, but emphasizes that this rate is affected by what is happening in adjacent regions.† The ratio hypothesis asserts that the neural event that underlies the color of gray perceived is one based upon the ratio, a neural interaction between the two intensities, as Wallach states it, or a cognizance of the ratio by a higher center of the brain to state it differently.

There are reasons for thinking that the lateral-inhibition explanation

---

*Another phenomenon discovered by Mach now attributed to lateral inhibition is the appearance of dark (or light) lines when a region of gradually decreasing (or increasing) reflectance abruptly decreases its rate of decrease (or increase). For a discussion of these "Mach bands," the reader is referred to von Békésy[32] and Ratliff.[33]

†For a lucid exposition of the role of lateral inhibition in the perception of neutral color and an explicit statement of the interpretation outlined here, see Cornsweet.[34]

of perceived neutral color is incorrect. When only a single region is visible in an otherwise completely dark field, it will never take on a surface color of a given nuance of gray no matter how weak its intensity of light. It will continue to appear luminous (although it will change in apparent brightness). That it has this appearance might be thought to follow from the inhibition explanation because there is now no inhibition on the single region from the surrounding dark field. But still the question arises as to why this should be true if the absolute rate of firing of neurons is the correlate of perceived neutral color. There should be some specific luminance value at which the isolated region will appear as a specific shade of gray.

Furthermore, when in daily life a surface is seen under different illuminations (or, in experiments, the absolute intensity of one pair of adjacent regions differs from that of another pair while the ratios of intensities remain the same for the two pairs), although the apparent shade of gray may be more or less constant, a difference in "brightness" is nevertheless perceived. Why should there be any perception of difference according to the lateral inhibition hypothesis? If the effective rate of discharging in a given region is maintained at a constant level by lateral inhibition, despite the actual change in physical light intensity, then why is the observer able to detect the change at all?*

A relatively recent discovery is receiving increasing attention as a fact which may reveal the mechanism underlying the perception of neutral color. In essence the discovery is that the difference in reflectance between two regions at the contour separating them determines the impression of achromatic colors extending throughout the two regions regardless of the reflectances in the remainder of the regions, for example even if these are in fact equal to one another.[35] This is illustrated in Fig. 11–23 *a* and *b*. In *a*, a disk is shown with a triangular dark sector containing a narrow light and dark spur. Without the spurs, the disk would look light gray throughout when rotated because the large white, and smaller black regions would alternate for any given region of the region. The spurs do create a difference in luminance which extends

---

*One final argument concerns the effect of a third region separated from a given region by a second region, for example, the effect of an outer ring, surrounding another ring, on a disk inside (as illustrated in Fig. 11–5B). This outermost ring should have the effect of lessening the inhibiting effect that the inner ring has on the disk by a process known as *disinhibition*. The outermost ring should have the effect of lowering the rate of neural firing in the inner ring and, therefore, the inner ring should no longer have as strong an inhibitory effect on the disk. Therefore, in the illustration on Fig. 11–5, the disk in *B* should appear lighter than the disk in *A*. In fact, however, it will appear darker. An explanation for this observation that is consistent with the ratio hypothesis is offered on p. 513.

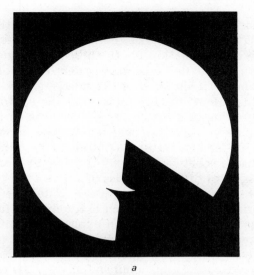

a

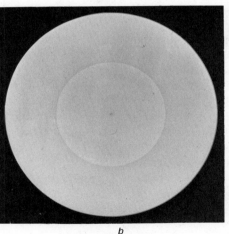

b

Figure 11-23

for only a short distance. Therefore one might expect to see narrow light and dark rings on a light gray disk. However what one perceives instead is a uniformly lighter disk inside a uniformly darker ring, *b*. Yet there is no difference between the physical mixture of black and white beyond the narrow regions of the spurs.

However when the disk is rotated the spurs simulate a contour in which the inside is lighter than the outside, i.e., a contour separating light and dark regions. For reasons which are not yet understood the colors perceived on the basis of this luminance difference at the contour are then extended by the perceptual system over the entire region of the disk. This means either that the luminance difference at a contour is the essential information for the perceived shades of gray over extended regions *or* that the perceptual system extrapolates this information and "assumes" it applies over extended regions. The reader can see for himself the role of the information at the contour by covering the contour with string or a narrow ring. Then the entire disk appears uniform in color again. Further evidence for the important role of a sharp luminance difference across a contour is the opposite fact, that very gradual transitions between regions of different luminance will not lead to an impression of different shades of gray on the two sides.

Based upon this discovery one might speculate that it is the lateral inhibition occurring at contours which is responsible for contrast and constancy effects. However if such an explanation in terms of lateral inhibition again reduces to one concerning the absolute rate of discharging of neurons (except now the crucial neurons are those stimulated at the border between contrasting luminances) then the criticisms raised here concerning lateral inhibition as an explanation of neutral color perception remain applicable. On the other hand, the effect may imply that the crucial information for neutral color is the ratio of luminances at a border, not the absolute rate of discharging of neurons as modified by lateral inhibition. According to this view, constancy would occur because the perceptual system receives the same information at borders regardless of the absolute level of luminances. Contrast would occur because, based on ratio, the border between gray and black would transmit a very different signal than the one between gray and white. (However this kind of information, whatever the mechanism underlying it, cannot be the whole story, because a region that is not directly contiguous with another region of lower luminance has at least some effect on the phenomenal color of the latter (see Fig. 11–5*a* versus *b*). Were this not true the effect of contrast ought to be expected to be much greater than it in fact is).

Perhaps the role of lateral inhibition is one of modifying the effective ratio of luminances across a contour. That is, the relative difference between luminances is the essential information for neutral color rather than absolute level of excitation. Lateral inhibition would simply have the effect of sharpening the relative difference by lowering or raising the rate of discharge of neurons. The shade of gray perceived would be a function of the ratio of rates of discharging of neurons stimulated by the neighboring regions, which rates are modified by lateral inhibition. This formulation avoids the implication that absolute rate of discharging of neurons determines the neutral color perceived and therefore must be assumed to be equalized wherever constancy prevails. Differences in absolute luminance may lead to differences in absolute rate of discharging of neurons and this may have certain consequences for perception.   As is suggested in the next section, absolute luminance may determine the perception of brightness.

It is probable that the presence or absence of a luminance difference across a contour has a bearing on some well-known phenomena of neutral color perception.   For example, the tendency toward constancy of a shadowed spot with a penumbra may result from the absence of a sharp contour between the inner and outer regions.   As would be predicted, covering that penumbra with a ring leads to an impression of a dark region on a lighter background (see p. 529).   The insensitivity to differences between reflectances when the transition between them is gradual has already been mentioned.   Possibly related to this fact is an effect illustrated in Fig. 11-26 where the gray ring is perceived as relatively homogeneous despite the fact that each half of the ring ought to be affected differently by contrast.   Introducing a sharp boundary at the midline of the ring (Fig. 11-25) changes the outcome.

Can Illumination Be Perceived?

When constancy prevails, so that an object is perceived to be a certain gray despite great differences in illuminations, one can still notice a difference in the appearance of the object.   For example, a white object in shadow looks different from one in sunlight, not in its white color, but in respect to what can perhaps best be described as brightness.   This term refers to a phenomenal impression and not to the objective intensity of light or luminance.   That a white object in sunlight looks "brighter" is generally attributed by the observer to stronger illumination. This attribution or interpretation may well be based on past experience since it is possible to imagine having the direct sensory impression of one object being "brighter" than another of the same apparent gray surface color without having any idea about why is this the case.   Also there are situations where impressions of brightness are not in any way correlated with interpretations about illumination, as, for example, in the case of a Ganzfeld.

For any surface there is ordinarily no way to distinguish physically between the component of light intensity reaching the eyes resulting from the reflectance of the surface and the component resulting from the illumination falling on the object.   Nevertheless, we typically perceive the reflectance correctly and we typically have an impression of "brightness" that is, roughly speaking, correlated with the intensity of illumination.* What makes this possible?

Constancy is not present for a single surface in an otherwise dark field. Thus, for example, under such experimental conditions, a black surface illuminated by a very intense beam of light might appear about the same as a white surface illuminated by a weak beam of light. This implies that the difference in illumination is also not perceived. The same is true when surfaces seen through a reduction screen are matched. However, when two or more adjacent surfaces are visible and the entire region is illuminated by a given source of light, then not only does constancy prevail but the observer is able to perceive differences in brightness and, therefore, to judge differences in illumination with a fair degree of accuracy.[36]

A simple answer to the problem, therefore, is that once the color of a surface is determined by the ratio of intensities of adjacent surfaces, any difference between its absolute intensity and that of another surface of the same perceived gray can be unambiguously perceived to refer to "brightness." Stated differently, the intensity of light reaching the eyes from any surface derives from two component sources, the surface's reflectance and the illumination falling on it. Once a "solution" is reached concerning one of these components, reflectance, by virtue of the ratio principle, then it becomes possible to "deduce" the other component, "brightness." An example will make this clear.

Suppose one object has a physical luminance of 100 units and another has a luminance of 10 units (see Fig. 11–24). Thus the intensity of light reaching the eyes from the first object is ten times that from the second object. With no further information, this state of affairs could result from various combinations of reflectances and illuminations. For example, the second object could be dark gray under illumination equal to that on the first object, which might be white, or both objects might both be white under very different illuminations. But the moment the observer correctly perceives the color of the objects (by virtue of the operation of the ratio principle), the difference in luminance can lead unambiguously to the perception of brightness, which corresponds with the actual condition of illumination. If both objects are perceived as white then it follows that the first is much

---

*It is probably correct to say that we are less aware of an object's "brightness" than of its neutral color. It may also be true that some observers pay more attention to "brightness" than others and, as a result, some individuals may find the task in a constancy experiment on matching neutral colors under different illuminations more ambiguous than do others. Also the instructions may be understood differently by different observers. Such differences may explain why individuals differ in matches in constancy experiments and why results may differ for adults and children or humans and animals. (See the footnote on p. 521.)

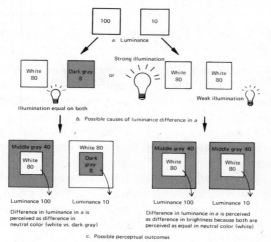

Figure 11-24

"brighter" than the second; if the first is white and the second is dark gray (equal, say to a reflectance value of 8 percent), then the difference in luminance is fully accounted for and the observer might have the impression that the two objects are under equal illumination.

In the explanation offered here it is not being suggested that the perception of the neutral color depends upon the perception of illumination, as is implied in the classical theory, for that approach leads to the difficulty of explaining how the illumination could be known prior to the shade being known, keeping in mind that illumination is generally only perceptually deducible from the light reflected by objects. Rather it is implied that the perception of neutral color generally is not a function of taking illumination into account, but is instead a direct function of ratio of intensities. In fact, the opposite is the case. "Brightness" can only be perceived (and illumination, therefore, only inferred from it) if the specific neutral color is first determined by ratio.

However, there seem to be special cases where the process works along the lines suggested by classical theory, namely, whenever information is directly available that two objects are receiving *different* intensities of illumination. Such seems to be the case when three-dimensional arrangements make it evident that one surface is in shadow whereas another surface is not; or where it is evident that two surfaces are oriented very differently from one another in relation to the source of light; or possibly where a penumbra suggests that a region is shadowed. In these cases it seems to be true—and logical considerations do not preclude it—that we *start* with certain impressions about differences in illumination between surfaces, and this in turn leads to interpretations about the color of these surfaces.

Effects of Perceptual Organization

In Fig. 11–25 contrast is illustrated in a somewhat different manner than it was in Fig. 11–8. The black and white fields are now in direct contact with one another and the gray regions are now halves of a ring. The contrast effect is clearly present although it is not quite as striking as in Fig. 11–8. However, in Fig. 11–26 very little effect of contrast is evident although the only change is in the elimination of the contour line in the center of the ring.

This effect, now known as the Koffka ring because of analogous experiments done by Koffka using chromatically colored backgrounds, is generally interpreted to mean that the tendency to perceive a figure as being unified opposes the effect of contrast.[37] When the vertical contour divides the ring into two distinct parts, there is no longer the same opposition to the contrast effect.

The gray region in these figures is in close proximity to both black *and* white, particularly the parts near the center of the ring. Therefore, we expect this fact to limit contrast and apparently it does.[38] From this point of view, the reason why the vertical contour line in Fig. 11–25 restores the full contrast effect is that it slightly reduces the effect of the black or white on the other side. According to this interpretation, figural unification has nothing to do with the effect. But then why is contrast so much stronger in Fig. 11–27 than it is in Fig. 11–26? Here the center parts of each half ring are in full proximity with the black or white on the other side of the contour. Therefore, the hypothesis of figural unity remains the most plausible. In this figure, the unity is completely eliminated by splitting the rings apart.

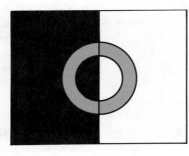

Figure 11–25

Figure 11–26

Another factor that influences contrast but is not reducible merely to the quantitative sum of black and white areas or to the physical proximity of these areas is illustrated in Fig. 11–28. Both gray triangles are surrounded by black on two homologous sides and by white on the hypotenuse side. Actually, triangle T2 has even more black near it than does triangle T1. Yet triangle T1 appears lighter than triangle T2.

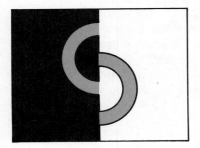

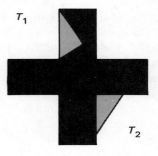

Figure 11-27   **Figure 11-28**

Benary[39], who investigated this phenomenon at Wertheimer's suggestion, interpreted this to mean that a figure contrasts more with a background to which it belongs than with one to which it does not belong. Triangle T1 is on the black cross; triangle T2 is on the white background. Therefore, triangle T1 contrasts more with black than does triangle T2 and is accordingly more lightened by it. Conversely, triangle T2 contrasts more with white than does triangle T1 and is accordingly more darkened by it. The same effect is shown in Fig. 11–29 where the gray triangle T1 on the large black triangle in *b* looks lighter than triangle T2 next to the black cross in *c*. The black triangle was formed by cutting it away from the black cross figure as shown in *a*. Consequently, it is quite clear that triangle T1 has less black in its vicinity than triangle T2. Yet triangle T1 appears lighter than triangle T2.

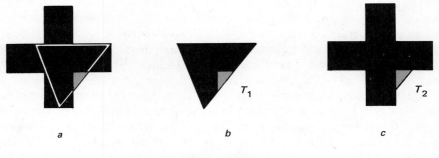

Figure 11-29

A further finding along this line is that a region perceived as figure undergoes more contrast with its surroundings than a region perceived as ground.[40] In a recent experiment, illustrated in Fig. 11-30, the observer judged the grayness of a circular region surrounded by a white (or black) ring.[41] By means of stereoscopic presentation, the central gray region in one case (*a*) was made to appear as background of a ring floating in front of it; in the other case (*b*) the central gray appeared as a figure floating in front of a larger circle in the background. The proximal stimulus distribution of white and gray (or black and gray) was essentially identical in the two cases. Yet the central gray region when perceived as figure, *b*, contrasted more strongly with the background than when it appeared as ground, *a*. In the illustration the central gray region appeared darker in *b* than *a;* when a black ring was used, it appeared lighter in *b* than *a*.

 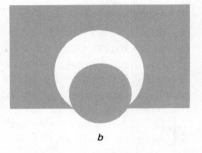

a   b

Figure 11-30

Organization of the field is also relevant to transparency effects.[42] Thus, for example, in Fig. 11-31 one has the impression of a white cross seen through a dark, narrow rectangular strip. Phenomenal transparency implies the simultaneous perception of two colors, one behind the other. However, there are no direct clues in the picture that the narrow rectangle is anything transparent such as might be present in looking through glass with both eyes. Apparently, the organization of the figure into cross and rectangle is important for the transparency effect. Compare this figure with Fig. 11-32, where there is no impression of transparency and the cross is seen as part white and part dark gray. Yet the only essential difference between the two figures is that in the first case the dark regions within the cross are perceived as be-

Figure 11-31

longing to a long strip extending beyond the cross on both sides. In this case, therefore, the perceptual system can arrive at the solution that a dark, transparent glass of uniform color is in front of a uniformly white cross.

In the examples of constancy in transparency situations discussed earlier (pp. 529ff), it was possible to explain the tendency toward constancy in terms of the ratio hypothesis. It was, therefore, irrelevant whether the observer did or did not have an impression of transparency. But in the present examples the focus of interest is on the experience of transparency and, furthermore, the examples suggest that constancy can depend upon whether or not an impression of transparency is present. One perceives the darkened section of the white cross as white in Fig. 11-31 but as gray in Fig. 11-32. The difference cannot be explained in terms of ratios because the gray section of the white cross is adjacent to the darker gray surrounding it in both cases.

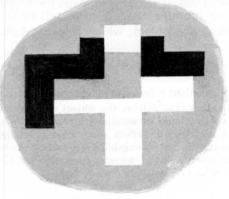

Figure 11-32

PLATE 4

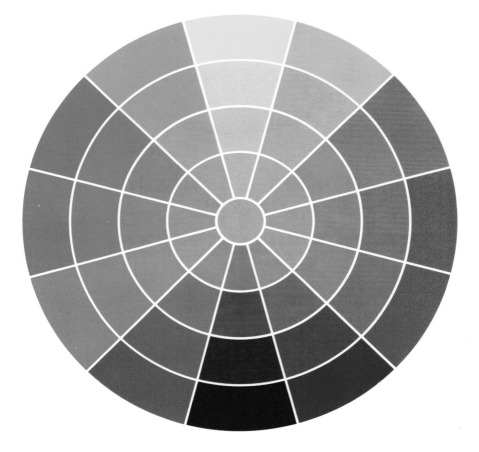

PLATE 5

PLATE 6

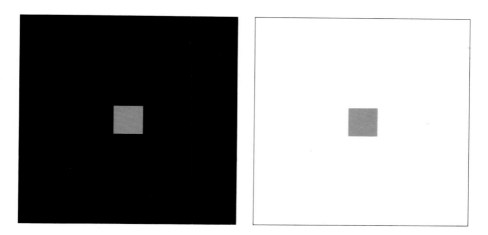

PLATE 7

flect predominantly blue-green light to the eye. But this leads to the same problem Hering raised about neutral color. How do we know that the background is not *actually* blue-green? And if it is, then there is no reason to assume that the object and surround are in blue-green light.

The fact that both object and surround must be visible for chromatic color constancy to occur has suggested that such constancy reduces to a contrast effect. A gray region surrounded by a colored region will tend to take on a color complementary to that of the surround. This is known as *simultaneous color contrast.* Consider again the situation of constancy just described, this time in terms of the proximal stimulus reaching the eye. The retinal image of the red object derives from neutral light; the image of the surround derives from blue-green light. But this is precisely the nature of the proximal stimulus in the contrast situation where, for example, a gray disk is surrounded by a blue-green background. Experiments have shown that the situations are indistinguishable and yield identical effects.[44]

This way of understanding chromatic color constancy is obviously analogous to the ratio explanation of neutral color constancy. In both cases the effect is a function of the relationship of the stimulus reaching the eye from one region to that reaching the eye from an adjacent or surrounding region, and in both cases it is unnecessary to refer to cognitive processes entailing the taking into account of the illumination. However, the analogy stops there, because in the case of neutral color, the hypothesis is that the ratio of intensities determines the perceived color, whereas in the case of chromatic color the notion of ratio of wavelengths does not seem appropriate.

The question arises as to the physiological mechanism that underlies chromatic color constancy and contrast. Of course, if the eyes move during inspection of the stimulus array, so that the colored surround stimulated the same region of the retina later stimulated by the gray sample, the simultaneous contrast effect can be considered to have been reduced to successive contrast that in turn can be explained on the basis of adaptation. The retinal cells that are most sensitive to the wavelength of the surround become fatigued so that the effective balance of neural discharging from that region of the retina shifts in the direction of the complementary color. But chromatic contrast occurs when the eyes are held stationary so that this explanation cannot be the answer. If lateral inhibition is to be considered the explanation, it would have to be the case that inhibition is selective, i.e. that stimulation by one wavelength in one region of the retina inhibits more strongly the discharging of those cells in an adjacent region which are primarily responsive to that wavelength, shifting the effective balance in the direction of the complementary color.

The color solid

Painted or dyed objects will generally reflect all wavelengths although one particular wavelength will be dominant. The purer the color, the less does it reflect other wavelengths and the more saturated it is. A saturated sample looks strongly or vividly colored. A desaturated color that reflects a high proportion of all wavelengths or "white light" in relation to the dominant wavelength appears weak or washed out. Plate 1 shows a continuum of saturation, from the maximal attainable with printing dyes to zero or neutral gray. One can imagine making up these various samples by starting with a quantity of red paint and a quantity of gray paint. The red paint alone would be quite saturated. By mixing a constant amount of the red paint with increasingly greater amounts of the gray, one could arrive at a decreasingly saturated mixture.

The hues can be arranged along the circumference of a circle according to the spectrum of wavelengths. Neighboring hues along this circle are experienced as similar to one another. If the saturation of each hue is represented along the radius of the circle, as is shown in Plate 5, then we end up with a circle full of many different possible color samples such as are encountered in daily life.

But there is another dimension not represented in the circle in which colors vary, that is particularly relevant to the topic of this chapter. In Plates 1 and 5 the desaturation is achieved by mixing a medium gray with the saturated colors. Suppose, instead, that white is used, as shown in Plate 2. Now, although we again create a series from maximally saturated to completely neutral or unsaturated, the entire series is *lighter*. Conversely, Plate 3 illustrates a series desaturated by the use of black paint. Here the entire series is darker. Therefore, it can be seen that several samples of *equal* degree of saturation of a given hue (for example, the middle region of Plates 2 and 3) will nevertheless appear different as a function of the *lightness* of the achromatic color used in the mixture. This dimension of lightness, therefore, gives rise to many different tints and shades of hues. Plate 4 illustrated for one hue how all these different tints and shades arise as a function of lightness (vertical dimension); also shown in the same color triangle are the varying colors achieved as a function of saturation (horizontal dimension). To represent in one figure the hues, saturations, and shades, a third dimension is necessary as is shown in Plate 6. Thus, we arrive at the color solid, the three-dimensional representation of all possible values that colors can appear to have.*

Of particular interest in the context of the present chapter is the fact just mentioned that variation of the achromatic component of a sample of any hue has the effect of altering not only the lightness of the sample (as it might appear to a color-blind person), but also of transforming the sample into different shades and tints of that hue. A green becomes dark green when mixed with black paint; an orange becomes brown when mixed with black; magenta becomes pink when mixed with white and so on. We have seen that neutral color is to a large extent a function not of the absolute intensity of light reflected but of intensity relative to that of surrounding objects. Thus, as noted previously, a white object looks white not directly because its reflectance value is 80 percent but indirectly because a reflectance of 80 percent will reflect proportionately more light than that of neighboring objects of other reflectance values. Therefore, what should matter in changing the lightness of an object of a given hue, by mixing different shades of neutrally colored paints with the saturated color, is that this step changes the *ratio* of total light reflected by an object to that reflected by the surround. Hence, it should follow that the various tints and shades of each hue can be produced merely by changing the intensity of light reflected by the region surrounding a given sample. This prediction is borne out and is illustrated in Plate 7.[45] A yellowish orange looks almost brown when the surrounding region is white instead of black. The difference is much greater when this experiment is performed in a dark room. The effect in the illustration is limited for the same reason that contrast, as illustrated in Fig. 11-8, is limited. The effect of the black surrounding one inner region is offset by the darkening effect of the white regions in the vicinity.

One final point about the vertical or lightness axis of the color solid is that it refers to surface color on the white-gray-black continuum and not to brightness. Although extreme changes in the level of illumination will produce certain changes in perceived color (for example, in dim light chromatic hues become difficult to detect and to discriminate from one another), these are not the changes of shades and tints that are implied in the color solid. A painted yellow object may well look dimmer in dim light, it may well look somewhat less saturated, but it will not

---

*The figure is spindle-shaped, tapering to a point at top and bottom, rather than a cylinder because there can only be one fully saturated sample of a given hue. Or to put it another way, starting with any nuance of gray, in increasing its saturation (by mixing it with more and more paint of the color in question), one necessarily changes it lightness. A black sample becomes lighter and a white sample becomes darker as more and more red is mixed with it.

appear to be olive. Whereas keeping the illumination constant and mixing dark gray or black paint with the yellow paint or brightening the region surrounding the yellow object *will* change its appearance from yellow to olive.

Summary

Since the intensity of light reflected to the eyes by any surface varies considerably, because the illumination falling on the surface varies, a central problem is to account for the veridical perception of neutral color, i.e., color on the white-gray-black continuum. The perception of neutral *color* must not be confused with perceived *brightness* since the same phenomenal gray may appear to be "bright" or "dim" depending upon conditions, and varying levels of brightness can be perceived even when there is no perception of a surface color. The correlate of perceived neutral color cannot be the intensity of reflected light (or luminance) because neutral color remains more or less constant when illumination varies. Two kinds of theories have been proposed. The classical theory holds that we take account of the strength of illumination and thereby "deduce" the reflectance property of a surface. The chief problem with this theory is that we have no unambiguous information about strength of illumination. The ratio hypothesis holds that neutral color is a function of the ratio of intensities of light reflected by adjacent surfaces. Ratios ordinarily do not change when illumination changes.

For the most part, at least for surfaces in one plane, the ratio hypothesis predicts and elegantly explains the facts observed. Whereas the classical theory, although generally predicting the same experimental outcomes, repeatedly encounters the difficulty of explaining how the strength of illumination can be "known." Among the major facts are these: Specific values of gray can be shown to derive directly from specific intensity ratios; changing such ratios alters the gray perceived as when the illumination changes on one region but is prevented from doing so on neighboring regions; simultaneous contrast is greatly increased if the gray on white and gray on black displays under comparison are separated from one another and viewed in an otherwise dark field (presumably because the presence of other ratios then no longer can have the effect of modulating the determination of neutral color by the ratio of white or black surround to gray sample); experiments have not always confirmed the ratio hypothesis when the absolute intensities are varied (particularly when they are made very high or very low) since the particular gray perceived varies somewhat although the ratio remains constant, *but* these experiments have not always been conducted appropriately and the instructions often do not distinguish between perceived neutral color and perceived brightness; in laboratory experiments on constancy in which the observer matches neutral colors under different illuminations, a high degree of constancy is obtained, but when the samples are viewed through a reduction screen, observers match on the basis of absolute intensities reflected to the eyes; both of these findings can be satisfactorily explained by the ratio hypothesis.

However, the amount of light reflected by a surface also depends upon the position and slant in the three-dimensional world—whether it is shadowed or receives light head on or at an angle—and to some extent at least such conditions of illumination seem to be taken into account by the perceptual system in assessing the reflectance property of surfaces. If the observer succeeds in "flattening out" the three-dimensional array, the perceived gray changes although no change in ratio occurs. Therefore, such facts are explicable in terms of the classical theory but are not easily accounted for by the ratio hypothesis. Some, but not all, demonstrations of constancy under conditions of transparency can be adequately explained by the ratio hypothesis.

The fact that constancy is evidenced by animals of various species and by young children certainly argues against the implication of the classical theory that the perception of neutral color depends upon a process of judgment. This is not to say that constancy could not be the result of learning, but at least in the case of the chicken, experimentation has now shown that constancy is present shortly after hatching, with no opportunity for learning.

Various sensory mechanisms have been suggested as a possible basis of neutral color constancy. Pupillary adjustments and retinal adaptation to light would have the effect of counteracting changes in level of illumination but, nevertheless, these mechanisms cannot adequately explain constancy and related facts. One sensory mechanism that conceivably could explain constancy, which in fact could account for the determination of the perceived gray by the ratio of intensities, is lateral inhibition. Since the rate of firing of neurons is attenuated by the firing of adjacent neurons, the increased illumination on a sample would tend to be counteracted by the increased inhibition resulting from the increased illumination on regions adjacent to the sample. Lateral inhibition can also account for simultaneous contrast. Although such inhibiting effects on perceived lightness can hardly be denied there are reasons for doubting that this mechanism does in fact explain the facts of constancy.

In addition to perceiving neutral color, we also perceive brightness, which we generally interpret as indicative of strength of illumination. It was argued that such perception is only possible because the neutral color is determined by ratio of intensities; i.e., once the particular color is unambiguously determined, differences in the intensity of light reflected by objects can then be attributed to differences in brightness. This conclusion, therefore, reverses the classical argument that we start with the awareness of strength of illumination and thereby deduce the shade of gray. Only in cases where there are definite indicators of differences in illumination received—as, for example, in three-dimensional arrays—is the classical argument tenable and probably to some extent at least, correct.

For reasons as yet unknown, perceptual organization affects neutral color. For example, the tendency toward the unification of figures can oppose if not completely eliminate contrast effects; the belongingness of a region to a "figure" will lead to greater contrast with that figure than its belongingness to the "ground" surrounding the figure; "figure" undergoes more contrast with its surroundings than "ground"; transparency effects depend upon perceptual organization.

Constancy also occurs with chromatic colors seen in chromatic light. Although it is possible to understand such effects on the basis of the classical theory—namely taking into account the hue of the light and mentally "subtracting" its contribution to the retinal image—it has been shown that these effects essentially reduce to simultaneous chromatic contrast. Thus the explanation is at least formally similar to the ratio explanation of neutral color constancy, namely, all that is required by way of explanation is reference to the effect of adjacent regions of reflected light upon one another.

Variations in the proportion of white light to that of a narrow band of wavelength determines the perceived saturation of a given hue. However, colors can be desaturated by white, gray, or black or, what amounts to the same thing, by variations in the intensity ratio of colored sample to surround. Such differences affect the perceived shades and tints of hues.

References

1. Katz, D. *The World of Colour*, Kegan Paul, Trench, Trubner & Co. 1935.

2. Helmholtz, H. von. *Treatise on Physiological Optics.* Vol. III Trans. from the 3rd German ed., edit. by J. P. C. Southall. Dover Publications, Inc., 1962. First publ. in the *Handbuch der Physiologischen Optik*, Voss, 1867.
3. Hering, E. *Outlines of a Theory of the Light Sense*, trans. by L. Hurvich and D. Jameson. Harvard University Press, 1964. Originally publ. in 1905 and 1907 as Grundzüge der Lehre vom Lichtsinn and reprinted by J. Springer, 1920.
4. Wallach, H. Brightness constancy and the nature of achromatic colors. *Journal of Experimental Psychology*, 1948, 38, 310–324; See also H. Wallach. The perception of neutral colors. *Scientific American*, 1963, 208, No. 1, 107–116.
5. Jameson, D. and L. Hurvich. Theory of brightness and color contrast in human vision. *Vision Research*, 1964, 4, 135–154.
6. Gelb, A. Die "Farbenkonstanz" der Sehdinge. In A. Bethe, G. V. Bergmann, G. Embden, and A. Ellinger, (eds.). *Handbuch der Normalen und Pathologischen Physiologie*, 12, J. Springer, 1929, Part I, 594–678.
7. Kardos, L. Ding und Schatten. *Zeitschrift fur Psychologie*, 1934, Ergbd. No. 23; R. B. MacLeod. An experimental investigation of brightness constancy. *Archives of Psychology*, 1932, No. 135,
8. Darlington, T. B. *Interaction in achromatic color contrast.* M. A. thesis, Swarthmore College, 1961.
9. Bezold, W. von. *The Theory of Color.* American ed. L. Prang and Co., 1876.
10. Festinger, L., S. Coren and G. Rivers. The effect of attention on brightness contrast and assimilation. *American Journal of Psychology*, 1970, 83, 189–207.
11. Hess, C. and H. Pretori. Quantitative investigation of the lawfulness of simultaneous brightness contrast, Trans. by H. R. Flock and J. H. Tenny. *Perceptual and Motor Skills*, 1970, 31, 947–969.
12. Heinemann, E. G. Simultaneous brightness induction as a function of inducing and test-field luminance. *Journal of Experimental Psychology*, 1955, 50, 89–96.
13. Jameson, D. and L. Hurvich. Complexities of perceived brightness. *Science*, 1961, 133, 174–179.
14. Freeman, R. B., Jr. Contrast interpretation of brightness constancy. *Psychological Bulletin*, 1967, 67, 165–187.
15. Katz, D. op. cit.
16. Brunswik, E. Zur Entwicklung der Albedowahrnehmung. *Zeitschrift für Psychologie*, 1929, 109, 40–115.
17. Thouless, R. Phenomenal regression to the real object. I. *British Journal of Psychology*, 1931, 21, 339–359.

18. Stewart, E. C. The Gelb effect. *Journal of Experimental Psychology*, 1959, 57, 235–242.
19. Mach. E. *The Analysis of Sensations.* Dover Publications, Inc., 1959.
20. Katona, G. Color contrast and color constancy. *Journal of Experimental Psychology*, 1935, 18, 49–63.
21. Beck, J. Apparent spatial position and the perception of lightness. *Journal of Experimental Psychology*, 1965, 69, 170–179.
22. Hochberg, J. and J. Beck. Apparent spatial arrangement and perceived brightness. *Journal of Experimental Psychology*, 1954, 47, 263–266; J. Beck. Apparent spatial position and the perception of lightness. *Journal of Experimental Psychology*, 1965, 69, 170–179; H. Flock and E. Freedberg. Perceived angle of incidence and achromatic surface color. *Perception & Psychophysics*, 1970, 8, 251–256.
23. Flock, H. R. Achromatic surface color and the direction of illumination. *Perception & Psychophysics*, 1971, 9, 187–192.
24. Gogel, W. C. and D. H. Mershon. Depth adjacency and simultaneous contrast. *Perception & Psychophysics*, 1969, 5, 13–17; D. H. Mershon and W. C. Gogel. Effect of stereoscopic cues on perceived whiteness. *American Journal of Psychology*, 1970, 83, 55–67.
25. Hering, E. op. cit. 1920.
26. MacLeod, R. The effects of "artificial penumbrae" on the brightness of included areas. In *Miscellanea Psychologica, Albert Michotte*, Librairie Philosophique, 1947.
27. Köhler, W. Die Farben der Sehdinge beim Schimpansen und beim Haushuhn. *Zeitschrift für Psychologie*, 1917, 77, 248–255.
28. Locke, N. M. Perception and intelligence: their phylogenetic relation. *Psychological Review*, 1938, 45, 335–345.
29. Gogel, W. C. A study of color constancy in the newly hatched chick by means of an innate color preference. Ph. D. dissertation, University of Chicago, 1951.
30. Helson, H. *Adaptation-level Theory.* Harper & Row Publishers, Inc., 1964.
31. Hartline, H. K., H. G. Wagner and F. Ratliff. Inhibition in the eye of Limulus. *Journal of General Physiology*, 1956, 39, 651–673.
32. von Békésy, G. *Sensory Inhibition*, Princeton University Press, 1967.
33. Ratliff, F. *Mach Bands: Quantitative Studies on Neutral Networks in the Retina.* Holden-Day, Inc., 1965.
34. Cornsweet, T. N. *Visual Perception.* Academic Press, Inc. 1970, Chapters 11 and 13.
35. This kind of effect was originally discovered by Kenneth Craik in

1940 but not published. It was later re-discovered by Vivian O'Brien. Therefore it is now referred to as the Craik-O'Brien effect. The particular illustration of the effect in Fig. 11-23 is known as the Cornsweet illusion. See K. J. W. Craik. *The Nature of Psychology.* Cambridge University Press, 1966, pp. 94–97; V. O'Brien. Contour perception, illusion and reality. *Journal of the Optical Society of America,* 1958, 48, 112–119; Cornsweet, op. cit., p. 273.

36. Beck, J. Stimulus correlates for the judged illumination of a surface. *Journal of Experimental Psychology,* 1959, 58, 267–274: Judgment of surface illumination and lightness. *Journal of Experimental Psychology,* 1961, 61, 368–375.

37. Koffka, K. Zur Grundlegring der Wahrnehumngspychologie. Eine Auseinandersetzung met. V. Benussi. *Zeitschrift für Psychologie,* 1915, 73, 11–190; Principles of Gestalt Psychology, Harcourt Brace Jovanovich, 1935. Benussi published a paper on this effect at around the same time (1916), and he credits a man by the name of Meyer working in Wundt's laboratory with the discovery. For more recent work on this problem, see P. W. Berman and H. W. Leibowitz. Some effects of contour on simultaneous brightness contrast. *Journal of Experimental Psychology,* 1965, 69, 251–256.

38. Cohen, H. H., J. C. Bill, and A. S. Gilinsky. Simultaneous brightness contrast: variations on Koffka's ring. *Proceedings, 76th Annual Convention,* APA, 1968.

39. Benary, W. Beobachtung zu einem Experiment über Helligkeitskontrast. *Psychologische Forschung.* 1924, 5, 131–142 and reprinted in W. Ellis. *A Source Book of Gestalt Psychology,* Selection 8, The Humanities Press, 1950.

40. Koffka, op. cit., 1935, p. 186.

41. Coren, S. Brightness contrast as a function of figure-ground relations. *Journal of Experimental Psychology,* 1969, 80, 517–524.

42. Metelli, F. The perception of transparency. *Scientific American,* 1974, 230, No. 4, 90–98.

43. Evans, R. M. *An Introduction to Color.* John Wiley & Sons, Inc., 1948: F. A. Geldard. *The Human Senses.* 2nd ed. John Wiley & Sons, Inc., 1972, Chapters 1–5; E. G. Boring. *Sensation and Perception in the History of Experimental Psychology.* Appelton-Century-Crofts, 1942, Chapters 3–6.

44. Wallach, H. and A. Galloway. The constancy of colored objects in colored illumination. *Journal of Experimental Psychology,* 1946, 36, 119–126.

45. Wallach, H. The perception of neutral colors. *Scientific American,* 1963, 208, No. 1, 107–116.

chapter 12

PRINCIPLES OF PERCEPTION

What general principles of perception emerge from our examination of the various topics in this book?

First, some characteristics of perception can be briefly summarized in the following statements:

1. The proximal stimulus array must be considered to be ambiguous concerning what it represents in the world.

2. Perception begins with a process of grouping and figure-ground organization of the proximal stimulus.

3. The organization achieved is based on a selection, decision, or preference on the part of the perceptual system for certain outcomes.

4. The central events that lead to particular perceptions are not themselves subjectively experienced, i.e., they are not conscious.

5. As a rule, what is perceived (or what is salient in what is perceived) does not simply correspond directly with the relevant feature of the proximal stimulus (for example, perceived movement with movement of the object's image or perceived size with the object's visual angle or perceived neutral color with the object's luminance.)

6. By and large, the facts of perception considered in these chapters cannot be adequately explained in terms of the operation of physiological detector-mechanisms such as are triggered by a particular stimulus impinging on the retina.

While there is fragmentary evidence that neural mechanisms may exist which respond to constant object properties rather than to constant proximal stimulus properties, there is also evidence that certain perceptions can occur in the absence of any relevant feature-detectors. Therefore it is difficult at this time to know what role these mechanisms play in perception since their activation is neither necessary nor sufficient to account for the perception of object properties. It is premature to try to explain most of the phenomena of perception in terms of current knowledge of neurophysiology.

7. What is perceived is generally, although by no means always, veridical.

8. Perception generally is not influenced by knowledge (in contrast to sensory information) i.e., what we perceive is not determined by or affected by what is known about the object.

9. Vision is dominant over other sense modalities so that not only does it tend to determine what is perceived when a sensory conflict occurs but it tends to "capture" and thereby distort the very experience of the object as given by that other modality.

Other general principles are discussed under the following headings.

The Tendency Toward Perceived Object Constancy

Two kinds of mechanisms appear to lead to object constancy. In the one case, perceptual constancy results from sensory information. In the other case, there is no such information and constancy must be considered to be the result of a preference on the part of the perceptual system.

Constancy based on sensory information

The perceptual constancies, such as those of size, shape, direction, velocity, position, orientation, and neutral color have in common that despite change of the relevant feature of the proximal stimulus (of size, shape, position, and the like) what is perceived is more or less constant and veridical.

For the most part, the evidence favors the conclusion that these constancies result from a process of taking-into-account of other sensory information: distance in the case of size and velocity constancy, slant in the case of shape constancy, eye position in the case of direction constancy, observer-movement in the case of position constancy, observer orientation in the case of orientation constancy, and differences in illumination under certain conditions in the case of neutral color constancy. (However, a different kind of explanation, based directly on certain stimulus relationships, has been offered with respect to some of these constancies, such as those of size, velocity, and neutral color. In the latter case the weight of evidence actually *favors* an explanation in terms of the maintenance of the same *ratio* of light intensities from adjacent regions despite varying overall illumination. The general importance of relational determination in perception is discussed under a separate heading.)

In the constancy situation, the relevant proximal stimulus varies while other co-varying information enables the perceptual system to correct the proximal stimulus and thus maintain constancy. (A corollary to this principle is that wherever the proximal stimulus remains constant—such as with an after-image—then the same process of taking-into-account the co-varying information—for example, distance—leads to *changing* perception. Thus, for every constancy there is an analogue of Emmert's law that is perfectly comprehensible in terms of the same mechanism that explains that constancy.)

In each of the constancies there is a dual aspect of perception. The salient perceptual property, to be sure, is the size, shape, position, velocity, orientation, and color that the object in the environment appears to have. But also present in perception is a less noticed, less attended to, aspect that is closely correlated with the relevant property of the proximal stimulus. Thus, for example, in size perception, there is, in addition to objective size, an impression of the object's *extensity* in the field based on its visual angle; in the case of shape, there is an impression closely corresponding to the shape of the object's retinal image, which might be referred to as one of *extensity-relations;* in the case of direction, there is an impression of *field location*, i.e., where in the momentary field of view the object is located; in the case of position, there may be an impression of *psuedomovement*, i.e., of "movement" of the object across one's field despite its stationary character in the visual world; in the case of velocity there is an awareness that a nearby object moves more rapidly through one's field although the objective speed is nevertheless veridically assessed; in the case or orientation, there is an impression of an object's *egocentric orientation* independent of its environmental orientation; and in the case of neutral color, there is an impression of *"brightness,"* as a function of illumination, despite the perceived constancy of the object's shade of gray.

Although these more directly determined "stimulus features" of perception are not dominant (and perhaps less accessible in animals and infants than in adults) their presence does have certain consequences. Only by recognizing the presence of such phenomenal attributes can one fully understand experiences such as the paradoxical impression of converging parallels in the case of a railroad track or the apparent "movement" of the world viewed from a moving vehicle. The compromise outcome of experiments on constancy may be explicable in terms of the conflict existing for the observer between the different impressions he obtains based on these dual aspects of perception. Individual differences in such experiments may reflect differences in emphasis on one or the other of these dual aspects.

Constancy based on a preference for that outcome

We have encountered a number of constancies where there is no separate sensory information available to the perceptual system that could be used to interpret the proximal stimulus changes but nevertheless, the outcome is one of constancy. One such example is the expansion pattern or "looming" effect where an expanding image is perceived as an object of constant size approaching (or a contracting image is perceived as an object receding). For this perception there need be no distance cues operating that indicate the change in the distance of the object from the observer. Therefore, the proximal stimulus change is ambiguous and, logically, could just as well lead to the impression of an object at a given distance changing its size.

Another example is the kinetic depth effect. Here a changing pattern, such as results from the shadow on a screen of a rotating three-dimensional object, is perceived as a constant object rotating rather than as an object whose shape is transforming.

Still another example is the impression one has when a figure is revealed through a narrow slit. When figures are used that have no discontinuities (such as the one shown in Fig. 7–5) and when its ends are not visible, then the proximal stimulus change of an element changing its slope and location within the slit could just as well lead to an impression of an element doing precisely that. But the preference for perceiving this change as representing a figure of a constant shape would seem to be another illustration of the kind under discussion.

Based on examples such as these the conclusion seems warranted that a basic law of perception is as follows: *Proximal stimulus transformations will, whenever possible, be perceived as representing a rigid object of unchanging physical properties that is undergoing some change in its location or orientation in the environment.*

It is possible that many phenomena, which in the past have been considered as illustrating a preference for the *simplest outcome*, can be better understood as manifestations of such a principle of object constancy. A rigid object is necessarily a simpler percept that a transforming object. Other examples that seem to illustrate a preference for simplicity can perhaps be understood either as resulting from an effect of past experience with regular objects or as resulting from a solution to the problem of what the proximal stimulus represents in the world in which the perceptual system favors symmetrical and regular organizations as "more probable." (See the section on the Intelligence of Perception.)

It is plausible to suppose that the first step in a very rapid process is a perception correlated with features of the proximal stimulus. This is followed quickly by the achievement of constancy by a process of constructing the phenomenal object either on the basis of other sensory information or on the basis of a preference for a constancy solution. The perception correlated with the proximal-stimulus features is then more or less superseded and less available in conscious awareness.

Relational Determination

There can be little argument with the conclusion that proximal stimulus relationships determine what we perceive in a wide variety of situations.   Among the examples we have encountered of relational determination are the following: The displacement of the image of an object with respect to that of other objects plays a fundamental role in the perception of movement and velocity. The orientation of an object with respect to others influences how it is perceived to be oriented in the environment. The size of an object relative to others affects its phenomenal size. The luminance of an object relative to that of neighboring objects is fundamental in determining its apparent lightness of color. Form itself is a function of the geometrical relationships of the parts of a figure with respect to one another. Various illusions are, by definition, a function of the relationship of test lines to that of inducing lines in the configuration.

In many situations, one object in the field assumes the role of *frame of reference.* That object will generally be one that encloses or is larger than other objects in its vicinity. The determining stimulus relationship then becomes one-sided in that the object is perceived with respect to the frame of reference but not the other way around. Thus, change of relative position between object and frame leads to perceiving the object as moving and the frame as stationary (regardless of which is actually moving). Or a line is seen as vertical if it is parallel to the sides of a large rectangle even if the rectangle itself is seen as tilted.

The frame of reference is interpreted by the perceptual system as representing the stable coordinate system of environmental space and that is why objects are perceived in terms of how they relate to it. Since the observer's body is itself an object in the environment, it too is perceived in terms of how it relates to the frame of reference. If a moving frame surrounds the observer and the observer is stationary, induced movement of the self occurs. The frame is then perceived to be stationary. If the frame is tilted, an observer inside it will perceive it as upright and himself as tilted.

However, unless the frame of reference is large so that the observer experiences himself as within it, it does not affect his perception of himself. That being the case, the tendency to perceive objects in terms of how they relate to other objects in the field may be opposed by or in conflict with information concerning how the object relates to the self. For example, in the case of induced movement, information is available that the stationary object is stationary with respect to the self. If the inducing object were to be removed, the stationary object would, of course, be perceived veridically. Therefore, one can think of this situation as one of sensory conflict in which *object-relative* information indicates movement of the stationary object and *subject-relative* information does not. From this point of view, the fact of induced movement implies a victory of object-relative over subject-relative determination.

Similarly, one can view the perception of a line's orientation in the environment when seen within a tilted rectangle as a conflict situation in which object-relative information indicates one thing and subject-relative information another. The strong effect of the tilted rectangle again suggests the great potency of object-relative determination, but the fact that the effect is only partial (i.e., the majority of observers do not set the line *parallel* to the tilted rectangle) demonstrates that subject-relative information is also influencing the outcome.

Even a property such as shape can be thought of in terms of object-relative and subject-relative information. Thus, what distinguishes a straight line from a curved one can be stated purely in terms of the internal geometry—whether or not the "segments" of the line are or are not parallel *to one another* (object-relative)—*or* in terms of direction with respect to the observer—whether or not all the points constituting the line are or are not straight ahead or at eye level (subject-relative).

Innate Determination Versus Past Experience

Despite over a century of interest and research on the problem of whether or not we learn to perceive, very little decisive evidence is available. It now does seem to have been established that the perception of distance is given innately but it is still not certain which cue or cues mediates this perception and it is quite probable that some of the pictorial cues to depth are acquired. There is some impressive evidence that perceived form is innately determined but there are examples of past-experience effects in form perception as well. There is now evidence of the presence of perceptual constancy very early in life but there is also some evidence that suggests a role of experience. Research on adaptation to prismatic distortion of various kinds suggests that the perception of radial direction, position constancy, egocentric orientation, specific (or absolute) size, specific line curvature, and depth based on binocular disparity are subject to learning. At the same time, it does not follow that such perceptions may not also be innately determined and in some of these examples there is at least the strong presumption based on logical considerations or evidence that this is the case. Moreover, the adaptation that has thus far been achieved in laboratory experiments in the case of egocentric orientation and specific line curvature is quite modest even following long periods of exposure to the prisms. Although some theories of the geometrical illusions assume that these are based on past experience, the evidence is not convincing and, in fact, these illusions are generally more pronounced in young children than in adults.

Where past experience effects have been demonstrated in certain instances of form and depth perception, a good case can be made for concluding that a two-stage process is responsible. The initial organization is achieved independent of prior experience and is, therefore, similar to the way the configuration was organized at a time prior to any experience. This perceptual organization is then recognized and identified as an object (or arrangement of objects or a feature of objects) so that it immediately is transformed, taking on the perceptual characteristics that that object was previously perceived to have. The previous perception was achieved on the basis of other information that was available then but is not necessary now. Presumably, an association has been established between the two possible perceptual organizations, the one that occurred spontaneously and did not depend on experience and the one that occurred only because other information was provided. Examples of this kind of two-stage process are the successful perception and identification of fragmented figures in a brief test exposure, the perception of certain kinds of ambiguous figures in a test exposure in accord with a prior training exposure, and the perception of depth on the basis of certain pictorial cues.

The Intelligence of Perception

We have seen in many examples that perception often seems to be intelligent, as if it resulted from a process of reasoning. To many investigators who are aware of this fact, it remains an unexplained curiosity, or it is considered to result from evolutionary adaptation to the environment. Many forms of animal behavior seem to be highly intelligent—for example, the spinning of a web by a spider or the building of a nest by a bird—but it does not follow from this that the behavior is in fact determined by intelligent thought. To the contrary, the student of animal behavior would say that such behavior is instinctual and is determined by specific internal states and external stimuli.

But it is possible that the intelligent character of perception does in fact result from a rapid-fire, unconscious, process of construction or problem solving. The problem is always this: What structure or event in the world could be giving rise to the proximal stimulus? Since that stimulus is generally ambiguous, there are always several possible solutions or hypothesis to the "problem."

We have encountered a great number of cases where such a problem-solving mechanism can explain what is perceived: Perceptual grouping, organization, and change of perceptual organization; perceptual constancy; depth perception based on motion parallax, binocular disparity, and various pictorial cues; form as revealed through a narrow slit; various aspects of movement perception including stroboscopic movement; and the perception of neutral color in certain situations where information is independently available concerning differences in illumination.

However, such an explanation in terms of perceptual problem solving is different from the classical theory of Wundt and Titchener, which sought to explain certain facts in terms of interpretation. One does not adequately describe stroboscopic movement perception by saying that we interpret the alternately flashing objects as moving (but do not really *see* movement). One does not do justice to the fact of position constancy by saying that we interpret the world as stationary when we move our eyes (but perceive it as moving). These phenomena are perceptual. There are cases where it *is* appropriate to speak of interpretation and where, contrary to the situation in perception, knowledge can play a role. Thus, for example, an airplane in flight looks small because there is inadequate sensory information about its distance. But we interpret it as a large object. On the other hand, when seen on the ground by an observer on the ground, where distance information is quite good, the airplane is *perceived* to be large, even when it is quite far away.

If, therefore, certain perceptions do result from a process of problem solving, where the solution *is* essentially an interpretation of the proximal stimulus, it is an interpretation of a proximal stimulus *supported by stimulus information.*

The rule that distinguishes cases of perceptual problem solving from nonperceptual interpretations seems to be that the solution (or construction) in perception must be such that it accounts for or "fits" the proximal stimulus both with respect to what is present and what is absent in the stimulus. Thus, for example, one *perceives* a figure with subjective contours (Fig. 7–4, p. 299) because if that figure were present it would produce the proximal stimulus that is given. But one does not perceive such a figure if certain features in the stimulus pattern do not "fit" (for example, if the visible segments of the "covered" triangle figure do not terminate at the edges of the contours of the subjectively achieved triangle); or if certain features in the stimulus pattern are absent (for example, if the pattern consisted of only one incomplete disk instead of three). For if such a triangle were actually present, certain parts of the contours of the hidden triangle would not be visible and there would be no reason provided for the absence of stimulation from its other two corners.

Perhaps it is necessary to think that the construction is a process rather like imagining which is imposed upon the proximal stimulus. For example, in subjectively achieved contours, we imagine an object that exactly fits the proximal stimulus pattern. In the kinetic depth effect we imagine that the object is rotating in depth in just the manner and at just the speed that would be producing the proximal stimulus change in its two-dimensional projection to the retina.

According to the classical sensation-interpretation theory, interpretations were based upon past experience. Whether perceptual problem solving as outlined here is or is not based on prior experience must remain an open question. Although it certainly helps to explain the availability of a "solution" if it derives from certain past experience in the life history of the individual, it is by no means logically necessary to argue that the solution must derive from such experience. This conclusion is similar to the one reached by the Gestalt psychologists in analyzing thinking. Some solutions to problems clearly derive from prior experience and some come directly from the perceived requirements of the problem.

There are both similarities and differences between perceptual problem solving and the problem solving that characterizes thought. In both cases one searches for a "hypothesis" that would explain certain observable facts (in the case of perception, the observable fact is the proximal stimulus or proximal stimulus transformation); in both cases, there are inelegant and elegant solutions; in both cases the "solution" often emerges suddenly in a flash of insight.

On the other hand, perceptual problem-solving is usually extremely fast; it is not conscious and not verbal (which is not to imply that thinking is necessarily slow, conscious, and verbal but often it is or at least is to some extent); it does not seem to require the strong motivation that sustained thinking requires; unlike many difficult problems of thought, perceptual problem-solving generally leads to correct solutions for most observers; finally, perceptual problem solving results in a percept rather than an idea.

In one respect, however, it might be said that perception is unintelligent. We often perceive what we know to be otherwise, or even what we know to be highly improbable if not impossible. For example, if a perspective reversal occurs for a stationary wire figure when the observer is moving, then the figure seems to be rotating. Or, if an observer moves his head in viewing a stereogram, the units at different phenomenal depths seem to move relative to one another although there is no change in the retinal images. One might consider these as examples of intelligent solutions to the problem of reconciling the perceived depth relationships with the parallax changes (or absence of such changes) of parts of the figures with respect to one another. But one might also say that it reveals the inflexibility of perception because we perceive what we know is not, in fact, occurring. And this perception is often obligatory. Since flexibility is one of the hallmarks of intelligence, in contrast to reflex or instinctual behavior, such examples contradict our characterization of perception as intelligent. However, perceptual solutions are based upon certain premises and rules and they seem to be intelligent within this framework. When they are not veridical, they can be considered as "good errors," in that they derive from correct deductions from these rules. Since these rules are concerned with sensory (or perceptual) information rather than with knowledge acquired less directly, what is perceived may occasionally contradict what is known about the situation.

It is doubtful if all perception can be understood along these lines. We have encountered various instances where a different kind of mechanism seems to be operating. For example, the perception of neutral color can, for the most part, be elegantly explained in terms of the ratio of adjacent luminances so that it would seem to be gratuitous to claim that a process of reasoning is necessary. Or, the aftereffect of movement can probably be explained in terms of a fatiguing of neural units sensitive to one direction of movement over the retina. Then there is the fact that perceptions that closely parallel those in humans undoubtedly occur in many lower species. If an insect behaves as if it is perceiving movement under conditions of stroboscopic flashing of stimuli, many would consider it highly improbable that such perception is based on a cognitive process such as that of thinking.

Therefore, the safest conclusion to reach at this stage of our knowledge is that different kinds of mechanisms underlie perception. In many cases a cognitive process of problem-solving is responsible for what is perceived. In other cases a sensory mechanism based more directly on the impinging proximal stimulus is responsible. Nevertheless, it has been argued throughout these chapters that this second kind of mechanism can only rarely do justice to the facts of perception in man.

SUBJECT INDEX

AUTHOR INDEX

People of the Ancient World

THE
ANCIENT
CELTS

WRITTEN BY
PATRICIA CALVERT

Franklin Watts
A Division of Scholastic Inc.
New York Toronto London Auckland Sydney
Mexico City New Delhi Hong Kong
Danbury, Connecticut

tic parents—and Irish mother, a Scottish father

Note to readers: Definitions for words in bold can be found in the Glossary at the back of this book.

Cover art by Dan Andreasen
Map by XNR Productions Inc.

Library of Congress Cataloguing-in-Publication Data

Calvert, Patricia.
    The ancient Celts / Patricia Calvert.
       p. cm. — (People of the ancient world)
Includes bibliographical references and index.
ISBN 0-531-12359-6 (lib. bdg.)   0-531-16845-X (pbk.)
1. Celts—Juvenile literature. I. Title. II. Series.
D70.C26 2005
930'.04916—dc22

2004026378